DIANA

INQUEST

THE

Untold

Story

John Morgan

PART 5:
WHO KILLED
PRINCESS DIANA?

First published in Australia by Shining Bright Publishing
Printed by Lightning Source

ISBN: 978-0-9807407-4-5

Cover Picture:
MI6 Headquarters in Vauxhall Cross, London
This building was officially opened by Queen
Elizabeth II in July 1994

Cover image reproduced from film footage in 2007 Francis Gillery documentary,
Requiem for a Princess

Diana Inquest: The Untold Story

Is dedicated

To

Diana, Princess of Wales

And

Dodi Fayed

Killed in a mindless tragedy

The crash in the Alma Tunnel, Paris, at 12.23 a.m., 31 August 1997

And

To those few in their and Henri Paul's families

Who have had the courage to fight for the truth to come out

Who have been confronted with an unconscionable
travesty of justice

Known as the official investigations

That commenced in Paris immediately after the crash

That concluded at 4.33 p.m. on 7 April 2008 in London's
Royal Courts of Justice

Other Volumes In This Series

Part 1: Diana Inquest: **The Untold Story** (2009)

Covers pre-crash events in the Ritz Hotel, the final journey and what happened in the Alma Tunnel

Part 2: Diana Inquest: **How & Why Did Diana Die?** (2009)

Covers possible motives for assassination and post-crash medical treatment of Princess Diana – including mistreatment in the ambulance

Part 3: Diana Inquest: **The French Cover-Up** (2010)

Covers the autopsies of the driver, Henri Paul, and the misconduct of the French investigation into the crash

Part 4: Diana Inquest: **The British Cover-Up** (2011)

Covers the post-death treatment of Princess Diana – including the embalmings and autopsies carried out in both France and the UK and the post-crash cover-up by UK authorities, including the Queen

Diana Inquest: **The Documents the Jury Never Saw** (2010)

Reproduces hundreds of key documents from within the British Paget investigation – all documents that the inquest jury were prevented from seeing

Other Books by John Morgan

Cover-Up of a Royal Murder: Hundreds of Errors in the Paget Report (2007)

Flying Free: A Journey From Fundamentalism To Freedom (2005)

Table of Contents

Special Acknowledgement	10
Preface	11
The Witnesses Not Heard	17
The Lawyers & Representation	22
The Organisations	23
Introduction	26
1 Was MI6 Involved?	28
1A MI6 Culture, Methods and Secret Operations	29
MI6 Culture	29
Secrecy and "Need to Know"	29
Deniability	30
Accountability	35
Queen and Country	38
Does MI6 Lie?	38
Conclusion	41
Relationship with Official Investigations	42
Richard Tomlinson's Affidavit	49
Does MI6 Frighten People?	51
Does MI6 Murder People?	54
MI6 Training	71
Heydrich Assassination: May 1942	81
Rubowitz Assassination: October 1947	82
Nasser Assassination Plot: September 1956	82
Grivas Assassination Plot: February 1959	86
Lumumba Assassination Plot: September 1960	87
Irish Assassination Plots: 1972	89

Gibraltar Assassinations: March 1988 — 91

Finucane Assassination: February 1989 — 91

20 Irish Assassination Plots: February 1991 to October 2000 — 96

Milosevic Assassination Plot: Summer 1992 — 99

Saddam Assassination Plot: June 1996 — 99

Gaddafi Assassination Plot: February 1996 — 101

The Increment — 148

Conclusion — 158

Independent Operations 180

Allegations Against MI6.. 185

Use of Powerful Flash Equipment 198

Involvement With Landmines.. 204

1B   MI6 in Paris: 30-31 August 1997 — 213

Sightings In and Around the Ritz Hotel...................................... 213

Bar Vendôme — 213

Place Vendôme — 228

Other Possible Sightings 229

Near Alma Tunnel — 229

MI6 Internet List.. 229

Movements of MI6 Officers 233

Richard Spearman and Nicholas Langman — 238

Embassy Tables — 273

Sherard Cowper-Coles — 287

Dr Valerie Caton — 306

Other MI6 Officers — 309

Conclusion 322

1C   Rosa Monckton — 326

Timeline of Events.. 327

Relationship with MI6 329

Meeting Diana.. 337

Bali-Moyo Island Holiday: August 1993..................................... 350

TABLE OF CONTENTS

Nature of the Diana-Rosa Relationship..............................361

Period of "Radio Silence".....................................366

Greek Islands Holiday: 15 to 20 August 1997 371

Final Phone Call..397

Philip-Diana Letters 400

Conclusion 446

1D   Other Intelligence Issues   451

Threats to Other People.......................................451

   Trevor Rees-Jones   451

   Hasnat Khan   453

Interference With Witnesses 453

   Bernard Lefort   453

   Clifford Gooroovadoo   454

Role of Other Agencies..454

   British-French Intelligence Relationship   458

   CIA-MI6 Relationship   461

   Was the CIA Involved?   462

1E   Conclusion   470

2   British Embassy in Paris   476

Embassy-Consulate Relationship...............................476

Embassy Reports..477

Phone Calls and Missing Records...............................480

Missing Notes 518

Communication with the UK 518

   FCO   518

   Scotland Yard   518

Role of Michael Jay 519

Location of Robert Fellowes....................................523

Knowledge of Diana's Presence in France 531

Evidence of Stephen Donnelly.................................542

Conclusion 543

3   The Royals   546

Timeline of Events.. 546

Anti-Landmine Speech: June 1997.. 548

Links to Intelligence Agencies.. 549

Way Ahead Group 559

Royal Motives.. 595

MI6 Report on the Fayeds.. 602

Prince Philip.. 616

"Dark Forces" 620

Other Evidence.. 649

    Arson Attack Against Burrell   649

    Queen's Perception of the Diana-Dodi Relationship   650

    Post-Crash Treatment of Diana's Staff   652

    Post-Crash Control of Diana's Belongings   652

    Queen's Request for Diana's Jewellery   653

Failure to Cross-Examine Royal Suspects 655

Conclusion 662

4   Role of British Government   664

Role of Tony Blair 664

    Timing of Crash Notification   668

    Prior Knowledge of Crash   676

Conclusion 678

5   Conclusion   681

Appendix 1   685

Bonn Embassy Political-Economic Staff List Comparison: 1996 to 1997
.... 685

Appendix 2   690

Paris Embassy Political-Economic Staff List Comparison: 1995 to 1996
.... 690

Appendix 3   693

British MP's Prediction of Princess Diana's Death 693

TABLE OF CONTENTS

Evidence, Maps, Diagrams & Photos   695

Bibliography   696

Index   706

Author Information   739

Notes   742

Special
Acknowledgement

This Part 5 has been the most difficult one in the series to research and write – primarily, as discussed in the book, because of the secretive and deceitful nature of the organisations being investigated.

To that end, I wish to acknowledge the uncompromising courage of the late Peter Wright[a], Richard Tomlinson, David Shayler and Annie Machon, who have all been prepared to go public to address important issues that would otherwise have remained officially buried and hidden from our collective understanding.[b]

---

[a] Peter Wright died in Australia in 1995, aged 78.
[b] General acknowledgements regarding the full series are included in Part 1 and the final volume.

Preface

Who killed Princess Diana and Dodi Fayed?

Some might believe no one ... deliberately. But the earlier four books in this series have shown that is not true.

These volumes of evidence – a tsunami of evidence – have revealed time and again that the 1997 car crash that took the lives of Diana and Dodi was no accident.

This crash was fully orchestrated.

And then after it occurred, one of the greatest and most extensive inter-governmental cover-ups of our time was set in motion.

It has been shown that the French government – including the police and elements of the judiciary – were fully involved in the cover-up.[a] And on the other side of the Channel, the senior royals – family and household, but led by the Queen – were very quick to illegally secure control over Princess Diana's body and the ensuing post-mortem.[b]

But that was only the start of the British side of the cover-up. It continued relentlessly over the years – the unbelievable delay in conducting any investigation; and then, when it did occur, it began with a deeply flawed police inquiry[c]; and culminated in one of the most corrupt inquests in modern history.

None of this evidence, though, has shown us who carried out this heinous act – who orchestrated it and who ordered it.

The evidence has pointed to several players[d] – Henri Paul, Claude Roulet, the several motorbike riders that pursued the Mercedes S280, Jean-Marc Martino, Arnaud Derossi, Dominique Lecomte, Gilbert Pépin and Jean Monceau – but nothing has clearly shown precisely who these people were working for.

---

[a] See Part 3.
[b] Thoroughly covered in Part 4.
[c] See the book: *Cover-Up of a Royal Murder: Hundreds of Errors in the Paget Report.*
[d] Players involved in the assassinations or the cover-up.

The reason for this is because people who carry out massive orchestrated assassinations of this nature are experts in covering their tracks. No one leaves clear – or even unclear – audit trails. There are no written instructions.

No person, group or organisation is going to put their hand up for the assassination of the "people's princess".

This is not like a terrorist bombing plot where some organisation is keen to claim responsibility. No one wants to be held responsible for the death of one of the most popular and loved persons of the 20th century – Diana, Princess of Wales.

Yet someone did do it. Someone was involved in orchestrating it. Someone did order this.

In the pages of this volume you will find evidence that identifies the perpetrators of this incredible crime – the organisations, and the individuals within those organisations, that planned and directed events in Paris and also the organisations and individuals that ordered this assassination to take place.

Evidence will be revealed that clearly points to the involvement of intelligence agencies – primarily MI6 – the British royal family and household – controlled by Queen Elizabeth II – and the British, French and US governments.

For many readers, the identification of these perpetrators would not be particularly surprising.

But what is surprising is the evidence – much of which has never previously been revealed – that leads to the identification of the assassins:

- top-level changes in named MI6 staff in Paris during the days leading up to the assassinations
- widespread involvement by British intelligence in assassination plots culminating in two plots by MI6 against world leaders in the year preceding the Paris crash
- a special meeting of the royal Way Ahead Group held just 39 days before Princess Diana was assassinated
- evidence that Paul Burrell lied about the Queen's "dark forces" statement
- the exposure of Rosa Monckton as an MI6 agent who spied on Princess Diana
- evidence showing British Prime Minister, Tony Blair, had prior knowledge of the assassination of Princess Diana.

This volume was particularly difficult to research, mainly because of the all-encompassing culture of secrecy and deception within the organisations being investigated – primarily, MI6, the royal family and household, the British embassy in Paris and the highest levels of the British government.

Who Killed Princess Diana? – this book does appear to answer that question. And in so doing, many issues are raised that demand official investigation. This increases the pressure for an independent inquest into the deaths of Princess Diana and Dodi Fayed – something which I believe is impossible to achieve on British soil.

Given that these assassinations were carried out on a multi-governmental level, this means that justice can only be found through a thorough and independent investigation by an international tribunal – such as the International Court of Justice[a] – with the power to summons witnesses from the UK, France and the United States.

At times this book refers to the "assassinations" – meaning Princess Diana and Dodi Fayed. The main focus of the volume is Princess Diana and that reflects the situation – Diana was clearly the prime target for assassination and the evidence shows that. But there is a possibility of an intention to remove both figures – Princess Diana and Dodi Fayed – and of course that is anyway what occurred. I suggest that had Dodi survived, he could have been an incredibly powerful witness of what took place[b] – that, I believe, was not an option for the perpetrators of this crime.

The evidence in Part 2 – which dealt with Diana's treatment in the SAMU ambulance – revealed there was a clear intention to completely eliminate Diana[c] – i.e. this crash was not just an intention to scare. Dodi died on impact, so it is not possible to know what approach the assassins would have taken, had he survived the crash itself.[de]

Diana Inquest: Who Killed Princess Diana? has drawn heavily on the information – 7,000 pages of transcripts and other evidence – that is on the official inquest website.

---

[a] The UK, US and France were involved – so it is unlikely justice will ever be achieved under their jurisdictions. The Baker inquest revealed that the UK judiciary is not independent of working on behalf of the rulers of the land – the Queen and the government – in a case such as this, where the stakes are so high. Cases in the ICJ are brought by nation states, but a state – such as Egypt. Pakistan or India – can bring a case on behalf of an individual. It is evident that this would be a special case, but the circumstances appear to be such that justice – which has been sought over the last 15 years – cannot be achieved in the courts of the countries that were involved in the assassinations and the ensuing cover-up. Relevant websites are: International Court of Justice: www.icj-cij.org ; International Criminal Court – ICC: www.icc-cpi.int

[b] Possibly even if he hadn't been a passenger in the Mercedes S280. Because of the significant amounts of time he had spent with Diana over the previous six weeks and their obvious deepening relationship (see Part 2) he could have been privy to information that no other witness was.

[c] Diana survived the crash itself, but died as a result of her deliberate mistreatment in the ambulance.

[d] This also is the case with Henri Paul, who would have been privy to a lot of retrospective knowledge regarding the assassination.

[e] The situation regarding Trevor Rees-Jones, who survived both the crash and ambulance trip, will be addressed in Part 6.

DIANA INQUEST: WHO KILLED PRINCESS DIANA?

In 2011 a decision was made at the Royal Courts of Justice to close down the official inquest website – which had been www.scottbaker-inquests.gov.uk Following that move, the inquest transcripts and evidence can now only be found in the UK National Archives. The easiest way to access them – at the time of writing – is using Google search with the words: "Diana inquest transcripts national archives".[a]

All quotes throughout this book have been fully referenced, and I encourage readers to look up the website[b] for the full transcript of any particular piece of witness evidence they need to view in its complete context.

This volume also uses material from the 2010 book *Diana Inquest: The Documents the Jury Never Saw* – often simply referred to as *The Documents* book. Generally the page number references from that book have been shown in the footnotes or endnotes in this volume.

Page numbers referenced to *The Documents* book relate to the UK edition. Readers who have the US edition of *The Documents* book will be able to locate the same excerpts within a few pages of the UK edition page number. For example, if the UK edition quote is from page 300, it will appear before page 310 in the US edition.

Extensive witness lists shown at the start of Part 1 have not been included in this book in an effort to save space. All witnesses mentioned in Part 5 have

---

[a] A simpler search, "Diana inquest transcripts", does not work. Also, this only works on Google, not Yahoo! The removal of the inquest website appears to be an attempt to cover up what has occurred by making it more difficult for members of the public to find the inquest transcripts. In this respect, it is significant that the RCJ failed to provide a redirection to the National Archives site – and despite repeated requests, still refuses to do so. It is also worth noting that the inquest transcripts can't be found by using the National Archives search engine. This was the situation through much of 2011 and into early 2012, when this book was written. Should the reader have difficulty locating the website using the method recommended, the following links may work:
http://webarchive.nationalarchives.gov.uk/20090607230718/http://www.scottbaker-inquests.gov.uk/
or:
http://webarchive.nationalarchives.gov.uk/20090607230252/http://www.scottbaker-inquests.gov.uk/ .
For those who still find themselves unable to locate the official inquest transcripts or wish to register a protest with the RCJ or the National Archives the phone numbers are: Royal Courts of Justice: +44 (0) 20 7947 6655; National Archives: +44 (0) 20 8876 3444.
[b] Now at the National Archives site – see address above.

been included in the index, and of course are also mentioned in the lists in Part 1.[a]

I have deliberately included verbatim inquest testimony in this book – it reveals the words of the witnesses themselves as they describe what they saw or heard.

Points to assist with the reading of *Diana Inquest* and accessing evidence:

Transcript quotes have been referenced through the book as follows:
Example:
Claude Garrec, Henri Paul's Closest Friend: 31 Jan 08: 124.15:
Hough: Q. Did he have any ambition to become the head of security?
A. No

Claude Garrec	= Witness name
Henri Paul's Closest Friend	= Witness' position or relevance
31 Jan 08	= Date of testimony at the inquest
124	= Page number – note that page numbers appear at the bottom of each page on the inquest website transcripts
15	= Line number on the page
Hough	= Lawyer doing the questioning – there is a list of lawyers and who they represent near the front of this book
Q	= Statement made by the lawyer or questioner
A	= Statement made by the witness or answerer

The inquest website[b] contains a large number of significant items of evidence: photos, documents, letters and so on. It is important to note that none of this evidence is stored in numerical or subject order – the easiest way to locate these items is by scrolling down the evidence list looking for the specific reference number you are seeking. The reference numbers, which always begin with the prefix code "INQ", will often be found in the footnotes or endnotes in this book.

In addition, the website has several interesting and useful videos that are available for viewing by the public. These are also not as easy to access as the transcripts. To reach the videos, click on "Evidence", then click on any date on the calendar, then scroll down or up until you come to an item of evidence that is obviously a video. When you click on that item, a page will open up that will give you access to all of the videos on the website.

Throughout this book underlining of words or phrases has been used as a means of emphasising certain points, unless otherwise stated.

---

[a] There are some additional "witnesses not heard" listed near the front of this volume.
[b] Now at the National Archives – see address above.

"Jury Didn't Hear" appears in bold before:
1) Any evidence that was not heard during the inquest
2) Written documents from the Coroner not seen by the jury.

"Jury Not Present" appears in bold before any statement made in court where the jury wasn't present.

There are several people who have provided invaluable support that has helped enable these volumes to be completed. Full acknowledgements are included in Part 1 and the final volume.

Word usage:

"Autopsy" and "post-mortem" are synonymous – "autopsy" is generally used in France, whereas "post-mortem" is generally used in the UK.

KP = Kensington Palace, Diana's home.

Sapeurs-Pompiers = Paris Fire Service

BAC = Blood Alcohol Concentration

"Cours la Reine", "Cours Albert 1er", "Avenue de New York" and "Voie Georges Pompidou" are all names for the same riverside expressway that runs into the Alma Tunnel. The parallel service road is also known as "Cours Albert 1er"

Fulham Mortuary = Hammersmith and Fulham Mortuary

Imperial College = Charing Cross Hospital[a]

MI6 = SIS = Secret Intelligence Service

MI5 = SS = Security Service

---

[a] Imperial College operates 5 hospitals in the area of West London, of which Charing Cross is one. Throughout this case the terms "Imperial College" and "Charing Cross Hospital" have been used interchangeably.

The Witnesses Not Heard

Parts 1, 2, 3 and 4 included lists of 221 witnesses not heard at the inquest. The following 36 witnesses should be added to that number, giving a new total of 257.[a]

Witness Name	Position or Relevance	French Investigation	British Investigation	Inquest
MI6-Related Evidence				
Sherard Cowper-Coles	Head of MI6 in France	Not interviewed	Not interviewed	No evidence heard
Cowper-Coles – Present in British Embassy 31 August 1997				
Valerie Caton	Head of Embassy Economic Dept	Not interviewed	Not interviewed	No evidence heard
Caton – Transferred into Paris in period prior to the crash				
Colin Roberts	MI6 Officer in Paris	Not interviewed	Not interviewed	No evidence heard
Caroline Copley	MI6 Officer in Paris	Not interviewed	1 statement	Statement only read out
Roberts, Copley – Paris-based MI6 officers at the time of the crash				
Nina Pillai	Rosa Monckton Contact	Not interviewed	Not interviewed	No evidence heard
Beatriz Flecha de Lima	Daughter of Lucia	Not interviewed	Not interviewed	No evidence heard
Pillai & Beatriz – Influential in introduction of Rosa to Lucia Flecha de Lima				

[a] Of the additional 36 listed here, 31 have never been officially interviewed or heard from. When added to the Parts 1 to 4 lists of 121, this gives a new total of 152. 4 others had previously given official statements or reports which were not read out at the inquest. When added to the Parts 1 to 4 lists of 55, this gives a new total of 59. There is one other who had excerpts of their report or statement only read at the inquest but should have been cross-examined. When added to the Parts 1 to 4 lists of 40, this gives a new total of 41.

DIANA INQUEST: WHO KILLED PRINCESS DIANA?

Witness Name	Position or Relevance	French Investigation	British Investigation	Inquest
Dominic Lawson	MI6 Agent & Rosa Monckton's Husband	Not interviewed	Not interviewed	No evidence heard
Lawson – Knowledge of Rosa Monckton's activities				
David Shayler	MI5 – Head of Libya Subsection	Not interviewed	1 statement	No evidence heard
Shayler – Made allegations of MI6 involvement in 1996 plot to assassinate Gaddafi				
Annie Machon	MI5 Officer & Shayler's Partner	Not interviewed	1 statement	No evidence heard
Machon – Close witness of events surrounding Shayler				
Anonymous MI6 Officer	Officer in Tunis Station Late-1995	Not interviewed	Not interviewed	No evidence heard
Tunis MI6 Officer – First contact with Tunworth regarding the Gaddafi Plot				
David Watson	MI6 Officer PT16/B	Not interviewed	Not interviewed	No evidence heard
Watson – Handled Tunworth and informed Shayler of the Gaddafi plot				
Richard Bartlett	MI6 Officer PT16	Not interviewed	Not interviewed	No evidence heard
Bartlett – Watson's direct line manager				
Jerry Mahoney	MI5 Officer G9A/1 to Dec 95	Not interviewed	Not interviewed	No evidence heard
Paul Slim	MI5 Officer G9A/1 after Dec 95	Not interviewed	Not interviewed	No evidence heard
Mahoney & Slim – Shayler's line managers; were briefed on Gaddafi plot developments				
MI6 Officer R/ME/C	Libyan Requirements Officer	Not interviewed	Not interviewed	No evidence heard
R/ME/C – Wrote up and despatched CX 95/53452 Report				

THE WITNESSES NOT HEARD

Witness Name	Position or Relevance	French Investigation	British Investigation	Inquest
Jackie Barker	MI5 Officer G9A/15	Not interviewed	Not interviewed	No evidence heard
Barker – Told of Gaddafi plot by Watson				
MI5 Officer G6A/5	Libyan Agent Handler	Not interviewed	Not interviewed	No evidence heard
MI5 Officer G6A/3	Libyan Agent Handler	Not interviewed	Not interviewed	No evidence heard
G6A/3 & G6A/5 – MI5 officers on recipient list for CX 95/53452 document				
Malcolm Rifkind	Foreign Secretary 1995 to 1997	Not interviewed	Not interviewed	No evidence heard
Rifkind – Gaddafi assassination plot occurred during his watch				
FCO Permanent Under-Secretary	CX 95/53452 Report Recipient	Not interviewed	Not interviewed	No evidence heard
Joint Intelligence Committee Head	CX 95/53452 Report Recipient	Not interviewed	Not interviewed	No evidence heard
FCO PUS & JIC Head – Both had prior knowledge of the Gaddafi assassination plot				
British Embassy				
Phil Whiteman	Security Manager	Not interviewed	Not interviewed	No evidence heard
Andrew Bishop	Security Manager	Not interviewed	Not interviewed	No evidence heard
Whiteman & Bishop – Responsible for Occurrence Logs, part of which have disappeared				
Keith Shannon	2nd Secretary Technology	Not interviewed	1 statement	No evidence heard
Shannon – Witness to embassy notification of crash				

DIANA INQUEST: WHO KILLED PRINCESS DIANA?

Witness Name	Position or Relevance	French Investigation	British Investigation	Inquest
Nicola Basselier	Asst Private Secretary to Massoni[a]	Not interviewed	Not interviewed	No evidence heard
Basselier – Massoni says she called Jay at about 12.50 a.m.				
Anonymous Male	Permanence, Elysée Palace	Not interviewed	Not interviewed	No evidence heard
Permanence – Called British Embassy at 1.10 a.m.				
Tim Livesey	Press Attaché	Not interviewed	1 statement	No evidence heard
Livesey – Made and received early post-crash phone calls				
Royal Issues				
Princess Anne	Diana's Ex-Sister-In-Law	Not interviewed	Not interviewed	No evidence heard
Prince Andrew	Diana's Ex-Brother-In-Law	Not interviewed	Not interviewed	No evidence heard
Prince Edward	Diana's Ex-Brother-In-Law	Not interviewed	Not interviewed	No evidence heard
Anne, Andrew, Edward – All attended Way Ahead Group meetings				
Michael Peat	Keeper of the Privy Purse	Not interviewed	Not interviewed	No evidence heard
Peat – Attended Way Ahead Group meetings				
Béatrice Humbert	Chief Nurse, La Pitié Hospital	Not interviewed	Not interviewed	No evidence heard
Humbert – Witnessed key events in the hospital				
British Government				
Anonymous FCO Officer	FCO Duty Officer	Not interviewed	Not interviewed	No evidence heard
FCO Officer – Made initial post-crash calls to Buckingham Palace and 10 Downing Street				

---

[a] Paris Prefect of Police.

THE WITNESSES NOT HEARD

Witness Name	Position or Relevance	French Investigation	British Investigation	Inquest
Nick Matthews	Downing St Duty Clerk	Not interviewed	Not interviewed	No evidence heard
Matthews – Witnessed crash notification times				
Tony Blair	British Prime Minister	Not interviewed	Not interviewed	No evidence heard
Blair – Had weekly meetings with the Queen				
Alistair Campbell	Blair's Press Officer	Not interviewed	Not interviewed	No evidence heard
Campbell – Close confidant of Tony Blair				

The Lawyers & Representation

Name[a]	Status	Representing
Ian Burnett	QC[b]	The Inquest
Ian Croxford	QC	President, Ritz Hotel
Tom de la Mare		President, Ritz Hotel
Henrietta Hill		Mohamed Al Fayed
Nicholas Hilliard		The Inquest
Richard Horwell	QC	Commissioner of Police
Jonathon Hough		The Inquest
Lee Hughes		The Inquest
Jeremy Johnson		SIS (MI6) & Foreign & Commonwealth Office
Richard Keen	QC	Henri Paul's Parents
Edmund Lawson	QC	Commissioner of Police
Jamie Lowther-Pinkerton		Princes William & Harry
Alison MacDonald		Mohamed Al Fayed
Duncan MacLeod		Commissioner of Police
Lady Sarah McCorquodale		Spencer Family
Michael Mansfield	QC	Mohamed Al Fayed
Martin Smith[c]		The Inquest
Robin Tam	QC	SIS (MI6) & Foreign & Commonwealth Office
Robert Weekes		Henri Paul's Parents

[a] Alphabetic Order
[b] Queen's Counsel
[c] Solicitor to the inquest

The Organisations

Abbreviation	Name	Definition or Function
BCA	Bureau Central des Accidents	Central Accident Bureau – French police
BJL	Hygeco or Bernard J. Lane	French embalming company – Subsidiary of PFG
	Brigade Criminelle	Department of French police dealing with murders, kidnappings and terrorism
BSC	British Security Coordination	North American branch of MI6 during WWII
CIA	Central Intelligence Agency	US Foreign Intelligence Service
DGSE	Direction Générale de la Securité	French Foreign Intelligence Service – French equivalent of MI6
DST	Directorate de Surveillance Territories	French Domestic Intelligence Service – French equivalent of MI5
	Elysée	Offices of the French Government
	Étoile Limousines	Provided chauffeured Mercedes to the Ritz as required
FBI	Federal Bureau of Investigation	Criminal investigative agency of the US Justice Department
FCO	Foreign & Commonwealth Office	UK Ministry of Foreign Affairs
FRU	Force Research Unit	British Military Intelligence Unit
GCHQ	Government Communications Headquarters	UK intelligence agency handling communications
IML	L'Institut Médico-Legal de Paris	Paris Institute of Forensic Medicine

Abbreviation	Name	Definition or Function
	Judicial Police	Department of French police dealing with judicial matters under direction of magistrates
LGC	Laboratory of the Government Chemist	Conducts chemical and DNA testing for the British Government
MI5	Security Service	British Domestic Intelligence Service
MI6[a] or SIS	Secret Intelligence Service	British Foreign Intelligence Service
MPS	Metropolitan Police Service	British Police – New Scotland Yard
NSA	National Security Agency	US Intelligence Service – handles communications
OCG	Organised Crime Group	MPS section dealing with terrorism, assassinations and organised crime
PFG	Pompes Funebres Generale	French Funeral Directors – Parent company of BJL
RG	Renseignements Généraux	Intelligence Gathering Arm of French Police – Equivalent to British "Special Branch"
SAMU	Service d'Aide Médicale d'Urgence	French Emergency Ambulance Service
	Sapeurs-Pompiers	Paris Fire Service
SB	Special Branch	Intelligence Arm of MPS[ba]

---

[a] MI stands for Military Intelligence.

[b] In March 2004 the British government outlined the close connection between Special Branch and the intelligence agencies, MI5 and MI6: "Special Branch exists primarily to acquire intelligence.... In particular, Special Branches assist the Security Service [MI5] in carrying out its statutory duties under the Security Service Act 1989 – namely the protection of national security.... Special Branch also supports the work of the Secret Intelligence Service (SIS) [MI6] in carrying out its statutory duties in support of national security....

"All intelligence about terrorism obtained by Special Branch is provided to the Security Service.... The Security Service sets the priorities for the gathering of counter terrorist and other national security intelligence by Special Branch....": Guidelines on Special Branch Work in the United Kingdom, Home Office, Communication Directorate, March 2004, pp8-9.

THE ORGANISATIONS

Abbreviation	Name	Definition or Function
SIS	See MI6	
SMUR[b]	Service Mobile d'Urgence et de Réanimation	French Emergency Ambulance Service
SOE	Special Operations Executive	Conducted sabotage and resistance during WWII[c]
TRL	Transport Research Laboratory	British Government agency concerned with road safety and accidents
WAG	Way Ahead Group	Policy discussion group of the royal family[d] – Inner circle of family members and key advisers

Special Branch was closely involved in the actions by authorities to suppress the evidence relating to the MI6 involvement in the 1996 plot to assassinate Muammar Gaddafi – see later in Chapter 1.

[a] In October 2006 Special Branch was merged with the Anti-Terrorist Branch forming Counter-Terrorism Command. According to the MPS website – in June 2011 – there are three commands under "Specialist Operations" – Protection, Counter-Terrorism and Security. "Intelligence" is one of four "strands" in the Counter-Terrorism Command. Sources: Sean O'Neill, Special Branch Absorbed into Counter-Terror Unit, The Times, 3 October 2006; www.met.police.uk/so/index.htm

[b] SMUR and SAMU are effectively the same organisation.

[c] After WWII the SOE was fused into MI6, becoming its Special Operations Branch.

[d] Chaired by the Queen.

Introduction

Who killed Princess Diana and Dodi Fayed?

Earlier volumes in this series have shown that the 31 August 1997 Paris crash that took their lives was no accident.

It was a premeditated, fully orchestrated event.

Diana did not die in the crash itself, but it has been shown[a] that later deliberate actions taken inside her SAMU ambulance culminated in her drawing her final breath six minutes after arriving at the hospital.

This evidence indicated that not only was the crash itself orchestrated, but also there was a medical-based back-up plan for just in case Diana survived it.

This then points to a highly organised and thorough operation. The complexity of the enterprise – as described in Parts 1 to 3 – indicates that this event was carried out by an organisation.

The assassination of Princess Diana was not the work of an individual[b] – it was instead a highly coordinated operation conducted by a well-resourced organisation or group.

The evidence has also shown us that whoever carried this out has done it with the support of – before the event, after the event, or both – the British and French police and governments. The French and British have both been clearly involved in the cover-up that has occurred – a cover-up that has taken the form of deeply flawed police and judicial investigations in both countries, culminating in a corrupt inquest conducted in the UK.

There would appear to be three main possibilities:

1) the assassination was carried out by an organisation, such as the royal family and household or the British government

2) the assassination was carried out by an organisation, such as MI6, working on behalf of orders from an individual or organisation, such as the Queen, the royal family, the British government

---

[a] In Part 2.

[b] Evidence in earlier volumes has revealed the coordinated involvement of several individuals who each fulfilled specific roles in the assassination and the initial cover-up – Henri Paul, Claude Roulet, James Andanson, Jean-Marc Martino, Arnaud Derossi. Dominique Lecomte, Gilbert Pépin, Jean Monceau. There were also unnamed players – the motorbike riders surrounding the Mercedes S280, the drivers of unidentified cars.

INTRODUCTION

3) the assassination was carried out by an organisation, such as MI6, or an independent group working within such an organisation, without orders from another individual or organisation.

The above possibilities need to be viewed in the light of the evidence relating to Possible Motives covered in the first section of Part 2.

That volume indicated that Princess Diana's high profile involvement in the anti-landmines movement may have been a significant factor in her premature death. This was supported by evidence in Part 3 that showed the incredible extent of French government involvement in the ensuing cover-up.

Part 4 revealed that the Queen took control of Diana's body immediately after her death. This action may have been to protect royal interests – it doesn't necessarily point to involvement by the Queen in events that occurred prior to the crash.

The following question demands an answer in this volume: Who killed Princess Diana and Dodi Fayed in Paris on 31 August 1997?

1   Was MI6 Involved?[a]

Coroner: Summing Up: 31 Mar 08: 10.15:
"There is no evidence that the Secret Intelligence Service or any other Government agency organised it."

If an order to assassinate Princess Diana had been made by a British authority, then it is likely they would use the Secret Intelligence Service, MI6, to carry out that act.[b]

Is there any evidence to indicate an involvement by MI6 – or other intelligence agencies – in the 31 August 1997 crash that took the lives of Princess Diana and Dodi Fayed?

---

[a] The primary focus is on MI6 – Britain's foreign intelligence service – but issues regarding other intelligence agencies are also covered in this chapter.

[b] MI6 would be used to carry out an assassination abroad – as happened with Diana. If there is a plan to assassinate a person in the UK, then it is more likely the domestic intelligence arm – MI5 – would be employed.

1A   MI6 Culture, Methods and Secret Operations

MI6 Culture

Secrecy and "Need to Know"

Secrecy of information is integral to operations conducted by MI6.
John Sawers, MI6 Chief, 2010, UK: 28 Oct 10 Public Speech:[a] **Jury Didn't Hear**:
"Secrecy is not a dirty word. Secrecy is not there as a cover-up. Secrecy plays a crucial part in keeping Britain safe and secure." [1]
Richard Dearlove, MI6 Director of Operations[b], 1994 to 1999, UK: 20 Feb 08: 26.23:
Burnett: Q. Is there a general approach to knowledge within the service that people only know what they need to know?
A. Well, the principle of "need to know" is applied throughout the organisation. Therefore your knowledge is compartmentalised in terms of the activity for which you are responsible, but of course the further up the service you go, the more you need to know what everyone else is doing.
Miss X, MI6 Administrator, UK: 26 Feb 08: 13.18:
Burnett: Q. Is that[c] because even though everyone in MI6 has developed vetting and is thus, one hopes, trustworthy, information is only accessible if you need to know it?
A. Absolutely. We operate on a terribly important "need to know" basis. So if I am in one area and somebody else is in another, even socially or anything else, we just don't discuss each other's work.
Coroner: The more people who know the information, the greater the risk there is –

---

[a] This speech – which was to the Society of Editors – was the first public speech ever made by a serving chief of MI6.
[b] Dearlove took over as Head of MI6 from 1999 to 2004.
[c] Referring to restrictions on access to information.

A. Absolutely.

Q. That there might just be an inadvertent slip of some sort?

A. Absolutely.

Coroner: And also the risks of perhaps putting two and two together from different places?

A. Yes, precisely, sir.

Comment: MI6 witnesses emphasised the importance of secrecy and restricting information on a "need to know" basis:

-   Dearlove: "the principle of 'need to know' is applied throughout the organisation"

-   Miss X: "we operate on a terribly important 'need to know' basis ... we just don't discuss each other's work".

Both Dearlove and X are talking about secrecy within MI6 itself – "throughout the organisation"; "each other's work".

I suggest that if MI6 apply such secrecy with their colleagues, then it seems likely they would be even less open in dealing with people outside of the MI6 organisation.[a]

This evidence indicates that if MI6 had any involvement in the Paris crash, then those outside of the organisation – particularly the general public – would not be included amongst those who "needed to know".

In other words, if MI6 assassinated Princess Diana, they are hardly going to admit it – particularly given their culture of secrecy.

This evidence also shows that if MI6 carried this out, then each person involved would have only known what they "needed to know".

This would help explain why a person like Henri Paul would carry out his role, even though it led to his death – the point being that he would not have known he was going to die. He may not have believed there was any risk at all to the Mercedes' occupants, if he had been only given "need to know" information.

It may be that other players – Claude Roulet particularly – had no idea that their actions would assist in bringing about the deaths of Princess Diana and Dodi Fayed.

Deniability

MI6 carry out operations that they can later deny involvement in.

Richard Tomlinson, Ex-MI6 Officer: 13 Feb 08: 90.2:

Mansfield: Q. Now, was [deniability] a concept that was discussed inside MI6?

A. Frequently, yes, making an operation deniable was always a consideration

---

[a] This also occurred at the inquest: real names of MI6 witnesses were provided to the coroner, but not to the jury investigating the deaths: 20 Feb 08: 1.7 and 26 Feb 08: 3.3.

so that, if things went wrong, you could plausibly demonstrate that the British Government had nothing to do with it.

Q. So it is not just a question of operating under cover, perhaps with a false cover; it is also operating in a way that nobody knows this is what you are doing and then, if it happens, denying that you have done it. That is what it comes to, doesn't it?

A. Yes.

Richard Dearlove, MI6 Director of Operations, 1994 to 1999, UK: 20 Feb 08: 116.6:

Mansfield: Q. Those concepts, "deniability", they are not culled out of the blue, are they, deniability?

A. Deniability of an operation carried out by SIS is a common concept which Tomlinson would have learned about on his training.

Q. What that involves – and he has given evidence about this last week – is this not right – is that ... the SIS themselves, as it were, don't dirty their own hands with tasks abroad. They employ an increment, do they not?

A. Can I cut to the quick, Mr Mansfield? I am not going to speculate on SIS's various operational capabilities. They are many and they are different and the court does not need to know about them. What the court does need to know is that all of these capabilities, every single one of them, were under my personal control as the chief of operations and subject to class 7 authorisations under the Act. So there are not any little offshore liars here that somehow do not fit into this pattern; they do not exist. Anything that is referred to, whether you have heard of it before or whether you have not heard of it before, whether it has a strange name or whether it has not got a strange name, was under the control of the director of operations. Let's be absolutely crystal clear about that and I think it is important that the jury understands that fact.

Q. Now, just going back to the question of deniability, the concept –

A. Some of these capabilities are, of course, deniable, but they are still under legal control. They still come under the Intelligence Services Act.

....Q. I am asking the question, starting in the tunnel, as to who was capable of causing a crash in the tunnel and then denying they had anything to do with it, which is why I am wanting to ask you about deniability. I want to ask this question, not at the official level but at any level; "deniability" means you can get in and out and deny what has happened, effectively?

A. But deniability is a basic concept of SIS activity –

Q. Yes.

A. – but under operational control and authorisation. It is just like secrecy, clandestinity. I do not think I can explain it any more than that.

At 162.13: Keen: Q. Tomlinson had disclosed that the document existed.[a] As Sir Richard said[b], there is the issue of deniability. Sometimes things are not capable of denial.

A. Deniability is not practised inside SIS or in SIS in relation to the Government, never, ever. That is a fundamental point of integrity. It is only practised in relation to its operations outside the Governmental context.

At 167.8: Mansfield: Q. Do you remember you gave an answer just before the break: "Deniability is not practised inside SIS or in SIS in relation to the Government, never, ever.... It is only practised in relation to its operations outside the Governmental context." What that means is you will deny it to everybody save members of your own service and the Government. Is that right?

A. No, that is not true.

Mr H, MI6 Direct Boss of Mr A[c], Balkans: 28 Feb 08: 133.16:

Mansfield: Q. Is there a policy of deniability within the department?

A. I think you already know that deniability is one of the techniques that we have as a service.

Q. Within the department?

Coroner: That is not very clearly put, Mr Mansfield. Sir Richard dealt with this. I mentioned the point yesterday. I think his evidence was to the effect that deniability to the world outside was one thing, but deniability inside was totally different and not acceptable.

Q. Quite. And that is why – You were aware of that, were you?

A. Absolutely.

Mr 6,[d] MI6 Officer. British Embassy, Paris: 29 Feb 08: 82.25:

Mansfield: Q. Was it part, this letter[e], of the culture of deniability?

A. I think deniability – and I know the various senses in which it has been bandied around during the process here – my understanding, what I mean when I talk about deniability, is our ability to act in a way in which other states will not know that we are doing it, but I do not accept that that means deniability in the context of internally, ie that you can deny things to one another or indeed that we deny things within Whitehall. So, the whole process of submissions is that this operation might be deniable, ie, we might want it to appear that we had not done it over here, but that is not the same as saying it would be invisible or deniable within Government. Within the UK

---

[a] Referring to a document related to the Milosevic assassination plot – this is covered later.

[b] Keen is addressing Baker here, then Dearlove answers.

[c] The role of A and H will be addressed later.

[d] It will later be shown that Mr 6 is Richard Spearman.

[e] Referring to a letter from the British Embassy to the French investigation into the crash.

Government, it would be seen and it would be recognised. So that is the split. It is an operational term of art, if you like, rather than a state of affairs.

Q. I appreciate that. It is a term of art, which would therefore mean that it would embrace denying it to a foreign Government, is that right?

A. It might.

Q. Yes?

A. And it would have to, if you think about that logically.

Stephen Dorril, Intelligence Consultant and Author: 2000 Book *MI6*: **Jury Didn't Hear**:

"A philosophy that ... was a particular hallmark of MI6 planning [is] plausible deniability. The use of third parties lessens the threat of any operation unravelling to reveal the hand of the sponsoring organisation." [2]

Comment: The evidence indicates that MI6 uses deniability, but not towards its own government. In other words, the indication is that if MI6 carried out an operation, then the UK government – if they asked – would be told about it.

The various witnesses have said:

- Tomlinson: "making an operation deniable was always a consideration"

- Dearlove: "deniability of an operation carried out by SIS is a common concept"

- Dearlove: "deniability is a basic concept of SIS activity"

- Dearlove: "deniability is ... only practised in relation to its operations outside the Governmental context"

- H: "deniability is one of the techniques that we have as a service"

- Mr 6: "deniability is our ability to act in a way in which other states will not know that we are doing it".

None of the witnesses denied that deniability is used by MI6.

There is a possible issue over who MI6 uses deniability against.

Dearlove is specific: "Deniability is not practised inside SIS[a] or in SIS in relation to the Government" and: "[Deniability] is only practised in relation to [MI6's] operations outside the Governmental context".

Yet when Mansfield restates this: "You will deny it to everybody save members of your own service and the Government", Dearlove replies: "No, that is not true" – but fails to explain why it is not true.

---

[a] This is supported by Mr 6: "I do not accept that that means deniability in the context of internally, ie that you can deny things to one another". There is an apparent conflict here with the principle of information – internally – supplied on a "need to know" basis (see earlier). I am suggesting that if a fellow MI6 colleague was asking about something he or she did not "need to know", then that could lead to deniability being used within the MI6 organisation.

H confirmed to Mansfield that "deniability to the world outside was one thing, but deniability inside was ... not acceptable".

6 confirmed that deniability "would embrace denying it to a foreign Government".

The general evidence then is that "deniability is a basic concept of SIS activity" and it involves carrying out operations that are deniable – i.e. difficult to trace to MI6 – then following the operation denying MI6 involvement to anyone outside of the UK government or MI6.

If one supposes for a moment that MI6 did carry out the assassination of Princess Diana, then how could we expect MI6 to conduct it, with regard to deniability?

There are two points:

1) Tomlinson said: "making an operation deniable was always a consideration". This indicates that deniability is part of the planning process.[a] This appears to point to the choice of the method used in carrying out an operation – choosing a method that is deniable.

In the case of Princess Diana: the decision to eliminate Diana in a car crash indicates deniability played a major role. An orchestrated car crash is extremely difficult to carry out – a lot of factors have to come together[b] – but it is very deniable.

Every day about 3,300 people die in road traffic accidents worldwide.[3c] When a person dies in a car crash, it is automatically presumed – unless proven otherwise – that it is an unfortunate and tragic accident.

Of all the forms of assassination, car crash may even be the most deniable.[de]

2) By definition, the MI6 culture of deniability means that if they are accused of carrying out an operation, they will deny it.[fa]

---

[a] I suggest this is also common sense.

[b] See Parts 1 to 3.

[c] This figure is based on an IRTAD (International Road Traffic and Accident Database) estimate from 2009 (see endnote) – the figure in 1997 would have been substantially higher than this. In 2008 there were 4,275 road deaths in France, whereas the equivalent toll in 2000 was 8,079. – and in 1990 there were 11,215 killed on French roads. Source: IRTAD Database, OECD Long-Term Trends, June 2010, www.internationaltransportforum.org/irtad

[d] There is a possibility – although it did not come up at the inquest – that the higher profile a target might be, the stronger the need to be able to deny MI6 involvement. This would fit with car crash being the chosen method to eliminate Diana.

[e] Former MI5 officer, Annie Machon, said in her 2005 book: "Vehicle 'accidents' are used as a way of assassination precisely because they are such a common cause of death.": Annie Machon, *Spies, Lies and Whistleblowers: MI5, MI6 and the Shayler Affair*, p215.

[f] Mr 6 supported this when he confirmed to Mansfield that deniability "would embrace denying it to a foreign Government".

If MI6 orchestrated the car crash that took out Diana and Dodi, they are hardly going to admit it to the outside world.

Accountability

Who does MI6 answer to?

Mr 6, MI6 Officer. British Embassy, Paris: 29 Feb 08: 77.9:

Mansfield: Q. You do agree that there is a need for accountability?
A. I do agree that there is a need for accountability, and again I can only talk to the years of experience that I have had within the organisation. The whole business of political submissions ... – which was going on long before we had the Intelligence Services Act in 1994, there was always a process by which, if you were undertaking an operation which – and before 1994 this was a political judgment about risk – you had to write it up and then get the Foreign Secretary to sign off on it. That is a process that has been in place for many, many years. Obviously, post the ISA[b], we have the statutory responsibilities ... we have the Intelligence Services Tribunal; we have the Parliamentary Oversight Committee; we have commissioners – we have a whole range of measures all in there designed to make sure we stay within the remit which we have been granted by the ISA.

Richard Tomlinson, Ex-MI6 Officer: 5 Apr 09 Interview: **Jury Didn't Hear**:

"I started to become aware of the substantial leeway for dishonesty that exists in the intelligence service.... Because there's no overall control at the very top, inevitably when people make a mistake, they're not held accountable for it – so their only accountability is ... how honest they are, if they're going to own up to making a mistake. That was one of the big faults of MI6. There was no overall accountability at the top. If the chief of MI6 wants to cover up for people below him, no one can go to him and hold him accountable for that. And that's one of the big ... problems at MI6, and that leads to a lot of their problems.... You can't sue MI6, no one can sue MI6.... It's like the police were 20 years ago, before the police were held accountable, and all the

---

[a] In his book, *Spycatcher*, Peter Wright indicated that MI6 will deny any operation not carried out by someone under the cover of the local British Embassy. In describing work done by his father, Maurice Wright, in Norway during WWI: "The MI6 station in the [British] Embassy [in Oslo] supplied him with communications and spare parts, but it was dangerous work.... He was not part of the diplomatic staff and would be denied if discovered.": *Spycatcher*, p9.
[b] Intelligence Services Act.

... injustices the police served upon the general public.... MI6 is still in that position, they're not held accountable at the very top....[a]

"If you wish to carry out ... a delicate operation ... it's only voluntary to put in a submission [to the foreign secretary]. There's no compulsion to put in a submission. If MI6 is absolutely convinced that it can carry something out without asking the foreign secretary – there's no possibility of him ever finding out – there's no compulsion for them to put it in....

"MI6 cannot be held accountable to the law. I can think of lots of examples of MI6 officers who, one way or another, have breached the law ... and they can never be held accountable for that. So that is the greatest failing of MI6. "They've tried to improve the accountability over the last 10, 15, 20 years and there is now what's called the ... Parliamentary Intelligence Security Committee who can make recommendations to the intelligence services but they can't order [them] to do anything or change anything. They can only recommend that they do so. So there is still a fair amount to go before MI6 is in the same degree of accountability to the government which any other intelligence service in the Western world is. Even the CIA is far more accountable to the American government than Britain's MI6 – also ... the Australian intelligence service, the NZ intelligence service, they're just streets ahead of MI6 in terms of legal accountability." [4]

Richard Tomlinson: 5 Apr 09 Interview: **Jury Didn't Hear**:
Regarding the situation if an MI6 officer has to provide evidence under oath at an inquest:
"He would know that he could never be held accountable to what he'd said. He could never be proven wrong or tried for perjury if what he'd said was wrong, because there's no way that MI6 would ever let him be hauled up in front of a court for perjury." [5]

Peter Heap, British Ambassador to Brazil, 1992 to 1995: 2003 Article: **Jury Didn't Hear**:
"Only very rarely ... is intelligence material subject to the same scrutiny, verification and testing as information governments receive from other sources. Naturally there are, by definition, genuine secrets in obtaining such material, but the whole process is wrapped around in an unnecessary aura of secrecy, mystery and danger that prevents those from outside the security services applying normal and rigorous judgments on what they produce. It is difficult to see why, for example, Sir Richard Dearlove, chief of MI6, should have given his evidence to the Hutton inquiry[b] by telephone. Everyone knows his name and what he does. Even his head office is probably

---

[a] Tomlinson outlines similar evidence on the MI6 Chief's lack of accountability in his book *The Big Breach,* pages 199 to 201.
[b] The inquiry into the circumstances surrounding the death of Ministry of Defence employee, David Kelly, on 18 July 2003.

not far behind the Houses of Parliament in its recognition factor. Yet the manner of his appearance merely enhances his mystique rather than protects national security." [6]

John Scarlett, MI6 Chief: Aug 09 BBC Interview: **Jury Didn't Hear**: "Our American allies know that we [MI6] are our own service, that we are here to work for the British interests and the United Kingdom. We are an independent service working to our own laws – nobody else's – and to our own values." [7]

Comment: Although Scarlett's aim is to distance UK methods from the US, he could also be talking about MI6 as an organisation when he says "we are an independent service working to our own laws".[a]

There was some focus at the inquest on MI6's accountability to the government and even the possibility of independent operations undertaken by rogue elements within MI6.

Although there is evidence pointing to a lack of accountability on the part of MI6[b], the later evidence will point to the majority of high-level assassination plots actually being undertaken with the blessing of – or even under the orders of – the government of the day. In those cases accountability – or actually, lack of accountability – is not an issue, because MI6 is fulfilling the wishes of the government.

The issue that then arises is the accountability of the British authorities – a) the government, and b) the Queen.

The answer to this might be, accountability to the people. In a modern democracy the government is accountable to the people and the judiciary. Parts 1 to 4[c] have already shown that in this particular case the judiciary have been shown to be corrupt.

The people make their judgement on the government at the next election. But if critical information is withheld from the people – for example, if the government were shown to be complicit in the assassination of Princess Diana – then the people have been prevented from being in a position to judge the government on their actions.

If the royal family is shown to be involved – for example, if Philip, Charles or the Queen gave the order to MI6 – then who are they accountable to?

At the inquest, even though some royals have been named as suspects, they were able to avoid producing any evidence – either by statement or

---

[a] Peter Wright was told in MI5 training in the 1950s: MI5's "work very often involves transgressing propriety or the law".: *Spycatcher*, p31.
[b] Tomlinson, Heap, Scarlett.
[c] And also later in this volume.

cross-examination. Nor have they ever been required to provide police statements in any of the investigations.

The significance and relevance of these issues will become clearer as this book progresses.

At this stage, I suggest that the issue may not be so much the accountability of MI6, which was addressed at the inquest, but instead the accountability of other organisations – the government, the royal family, the judiciary – and this was not addressed at the inquest.

Queen and Country

Richard Tomlinson, Ex-MI6 Officer: 13 Feb 08: 94.4:
Mansfield: Q. In relation to those days – and we are talking about the 1990s as opposed to since 2000 – if an MI5 officer – and if there is an objection, please say – if a MI5 officer or an MI6 officer felt that what was happening in the United Kingdom or elsewhere was [not] in[a] the interests of the United Kingdom and was subversive, undermining the state or the Monarchy, that might generate discussion about what to do about it, mightn't it, then?
A. I think that is possibly the case, yes. I think that is the case, yes.

Does MI6 Lie?

Does MI6 lie?
Richard Tomlinson, Ex-MI6 Officer: 2001 Book: **Jury Didn't Hear**:
"On Tuesday, 30 March 1909, a sub-committee of the Committee of Imperial Defence met in a closed session in Whitehall. Colonel James Edmonds was the first speaker. He was the head of MO5[b], the forerunner of today's MI5, whose job was to uncover foreign spies in Britain with his staff of two and a budget of £200 per year. Edmonds had ambitious plans and wanted to extend his service to spy abroad, primarily in Russia and Germany. But Lord Esher, the chairman of the committee, disbelieved Edmonds' tales of German spying successes in England and insisted that Edmonds prepare a detailed list of cases to back his arguments.
"Rather than back down, Edmonds ... fabricated evidence to support his case. He provided Esher with a fictional list of spies drawn from a contemporary best-selling novel, *Spies of the Kaiser* by William LeQueux. When Esher asked for corroboration of his evidence, Edmonds claimed that such revelations would compromise the security of his informants.... It was enough for Edmonds to win his argument and with it the budget to expand MO5 to form the Secret Service Bureau....

---

[a] The transcript reads "was in", but it probably should read: "was not in".
[b] MO5 ran the "Special Section" of the War Office.: Christopher Andrew, *Secret Service*, p88.

"Through both world wars the Secret Service Bureau survived and thrived, eventually being named MI6 in 1948."[8a]

Richard Tomlinson: 13 Feb 08: 49.24:

Mansfield: Q. You were given practical tests of how under cover in the United Kingdom you might pretend to be somebody other than you are in order to obtain information; is that right?

A. That is correct, yes.

Q. In other words ... you were being authorised to deceive people into providing you with material information, is that right?

A. You could certainly put it in those terms, yes. It was not put to us in those terms when we were training. We, at the time, believed that we were doing it for a good cause, but – yes, I suppose, you could use that word, exact word, yes.

Q. In other words, if it is considered to be in the national interest, it was permissible to deceive?

A. Yes.

Richard Tomlinson: 2001 Book: **Jury Didn't Hear**:

"The IONEC[b] was designed to train a recruit to a level of proficiency to step into a junior desk job in MI6.... 'Perfect Stranger' [was] the first of many increasingly complicated tests that were to form the backbone of the course. "Our brief was simple.... We were each assigned a pub in downtown Portsmouth in which we had to approach a member of the public and, using whatever cunning ruse we could invent, extract their name, address, date of birth, occupation and passport number. We were given an alias, but had to use our initiative to invent the rest of our fictional personality....

"I fabricated everything on the spot.... It was alarming that the art of deception came so easily and surprising how gullible strangers could be.... "[Afterwards] I climbed [back] into the minibus[c].... The others, some a bit tipsy, were elatedly describing how they conned innocent pub-goers into providing personal details....

"For a moment, sitting quietly in the back of the bus, I pondered the morality of my actions.... Was it right to dupe members of the public so casually? As we drove through the ... entry to ... our main base for the IONEC, I dismissed

---

[a] This account in Tomlinson's book – that organised British intelligence was set up as a result of lies and fiction – is supported in Christopher Andrew's book *Secret Service: The Making of the British Intelligence Community*, pp88-102 and Andrew Green's book *Writing the Great War: Sir James Edmonds and the Official Histories, 1915-1948 (Military History and Policy)*, pp31-33.

[b] Intelligence Officer's New Entry Course – the six month training program.: *The Big Breach*, p44.

[c] That had carried the MI6 trainees to the location.

such concerns. We were lying for Britain and that was sufficient justification. Unwittingly, I took the first step down the long path of indoctrination towards becoming an MI6 officer." [9]

Richard Tomlinson: 13 Feb 08: 115.6:

Mansfield: Q. Is there a department within MI6 or MI5 that is concerned with the production and dissemination of disinformation? Don't answer for the moment. Of course, if the department is here, probably ...

Tam:[a] There are actually two problems with that question. One is relevance, which is not apparent to us, but there is also an objection because this is going to – well, I can see what the allegation is going to be that follows on from it and it would be exploring a part and a mechanism of how the intelligence agencies do their work, and that is crossing the line there.

Coroner: I am pretty doubtful about its relevance anyway. You might try it again with Sir John Dearlove[b] next week.

Q. Well, I give due warning. I will want to try it again. I will not deal with it with this witness.

Miss X, MI6 Administrator, UK: 26 Feb 08: 80.24:

Mansfield: Q. You did approach this with an open mind, did you, this whole matter of research?

A. Yes, I did.

Q. Because all sorts of people may be telling taradiddles, mightn't they?

A. I am sorry, may be telling ...?

Q. I am sorry, it is an old-fashioned phrase. Maybe a phrase which I know is familiar in the service, "economic with the truth". People may do that, may they not?

A. Not to the best of my knowledge.

Gerald Posner, Investigative Writer and Journalist, USA: 28 Feb 08: 182.15: "In my dealings with intelligence agencies, primarily here in the United States, they will often obfuscate, lie, hold back information, refuse to release it until they are absolutely forced to years or decades down the road. They are their own worst enemies in providing information to the public. They create the fodder and the groundwork for conspiracy theories because they hold on to information and people believe they have something to hold on to because they have a secret or they are lying."

Coroner: Summing Up: 31 Mar 08: 64.2:

"[Tomlinson] says he finds the idea of a document containing A's proposal[c] being destroyed as completely unbelievable. He thinks it was destroyed when the Stevens inquiry began and MI6 realised they would have to disclose it.

---

[a] MI6 lawyer, Robin Tam.
[b] This should be Richard Dearlove.
[c] This is addressed later.

Members of the jury, if that were right, then every MI6 witness who gave evidence lied to you."
Comment: Does MI6 lie?

It seems logical that the self-admitted concept of deniability – which includes MI6 denying they were responsible for events they were responsible for – indicates that MI6 must lie.

I suggest it is no coincidence that the very first test MI6 trainees underwent was one that was focused on each individual being required to explicitly deceive unsuspecting members of the public.[a] This could have been designed to set the scene for each recruit's future in the organisation.

When Mansfield wanted to address the issue of disinformation – information which is intended to mislead[b] – he is prevented from doing so, by Tam and Baker.

Both claim lack of relevance – Baker: "I am pretty doubtful about its relevance" – yet I suggest its relevance to this case is obvious. If MI6 carried out the assassination of Diana, the question is: Has MI6 provided post-crash disinformation to distance itself from the crash?

Mansfield expressed a clear interest in addressing this issue: "I give due warning – I will want to try it again". Yet that did not happen.

Why? Did Baker – "I am pretty doubtful about its relevance" – prevent Mansfield from doing so?

This issue of disinformation was never raised again in the remaining two months of the inquest.

The fact that Tam intervened at that point in the cross-examination appears to indicate that there may be "a department within MI6 or MI5 that is concerned with the production and dissemination of disinformation".

If no such department existed then I suggest that Tam would have left the question to be answered.

Conclusion

Both past and present officers of MI6 have spoken:
-    Sawers: "secrecy plays a crucial part in keeping Britain safe and secure"
-    Dearlove: "the principle of 'need to know' is applied throughout the organisation"
-    X: "we operate on a terribly important 'need to know' basis"
-    Tomlinson: "if it is considered to be in the national interest, it was permissible to deceive" – confirmed to Mansfield

---

[a] Tomlinson.
[b] Oxford definition.

- Tomlinson: "making an operation deniable was always a consideration"
- Dearlove: "deniability is a basic concept of SIS activity"
- H: "deniability is one of the techniques that we have as a service"
- Spearman[a]: "deniability is our ability to act in a way in which other states will not know that we are doing it"
- Scarlett: "we are an independent service working to our own laws – nobody else's".

We end up with an organisation, MI6, that is – by its own admission – secretive, deceptive, dishonest and not accountable.

At the inquest, evidence was heard from ten MI6 officers – Dearlove, Spearman, A, E, H, I, X, 1, 4 and 5.[b]

The above evidence places serious question marks over the validity or honesty of the testimony provided by them.

Relationship with Official Investigations

MI6 have said that they opened up their files fully to the British police.
Miss X, MI6 Administrator, UK: 26 Feb 08: 41.23:
Burnett: Q. Were Lord Stevens' officers denied access to anything they wished to see?
A. No, they were not.
.... Q. Within SIS, did anyone else have unrestricted access to the whole of the information, electronic and paper, that is contained there?
A. Yes. Obviously – am I able to answer this in terms of – I can say the three most senior members of our organisation.
....Q. It is called what?
A. "God's access".
Q. So there is a very small number of people who have God's access to information within SIS. To enable proper searches to be made by you and by Paget, what arrangements were made?
A.... Rather unusually – and I do not think it happens very often – my director said, "Okay, fine, no problem, I will give you the accesses and you just show them everything that they would wish to look at".
Q. So essentially you got God's access too?
A. I got God's access and it bypassed the need to clear individual documents.
Paget Report, pp753-4: **Jury Didn't Hear**:
"In 2004 Operation Paget contacted the SIS, outlining the areas of interest to the inquiry and sought their assistance in answering specific questions. Claims had been made against the SIS, and individuals allegedly within it,

---

[a] Mr 6 – see later.
[b] See Witness list at beginning of Part 1. The evidence of these witnesses is addressed in this chapter.

but co-operation would be voluntary. The MPS had no grounds to coerce or force the SIS or individuals working for the organisation to provide information.

"The SIS had a meeting with the Operation Paget team, led by the then Commissioner of the Metropolitan Police Service, Sir John Stevens (now Lord Stevens.) At this meeting in 2004 the SIS offered full co-operation to Lord Stevens and two senior members of the team. They agreed to identify those individuals referred to in Richard Tomlinson's claims only by code, pseudonym or description.[a] Details of all SIS officers that had worked in Paris at the relevant time were also provided. All, still serving or retired, were subsequently made available for interview. The SIS also agreed to provide access to SIS databases, together with any supporting documentation, for independent search by Operation Paget officers having the necessary security clearance.

"The detail of who was interviewed, how the enquiries were undertaken, the security protocols put in place and the extent of searching SIS databases is held securely by Operation Paget....

"The nominated Operation Paget officers interviewed SIS personnel or examined databases and documentation for a total of 18 working days over a period of two months.

"The arrangements and protocols were also used at the Security Service (MI5). They offered the same assistance to Operation Paget even though there were no specific allegations or claims made against them. The Operation Paget officers undertook those enquiries in six working days over a period of six months."

Paget Report, p770: **Jury Didn't Hear**:

"Operation Paget officers have searched the databases at SIS Headquarters in London, having first acquired a good understanding of the databases and associated operating systems. Full access was enabled. Details of all current and historical databases were provided, including how the systems had developed and changed over time. As a part of this process Operation Paget officers interviewed an SIS IT system controller, focusing on the internal audit set-up of the systems and different databases. The Operation Paget officers are confident about the integrity of the results achieved from their interrogation of the databases."

Paget Report, p817: **Jury Didn't Hear**:

"There is no evidence that any SIS officer of any designation was involved in the events surrounding the crash in the Alma underpass."

---

[a] This could be a conflict with the claim that Paget was provided "full access" – see below.

Richard Tomlinson, Ex-MI6 Officer: 5 Apr 09 Interview: **Jury Didn't Hear**:

"I was absolutely amazed when the police investigating were ... allowed into the MI6 building and were allowed access to some of the files.... I very much doubt that the police were allowed unfettered access to everything they wanted to see. It's impossible really to know, but I can't imagine that the police were allowed to walk into any room in the whole of MI6 and walk up to any filing cabinet, open it up, and say 'I want to read that'. Very unlikely to my view." [10]

Comment: The evidence from X and Paget is consistent:
- X: "just show [Paget] everything that they would wish to look at"
- Paget: "full access was enabled".

The question is: If MI6 did the assassination, would they be telling Operation Paget?

There would appear to be three main possibilities:

1) MI6 did it but has lied – they told Paget that the files were completely opened up, but they weren't

2) MI6 did it, and there has been collusion between MI6 and Operation Paget. Paget know MI6 was involved but have pretended in their report that MI6 did not do it

3) MI6 didn't do it and both Paget and MI6 have told the truth.

Some of these issues won't be resolved until the evidence – yet to be covered – can be looked at as a whole.

Later evidence will reveal that neither MI6 nor the MPS[a] have been honest in their evidence and activities relating to this case.

Coroner: Summing Up: 31 Mar 08: 11.9:

"One reason, perhaps the reason, why the conspiracy has shifted from the original allegation that the Duke of Edinburgh was its mastermind is the unprecedented manner in which the Secret Intelligence Service and indeed others have been prepared to open their doors and give evidence about their inner workings. No longer can it be said, as Mohamed Al Fayed has frequently complained, that there was a steel wall that it was completely impossible to penetrate."

Comment: Scott Baker has misled the jury here on two counts:
- Mohamed Al Fayed has consistently alleged that the Duke of Edinburgh was behind the assassination and this did not change at the inquest – see below
- MI6 was actually quite secretive at the inquest and closed down several key avenues of questioning throughout the proceedings.

---

[a] MPS actions are addressed in Part 6. The 2007 book *Cover-Up of a Royal Murder: Hundreds of Errors in the Paget Report* has revealed that the MPS did not carry out an honest investigation into the crash.

Further than this, Baker has deftly linked the two points together – he has used the supposed openness of MI6 to remove any focus on Prince Philip as a possible suspect.

In other words, Baker has suggested that because MI6 have been so open, the allegation that Philip masterminded the assassination is no longer being put forward.

Baker is wrong on both points – MI6 was not open at the inquest (see later); Mohamed did not withdraw the allegation regarding Philip.

Mohamed Al Fayed: 18 Feb 08: 55.22:

Q. [In your 2005 statement] you say ... I think it is clear already that you would adhere to this view: "I am in no doubt whatsoever that my son and Princess Diana were murdered by the British security services on the orders of Prince Philip, Duke of Edinburgh." That remains your view and you have expanded upon it.

A. Definitely.[a]

Inquest "Housekeeping": 20 Mar 08: 7.12: **Jury Not Present**:

Mansfield: The last occasion the jury were here, on 18th March, this week, they came back in to court during the time that there was a question over what was happening in the Administrative Court.

Coroner: Yes.

Mansfield: ... There is a passage where you[b] say this: ".... Just to deal with this, Mr Mansfield, again so there is no doubt about it. The legal representatives of Mohamed Al Fayed made clear that there is no evidence to support an allegation that (a) the Duke of Edinburgh played any part in the deaths of Princess of Wales and Dodi Al Fayed and (b) that MI6 played any part likewise." Then I ask to defer the matter. The problem is – because I have the transcript – what had actually been said in court –

Coroner: I was putting to you the matter that the Divisional Court was asking whether that could be said in public and I raised the question that the word "direct" was missing.

Mansfield: I understand that.... The problem is ... that when the jury came back, those words were still on the screen and certainly at least one person noticed. They were certainly on our screens, unless it was not on their screens and Mr Smith cannot assure me that that is the case. In other words, that what we could read on our screens was on their screens and it was noticed that they were reading what was on their screens. Now, I am very concerned about that, irrespective of any decisions that you may make today in relation

---

[a] The involvement of Prince Philip was actually one of the central themes of Mohamed's inquest testimony.

[b] Mansfield is talking to Baker.

to verdict that they will read what is actually not an accurate ... reflection of what had been said.... We appreciate it is not on the website and it is not in the transcripts that they will be given. The problem does not lie there. It lies in the fact that it was on screen.

Coroner: Yes. I think the question is whether you want me to say anything to the jury about it at some point and if so, what.

Mansfield: I think in fact –

Coroner: Least said soonest mended is often the rule in these circumstances.

Mansfield: I would always agree with that. For example, when something is said in the press, you can probably overlook it these days. On the other hand, when it is part of an official transcript, it may have been of interest to them to read what may have just been said before they came back in.

Coroner: Summing Up: 1 Apr 08: 5.22:

"I ruled that ... the Duke of Edinburgh should not be called to give oral evidence to you in this court." [a]

Comment: At the inquest Mohamed confirmed to Burnett his assertion that "my son and Princess Diana were murdered ... on the orders of Prince Philip".

In fact, it was requested that Philip be subjected to cross-examination – this call was rejected by Baker: "I ruled that ... the Duke of Edinburgh should not be called". [b]

On the last day that the jury heard evidence – 18 March 2008 – the jury returned from a break to see on their transcript screens the following words spoken by Scott Baker: "The legal representatives of Mohamed Al Fayed made clear that there is no evidence to support an allegation that (a) the Duke of Edinburgh played any part in the deaths ... and (b) that MI6 played any part likewise."

Mansfield's reaction to this suspicious incident indicates that he did not agree with this – he states: "I am very concerned about that"; "[the jury] will read what is actually not an accurate ... reflection of what had been said".

It may not be a coincidence that Baker appears to resurrect this false perception in his Summing Up – see above – linking the openness of MI6 to a fictitious dropping of claims against Philip.

In doing this, Baker has misled his own jury.

Coroner: Summing Up: 31 Mar 08: 74.22:

"One of the consequences of an organisation operating largely in secret, as does MI6 and the other agencies, MI5 and GCHQ, is that it is inevitable that ill-informed speculation about their activities abounds. Yet, having seen the

---

[a] Despite preventing the jury from hearing any evidence from Philip, Baker told them, in his Summing Up: "There is no evidence that the Duke of Edinburgh ordered Diana's execution". Baker never explained how it was possible to know this, without hearing any evidence from the suspect – Prince Philip.

[b] This issue is readdressed in the chapter on The Royals.

way in which MI6 works through the evidence of Witness X, Dearlove and others, you will have gathered how far removed the reality is from the myth."

Comment: Baker admits that MI6 operates "largely in secret", but goes on to say that X and Dearlove have shown us "the way in which MI6 works".

But how open was the evidence from the MI6 officers? The excerpt below is an example of how much information Dearlove was prepared to divulge at the inquest.

Richard Dearlove, MI6 Director of Operations, 1994 to 1999, UK: 20 Feb 08: 140.5:

Mansfield: Q. The British security services abroad used paparazzi as a cover for gaining information about the movement of people they are interested in. There is a group – and I am going to give it, since it has been given in public – UK/N, to which such people are attached from time to time. Is there any truth in that?

A. There is no truth in the allegation that SIS use paparazzi and I have – that is, I am afraid, Tomlinson again elaborating. I am not going to talk to the court about what you refer to as "UK/N". It is another one of the capabilities to which I have made a general reference.... As it happens, in the context of this court, I am quite happy to say categorically that there is no link with paparazzi and that is an invention.

Q. But as far as UK/N is concerned, the group itself, are you prepared to say this – we have had it from another witness – that group does exist?

A. I am not going to confirm its existence or not. That is going down a route which I am not prepared to go down, but I have said to you that there are a variety of capabilities of different types, some of which you have vague references to, some of which you do not know about, and as I have said, all of these come under the control of the operational director.

Comment: Dearlove made comments such as:
- "I am not going to talk to the court about what you refer to as 'UK/N'"
- "I am not going to confirm its existence or not"
- "that is going down a route which I am not prepared to go down".

These remarks conflict with Baker's: "the Secret Intelligence Service ... have been prepared to open their doors and give evidence about their inner workings".

If MI6 were genuinely concerned about making information about their role available to the jury – but not the public – why didn't they give some of this evidence in closed court?

Instead what we see is Dearlove refusing to answer and several other cases – see later – of the MI6 lawyers shutting down potentially critical lines of questioning.

Coroner: 14 Feb 08: 1.4:

"Members of the jury, you may remember, when I opened this case to you last October, that I mentioned that the conclusions of [the] Paget inquiry ... were neither here nor there and that the facts are for you on the evidence that you hear in these inquests."

Comment: Operation Paget has told us that "full access was enabled" by MI6.

But when it comes to the inquest, full access is <u>not enabled</u>.

Baker tells us that the Paget conclusions are "neither here nor there". In other words it is the conclusions from the inquest that count – not Paget.[a]

This raises a separate issue: What is the point in holding a three year police inquiry[b], if the judge is then allowed to tell the jury to take no notice of it – it is "neither here nor there"? This is addressed in Part 6.

The question at the moment is: Why is Paget – which doesn't count – provided full access to MI6 files, but the inquest – which does count – is not provided full access?

And why does Baker say that MI6 "have been prepared to open their doors and give evidence about their inner workings", when that is not the case?

This evidence raises the possibility of a cover-up of evidence regarding MI6 at the inquest.

Statements that reveal the inquest was not afforded full access are:

- "I am not going to start answering questions about SIS training" – Dearlove: 20 Feb 08: 71.9
- "I think that [question] is probably edging closer to the area ..." – Miss X: 26 Feb 08: 146.21
- "the 'neither confirm nor deny' principle would apply there as well" – Tam: 26 Feb 08: 146.23
- "I am not going to speculate on SIS's various operational capabilities. They are many and they are different and the court does not need to know about them" – Dearlove: 20 Feb 08: 116.16
- "it would be exploring a part and a mechanism of how the intelligence agencies do their work, and that is crossing the line there"[c] – Tam: 13 Feb 08: 115.15.

---

[a] Soon after being designated coroner of the case, Baker removed the link to the Paget Report from the official inquest website.

[b] From January 2004 to December 2006.

[c] This is in conflict with Baker's false assertion – see above – that the inquest was provided "evidence about [the] inner workings" of MI6.

Richard Tomlinson's Affidavit

Tomlinson provided the following affidavit to the French investigation. **Richard Tomlinson**, Ex-MI6 Officer: 12 May 99 Affidavit: **Jury Didn't Hear**:

"I firmly believe that there exist documents held by the British Secret Intelligence Service (MI6) that would yield important new evidence into the cause and circumstances leading to the deaths of the Princess of Wales, Mr Dodi Al Fayed, and M. Henri Paul in Paris in August 1997.

"I was employed by MI6 between September 1991 and April 1995. During that time, I saw various documents that I believe would provide new evidence and new leads into the investigation into these deaths. I also heard various rumours – which though I was not able to see supporting documents – I am confident were based on solid fact....

"In Paris at the time of M. Paul's death, there were two relatively experienced but undeclared MI6 officers. The first was Mr Nicholas John Andrew Langman, born 1960. The second was Mr Richard David Spearman, again born in 1960. I firmly believe that either one or both of these officers will be well acquainted with M. Paul, and most probably also met M. Paul shortly before his death.

"I believe that either or both of these officers will have knowledge that will be of crucial importance in establishing the sequence of events leading up to the deaths of M. Paul, Dodi Al Fayed and the Princess of Wales. Mr Spearman in particular was an extremely well connected and influential officer, because he had been, prior to his appointment in Paris, the personal secretary to the Chief of MI6 Mr David Spedding. As such, he would have been privy to even the most confidential of MI6 operations. I believe that there may well be significance in the fact that Mr Spearman was posted to Paris in the month immediately before the deaths.

"In 1992, as the civil war in the former Yugoslavia became increasingly topical, I started to work primarily on operations in Serbia. During this time, I became acquainted with Dr Nicholas Bernard Frank Fishwick, born 1958, the MI6 officer who at the time was in charge of planning Balkan operations.

"During one meeting with Dr Fishwick, he casually showed to me a three-page document that on closer inspection turned out to be an outline plan to assassinate the Serbian leader President Slobodan Milosevic. The plan was fully typed, and attached to a yellow 'minute board'....

"Fishwick had annotated that the document be circulated to the following senior MI6 officers: Maurice Kendwrick-Piercey, then head of Balkan operations, John Ridde, then the security officer for Balkan operations, the SAS liaison officer to MI6 (designation MODA/SO, but I have forgotten his name), the head of the Eastern European Controllerate (then Richard Fletcher) and finally Alan Petty, the personal secretary to the then Chief of MI6, Colin McColl.

"This plan contained a political justification for the assassination of Milosevic, followed by three outline proposals on how to achieve this objective. I firmly believe that the third of these scenarios contained information that could be useful in establishing the causes of death of Henri Paul, the Princess of Wales, and Dodi Al Fayed. This third scenario suggested that Milosevic could be assassinated by causing his personal limousine to crash.

"Dr Fishwick proposed to arrange the crash in a tunnel, because the proximity of concrete close to the road would ensure that the crash would be sufficiently violent to cause death or serious injury, and would also reduce the possibility that there might be independent, casual witnesses. Dr Fishwick suggested that one way to cause the crash might be to disorientate the chauffeur using a strobe flash gun, a device which is occasionally deployed by special forces to, for example, disorientate helicopter pilots or terrorists, and about which MI6 officers are briefed about during their training.

"In short, this scenario bore remarkable similarities to the circumstances and witness accounts of the crash that killed the Princess of Wales, Dodi Al Fayed, and Henri Paul.

"I firmly believe that this document should be yielded by MI6 to the Judge investigating these deaths, and would provide further leads that he could follow.... [a]

"The lengths which MI6, the CIA and the DST have taken to deter me giving this evidence and subsequently to stop me talking about it, suggests that they have something to hide....

"Whatever MI6's role in the events leading to the death of the Princess of Wales, Dodi Al Fayed and Henri Paul, I am absolutely certain that there is substantial evidence in their files that would provide crucial evidence in establishing the exact causes of this tragedy. I believe that they have gone to considerable lengths to obstruct the course of justice by interfering with my freedom of speech and travel, and this in my view confirms my belief that they have something to hide. [b]

"I believe that the protection given to MI6 files under the Official Secrets Act

---

[a] During Tomlinson's inquest evidence Michael Mansfield read out the contents of a September 1998 letter (attached to a letter to his solicitor, John Wadham) from Tomlinson, that was in the possession of the MPS – see transcripts for 13 Feb 08: 83.16 to 92.25. The contents of that letter are similar to what is in Tomlinson's affidavit, except that the names of the recipients of A's proposal were not read out (due to MI6 secrecy at the inquest).

[b] The MI6 treatment of Tomlinson is addressed in a later footnote.

should be set aside in the public interest in uncovering once and for all the truth behind these dramatic and historically momentous events."

Does MI6 Frighten People?

Michael Mansfield, lawyer for Mohamed Al Fayed, canvassed the possibility that the Paris crash was a result of an attempt to frighten.

Mansfield asked E if MI6 would deliberately frighten a target.

Mr E, MI6 Controller of Central and Eastern Europe: 29 Feb 08: 22.21:

Mansfield: Q. If an officer perceives a threat ... in other words identifies a potential threat in his area of work and then conceives of a way of nullifying the threat, which may stretch from the ultimate, in other words, annihilation, to nullification, in other words, you nullify not by killing, but by frightening, shocking or doing something else; do you follow? It is that range. That is all entirely appropriate thinking for an operative at that time, isn't it?

A. Yes, I would have to qualify that by saying one would have to see the detail in such a proposal, but short of saying – asking that as a caveat, my answer, I would say, yes, a broad spread of imaginative ideas.

Coroner: There are lots of ways of getting rid of a threat apart from killing an individual.

A. Indeed, sir.

Coroner: For example, you could stop up the information getting to the threat.

A. Indeed.

Q. Or you could give the threat such a shock that the threat goes away; you could frighten the person –

Coroner: Where is this getting us, Mr Mansfield?

Q. I will put it precisely. One of the possibilities – I have already floated it with another witness – is a plan or proposal that does not intend killing but does intend that the person who is, as it were, the target is frightened into withdrawing from a situation in the tunnel.... These would have been entirely within the scope of the thinking of operatives who were being creative at the time; do you agree?

A. Again, with the caveat that one would have to see the whole proposal. I think to talk in generalities of this nature about operational work is very difficult, to give a generic "yes" or "no" answer. I think when you are dealing with intelligence operations or intelligence planning, the devil is really in the detail, and I would not want to give anybody in this room the idea that there was a sort of – you know, you could have –

Q. A licence?

A. – a licence to do any of these things. Thank you. That is the word I was looking for.

Coroner: Mr Mansfield, are you really suggesting that the collision was a plan to scare that went wrong and it was a plan that could have been orchestrated by somebody in MI6? Is that what you are really getting at? Because I think the witness ought to have a chance of dealing with reality rather than amorphous[a] speculation.

Q. I appreciate it is speculation. As you are aware, of course, we were not there. Mr Mohamed Al Fayed was not there. He was not a member of any of these organisations. What the jury will have to consider, looking at events in the tunnel first, is clearly whether it was an accident, and if it was not an accident – I take it in stages – then what was it and how could it have been organised and for what reason. There are a range of questions.

Coroner: They have to work on the basis of evidence, not speculation.[b]

Comment: The most significant aspect of this exchange between Mansfield, Baker and E might be E's initial response, apparently given without hesitation.

Mansfield asked: "Frightening, shocking.... That is all entirely appropriate thinking for an operative ... isn't it?" E answers: "Yes, ... [but] one would have to see the detail in such a proposal".

Baker apparently was not comfortable with E's answer. It does not fit at all with Baker's Summing Up description of MI6's activities: "national security, the economic well-being of the United Kingdom and the prevention or detection of serious crime"[11] – so he intervenes.

Baker comes up with "[stopping] up the information getting to the threat" to "[get] rid of a threat" – this is despite E already acknowledging that in certain circumstances they would frighten or shock the target.

Mansfield then reintroduces the words "shock" and "frighten", but instead of letting E answer, Baker again doesn't even let Mansfield finish the question – Baker: "Where is this getting us, Mr Mansfield?"

Baker next suggests Mansfield is entering into "amorphous speculation".

The point here is that E – who is a senior MI6 officer – had already answered in the affirmative that MI6 would contemplate "frightening [and] shocking" a target in certain circumstances.

Since MI6 had clearly been alleged to be a prime suspect in the Paris crash, it was then a natural line of inquiry for Mansfield to ask questions to establish if MI6 would have considered frightening or shocking any of the occupants in the Mercedes S280.

The fact that Baker then intervened three times in this short period of cross-examination appeared to indicate he was neither comfortable with E's initial response nor Mansfield's subsequent line of questioning.

---

[a] "Without a definite shape or form" – Oxford.
[b] There is further discussion between Mansfield and Baker on this point – it starts on the inquest website at 25.19.

I suggest that Scott Baker should have left E to answer the questions that were raised.

The evidence from Part 2 – the mistreatment of Princess Diana inside the ambulance – indicates that the perpetrators of the crash were intent on murder, not just an attempt to frighten.

It is significant that Mansfield only introduced frightening the target as "one of the possibilities".

Later during E's cross-examination, MPS lawyer Richard Horwell took this scenario on board: "There has been an important statement this morning. We are moving away from a planned assassination, it seems, to a planned scare of occupants in a car." Horwell continued: "The suggestion now is that the Duke of Edinburgh ... orders that MI6 scares the occupants of a car in Paris that night".[12a]

Baker reinforced this false perception – that the allegation had changed from assassination to frightening – during his final Summing Up to the jury: "One thing that is not suggested is that Henri Paul was a knowing participant in a plot to kill or, as is now suggested, merely to injure or frighten Diana and Dodi."[13b]

Mansfield never did change the allegation – he had only ever introduced an attempt to frighten as "one of the possibilities".

In suggesting otherwise, both Horwell and Baker lied to the inquest.
John Scarlett, MI6 Chief: Aug 09 BBC Interview: **Jury Didn't Hear**: "Obviously a new recruit is always going to ask the question, 'Do we blackmail people, do we seek to compromise them, do we seek to put pressure on them?'
"No, is the answer."[14]

---

[a] This is looked at again in the later section on Independent Operations.

[b] In his Summing Up Baker also said: "It has been suggested to a number of witnesses that perhaps the intention was to do no more than frighten the occupants of the car." 31 Mar 08: 53.12. The use of the term "a number" can mean different things to different people, but Mansfield only canvassed the "frighten" possibility with two witnesses, E (see above) and Tomlinson (13 Feb 08: 94.16).

Does MI6 Murder People?[a]

Coroner: Summing Up: 31 Mar 08: 66.25:

"Do MI6 kill people?... Its concerns are national security, the economic well-being of the United Kingdom and the prevention or detection of serious crime."

At the inquest MI6 officers claimed that their organisation does not carry out assassinations.

Richard Tomlinson, Ex-MI6 Officer: 13 Feb 08: 74.6:

Coroner: Q. When you were trained by MI6[b], were you instructed that MI6 agents were required to operate within the restraints of the criminal law?

A. Yes, we were. We were advised that, yes, but at the same time there are various facets to that because when you are overseas, whether that is the case or not, which legal system you come under when you are overseas, and there was definitely, during our training, a sufficient amount of speculation within the group of officers who were training together that we would talk about it amongst ourselves, and we were never entirely sure if what we were being told was always strictly held to and accounted to. I do remember during my training programme another trainee specifically asked a question to a senior officer about whether MI6 do break the law or do kill people. The senior officer – and this was in one of the training talks that we were given – and the senior officer evaded the question and did not answer directly. His entire countenance and bearing towards this question was such that he did not want to answer it in any more detail. This led to a lot of speculation amongst us afterwards: "well, what is the case, do we keep always within the law or do we not?".... There were other occasions – I can remember talking to another senior officer and asking them about the death of someone in circumstances which were slightly odd. Again the answer was not direct – was not a direct, "Absolutely no way do we get involved in that sort of thing". It was an obfuscated answer.[c] So I think it is fair to say – I am sure now, and we are now in 2008, that MI6 is probably very, very accountable because the laws in

---

[a] This is not about the rights or wrongs of murder. In some cases it can be argued that a targeted assassination of a wayward dictator – e.g. Adolph Hitler, Robert Mugabe – could be a desirable outcome for society. The issue here is whether British intelligence has been involved in targeted assassination plots. At the inquest – see below – the general MI6 witness evidence was that they never entertained thoughts of assassination.

[b] In his book Tomlinson describes just nine trainees (including himself) present at his training sessions, which started in late 1991.: *The Big Breach*, pp44, 53.

[c] Obfuscate means "make something hard to understand" – Oxford.

accountability have been tightened and that is the case with the American intelligence agencies and other intelligence agencies, but I was there when there was a period of transition and I think there was a lack of clarity at the time.

At 184.21: Hilliard: Q. Do you remember that you said that during the training programme that another trainee, you said, had asked the question about "do we" meaning SIS, "act within the law or kill", and you said the person that that question was asked of evaded it and did not answer directly. Do you remember telling us that?

A. Yes.

Q. Tell me, was that in the new entrants course?

A. That is correct, yes.

Q. Was the person who was asked a DS; one of the directing staff? Is that what they are called?

A. No, it was – sorry, it was not one of the teaching staff. We had visiting officers from the head office who would come down and give us lectures on all sorts of things, regularly. Look, I cannot remember the name of the person.

Q. It is all right.

A. I remember more discussing it with colleagues in the bar afterwards and we were sort of mildly uncomfortable with the idea that the question had not been answered directly.

Q. As you say, the person evaded it and did not answer it directly. The reason I ask is just that there is a passage in *I Spy*[a] – do you remember, the draft that I was asking you about, it must seem like hours ago, this morning –

A. Indeed, yes.

Q. – in which you explained that you had been on this new entrants' course. I think it must be the one that you are telling me about, and you said that the question was "Did SIS ever assassinate a peacetime target?" You said, "Nobody quite dared to ask in front of the other students", but that then one evening at the Fort bar – because you explain in your book this place was called the Fort – when nobody else was listening, you had asked about it. You said that you were given the answer: "'Absolutely not, never.' [He] replied." I will leave the name out: "His face puckered with sincerity and severity." Now, I do not know, is your memory playing tricks because "Absolutely not, never" is –

A. No. I do remember another officer saying quite definitely that they did not, yes. Yes, so there were two conflicting opinions there.

---

[a] This was the title of an early draft of Tomlinson's book, which was later published as *The Big Breach* – see Bibliography.

Q. Did you put anything in your book about the person who evaded the question?

A. I do not think I did, from memory, no.

Richard Tomlinson: 2001 Book: **Jury Heard Part Only**:

"Has MI6 ever assassinated a peacetime target? It was a question that a few of us sometimes discussed on the IONEC[a] but nobody quite dared to ask one of the DS[b] in class. It was a taboo subject, left unsaid by the DS and unasked by the students. One evening down in the Fort bar, when nobody else was listening and after several pints of beer, I asked Ball[c] about it. 'Absolutely not, never,' he replied, his face puckered with sincerity. I was not very sure, however, as he had already proved himself a convincing liar. In any case, if an assassination were plotted, only a tiny handful of officers would know about it and even if Ball were one he would not make a lowly IONEC student privy to such sensitive information."[15de]

---

[a] Intelligence Officer's New Entry Course.

[b] Directing Staff.

[c] Jonathan Ball, who was the principal teacher during Tomlinson's training.: *The Big Breach*, p45.

[d] Hilliard said that he was quoting from a draft of Tomlinson's book, but there is no reason to suggest that it would differ substantially from the final version, shown here. There appears to be key information in the book account that Hilliard may have deliberately neglected to remind Tomlinson of, during this period of cross-examination: a) Tomlinson says in his book that the question was asked "after several pints of beer"; b) Tomlinson wrote that Ball – the person he questioned – "had already proved himself a convincing liar"; c) Tomlinson wrote: "if an assassination were plotted, only a tiny handful of officers would know about it"; d) Tomlinson wrote: "Ball ... would not make a lowly ... student privy to such sensitive information". None of these four points were included in Hilliard's account of Tomlinson's book and they all detract from the credibility of the answer – "Absolutely not, never" – that Tomlinson received from Ball.

[e] There is an apparent conflict in Richard Tomlinson's evidence: at the inquest he said he remembered "another trainee specifically asked a question ... about whether MI6 do ... kill people ... in one of the training talks that we were given". Yet it his 2001 book, Tomlinson said: ""Has MI6 ever assassinated a peacetime target?... Nobody quite dared to ask one of the DS in class. It was a taboo subject, left unsaid by the DS and unasked by the students". There are a couple of differences – the question in the book is very specific about assassinating a peacetime target, whereas at the inquest the topic described by Tomlinson was more general: "whether MI6 do break the law or do kill people"; in the book Tomlinson specifically says the students didn't dare to ask the DS, the directing staff, but at the inquest the question was asked of someone who was not DS: "not one of the teaching staff – we had visiting officers from the head office". Tomlinson was not asked to clarify this conflict, but I suggest it is possible that students could be afraid to ask teachers about assassinating peacetime targets, but still feel able to ask a more general question about killing people.

Richard Dearlove, MI6 Director of Operations, 1994 to 1999, UK: 20 Feb 08: 19.25:

Burnett: Q. The Secretary of State – that is to say the Foreign Secretary – can personally grant an authorisation so that acts which might otherwise be unlawful can be rendered lawful?

A. That is precisely the case, yes.

At 27.20: Q. During the whole of your time, Sir Richard, with SIS, 1966 through to 2004, were you ever aware of the service assassinating anyone?

A. No, I was not.

At 70.7: Mansfield: Q. So are you saying that during their training, officers are clearly told that thoughts of assassination on behalf of the British Government are out of the question?

A. They are told that assassination is not part of the service's activities.

Q. I want to be clear: out of the question?

A. Not part of – well, that is your choice of words. I used a slightly different formulation.

Q. I am being very careful because, as we shall see when I come to various letters, the way things are worded in public is very careful, and if I may put it to you, sometimes weasel words are used so that unless you ask the right question, you don't get the answer. Do you follow what I am saying here? Do you follow that?

A. Yes.

Q. Right. Are the officers told that under no circumstances must assassination be considered, let alone carried out?

A. Again, those are your words, not mine.

Q. What is the answer?

A. That phrase might be used, yes.

Q. I am sorry? Might be used? Sir Richard, this is a very simple and initial question. The follow-up question is this: if you don't remember what they are told, is there a training manual for officers in the SIS?

A. I am not going to start answering questions about SIS training, which is rather specific.

Q. No, I have not even got to that and I am not even asking about method. I said that at the beginning. Is there a training manual? That is a very simple question.

A. There are training manuals, obviously.

Q. Given that it is not Government policy to even consider it[a], let alone carry it out, do any of the training manuals make that clear?

A. This would be made clear orally to trainee officers.

---

[a] Referring to assassination.

Q. So what is the answer to the question?

A. The answer that I have given you, that this would be made clear orally.

Q. You see, I am going to ask you the question again so that we may get a direct answer from you, Sir Richard. I will make it easier for you by actually indicating the answer in the question. Is it right to say that there is no training manual that indicates clearly in writing that contemplation or consideration of assassination, let alone its execution, is to be considered or whatever? Is that right?

A. I do not think there is a training manual in which this is written down, if that is what you are driving at.

....Q. What is in writing about the policies of assassination or no assassination that they will receive in writing? At the moment, the position is they get nothing in writing, is that right?

A. I think that is probably true, but I have been retired for four years.

Q. In your time, I mean.

A. In my time, I think I can say that they received nothing in writing.

Q. The reason I am asking you this is very particularly that Mr Tomlinson indicated that, in fact, when questions like this were raised during training, there was obfuscation and no real answer was given; in other words, they were not told that it was out of the question. Do you follow?

Coroner: Well, I think that is not precisely accurate of what his evidence was. I think he said that there were two occasions when this was raised, not perhaps in the training session itself but in the bar afterwards, and that on two occasions, he got a blank stare rather than an answer, or at least no answer, but there was another occasion when he said that he did ask the question and he got the firm answer that it was not on.

Q. He also used the word "obfuscation", so ...

Coroner: We can get the detail off the LiveNote transcript if necessary.

Q. Yes, I have them here. What I want to ask you is this: is that your recollection of the oral position, namely that there were no clear instructions being given during the oral training?

A. There are clear instructions given orally.

Q. That is your understanding, is it?

A. That is certainly my memory and understanding.

Q. How long is the training normally? How long was it at that time, just roughly speaking?

A. Months.

Q. A month?

A. Months, several months.

Miss X, MI6 Administrator, UK: 26 Feb 08: 80.4:

Mansfield: Q. When you typed in "Milosevic" and you got a fair amount of material, did any of the material relate to assassination?

A. I honestly – I hope this is not a difficult answer here – I honestly don't remember.

At 82.25: Q. Did you look, within the material headed "Milosevic", for anything that could be associated with the word "assassination"?

A. I do not believe I did, no.

Q. Why not?

A. Just speaking quite carefully here, but the – it became very apparent very early on that the name in question in connection with this particular idea was not Milosevic. So frankly I had an awful lot of other searches to do, so I concentrated my searches on the area surrounding not only the name of the person that did figure in the idea, but the other researches that the Paget team were going to need.

Coroner: But did you look at the material that was thrown up by the request "Milosevic"?

A. I looked at it as far as the carding of the name went and any hits that brought up, but I did not take it any further to carry out a file search, sir.

Coroner: When did you[a] look at it, to the extent that you did, what were you actually looking for?

A. In that instance, yes, I was looking for anything which might associate Milosevic with assassination or anything like that or anything that might have been – might have thrown up any information about that idea, yes. But I have to stress that that was a narrower search than it would have been if I had done a very big, full research job on it.

Q. Did the Paget team ever engage in this exercise that I am now asking about in relation to the name "Milosevic" and any connection with assassination of any kind? Did the Paget team, in your presence, that you are aware of, ever do that?

A. Yes, we certainly discussed it.

Q. No. Sorry, the question was: did they ever do it, as far as you are aware?

A. I am wanting to be absolutely precise. I do recall that I had a card on that individual and I am pretty certain that we may have checked something, but I might have got that wrong. I definitely know that we had discussions about it and the way of looking into it and so on.

Q. You see we have a report. I do not have every document that they have. At the moment – I will be corrected – there does not appear to be a reference to a search under the name "Milosevic" and whether it did or did not produce anything. You see, I do not have a document to that effect so I am having to ask you obviously for your memory and I am sorry about that. So is the

---

[a] This probably should read: "When you did".

position really that you now don't know whether the search under the name "Milosevic" produced any reference to assassination or not? Is that fair?

A. As far as the initial carding papers, the papers related to the card that I searched, they had no reference to assassination.

Q. You know that, do you?

A. Yes, because I looked at those.

Q. You did? Because I started off with this question. You now say they did not. Is that what you are saying; that the Milosevic material you looked at on the cards did not have any reference to assassination?

A. No, it did not, but those are – as I am just wanting to absolutely make clear for the jury and you, sir, I did not do the widest possible search on that. I did not put them into our filing system, for example, and then go and physically check any files we might hold. I would not want anyone to think that it was that detailed.

At 138.6: Q. In 1997 and going back to 1993 and 1992, the time when Mr Tomlinson, as you have indicated, had his original training, was there a training manual?

A. We did not tend to have a composite manual as such, but we had lots of sort of – I do not know what you would call them, but just things on subjects. Do you know what I mean? So different lectures would be given and different booklets would be handed out, papers and so on.

Q. Was there one on the use of force or the threat of force abroad in pursuit of certain objectives?

A. I have never come across anything like that.

Q. No. So nothing was ever said in a document to anyone about the use of force?

A. No. Certainly to the best of my knowledge that is something we have always kind of soaked up as a kind of – I cannot think of the word I am looking for now, but, you know – I do not recall there being a lecture, "You will not go around killing people", but at the same time there were always discussions about that from a kind of morality/ethics point of view.

Q. So there were discussions about that between the person giving the lecture or the training session and those on the course?

A. Yes, and I think anybody else that students would care to ask. They come across a great many senior and junior people and anybody – they are quite at liberty to ask what people's views are on that.

Q. Were the views actually rather blurred – do you follow what I am putting – in other words there was not any clear line being put out on this issue?

A. You mean other than those laid down by Parliament and everything like that?

Q. Oh yes. I am talking about the soaking up. It is not in any written training document; you said that you soak it up. What did you soak up in these sessions?

A. Well, just the fact that we don't go around killing people. It is simply not done.

Q. It is simply not done?

A. No.

Q. So if somebody starts to think about it and suggests that it goes to the controllerate, that really would be exceptional, would it?

A. You know, it has never happened in my time, other than hearing about this.[a] It is an unusual way of doing things – you know, putting something forward like that would be unusual, highly, highly unusual, within the service. However, people are taught to think a little bit outside the box rather than –

Q. Right. "Thinking laterally" it has been called.

A. Thinking laterally, okay.

At 146.20: Keen: Q. Has that other person[b] since been assassinated, Miss X?

A. I think that is probably edging closer to the area –

Tam: Sir, I have thought about that for a moment because the "neither confirm nor deny" principle would apply there as well.

Coroner: Yes.

Tam: The name itself is sensitive. I think everyone here recognises that. If questions are asked about what has happened to that individual since, it could tend to identify him.

Coroner: Yes.

At 151.8: Q. An alleged plot to assassinate Colonel Gaddafi.... If there was a P file for that individual and a proposal for an assassination, presumably the P file would contain a record of that proposal?

A. If something like that had ever existed, yes, it would be on that file.

Q. So, again, that would be a simple way of checking whether or not, in fact, at the relevant time, the Secret Intelligence Service did advance such proposals beyond the wild imaginings of Mr A?

Coroner: This is not an issue in these inquests.

Mr A, aka Nicholas Fishwick[c], MI6 Head of Balkan Target Team: 26 Feb 08: 189.4:

Burnett: Q. If the whole ethos of SIS was against using assassination, how on earth did you come to make the proposal[d] in the first place?

A. It is true that the ethos of the service was against assassination, it is true that whenever you spoke to an experienced officer, then they would say that

---

[a] "This" being the Milosevic plot.

[b] Referring to the other person MI6 claim was the target – i.e. not Milosevic.

[c] Known as Mr A during the inquest but named in Richard Tomlinson's affidavit to the French investigation.

[d] The Milosevic proposal.

that is against the service's policy. The reason why I considered it was because I had been brought up and trained in a service that dealt with peaceful cold war, if I can use the phrase, spy games. Suddenly here I am confronted by a situation where we are dealing with a bloody civil war in the centre of Europe, where tens of thousands of innocent people are being killed. So it seemed to me appropriate that we should at least revisit that dictum of the services and see if we felt obliged to revise it in an exceptional case.

At 208.15: Mansfield: Q. Now, in relation to this proposal, would it be right that it is perfectly proper for you and for others working in a similar way in MI6, in the mid-1990s, to think – and the way it has been described – either laterally, creatively or outside the box. I think you understand all those phrases?

A. I do.

Q. You were expected to do that, weren't you?

A. Within obvious parameters, yes.

Q. Yes, but the parameters permitted you to think, where it was considered necessary by you, about the possible employment of force. Correct?

A. That was what I thought about, yes.

....Q. When you went on training, you had various training manuals given to you, didn't you?

A. No, we did not.

Q. You did not?

A. No.[a]

Q. Oh right. Well what were you told then – leaving aside the absence of written manuals, what were you told about the use of force on the training that you had?

A. Virtually nothing because the use of force did not figure in the training.

Q. But there were discussions, were there not, informally about whether in fact the use of force could be contemplated in some circumstances?

A. You are asking me, sir, about conversations that took place during my training course?

Q. That is right. At a very early stage. The witness this morning – so you understand the context here – was talking about this sort of thing not being written down – you say there were not any manuals anyway – but that she "soaked it up" during discussions, what the ambiance or the feeling of the service was towards certain concepts. So what I am suggesting is that

---

[a] Mr A later stated: "The training staff had different manuals..... So there were not, as far as I remember, manuals that were given to us. I have never been a training officer, but the training officers may have had manuals that they referred to.": 26 Feb 08: 210.13. This clarification may have been a result of A becoming aware that his evidence conflicted with others – Mansfield appeared to imply a conflict when he told A: "you say there were not any manuals anyway" (see below).

although nothing was said formally, informally the parameters were blurred a bit about whether in fact force would be used when it was thought to be necessary. Is that a fair observation?

A. I do not think it is completely fair, sir.... I actually do not recollect any conversations about the use of force that I had during my training course, which actually was about 25 years ago.

At 214.7: Q. When you first approached E before you wrote it[a] down for him for action, can you recall, what is it that you told him which prompted him to say, "Write it down"?

A. It is very difficult to recollect what it was that I said to him, but I think I said that I was worried about the possibility of this man taking power in Serbia or Yugoslavia and I think that we ought to think about having a contingency plan to assassinate this guy.

....Q. The one thing he does not do is say, "What a load of nonsense, you know that is against policy, don't even bother to think about it". He doesn't say any of that, does he?

A. He did not say that, no.

Mr H, aka Maurice Kendwrick-Piercey[b], MI6 Direct Boss of Nicholas Fishwick (Mr A), Balkans: 28 Feb 08: 115.7:

Burnett: Q. You were able to see that it was a proposal for a contingency plan for an assassination?

A. Yes.

Q. Was it obvious to you, without whatever E might have said, that such a thing was not to be countenanced?

A. Yes, absolutely.

Q. And why was it obvious to you?

A. It is against the ethos of the service. And I had grown up throughout my time in the service knowing, if you like, that this is the sort of thing we don't do. I do not even think I remembered the fact that we had had the House of Lords discussion about it. It was simply not done. So it was straightforward to me. There is one point in addition I might make which is, about three or four years earlier, I remember being in touch with our training department and going over and attending one of the lectures given by our head of training department to new entrants. This was very early on in the course. It must have been the first week. And he made it absolutely clear, clear to the new entrants, that assassination was something that we did not countenance. It was done in one sentence and moved on very quickly from there, we didn't

---

[a] The Milosevic proposal.
[b] Known as Mr H during the inquest but named in Richard Tomlinson's affidavit to the French investigation.

hang around on it, it was not a matter for discussion or debate. It was just stated.

Q. When did you join SIS?

A. In the 1970s.

Q. And in that time, since you joined in the 1970s, had you ever seen or heard of any other proposal that involved assassination?

A. Neither before nor, I know you haven't yet asked me – nor since.

At 137.20: Mansfield: Q. Now, on the training course, do you know what [Mr A] said about what was being said in relation to the "use of force", is how I put it to him?

A. Sorry, could you repeat that? On the training course –

Q. Yes. You have indicated in your statement and today that in fact assassination or the use of lethal force, however you put it, was explained from day one and everybody is very clear about it. Is that right?

A. I can only say about the time that I was there. I was there on a couple of occasions, in 1987 I think it was.

Q. Well, we have had two witnesses dealing with this. Tomlinson is one but I will leave him out of it. I am dealing with A, one of your staff. He told us that on the training course, one, he did not get a training manual but I leave that to one side; and when asked about the advice that he got on the use of force, he said "virtually nothing". Is he right?

A. Who said "virtually nothing"?

Q. A has said that on the training course virtually nothing was said about the use of force?

A. Are you asking me about my training course back in the 1970s?

Q. No. Not yours. He obviously went on one, I can't put to you exactly when he went on one, we have the dates, but it was later than that.

A. Sorry, I went on a training course in the 1970s.

Q. All right. It is obvious that you are not familiar with what training courses that he went on might have said?

A. That Witness A went on?

Q. Yes.

A. I was not there. It was his course, I am sorry.

At 156.18: Burnett: Q. My learned friend Mr Mansfield put to you an observation by Witness A that on his training course he was told virtually nothing about the use of force. You remember Mr Mansfield putting that to you?

A. Yes.

Q. Do you remember what Witness A went on to say, to explain the use of the words "virtually nothing"?

A. No, I do not, I am sorry.

Q. Let me see if I can jog your memory. He added: "Because the use of force did not figure in the training." Does that sound right, even at the time you were trained?

A. Most certainly, most certainly.

Mr E, aka Richard Fletcher[a], MI6 Controller of Central and Eastern Europe, 1992-94: 29 Feb 08: 7.13:

Burnett: Q. If Witness A had said to you orally, face to face, that he had a plan that involved assassinating somebody, would you have asked him to write it down?

A. If the word "assassination" had been used to me in those terms, absolutely not.... The whole idea of SIS being involved in targeted assassinations is repugnant to the ethos of the service and certainly repugnant to me personally.

.... Q. Now you have said that assassination is no part of the ethos of SIS and we have heard that from others. When did you join SIS, E?

A. 1968.

Q. In the time that you have been there, so, however long your service was – I do not need to ask you whether you are still there or not – but during your time there, are you aware of any assassination having been carried out?

A. Categorically no.

Q. Or any proposal that there be an assassination?

A. Categorically no.

Q. That being the case, it might be thought surprising that you have no memory of such a unique proposal having crossed your desk.

A. I cannot give an answer to that, other than to say it is probably surprising, but the fact is that I do not – I did not recall this. When I gave the statement to Lord Stevens' police inquiry, I did not recall the incident having happened then and I still don't. Of course, subsequently, all these different pieces of testimony have arrived, which puts in doubt the calibre of my memory, but it would be untruthful to say that what I have said on the record is anything other than the whole truth.

At 10.12: Mansfield: Q. Would you have a look at your statement, please?....: "Furthermore, I can say that I have never seen any proposal relating to any targeted assassination." That is put in very clear terms, isn't it?

A. Yes.

Q. And it is wrong.

A. In what way is it wrong?

....Q. It is one thing to say "I do not remember"; it is quite another to say "I have never seen". There is a difference, you will appreciate, isn't there?

A. Yes, but I have – I still have never seen – this was in relation to the time

---

[a] Known as Mr E during the inquest but named in Richard Tomlinson's affidavit to the French investigation.

of the inquiry and I have not seen anything put in front of me related to flashing lights and everything of that nature.

Mr I, aka Alan Petty[a], MI6 Chief Colin McColl's Private Secretary[b], 1992-93: 29 Feb 08: 30.2:

Burnett: Q. In your time in SIS, have you ever seen a proposal that involves assassination?

A. Never.

Q. To your knowledge, has any assassination during your period been carried out by SIS?

A. No.

Richard Tomlinson, Ex-MI6 Officer: 5 Apr 09 Interview: **Jury Didn't Hear**:

"The fact remains that they did actually put out a plan to assassinate this particular target[c].... I don't know everything that went on at MI6.... It does seem very likely that they've been involved in torturing as well.... It could well be that they are involved in assassinations and I wouldn't necessarily know about it."[16]

John Stevens, MPS Commissioner: 17 Apr 03 Stevens Enquiry Report on Northern Ireland: **Jury Didn't Hear**:

"I conclude there was collusion in both murders and the circumstances surrounding them. Collusion is evidenced in many ways. This ranges from the wilful failure to keep records, the absence of accountability, the withholding of intelligence and evidence through to the extreme of agents being involved in murder.

"The failure to keep records or the existence of contradictory accounts can often be perceived as evidence of concealment or malpractice. It limits the opportunity to rebut serious allegations. The absence of accountability allows the act or omissions of individuals to go undetected. The withholding of information impedes the prevention of crime and the arrest of suspects. The unlawful involvement of agents in murder implies that the security forces sanction killings."[17]

Gordon Thomas, Intelligence Author: 2010 Book *Inside British Intelligence*: **Jury Didn't Hear**:

In the 1950s, inside "the MI6 Registry was a copy of a CIA manual written by Dr Sidney Gottlieb, the director of the agency's Technical Services Division. Its 88 pages were titled 'Assassination Methods', and it was the first handbook for state-sponsored murder. It included a warning: 'Decisions and instructions should be confined to an absolute minimum of persons and

---

[a] Known as Mr I during the inquest but named in Richard Tomlinson's affidavit to the French investigation.

[b] Dorril describes Petty as McColl's assistant: *MI6*, p759.

[c] This is the target that at the inquest, and in his earlier affidavit, Tomlinson said was Milosevic.

ideally only one person will be involved, whose death provides positive advantages."'[18a]

David Cornwell[b], Ex-MI6 Officer: *Sunday Telegraph Seven* Interview: 29 Aug 10: **Jury Didn't Hear**:

"Certainly, we did very bad things. We did a lot of direct action. Assassinations. Although I was never involved. But there is a big difference in working for the West and working for a totalitarian state. I promise you that even when quite ruthless operations are being contemplated, the process of democratic consultation was still relatively intact and decent humanitarian instincts came into play."[19]

Nicholas Anderson[c], Former MI6 Officer: 2009 Book *NOC*: **Jury Didn't Hear**:

"I first joined SIS ... from the Royal Navy in 1973 following extensive training, I was originally assigned to the Special Political Action section ... [and was later] integrated into a ... secret sub-division ... externally known as "Operational Support Branch" ... which specialised in sabotage....

"We were institutional killers that undertook disruptive actions.... We made illegal entries across borders to perform dirty work....

"A licence to kill is known at SIS as 'supreme breach of law' [and] was written in the employment contract[d] as: 'In extreme situations ... laws may be disobeyed if said disobedience is deemed legitimate and in furtherance to the cause'....

"It slowly dawned on me that I was being employed by a criminal organisation – they believe they had the right to be above the law." [20]

---

[a] The CIA assassination manual is addressed in the later section on CIA involvement.

[b] Cornwell worked for British intelligence from 1950 (MI5 from 1952) and specifically for MI6 from 1960, retiring to pen novels in 1964. He writes spy thrillers under the pseudonym John le Carré.

[c] Pseudonym.

[d] This is in conflict with Richard Tomlinson who, discussing his dismissal from MI6, in a 2009 interview, said: "I was absolutely devastated when they ended my – well, they didn't end my contract, because I didn't even have a contract, we didn't have contracts". This may be because Tomlinson was employed in the 1990s – it is possible that MI6 did have a contract when Anderson commenced employment in 1973, but had dispensed with it by the early 1990s. Anderson appears to have provided a direct quote from within the employment contract. Source: Interview with Richard Tomlinson conducted by Paul Sparks at Arles, France on 5 April 2009.

Daphne Park, Ex-MI6 Officer:[a] 10 Aug 09 BBC Documentary Interview: **Jury Didn't Hear**:

"Well, there have been other times in my life where I have been involved in death, yes, but I can't talk about that." [21]

John Scarlett, MI6 Chief 2004 to 2009: Aug 09 BBC Interview: **Jury Didn't Hear**:

"This, the 'license to kill' issue. No, we do not. We do not have license to kill." [22]

Stephen Dorril, Intelligence Consultant and Author: 2000 Book *MI6*: **Jury Didn't Hear**:

"The modern conception of the world of the secret intelligence services and assassinations derives partly from the fictionalised activities of James Bond. The licensed-to-kill operative is the model for the secret service agent of the public's imagination. While this is a fantasy, the former naval intelligence and one-time MI6 asset Ian Fleming based the plots and details for his 007 books on incidents in his own life and information he picked up during his career in the secret world. However fantastic the story, there is always an element of truth in Bond...."[b]

---

[a] Daphne Park died on 24 March 2010, aged 88. She worked for British intelligence during WWII and at the conclusion of the war, took up employment with MI6, staying with them for 34 years, retiring in 1979.

[b] This is supported by John Pearson in his 1966 book on the life of Ian Fleming. Fleming worked in the Admiralty, including several years in Naval Intelligence, throughout WWII. During this time Fleming conducted secret missions for British intelligence: "A ... sophisticated little weapon that ... appealed to Fleming was a fountain pen which could eject a sizeable cloud of tear gas when you pressed the clip. He sometimes carried one with him. 'Of course, ' he explained to another member of NID [Naval Intelligence Division] 'you're not confined to tear gas. It will take a cyanide cartridge too, but naturally you don't fit one of those except on really dangerous missions.' The pen was kept loaded with tear gas on the off-chance of his meeting an enemy agent face to face.... His routine contacts with the undercover society of Special Operations made him an ex-officio member of the cloak-and-dagger world, where all this was rather taken for granted.

"Fleming ... seems to have become very much involved in spirit with the 'black' world of the Special Operations Executive. His brother Peter had ... been recruited by the SOE for special work in the Middle East....

"According to Fleming's close friend, Ivar Bryce, who was ... working for Sir William Stephenson [Head of SOE] 'Ian wrote out the charter for the American COI [Coordination of Information, forerunner of today's CIA] at General William Donovan's [Head of COI] request. He wrote it in long-hand in a room in the British Embassy and it took him just over two days.

"On leaving NID in December 1942 [Admiral] Godfrey acknowledged that Fleming 'had contributed very largely to the development and organisation of the Naval Intelligence Division during the war'." John Pearson, *The Life of Ian Fleming*, pp106,114-5,127,136.

"Just before the CIA's William Harvey, who had been presented to President Kennedy as the agency's own 'James Bond', began recruiting members of the Mafia to help organise assassination plots against Fidel Castro, Harvey queried MI5's technical officer, Peter Wright, on ideas. 'Have you thought of approaching [William] Stephenson[a]?' Wright enquired, 'A lot of the old-timers say he ran this kind of thing in New York during the war. Used some Italian, apparently, when there was no other way of sorting a German spy. Probably the Mafia.' It turns out that Wright was correct. Before he died in 1990, former BSC[b] officer H. Montgomery Hyde revealed on Channel Four's *After Dark* programme that the BSC had assassinated a German seaman who was operating as a spy in New York....

"The Special Operations Executive[c] (SOE) had an assassination capability that to some extent did correspond with a James Bond world. According to historian, M.R.D. Foot, 'SOE was the only body competent enough to fake an accident'. SOE operational head, Colin Gubbins, appears to 'have seen no particular objection to SOE being implicated in a political assassination'.... When SOE proposed assassinating an important German figure in the Middle East, Gubbins told the minister controlling SOE that there was 'really no need for him to know about such things'....

"According to Kenneth Younger, a minister of state for foreign affairs under Ernest Bevin in the late forties and a senior MI5 officer during the war, serious thought was given to the assassination of the Mufti of Jerusalem, the Indian nationalist leader Chandra Bose, and an unnamed Balkan monarch. These thoughts never proceeded beyond the planning stage because it was concluded that 'nothing would be gained by making martyrs of such people'.

"SOE's assassination capability was, apparently, officially closed down at the end of hostilities[d], but since elements of SOE were later subsumed within MI6 into the Special Operations Branch it is clearly possible that the relevant expertise did not go to waste. Assassination as a policy was openly discussed in the post-war years. Sponsored murder gangs operated among the exiles in

---

The COI started in 1941, the following year it became the OSS (Office of Strategic Services) which was replaced by the Central Intelligence Group in 1946 and finally became the CIA in 1947.

[a] Head of the BSC – British Security Coordination.

[b] British Security Coordination – a branch of MI6 set up in New York in 1940 to handle covert operations in North America during WWII.

[c] Special Operations Executive – an organisation established in 1940 to conduct operations involving sabotage and resistance. After WWII it became the "Special Operations Branch" of MI6.

[d] World War 2 – 1945.

the DP[a] camps in Germany and Austria. Many of these operatives, known as 'mechanics', were sponsored by the Allied intelligence services but their activities were always arm's-length operations. By 1950, the idea of assassination as a serious policy had been shelved, though within MI6 ... the concept was not dead. It was in the Middle East that MI6 seriously considered using it as an option." [23]

William Stephenson, Head of SOE: Quoted in 1966 Book: **Jury Didn't Hear**:

Describing an SOE training procedure: "One of the instructors I'd recruited was this top armed combat man with the Shanghai police.... We used to book him a room in a cheap downtown hotel in Toronto – nothing but a table and a chair and a single light bulb – and then we'd give the trainee the name of this hotel and the room number and say that the man staying there was a dangerous enemy agent who had to be destroyed. It would all be as realistic as possible – after all, this was exactly the sort of mission an agent might be called on to perform in the field – and we'd try to pressure him into thinking that it was a genuine killing. It was a test of nerve really, a test to decide whether he really was ruthless enough to kill a man when it came down to it.... The trainee would have his instructions and a normal police .38 revolver which he'd load himself. From then on we'd watch him to see exactly what he did – we even had a peep-hole through the wall into the hotel bedroom where the instructor was waiting. Now one of the tricks this instructor had picked up was the ability to dodge a bullet.... If you fired at him from five yards he knew how to divert you sufficiently for the shot to go wide. Extraordinary man." [24]

Annie Machon, ex-MI5 Officer: 2005 Book: **Jury Didn't Hear**:

"Under the 1994 Intelligence Services Act, the real James Bonds do have a licence to kill or immunity for criminal acts carried out abroad in the course of their work, provided they gain the permission of the Foreign Secretary." [25]

Intelligence Services Act 1994, s7: **Jury Didn't Hear**:

"Authorisation of Acts Outside the British Islands.

"If ... a person would be liable in the United Kingdom for any act done outside the British islands, he shall not be so liable if the act is one which is authorised to be done by ... the Secretary of State[b]...."

Criminal Justice (Terrorism and Conspiracy) Act 1998, s5: **Jury Didn't Hear**:

"England and Wales....

"Conspiracy to Commit Offences Outside the United Kingdom....

"Nothing in this section ... imposes criminal liability on any person acting on behalf of, or holding office under, the Crown."

---

[a] Displaced Person.
[b] Foreign Secretary.

Comment: At the inquest the issue wasn't just whether MI6 were involved in the assassination of Princess Diana and Dodi Fayed. MI6 officers actually claimed that they would never consider targeted killing of anyone under any circumstances.

Two issues are covered in the evidence:
a)   What MI6 trainees are told about the policy on assassination
b)   What actually happens in practice out in the field.

MI6 Training

During the cross-examinations a significant issue cropped up: Does MI6 give training manuals out to students? This is important because there is a critical difference between something in writing as opposed to verbal. A written training manual – if made available – could be used as documentary evidence. If the training is just oral then it can come down to just one witness' word against another's.

However, there was conflict on even this – whether MI6 has training manuals.

The witness evidence is:
-   Dearlove: "there are training manuals, obviously" – 20 Feb 08
-   Miss X: "we did not tend to have a composite manual as such.... Different booklets would be handed out, papers and so on" – 26 Feb 08
-   A: "we did not" have training manuals – 26 Feb 08.

So three witnesses and three completely different answers: Dearlove – manuals; X – booklets and papers; A – no manuals.

Why?

Is someone lying?

The subject was initially broached by Mansfield to Dearlove: "Is there a training manual for officers in the SIS?" Dearlove's response is fascinating: "I am not going to start answering questions about SIS training".

That type of answer indicates that this could be a sensitive question.

When Mansfield challenged this, Dearlove immediately submitted: "There are training manuals, obviously".

Well, no, it's apparently not obvious to X or A: "we did not ... have a ... manual"; "we did not" have manuals.

Although both X and A have conflicted with Dearlove's evidence, it is significant that Dearlove's first response was not to answer the question: "I am not going to start answering questions about SIS training".

Neither Tam – the MI6 lawyer – nor Baker came to Dearlove's defence. It may be that they didn't see the significance of the question. Mansfield applied pressure: "That is a very simple question". And Dearlove capitulated: "There are training manuals, obviously".

71

Back to the issue which led to the discussion on manuals: What are MI6 trainees told about the policy on assassination?

The general evidence – including Tomlinson – is that there was nothing on this subject in writing. When Tomlinson addresses this issue – on 3 occasions – each one is verbal, whether in a lecture session or in private (see below).

Tomlinson has indicated that there were conflicting answers from the MI6 trainers:

- "a question to a senior officer about whether MI6 do ... kill people.... The senior officer ... did not answer directly [and] ... he did not want to answer it in any more detail"

- "asking [a senior officer] about the death of someone in circumstances which were slightly odd. Again the answer was not direct.... It was an obfuscated answer"

- "the question was 'Did SIS ever assassinate a peacetime target?' ... You were given the answer: 'Absolutely not, never.'" – confirmed to Hilliard.

So, three different senior officers or trainers – two are evasive with indirect answers regarding whether MI6 kill people and the third gives a direct response that MI6 never "assassinate a peacetime target".

When Dearlove is asked by Mansfield if MI6 trainees "are clearly told that thoughts of assassination ... are out of the question", Dearlove himself answers evasively.

Mansfield never actually gets an answer – instead he is told:

- "they are told that assassination is not part of the service's activities"
- 'out of the question' "is your choice of words"
- 'under no circumstances' "are your words, not mine"
- "that phrase ['under no circumstances'] might be used"

Then this: "I am not going to start answering questions about SIS training", when asked: "Is there a training manual?" Then Dearlove does an about-flip: "There are training manuals, obviously".

After more of Dearlove's evasive to-ing and fro-ing – see above – Dearlove's position ends up as: a) "they received nothing in writing" regarding assassination; b) "there are clear instructions given orally" regarding assassination.

Reading through the cross-examination, one could argue that by that stage the jury may have been confused as to precisely what Dearlove's position was on this – and that may be how he wanted it.

The MI6 witnesses have said:

Dearlove: "they are told that assassination is not part of the service's activities"

Dearlove: "there are clear instructions given orally"

Miss X: "I do not recall there being a lecture [saying] 'You will not go around killing people'"

Miss X: "there were always discussions about that from a kind of morality/ethics point of view"

Miss X: I "soaked up ... that we don't go around killing people"

Mr A: "the use of force did not figure in the training"

Mr A: "I actually do not recollect any conversations about the use of force"

Mr H: "our head of training department to new entrants ... made it absolutely clear ... that assassination was something that we did not countenance.... It was not a matter for discussion or debate".

All witnesses – including Tomlinson – appear to agree that there is nothing put down in writing. I suggest that that in itself is a concern – if MI6 has such a clear policy against the use of force or assassination, why is it not prepared to put it in writing – so that new entrants would have that to refer to when familiarising themselves with MI6 policy?

The lack of a written document then leaves us with a comparison of witness evidence on what was verbally stated on this in training.

And again – as with the existence of training manuals (see above) – we see substantial conflict.

H and Dearlove tell of a clear instruction – H: "absolutely clear", "not a matter for discussion"; Dearlove: "clear instructions".

X says: "there were always discussions about that"; information was "soaked up".

A states that not only was there no mention of assassinations, but even "the use of force did not figure".

X has stated the opposite to both H and A – she says "there were always discussions", but H says it was "not a matter for discussion" and A did "not recollect any conversations".

When there are conflicts on very basic issues like this – as with the training manual accounts – it indicates there are people lying.

Is there an issue with the timing of witness experiences? In other words, did MI6's teaching techniques change over time? [a]

Dearlove's training would have been when he joined MI6 in 1966. From 1984 to 1987, he was deputy head of MI6's personnel department and in 1993 he was promoted to become the director of personnel and administration. The following year, 1994, Dearlove became Director of

---

[a] This is intimated by H to Mansfield – see above and below.

Operations until 1999, when he took over as MI6 Chief. He retired in 2004. From 1993 to 2004 Dearlove was a member of the MI6 board.[a]

This evidence indicates that Dearlove would have been aware of MI6's training policies – I suggest particularly issues like training regarding assassinations – around 1966, but also when he was involved with personnel from 1984 and later moved into very senior roles.

X joined MI6 in 1982 and had worked in administration for 25 years[b], initially as a personal assistant.[26] She may have undergone training in 1982 and possibly has had a broad knowledge of MI6 operations throughout her period of employment.[cd]

A stated that his training took place "about 25 years ago" – around 1983.

H said that he joined MI6 "in the 1970s", but also remembered "about three or four years earlier [than 1992[e]] I remember ... attending one of the lectures given by our head of training department to new entrants ... very early on in the course." H later clarified that this occurred in 1987.[f]

Dearlove and X are the two witnesses who would appear to have a more general knowledge of the training spanning over decades – Dearlove, initially in 1966 but later from 1984 to 2004; X, from 1982 to 2008.

H's knowledge relates to "the 1970s" and 1987. A's experience is limited to around 1983.

Neither Dearlove nor X have ever suggested that there were any changes at any point in the MI6 training on this issue. If there had been, considering the importance and relevance of the subject – assassination – one would have expected they should have said.

Given that Dearlove and X are referring to a similar period – the 80s through to the 00s – their evidence should be directly comparable.

They conflict.

Dearlove says there were "clear instructions". X says "there were always discussions about that" and information was "soaked up" – so not "clear instructions".

H and A also refer to a similar period – H refers to the 1970s, A to 1983, then H again to 1987. They also conflict with each other.

---

[a] Dearlove's background was covered on 20 Feb 08: 4.4 to 5.15.

[b] At the time of the inquest.

[c] X was involved in showing MI6 files to Operation Paget and at that time was given "God's access" to all files – see earlier.

[d] In her evidence, X said "there were always discussions about that" – as though she could have had experience of training sessions over a period, as a result of her role in administration.

[e] The year of A's assassination proposition – see later.

[f] "I was there [at the training sessions] on a couple of occasions, in 1987 I think it was".

H specifically recounts that in 1987 "our head of training department to new entrants ... made it absolutely clear ... that assassination was something that we did not countenance. It was done in one sentence and ... it was not a matter for discussion".

A says that around 1983 there was "virtually nothing" about the use of force "because the use of force did not figure in the training".

So, H recounts an "absolutely clear" statement on assassination, whereas A says that even "the use of force did not figure".

Either MI6 have regularly changed their policy on what they teach recruits, or we have MI6 witnesses lying under oath.

The general evidence from Dearlove and X indicates that the training policy is not something that changes on such a critical issue – otherwise one presumes they would have said.[a]

When this evidence is put together with the conflicting evidence on the training manuals, a picture is emerging of extremely inconsistent evidence between MI6 officers.

During Mansfield's cross-examination of Dearlove he stated that "Tomlinson indicated that ... when questions like this were raised during training, there was obfuscation and no real answer was given; in other words, they were not told that it was out of the question".

Baker immediately intervened saying: "Well, I think that is not precisely accurate of what [Tomlinson's] evidence was. I think he said that there were two occasions when this was raised, not perhaps in the training session itself but in the bar afterwards, and that on two occasions, he got a blank stare rather than an answer, or at least no answer, but there was another occasion when he said that he did ask the question and he got the firm answer that it was not on."

There are problems associated with Baker's intervention on this.

Tomlinson related three instances:

1) "another trainee specifically asked ... a senior officer about whether MI6 do break the law or do kill people.... This was in one of the training talks that we were given – and the senior officer evaded the question and did not answer directly. His entire countenance and bearing towards this question was such that he did not want to answer it in any more detail"

2) "I can remember talking to another senior officer and asking them about the death of someone in circumstances which were slightly odd. Again the answer was not direct.... – it was an obfuscated answer."

---

[a] The presumption is that Dearlove and X should have been trying to present a true overall picture to the court.

3) Described by Hilliard who quoted from Tomlinson's book: "You said that the question was 'Did SIS ever assassinate a peacetime target?' ... One evening at the Fort bar ... you had asked about it. You said that you were given the answer: "'Absolutely not, never,' [he] replied. His face puckered with sincerity and severity."

There are several issues:

a)   The circumstances of the question and answer.

Mansfield has specifically referred to Tomlinson's evidence regarding "when questions like this" – about assassination – "were raised during training". Mansfield doesn't specify whether this was actually in training sessions or after a class.

Baker has stated that the "two occasions when this was raised [were] not perhaps in the training session itself but in the bar afterwards" and then "another occasion" where Baker doesn't specify the circumstances, where Tomlinson "got the firm answer that [assassination] was not on".

This shows that Baker has switched the circumstances.

Tomlinson says the circumstances for instance 1 (above) was "this was in one of the training talks". For instance 2 he doesn't specify. Then instance 3 – where the answer was "Absolutely not, never." – was "at the Fort bar".

Baker has falsely stated that the first two were "in the bar afterwards" – even though the first was in a training session and the second is not specified – and Baker has then gone on to fail to specify the circumstances of the third instance, even though Tomlinson had stipulated it was in the bar.

In doing this, Baker has made out that the two cases when Tomlinson heard indefinite answers were in the bar – whereas the opposite is the case: only the time Tomlinson heard a definitive answer was in the bar.

b)   The nature of the answer.

Tomlinson has described the answers on the three occasions as follows: 1) "the senior officer evaded the question and did not answer directly. His entire countenance and bearing towards this question was such that he did not want to answer it in any more detail"; 2) the answer was not direct – was not a direct, 'Absolutely no way do we get involved in that sort of thing'. It was an obfuscated answer"; 3) "'Absolutely not, never.' [He] replied. His face puckered with sincerity and severity".

Baker has said "that on two occasions, [Tomlinson] got a blank stare rather than an answer, or at least no answer, but there was another occasion when he said that he did ask the question and he got the firm answer that it was not on".

Tomlinson has said that on the first two occasions the answer was not direct – "the senior officer ... did not answer directly"; "the answer was not direct".

Baker has said the first two occasions were in a bar (see above) and there was "no answer" – this implies silence.

Baker's description is again completely false – he says "no answer", when clearly Tomlinson described indirect answers on both occasions.

Baker correctly states that Tomlinson "got the firm answer that it was not on" on the third occasion, but he fails to state it was in the bar.

So Baker presents the jury with a situation where there was silence for the first two answers in the bar, then an unequivocal disowning of assassination on the third occasion, not in a bar.

The point here is that silence is completely different to an indirect, evasive or obfuscated answer. The latter indicates that there could be something being covered up – that assassinations could occur but the senior officer is not prepared to say so.

Silence, on the other hand, could mean anything. It is like the saying "It is better to remain silent and be thought a fool, than to open one's mouth and remove all doubt". No one knows what a person is thinking if they remain silent.

But whatever the silence in the bar meant, Baker then brings in the third occasion – by implication, not in a bar – to show that there was "the firm answer that it was not on".

Out of the three occasions Baker states there was only one answer: assassination is "not on".

But that is a fictional account of what Tomlinson actually said.

Baker's account of a "blank stare" from the senior officer on the first two occasions is also fictional. On the first occasion Tomlinson describes: "His entire countenance and bearing towards this question was such that he did not want to answer it in any more detail". Tomlinson does not describe facial features on the second occasion. On the third occasion – in the bar – Tomlinson recounts: "His face puckered with sincerity and severity".

c)   The circumstances of Baker's intervention.

Mansfield stated that he was addressing the occasions when the "questions ... were raised during training" – he doesn't deal with the incident in the bar.[a] Tomlinson doesn't specify the precise circumstances of the second occasion, but the context indicates it was a conversation he had with a senior officer around the time of his training. There is no mention of a bar.

Mansfield went on to describe the answers: "there was obfuscation and no real answer was given; in other words, they were not told that it was out of the question".

---

[a] One could argue that Mansfield should have included that one, but it did occur in the bar, and in Tomlinson's book – not heard by the jury – he said that it was "after several pints of beer" and that the officer who told him was "a convincing liar".

Tomlinson only uses the term "obfuscated" to describe the second occasion, but he said the answer on the first occasion was evasive and indirect. The word meanings are similar.[a]

Mansfield appears to have basically presented a truthful – albeit paraphrased and summarised – account of Tomlinson's evidence.

This raises the question: Why has Baker intervened – making out that Mansfield had misrepresented Tomlinson's evidence[b] – when Mansfield had not misrepresented it?

After falsely stating what Tomlinson "said", and Mansfield correctly insists Tomlinson "used the word 'obfuscation'"[c], Baker then goes on to say: "We can get the detail off the LiveNote[d] transcript if necessary".

Why didn't Baker look at the LiveNote <u>before</u> he recounted what Tomlinson had said, falsely contradicting Mansfield's account?

Mansfield indicates that he was already using the LiveNote transcripts – "Yes, I have them here".

H was asked by Burnett: "Why was it obvious to you" that assassination "was not to be countenanced?"

H answered the question: "it is against the ethos of the service" and "it was simply not done – so it was straightforward to me". But then H continued with unsolicited information that was not directly connected to the question: "There is one point in addition I might make which is, about three or four years earlier, I remember being in touch with our training department...."

This is where H provides his evidence – addressed above – about what was taught to new recruits about assassination: "assassination was something that we did not countenance – it was done in one sentence".

Why did H provide this unsolicited account?

It may be significant that H was the final MI6 witness to provide an account of what was taught during training – Dearlove was first on Wednesday, 20 February 2008; X was next on Tuesday, February 26; then A later on the same day, the 26th. H was heard two days later on Thursday, February 28.

The inquest was closed on Wednesday, 27 February 2008 – according to Baker this was because a jury member had to attend a family funeral.[27] It is possible that MI6 used this day off to review their evidence – if they did, they would have found that there were three conflicting accounts on what MI6 told trainees about assassination: Dearlove, X and A (see above).

---

[a] "Obfuscate" means "to make something hard to understand": Oxford.

[b] "That is not precisely accurate of what [Tomlinson's] evidence was".

[c] The actual word used by Tomlinson was "obfuscated".

[d] The LiveNote was the inquest transcripts, which the judge and lawyers had in front of them on computer screens during the inquest sessions.

I suggest that it is possible that H was given the job of "fixing" this by providing evidence that directly supported Dearlove's account – it also is the account that could be seen to show MI6 in the best light: trainees are told "assassination was something that we did not countenance", or as Dearlove put it, "they are told that assassination is not part of the service's activities".

What's possibly more significant is that this evidence from H supporting Dearlove's version is also directly contrary to the account put forward by Tomlinson:

a) Tomlinson said that "another trainee specifically asked" the question about killing people – this indicates that the issue hadn't been addressed by the lecturers.

H's account is that in "the first week [the head trainer] made it absolutely clear ... to the new entrants" about assassination. "It was done in one sentence and moved on very quickly.... It was just stated."

Tomlinson says the subject was broached by the trainee, whereas H says MI6 make it very clear very early on – therefore there would be no opening or need for a trainee to raise the subject.

b) Tomlinson says "the senior officer evaded the question and did not answer directly".

In contrast, H presents a picture of no hesitation at all – and he emphasises this in 6 different phrases:

- "he made it absolutely clear"
- "it was done in one sentence"
- he "moved on very quickly from there"
- "we didn't hang around on it"
- "it was not a matter for discussion or debate"
- "it was just stated".

Considering that this response was unsolicited (see above), such a degree of emphasis by H on this point is quite incredible. It runs directly counter to the evidence of Tomlinson.

Later Mansfield recounted to H the evidence A had provided about his MI6 training – "when asked about the advice that [A] got on the use of force, he said 'virtually nothing'". This directly conflicted with H's above evidence.

H – who was A's MI6 boss – then became evasive. H suddenly showed signs of either severe deafness, or acute distraction.

Initially Mansfield simply asked if H knew what A had testified about what was said in training regarding the use of force. H replied: "Sorry, could you repeat that?"

Before repeating it, Mansfield seeks to reclarify H's position: "You have indicated ... that ... assassination ... was explained from day one and everybody is very clear about it. Is that right?"

H now qualifies his earlier evidence: "I can only say about the time that I was there [at the training]. I was there on a couple of occasions, in 1987 I think it was."

H appears to have introduced this qualification – "I can only say about the time that I was there" – in direct response to Mansfield challenging him with A's account.

There is one problem with this: up to this point in the cross-examination Mansfield hasn't put A's account. All that's happened is that Mansfield has asked: "do you know what [A] said about ... use of force"?

And H had indicated he didn't hear that anyway: "Sorry, could you repeat that?"

H's qualification of his training account – "I can only say about the time that I was there" – indicates that not only did H actually hear Mansfield's question, but he also knew what A's training evidence was.

Mansfield then goes on to explain to H what A had testified – "when asked about the advice that he got on the use of force, he said 'virtually nothing'".

This time H again feigns deafness or distraction: "Who said 'virtually nothing'?"

Mansfield repeats the evidence from A.

Now H completely changes tack – it may be that he has suddenly realised that A's training may have been relatively close timewise to his own stated 1987 encounter.[a] H no longer talks about his 1987 experience – he asks Mansfield: "Are you asking me about my training course back in the 1970s?"

Mansfield replies: "No. Not yours." Mansfield is asking about A's course in the 1980s.

But H has found his way out of answering the question, so he now sticks to it: "Sorry, I went on a training course in the 1970s."

It's like H's evidence about attending training course lectures in 1987 has now evaporated into thin air. H's only experience now is "back in the 1970s".

Then H finishes off the issue with: "I was not there. It was [A's] course, I am sorry."

The next question was: What happens regarding assassination out in the field? This question is fully addressed in the remaining part of this chapter.

This issue is central to MI6's defence. They have said time and again at the inquest – see earlier – that MI6 has never gotten involved in, or contemplated, assassinations. That, in turn, leads to the natural conclusion that MI6 could not have been involved in the assassination of Princess Diana.

The following evidence of British intelligence assassination plots tells a different story. The events are shown in time order.

---

[a] Earlier evidence indicated that A's training could have been around 1983.

Heydrich Assassination: May 1942

William Stevenson[a], Author: 1976 Book *A Man Called Intrepid*: **Jury Didn't Hear**:

"Plans for the assassination of ... [Reinhard] Heydrich were begun in New York at the beginning of August 1941....

"An order by Reich Commissioner for Jewish Affairs, Hermann Göring ... instructed Heydrich 'to ... make all ... preparations for a comprehensive solution of the Jewish question'....

"The specialists called to a [BSC[b]] conference in Room 3553 knew nothing of the order.... Papers and drawings were distributed singly.... It was the job of ... Captain Herbert Rowland to make sure they did not compare notes....

"Josef Gabcik and Jan Kubris were two of the agents selected to kill Heydrich..... Gabcik carried a Sten under the raincoat draped over his arm as he stood waiting at the hairpin bend outside Prague on the morning of May 27 [1942]. Kubris had a grenade in the deep poacher's pocket of his jacket. One hundred yards away ... stood a third man known as Valcik. And another two hundred yards farther on, the man called Jemelik waited on the opposite side of the road. He would be the first to see the open green Mercedes in which the Protector [Heydrich] rode to his office.... The four agents had parachuted [in] near the Polish border....

"At 10.25 [a.m.] Gabcik heard four sharp whistles – H in Morse code – the signal. A moment later an open Mercedes swept down the hill.... Gabcik dropped his coat.... He brought up the Sten and squeezed the trigger. Nothing happened.... The ... streetcar rattled into the bend. Kubris, seeing his companion trying to clear the Sten, tossed his grenade against the side of the ... car. There was an explosion. Out of the billowing smoke emerged Heydrich, vaulting over the stuck door, firing at the assassins.... They began to run.

"Heydrich staggered to the sidewalk.... An hour later, Heydrich was delivered in a commandeered baker's van to Bulovka Hospital....

"Hitler telegraphed around Europe for the best physicians. Specialists flew in from a half-dozen capitals.... Heydrich ... died a full week after the attack on him....

"The assassins' ... escape plan was never completed."[28]

---

[a] William Stevenson – the author – has written about events involving William Stephenson – the head of SOE. The two men are separate people and their surnames are spelt differently.
[b] British Security Coordination.

Rubowitz Assassination: October 1947

Nigel West, Military Historian: 1990 Book *The Friends*: **Jury Didn't Hear**:
In late 1944 "the Colonial Office requested SIS assistance [in Palestine].
Stewart Menzies[a] was asked to help achieve ... the formation of a counter-
terrorist intelligence group to operate within Palestine.... The plan had the
support of the ... Foreign Secretary, [Ernest] Bevin, who approved the
creation of a small unit headed by General Sir Bernard Fergusson.... He was
given carte blanche to identify and eliminate the fanatics....
"[Roy] Farran [was] recruited by Fergusson....
"In October 1947 [Farran] was charged with the torture and murder of an
Irgun[b] suspect named Alexander Rubowitz....
"[Farran] was acquitted, but a price was put on his head by the Irgun. A year
after these events, his younger brother Rex was killed when he opened a
parcel-bomb addressed to 'R. Farran'."[29]

Nasser Assassination Plot: September 1956

British Prime Minister Anthony Eden and MI6 joined forces in several
attempts to eliminate the Egyptian leader, Gamal Abdel Nasser.
Gordon Thomas, Intelligence Author: 2010 Book *Inside British
Intelligence*: **Jury Didn't Hear**:
"In the summer of 1956 the issue of what to do with Nasser had become a
renewed matter of urgency....
"In London the idea that Nasser should be assassinated was increasingly a
matter of discussion. MI6's legal department concluded that under its royal
prerogative to defend the realm, it would be permissible to murder a head of
state when the very security of Britain was under threat. The CIA
assassination manual was consulted, and George Young met with CIA officer
James Eichelberger.... Afterward the CIA officer hurried to his office in the
American Embassy and sent a coded cable to Allen Dulles[c]. '[Young] talked
openly of assassinating Nasser instead of using a euphemism like liquidating.
He said his people had been in contact with suitable elements in Egypt....'" [30]
Stephen Dorril, Intelligence Consultant and Author: 2000 Book *MI6*: **Jury
Didn't Hear**:
"On 26 July [1956] in Alexandria ... Nasser made his nationalisation [of the
Suez Canal Company] announcement.... The Iraqi PM's[d] advice [to Anthony
Eden[e]] was 'You have only one course of action open and that is to hit, hit
hard and hit now. Otherwise it will be too late.' Once his guests had left,

---

[a] MI6 Chief from 1939 to 1952.
[b] Irgun Zvai Leuni: a Jewish underground terrorist organisation.
[c] CIA Director, 1953 to 1961.
[d] That night the Iraqi Prime Minister, Nuri es-Said, was visiting 10 Downing St.
[e] British Prime Minister.

Eden summoned a council of war.... An emotional Prime Minister told his colleagues that ... the 'muslim Mussolini' must be 'destroyed'. Eden added: 'I want him removed and I don't give a damn if there's anarchy and chaos in Egypt.'[a] ...

"Eden immediately established the 'Egypt committee' to supervise a response....

"It was agreed that the more formidable a response, the better the chance that Nasser could be overthrown or even murdered by his own countrymen, if his nerve broke....

"During the spring of 1956, at the request of Eden, the IRD[b] had stepped up its propaganda efforts in the Middle East with a special emphasis given to radio broadcasting.... The IRD ... had arranged for more 'black' propaganda....

"One of the black radio stations set up in Aden, masquerading as the 'Voice of Free Egypt', began broadcasting on 28 July.... An Iraqi announcer made vituperative attacks on Nasser, called for his assassination, and gave out a series of cryptic messages to alleged agents inside Egypt....

"MI6's new chief, Dick White, was ... briefed by George Young, who informed him that he and the SPA[c] branch had been personally chosen by the Prime Minister to 'bump Nasser off'....

"Although the Queen did see all the 'special bulletins', only a few senior Cabinet ministers and Foreign Office officials were let into the inner ring of secrecy.... Geoffrey McDermott was ... part of a three man team with Dean and Kirkpatrick in receipt of 'clear and unusual' orders from Eden, involved in intelligence and military contingency planning for Egypt. The first plan was called 'Hamilcar' and was based on a landing at Alexandria which McDermott saw as clear proof that the real intention was to topple Nasser....

"An angry Eden told Conservative MP Robert Boothby that 'we must crush this man at all costs'.... According to one Cabinet colleague, Eden was now 'intoxicated with drugs'.

"MI6's main task was to 'support any armed forces intervention with internal action against Nasser'.... In early August, CIA liaison officer Chester Cooper had a meeting with Young ... at which the MI6 director had a go at the Americans for knocking down 'every proposal for bashing the Gyppos'. At another meeting, Young told Eveland[d] that Britain and Iraq would proceed with plans for a coup in Syria....

---

[a] At this time Eden was taking large doses of prescription drugs.
[b] Information Research Department, a part of the Foreign Office.
[c] Special Political Action.
[d] Wilbur Eveland, CIA officer.

"Under the general mandate given by Eden, MI6 began to construct a 'shadow government' for Egypt without consulting the Foreign Office....

"It was said the Gen. Mohammed Neguib would ... take the presidency and that dissident officers were conferring with civilians about the assassination of Nasser and his ministers....

"At a meeting with ... Patrick Reilly[a], White confided, 'We've got a group of dissident military officers who will go against Nasser'. He further explained that the MI6 plan was for that group to murder the Egyptian leader....

"MI6 did not believe ... that it was necessary to have an alternative [government] in place. The Service was confident that once Nasser was overthrown suitable candidates would emerge....

"There was little the Foreign Office could do to control events, since MI6 was working via back channels to Eden....

"In late August, MI6 suffered a setback when the Egyptian secret police, the Mukhabarat, raided the offices of its front, the ANA[b]. On the 27th the Egyptians announced at a press conference that a British espionage ring had been rolled up and ... James Swinburn, the business manager of ANA, had been arrested and had promptly confessed to being in charge of the ring.... Also arrested were Charles Pittuck ... and James Zarb....

"Other Britons [were] accused and tried in absentia.... Eleven Egyptians were accused of espionage.... Two British diplomats involved in intelligence-gathering were expelled.... Swinburn confessed that they were planning a coup d'état....

"On 30 August, CIA director Allen Dulles reported to his brother at the State Department on his talks with MI6 officers, who were persisting in their plans to overthrow Nasser....

"With no assets left in the country, MI6 had to use outside agents for its assassination plans. [Journalist] James Mossman ... who had worked for MI6 during the war, was posted to Egypt as the *Daily Telegraph* correspondent in 1956. In Cairo he was approached by an MI6 officer in the local embassy.... Although Mossman said he had finished with intelligence work, the officer appealed to his patriotism, telling him that 'you must do this because we are just about to go to war with Egypt'. Agreeing to cooperate, Mossman was asked to drop off a package from the boot of his Morris Minor at the twelve-mile post outside Cairo. Given a telephone on which to confirm safe delivery, Mossman discovered that he had contacted the wrong man. The package had contained £20,000 in English banknotes which was intended as a bribe to Nasser's doctor to poison Nasser.

"The poison was organised by the head of the Service's 'Q' Ops Department, Major Frank Quinn.... On one occasion Quinn was asked to inject lethal

---

[a] Deputy Under-Secretary at the Foreign Office.
[b] Arab News Agency.

poison into some popular Egyptian Kropje chocolates. A dozen boxes were obtained from Cairo.... After trial and error, in which six boxes were destroyed, Quinn found the correct formula.... The chocolates were handed over, though it appears they never reached their intended destination.

"One plan was drawn up ... [involving] nerve gas[a]....

"By [October 1956] ... it was decided that a three-man hit team would be sent by the SPA group from London as 'a Special Service to assassinate Nasser'. They apparently did enter Egypt but got 'cold feet and left'. At the same time, the Egyptian security service had been tipped off about the presence in Cairo of a German mercenary who had been hired by MI6 for a 'wet job'. He disappeared before the security net was closed and was believed to have been smuggled out of the country under diplomatic cover. There was also a British plan to use SAS troops in the run-up to the invasion to kill or capture Nasser...."[31b]

Peter Wright, ex-MI5 Officer: 1987 Book *Spycatcher*: **Jury Didn't Hear**: "At the beginning of the Suez crisis, MI6 developed a plan, through the London station, to assassinate Nasser using nerve gas. [Anthony] Eden initially gave his approval, but later rescinded it.... Eden [later] reactivated the assassination option a second time. By this time virtually all MI6 assets in Egypt had been rounded up by Nasser, and a new operation, using renegade Egyptian officers, was drawn up, but it failed lamentably, principally because the cache of weapons which had been hidden on the outskirts of Cairo was found to be defective....

"I was consulted about the plan by John Henry and Peter Dixon, the two MI6 Technical Services officers from the London Station responsible for drawing it up....

"Both MI5 and MI6 ... wanted to know a lot more about the poisons being developed at Porton[c], though for different reasons. I[d] wanted the antidotes, in case the Russians used a poison on a defector in Britain, while MI6 wanted to use the poisons for operations abroad.

"Henry and Dixon both discussed with me the use of poisons against Nasser, and asked my advice. Nerve gas obviously presented the best possibility,

---

[a] See Peter Wright's account below. Dorril also includes the poison dart story which was described by Wright.

[b] Richard Belfield states: "MI6 concocted a plan to assassinate [Nasser] by pumping cyanide gas through the U-bend of his toilet....": *The Secret History of Assassination*, p254.

[c] Porton Down, the UK government's chemical and biological Weapons Research Establishment. Today it is home to the UK government's Defence Science and Technology Laboratory.

[d] In this, Wright represented MI5.

since it was easily administered. They told me that the London Station had an agent in Egypt with limited access to one of Nasser's headquarters. Their plan was to place canisters of nerve gas inside the ventilation system, but I pointed out this would require large quantities of the gas and would result in massive loss of life among Nasser's staff.... Henry told me later that Eden had backed away from the operation....

"After the gas canisters plan fell through, MI6 looked at some new weapons. On one occasion I went down to Porton to see a demonstration of a cigarette packet which had been modified by the Explosives Research and Development Establishment to fire a dart tipped with poison." [32]

Comment: None of MI6's attempts to assassinate Nasser succeeded – he finally died from a heart attack in Cairo 14 years later.

Grivas Assassination Plot: February 1959

Georgios Grivas, formerly a general in the Greek army, led a guerrilla campaign in the 1950s aimed at ending British rule in Cyprus.

Peter Wright, ex-MI5 Officer: 1987 Book *Spycatcher*: **Jury Didn't Hear**: "In 1958, [Colonel Georgios] Grivas stepped up his guerrilla campaign [in Cyprus] in an effort to thwart the determined efforts to achieve a political solution being made by the new Governor, Sir Hugh Foot....

"Grivas needed to be located, isolated and neutralised before political negotiations stood a chance....

"Foot ... agreed to call in MI5 as the situation was rapidly deteriorating. From the start we were in a race: Could we find Grivas before the Colonial Office stitched up a ramshackle [peace] deal?

"I was to ... plan and execute the technical side of the operation, which was given the code name 'Sunshine'.

"It would be too crude to say that Sunshine was an assassination operation. But it amounted to the same thing. The plan was simple: to locate Grivas and bring up a massive concentration of soldiers. We knew he would never surrender and ... he would die in the shoot-out....

"We estimated that Sunshine would take six months to complete, but just as we moved into top gear, in late February 1959, the Colonial Office hurriedly settled the Cyprus problem at a Constitutional Conference at Lancaster House. The carpet was roughly pulled out from under our feet, and the entire Sunshine plan aborted overnight....

"Looking back, I am certain that, had we been allowed to implement Operation Sunshine when we first lobbied for it, in 1956, we could have neutralised Grivas at the outset." [33]

Nigel West, Military Historian: 1990 Book *The Friends*: **Jury Didn't Hear**: "It was Gamal Abdel Nasser's [1954] demand for the return of Britain's base in the Suez Canal Zone that transformed Cyprus's rather dubious strategic value....

"From the intelligence viewpoint, Cyprus [was] designated the new home for SIS's regional base....

"By 1958, the level of violence [in Cyprus] had reached a peak.... The British response was a reorganisation of the security apparatus, with Sir John Prendergast brought in from Kenya ... to take over a new coordinating post of Chief of Intelligence.... Supporting Prendergast was Philip Kirby Green (known as 'K-G'), one of Britain's most remarkable secret warriors....

"Prendergast and K-G were a formidable team and, with Magan's[a] support, they devised a joint MI5-SIS scheme code-named Operation Sunshine to trace Grivas to his hiding place and eliminate him. John Wyke and Peter Wright made all the technical arrangements... while Sir Stephen Hastings[b] was transferred from the Paris station to be 'in at the kill'....

"Before Sunshine could be executed, it was scrapped because, against all the odds, the politicians began to make progress." [34]

Lumumba Assassination Plot: September 1960

Ian Black, Journalist: 28 Jun 01 *Guardian* Article: **Jury Didn't Hear**:
"Britain backed Belgium and the US in their desire to eliminate Patrice Lumumba, the radical prime minister of Congo who was murdered in 1961, according to newly-discovered documents.

"Ludo de Witte, a Flemish historian, reveals that while the US and Belgium actively plotted to murder the African nationalist leader, the British government secretly believed that Lumumba posed a serious threat to western interests and wanted him 'got rid of'.

"Within days of its independence in June 1960, Congo was in chaos....

"On September 19 1960, President Dwight Eisenhower discussed the Congo crisis with Lord Home, the then foreign secretary. 'The president expressed his wish that Lumumba would fall into a river full of crocodiles,' a declassified US document records....

"The minutes suggest that the British government could have known of the CIA's plans to kill Lumumba, Mr De Witte says.

"Just a week later, Eisenhower met the Conservative prime minister, Harold Macmillan, with the foreign secretary again in attendance.

"'Lord Home raised the question why we are not getting rid of Lumumba,' the US account of the talks reports. 'He stressed that now is the time to get rid of Lumumba.'

---

[a] Bill Magan, MI5 officer. Both Magan and K-G later became Directors on MI5's board.: *The Friends*, p23.
[b] MI6 officer who became Conservative MP for Mid-Bedfordshire in 1960.: *The Friends*, p102.

"The Congolese leader's public denunciation of racism and exploitation under 80 years of colonial rule and his overtures to the Soviet Union in the midst of the cold war had made him powerful enemies.

"At the end of September 1960, when Lumumba had already been dismissed by the Congo's president and the army commander moved to arrest him, Howard Smith, a senior Foreign Office official who was later to become the head of MI5, led a discussion recorded in a document released by the Public Record Office last year.

"'I can see only two possible solutions to the problem,' Mr Smith said. 'The first is the simple one of ensuring Lumumba's removal from the scene by killing him. This should solve the problem...'" [35]

Richard Belfield, Investigative Author: 2008 Book: **Jury Didn't Hear:**[a]

"A senior official, career diplomat H.F.T. Howard Smith sent a memo ... dated 28 September 1960, with the word 'Secret' written by hand ... simply entitled 'The Congo'....

"[It read] 'I see only two possible solutions to the problem. The first is the simple one of ensuring [Patrice] Lumumba's removal from the scene by killing him. This should in fact solve the problem since, so far as we can tell, Lumumba is not a leader of a movement within which there are potential successors of his quality and influence. His supporters are much less dangerous material.' Smith made it very clear that this was his preferred option. He wanted 'Lumumba to be removed from the scene altogether, because I fear that as long as he is about his power to do damage can only slightly be modified.'[b]...

"Smith's memo was circulated around Whitehall.... There is no evidence on the memo that [anyone who read it] raised any objections, moral, ethical or legal to Smith's preferred wish to kill a democratically elected prime minister of a sovereign state." [36c]

---

[a] Belfield's account is sourced from the British National Archives, Reference FO371/146650. Belfield also said: "The Foreign Office was being encouraged to take action by their man in Leopoldville. MI6 was also being prodded into action by reports from their Congo station chief, Daphne Park, who argued that Lumumba was going to take the Congo into the Russian camp.": *The Secret History of Assassination*, p24.

[b] Belfield states: "The second option was to bring in a constitution taking power away from Patrice Lumumba as prime minister and giving it to the president.": *The Secret History of Assassination*, p25.

[c] Patrice Lumumba was assassinated, but not by the British. Belfield wrote: "The CIA dispatched an agent to the Congo armed with a deadly virus with which to kill Lumumba, but it was the Belgians who got there first, shooting him dead after days of brutal and inhumane treatment.": *The Secret History of Assassination*, p26.

Irish Assassination Plots: 1972

Richard Bennett, Intelligence Analyst, AFI Research: 13 Jun 03 *Asia Times* Article[a]: **Jury Didn't Hear**:

"The Littlejohn brothers [Keith and Kenneth] were recruited in 1972 by John Wyman of MI6, who handled a number of agents in Northern Ireland and paid them substantial sums of taxpayers' money to infiltrate the IRA and to act as agent provocateurs, organizing and conducting bank robberies and bomb attacks in the Republic of Ireland. Wyman told them that there was 'going to be a policy of political assassination' for which they were to make themselves available. 'If I was told about any illegal act before it happened, I would always discuss it with London. I was always told to go ahead,' said Kenneth Littlejohn, who went on to claim that the MI6 officer told him, 'If there is any shooting, do what you've got to do.'

"Wyman ... gave the Littlejohns a list of IRA leaders to assassinate; these included Seamus Costello[b], Sean Garland[c] and Sean MacStiofain[d]. After Littlejohn passed on the name of Joe McCann, a leading Republican, to his MI6 handler, McCann was shot dead by British paratroopers a few days later as he walked, apparently unarmed, through the Belfast market area[e]." [37]

Ireland's Own: 27 Dec 01 History Article: **Jury Didn't Hear**:

"[John] Wyman, who used various aliases, was [a] member of the British secret service agency, MI6, and was ... important ... in the British intelligence network in Ireland....

"Included in ... Wyman's spy network were the Littlejohn brothers, Keith and Kenneth. These were two English criminals on the run in Ireland during 1969, with whom British intelligence made contact....

"The Littlejohns were told to infiltrate Republican circles [and] kill Republican leaders....

"In November 1972, Fianna Fail Justice Minister Dessie O'Malley brought the draconian Offences Against the State (Amendment) Bill before Leinster House deputies. In the early hours of 2 December, as the bill was being

---

[a] In June 2003 this article – entitled *Assassination and the License to Kill* – was submitted as written evidence to the Select Committee on Foreign Affairs in the House of Commons, by Dr Martha Mundy, Senior Lecturer in Anthropology (Specialist in the countries of the Arab East) London School of Economics.: www.publications.parliament.uk/pa/cm200203/cmselect/

[b] Leader of the Official Irish Republican Army (OIRA) assassinated in Dublin on 5 October 1977.

[c] Member of the OIRA. He survived an attempted assassination on 1 March 1975.: Wikipedia under "Sean Garland".

[d] First chief-of-staff of the Provisional IRA. He died on 17 May 2001, aged 73.

[e] This occurred on 15 April 1972.

debated in the Dail chamber, British military intelligence agents exploded a number of bombs in Dublin City, killing two people and seriously injuring 127 others. Within hours of news that bombs were exploding on the streets outside, the bill was passed by a large majority.

"The Littlejohns were arrested in London on December 20th. The following day Wyman and Crinnion[a] were arrested in London.... The 26 authorities acted, it appears, out of knowledge that ... the British agents were planning a campaign of political assassinations in the 26 counties.[b]

"With the loss of two key agents, the British opted to sacrifice the Littlejohns in exchange for Wyman and Crinnion." [38]

Gordon Thomas, Intelligence Author: 2010 Book *Inside British Intelligence*: **Jury Didn't Hear**:

"Kenneth Littlejohn ... claimed, '[John Wyman] said he would like us to carry out political assassinations of IRA leaders. He gave me a list that included Seamus Costello and Joe McCann.' [c]

"It was agreed McCann would be the first target. Before the Littlejohns could assassinate the IRA man, however, he was shot dead by a British patrol in Belfast." [39]

Stephen Dorril, Intelligence Consultant and Author: 2000 Book *MI6*: **Jury Didn't Hear**:

"The explosion of two bombs in Dublin on 1 December 1972 aided the passage of an anti-terrorism bill.... The Irish Gardai Special Branch presented fragmentary evidence that the bombers had been ... aided by British intelligence in planting the devices. On 19 December, the Irish rounded up an MI6 intelligence network. This included John Wyman, who had recruited an agent inside the Gardai[d]...." [40]

---

[a] DS Patrick Crinnion, member of the Irish SB, recruited as an agent by John Wyman.

[b] "26 counties" is a term used by the Irish to describe the Republic of Ireland, which comprises 26 counties.

[c] There is a conflict between Thomas' and Bennett's account. Bennett says that "Littlejohn passed on the name of Joe McCann" to Wyman. Thomas says that Wyman included McCann on the assassination list he gave to Littlejohn. Although the latter would seem most likely, the main issue here is that the overall evidence points to MI6 being involved in a proactive campaign of targeted assassinations in Ireland in the early 1970s.

[d] Irish National Police Service. Dorril is probably referring here to Patrick Crinnion.

Gibraltar Assassinations: March 1988

Richard Norton-Taylor, Intelligence Journalist: 1990 Book: **Jury Didn't Hear**:

"[In 1988][a] four SAS men shot dead three unarmed IRA terrorists in Gibraltar....

"The Gibraltar operation was controlled by MI5, though the SAS would not have acted without the personal authority of [Margaret] Thatcher[b].

"Two years after the incident[c] ... questions remain unanswered. If, as the Spanish Government and police maintain, the three terrorists – Danny McCann, Sean Savage, and Mairead Farrell – were followed up to the Gibraltar frontier, why were they not arrested?... Spanish police sources ... [said] that the three were unarmed and had crossed the border without explosives. Why then did the MI5 officers tell the SAS soldiers ... that the three were most certain to be armed ... [and] were also likely to have on them a remote-control detonator enabling them to trigger a bomb they had left, primed, down-town?...

"The SAS soldiers were heavily briefed by MI5 officers who told them they were following highly dangerous terrorists who could be expected to be ruthless and deadly.... Anonymous MI5 officers, shielded from view, gave evidence at the inquest. But the jury was prevented from hearing crucial evidence about the MI5 operation and MI5's state of knowledge by public interest immunity certificates signed by government ministers. The MI5 officer in charge of the operation, the man who briefed the SAS soldiers, did not give evidence at all." [41]

Finucane Assassination: February 1989

British agents were involved in the assassination of Patrick Finucane[d] in Northern Ireland.

John Stevens, MPS Commissioner: 17 Apr 03 Stevens Enquiry Report on Northern Ireland: **Jury Didn't Hear**:

"Patrick Finucane was murdered in front of his wife and three children in his home on Sunday 12th February 1989. He was 39 years old....

"By November 1989 the murder remained unsolved and the investigation had effectively ceased. However in 1990 a journalist, Mr Neil Mulholland, provided new information about the Finucane murder from a man claiming to

---

[a] This occurred on 6 March 1988.
[b] British Prime Minister at the time.
[c] Norton-Taylor was writing in 1990.
[d] An IRA lawyer.

be both a quartermaster for the Ulster Defence Association and an agent of the RUC[a] Special Branch. This man was William Stobie....

"Stobie was recruited as an agent by the RUC Special Branch in November 1987 following his arrest for the murder of Brian Adam Lambert for which he was released without charge. He was tasked by Special Branch until 1990 when as a result of Mulholland's information he was arrested by the RUC for the Finucane and Lambert murders.... His activities, whilst an agent, clearly indicate his central role in the commission of serious offences from at least July 1988 onwards.

"It has now been established that before the murder of Patrick Finucane, Stobie supplied information of a murder being planned. He also provided significant information to his Special Branch handlers in the days after the murder. This principally concerned the collection of a firearm. However this vital information did not reach the original murder enquiry team and remains a significant issue under investigation by my Enquiry team....

"My Enquiry team ... reviewed William Stobie's and Brian Nelson's roles in the murder of Patrick Finucane. Nelson, an Army agent, had been identified as a suspect during my first Enquiry. He was charged with thirty-five serious terrorist offences and later convicted. He was imprisoned for ten years....

"Nelson was aware and contributed materially to the intended attack on Finucane. It is not clear whether his role in the murder extended beyond passing a photograph, which showed Finucane and another person, to one of the other suspects....

"Brian Nelson's role also raised a number of issues arising from the work of the Force Research Unit (FRU), the Army's agent-handling unit in Northern Ireland...." [42b]

---

[a] Royal Ulster Constabulary.
[b] On 19 November 2000 the *Sunday Herald* published an interview by Neil Mackay with an FRU officer who spoke out on condition of anonymity. He stated: "My unit was guilty of conspiring in the murder of civilians in Northern Ireland, on about 14 occasions." The article states: "The FRU was under the command of Brigadier Gordon Kerr. Kerr ... was in charge of this shadowy network of British army agents, who quite simply collaborated with their loyalist informers to murder civilians in Ulster, between 1987 and 1991.... The FRU officer ... said Kerr was in charge of the day-to-day handling of loyalist informers. He knew his officers were handing information to UDA [Ulster Defence Association] terrorists to be used to kill Republicans. The source worked with Kerr before and after [Patrick] Finucane's death." The source continued: "Under Kerr's command, the FRU were giving information to [Brian] Nelson to help him prepare intelligence for attacks. The mind-set was one of 'the right people would be allowed to live and the wrong people should die'.... What was happening may have been occurring outside the law but the establishment knew what was happening.... I can say with dead certainty that the FRU did conspire to murder certain individuals with loyalist terrorists through our work with UDA informers. And Kerr knew about it." Mackay also quoted a "security

Martin Ingram & Greg Harkin, 2004 Book *Stakeknife*: **Jury Didn't Hear**: "The FRU provided [agent Brian] Nelson with photographs and detailed maps of Finucane's home.... [FRU] handlers were also involved in reconnaissance missions at the Finucane family home. There was at least one occasion when a FRU officer drove Brian Nelson to Fortwilliam Drive to see the Finucane's house. Another time, a FRU officer posed as a window cleaner with Nelson and they offered their 'services' to a neighbour of the Finucanes so they could check out the rear of their target's home....

"[Tommy] Lyttle[a] told me[b] that ... all the UDA members involved in the [Finucane] killing attended a 'celebration' party held in [Lyttle's] house after the murder. FRU informer Brian Nelson, Special Branch informer Jim Spence and Ken Barrett[c] were among the guests at this macabre gathering." [43]

Owen Bowcott, Journalist: 26 Jun 07 *Guardian* Article: **Jury Didn't Hear**:

"No policemen or soldiers are to be charged in connection with the loyalist murder of the solicitor Pat Finucane, the prosecution service said yesterday.

"The decision to take no action against senior officers in military intelligence and the Royal Ulster Constabulary effectively marks the end of an 18-year investigation to prove in court that there was organised collusion between the security forces and loyalist paramilitaries....

"The latest evidence reviewed by the Public Prosecution Service of Northern Ireland came out of the third inquiry conducted by the former Metropolitan police commissioner Lord Stevens into agent-handling in Northern Ireland during the late 1980s and early 1990s.

---

source": The people who should be charged as a result of the Stevens inquiry "are so high-ranking that the establishment will have to cover-up for them. If they go down, the stink of what was happening will reach right to the top of government." The FRU source stated: "'Lie upon lie has been told and documents have been destroyed or not handed over. The police are spotting that the story they were given by the FRU in the early stages of the [Stevens] inquiry do not tally with what they now know. The police know there's been a cover-up and they know how it all worked.": Neil Mackay, "My Unit Conspired in the Murder of Civilians in Ireland", *The Sun-Herald*, 19 November 2000. Gordon Kerr has never been charged. According to the "British Army Killings" website (in June 2011) "Brigadier Gordon Kerr is now in charge of the Special Reconnaissance Regiment (SRR) to provide covert surveillance expertise for operations by the SAS and Special Boat Service in Afghanistan and other UK overseas interests.": http://britisharmykillings.org.uk

[a] A senior UDA official working for Special Branch on the weekend of the Finucane assassination.

[b] Greg Harkin.

[c] UDA hitman.

"In a statement the prosecution service said there was insufficient evidence to bring cases to trial. It cited problems with missing records, witnesses who have died and the difficulties of ascertaining 'the role and responsibilities that individuals played in specific events'. It also had to take account of potential abuse of process arguments by the defence that any trial at this stage would be unfair.

"The main thrust of what was known as Stevens III was the role of the army's surveillance operations in Northern Ireland, in particular the Force Research Unit (FRU). Nine former members of the unit, including its former head, Brigadier Gordon Kerr, were questioned, as well as seven police officers and a civilian. The prosecution service said: 'There was insufficient evidence to establish that any member of FRU had agreed with Brian Nelson [an agent run by FRU] or any other person that Patrick Finucane should be murdered or had knowledge at the relevant time that the murder was to take place.'

"It added: 'Lord Stevens ... stated that he believed there had been collusion between loyalist paramilitaries and elements of the security forces. While an investigator may properly reach general conclusions on collusion, the prosecutor's role is different.'...[ab]

---

[a] The Public Prosecutor's report is not publicly available. According to David Sharrock, writing in *The Times* in 2007, the statement to the press was made by Pamela Atchison, assistant director of Northern Ireland's Public Prosecution Service: "In a statement, Ms Atchison said that prosecutors had spent years considering whether to bring murder charges against former members of the ... FRU and the Royal Ulster Constabulary. But she said that too much time had passed and key witnesses had been killed or died...." This is an incredible statement – "prosecutors had spent years considering whether to bring murder charges" followed by "too much time had passed and key witnesses had been killed or died". The authorities "spent years considering" then concluded that "too much time had passed" for justice to occur. This appears to be another case of deliberate delay by the authorities and then in the end, true justice is denied. As has been discussed in earlier volumes and is specifically addressed later, the Diana inquest was delayed for ten years to a time when justice was much less likely to take place. The saying is: "Justice delayed is justice denied".: Source: David Sharrock, No Charges Against Security Forces for Finucane Murder, *The Times*, 26 June 2007.

[b] Martin Ingram, alias Jack Grantham, "who spent ten years operating in Ireland as a handler" spoke to *Politico* in 2006. "He was a senior member of the Force Research Unit a ... branch of British Military Intelligence.... In the 1990s Ingram left ... the notorious Force Research Unit after being disillusioned with how his superiors 'ran' agents. He says that in too many cases informers were allowed to carry out multiple murders without any fear of prosecution. In 2003 [Ingram] helped expose the activities of Freddie Scappaticci, a British agent inside the IRA since the 1970s who [he] believes killed more than a dozen people.": Colm Heatley, British Spies in Irish Parties, Claims Former British Spook, *Politico*, 5 January 2006.

"Alex Maskey, a Sinn Féin assembly member who was also targeted by Nelson, said yesterday: 'It has to be remembered that the DPP [prosecution service] is simply another level in the policy of collusion and the policy of concealment and cover-up.'

"The Police Service of Northern Ireland issued a statement on Lord Stevens's behalf, saying: '[He] notes the statement made by the public prosecution service. It is a matter for them.'

"British-Irish Rights Watch, the organisation whose report triggered the Stevens III inquiry, said it was 'disappointed but not surprised' at the decision.

"The MoD[a] said: 'We welcome the decision. Soldiers have been criticised for long enough and should be left to get on with their lives. The MoD has cooperated fully with the Stevens inquiries.'

"The government has said it is committed to holding a public inquiry into the Finucane murder but, it is believed, has been unable to find a judge to chair it....

"In 1987 Gordon Kerr, a lieutenant-colonel and veteran of army intelligence, now retired, was appointed head of the Force Research Unit. He oversaw the recruitment of Brian Nelson and his infiltration of the Ulster Defence Association. Nelson took up a key position as a gatherer of intelligence on potential republican targets. At Nelson's trial in 1992 Col Kerr defended his former agent's role, declaring: 'There were several occasions when targets for assassination were brought to our notice by Nelson.' Col Kerr has insisted his operation saved lives and that Nelson never told the FRU that Finucane was going to be killed." [44]

Comment: The main point here is that Finucane was not the sole assassination. The Northern Ireland Ombudsman's report – see below – established that there were 20 separate assassination plots between 1991 and 2000, and the anonymous evidence (see above footnote regarding the 2000 *Sunday Herald* article) indicates at least 12 others between 1987 and 1991.

Why has the Ombudsman's report been ignored?

Why did John Stevens[b] focus his investigation on one assassination – Finucane – when other evidence indicates there were up to 32 others?

Why have no members of British intelligence been charged for assassinations they have been shown – by Nuala O'Loan's report (below), by the Stevens report – to have been involved in?

---

[a] Ministry of Defence.

[b] Stevens oversaw the incredibly flawed Paget Report into the deaths of Princess Diana and Dodi Fayed. See the 2007 book: *Cover-Up of a Royal Murder: Hundreds of Errors in the Paget Report*.

20 Irish Assassination Plots: February 1991 to October 2000

An investigation by the Northern Ireland Police Ombudsman into the 9 November 1997[a] assassination of Raymond McCord Junior[b] uncovered widespread involvement by Special Branch agents in 20 assassination plots. The investigation also revealed a culture of collusion and cover-up of the plots by Special Branch officers.

Nuala O'Loan, Police Ombudsman for Northern Ireland: 22 Jan 07 Investigative Report: **Jury Didn't Hear**:

"Intelligence reports and other documents within the RUC[c] and the PSNI[d] ... linked informants, and in particular one man who was a police informant (referred to in this report as Informant 1) to the following ten murders:

• **Mr Peter McTasney** who died on 24 February 1991;
• **Ms Sharon McKenna** who died on 17 January 1993;
• **Mr Sean McParland** who was attacked on 17 February 1994, and died on 25 February 1994;
• **Mr Gary Convie** who died on 17 May 1994;
• **Mr Eamon Fox** who died on 17 May 1994, in the same attack as Mr Gary Convie;
• **Mr Gerald Brady** who died on 17 June 1994;
• **Mr Thomas Sheppard** who died on 21 March 1996;
• **Mr John Harbinson** who died on 18 May 1997;
• **Mr Raymond McCord Junior** who died on 09 November 1997
• **Mr Thomas English** who died on 31 October 2000

"Intelligence was also found linking police informants, and in particular Informant 1, to ten attempted murders between 1989 and 2002." [45]

"Whilst undoubtedly Special Branch officers were effective in preventing bombings and shootings and other attacks, some informants were able to continue to engage in terrorist activities including murders without the Criminal Investigation Department having the ability to deal with them for some of those offences.

"On occasions this also resulted in crimes being committed by informants with the prior knowledge of Special Branch officers. Informants engaged in such crimes were not subject to any of the controls inherent in the system.... On occasion ... [Special Branch] police ... watched as serious terrorist crimes were committed by their informants....

"The evidence clearly shows that Informant 1's behaviour, including alleged murder, was not challenged by Special Branch, and the activities of those

---

[a] Just over 2 months after the deaths of Princess Diana and Dodi Fayed.
[b] The investigation was requested by the father of the victim, Raymond McCord Senior.
[c] Royal Ulster Constabulary.
[d] Police Service of Northern Ireland.

who sought to bring him to justice were blocked repeatedly. Records were minimized, exaggerated, fabricated and must also have been destroyed. Informant 1 would have been well aware of the level of protection which he was afforded.

"It is also the case that whilst he was engaged in drug dealing and other money making activities, Informant 1 was not only protected by Special Branch but he was also given large sums of public money in return for such services as he provided.... The total amount estimated to have been paid to Informant 1 over 12 years is in excess of £79,000.

"This investigation demonstrates graphically the dangers of a separated and effectively unaccountable specialist intelligence department with extensive and largely uncontrolled powers....

"In many ... crimes described in this report there were witnesses, who either drew police attention to a crime or volunteered to give evidence, some of it quite specific.... The Police Ombudsman has found that on a number of occasions the police did not use these opportunities to further their investigations. This had two consequences: firstly the investigation did not proceed, and secondly [this] failure by police to use evidence tendered by witnesses ... must have given rise to a lack of confidence among the people that there was any point in assisting the police when such crimes were committed...." [46]

Dermot Ahern, Irish Minister for Foreign Affairs: 22 Jan 07 Press Release: **Jury Didn't Hear**:

"The Police Ombudsman's Report is a deeply disturbing and shocking exposé of the activities of loyalist paramilitaries and their relationship with the RUC Special Branch.

"The report's findings are damning....

"The Ombudsman has found that RUC officers colluded in crimes by their failure to tackle the most serious activities of their informants – including murder. Clearly, elements of the RUC Special Branch had lost all moral compass at that time. I note that there are to be further investigations on foot of this report. Police officers implicated in these appalling acts must be held accountable for their actions.[a]

"These findings confirm what many observers feared about the conduct of RUC Special Branch." [47b]

---

[a] This has never occurred.

[b] In addition to these Irish assassinations listed above, former British intelligence officer Martin Ingram (pseudonym) and Belfast journalist Greg Harkin revealed the details of many other assassinations in Ireland involving British intelligence, in their 2004 book, *Stakeknife*. These took place between 1980 and 1996 and generally involved the British military intelligence unit, the FRU. Ingram points out that the

assassinations were carried out with either the involvement or full knowledge of MI5: "A member of MI5 who was based in the FRU operations office, saw all the material generated by FRU and channelled it upwards.... MI5 brought their agent handling and electronic technical expertise to the table." (pp30-31). Stakeknife – codename for Freddie Scappaticci – worked for British intelligence from 1978 and was ensconced in the IRA's internal security department, known as the Nutting Squad, from 1980.

The people assassinated during Stakeknife's time in the Nutting Squad follow. At the least British intelligence would have been aware of these killings as Stakeknife was passing on intelligence to them. The evidence also indicates that some – and possibly a majority – would have been assassinated on the orders of British intelligence, even though they have mainly been attributed to the IRA and were mostly executed by IRA personnel.

The people assassinated are: Paul Valente – killed November 1980; Maurice Gilvarry – January 1981; Patrick Trainor – February 1981; Vincent Robinson – June 1981; Anthony Braniff – September 1981; John Torbett – January 1982; Seamus Morgan – February 1982; Patrick Scott – April 1982; James Young – February 1984; Brian McNally – July 1984; Kevin Coyle – February 1985; John Corcoran – March 1985; Catherine and Gerard Mahon – September 1985; Damien McCrory – October 1985; Frank Hegarty – May 1986; Patrick Murray – August 1986; David McVeigh – September 1986; Charles McIlmurray – April 1987; Thomas Wilson – June 1987; Eamonn Maguire – September 1987; Anthony McKiernan – January 1988; Joseph Fenton – February 1989; John McAnulty – July 1989; Paddy Flood – July 1990; Ruari Finnis – June 1991; Tom Oliver – July 1991; Greg Burns, John Dignam, Aidan Starrs – July 1992; Robin Hill – August 1992; Gerard Holmes – November 1992; Christopher Harte – February 1993; James Kelly – March 1993; John Mulhern – June 1993; Michael Brown – April 1994; Caroline Moreland – July 1994.

Ingram and Harkin also "detail those who died as a ... result of" FRU agent Brian Nelson's activities: Gerry Adams (attempted assassination – received bullet wounds) – March 1984; Edward Campbell – July 1987; Patrick Hamill – September 1987; Jim Meighan – September 1987; Francisco Notorantonio – October 1987; Adam Lambert – November 1987; Terence McDaid – May 1988; Brendon Davison – July 1988; Gerard Slane – September 1988; John Joe Davey – February 1989; Patrick Feeney – February 1989; Gerard Casey – April 1989; Liam McKee – June 1989; Loughlin Maginn – August 1989. (Ingram-Harkin also include Patrick Finucane in this list – his assassination has been covered separately in this book).

There were other assassinations with British-intelligence involvement, recorded by Ingram and Harkin, that were not carried out by Brian Nelson or the IRA's Nutting Squad: Sean Burns, Eugene Toman, Gervaise McKerr – November 1982; David Ead – April 1987; Peter Duggan (attempted assassination) – January 1988; Margaret Perry – June 1991.

In their book Ingram and Nelson provided detailed support for the allegations of British intelligence involvement in all the assassinations or plots listed above.

Source: Martin Ingram & Greg Harkin, *Stakeknife: Britain's Secret Agents in Ireland*, 2004.

Milosevic Assassination Plot: Summer 1992[a]

Ex-MI6 agent Richard Tomlinson has stated that he was shown evidence – by Nicholas Fishwick[b] – of an MI6 plot to assassinate Serbian leader Slobodan Milosevic. It was a two page document outlining the justification for and methods of execution of the plot. The third method involved a car crash in a tunnel and a strobe flash gun to disorientate the driver.

The evidence from the seven MI6 witnesses was that there was a documented proposal[c], but the assassination target was someone other than Milosevic[d] – someone whose identity can't be revealed – and the idea was quashed early because such a proposal was outside the ethos of MI6.

According to MI6 witnesses the documentary evidence has since been destroyed.

Saddam Assassination Plot: June 1996

James Risen, *Los Angeles Times* Journalist, USA: 15 Feb 98 Article: **Jury Didn't Hear**:
"A ... CIA covert action program, designed to attract and recruit Iraqi officers to foment a military coup, was ... destroyed by [Saddam] Hussein, in June 1996.
"That CIA program, operated jointly with MI6, the British intelligence service, was based in Jordan, using a front group called the Iraqi National Accord....
"CIA sources now say this ... covert program was thoroughly penetrated by Iraqi double agents, who betrayed the Iraqi military officers who dared to sign up to work with the CIA and MI6.
"Hussein executed at least 100 military officers and others who had cooperated with the Americans and the British." [48]
Patrick Cockburn, *The Independent* Journalist, UK: 17 Feb 98 Article: **Jury Didn't Hear**:

---

[a] For reasons that are addressed later, the detail of the evidence relating to the Milosevic plot is not covered in this book. It can be found in the Paget Report pp754 to 764 and Inquest Transcripts: Richard Tomlinson – 13 Feb 08; Richard Dearlove – 20 Feb 08; Miss X and Mr A – 26 Feb 08; Mr H – 28 Feb 08; Ms F, Mr E, Mr I – 29 Feb 08. Also relevant is the full affidavit of Richard Tomlinson given to Judge Stéphan in May 1999 – this can be viewed at
http://www.conspiracyplanet.com/channel.cfm?channelid=41&contentid=88
[b] Known at the inquest as "A".
[c] Some of the details of the proposal differed in the MI6 witness evidence, but no one denied that it was an assassination plot.
[d] It will be shown later that MI6 appear to have lied when they state that the target was someone other than Milosevic.

"MI6 in Plot to Kill Saddam

"A plot by MI6, Britain's Secret Intelligence Service, to topple President Saddam Hussein collapsed in ignominy, triggering one of the worst defeats in its history.

"The coup, organised by intelligence officers in Amman, Jordan, was crushed by the Iraqi leader, who executed as many as 80 conspirators and arrested hundreds more.

"The revelation will be widely seen as contradicting British and American claims that they are not planning to topple the leadership in Baghdad. They have claimed repeatedly that the only issue at stake is the entry of UN weapons inspectors. Yet 18 months ago MI6 and the CIA joined in trying to foment a military coup against President Saddam in Iraq....

"CIA agents, angry that the White House stopped them from backing an attempt to assassinate President Saddam or mount a military attack on him, have confirmed for the first time to the *Los Angeles Times* that the attempted coup was a joint operation by MI6 and the CIA.

"The two intelligence agencies chose a group called the Iraqi National Accord, recruited from Iraqi army, party and intelligence officers, as the instrument through which to organise a military coup in Baghdad....

"Other sources say that the London station of the CIA along with MI6 played a key role in choosing the Accord to overthrow the Iraqi government. With money from the intelligence agencies it moved its headquarters to Jordan in early 1996 and tried to recruit serving Iraqi officers to act against President Saddam....

"Starting in late June and early July 1996, there was a wave of arrests and executions of senior officers in an elite formation. The number of those killed is not known but may be as high as eighty.

"The CIA's attempt to overthrow President Saddam has received some publicity in the US, but the role of MI6 in the failed coup has hitherto been kept secret." [49]

Stephen Dorril, Intelligence Consultant and Author: 2000 Book *MI6*: **Jury Didn't Hear**:

"In 1996, MI6 cooperated with the CIA's station chief in London, Thomas Tweeten, in a botched operation in northern Iraq.... A meeting in January 1996 of CIA and MI6 officers and intelligence officers from Jordan and Saudi Arabia agreed to back the INA[a] as the vehicle to overthrow Saddam. The CIA and MI6 invested millions of dollars in the London-based INA ... which ran the operation from lavish offices in Amman. The conspirators were supplied with weapons and explosives, and were provided with a powerful radio transmitter taken from Croatia. Unfortunately for MI6, the INA was riddled with informers and double agents.

---

[a] Iraqi National Accord.

"During late June and July there were a spate of arrests of senior army officers, including a number from the élite Special Republican Guard which protects the Iraqi leader, who were said to be party to a plot to start a mutiny. It is not known how deeply implicated MI6 officers were, but a number of CIA officers were deemed to be 'out of control'. Organising the opposition from Kurdistan, they planned without authorisation the assassination of Saddam.... On 31 August Saddam sent his tanks ... into Kurdistan, crushing the opposition and destroying the headquarters of the Iraqi National Congress." [50]

Gaddafi Assassination Plot: February 1996 [a]

Coroner: 26 Feb 08: 152.1:
"This is not an issue in these inquests. We are not looking into newspaper reports into what might or might not be going to happen to Colonel Gaddafi."

In early 1996 a roadside bomb exploded underneath a vehicle in a motorcade carrying Colonel Muammar Gaddafi, the leader of Libya. Several people died as a result of the blast, but Gaddafi survived – he was severely shaken but not injured.

There is evidence indicating that on that day Gaddafi was the target of an attempted assassination and there is conflicting evidence over the degree of MI6's involvement in the operation.

Richard Dearlove, MI6 Director of Operations, 1994 to 1999, UK: 20 Feb 08: 64.8:
Burnett: Q. Now, there is a very well-known allegation of planned assassination that I wish to ask you about. It has been suggested widely and publicly that, in February 1996, SIS conspired with one of its Libyan agents to assassinate Colonel Gaddafi. Now, first of all, just to locate that in time, you were head of operations at the time.
A. I was indeed head of operations at the time.
Q. Were you the chief of the service when that allegation emerged publicly?
A. Yes, I was.
Q. Is it true?

_____

[a] It will be shown later that the inquest focused on the 1992 Milosevic plot – which never passed the proposal stage and revolved around a single document which has since been destroyed. The Gaddafi evidence will reveal that this was the plot the inquest should have addressed – it reached execution stage and its existence is supported by a substantial amount of evidence.

A. No, it is not true, and I think one should add that – this is an allegation that was made by a former Security Service officer, David Shayler. It was fully investigated by the Metropolitan Police, who sent a team into SIS. They were given full access, full cooperation, and it was shown as a result of their investigation that Shayler's allegations were without substance.

Q. Now, Shayler, you say, was a former Security Service officer; that is MI5 –

A. MI5.

Q. – not MI6, as it happens.

A. Not MI6.

Q. So investigated by the Metropolitan Police?

A. An independent police investigation, which was ordered by the Crown Prosecution Service.

Q. You have said what its conclusions were. Did you obviously, as chief, take a close interest in that?

A. I took an exceptionally close interest.

Q. Do you have any doubts about the correctness of that conclusion?

A. I have no doubts whatsoever, nor did I from the start of the investigation.

Miss X, MI6 Administrator, UK: 26 Feb 08: 151.8:

Keen: Q. An alleged plot to assassinate Colonel Gaddafi.... If there was a P file[a] for that individual and a proposal for an assassination, presumably the P file would contain a record of that proposal?

A. If something like that had ever existed, yes, it would be on that file.

Q. So, again, that would be a simple way of checking whether or not, in fact, at the relevant time, the Secret Intelligence Service did advance such proposals beyond the wild imaginings of Mr A?

Coroner: This is not an issue in these inquests. We are not looking into newspaper reports into what might or might not be going to happen to Colonel Gaddafi, and we also have Sir Richard's evidence on this.

Q. With respect, sir, Sir Richard's evidence was that, as a matter of principle, the Secret Intelligence Service would never contemplate such an action or operation, and that was challenged by my learned friend, Mr Mansfield, and the issue that arises is whether there is in fact evidence to show that that in fact is the case and that there have been occasions where such operations have been contemplated by the Secret Intelligence Service.

Burnett: Maybe I shall waste time – I am sorry if I do – but my recollection of Sir Richard's evidence[b], which I do not have up in front of me at the moment, was that he explained to the jury that following those public

---

[a] MI6 has a "P file" for each individual it deals with or has a relationship with. In that file information relating to the individual is kept. They are referenced by a "P" followed by a number, e.g. P12345. Sources: Tomlinson: 13 Feb 08: from 31.9; Dearlove: 20 Feb 08: from 136.9; Miss X: 26 Feb 08: from 17.1.

[b] Dearlove's evidence regarding the Gaddafi plot is above.

allegations made in newspapers – and I think he attributed them to a former MI5 officer, there was a police investigation –

Coroner: I think we know who he was.

Burnett: I am sure he named him.

Coroner: Yes.

Burnett: – there was a police investigation, and the police then consulted the CPS and the conclusions were negative. I have a fairly vivid recollection of Sir Richard indicating that he always knew that they would be because he was the head of operations at the time alleged and he knew there was nothing in it. So it may well be that this witness cannot add anything to that.

A. I cannot add anything to what you have already said there.

Burnett: It is at Day 73[a], pages 64 and 65.

Q. Given that there was an investigation of that alleged conspiracy to murder, have you any explanation as to why there wasn't a similar investigation in respect of Mr A's proposal?

A. Only that Mr A's proposal, I do not think, ever really got beyond being just an idea.

Q. Is an idea not sufficient?

A. An idea that does not become in any way substantive is not recorded formally anywhere or anything like that and is quashed right from the word go, no.

Q. And Tippexed out of the record?

A. That was a normal way of treating correspondence.

Annie Machon[b], Ex-MI5 Officer: 2005 Book *Spies, Lies & Whistleblowers*: **Jury Didn't Hear**:

"In summer 1995 ... David [Shayler] was first briefed on the plot. David Watson [code PT16/B], David's counterpart in MI6, asked to meet to discuss an unusual case which he could not mention over the phone. At the subsequent meeting PT16/B told David that:

- a senior member of the Libyan military intelligence service had walked into the British embassy in Tunis and asked to meet the resident MI6 officer

- the Libyan 'walk-in' had asked for funds to lead a group of Islamic extremists in an attempted coup, which would involve the assassination of Colonel Gaddafi, the head of the Libyan state

- although the Libyan military intelligence officer led the group, he had said he was not an Islamic extremist himself

---

[a] 20 Feb 08.

[b] Annie Machon and David Shayler met while both were working for MI5. According to the 1999 book, *Defending the Realm*, by August 1997 they had been partners for 4½ years – since early 1993.: Mark Hollingsworth and Nick Fielding, *Defending the Realm:MI5 and the Shayler Affair*, p165.

- the Libyan had a brief MI6 record, which PT16/B thought was enough to confirm that the Libyan did have the access to the regime that he claimed. "In exchange for MI6's support, the Libyan offered to hand over the two Lockerbie suspects after the coup....

"In the following weeks, PT16/B told David that the Libyan was codenamed Tunworth. At some point in the following weeks David briefly saw the printout of MI6's record of him. It contained around two or three separate mentions. They supported his claim to be a senior member of Libyan military intelligence....

"David takes up the story: 'Throughout this process, I briefed my line manager, G9A/1 – Jerry Mahoney until December 1995, Paul Slim after that – about these developments....

"'It is inconceivable that G9A/1 did not think an MI6-funded plot to engineer a coup in Libya was worthy of mentioning to his line manager, G9/0, Paul Mitchell. In turn, it is unthinkable that Mitchell did not raise the matter with his line management who would have informed his boss until the DG[a] herself [Stella Rimington] had been made aware....'

"In December 1995 ... R/ME/C at MI6, circulated CX95/ 53452 report[b] to Whitehall and other addressees, warning of a potential coup in Libya.... The report clearly demonstrated that Watson knew that Tunworth was planning terrorism and his group had already been involved in attempts on Gaddafi's life....

"David remembers another MI6 CX report being issued about the plot in early 1996. It was a shopping list of the group's requirements to carry out the coup, including the supply of weapons and basics like jeeps and tents.

"Around the same time, Christmas 1995, Watson told David that he had met Tunworth, in Geneva and paid him $40,000. Jackie Barker, who had replaced Jane Thomas as G9A/15, told him that Watson had told her the same information 'in confidence'. During routine G9/PT16 meetings around this time, officers occasionally mentioned the plot. Watson then met Tunworth on two further occasions early in 1996 in Geneva.... Watson mentioned [to David] that he had paid 'similar sums' to Tunworth on each occasion. Although PT16/B never specifically mentioned it, it was tacitly understood that Watson was working with the approval of his direct line manager, PT16, Richard Bartlett.

"At some point ... Watson mentioned that the submission – MI6 jargon for the letter requesting permission from the Foreign Office for otherwise illegal operations – was going to go 'all the way to the top'. In about January 1996, Watson told him that the submission had been successful, indicating that the

---

[a] Director-General.
[b] Reproduced later.

Foreign Secretary himself had signed the document permitting the operation....

"Then, in either February or March 1996, David read two, possibly three intelligence reports quoting independent sources – the Egyptian and Moroccan intelligence services. They all stated that an attack had been made on Colonel Gaddafi in Sirte, Libya. Two of the reports indicated that the attackers had tried to assassinate Gaddafi when he was part of a motorcade but had failed as they had targeted the wrong car. As a result of the explosion and the ensuing chaos in which shots were fired, civilians and security police were maimed and killed.

"'At a meeting shortly after, Watson ventured to me[a] in a note of triumph that Tunworth had been responsible for the attack. "Yes that was our man. We did it," was how he put it. He regarded it, curiously, as a triumph even though the objective of the operation had not been met, and reporting indicated there had been civilian casualties....'" [51]

Paget Report, p811: **Jury Didn't Hear**:

"[David Shayler's] assessment that the SIS was involved in the crash in the Alma underpass was based largely on his knowledge of a plot involving a bomb or grenade being placed under a car in a cavalcade in Libya in order to kill Colonel Gadaffi – i.e. it involved attacking a car in a foreign country using what he described as 'surrogates' (cut-outs) to do the killing.

"By David Shayler's account this was an overt attack involving no apparent attempt at disguise. He stated that an SIS officer briefed him on this and he saw corroboration of the plot in GCHQ material in terms of timings, intent etc. He claimed that the attack took place on the wrong car and that innocent people were killed.

"There was an independent investigation by the MPS into the 'Gadaffi allegation'. Operation Paget enquiries have shown there is no evidence to support [Shayler's] assessment that there is any link to this investigation."

Note: The following items of evidence, media reports, interviews and comment pertaining to the Gaddafi plot are shown in chronological order.[b]

Mail on Sunday, 31 Aug 97 Article: **Jury Didn't Hear**:[c]

"Gaddafi Plot Credible, Says US

"David Shayler's revelations that MI6 tried to blow up Colonel Gaddafi were given strong credence by US intelligence sources yesterday.

---

[a] Shayler.

[b] The order in which they were published or appeared.

[c] This article was published on the day of the Paris crash involving Diana and Dodi.

"They insisted that, despite claims to the contrary, the British secret service was financing the group behind the attempt on the Libyan leader's life in February 1996.

"A bomb was planted under Gaddafi's motorcade as he travelled 210 miles south-east of the capital, Tripoli. Several people were killed but Gaddafi survived, although he is reported to have been so badly shaken that he needed hospital treatment.

"Shayler, who was working on the Libya desk at the time of the attack, gave a detailed account of British involvement in the affair to the *Mail on Sunday* and the BBC's *Panorama*.[a]

"British government officials have since declared that the assassination story is false. But the American sources, speaking on the understanding that they are not identified, claimed there could be at least some truth in what Shayler says.

"In 1990, they said, the US, Britain and others staged a joint intelligence effort that closed down a Libyan chemical weapons plant in Rabta. But by the end of 1992, drawing on satellite photos and reports from spies – some through British intelligence – the CIA had constructed a computer model of a second nerve gas plant Gaddafi was building.

"A secret conference at CIA headquarters in Langley, Virginia – to which British intelligence representatives were invited – decided to wage a covert battle to prevent Gadaffi from finishing his new factory.

"The intelligence community agreed, as a preliminary step, to bog down construction by stopping the delivery of machinery needed for the building. Congressional forces say that in 1995, and again in 1996, the CIA provided classified briefings on Libya during which it was said that Gadaffi was vulnerable on the home front with religious unrest spreading into the armed forces.

"The CIA was financing at least one tribal group and encouraging it to revolt. But according to a Washington-based Middle East expert: 'The CIA is notoriously weak in recruiting humint (human intelligence) assets, especially in the Middle East.'

"This is not true of MI6 and, say the Americans, the British service turned to the Fighting Islamic Group (FIG) and its leader, Abu Abdullah Sadeq, who was living in London. It was this group that was behind the failed assassination attempt.

"Last week a former senior analyst with American intelligence said: 'I'm sure that British intelligence has all the plausible deniability that it needs. Certainly there were contacts between MI6 and FIG.'

---

[a] At this stage *Panorama* had conducted the interview, but it didn't go to air until 1998 – see below.

"Another source in Washington said that he understood MI6 had 'provided various kinds of support' to FIG, including financial help." [52]

Mark Hollingsworth & Nick Fielding, 1999 Book *Defending the Realm*: **Jury Didn't Hear**:

On 2 August 1998 "hints of a story about Gaddafi surfaced in the *Sunday Times*. It was clear that the story was beginning to leak out, but with the government injunction in force it would not appear in Britain. Lord Williams, the Home Office minister, appeared on BBC Radio 4 to deny that there had been an 'official plot' to kill Colonel Gaddafi. His comments only fuelled speculation that there had been an unofficial plot. The Foreign Office would say only that 'the central claim that there was an official plot to kill Gaddafi is untrue'.

"The following week ... the *New York Times* published a version of the story.... [It] was brief but accurate." [53]

Sarah Lyall, *New York Times* Journalist, USA: 5 Aug 98 Article: **Jury Didn't Hear**:

"Are Britain's Covert Operatives Messing Up? Don't Even Ask

"Did the British Government try to assassinate Col. Muammar el-Qaddafi, the Libyan leader, in February 1996 by planting a bomb under his motorcade?...

"A sweeping injunction has barred [UK] newspapers and television news programs from publishing the embarrassing allegations about the inner workings of Britain's security services, brought up by a disgruntled former officer [David Shayler]....

"'I've known these things for something like 16 months, and I am not allowed to publish any of it,' said Jonathan Holborow, editor of *The Mail on Sunday*....

"The Labor Government has taken the harshest possible stand against the news media. 'The thinking behind the injunction is that because of the nature of [Shayler's] work, it's possible that national security can be damaged', said a spokeswoman for the Home Office who spoke on condition that her name not be used.

"Strangely enough, the Government told the press earlier this week that it could report the allegation about the Qadaffi assassination plot in the vaguest possible terms because, the Home Office spokeswoman said, 'it is untrue.'

"But it forbade reporting of related details, like the allegations that the agent in charge had ties to a shady right-wing fundamentalist group in Libya, and that he was paid $160,000....

"'As a journalist in a free democracy,' said Mr. Holborow, of *The Mail on Sunday*, this censorship 'makes me feel pretty sick.

"'We haven't had this sort of thing since the war,' he said." [54]

BBC Panorama, 7 Aug 98[a] Documentary: **Jury Didn't Hear**:
David Shayler: The Libyan section [of MI6 and MI5] ... had regular three-month meetings....
Mark Urban, BBC Diplomatic Editor: At one of the joint meetings[b] Shayler learnt of the existence of an Arab agent, who was given the very English code name, Tunworth. That informer and his SIS case officer are the key figures in Shayler's allegations.... MI5 and SIS[c] each sent two or three officers to the meetings. The MI5 ones, who *Panorama* has established were present, were G9A/1, Shayler himself, two others using the MI5 internal acronym, G9A/15.[d] The SIS ones were called, in their service jargon, PT16, PT16 ops B and the man meeting and running Tunworth, PT16/B. At one of these meetings Shayler discovered that PT16/B's new agent was much more than a simple supplier of information.
Shayler: PT16/B, who was my kind of opposite number in SIS ... we'd talk about how [Tunworth] was involved ... in trying to plan an assassination attempt on Gaddafi, using a Libyan Islamic extremist group[e]. Basically ... this was what [Tunworth] was coming up with, with SIS. I mean that was the

---

[a] The BBC interview with Shayler was conducted by Mark Urban in 1997, but the government had imposed an "injunction designed to protect national security".: Sources: BBC News, BBC Screens Shayler Interview, 8 August 1998; Annie Machon, *Spies, Lies and Whistleblowers:MI5, MI6 and the Shayler Affair*, page 243.
[b] There is an apparent conflict with the account in Annie Machon's book: "In summer 1995 ... David [Shayler] was first briefed on the plot. David Watson [code PT16/B], David's counterpart in MI6, asked to meet to discuss an unusual case which he could not mention over the phone." According to *Panorama,* Shayler first heard about the plot in one of the three-monthly joint meetings between the MI5 and MI6 Libyan sections. It could be significant that this account doesn't come from Shayler, but is from the reporter, Mark Urban. I suggest that the Machon account is more likely to be accurate because: a) it is probable that an issue of this nature could be dealt with secretly, i.e. a one-on-one meeting rather than an open discussion; b) Machon was very close to the events and there does not appear to be any reason for her not to be truthful on this. Machon later mentions in her book: "During routine G9/PT16 meetings around this time [December 1995], officers occasionally mentioned the plot." This does not necessarily indicate discussion in these meetings of MI6's role in the plot.
[c] MI6.
[d] Normally there would only be one person holding each designation. Annie Machon stated, in an email to the author: "During David's tenure of the Libya desk, the first G9A/15 was moved on and replaced.... Both were officially briefed about the Gaddafi Plot.": Annie Machon, Email to John Morgan, 25 April 2011.
[e] Islamic Fighting Group.

reason for the initial walk-in[a] and so on. He was: "I've got a plan, I've got people behind me. What I also need is the money to buy the things I need."

Urban: Tunworth's intelligence was, we're told, shared with a small number of key officials. These reports are known in the secret jargon of Whitehall as CX. Shayler says a special CX report of Tunworth's information was put out. It contained details of what was brought together for the plan to kill Gaddafi. As is normal procedure the CX report was sanitised – it didn't explicitly spell out that PT16/B's agent was himself a part of the conspiracy to kill Gaddafi.

Shayler: When I first heard this story I thought this was Boy's Own, James Bond, SIS stuff, and we'll probably hear about it for a month, then it will disappear and we'll never hear anything about it again.... They were actually put out as a CX report to Whitehall, probably to the Foreign Office, and certainly obviously to us, probably to GCHQ, may not be to GCHQ.

Urban: So they're obviously very excited about this.

Shayler: Very excited about it, well, but even then my thinking still was, ok, I mean, they've put this out, they're obviously not saying they're involved at the moment, because what they're saying is they've got a source reporting on somebody else doing it, which is one of the ways of hiding the source of your intelligence. My thinking even then was this is still Boy's Own stuff. And I don't think this is going to happen. It's like so many things they've told me – it's not going to happen.

Urban: As the plan to kill Gaddafi took shape inside Libya, the SIS officer PT16/B met his agent Tunworth again. As SIS' relationship with Tunworth deepened a substantial sum of money was changing hands.

Shayler: So we're talking about sort of like a hundred thousand pounds[bc] to fund the assassination attempt against Gaddafi, which of course will come from the British taxpayer.

Urban: Britain's agent Tunworth was a part of a conspiracy. He became SIS' link with a militant Islamic group, a hardline organisation headed by Abdullah Al Sadiq. In the past several Arab countries have said that Britain is

---

[a] This was the walk-in to the British Embassy in Tunis, mentioned in Machon's book – see earlier.

[b] The evidence in Machon's book (p171) indicates an initial payment of $US40,000, with payment of "similar sums" on "two further occasions". The exchange rate in December 1995 hovered around $1.50 to the pound, so the equivalent of around £80,000 in total was paid out.

[c] Putting this into some perspective, according to Dorril, by 1993 the largest portions of the MI6 budget went evenly to the Middle East and Russia, with 15% of the entire MI6 budget spent on the Middle East – the same percentage as Russia: Stephen Dorril, *MI6*, p760.

harbouring Islamic militants.... Libya has publicly accused Britain of giving refuge to the leader of [this] militant Islamic group. In response to our enquiries the Foreign Office remarkably says it doesn't know if Abdullah Al Sadiq is in this country.

Late in February 1996 the militant Islamic group went into action. They had learnt that Colonel Gaddafi's car was going to pass on a road near the city of Sirte. The terrorists had put a bomb under the road and waited. They set it off. Several bodyguards are thought to have died. In the gun battle which followed three members of the militant Islamic group were also reportedly killed. Shortly after the attack failed, intelligence reports were received and sent back to London where they ended up on David Shayler's desk.

Shayler: [The reports were] ... saying an attempt had been made on Gaddafi's life, that in fact a bomb had been put under a car in a cavalcade. Gaddafi was travelling in the cavalcade, but in a different car, so the explosion's gone off and there'd been various casualties and fatalities, but in fact they'd got the wrong people.[a] Now even then I was still thinking this

---

[a] There appears to be some conflict over exactly what occurred in February 1996:
- Machon's book: "as a result of the explosion and the ensuing chaos in which shots were fired, civilians and security police were maimed and killed"
- Urban on *Panorama*: "several bodyguards are thought to have died. In the gun battle which followed three members of the militant Islamic group were also reportedly killed"
- Shayler on *Panorama*: "the explosion's gone off and there'd been various casualties and fatalities, but in fact they'd got the wrong people"
- Paget Report: "innocent people were killed".

It is possible that all of these accounts are correct – that several of Gaddafi's bodyguards or security police were killed in the initial explosion and then in the ensuing chaos three of the IFG died along with innocent civilians caught up in the crossfire.

In their book Hollingsworth and Fielding state: "Early in September 1998 Libya showed television footage of what it said had been an assassination attempt in 1996 on Gaddafi. The images were broadcast by the London-based Arab satellite TV channel ANN during a live interview with Gaddafi from Tripoli.

"The footage shows Gaddafi being greeted by large crowds at a rally in Wadi Achatt ... about 200 miles south of Sirte. First he is shown being driven along in a jeep. Later he gets down and walks amongst the crowd. Suddenly an object can be seen flying through the air and landing at [Gaddafi's] feet. Gaddafi and his entourage bend over to examine it then walk away. According to the Libyan authorities, this was a grenade, thrown by a man in the crowd. As Gaddafi walks away, closely surrounded by bodyguards, other guards move in to arrest the man. According to the commentary with the film, the man was 'an agent of British intelligence'." Annie Machon makes a similar description of the Libyan footage in her book and then states: "Libyan TV named the assailant as Abdullah Radwan, a partner of Abu Abdullah Sadiq, the leader of the IFG."

could be the result of Islamic extremists ... in Libya in general.... There was another intelligence report which wasn't quite as detailed, but this again was supporting the fact that the thing had happened.

Urban: A few days later, at the offices of an Arabic newspaper in London a fax arrived at the desk of Camille Tawil. In it the militant Islamic group claimed responsibility for the attack. They also identified the members of its team who they said had been martyred in a bid to kill Gaddafi.

Camille Tawil, Journalist, Al-Hayat: I remember receiving a statement by fax from this group, Islamic Fighting Group, saying that they are responsible for an assassination attempt on the life of Gaddafi. I read the statement. It contained several names. The statement claimed that they were involved in the assassination attempt. I felt it was credible information given to me, but I wanted to verify the story. I contacted other Libyan groups and they gave me a similar account of what had happened. This is why I decided to publish the story.

Urban: Shayler didn't realise the full implications of the intelligence report until the next meeting of the joint group. It was MI5's turn to host. Officers filed into Room 470 at Thames House. Once again PT16/B, the MI6 man who ran Tunworth was there.

Shayler: It was only when I met PT16/B, discussing other matters with him, that he mentioned this thing in a kind of note of triumph saying, "Yes you know, we've done it.... We are the kind of intelligence service that people think we are, almost." My reaction was one of total shock. I mean, this was kind of really against ... what I thought I was doing in the intelligence services and against ... what I'd been telling people. In my job at MI5 I knew quite a few journalists, because I used to be a journalist. From time to time in conversations it would come up about work with the intelligence services and so on. I would say these stories are rubbish or, you know, somebody's completely misunderstood what's going on. Yeah, the intelligence services don't get up to the things that were reported.... I [was] very determined to tell these people this sort of thing didn't go on, but this was a refutation of that. Suddenly this sort of thing does go on. I was absolutely astounded when I heard this was the case. Because as I say my thinking on the SIS was that they were involved in a Boy's Own comic. This was very real. Suddenly

---

Although it has been claimed by some that this is a recording of the incident described by Shayler, this does not appear to be the case – Shayler described a roadside bomb attack, whereas the Libyan footage allegedly shows a grenade being thrown. Sources: Mark Hollingsworth & Nick Fielding, *Defending the Realm: MI5 and the Shayler Affair*, p151; Annie Machon, *Spies, Lies and Whistleblowers:MI5, MI6 and the Shayler Affair*, p253. A sequence of still photos of the Libyan footage appears in the Hollingsworth/Fielding book, between pages150 and 151.

we're talking about tens of thousands of pounds of taxpayer's money being used to attempt to assassinate a foreign head of state.

Urban: So, is that shocking claim about what went on in the key meeting here [at MI5 HQ] true? In the course of investigating Shayler's allegations, I have corroborated many of the key facts. There were indeed a series of meetings involving Shayler and the SIS officer PT16/B. Britain did have advance knowledge of the attempt on Colonel Gaddafi's life. And British intelligence was using its Arab agent Tunworth as a cut-out or go-between with Islamic militant groups in Libya.

All of this begs the question: Just exactly who knew what SIS was up to? SIS' foreign operations are governed both by law and Whitehall convention. A sensitive foreign operation requires the intelligence agency to draw up a submission. This is sent across the Thames to the Foreign Office where officials may alter it. It then goes to the desk either of a junior minister or the Foreign Secretary himself.

Shayler: In this case obviously because you are giving money to a group to assassinate a foreign head of state they actually said to me, we're going to submit, but we think it's going all the way to the top.

Urban: And it did?

Shayler: Yes ... that's what he was saying. I mean the law, obviously not at the same time, but later on they said it had gone to the top and they got authority from the top.

Urban: But did they get authority from their political masters here at the Foreign Office? Well, two well-placed people have told me that the Tory ministers running this department at the time gave no such authorisation. This is open to several possibilities. The SIS man, PT16/B was lying at those crucial meetings, perhaps to try and impress his MI5 colleagues. Or that an assassination operation went ahead without any kind of political approval. In short, Britain's intelligence service was operating completely out of control. There are precedents for SIS using Arab assassination groups. In the 50s they organised a group of Egyptians for an attempt to kill President Nasser. It wasn't authorised by ministers[a] – it was discovered by Nasser, and after this scandal the current procedures were put in place. More recently there's considerable evidence that Britain cooperated with the CIA in an attempt to overthrow Saddam Hussein. In this case though, the plots were authorised by ministers....

For Shayler, there's little doubt that SIS masterminded the Gaddafi operation and that he's morally justified in revealing it.

Shayler: Essentially you're paying, like in the region of a hundred thousand pounds ... to carry out the murder of a foreign head of state....

---

[a] It was authorised by the prime minister – see earlier.

Urban: It is true of course that Shayler's knowledge of this affair depends entirely on what the SIS man, PT16/B, told him at their meetings. But certain pieces of this Libyan jigsaw cannot easily be argued away by SIS.
There was an assassination attempt. Numerous Libyan sources confirm it. Britain did have a relationship with Tunworth. Any inquiry into David Shayler's allegation will be able to find the key CX report which detailed the plot against Gaddafi, so showing Tunworth's inside knowledge.
Shayler: Obviously [the CX report] wasn't saying we have an agent who was going to go and assassinate Gaddafi – what [it] was saying is there is an agent reporting that there is a group who have ... taken certain steps towards the assassination of Gaddafi. But ... it was much longer than the sort of stuff you normally got from SIS. Whereas the actual report would normally be a sheet of A4, two sheets of A4 at the most and this was 3 or 4 sides of A4.[a]
Urban: Somewhere in Whitehall then there should be copies of that secret memo, detailing SIS' advance knowledge of the plot and proximity to it. As for MI5's copy, Shayler tells me he remembers the file number....
This week the government has denied the suggestion that there was any authorised – and they stress the "authorised" – operation to kill Colonel Gaddafi.
MI6, or SIS', defence against these serious allegations may well involve some sort of play with words. Their man, PT16/B, could well argue that he was just paying his Arab agent for information – the sort of routine intelligence work which does not require specific ministerial approval. So when the government says, as it has during recent days, that no authorisation was given to a plot to kill Colonel Gaddafi, they may well be right.
But only a thorough-going inquiry would stand a chance of getting to the bottom of whether some intelligence officers played fast and loose with the rules. David Shayler has provided *Panorama* with other details about the Libyan operation and the people connected with it. Combined with our own information, it suggests that SIS have a very serious case to answer. Only somebody [with the] power to delve into their most secret archives could stand a real chance of getting to the bottom of what exactly they thought they were buying when they handed over £100,000 to agent Tunworth.
BBC News, 8 Aug 98 Article: BBC Screens Shayler Interview: **Jury Didn't Hear**:
"The BBC has broadcast an interview with the former MI5 officer David Shayler in which he spoke about an alleged plot by the UK's Secret Intelligence Service to kill Libyan leader Colonel Gaddafi.

---

[a] The CX report, shown later, prints out on three A4 sides.

"The interview [was] with *Panorama*.... In it, he told how a £100,000 payment to an agent 'Tunworth' funded a militant plot to murder Gaddafi. "The film was not broadcast until Friday because the government has an injunction designed, it says, to protect national security. The BBC decided to go ahead with the transmission after parts of the script were submitted to government solicitors, who gave authority to proceed....

"Mr Shayler joined MI5 in 1994, as part of the G9 section dealing with Libya. At a joint meeting on Libya with the SIS he heard of an agent known as Tunworth. Also at the meeting was PT16/B, who controlled Tunworth and detailed Tunworth's collaboration with an extremist group in Libya trying to kill Colonel Gaddafi.

"However the CX Report, circulated to officials, GCHQ and the Foreign Office, did not say that Tunworth was actively involved in the plot.

"Mr Shayler later learned that as the assassination plot gathered pace, about £100,000 was given to Tunworth.

"In February 1996 a bomb was planted under Gaddafi's motorcade, but it exploded under the wrong car. Several bodyguards were killed and in the ensuing gun battle three extremists were reportedly killed....

"Mr Urban obtained evidence that meetings did take place with PT16/B, that Britain had advance knowledge of the attempt on Gaddafi's life and that Tunworth was a go-between with Islamic militant groups in Libya.

"However, Foreign Office ministers at the time of the affair said they had not given any authorisation for a murder attempt.

"Mr Urban concluded that one answer was that security services had acted without any political authority.

"He said that the BBC had obtained other evidence of SIS activities, but these were withheld for security reasons." [55]

Robin Cook, UK Foreign Secretary, 1997 to 2001: 9 Aug 98: **Jury Didn't Hear**:

"The tale about the MI6 plot to assassinate Gaddafi is fantasy.... I have pursued these allegations. I am absolutely satisfied that the previous Foreign Secretary did not authorise any such assassination attempt. I'm perfectly satisfied that MI6 never put forward any such proposal for an assassination attempt. Nor have I seen anything in the 15 months I have been in the job which would suggest that MI6 has any interest, any role or any experience over the recent decade of any such escapade. There was no Government-inspired plan to assassinate Gaddafi. It is pure fantasy.

"I have already made my own enquiries. I have satisfied my mind. I see no basis for the reports in today's papers about any forthcoming enquiry. There was no SIS proposal to do it, and I'm fairly clear there has never been any SIS involvement. I do wish people would recognise that somebody who has left another service – not the Secret Intelligence Service MI6, he was never in MI6 – is making allegations, no doubt for his own reasons....

"I'm perfectly clear that these allegations have no basis in fact. And secondly, I am quite clear that the SIS operations I have authorised have nothing remotely to do with the kind of fantasy that has been produced over the last two days." [56a]

Nicholas Rufford, *Sunday Times* Journalist, UK: 13 Feb 00 Article: **Jury Didn't Hear**:

"Revealed: Cook Misled Public Over Libya Plot

"A top-secret report[b] linking MI6 with a failed attempt to assassinate Colonel Gadaffi appeared on an American internet site yesterday, refuting Robin Cook's claim that British intelligence was not involved.

"The document, marked 'UK Eyes Alpha', details contacts between MI6 and a group of Middle Eastern plotters who tried unsuccessfully to blow up Gadaffi's motorcade.

"It reveals that British intelligence knew of the 1996 assassination attempt at least two months in advance. A member of the rebel group gave detailed intelligence to his MI6 handler in anticipation of help from Britain.

"The foreign secretary, who said 18 months ago that MI6 had 'no interest' in any such plot, faced calls for a parliamentary inquiry.

"The report, coded CX95/ 53452, was passed to senior Foreign Office officials. It revealed when and where the assassination attempt was due and said that at least 250 British-made weapons were distributed among the plotters.

"Allegations of a plot to kill Gadaffi, said to involve MI6, emerged 18 months ago. British newspapers were prevented from publishing the claims, but details later appeared in *The New York Times*.

"Arab newspapers reported that the Libyan leader had only narrowly survived. A number of his bodyguards and would-be assassins died....

"There will be speculation, that the intelligence services were out of control, or that Cook was not told the full facts by Foreign Office staff....

"Francis Maude, the shadow foreign secretary, called for an immediate investigation: 'Did Cook conceal the truth? Was it kept from him, or did he ignore it?' he said....

"A Foreign Office spokesman defended Cook's conduct. 'The foreign secretary did not mislead the public,' he said. 'At the time of the Frost interview he was not asked if MI6 knew about the plot. He was asked whether MI6 instigated it or was involved in it. Those were the allegations around at the time.'...

---

[a] Speaking on the BBC's *Breakfast With Frost* program.
[b] The report is reproduced in full below.

"The four-page CX document, published on the Yahoo! website, carries a
coded header sheet that appears to confirm its authenticity.... It reveals that in
November 1995 links were established between a plotter and 'HMG' – Her
Majesty's government....

"The text published on the web is blanked out at one point and the words
'removed to protect Tunworth's identity' inserted. Tunworth is the codename assigned to the source....

"The report was passed to Sir John Coles, then the most senior civil servant
in the Foreign Office, as well as to GCHQ, the government listening station,
MI5 and the Ministry of Defence. It was also relayed to British stations in
Tunis, Cairo and Washington....

"The claim that MI6 was involved in trying to kill Gadaffi was first made in
August 1998 by David Shayler....

"Accounts published in Arab newspapers confirmed that an assassination
attempt had taken place. Al-Hayat, the London- based Arab newspaper,
reported that rebels had attacked Gadaffi's motorcade near the city of Sirte in
February 1996. Several bystanders were said to have been killed....

"The leaking of the CX report raises wider questions about the control of
secret government material which finds its way onto the internet....

"The *Sunday Times* has complied with a request by Rear-Admiral Nick
Wilkinson, secretary of the government's defence, press and broadcasting
advisory committee, not to print the address of the website on which the CX
report is published...." [57]

Martin Hickman, *The Independent*, UK: 13 Feb 00 Article: **Jury Didn't
Hear**:

"An intelligence report placed on the world wide web has reportedly
disclosed that British intelligence knew at least two months in advance that
there would be an attempt to blow up Gaddafi....

"CX reports reportedly summarise MI6's key intelligence findings and are
circulated to the Prime Minister, the Cabinet Office and the Joint Intelligence
Committee.

"Whitehall sources confirmed to *The Sunday Times* that the four page report
– which carried a coded header sheet – was genuine....

"In a statement, the Foreign Office declined to state that the intelligence
report was a fake. And it conceded that the British Government had known of
plots against Gaddafi.

"The statement read: 'In August 1998, interviewed on *Breakfast With Frost*,
the Foreign Secretary said: "... I am absolutely satisfied that the previous
Foreign Secretary did not authorise any such assassination attempt ... nor
have I seen anything which would suggest that SIS has any interest, any role,
or any experience over the recent decade of any such escapade."

"'The Foreign Secretary went on: "... there was no Government-inspired plot
to assassinate Gaddafi, there was no SIS proposal to do it".'

"The statement added: 'Nothing in the alleged intelligence report posted on the Internet invalidates what the Foreign Secretary said. Nor have we ever denied that we knew of plots against Gaddafi.'

"However, a storm is likely to engulf the Foreign Secretary over the disclosure that British intelligence apparently knew about the plot in advance." [58]

BBC News, 15 Feb 00 Article: **Jury Didn't Hear**:
"Robin Cook has denied misleading the public following the publication of a document on the internet alleging British involvement [in a plot to assassinate Gaddafi]. He said he was 'satisfied' that the intelligence services had no involvement in an 'escapade' to kill the Colonel.

"Mr Cook also denied two years ago that British security services had been involved in a bombing which narrowly failed to kill Colonel Gaddafi and overthrow his regime....

"The document published on the internet and marked 'UK eyes alpha' alleges that MI6 had been told of the plot two months before it was said to have taken place in February 1996.

"But Mr Cook told the BBC: 'I accept absolutely nothing in the way of having misled the British public. What I said two years ago was that I was absolutely satisfied that the previous foreign secretary did not authorise an assassination attempt, that the SIS never put forward such a proposal and in my time in office I have never seen any evidence that the SIS had any interest in such escapades.

"'There is absolutely nothing in this supposed intelligence document which would suggest otherwise. Indeed this document ends with the contact telling the SIS that the other plotters are unhappy about him even telling SIS, which rather proves that SIS were not manipulating this coup attempt.'

"Mr Cook refused to confirm whether the document was genuine or a forgery. But despite this, Rear Admiral Nick Wilkinson, secretary of the D notice committee which operates an agreed self-censorship system with the media on matters of national security, asked journalists not to publish the document's website address....

"Shadow foreign secretary Francis Maude said that the documents raised 'serious questions' over Mr Cook's previous comments and demanded an immediate inquiry.

"And the Liberal Democrat's foreign affairs spokesman Menzies Campbell said: 'Knowing that there were plots against Gaddafi is one thing, but being involved in them is something entirely different.'

"The Libyan government has summoned Britain's ambassador to ask to take part in any investigations over the plot." [59]

Nick Cohen, *Observer* Journalist, UK: 12 Mar 00 Article: **Jury Didn't Hear**:

"The 'friends of Robin Cook', as we polite journalists call the Foreign Secretary when we want to be discreet, are apprehensive. He's 'very edgy about Shayler,' they/he are whispering. 'He knows he hasn't been told the whole truth by MI6'....

"David Shayler alleged in 1998 that MI6, the Secret Intelligence Service, had been involved in an attempted coup against Gadaffi.... Cook's response was firm and suspiciously fast. MI6 had investigated the disillusioned spook's Libyan accusations in the space of a few hours. He could assure the nation that they were nothing more than 'pure fantasy'.

"Earlier this year, an MI6 report headed 'UK Eyes Alpha', was placed on the Internet. It said MI6 was indeed told by a 'delicate source' about a plot to kill the Libyan leader two months before a bungled coup took place in February 1996....

"It is possible that Robin Cook was fibbing when he said that Shayler was a fantasist, but not, in my view, likely. Cook's 'friends' say that MI6 told him the allegations were nonsense, and he thus backed the Foreign Office's covert wing in good faith. What else was he meant to do? Malcolm Rifkind, the Foreign Secretary in 1996, was equally gullible. When the Libyan document was leaked in February, he was dismissive. Even MI6 has not tried to pretend it is anything but genuine, but Rifkind said: 'SIS has never put forward such a proposal for an assassination attempt and in my time in office I have never seen any evidence that SIS is interested in such an escapade.' Richard Norton-Taylor of the *Guardian*, who knows more about the espionage bureaucracies than most, discovered with ease the service's contempt for mere elected politicians. A 'well-placed source' told him Rifkind would have been kept in ignorance. 'It was up to MI6 to judge what to tell Ministers about their activities,' the spy smugged." [60]

Mark Hollingsworth, *Guardian* Journalist and Author, UK: 17 Mar 00 Article: **Jury Didn't Hear**:

"We were sitting in a secluded office. 'Do you have any documents to back up what you are saying?' I asked David Shayler, the since-famous MI5 whistleblower. It was Wednesday, August 20 1997.... To my astonishment, he admitted there were indeed some papers.

"The next day a package of 28 documents arrived. Most were photocopies, although at least one was an original with a circulation sheet still attached. They were mainly internal MI5 reports, marked 'Top Secret UK Eyes Alpha Umbra Gamma' ... 'UK-US Eyes Only' ... 'Confidential', and so on. These included papers about Libyan dissidents by Shayler himself; a report entitled 'Investigation of Subversive Organisations'; and details of meetings between foreign office and Libyan officials in Cairo....

"Shayler had been careful ... not to take any 'raw' intelligence reports that might identify agents or informers. His exercise was purely to demonstrate his credibility....

"One important document, however, was absent from that dossier: the intelligence report which specifically links MI6 with the attempt to assassinate Colonel Gadafy. The recent leak of this document, on an American internet site, was devastating because it showed that British intelligence knew of the murder plot two months in advance, although the foreign secretary, Robin Cook, had described Shayler's original allegation as 'pure fantasy'. An Arab dissident was passing detailed information to his MI6 handler in anticipation of British assistance....

"Clearly, MI5 and MI6 are now terrified about more humiliating leaks. But the really interesting question is: who leaked that MI6 document?

"Shayler himself did not have this report in his own dossier in 1997. (If he had hidden it from us all at the time, he would certainly have distributed it 18 months ago when the foreign secretary first denounced him as a fantasist.) The logical conclusion is that the MI6 document may have been separately leaked from within the intelligence community or the foreign office. This has frightening implications for those bodies. It suggests there is another mole and that Shayler has more support in Whitehall than has been realised.

"And it corroborates my own information that there are other MI5 and MI6 officers who agree with Shayler's analysis. (The fact that half of the 1991 intake of MI5 officers had resigned by 1996 shows that Shayler was hardly a lone voice.)" [61]

```
5C2C IDP225 O24276 GG9613 NG0044 04122114 1CA952 91.13
```

```
      OO GG6 GG9 NDO LOG
      .5 G4 LEDGER
      LEX095
      AAAA
      041807Z DEC 95          Names and tel nos removed
      FM LONDON               to protect security
      TO PUSD 185 IMMEDIATE
      TO RESEARCH DEPT 234 IMMEDIATE
      TO MOD 913 IMMEDIATE
      TO CABINET OFFICER 721 IMMEDIATE
      TO SECURITY SERVICE 100 IMMEDIATE
      BT


      IMMEDIATE

      LEDGER   UK S E C R E T/DELICATE SOURCE/UK EYES ALPHA

      REQUIREMENTS: 2LIAPX01

      LEDGER DISTRIBUTION:
      FCO - PUSD

            DICTD
            NENAD
      RAD - ME
      MOD - DI(I AND W)
            DI (ROW)A
      CABINET OFFICE - JIC (ASSESSMENTS STAFF
      GCHQ - E1GA2
      SECURITY SERVICE - G9A5, G6A5 AND G6A3

      BRITISH AUTHORITIES INFORMED:
      CAIRO
      TUNIS
      WASHINGTON

      CX 95/53452(R/ME/C) OF 04 DECEMBER 1995 (GTN [-----]
EXT [----])

      /REPORT
```

PAGE TWO   UK S E C R E T/DELICATE SOURCE/UK EYES ALPHA

REPORT NO: 95/53452 (R/ME/C)

   TITLE: LIBYA: PLANS TO OVERTHROW QADAHFI IN EARLY
1996 ARE WELL ADVANCED

   SOURCE: A NEW SOURCE WITH DIRECT ACCESS WHOSE
RELIABILITY HAS NOT BEEN ESTABLISHED

SUMMARY

   5 Libyan colonels in charge of plans to overthrow
QADAHFI, scheduled to coincide with the next General
Peoples Congress in February. Coup will start with
unrest in Tripoli, Misratah and Benghazi. Coup plotters
are not associated with Islamic fundamentalists.
MUSA QADHAR AL-DAM murdered by coup plotters in June.
Attempt to assassinate QADAHFI in August thwarted by
security police.

DETAIL

1.   In late November 1995 [Removed to protect
TUNWORTH's identity]described plans, in which he was
involved, to overthrow Colonel QADAHFI. He said that 5
colonels from various parts of the armed forces were in
charge of the coup plot. these included [blank---
---------------blank] The latter was most likely to
take overall control.

2.   The coup was scheduled to start at around the time
of the next General Peoples Congress on 14 February 1996.
It would begin with attacks on a number of military and
security installations including the military
installation at TARHUNA. There would also be
orchestrated civil unrest in Benghazi, Misratah and
Tripoli. The coup plotters would launch a direct attack
on QADAHFI and would /either

DIANA INQUEST: WHO KILLED PRINCESS DIANA?

either arrest him or kill him.

3.   The coup plotters had 1275 active sympathisers in
the following areas: TRIPOLI 240 persons; BENGHAZI 135;
TOBRUK 114; MISRATAH 148; SIRTE 40; AL-ZAMIYA 180; AL
ZUMARAH 300; AL KHUMS 28; GHADAMIS 50. Their occupations
ranged from students, military personnel and teachers
throgh to businessmen, doctors, police officers and civil
servants. The plotters were divided into 5 groups, each
with 5 officers in charge. Messages to members of each
group were passed via schools and Mosques. The start of
the coup would be signalled through coded messages on
television and radio. The coup plotters had sympathisers
working in the press, radio and television.

4.   The military officer said that the plotters would
have cars similar to those in QADAHFI's security
entourage with fake security number plates. They would
infiltrate themselves into the entourage in order to kill
or arrest QADAHFI.

5.   One group of military personnel were currently
being trained in the desert area near KUFRA for ther role
of attacking QADAHFI and his entourage. The aim was to
attack QADAHFI after the GPC, but before he had returned
to SIRTE. One officer and 20 men were being trained
especially for this attack.

6.   The coup plotters were not associated with the
Islamic fundamentalists who were fermenting unrest in
Benghazi. However, they had had some limited contact
with the fundamentalists, whom the military officer
described as a mix of Libya veterans who served in
Afghanistan and Libyan students. The coup plotters also
had limited contact with the Algerian and Tunisian
governments, but the latter did not know of their plans.
/7.

PAGE FOUR   UK S E C R E T/DELICATE SOURCE/UK EYES ALPHA

95/53452

7.   The coup plotters were responsible for the death of [blank,- Names removed to protect security---------blank] was about to take up the position as head of Military Intelligence when he was forced off the Tripoli-Sirte road and was killed. The 2 coup plotters involved escaped unhurt. In August 1995, 3 army captains who were part of the coup plot attempted to kill Colonel QADAHFI. However, security police caught them waiting at the roadside on the Tripoli-Sirte road awaiting QADAHFI's entourage. Both men escaped to TUNISIA.

8.   The plotters had already distributed 250 Webley pistols and 500 heavy machine guns amongst the groups.

SOURCE COMMENT

A.   The coup plotters expected to establish control of Libya by the end of March 1996. They would form an interim government before discussions with tribal leaders. The group would want rapproachment with the West. They hoped to divide the country into smaller areas, each with a governor and a democratically elected parliament. There would be a federal system of national government.

B.   The officer was disclosing this information in the hope that if the coup was successful, the new government could enlist HMG support. Other plotters were aware of the officer's contact with HMG, but did not entirely approve of it.

GRS C0616

Figure 1

Replica of an MI6 document that appeared anonymously on a US internet site on 14 February 2000. The issue of authenticity is discussed in the next Comment section. Ex-MI5 officer, David Shayler, has stated that the document is one that he received a copy of in December 1995 during his time in charge of the MI5 Libya desk. A listing of explanations of codes and abbreviations appears below.

ab

Explanation of codes and abbreviations found in the above MI6 document:[c]

GG6 = MI5 agent running the counter Mid-East terrorism section

GG9 = MI5's counter Mid-East terrorism section

NDO = MI5 Night Duty Officer

041807Z DEC 95 = Time the telegram arrived: 1807 or 6.07 p.m. on 4 December 1995; Z = Zulu time or GMT (Greenwich Mean Time)

FM London = From London – the London station of MI6 HQ at Vauxhall Cross

TO PUSD = To Permanent Under-Secretary's Department in the FCO[d]

185 = 185th telegram in 1995 from London to PUSD[e]

Research Dept = Research Department of the FCO

MOD = Ministry of Defence

Security Service = MI5

Immediate = 2nd level of urgency – the 4 levels are: Flash, Immediate, Priority, Routine

UK Secret = UK only – not to be shared with agencies in other countries

Delicate Source = A sensitively placed human source is involved

UK Eyes Alpha = Limited to certain departments within the UK

2LIAPX01 = Joint Intelligence Committee requirement code

DICTD = Drugs, International Crime and Terrorism Department in the FCO

NENAD = North-East and North Africa Department in the FCO

RAD – ME = Research and Analysis Department – Middle East

DI = Defence Intelligence within the Ministry of Defence

JIC = Joint Intelligence Committee

---

[a] The above document appeared on the Yahoo! website: www.geocities.com/byanymeans_2000/document.html on 14 February 2000. It was later removed.

[b] The person who posted the CX document onto the internet also stated: "I've just about had it up to here with the lies of ministers. It is difficult to imagine a more serious abuse of power than MI6 funding our terrorist enemies with the result that innocent people are murdered in cold blood. If there had been a legal way of presenting that document to independent investigators, I would have used it. As there was not, I had to resort to the Internet. Thank God for modern technology.": Annie Machon, *Spies, Lies and Whistleblowers:MI5, MI6 and the Shayler Affair*, p255.

[c] This list is primarily based on information from David Shayler – his explanation of codes and abbreviations within this document can be found at http://cryptome.orh/shayler-gaddafi.htm

[d] The PUSD is "responsible for liaison between the FO [Foreign Office] and the UK's intelligence agencies": Source: Release of PUSD records to The National Archives on 1 April 2005: http://collections.europarchive.org.tna

[e] This numbering would also appear to apply to the next 4 lines: Research Dept, MOD, Cabinet Office and MI5. e.g. this is the 234th telegram to the Research Dept.

GCHQ = Government Communications Headquarters

G9A5[a] = David Shayler – Head of Libyan desk

G6A5 and G6A3 = MI5 handlers of Libyan agents

CX[b] = Intelligence Report

95/53452 = Unique reference number for the report[c]

R/ME/C = Libyan requirements officer in MI6 – the person who writes up and sends the report

GTN = Government Telephone Network

Comment: Scott Baker said that the Gaddafi plot "is not an issue in these inquests".

When Baker made the decisions on what material the inquest would cover, one of the key issues he had to confront was the possible involvement of MI6 in the 1997 Paris crash. In fact, in his Opening Remarks to the jury, Baker laid down eight questions that he said the inquest must address – one of these was: "Whether the British Security Services or any other country's security services had any involvement in the collision".[62]

Allegations had been made:

-   Richard Tomlinson: "I am absolutely certain that there is substantial evidence in [MI6's] files that would provide crucial evidence in establishing the exact causes of this tragedy" – 1999 affidavit

-   David Shayler: "Having looked at the available evidence I am personally inclined to think that MI6 paid to have Diana and Dodi involved in an accident, in the same way they paid to have Gaddafi assassinated, using a 'surrogate'" [63]

-   Mohamed Al Fayed: "I am in no doubt whatsoever that my son and Princess Diana were murdered by the British Security Services...." [64]

Given that MI6 is such a secretive organisation – see earlier – it is logical that if they assassinated Princess Diana and Dodi Fayed, they are hardly going to put their hand up and announce that to the inquest.

In this situation, circumstantial evidence becomes very significant – as does the answer to the question: Is there any evidence that could link MI6 to other assassinations in a similar time frame to the Paris crash?

Prior to the inquest there were three publicly known allegations of MI6 involvement in assassination plots in the 1990s:

---

[a] G = Terrorism; G9 = Middle East Terrorism.

[b] The use of CX to describe reports dates back to the time of the first MI6 Chief, Mansfield Cumming (1909 to 1923), who was referred to as C. Secret intelligence reports were sent to him and were marked CX, standing for "Exclusive for C". Sources: "Glossary" on MI6 website: www.sis.gov.uk and Richard Tomlinson, *The Big Breach*, p59.

[c] I suggest that the "95" would stand for the year of despatch, 1995.

DIANA INQUEST: WHO KILLED PRINCESS DIANA?

1) the Tomlinson claim regarding a 1992 plot to assassinate Slobodan Milosevic, leader of Serbia

2) the Shayler claim regarding the early 1996 failed plot to assassinate Colonel Gaddafi, leader of Libya

3) claims by CIA agents of a failed mid-1996 plot to assassinate Saddam Hussein, leader of Iraq.

In the months leading up to the 2007 inquest the judge, Scott Baker, had to make a decision about how this issue of MI6 assassination plots would be handled in the evidence the jury would hear.

Baker had several choices – he could ignore the issue of alleged assassination plots altogether; he could address one or two of the cases (Milosevic, Saddam or Gaddafi); or he could have addressed all three cases.

If Baker had ignored all of these plots, he would have opened himself up to criticism that he had failed to deal with one of the most important aspects of the Diana case: possible evidence of high-level assassination plots in a similar time-frame by the prime suspect (MI6) named in the allegations (see above).

The decision Baker made was to deal with the Milosevic case, but ignore the Gaddafi and Saddam plot evidence. Baker was very determined in this – as we have seen, when the issue of MI6 involvement in the Gaddafi plot came up, Baker was quick to close it down: "This is not an issue in these inquests."

Instead Baker used up three or four inquest days[a] addressing the evidence relating to the Milosevic plot.

The question is: Why did Baker choose to address the Milosevic plot and ignore the Gaddafi and Saddam plots?

There are critical differences between the three plots:

a) The Gaddafi plot was a fully-fledged plan that was carried out to execution. It apparently only failed because the wrong vehicle was targeted.

The Saddam plot didn't reach the execution stage, but was very advanced – a base had been set up in Jordan and up to 80 people were executed after Saddam found out about it.

The Milosevic plot was a single proposal document which appeared to get no further than that and according to MI6 it was destroyed.

b) The Gaddafi and Saddam plots both occurred in 1996 – the year preceding the Alma Tunnel crash, whereas the Milosevic document was drawn up in 1992.

---

[a] Spread between 13, 20, 26, 28 and 29 February 2008. Inquest weeks were mostly just 4 days – Monday to Thursday. So this was the equivalent of nearly one week out of the 21 weeks of testimony that the jury heard.

c) There is detailed documentary evidence of the Gaddafi plot – the CX report – whereas there is no known existing documents supporting the Milosevic or Saddam plots.

d) There is conflict over the target in the Milosevic plot – according to MI6 it was not Milosevic, but someone else[a], whereas the targets in the Gaddafi and Saddam plots are very definite – Gaddafi and Saddam.

e) The CX report indicates that the FCO, Cabinet Office, MOD, MI5 and JIC were all provided detail regarding the Gaddafi plot prior to its execution.

There is no evidence of UK-based prior knowledge of the Milosevic or Saddam plots outside of MI6.

f) Prior to the inquest, MI6 had admitted there was a plan to assassinate an "extremist leader" in the Balkans[65b], but they have never acknowledged any involvement in the Gaddafi or Saddam plots.

There is a likelihood that MI6 would have been more comfortable dealing with the Milosevic plot, rather than the Gaddafi or Saddam plots, at the inquest.

The Paget report addressed the MI6 response to the Milosevic allegation[66], but when it came to addressing the Gaddafi plot, it says: "There was an independent investigation by the MPS into the 'Gadaffi allegation'. Operation Paget enquiries have shown there is no evidence to support [Shayler's] assessment that there is any link to this investigation."

Paget stated their assessment that "there is no evidence ... [of] any link to this [Diana] investigation". Paget does not indicate that there is nothing to the Gaddafi allegations – just that they believe there is no link between that plot and the Paris crash.

Paget completely ignored the existence of the plot to assassinate Saddam Hussein.

In December 2000, just 10 months after the CX report was placed on the internet, the British police interviewed David Shayler. The MPS' final report was completed 9 months later, in September 2001.

The police wrote to Shayler on 9 November 2001: "As you know, the Metropolitan Police Service undertook an assessment of the available material and submitted two reports to the Crown Prosecution Service, an interim report in February 2001 and a final report in September 2001. The police enquiry has been extremely thorough, examining all relevant

---

[a] Tomlinson, who was the first to give evidence of the plot, says it was Milosevic. Later evidence – in the Conclusion section of Assassination Plots – will indicate that the MI6 claim that the target was someone else could be false.

[b] MI6 appear to be comfortable with this admission because they say the plan was put forward by one wayward individual, but was immediately quashed – this was covered extensively in the inquest and also in the Paget Report, pp762-4.

material…. Final advice from the Crown Prosecution Service has now been received, saying that the material does not substantiate the allegation made by David Shayler." [67]

It is significant that although the MPS inquiry took 9 months – from December 2000 to September 2001 – no detail from it has ever been made public.

The following table compares the strength, clarity and relevance of evidence in the Milosevic, Gaddafi and Saddam plots.

Comparison of 1990s MI6 Assassination Plots			
Aspect	Gaddafi Plot	Saddam Plot	Milosevic Plot
Stage Reached	Final execution	Advanced; Jordan base; Up to 80 persons involved	Proposal document raised
Time Before Paris Crash	18 months	14 months	5 years
Documentary Evidence	Detailed CX report	None available	None available
Assassination Target	Very clear	Very clear	Conflicting evidence
UK-Based Prior Knowledge Outside MI6	FCO, Cabinet Office, MOD, JIC, MI5, GCHQ	None known	None
MI6 Admission	None	None	Yes, but limited
Similarities to Paris Crash	VIP target; use of local agents; vehicle targeted	VIP target; use of local agents	VIP target; car crash in tunnel; light flash

When the three plots are compared – as in the above table – it becomes obvious that the stronger and clearest case indicating MI6 involvement in an advanced assassination plot is the 1996 Gaddafi plot, then the Saddam plot – not so much the Milosevic plot.[a]

The main argument supporting the relevance of the Milosevic plot is the similarities in methodology to the Paris crash – a crash in a tunnel using a strobe flash light to disorientate the driver. This indicates that the Milosevic plot should have been addressed at the inquest, but certainly not at the exclusion of either the Gaddafi or Saddam plots. Given that MI6 were prime

---

[a] This is not to say that there is no evidence of MI6 involvement in an assassination plot regarding Milosevic – it's just that the plot was not advanced and the available evidence is not as strong or clear.

suspects in the Paris crash, the evidence regarding all three plots should have been dealt with in front of the jury.

That did not occur.

This was the situation Scott Baker was confronted with in 2007, whilst deciding which evidence to cover at the upcoming inquest. The fact that Baker chose not to address the evidence relating to the Gaddafi or Saddam plots is a further indication that Baker is a corrupt judge.

This evidence also raises the possibility of collusion between Baker and MI6.

The inquest spent around three days dealing with the Milosevic plot.[a] There was no existing documentary evidence – it was simply the word of ex-MI6 agent Richard Tomlinson against a stream of former and current MI6 officers: Dearlove, Miss X, Mr A, Mr H, Ms F, Mr E and Mr I.

The jury heard Tomlinson give evidence on 13 February 2008, then over the next two to three weeks – finishing on February 29 – they heard a succession of seven MI6 witnesses disputing his account.

The jury would probably have come away believing the MI6 accounts, but when one considers the earlier and later evidence on the honesty of MI6 officers, serious questions are raised about whether their evidence can be relied on.

Richard Keen's cross-examination of X regarding the Gaddafi plot could be significant. Keen suggested to X that a search of the MI6 P file relating to Muammar Gaddafi "would be a simple way of checking whether or not ... the Secret Intelligence Service did advance ... proposals" for assassinations.

This is when – as earlier stated – Baker quickly tried to close this line of questioning down: "this is not an issue in these inquests". Baker went on to say: "we also have Sir Richard [Dearlove]'s evidence on this".

Keen correctly replies by describing Dearlove's evidence on the central issue here – whether MI6 assassinates people. Keen states that Dearlove said "the Secret Intelligence Service would never contemplate such an action or operation, and that was challenged by my learned friend, Mr Mansfield". Keen explains that his intent is to establish whether "there have been occasions where [assassinations] have been contemplated by the Secret Intelligence Service".

---

[a] The detail of the Milosevic plot and the witness evidence is not covered in this book. It can be found in the Paget Report pp754 to 764 and Inquest Transcripts: Richard Tomlinson – 13 Feb 08; Richard Dearlove – 20 Feb 08; Miss X and Mr A – 26 Feb 08; Mr H – 28 Feb 08; Ms F, Mr E, Mr I – 29 Feb 08.

This argument by Keen appears to put Baker in a difficult spot[a] – why wouldn't the evidence regarding the Gaddafi plot be looked at, if we are interested in determining the MI6 approach towards assassinations?

This is when Ian Burnett, the inquest lawyer, chimes in to rescue Baker, by completely changing the subject – instead of dealing with the issue of Dearlove's evidence regarding MI6's approach to assassinations, Burnett starts fully relating Dearlove's account of the handling of the Gaddafi plot by MI6 and the MPS investigation.

At the conclusion of Burnett's recount of this, X – no doubt relieved that she too has been rescued from dealing with the Gaddafi plot – states: "I cannot add anything to what you have already said there".

Although Keen has been forced – by Baker and Burnett acting together – to abandon his original line of cross-examination, he still manages to include the Gaddafi plot in his next question: "Given that there was an investigation of that alleged conspiracy to murder [Gaddafi], have you any explanation as to why there wasn't a similar investigation in respect of Mr A's proposal?"

X's answer is significant: "Only that Mr A's proposal, I do not think, ever really got beyond being just an idea."

X appears to have inadvertently admitted that the Gaddafi plot was "beyond being just an idea" – otherwise there would not have been an MPS investigation.

In other words: the proposal of Mr A never "really got beyond being just an idea", so there was no investigation. By implication though, in the case of the Gaddafi plot, there was an investigation, therefore it must have got beyond just being an idea.

At the inquest Baker went to great lengths to investigate the Milosevic plot, knowing that it revolved around a document that no longer existed – to this end, he arranged for the cross-examination of Tomlinson, Dearlove, X, A, E, H and I, and the reading of the statement of F.

Of more importance were the accounts of officers involved in the Gaddafi plot – a plot that led to a full-fledged attempt on the life of Muammar Gaddafi.

There are 15 people who could and should have been cross-examined. They were:
-   David Shayler – he made the allegations of MI6 involvement in the plot

---

[a] This is only a difficult spot for Baker because he appeared to have no interest in really getting to the bottom of the evidence regarding MI6's attitude towards assassinations – despite its centrality to the Diana case. Had Baker been determined to uncover the evidence, he would not have attempted to shut down discussion about the Gaddafi plot in the first place.

- Annie Machon – as Shayler's partner and also an ex-MI5 officer, she was close to the events and wrote a book about them
- Richard Spearman[a] – Tomlinson said Spearman "had been, prior to his appointment in Paris, the personal secretary to the Chief of MI6 Mr David Spedding". Spedding was head of MI6 from 1994 to 1999 – this covered the period of the Gaddafi and Saddam assassination plots, along with the Paris crash[b][c]
- the unnamed MI6 officer in Tunis who was originally told of the Gaddafi plot by Tunworth in the summer[d] of 1995[68]
- David Watson – MI6 officer PT16/B – Shayler says he was briefed by him on the plot as it unfolded[69]
- Richard Bartlett – MI6 officer PT16, Watson's direct line manager – Shayler said "it was tacitly understood that Watson was working with the approval of ... Richard Bartlett" [70e]
- Jerry Mahoney – MI5 officer G9A/1 until December 1995 – Shayler says: "Throughout this process[f], I briefed my line manager ... Jerry Mahoney ... about these developments" [71]
- Paul Slim – MI5 officer G9A/1 after December 1995 – Shayler says he briefed Slim after he replaced Mahoney[72]
- MI6 officer R/ME/C, Libyan requirements officer[g] – he authored and sent the CX 95/53452 report
- Jackie Barker – MI5 officer G9A/15 after spring 1995[73] – Machon says: "Jackie Barker ... told [Shayler] that Watson had told her the same information[h] 'in confidence'" [74i]
- G6A/5 and G6A/3 – these two MI5 officers handled Libyan agents according to Shayler. They both were recipients of the CX 95/53452 document

---

[a] Spearman was cross-examined at the inquest – under the codename "Mr 6" or "Witness 6" – but he was never asked about his knowledge of the Gaddafi plot.
[b] David Spedding died in 2001, aged 58, from lung cancer.
[c] Spedding specialised in the MI6 role in the Middle East – this is discussed in the Comment below.
[d] Northern hemisphere.
[e] It will be suggested later in this Comment that it would be very unlikely Watson was working alone.
[f] The whole Gaddafi plot operation.
[g] See earlier explanation of codes on the CX document.
[h] About a payment of $40,000 made to Tunworth by Watson around Christmas 1995.
[i] The *Panorama* evidence also showed that G9A/15 was present during the joint meetings between MI5 and MI6.

- Malcolm Rifkind – Foreign Secretary – this occurred under his watch and he should have been cross-examined about his level of knowledge and accountability
- Permanent Under-Secretary in the FCO – on the recipients list of the CX 95/53452 document
- Head of the Joint Intelligence Committee – on the recipients list of the CX 95/53452 document.[a]

The point is that evidence indicating MI6 could have been involved in assassination attempts in the year prior to the Paris crash was of critical importance to this inquest. If Baker had been serious about finding out if MI6 had a role in the assassination of Princess Diana, he should have made it his business to establish whether Shayler's claims were credible. Cross-examination of MI6 and MI5 officers could have helped in this.

None of this ever occurred – instead Baker said: "This is not an issue in these inquests."

Why?

It could be significant that the British government has made immense efforts to suppress David Shayler's evidence – this has included:

- 29 August 1997: Special Branch officers broke into Shayler and Machon's unoccupied Pimlico flat[b], armed with a warrant, and spent two days[c] inside searching for material[75de]

---

[a] Richard Tomlinson described "Exercise Solo", one of the final parts of his 1992 MI6 training program, in his 2001 book: "The decision to base 'Solo' in Italy was taken for political reasons in both countries [UK and Italy].... Recent developments had brought MI6 and SISMI [the Italian secret service] closer. SISMI was doing some good work against its recalcitrant southern neighbour, Libya, and MI6 wanted access to this intelligence.": *The Big Breach*, p78. Tomlinson was cross-examined at the inquest and he should have been asked what he knew about MI6's interest in Libya in the early to mid-1990s.

[b] *Defending the Realm* has a photo of the inside of the flat taken following the departure of the officers – see photos between pages 150 to 151.

[c] From Friday at 4.30 p.m. to Sunday 4 p.m. The departure of the Special Branch officers at around 4 p.m. on Sunday 31 August 1997 occurred just over 16 hours after the crash in the Alma Tunnel.

[d] Machon states that she and Shayler – who at that time were in self-imposed exile in first, Holland, then France – were unaware of the Special Branch search until a month after it had occurred: *Spies, Lies & Whistleblowers*, p212.

[e] It may not be a coincidence that Richard Tomlinson's flat in Wavendon [a village in Milton Keynes, Buckinghamshire] was burgled around the same time period – close to the deaths of Diana and Dodi. Tomlinson describes his break-in occurring on the morning of 8 September 1997, while he was at work: "A token attempt had been made to disguise [it] as a normal burglary, the contents of the fridge were strewn across the floor and my bookcase had been overturned. But the identity of the culprits was not hard to guess as the only item of value that had gone was the laptop

- 29 August 1997: visit by Special Branch officers to the BBC offices seeking details of any payment to Shayler for his appearance on *Newsnight* on August 26[76]

- 30 August 1997: temporary injunction, sought and granted[a], that prevented the *Mail on Sunday*, other British media and Shayler from publishing or disclosing information that Shayler had gained from his work at MI5[77b]

- 2 September 1997: visit by Special Branch officers to the *Mail on Sunday* offices seeking details of any payment to Shayler for interviews[c]

- 4 September 1997: judicial order to continue the temporary injunction set up on August 30[78d]

- 20 September 1997: Machon is arrested by 5 Special Branch officers at Gatwick Airport[e], on suspicion of breaking the Official Secrets Act and money laundering[79fg]

- 22 September 1997: two of Machon and Shayler's friends – Matt Guarente and Graham Dunbar – are arrested in early morning raids, on suspicion of money laundering[80h]

---

containing the [book] draft. The TV, stereo, video-recorder and even small valuables had not been touched. The police arrived to have a poke around but they were not interested in taking any forensic evidence.": *The Big Breach*, pp225-6.

[a] This was granted at 4.30 p.m. on the Saturday, just 7 hours ahead of the crash in Paris: *Defending the Realm*, p177.

[b] This injunction wasn't lifted until the BBC ran the *Panorama* program nearly a year later, on 7 August 1998 – see earlier.

[c] The *Mail on Sunday* published some of Shayler's revelations on 24 August 1997 – these did not include information relating to the Gaddafi plot. The Gaddafi plot story was published by the *Mail* on August 31, based on information from sources in US intelligence – see earlier.

[d] According to Annie Machon the injunction against Shayler was still in place when she wrote her book in 2005: *Spies, Lies & Whistleblowers*, pp211-2

[e] There is a photo of this arrest in *Defending the Realm* – photos between pages 150 and 151.

[f] This was related to the transfer of proceeds from interviews by Shayler and Machon to friends' accounts to avoid the money being seized by authorities. Those authorities viewed the money as proceeds from crime.: *Spies, Lies & Whistleblowers*, p217; *Defending the Realm*, p182.

[g] From this point Machon was on police bail until 27 March 1998, when she was cleared: *Defending the Realm*, p196. Police bail does not require a payment, but it means the police are still investigating and the person could be asked to return to the station for further questioning.: Home Office website: www.homeoffice.gov.uk/police/powers

[h] See previous footnote.

- October 1997: David Shayler's brother, Phil, is arrested on suspicion of money laundering[81]
- February 1998: a package of 28 documents, comprising of internal MI5 reports Shayler had provided to Hollingsworth and Fielding[a] in August 1997, were handed back to MI5, after pressure from Special Branch[82]
- 29 July 1998: three days after Shayler has started setting up a website, www.shayler.com it is professionally hacked into, before it is up and running[83]
- 1 August 1998: David Shayler is arrested in a Paris hotel by the French DST – responding to a faxed arrest warrant for two offences relating to the Official Secrets Act. Shayler is then jailed in Paris – he is prevented from access to a lawyer for over two days and Machon could not visit him for over two months. He was prevented from applying for bail for two months – when he did, it was refused. Shayler was incarcerated for 110 days and was released on November 18 after the British authorities lost their case for extradition[84]
- 8 August 1998: Foreign Secretary, Robin Cook, publicly denies the veracity of Shayler's allegations, describing them as "pure fantasy"[b]
- February 2000: British government issues a writ against Shayler for breaches of confidence, contract and copyright laws on files held by MI5 and MI6[85]
- 6 March 2000: Special Branch officers arrest Julie Ann Davies, a 35 year old university student and supporter of Shayler, under the Official Secrets Act, during a lecture[86c]
- April 2000: a court order is granted to Special Branch enabling them to search for and seize material from *The Observer*[d] and seize a letter from *The Guardian* relating to the Shayler case[87]
- 21 August 2000: Shayler is charged under the Official Secrets Act immediately after his voluntary return to the UK[88]
- 16 May 2001: a judge rules that Shayler is unable to argue his defence that his revelations to the media served the public interest and didn't damage national security[89]
- 20 September 2001: Appeal Court upholds the May ruling that Shayler cannot argue his defence[90]

---

[a] Authors of *Defending the Realm*.
[b] This is addressed later.
[c] Davies was questioned for several hours then was released, but was under police bail for over five months – the bail was lifted on the same day Shayler returned and was arrested in the UK: *Spies, Lies & Whistleblowers*, p274; Email correspondence from Julie Ann Davies to John Young, 22 August 2000, reproduced on http://cryptome.sabotage
[d] The decision against *The Observer* was later overturned in a higher court, on 19 July 2000: *Spies, Lies & Whistleblowers*, p278.

- 21 March 2002: House of Lords upholds the May ruling that Shayler cannot argue his defence[91]
- 7 October 2002: the judge in the Shayler trial rules that the media cannot report parts of Shayler's evidence, including anything relating to the activities of MI5 and MI6[92a]
- 4 November 2002: Shayler is convicted – found guilty on three counts of exposing official secrets[93]
- 5 November 2002: Shayler is sentenced to 6 months jail[94b]
- 29 July 2003: the appeal court refuses Shayler's application to appeal the 4 November 2002 judgement.[95c]

---

[a] This was after Public Interest Immunity Certificates had been signed by the relevant government ministers, Jack Straw (Foreign Secretary) and David Blunkett (Home Secretary): Paul Daley, *Media Gag on Alleged Plot to Kill Gaddafi*, The Age, 10 October 2002.

[b] Shayler was released after serving around 7 weeks in jail: BBC News, Timeline: *Shayler Spy Row*, 4 November 2002.

[c] Richard Tomlinson was mistreated by MI6 after he was fired in April 1995. When viewed in the light of David Shayler's MI5 experience, it indicates that British intelligence have a problem with their treatment of people who leave the organisation in difficult circumstances. Peter Wright didn't leave in difficult circumstances, yet after 20 years of dedicated service, he was left with poor health and a pension he described as "derisory" – promises made to him were not honoured: *Spycatcher*, pp367, 381.

Tomlinson provides a detailed account of his post-MI6 treatment in his 2001 book, *The Big Breach*: He describes being bullied into signing a one-sided unfair termination agreement, February 1997 (pp217-9); flat ransacked and laptop stolen, 8 September 1997 (pp225-6) (see earlier footnote); arrested, handcuffed, strip-searched, all in his flat, which was thoroughly searched and a large box of "items of interest" taken away, his workplace PC taken and his parents' home in Cumbria searched, all three operations conducted simultaneously. Tomlinson was then taken handcuffed to Charing Cross station where he was locked up and again strip-searched, 30 October 1997 (pp226-8); after being imprisoned for 2 to 3 days and prevented from showering or shaving, he was again strip-searched before a court hearing on 2 November 1997, where bail was refused (pp229-232); Tomlinson was imprisoned for around six months, mostly in Belmarsh (heavy security), and released on 1 May 1998, with strict probation – confiscation of passport, no use of internet or email and no contact with the media (pp267-9); he receives most of his possessions back but with all the data erased on his Psion organiser (p270); assaulted and arrested by the French police in his Paris hotel room – "cartwheeling me backwards, smashing my head on the desk and crushing me to the floor ... blows still rained down on the back of my head" – he is left with a cracked rib, handcuffed, his possessions again taken, locked up and interviewed by DST with British Special Branch initiating the questions. Within 48 hours he is released and is told that "the

English ... said that you were a terrorist and dangerous – that is why we beat you up", late July 1998 (pp281-7); SB officers "burst into the ... flat of Kathryn Bonella [a journalist Tomlinson had job interviews with] pulled her out of bed and took her down to Charing Cross police station for questioning", late July 1998 (p288); Tomlinson's laptop and Psion are despatched from Paris to London – the laptop is returned around Christmas 1998, but he never sees the Psion again (p287); after arriving in NZ an injunction is served to prevent him talking to the media, late July or early August 1998 (p288); at Auckland airport taken off a flight destined for Sydney and prevented from travelling to Australia, 7 August 1998 (p290); NZ police enter Tomlinson's hotel room – "the door smashed to its limit against the chain ... 'Police, police, open the fucking door'" – with a search warrant. Tomlinson is strip-searched. Two British SB officers were also present. A Psion disk is taken away, 7 August 1998 (pp291-2); immigration officials handcuff Tomlinson and remove him from a flight that had just landed at JFK airport in New York. He is then manacled with leg irons and is prevented from entering the US for an NBC *Today* interview scheduled for the first anniversary of the Paris crash, 30 August 1998 (pp295-8); Tomlinson, who had moved to Switzerland, is shown by friendly Swiss police "MI6's ... requests to have me arrested and deported to Britain or ... expelled from Switzerland", late 1998 (p299); telegram from MI6 to ASIO (Australian Security Intelligence Organisation) requesting a ban on Tomlinson entering Australia, 2 November 1998 (p301); Tomlinson, travelling with his parents, is stopped at the border trying to enter France for a skiing holiday. He is held by customs and later handcuffed and interviewed by DST officers who ban him from entering France, 6 January 1999 (pp299-301); Tomlinson sets up websites on Geocities which are closed down due to a "complaint from a third party", early May 1999 (p302); Foreign Secretary, Robin Cook, holds a press conference where he accuses Tomlinson of posting an MI6 officer list onto the internet – this appears to be a false accusation (see later section on MI6 Internet List) mid-May 1999 (pp302-3); apparently as a result of the MI6 internet list, Tomlinson is deported from Switzerland to Germany and banned from reentering Switzerland for five years, 8 June 1999 (pp303-5); Tomlinson travels to Austria and mistakenly strays into a Swiss border post. He is locked up and police strip-search and handcuff him before holding him overnight, late September 1999 (pp307-8); Tomlinson illegally enters France for a two week skiing holiday, but he is notified by his landlord that his flat in Germany was searched by four German police officers, with a warrant to confiscate his computer, February 2000 (p308); Tomlinson had moved to Italy and local police burst into his flat – "'Up against the wall' screamed the two heavies who led the charge, their pistols drawn and pointing at my chest" – accompanied by two British SB officers. They took his computer, Psion, entire music and software CD collection, mobile phone and TV remote back to London and never returned any of this, 17 May 2000 (pp309-311); on a visit to Monte Carlo for a job interview Tomlinson is arrested by the Monaco Special Investigations Unit. He is locked up and MI6 asked the Monaco officers to confiscate Tomlinson's Psion and mobile phone, but after checking with DST they decide to release him on the proviso he returns straight away to Italy, June 2000 (p313); Tomlinson's real estate agency is visited by two men

In early August 1998, when Cook refuted Shayler's allegations he said:
- "the tale about the MI6 plot to assassinate Gaddafi is fantasy"
- "I am absolutely satisfied that the previous Foreign Secretary[a] did not authorise any such assassination attempt"
- "I'm perfectly satisfied that MI6 never put forward any such proposal for an assassination attempt"
- "nor have I seen anything ... which would suggest that MI6 has any interest, any role or any experience over the recent decade of any such escapade"
- "there was no Government-inspired plan to assassinate Gaddafi"
- "it is pure fantasy"
- "there was no SIS proposal to do it"
- "I'm fairly clear there has never been any SIS involvement"
- "I'm perfectly clear that these allegations have no basis in fact"
- "I am quite clear that the SIS operations I have authorised have nothing remotely to do with the kind of fantasy that has been produced over the last two days".

All of Robin Cook's statements were categorical – "the tale ... is fantasy"; "absolutely satisfied", "perfectly satisfied", "nor have I seen anything", "there was no", "it is pure fantasy", "I'm perfectly clear", "I am quite clear" – except for one:

"I'm fairly clear there has never been any SIS involvement".

Cook is categorically denying the receipt by the government of a proposal from MI6, but he appears to leave open the possibility of MI6 involvement without notifying the government of the day.

In 2000, Malcolm Rifkind – the 1996 Foreign Secretary – also denied knowledge of a proposal to government by MI6: "SIS has never put forward such a proposal for an assassination attempt and ... I have never seen any evidence that SIS is interested in such an escapade."

---

claiming to be police officers, who ask questions about him and tell them that Tomlinson is a paedophile, June 2000 (p313).
Tomlinson was raided again on 27 June 2006 in his Cannes home on the French Riviera – five years after his book was published and just six months before the publication of the Paget Report. Tomlinson said: "At 6.27am on Tuesday, 12 police were outside my home with an EU arrest warrant. They took every bit of computer equipment, all my phones, my emails, all my personal files, my Psion organiser with my bank account details." Tomlinson said that they then searched his boat and British police wanted to take away the files in his office and both his passports but their French colleagues prevented them. Source: Richard Norton-Taylor, Police Raid Riviera Home of Former MI6 Officer, *The Guardian*, 29 June 2006.
[a] Malcolm Rifkind.

The issue of how high this proposal went is discussed later.

After the emergence of the CX document in February 2000, Cook was challenged on what he had said in 1998. Cook insisted that he hadn't "misled the British public" and restated his 1998 position for the media: "What I said two years ago[a] was that I was absolutely satisfied that the previous foreign secretary did not authorise an assassination attempt, that the SIS never put forward such a proposal and ... I have never seen any evidence that the SIS had any interest in such escapades."

In restating his 1998 position, Cook actually proceeded to mislead the public by missing out his most significant statements: "the tale about the MI6 plot to assassinate Gaddafi is fantasy"; "I'm perfectly clear that these allegations have no basis in fact" and "it is pure fantasy".

When, in February 2000, the Foreign Office made its official statement outlining what Cook had said two years earlier, it also proceeded to mislead the public.[b] The Foreign Office also chose to omit Cook's most critical comments: "the tale about the MI6 plot to assassinate Gaddafi is fantasy"; "I'm perfectly clear that these allegations have no basis in fact" and "it is pure fantasy".

Cook also said in 1998: "I do wish people would recognise that somebody who has left another service – not the Secret Intelligence Service MI6, he was never in MI6 – is making allegations, no doubt for his own reasons."

Cook appears to be suggesting that because Shayler was not in MI6 – he was head of the Libyan subsection of MI5[96] – he wouldn't be privy to an MI6 operation.

Inquest lawyer Ian Burnett and Richard Dearlove also focused on this at the inquest:

Dearlove: "This is an allegation that was made by a former Security Service officer, David Shayler...."

Burnett: "Now, Shayler, you say, was a former Security Service officer; that is MI5."

Dearlove: "MI5."

Burnett: "Not MI6, as it happens."

Dearlove: "Not MI6."

In contrast, in Shayler's *Panorama* interview he provided a detailed account of regular meetings between MI5 and MI6.[c]

---

[a] In 1998.

[b] The Foreign Office statement is quoted earlier in the Martin Hickman article in *The Independent*.

[c] This is supported in Annie Machon's book: "During routine G9/PT16 meetings around this time, officers occasionally mentioned the plot." G9 being MI5's Middle East terrorism section and PT16 being the equivalent section from MI6. Source: *Spies, Lies & Whistleblowers*, p171.

Shayler's evidence is supported by Stephen Dorril in his book *MI6: Fifty Years of Special Operations*. Dorril describes changes made in January 1993 under the directorship of Colin McColl: "Changes included closer cooperation with [MI6's] traditional rival, the Security Service (MI5), including the establishment of joint sections to cover the Middle East and Russia, particularly in the area of terrorism, and a shared research and development department...." [97]

So although Cook, Burnett and Dearlove[a] imply that Shayler, as head of the MI5 Libyan subsection, would not be a reliable witness of an MI6 operation in Libya, Dorril shows that just three years earlier a decision had been made to create a "joint [MI6-MI5 section] to cover the Middle East".

In the February 2000 declaration from the Foreign Office they said in reference to the CX document: "Nor have we ever denied that we knew of plots against Gaddafi."

The issue here is that the CX document was raised on 4 December 1995 and the plot took place in February 1996 and since the document included FCO addressees, the issue of prior knowledge arises.

This statement appears to be an admission on the part of the FCO of prior knowledge of the plot to assassinate Gaddafi.

There appear to be only three possible positions the FCO could have in relation to the plot:
1) they had no prior knowledge of the plot to assassinate Gaddafi
2) they had prior knowledge of the plot to assassinate Gaddafi
3) they had knowledge of MI6 involvement in the plot to assassinate Gaddafi.

The sudden appearance of the CX document in early February 2000 appeared to eliminate the first possibility – the document indicates that the FCO was provided prior knowledge of the plot from MI6.

Is the CX 95/53452 document authentic?
The evidence is:
-   On *Panorama* Urban described Shayler's account: "Shayler says a special CX report of Tunworth's information was put out. It contained details of what was brought together for the plan to kill Gaddafi. As is normal procedure the CX report was sanitised – it didn't explicitly spell out that PT16/B's agent was himself a part of the conspiracy to kill Gaddafi".

---

[a] The transcript appears to show Burnett pushing this line, with Dearlove not quite so keen – this could be a reflection of Dearlove's knowledge that Shayler, in his position, could have been aware of an MI6 operation in Libya. Had Dearlove been providing honest and open evidence one would think, after Burnett pushed the issue, he would have outlined that to the jury – he didn't.

Shayler said, in the same program: "They were actually put out as a CX report to Whitehall, probably to the Foreign Office, and certainly obviously to us [MI5], probably to GCHQ, may not be to GCHQ."

The CX report reads: "In late November 1995 [Tunworth] described plans, in which he was involved, to overthrow Colonel Qadahfi.... The coup plotters would launch a direct attack on Qadahfi and would either arrest him or kill him."

It also states that the report was sent to Whitehall, the FCO, MI5 and GCHQ.

Urban stated that the CX report "didn't explicitly spell out that PT16/B's agent [Tunworth] was himself a part of the conspiracy to kill Gaddafi", yet the report does say that Tunworth "described plans, <u>in which he was involved</u>, to overthrow Colonel Qadahfi".

This is a direct conflict.

There are four main possibilities:
1) Urban has misstated Shayler's account
2) Shayler has incorrectly recalled the content of the CX report on a key point
3) the CX report – released on the internet in February 2000 – is not authentic
4) the CX report never existed – both Shayler's account and the released report are false.

Before establishing which of these is correct, it is essential to view this issue in the context of the other evidence relating to the authenticity of the CX report:

- MI6, MI5, Cook, Rifkin and the FCO have all avoided declaring the CX document invalid or not authentic[a]

- the 2000 FCO statement said: "Nothing in the alleged intelligence report[b] posted on the Internet invalidates what the Foreign Secretary said. Nor have we ever denied that we knew of plots against Gaddafi."

This shows that instead of attempting to deny the authenticity of the CX document the FCO tried to address the issues the document raised.

- Cook said: "Indeed this document ends with the contact telling the SIS that the other plotters are unhappy about him even telling SIS, which rather proves that SIS were not manipulating this coup attempt."

This comment reveals that Cook addressed the CX document as though it was authentic.[c]

---

[a] Martin Hickman reported: "Whitehall sources confirmed ... that the four page [CX] report – which carried a coded header sheet – was genuine".

[b] The CX document.

[c] The veracity of this comment by Cook is addressed below.

- according to the document, there were up to 11 copies sent to people outside of MI6[a][b] – all it would need is for one person who had access to a copy and was disaffected to the point of saying: "I've just about had it up to here with the lies of ministers".[c]

These points raise the following questions: If the CX document is not authentic then why was it addressed as though it was authentic by Cook and the FCO? And why hasn't any one of the involved organisations or people – MI6, MI5, Cook, Rifkin, the FCO – disowned the document?

Returning now to the above conflict between the *Panorama* program and the CX document.

In 1998 Urban, presumably paraphrasing Shayler, said the CX document did not explicitly show Tunworth as "part of the conspiracy" but in 2000 the CX document said Tunworth "was involved".

There are a couple of points:

a) The *Panorama* interview was conducted at a time prior to 31 August 1997[d] but the CX document would have been read by Shayler in early December 1995[e] – so there is a lapse of around 18 months. There is a possibility that this is a point that Shayler had simply forgotten – a lot had transpired in that period and Shayler was in exile in Paris at the time of the interview.

b) One could argue that the fact Shayler got this point wrong is evidence that Shayler did not possess a copy of the document after leaving MI5, as he would have consulted it prior to giving the *Panorama* interview.

This view is also supported in Shayler's difficulty in recalling during the interview precisely who the CX document was addressed to – "probably to the Foreign Office ... probably to GCHQ, may not be to GCHQ".

---

[a] Recipients were in the FCO, RAD, MOD, JIC, GCHQ, MI5 – see explanations of abbreviations immediately following the earlier reproduction of the CX document. The British embassies listed in the document appear to have been "informed" without actually receiving a full copy – the level of information supplied to them is not explained.

[b] In her book Machon says the CX document was released by a "former intelligence officer" – it is not known how she knew this: *Spies, Lies & Whistleblowers*, p255.

[c] See earlier footnote for full statement made by the person who posted the document on the net.

[d] The interview is referred to in the *Mail* article dated 31 August 1997 (shown above), but it didn't go to air until early August 1998 – see earlier. According to Hollingsworth and Fielding the *Panorama* program was recorded in the "spring of 1998", but that appears to be wrong.: *Defending the Realm*, p208.

[e] The document is dated 4 December 1995.

In fact, the document was addressed to the FCO and GCHQ, among the other recipients.

Hollingsworth also pointed out[a] that it was unlikely Shayler had possession of the CX document – and therefore he would not have been in a position to arrange its appearance on the worldwide web: "Shayler himself did not have this [CX] report in his own dossier in 1997. (If he had hidden it from us all at the time, he would certainly have distributed it 18 months ago when the foreign secretary first denounced him as a fantasist.)"

c) Earlier evidence has indicated instances of Urban possibly misstating Shayler's account.

Regarding the four possibilities – listed above – explaining the conflict of evidence relating to Tunworth's involvement, I suggest that the CX document did exist and the evidence points to it being authentic. I further suggest that either Shayler had an incorrect recall or Urban, on the program, has misstated Shayler's position.

As shown above, after the unexpected release of the CX document, Cook said: "Indeed this document ends with the contact[b] telling the SIS that the other plotters are unhappy about him even telling SIS, which rather proves that SIS were not manipulating this coup attempt."

Is this true?

Is it true that the fact that "the other plotters are unhappy about [Tunworth] ... telling SIS ... proves that SIS were not manipulating this coup attempt"?

The truth is that there is no connection between the other plotters being unhappy with Tunworth telling MI6 and whether MI6 are involved or "manipulating" the assassination plot.

Cook's statement on this is completely bereft of logic.

When one considers that these government statements on serious issues are presumably well thought through, this glaring lack of logic indicates the possibility that Cook panicked following the CX document release – possibly as a result of his earlier "no basis in fact" and "it is pure fantasy" comments.

In summary, Cook has made two very basic errors in his short 2000 statement – both of which could have misled the public:[c]

- Cook misquoted himself – in outlining what he had said in 1998 he left out his most significant comments

- Cook falsely connected the other plotters being unhappy about Tunworth's communications with MI6, to MI6's role in the assassination plot.

---

[a] In his March 2000 article in *The Guardian*.

[b] Tunworth.

[c] Ironically, in the same 2000 statement, Cook said – referring to his 1998 statement – "I accept absolutely nothing in the way of having misled the British public".

Was MI6 involved in the 1996 plot to assassinate Muammar Gaddafi?

The CX document reveals that Tunworth was supplying information to MI6.

The question is: Why?

Why would Tunworth supply information to MI6?

The CX report reads: "The officer was disclosing this information in the hope that if the coup was successful, the new government could enlist HMG[a] support."

Machon explains: "As a CX report going out to ministers, it could not detail the illegal payments" from MI6 to Tunworth.[98b]

The fact that Tunworth was supplying intelligence information to MI6, automatically makes him an MI6 agent and it is obvious that Tunworth would not have provided the intelligence in the CX report without receiving something in return.[c]

Whether MI6 provided material or monetary support for the assassination plot, or personal benefits to Tunworth, or both, the evidence – Shayler, Machon, the CX report – indicates that an MI6 agent, Tunworth, was involved in the February 1996 plot to assassinate Muammar Gaddafi.

Since Tunworth was involved and Tunworth was an MI6 agent, then that means MI6 was involved.

There are other factors – outside of the accounts from Shayler and Machon – that link MI6 to the Gaddafi assassination plot:

---

[a] Her Majesty's Government – UK.

[b] This is based on the presumption that MI6 did not have FCO approval. Later evidence indicates that this presumption could be incorrect. This description of the reason Tunworth provided the intelligence – which is in the final paragraph of the CX report – could be there for other reasons, including: a) The CX report, dated 4 December 1995, could have predated FCO approval; b) it may have been misinformation for readers of the CX report who didn't "need to know" the full extent of the MI6 involvement in the Gaddafi plot.

Machon also mentions in her book: "David remembers another MI6 CX report being issued about the plot in early 1996. It was a shopping list of the group's requirements to carry out the coup, including the supply of weapons and basics like jeeps and tents." This could support possibility a) above, and is a possible indication that by early 1996 FCO approval had been obtained and a "shopping list" – which would support the outlay of government money – was being circulated.

[c] In other words, Tunworth was not providing a charitable service in passing on intelligence information to MI6. Hollingsworth put it like this in his *Guardian* article: "An Arab dissident [Tunworth] was passing detailed information to his MI6 handler [PT16/B] in anticipation of British assistance...."

-   in 1997 two separate sources within US intelligence stated: "Certainly there were contacts between MI6 and FIG" and MI6 had "provided various kinds of support" to FIG, including financial help
-   the huge effort by the British authorities to suppress Shayler's evidence and prevent it reaching the public arena – see earlier list of 23 actions taken over six years, between 29 August 1997[a] and 29 July 2003
-   the failure by Scott Baker to call on key MI6 and MI5 personnel and other witnesses for cross-examination at the Diana inquest.

The above evidence – the implications of the information in the CX report, the US intelligence corroboration, the British suppression – indicates that David Shayler[b] was telling the truth when he went to the media in 1997 with his allegations of MI6 involvement in the Gaddafi assassination plot.

There are key aspects of Shayler's evidence that cannot easily be independently verified – e.g. the allegation that MI6 paid Tunworth $US120,000 in three instalments cannot be supported without witness evidence from key officers in MI6 and MI5, Tunworth or an independent review of the financial records of MI6.

But this failure to investigate does not render Shayler's evidence false – in fact, it suggests the opposite. The indication is that the authorities have not allowed the evidence to become public knowledge because it is not in the interests of the British Establishment.

How high did the knowledge and authorisation of the Gaddafi assassination plot go – in MI6, MI5, the FCO and the Tory government?

Shayler stated: "Throughout this process, I briefed my line manager, G9A/1 – Jerry Mahoney until December 1995, Paul Slim after that – about these developments.... It is inconceivable that G9A/1 did not think an MI6-funded plot to engineer a coup in Libya was worthy of mentioning to his line manager, G9/0, Paul Mitchell. In turn, it is unthinkable that Mitchell did not raise the matter with his line management who would have informed his boss until the DG herself [Stella Rimington] had been made aware...."

Because there were no personnel from MI5 cross-examined or heard from during the inquest, it is impossible to verify Shayler's account of this – except to say, it appears logical. It is logical that an issue of this significance – MI6 involvement in a plot to assassinate a foreign leader – would have gone to the top of MI5.

And if it didn't, one could be justified in asking: "Why didn't it?"

Annie Machon says in her book: "Although PT16/B never specifically mentioned it, it was tacitly understood[c] that Watson[a] was working with the approval of his direct line manager, PT16, Richard Bartlett."

---

[a] Just two days before the Paris crash.
[b] Supported by Annie Machon.
[c] By Shayler.

An MI6 operation of this nature – which included the payment of around $US120,000 – would have required the knowledge of the financial section of the organisation. I suggest that it would have been impossible for PT16/B to raise cheques or cash totalling $US120,000 without someone else in MI6 being aware of it – either ahead of time, at the time, or after the event.

I also suggest that, in a similar way to Shayler's description of the upline contact in MI5, the knowledge of this operation would have gone all the way to the top – MI6 chief, David Spedding.[bcd]

Again, there is no easy way to confirm this because, although Baker allowed some MI6 officers to be cross-examined during the inquest, it was not regarding the Gaddafi plot, but instead the Milosevic plot – see earlier.

The evidence that David Watson was sharing this information on the Gaddafi plot with Shayler and also Jackie Barker[e] in MI5 is another indication that he would have spoken to others in MI6 about it.

Added to this evidence is the clear existence of the CX report and Shayler's recollection of a later CX report "shopping list".

Did MI6 seek authorisation from the Foreign Secretary, Malcolm Rifkind?

---

[a] PT16/B.

[b] Spedding was Chief during the Gaddafi, Saddam and Diana plots.

[c] Spedding's personal secretary, Richard Spearman, was transferred from London to Paris on 26 August 1997, just 5 days ahead of the Paris crash. This issue is dealt with later in the book.

[d] After Spedding was recruited into MI6 in 1967 (aged 24) he became an Arab specialist, studying for two years at the Middle East Centre for Arabic Studies – known as the "school for spies" – at Shemlan in Lebanon. Spedding then served a stint as Second Secretary to the MI6 station in Beirut. Later, in the 1970s Spedding became head of the MI6 station in Abu Dhabi, then was transferred to London and held a senior position in the Middle East Directorate. In the mid-1980s Spedding moved back to the Middle-East where he took over as head of the MI6 station in Amman, Jordan. On his return to London in 1986, he became head of a joint MI5-MI6 section responsible for tracking terrorists and spies throughout the Middle East. This led to Spedding being put in charge of MI6's entire Middle East section. I suggest that David Spedding's thorough grounding and decades of involvement in MI6's Middle East operations, is further indication that he would have been aware of MI6 involvement in the 1996 plot to end Gaddafi's life.: Sources: Richard Norton-Taylor, Sir David Spedding: MI6 Chief Behind Post-Cold War Change of Role, *The Guardian*, 14 June 2001; Sir David Spedding, *The Telegraph*, 14 June 2001.

[e] "Jackie Barker, who had replaced Jane Thomas as G9A/15, told him that Watson had told her the same information 'in confidence'.": Annie Machon, *Spies, Lies & Whistleblowers*, p171.

Machon states: "At some point ... Watson mentioned that the submission – MI6 jargon for the letter requesting permission from the Foreign Office for otherwise illegal operations – was going to go 'all the way to the top'. In about January 1996, Watson told [Shayler] that the submission had been successful, indicating that the Foreign Secretary himself had signed the document permitting the operation."

On *Panorama* Shayler said: "They actually said to me, 'we're going to submit, but we think it's going all the way to the top'." Urban then asked: "And it did?" Shayler: "Yes ... that's what he was saying.... Later on they said it had gone to the top and they got authority from the top."

Machon referred to a second CX report: "David remembers another MI6 CX report being issued about the plot in early 1996. It was a shopping list of the group's requirements to carry out the coup, including the supply of weapons and basics like jeeps and tents."

This circulation of FIG's shopping list for the coup is a possible further indication that FCO approval had been sought and granted.

In conflict with the above evidence, Mark Urban, the *Panorama* journalist stated: "Two well-placed people have told me that the Tory ministers running this department[a] at the time gave no ... authorisation" for the Gaddafi assassination plot.

Malcolm Rifkind, the Foreign Secretary in 1996, has said: "SIS has never put forward such a proposal for an assassination attempt".

Rifkind's successor, Robin Cook, supported this: "I'm perfectly satisfied that MI6 never put forward any such proposal for an assassination attempt".[b]

But then, we have already seen that Cook misled the British public on at least three occasions: 1) in 1998, when he called MI6 involvement in the Gaddafi plot a "fantasy" three times in the one statement; 2) in 2000, when he misquoted his earlier 1998 statement, deliberately leaving out any mention of "fantasy"; 3) in 1998, by indicating that Shayler couldn't have known about an MI6 operation, because he was an MI5 officer.

There is a possibility that both Cook and Rifkind have lied in their denials that MI6 sought authorisation for their involvement in the Gaddafi plot.

Urban has stated that "two well-placed people" told him that the Foreign Secretary "gave no ... authorisation" for the plot.

Why have these two people remained anonymous? All they are doing is stating the government line, so why – if they are telling the truth – was it necessary for them to remain anonymous?

---

[a] FCO.

[b] It is interesting that the wording of the Rifkind and Cook statements on this is very similar: Rifkind: "never put forward such a proposal for an assassination attempt" compares with Cook: "never put forward any such proposal for an assassination attempt". The only difference in these words is Rifkind uses "such a" and Cook uses "any such".

I suggest that if the Tory government did provide authorisation for this ill-fated plot, then it would be a very brave official indeed, who would confirm that to the media. In other words, I suggest that FCO officials could have to abide by a similar requirement to MI5 and MI6 officers – to speak in the national interest, even if that involves the telling of lies (see earlier).

In summary, Shayler's 1997 account, based on his communications with MI6 officer, David Watson – made public in 2000 – essentially stacks up when it is compared to the documentary evidence from the CX report (this has been covered above).

I suggest there is no reason to disbelieve Shayler's additional evidence – from the same source – that a) a sum of approximately $US120,000 was supplied to Tunworth, and b) that the Gaddafi assassination operation was approved by the Foreign Secretary of the day, Malcolm Rifkind.[a]

Conversely, I suggest that it is very plausible that the information from Cook, Rifkind and employees of the FCO is misinformation – designed to quell any potential public disquiet over the actions of the British government.

These people should have been subjected to cross-examination in a public forum – such as the Diana inquest – but that has never occurred.[bc]

---

[a] In Richard Tomlinson's 2001 book *The Big Breach*, on p184, he describes the situation in mid to late 1995: "Writing submissions for Douglas Hurd was a time-consuming task, requiring flawless reasoning and perfect prose, but Rifkind was already renowned for looking favourably on whatever MI6 put in front of him." Rifkind took over (as Foreign Secretary) from Hurd in July 1995 – just 7 months before the execution of the Gaddafi assassination attempt.

[b] In 2007 Shayler's life took a bizarre twist when he made claims of being Christ the Messiah – he said in an interview in August 2007: "I am the Messiah and hold the secret to eternal life". By 2009 Shayler had moved in with squatters and started cross-dressing, calling himself Delores Kane. Annie Machon, his former partner, has said: "I believe David ... has had some sort of severe breakdown.... I do blame the government and the intelligence agencies for what he has become and they have ruined his life."
There is no evidence to suggest that these more recent events have any bearing on what occurred during Shayler's time in MI5, over a decade earlier, and on his allegations made initially in 1997, the year following the failed plot. Sources: Jane Fryer, The MI5 Messiah: Why David Shayler Believes He Is the Son of God, *Daily Mail*, 15 August 2007; Christian Gysin, Call Me Delores, Says MI5 Whistleblower David Shayler, *Daily Mail*, 16 July 2009.

[c] Robin Cook died from a heart attack in August 2005 – two years before the inquest commenced. It will be shown in Part 6 that the inquest was delayed by nearly ten years. Cook's evidence should have been heard, had the inquest not been delayed.

The Increment

The inquest heard that MI6 employs elements of the Special Air Service (SAS) and Special Boat Service (SBS) to carry out missions on its behalf.
Richard Tomlinson, Ex-MI6 Officer: 13 Feb 08: 51.4:
Mansfield: Q. Now MI6 or SIS, could it be described in this way in terms of its general role? Part of it was the acquisition and collation of information from a variety of sources. That is one role. The other role was to oversee objectives which might be carried out by others?
A. Yes, that is the case, yes....
Q.... In relation to the tasks that might be carried out by others, is that generally termed "the increment"?
A. Yes, okay – obviously I do not want to say too much on this subject, but I agree, yes.
Q. That covers – it may cover more – two of the organisations you have already mentioned, the SAS, Special Air Service – is that right?
A. That is correct, yes.
Q. – and SBS, Special Boat Service?[a]
A. Yes.
Q. Because MI6 itself does not contain operatives with the relevant skills to carry out particular practical tasks abroad?
A. That is exactly the case, yes.
At 91.2: Q. [Quoting from a September 1998 letter by Tomlinson] "The second method[b] was to use the increment ... a small cell of the SAS or SBS which is especially selected and trained to carry out operations exclusively for MI5/MI6 to infiltrate Serbia and attack Milosevic, either with a bomb or sniper ambush. [A] argued that this plan would be the most reliable, but would be undeniable if it went wrong." Does it follow that if it went right, it would be deniable?
A. Well, if it went right anonymously, they would have got out of the country anonymously so there would never have been any question of them being caught and interrogated. But clearly, if it went wrong and they were caught and interrogated, it would be very difficult to deny them because no British Government would really leave their highly trained and very loyal soldiers to be imprisoned in that fashion, so the British Government would have to be involved if they were, for some reason, compromised and caught.
Richard Dearlove, MI6 Director of Operations, 1994 to 1999, UK: 20 Feb 08: 116.12:
Mansfield: Q. The SIS themselves, as it were, don't dirty their own hands with tasks abroad. They employ an increment, do they not?

---

[a] There is official information on the SBS at www.specialboatservice.co.uk
[b] This is the second out of three possible methods in A's proposal to assassinate President Milosevic.

A. Can I cut to the quick, Mr Mansfield? I am not going to speculate on SIS's various operational capabilities. They are many and they are different and the court does not need to know about them. What the court does need to know is that all of these capabilities, every single one of them, were under my personal control as the chief of operations and subject to class 7 authorisations under the Act. So there are not any little offshore liars here that somehow do not fit into this pattern; they do not exist. Anything that is referred to, whether you have heard of it before or whether you have not heard of it before, whether it has a strange name or whether it has not got a strange name, was under the control of the director of operations. Let's be absolutely crystal clear about that and I think it is important that the jury understands that fact.

At 120.15: Q. What I wanted to put to you is deniability means this, doesn't it: it means there will be a secret operation abroad, carried out by an increment, not SIS officers but SAS officers or SBS officers –

Coroner: But under the approval of SIS?

Q. Well, yes.

Coroner: The whole point is that this plan is not one officer on a frolic of his own going to carry it out on his own. It has been put up through the system for approval.

Q. Oh yes, this one is[a], yes.

Coroner: So I do not really see why we are spending so long on this, on a matter which really must be speculation.

Q. Sir, it is not speculation because I submit that Tomlinson obviously regarded it – and I would submit to you and to the jury – that it was of some importance that what he remembered – obviously Sir Richard has his own views about it – but what he[b] remembered bore a resemblance to what happened in Paris, which is why he went to the French juge....

Coroner: I think we need to focus on what happened in the tunnel, not on other ephemeral matters.

At 124.14: Mansfield: Q. [Quoting Tomlinson's letter] "The second method[c] was to use the increment, a small cell of SAS and SBS which is especially selected and trained to carry out operations exclusively for MI5 and MI6." He is right about that, isn't he?

A. I am not going to speculate or comment.

Q. If it is going to be suggested that this is a construct of some kind that he fabricated out of nowhere, I want to put to you very clearly that there was a

---

[a] Baker and Mansfield are referring to the Milosevic assassination plot.
[b] Tomlinson.
[c] In the Milosevic assassination proposal.

small cell called the "increment" that was employed by the security services, SIS and SBS, abroad; correct?

A. Mr Mansfield, I have told –

Tam: I have been very –

Coroner: I think the witness is looking after himself at the moment, Mr Tam.

Tam: I do want to say that this is the point at which my learned friend is getting into operational details and methods which are sensitive and should not be asked about.

A. I am happy to comment as I commented before, Mr Mansfield. There are a number of capabilities that SIS has, but what I am going to say – and I am going to repeat this because I do find your line of questioning on this rather tedious – that there is no part of SIS, whether it is deniable or not, which does not come under the terms of the Official Secrets Act which is not fully under the control of the operational director of SIS. There is not a bit of SIS that acts independently or goes off and does its own thing. This does not exist, whatever it may be called, however it is composed, however it is trained, wherever it is found in the world. I do not know how many times I am going to have to emphasise this – I have said it four or five times already[a] – so I would be grateful if we moved on to a different line of questioning because it is unproductive to go on banging on about this point.

Q. Well, I am sorry to be tedious and ask you questions about policy and also observations about the capability because one of the points that the jury will have to consider is whether members of SIS, acting without authority, would be aware of the capability. Can I just explain the context? Mohamed Al Fayed believes ... that there was a conspiracy to cause this crash. One of the questions that Lord Stevens had to consider is motive, opportunity and capability. These are the features that this jury will have to look at. Are you following me?

A. I am.

Q. So, therefore, capability is important. Do you understand that?

A. The service's capability is the service's capability, but I do not think that has anything to do with this inquest into the death of Princess Diana.

Q. Well, I am not going to persist if that is your answer, that "the service's capability is the service's capability". I will leave the jury to decide what that means and I am going to ask you about another topic.

Mr A, MI6 Head of Balkan Target Team: 26 Feb 08: 210.25:

Mansfield: Q. You were certainly made aware during the training courses of what has been called the increment or the use of military agents, whether they be SAS or SBS. You were made aware of that, were you not?

A. I was made aware of a variety of capabilities.

---

[a] Dearlove had actually only said it twice – and that was in one answer – prior to his current repetition of it.

Richard Tomlinson, Ex-MI6 Officer: 2001 Book: **Jury Didn't Hear**:
"The army provides a detachment from the SAS regiment, called Revolutionary Warfare Wing[a] in Hereford, and the navy provides a small detachment from their Special Boat Service in Poole. Both have similar roles as far as MI6 is concerned and are known collectively within the service as the 'increment'. To qualify for the increment, SAS and SBS personnel must have served for at least five years and have reached the rank of sergeant. They are security vetted by MI6 and given a short induction course into the function and objectives of the service.... They learn how to use improvised explosives and sabotage techniques...." [99]

Stephen Dorril, Intelligence Consultant and Author: 2000 Book *MI6*: **Jury Didn't Hear**:
"As Chief of MI6, [Maurice Oldfield[b]] 'insisted that if an intelligence service was to be respected, it should never confuse the collection of information with sabotage and assassinations'. 'Disruptive actions' were continued, but more at arm's length under the umbrella of a 'General Support Branch' which liaised closely with the SAS. A Defence Intelligence Staff officer as

---

[a] The existence of the Revolutionary Warfare Wing (RWW) is supported from various sources. In March 2011 the *Daily Record* stated that the RWW were involved on the ground in the 2011 Libyan revolution: "British Special Forces are already helping to direct the revolt against Colonel Gaddafi. A dozen soldiers from the SAS's ultra secret 'Revolutionary Warfare Wing', who specialise in masterminding uprisings, are advising [Libyan] rebel forces from their Benghazi stronghold." In March 2007, Thomas Harding reported on British intelligence involvement in the monitoring of 15 prisoners held by Iran: "As the intelligence-gathering resources run at full tilt, the SAS will be preparing to put in troopers. An adviser from the regiment's Revolutionary Warfare Wing has been moved to the Gulf to assist diplomats and MI6 agents." According to *The Herald* (Glasgow) they were also present in a hostage rescue in Magbeni, Sierra Leone, in September 2000: "The team tasked with putting together a plan for the armed rescue also debriefed the five Royal Irish Regiment hostages freed last week. These soldiers were interrogated by members of the SAS Counter Revolutionary Warfare Wing." The SAS website admits to the existence of a "Counter Revolutionary Wing (CRW)" which "came into being in the early [19]70s literally overnight." It goes on to say that "the CRW is active all over the world".: Sources: Martin Fricker, Scots Battalion The Black Watch on 24-Hour Standby to Enter Libya in Humanitarian Mission, *Daily Record*, 5 March 2011; Thomas Harding, Intelligence Assets Listen In To Tehran, *The Telegraph*, 26 March 2007; Ian Bruce, Smash-and-Grab Rescue Comes After Fortnight Spying on Captors, *The Herald*, 11 September 2000; SAS Website: www.sasregiment.org.uk/crw.html
[b] MI6 Chief from 1973 to 1978.

part of ... the MoD stationed at Century House[a] arranged the employment and deployment of members of the SAS and Special Boat Squadron[b] (SBS) as 'contract labourers'."[100]

Jonathan Bloch & Patrick Fitzgerald, Intelligence Writers: 1983 Book: **Jury Didn't Hear**:

"Covert operations of a military nature ... are not carried out by MI6, but by the Special Air Service (SAS), three army regiments with ... an inherently political function beyond that of the British armed forces as a whole....

"Close cooperation is required between MI6 and the SAS before and during overseas campaigns and SAS squadrons receive briefings from MI6 before departure....

"The SAS have been extensively deployed in Northern Ireland.... Persistent reports of SAS assassinations are invariably dismissed because they come from republican sources.... Simultaneously their justifiable reputation for ruthlessness – one former British soldier who worked with [the SAS] in the Middle East described them as 'the coolest and most frightening body of professional killers I have ever seen' – is believed by the army to be a powerful ... deterrent to some forms of IRA activity."[101]

Richard Norton-Taylor, Intelligence Journalist: 1990 Book: **Jury Didn't Hear**:

"The Special Air Service (SAS) is ... now firmly established as a highly-trained, armed unit permanently available to the security services and the prime minister.

"The SAS has become the armed military wing of the security and intelligence services."[102c]

Comment: The evidence on the role of SAS and SBS in fulfilling MI6 objectives is:

- Tomlinson: "the increment [is] ... a small cell of the SAS or SBS which is especially selected and trained to carry out operations exclusively for MI5/MI6" – in letter read to inquest

- Tomlinson: "the increment, SAS and SBS personnel ... are security vetted by MI6 and ... learn how to use improvised explosives and sabotage techniques" – in 2001 book

- Dorril: "[MI6-controlled] 'disruptive actions' were continued ... at arm's length.... A Defence Intelligence Staff officer ... stationed at Century House arranged the employment and deployment of members of the SAS and ... SBS as 'contract labourers'"

---

[a] Headquarters of MI6 from 1966 to 1995.
[b] Later changed to Special Boat Service.
[c] Norton-Taylor also quoted from Hansards on 19 May 1988 (col. 1095): Margaret Thatcher in the House of Commons: "We do not discuss matters relating to the SAS, and no one would want to do so unless he wished to undermine the security of this country.": *In Defence of the Realm?*, p64.

- Bloch & Fitzgerald: "covert operations of a military nature ... are ... carried out by ... the ... SAS.... One former British soldier ... described them as 'the coolest and most frightening body of professional killers I have ever seen'"

- Norton-Taylor: "the SAS has become the armed military wing of the security and intelligence services".[a]

It must be realised that this is a subject about which there is little publicly known knowledge, primarily because the authorities withhold information on it – witness Dearlove's contribution, discussed below. Even Tomlinson was reticent to speak on it – he told Mansfield: "obviously I do not want to say too much on this subject".

The evidence that is available – primarily from books by intelligence analysts or writers – essentially supports Tomlinson's account.[b]

Tomlinson's basic assertion is that MI6 uses people from within the SAS and SBS "to carry out operations" which may involve the use of "improvised explosives and sabotage techniques". This is "because MI6 itself does not contain operatives with the relevant skills to carry out particular practical tasks abroad".

In other words, MI6 uses the SAS and SBS to do its dirty work.

There are two key aspects to this: a) the nature of the work done; and, b) the work is done on behalf of MI6 by the SAS or SBS.[c]

a) the nature of the work done

Dorril refers to "disruptive actions"; Bloch & Fitzgerald: "covert operations of a military nature"; Norton-Taylor: "the armed military wing".

All of these descriptions fit with Tomlinson's, the use of "improvised explosives and sabotage techniques".

b) the work is done on behalf of MI6 by the SAS or SBS

Dorril's context is MI6[d] and he states that the officer involved in organising the SAS and SBS deployments was based at Century House – MI6 headquarters during the period he is referring to.

Bloch and Fitzgerald don't spell this out so clearly, but their context is the roles of MI6 and SAS and they also refer to the requirement for "close cooperation ... between MI6 and the SAS". They mention the SAS

---

[a] Martin Ingram also confirmed the involvement of SAS in intelligence operations in Ireland – "22 Squadron ... undertook 'executive actions'": *Stakeknife*, p31.

[b] See also the earlier footnote relating to the "Revolutionary Warfare Wing".

[c] The SBS has a much lower profile than the SAS – the SBS website reads: "The Royal Navy's Special Boat Service ... is the lesser known sister unit of the British Army's Special Air Service." In this connection, two of the sources – Bloch & Fitzgerald and Norton-Taylor – refer only to the SAS.

[d] See the full statement above. Dorril's book is entitled *MI6*.

involvement in Northern Ireland – other evidence earlier in this book shows that the SAS activities in Northern Ireland were controlled by MI6 up to 1973, when MI5 took over.

Norton-Taylor confirms that the SAS worked on behalf of "the security and intelligence services" – this indicates both MI5 and MI6.

Tomlinson describes the SAS and SBS operatives used by MI6 as "the increment". This is not a term that has been used by the other sources, but Tomlinson does specify in his book that the increment is the name they are known by "within the service". The other sources do not have experience from within MI6.[a]

Michael Mansfield asked Richard Dearlove – who has a great deal of inside MI6 experience[b] – about the increment, on four occasions.

It may be significant that Dearlove initially reacted very strongly, on the second occasion Baker intervened, on the third Dearlove simply refused to comment and on the fourth Tam intervened:

1st instance: Dearlove: "can I cut to the quick, Mr Mansfield? I am not going to speculate on SIS's various operational capabilities...."

2nd instance: Baker: "I do not really see why we are spending so long on ... a matter which really must be speculation"

3rd instance: Dearlove: "I am not going to speculate or comment"

4th instance: Tam: "my learned friend is getting into operational details and methods which are sensitive and should not be asked about" followed by Dearlove: "the service's capability is the service's capability".

There are several serious concerns about what occurred during this critical period of cross-examination:[c]

1) Speculation.

Dearlove's initial reaction, when Mansfield suggested that MI6 "employ an increment" for "tasks abroad", was "I am not going to speculate on SIS's various operational capabilities".

Baker later supported that: "I do not really see why we are spending so long on this, on a matter which really must be speculation".

---

[a] It is very rare for ex-MI6 officers to write books or speak out – David Shayler, Annie Machon, Peter Wright and Stella Rimington are all ex-MI5.

[b] See earlier.

[c] The reader should bear in mind that this subject – the use of others, e.g. the SAS, to carry out operations for MI6 – is possibly central to the Paris crash. There is a realistic possibility that, if MI6 were involved, they would have used other people to operate on their behalf. Other evidence in Parts 1,2, 3 and 4 have shown that on the night of the crash and the following day people such as Henri Paul, Claude Roulet, Jean-Marc Martino, Dominique Lecomte, Gilbert Pépin and Jean Monceau appeared to be working on behalf of an outside organisation. There is also extensive witness evidence of riders on powerful motorbikes pursuing the Mercedes S280 – none of these riders have been identified.

Just in case we didn't get it, Dearlove repeated it: "I am <u>not going to speculate</u>".[a]

Speculation[b] – the point here is that Richard Dearlove is on the stand. Dearlove: 38 years experience in MI6, Director of Operations for 5 years and MI6 Chief for another 5 years, 11 years on the MI6 board.[c]

Dearlove is being questioned on a key aspect of MI6 operations – critical to the current case[d] – so it is ridiculous to suggest that any answer on this from him would be speculative. Yet we have both Dearlove and Baker suggesting just that – "I am not going to speculate"; "a matter which really must be speculation".

2) MI6 capabilities.

Dearlove states that "the court does not need to know about ... [the] SIS's various operational capabilities". And later: "I am not going to confirm or deny whether the [capabilities] you are mentioning are part of the service's capabilities".

Dearlove finished up by stating: "the service's capability is the service's capability".

The inquest jury were investigating the circumstances of the Paris crash. MI6 had been named as a prime suspect for having orchestrated it. Yet Dearlove is trying to tell the jury they are not entitled to be told about MI6's "operational capabilities".

This type of evidence tends to make a sham out of even having MI6 witnesses cross-examined at this inquest. If the jury aren't allowed to know about the capabilities of a prime suspect in the investigation[e], then how can they be expected to reach an informed verdict on the circumstances of the crash?[f] If there were concerns that national security was threatened by revealing this information, then why wasn't it told to the jury in a closed court?

---

[a] On the third occasion "the increment" came up.

[b] To speculate is to "form a theory or opinion without firm evidence" – Oxford.

[c] Dearlove joined MI6 in 1966: 20 Feb 08: 4.4. Dearlove's experience is covered in the earlier section on MI6 Training.

[d] See earlier footnote regarding the use of others.

[e] MI6.

[f] One of the key questions regarding the crash was: Was it possible for a crash of this complex nature to be orchestrated? In other words, was there any organisation that would actually have the capabilities to pull such an operation off? In that light, it was important that the jury got to hear this type of critical information. Linked to this was the knowledge – indicated by the accumulated facts of the case – that various operatives appeared to be working for an outside organisation. This is addressed in an earlier footnote.

3) Dearlove's control.

Dearlove strongly states on three occasions that the jury needed to know that he was in control:

- "what the court does need to know is that all of these capabilities, every single one of them, were under my personal control"
- "anything that is referred to ... was under the control of the director of operations"
- "there is no part of SIS ... which is not fully under the control of the operational director".[a]

Dearlove appears to be suggesting that everyone should rest easy because in 1997 – at the time of the deaths of Princess Diana and Dodi Fayed – the operational capabilities of MI6, whatever they may be, were under Dearlove's personal control.

What Dearlove, or anyone else, fails to tell the jury is that in the previous year, 1996, under Dearlove's watch as Director of Operations, MI6 had been deeply involved in two high-level assassination plots – Gaddafi and Saddam.[b]

What this means is that the knowledge that Dearlove was in control at the time of the Paris crash is not a cause for comfort, but instead a cause for concern.[c]

It raises the inevitable question: If Dearlove – and Chief Spedding[d] – presided over the assassination plots of Muammar Gaddafi and Saddam Hussein, did these same men also preside over the assassination of Princess Diana?

4) Subject change.

On the second occasion that Mansfield mentioned the increment, Baker interrupted him midstream, pointing out that even if the increment was used an operation would still be "under the approval of SIS" and then continued: "the whole point is that this [Milosevic] plan is not one officer on a frolic of his own going to carry it out on his own. It has been put up through the system for approval."

---

[a] Dearlove used various phrases to emphasise this point: "every single one"; "whether you have heard of it before or whether you have not heard of it before, whether it has a strange name or whether it has not got a strange name"; "let's be absolutely crystal clear"; "it is important that the jury understands that"; "I am going to repeat this"; "whether it is deniable or not"; "I do not know how many times I am going to have to emphasise this"; "I have said it four or five times already"; "it is unproductive to go on banging on about this".

[b] See earlier.

[c] The jury would not have realised this because they were prevented from hearing about the Gaddafi and Saddam plots.

[d] David Spedding was MI6 Chief for the same period as Richard Dearlove was Director of Operations – 1994 to 1999. Spedding was never interviewed in any police investigation. He died in 2001.

If we go back to Mansfield's question, we can see that it has nothing to do with what Baker is suggesting: "What I wanted to put to you is deniability means this, doesn't it: it means there will be a secret operation abroad, carried out by an increment, not SIS officers but SAS officers or SBS officers – "[a], at which point Mansfield was cut off by Baker.

Mansfield's question focuses on the issue of deniability and he mentions just before this – see previous footnote – "I am asking ... whether in 1993 there were discussions which involved the concept of deniability". He then puts it to Dearlove that deniability "means there will be a secret operation abroad, carried out by ... SAS officers or SBS officers".

This is where Baker cuts Mansfield off and changes the subject to the issue of: "one officer on a frolic of his own".

Mansfield was not suggesting anything like that – he was describing a "secret operation abroad, carried out by an increment" on behalf of MI6, which could later though, if necessary, be denied by MI6: the issue of deniability.

Mansfield was effectively describing a possible scenario for the way the Paris crash could have been organised, had MI6 done it – a deniable operation.

Yet we next find Baker saying: "I think we need to focus on what happened in the tunnel, not on other ephemeral matters." [b]

In doing this, Baker was able to deftly – but dishonestly – shut down Mansfield's line of questioning and he was forced to move on to the next subject.[c]

Later, when Mansfield brings up the increment for the fourth time, Dearlove then emphasises his argument by appearing to copy a similar line from Baker: "There is not a bit of SIS that acts independently or goes off and does its own thing. This does not exist...."

---

[a] The full question started at 120.10: "But now you see why I am asking the questions about what discussions even take place at an official level. That is all I am asking, whether in fact – before we even get to unofficial levels, whether in 1993 there were discussions which involved the concept of deniability. What I wanted to put to you is deniability...." For the full context, refer to the inquest website. The fuller context does include discussion regarding MI6 officers conducting independent operations, but by the time Mansfield asked this question he was focusing on the issue of deniability "at an official level" – see discussion below.

[b] This is from the person who spent around three days of the inquest focusing on the Milosevic plot, where the only documentary evidence was apparently destroyed by MI6.

[c] And Dearlove was saved from having to address the increment ... until Mansfield's next attempt.

The point is that no one has ever suggested that the increment – the use of the SAS or SBS to conduct operations for MI6 – was ever acting independently. In all the mentions of this in the literature, including Tomlinson, the actions of the SAS and SBS – when operating on behalf of MI6 – are under the control of MI6.

If the SAS conducts an operation for MI6, then the fact that MI6 is not directly carrying it out makes it easier for them to deny involvement. That does not however mean that MI6 is not in control of the conduct of that operation.

5) Relevance.

Both Baker and Dearlove suggested that the issue of the increment had nothing to do with the current case – the deaths of Princess Diana and Dodi Fayed:

- Baker: "I think we need to focus on what happened in the tunnel, not on other ephemeral[a] matters"

- Dearlove: "I do not think [MI6's capabilities] has anything to do with this inquest into the death of Princess Diana".

As has been mentioned, MI6 was alleged to be one of the prime suspects for the orchestration and conduct of the Paris crash. Therefore, if the jury were to be allowed to do a proper job of determining the cause of the deaths of Diana and Dodi, it would be imperative for them to understand the capabilities – including use of the increment – of MI6.[b]

Baker, who was in control of the inquest, appeared very determined – with the help of Tam and Dearlove – to ensure that his own jury were not privy to such information.

Why is this?

Despite the refusal by Baker, Dearlove and Tam to divulge this to the jury, other evidence, mostly not heard at the inquest – Tomlinson, Dorril, Bloch and Fitzgerald, Norton-Taylor – reveals that the SAS and SBS are used to conduct operations on behalf of MI6.

Conclusion

The earlier question was: What happens regarding assassination out in the field?

Does MI6 involve itself in assassination plots?

As usual, the evidence is conflicting:

- Dearlove: "no, I was not ... ever aware of the service assassinating anyone ... from 1966 through to 2004" – confirmed to Burnett

---

[a] Ephemeral was a favoured word by both MI6 and Baker – it means: "lasting or living for a very short time": Oxford.
[b] Even if this meant that such evidence should be heard in closed court, to protect national security.

- X: an assassination proposal "has never happened in my time, other than hearing about this" proposal from A
- A: "the ethos of the service was against assassination"
- A: "it seemed to me appropriate that we should ... see if we felt obliged to revise [the "against assassination" ethos] in an exceptional case" [a]
- H: "this is the sort of thing we don't do ... [assassination] was simply not done"
- H: "neither before [A's proposal] nor ... since" had he seen a proposal for an assassination
- E: "the whole idea of SIS being involved in targeted assassinations is repugnant to the ethos of the service"
- E: "categorically no" when asked, "during your time [at MI6 from 1968] are you aware of any assassination having been carried out ... or any proposal that there be an assassination?" – at inquest
- E: "I have never seen any proposal relating to any targeted assassination" – statement [b]
- I: "no" to Burnett's: "has any assassination during your period been carried out by SIS?"
- I: "never" in response to "in your time in SIS, have you ever seen a proposal that involves assassination?"
- Scarlett: "we do not have license to kill"
- Machon: "the real James Bonds do have a licence to kill"
- Anderson: "we were institutional killers that undertook disruptive actions"
- Anderson: "a licence to kill ... was written in the employment contract"
- Cornwell: "we did ... assassinations, although I was never involved"
- Park: "I have been involved in death, yes, but I can't talk about that"
- Stephenson: an assassination "was exactly the sort of mission an agent might be called on to perform in the field"
- Dorril: "H. Montgomery Hyde revealed ... that the BSC had assassinated a German seaman who was operating as a spy in New York"
- Foot: "SOE operational head, Colin Gubbins ... proposed assassinating an important German figure in the Middle East" – quoted by Dorril
- Dorril: "Kenneth Younger ... [said] serious thought [by SOE] was given to the assassination of the Mufti of Jerusalem, the Indian nationalist leader Chandra Bose, and an unnamed Balkan monarch"

---

[a] A stated: "Whenever you spoke to an experienced officer, then they would say that [assassination] is against the service's policy". This appears to be an admission that the issue was the subject of discussion within MI6.

[b] Confirmed by E at the inquest.

- Dorril: "assassination as a policy was openly discussed in the post-war years"
- Dorril: "it was in the Middle East that MI6 seriously considered using [assassination] as an option"
- Dorril: "there is always an element of truth in Bond" [a]
- Dorril: "sponsored murder gangs operated among the exiles in the DP camps in Germany and Austria"
- Thomas: "in the MI6 Registry was a copy of a CIA manual ... titled 'Assassination Methods'"
- Stevens: In his Northern Ireland report: "I conclude there was collusion.... Collusion is evidenced in many ways. ... [including] agents being involved in murder.... The unlawful involvement of agents in murder implies that the security forces sanction killings"
- Intelligence Services Act: "a person ... shall not be so liable if the act is ... authorised ... by ... the Secretary of State"
- Dearlove: "the Foreign Secretary can personally grant an authorisation so that acts which might otherwise be unlawful can be rendered lawful" – confirmed to Burnett.

---

[a] Christopher Andrew in his 1986 book: "Of all SIS agents, the buccaneering [Mervin] Minshall probably came closest to the fictional stereotype of James Bond and may well have given his friend and Bond's creator, Ian Fleming, some of his raw material.": Christopher Andrew, *Secret Service: The Making of the British Intelligence Community*, pp662-3. Minshall's activities are described in a footnote below.

Table: Known Specific British Intelligence Assassination Plots[a]

Time	Target	Group Involved	Stage Reached	Evidence
[b]				
May 1942	Reinhard Heydrich	BSC[c]	Target Killed	William Stevenson
During WWII	Adolf Hitler	SOE[d]	Serious Scrutiny	John Pearson[efg]
During WWII[h]	Chandra Bose	SOE	Serious Thought	Kenneth Younger[a]

---

[a] This table list is not comprehensive – see footnote following the table – but I believe the main ones are included here. It is also probable that British intelligence have carried out assassinations that are not known about.

[b] In chronological order.

[c] British Security Coordination – a branch of MI6 set up in New York in 1940 to handle covert operations in North America during WWII.

[d] Special Operations Executive – an organisation established in 1940 to conduct operations involving sabotage and resistance. After WWII it became the "Special Operations Branch" of MI6.

[e] John Pearson in his 1966 book: "Blowing up the Iron Gates and assassinating Hitler were both SOE pipedreams which were scrutinised in complete seriousness in the earlier days of the war".: John Pearson, *The Life of Ian Fleming*, p106. Fleming was involved with the SOE during the war.

[f] Pearson assisted Fleming on the "Atticus" column in the *Sunday Times*. Earlier he had worked on the Economist Intelligence Unit. Later he went on to write the book mentioned in the previous footnote, which was the only authorised biography of Ian Fleming.: Random House Author Details on John Pearson, www.randomhouse.com.au/Author

[g] M.R.D. Foot refers to a separate incident: "An attempt in March 1943 by some of Hitler's entourage to kill him – using SOE's material, but without benefit of SOE's advice – failed to work. The would-be assassin, von Tresckow, used a home-made bomb composed of two of SOE's portable clams ... disguised as a bottle of Cointreau slipped into Hitler's aircraft as a present for one of his staff. It took some nerve to recover the package ... and ... unravel the faulty fuse.": M.R.D. Foot, *SOE*, p73.

[h] Christopher Andrew describes other possible wartime assassinations and plots by MI6: "By his own (never understated) account, [MI6 agent Mervin] Minshall actually exercised his licence to kill while travelling on the Orient Express....
"[Minshall] was given diplomatic cover as vice-consul in Bucharest and supplied with plastic explosive through the diplomatic bag. His ... scheme to disrupt Danube navigation by bribing 40 of the 50 Iron Gates pilots to leave the country for 500 gold sovereigns each and having the remainder 'unobtrusively bumped off' fell through

DIANA INQUEST: WHO KILLED PRINCESS DIANA?

Time	Target	Group Involved	Stage Reached	Evidence
October 1947	Alexander Rubowitz	MI6	Target Killed	Nigel West
September 1956	Gamal Abdel Nasser	MI6	5 Failed Attempts	Peter Wright
February 1959	Georgios Grivas	MI5/MI6	Aborted Before Fruition	Peter Wright
September 1960	Patrice Lumumba	FCO	Target Killed by Belgium	British National Archives; Ian Black; Richard Belfield
1972	Various Irish Targets	MI6	Orders Given	Ireland's Own; Richard Bennett; Gordon Thomas
March 1988	3 Targets in Gibraltar	MI5/SAS	Targets Killed	Richard Norton-Taylor
February 1989	Patrick Finucane	SB/FRU	Target Killed	John Stevens
February 1991 to October 2000	20 Civilians[b]	SB	10 Targets Killed; 10 Failed Attempts	Nuala O'Loan
Summer 1992	Slobodan Milosevic	MI6	Written Proposal	Richard Tomlinson[c]
February 1996	Muammar Gaddafi	MI6	Failed At Point of Execution	David Shayler; CX 95/53452 Report

for lack of sovereigns." Christopher Andrew, *Secret Service: The Making of the British Intelligence Community*, p663.

[a] Ex-MI5 senior officer and post-war Minister of State for Foreign Affairs.

[b] Ten civilians – named earlier – were assassinated over the ten year period. A further ten attempted assassination plots failed – the targets of these failed plots, which occurred in a similar time frame, are not named in the 2007 Ombudsman's Report, but other details about the plots are included. There is also a list on page 3 of the report. See Bibliography for details of the report.

[c] Tomlinson's evidence of a documented proposal was supported by other witnesses, but they said the target was different – see earlier and inquest transcripts referred to in an earlier footnote. It will be shown later that the evidence points to Tomlinson being correct.

Time	Target	Group Involved	Stage Reached	Evidence
June 1996	Saddam Hussein	MI6[a]	Local Agents Killed by Saddam	CIA Sources

[b]

---

[a] Joint project with the CIA.

[b] There are other allegations of assassination plots that have not been included because they are unconfirmed or the details are not specific:

- BSC officer "Cynthia" (cover name) put forward a proposal for the assassination of Dr Gerhard Westrick, a Nazi who was operating among French industrialists during the German wartime occupation: William Stephenson, *A Man Called Intrepid*, pp362-3

- Admiral Jean-François Darlan, deputy to the French President, was assassinated by an SOE officer, Ferdinand Bonnier de la Chapelle, just outside Algiers on 24 December 1942: M.R.D. Foot, *SOE*, pp150-1, 218-9; History Learning Site www.historylearningsite.co.uk

- in July 1944, following D-Day, the SAS were assigned the job of either kidnapping or killing the German General Erwin Rommel, who was at a French chateau: "In [an SAS] document marked 'Secret' and under the heading 'Method' the orders state: 'The following points should be borne in mind: If it should prove possible to kidnap Rommel and bring him to this country [UK] the propaganda value would be immense and the inevitable retaliation against the local inhabitants might be mitigated or avoided. Such a plan could involve finding and being prepared to hold for a short time if necessary a suitable landing ground. To kill Rommel would obviously be easier than to kidnap him and it is preferable to ensure the former rather than to attempt and fail in the latter.' However, the day before the SAS team was due to parachute in, Rommel returned to Germany having been seriously injured when his staff car was hit by RAF planes.": Thomas Harding, Forgotten SAS Diary Reveals Mission to Capture Rommel, *Daily Telegraph*, 24 September 2011, quoting from *The SAS War Diary 1941-45*.

- M.R.D. Foot relates a wartime incident in Toulouse, France, where a Jew, codename "Felix", was an assistant wireless operator for a British SOE agent, codename "Alphonse". After alighting from a train Felix, who was carrying a transmitter in a suitcase was confronted with a German SS baggage search. Felix "held the suitcase high and called in authoritative German, 'Get me a car at once, I have a captured set.' He was driven away in a German-requisitioned car, had it pull up in a back street, killed the driver, and reported to Alphonse with the set for orders.": M.R.D. Foot, *SOE*, p111

- the assassination by MI6 in the 1970s or early 80s of "an officer working on the Czechoslovak desk" after he was "revealed as a double agent": Jonathan Bloch & Patrick Fitzgerald, *British Intelligence and Covert Action*, 1983, p40

- the assassination of terrorists by the SAS in the Iranian Embassy in London in May1980. Peter Taylor in *The Guardian*: "Robin Horsfall was one of the counter terrorist team's crack shots.... When I asked [him] if he wanted the negotiations to succeed, he gave a brutally honest reply. 'We didn't want them to surrender. We wanted them to stay there so we could go in and hit them. That was what we lived for and trained for.... We didn't want the negotiators to be successful. Ultimately, we wanted to go in there and do the job.'...

"Just before the SAS team went in, Tom [surname not given] claims that a highly sensitive message was passed from [British Prime Minister, Margaret] Thatcher. He says that nothing was written down and it was relayed off the record, verbally, to the assault team. 'The message was that we had to resolve the situation and there was to be no chance of failure, and that the hostages absolutely had to be protected. The prime minister did not want an ongoing problem beyond the embassy – which we took to mean that they didn't want anybody coming out alive. No surviving terrorists.'

"Although, 22 years later, Tom is not 100% sure of the precise words, he stands by his recollection and has no doubt what it meant. However, Tom's counter terrorist team-mates do not share his recollection and the SAS and the Ministry of Defence refuse to comment. If a message was received, 'an ongoing problem' could be open to wide interpretation....

"The most controversial killings took place in the embassy's telex room, where two of the gunmen, Shai and Makki, were guarding most of the Iranian hostages.... [Hostage] Ahmad Dadgar ... says that the hostages persuaded the gunmen to surrender rather than be killed. According to his account, Shai and Makki agreed, threw down their weapons and sat on the floor with their hands on their heads. As the television pictures show, weapons were thrown out of the window and a white flag of surrender appeared. When the SAS entered the room, they demanded to know who the gunmen were. Dadgar remembers: 'They then took the two terrorists, pushed them against the wall and shot them. They wanted to finish their story. That was their job.' He said that they might have 'had something in their pockets but certainly had no weapons in their hands at the time'.

"Dadgar's account is confirmed by two of the other Iranian hostages who were witnesses in the telex room at the time....

"Five of the six gunmen died in a hail of SAS bullets. One, Fawzi Nejad, survived by passing himself off as a hostage. Once 'rescued' and taken outside the embassy, he was identified as a gunman by a real hostage and almost joined his dead comrades. One SAS soldier appeared to be about to drag him back inside the building until Horsfall advised him against it since the world was watching....

"The SAS then retired to Regents Park barracks for a beer, a debrief and a congratulatory visit from Margaret Thatcher and Denis....

"Tom distinctly recollects ... that Denis was 'quite upset' that one of the terrorists had survived. 'He told us in no uncertain terms that we had failed in some respects,' Tom says. 'He had a big grin on his face and said, "You let one of the bastards live."'": Peter Taylor, Six Days That Shook Britain, *The Guardian*, 24 July 2002. Richard Belfield briefly describes the same incident: "The recollection of one of the SAS soldiers involved in the hostage release ... was that their off-the-record verbal

The above table includes a few of the assassination plots that were considered or executed during the second world war, but more importantly, it shows that the British intelligence appetite for assassinations did not dissipate at the conclusion of hostilities in 1945. If anything, it appears to have grown.

There were at least two targets in the 1950s – Nasser and Grivas – then an upsurge through the 1970s[a], 80s[b] and 90s, culminating in three high profile world leaders in the 1990s – Milosevic, Gaddafi and Saddam Hussein.

So in the five year period leading up to the death of Princess Diana, there were three known top-level assassination plots involving MI6 – Milosevic, Gaddafi and Saddam.[c]

The table does indicate that British intelligence is not particularly good at carrying high profile assassinations through to completion – none of the three known proposed top-level assassinations in the 1990s were successfully executed.

One could argue that this high failure rate would indicate that MI6 were unlikely to have been involved in the assassination of Princess Diana, which was a highly complex, yet successful operation.[d] This issue is addressed later in this book.

---

orders were clear – 'they didn't want anybody coming out alive. No surviving terrorists.' He believed an order was passed down from Mrs Thatcher. One did escape with the hostages and the SAS tried to drag him back into the building for summary execution, only to be stopped by the police.": *The Secret History of Assassination*, p27

- an assassination plot against Robert Mugabe, leader of Zimbabwe: "The British tried to assassinate ... Mugabe shortly after he became the ... leader, but missed him.": *The Secret History of Assassination*, p246

[a] On 17 May 1974 four bombings occurred in Dublin and Monaghan in Ireland, taking the lives of 33 innocent civilians (including one pregnant woman). The official inquiry report, published in December 2003, stated in its conclusions: "A number of those suspected for the bombings were reliably said to have had relationships with British Intelligence and/or RUC Special Branch officers.... There are grounds for suspecting that the bombers may have had assistance from members of the [British] security forces.": The Report of the Independent Commission of Inquiry into the Dublin and Monaghan Bombings, December 2003, pp355,356.

[b] Tony Collins' 1990 book, Open Verdict, details 25 unexplained deaths that occurred in the UK defence industry, most of them in a three year period from 1986 to 1988.

[c] When combined with the increasing assassinations in Ireland in the late 80s and 90s, it seems the British intelligence role in assassinations was increasing in the period leading up to the 1997 assassination of Princess Diana.

[d] See Parts 1 to 3.

What quickly becomes clear, in assessing the earlier witness evidence on MI6 and assassination, is that at the inquest the MI6 witnesses – Dearlove, X, A, H, E, I – presented a united front. To the last man, or woman, they swore on oath that, as employees of MI6, they had not seen any evidence of MI6 involvement in any assassination plots:

- Dearlove: "not ... ever aware of the service assassinating anyone" in his time
- X: an assassination proposal "has never happened in my time ... other than ..." A's
- A: "the ethos of the service was against assassination"
- H: assassination "was simply not done"
- E: "I have never seen any proposal relating to any targeted assassination"
- I: never in his time had he ever "seen a proposal that involves assassination".

All this is despite the admission from these same people that A had drawn up a proposal for the assassination of a Balkan identity.

John Scarlett, speaking in 2009 in his role as MI6 chief, supported the inquest accounts: "we do not have license to kill"[a] – but he is a lonely voice.

When we look outside of the inquest evidence, to ex-intelligence officers or intelligence experts and historians – none of which was heard by the jury – there is a major divergence from the inquest line.

That evidence is:

- Machon: "the real James Bonds do have a licence to kill"
- Anderson: "a licence to kill ... was written in the employment contract"
- Cornwell: "we did ... assassinations"
- Park: "I have been involved in death"
- Foot: "Gubbins ... proposed assassinating an important German figure"
- Dorril: "assassination as a policy was openly discussed in the post-war years"
- Thomas: "in the MI6 Registry was a copy of a CIA manual ... titled 'Assassination Methods'"
- Stevens: "I conclude there was collusion ... [including] agents being involved in murder".

So a huge contrast in the evidence: at the inquest "MI6 assassination" is an oxymoron, but outside of the inquest a considerable amount of evidence indicates that MI6 does involve itself in assassination plots.

---

[a] Taken literally, this statement does not necessarily preclude the conduct of assassinations. Saying, "we do not have license to kill", is not the same as saying "we never assassinate anyone".

This latter view is then strongly supported by the evidence already looked at showing MI6 involvement in various assassination plots – some WWII identities, Nasser, Milosevic, Gaddafi and Saddam.

The Intelligence Services Act states that if the Foreign Secretary authorises an illegal action outside the UK then that act is legal. In other words, an assassination[a] sanctioned by the Foreign Secretary is legal under British law.

Although that is a 1994 law, the accounts included in Peter Wright's book – he was an MI5 officer from 1955 to 1976 – indicate that it was also a requirement to run illegal operations past the Foreign Office, well before 1994. Wright's book includes evidence of that rule being flouted: on page 310, referring to an event in the mid-1960s: "the plan was put up to F.J.[b], who gave his consent, although the operation[c] was kept secret from the Foreign Office, on the grounds that they would very likely veto it" [103d]

Wright's account raises a serious concern: the possibility that there was a culture of hiding a planned operation from the FCO, if MI5 felt it would be rejected. This appears to defeat the purpose of FCO oversight – the FCO are only shown operations which MI5 think will be authorised.

If MI5 were doing this, it is possible that MI6 were too.

There were two major assassination plots in the 18 months leading up to the Paris crash – Saddam and Gaddafi.

The Gaddafi evidence – see earlier – indicates that FCO authorisation was sought and obtained, but in the case of the Saddam assassination plot, it is not possible, from the available evidence, to ascertain if this occurred.

The Wright evidence certainly indicates the possibility of an earlier culture of ignoring the FCO on "difficult" operations.[ef]

---

[a] Outside the UK.

[b] MI5 Director General, Martin Furnival-Jones.

[c] This was an entrapment operation involving lining up a "high-class call girl" with a Russian agent in the hope that it would lead to an affair – British intelligence would then offer the compromised agent an "opportunity" to defect.

[d] Wright also said on p349 of *Spycatcher*: "there were many secrets which MI5 had kept from their political and Civil Service masters".

[e] In 1956, during the plotting to assassinate Gamal Abdel Nasser, MI6 worked in tandem with the Prime Minister and bypassed the FCO.

[f] This was supported in 2003 by the findings of the Commission of Inquiry into the 1974 Dublin and Monaghan bombings: In referring to any possible role of the British "security forces": "There is evidence that the Secretary of State [for Northern Ireland] of the day was not fully informed on matters of which he should have been made aware. On that basis, it is equally probable that similarly sensitive information might be withheld from the present holder of that office.": The Report of the

The 1994 Intelligence Services Act indicates that MI6 officers or agents are not liable if the illegal act has the Foreign Secretary's authorisation. But, if MI6 is found later to have acted illegally without that authorisation, what then is the penalty?[a] And, would there anyway be any will within government circles to punish perpetrators working for MI6?

It could be significant that in 1998 – the year following the Diana crash – the Criminal Justice Act was passed. It appears to extend the rights of MI6 officers: there is no criminal liability for offences committed outside the UK, if the person is "acting on behalf of, or holding office under, the Crown".

No mention there of a requirement for the Foreign Secretary's authorisation.

This evidence suggests that if MI6 were involved in the Paris crash, it may or may not have had the authorisation of the FCO – in other words, it is possible, regardless of the legislation, for MI6 to conduct an illegal operation without government approval.

So the evidence the jury heard – mostly witness evidence from inside the organisation – strongly supported the view that MI6 <u>does not contemplate</u> assassinations – outside of A's proposal.

The evidence the jury didn't hear – witnesses from outside of MI6, ex-officers, the evidence of various specific plots, including the published CX report – just as strongly supports the view that <u>MI6 does involve itself</u> in assassination plots.

I suggest that on balance, to any unbiased observer, the evidence shown in the earlier pages is overwhelming in indicating that MI6 has been involved in assassination plots.

Does this mean that the MI6 witnesses all lied on this point at the inquest?

Not necessarily – it depends on: a) what each one actually said; b) their role in the organisation[b]; and c) their period of service:

- Dearlove was asked by Burnett: "During ... 1966 through to 2004[c], were you ever aware of the service assassinating anyone?" He answered: "No, I was not."

That could be careful questioning: Dearlove wasn't asked if he knew of any plots – only if he knew of any successful assassinations.[d]

Independent Commission of Inquiry into the Dublin and Monaghan Bombings, December 2003, p355.

[a] The Act doesn't appear to make any reference to penalties.

[b] Because of the "need to know" rule regarding information – see earlier. It is possible that a section of MI6 could be involved in an assassination plot, but a person working in a completely different area would not necessarily be made aware of it.

[c] Dearlove's period of service.

[d] Dearlove was made Director of Operations in 1994 and later became Chief. So it is reasonable to assume that from 1994 Dearlove should have been aware of any assassination plots.

As pointed out earlier, the table shows that MI6 are not particularly successful at converting known plots into actual assassinations.

Ostensibly the jury were there to determine if Princess Diana and Dodi Fayed were assassinated[a], so even if MI6 had done it, Dearlove – who was Director of Operations at the time – would be most unlikely to put his hand up for it during questioning.

Effectively, Dearlove may have told the truth, if MI6 weren't involved in Diana's assassination. If they were involved, then he has lied under oath.

-    Miss X was asked by Mansfield: "If somebody starts to think about [assassinating someone] and suggests that it goes to the controllerate, that really would be exceptional, would it?" X replied: "You know, it has never happened in my time, other than hearing about this [assassination proposal from A]".

X joined MI6 in 1982[104] and in 2008[b] – when cross-examined – confirmed that she had "started ... there as a ... personal assistant, but ... some time ago" had risen to "middle management". X is evidently a trusted employee, because during the Paget investigation she was provided with "God's access" – unrestricted access to all MI6 files (see earlier[c]).

It is significant that X appears to speak with authority on this subject. She says: "it has never happened in my time" – not qualifying it with "from my experience" or "to the best of my knowledge".

This indicates then that X has lied when she says an assassination proposal – other than A's – "has never happened in my time".

-    H was asked by Burnett: "Since you joined in the 1970s, had you ever seen or heard of any other proposal[d] that involved assassination?" H replied: "Neither before nor – I know you haven't yet asked me – nor since" A's proposal.

H was A's line manager in 1992, and at that time A was Head of the Balkan Target Team[105]. H's immediate boss was E, Controller of Central and Eastern Europe. According to Tomlinson's affidavit,[e] H was the Head of Balkan Operations. That was a senior position, but it is impossible to know how high H had been promoted in the organisation by 2008 – or even if he was still at MI6 – when he was cross-examined.

---

[a] Just prior to the jury leaving to deliberate on a verdict, in a surprise move, Scott Baker actually withdrew murder or assassination as a possible verdict. This has been addressed in Part 1.

[b] X was still employed by MI6 at the time of the inquest: 26 Feb 08: 3.19.

[c] In the section on Relationship With Official Investigations.

[d] Other than A's.

[e] Shown earlier. This is also referred to in a letter read out during the inquest: 13 Feb 08: 87.19.

It is then not possible to know what access H would have had to information – and therefore whether he was lying – when he confirmed to the inquest he had never "seen or heard of any ... proposal that involved assassination" other than A's.

- E was asked two questions by Burnett: "During your time there [at MI6][a], are you aware of any assassination having been carried out?" and secondly, "Or any proposal that there be an assassination?" E responded with a firm: "Categorically no." to both questions.

E's position in 1992 was Controller of Central and Eastern Europe.

Mansfield correctly pointed out that when E said in his Paget statement that he had "never seen any proposal relating to any targeted assassination", that could not be true – other evidence at the inquest had shown E had seen A's assassination proposal.

E gave a muddled response: "Yes, but I have – I still have never seen – this was in relation to the time of the [Paget] inquiry and I have not seen anything put in front of me related to flashing lights and everything of that nature."

E gave two defences: a) "this was in relation to the time of the [Paget] inquiry", and b) "I have not seen anything put in front of me related to flashing lights".[b]

The issue though was that E had categorically stated: "I have never seen any proposal relating to any targeted assassination". Whether the statement was made to the Paget inquiry or included flashing lights is actually irrelevant.

Burnett had earlier asked E: "Are you aware of ... any proposal that there be an assassination?"[c] There is no qualification here – Burnett does not say "any proposal other than A's".

One of E's defences to Mansfield was that his statement was made at "the time of the [Paget] inquiry". E admitted to Burnett: "When I gave the statement to Lord Stevens' police inquiry, I did not recall the incident.... Of course, subsequently, all these different pieces of testimony have arrived, which puts in doubt the calibre of my memory...."

If E was unaware that he had seen this proposal at the time of Paget, E's awareness of "all these different pieces of testimony"[d] reveals that he must have been aware that evidence indicated he had seen the proposal, by the

---

[a] From 1968, but it is not known if E was still there in 2008.

[b] Tomlinson's account was that A's plot proposal included "disorientating Milosevic's chauffeur using a blinding strobe light": 13 Feb 08: 92.2. This was disputed by the MI6 witnesses.

[c] E answered: "Categorically no" – see above.

[d] This refers to other witness accounts of what occurred. That is not covered in this book, but is included in the inquest transcripts relating to the Milosevic plot – details of the relevant transcripts have been shown earlier.

time he was asked this question by Burnett. Yet E responds: "Categorically no."

I suggest that when E responded with "Categorically no", to "Are you aware of ... any proposal that there be an assassination?" E has either misunderstood the question, or has lied.

When this is viewed in the light of his muddled or evasive answer – introducing flashing lights and the timing[a] – to a straightforward question from Mansfield, it raises the possibility that E has lied to Burnett.

- Mr I, MI6 Chief Colin McColl's[b] private secretary, was asked by Ian Burnett: "In your time in SIS[c], have you ever seen a proposal that involves assassination?" Mr I replied, "Never." Then Burnett asked: "To your knowledge, has any assassination during your period been carried out by SIS?" Mr I said: "No."

In Tomlinson's affidavit – shown earlier – he included Mr I[d] on the circulation list for A's proposal. Mr I has stated: "I have no memory of having seen or heard of such a proposal."[106] The general evidence the inquest heard was that A's assassination proposal document was destroyed before it reached Mr I.

Would Mr I have seen the evidence of other MI6 assassination attempts, such as the 1996 Gaddafi and Saddam plots?

Mr I confirmed to Burnett that he was in "a position which oversaw a number or all aspects of the work of SIS in 1992 and 1993 because ... [he was] on the central staff ... [and was] also secretary to the board of directors".[107] Mr I also told Mansfield: "I had left SIS by 1998".

One can't know for sure whether Mr I was still working for MI6 in 1996.

Burnett's questioning appears to be careful – he only asks Mr I if he has "seen a proposal" – not whether he knew of one. Then Burnett asks if he had "knowledge" of any actual assassination. As we know from earlier, there is a big difference between an assassination proposal and a successful assassination – MI6 do not have a high conversion rate.

So Burnett has limited Mr I's questioning – a significant witness because of his central position – to the sighting of a proposal document. It is possible that Mr I could have heard of an assassination proposal without actually seeing the document.

There is another serious flaw in Burnett's methods of questioning the MI6 witnesses on this issue – knowledge of assassination proposals or assassinations. In some cases Burnett has failed to ascertain the precise

---

[a] At the time of the Paget investigation.
[b] McColl was Chief from 1989 to 1994.
[c] Mr I started in 1975 and had left by 1998: 29 Feb 08: 29.25 & 31.13.
[d] Alan Petty.

171

periods that the MI6 employees worked for the organisation. This is significant because the jury were expected to decide on the alleged assassinations of Princess Diana and Dodi Fayed, which occurred in August 1997. Burnett asked the MI6 witnesses questions about what they knew or saw about assassination plots, but then neglected to establish whether these people were even at MI6 in August 1997.

- Burnett asked Mr I: "When did you join SIS?" Mr I said: "In 1975." [108] Burnett then went straight into his questioning[a] on assassinations and plots, starting off: "In your time in SIS...." He did this without finding out when Mr I left MI6. It is only later, when Mansfield is questioning Mr I about something that occurred in 1998, and Mr I volunteers: "I should point out that I had left SIS by 1998" [109]

Even then, the jury are not that much wiser, as Mr I has not told precisely when he left – just that he was gone by 1998. The jury heard only that Mr I worked for MI6 from 1975 to 1993[110], but he could have left the organisation in any year from 1994 to 1997.

The inquest jury also couldn't have known whether Mr I was still working in MI6 during the 1996 Gaddafi and Saddam plots.[b] But then, they wouldn't have even been asking the question – the inquest heard nothing about the Saddam plot and then was told by Baker that the Gaddafi plot was "not an issue in these inquests".

The jury could not then ascertain whether Mr I was present at MI6 during the Saddam, Gaddafi or Diana assassination plots.

- Burnett asked E: "When did you join SIS, E?" E: "1968." Then Burnett: "In the time that you have been there, so, however long your service was – I do not need to ask you whether you are still there or not – but during your time there...."

So again, Burnett goes on to ask questions of E about his knowledge of assassinations and plots, but deliberately failing to establish what time period E is able to witness about. We know from the general evidence that E was still at MI6 in 1992. There is also evidence of an MI6 document signed by E in January 1994.[c]

It wasn't until the following day, when E was asked by Mansfield about an event in 1998, that E then volunteered: "[That] was just before I retired".[d]

---

[a] Shown above.
[b] Both plots occurred in the year preceding the Paris crash.
[c] This came up during MI6 lawyer, Robin Tam's questioning of X, two days previously: 27 Feb 08: 165.12.
[d] This fits with an MI6 officers list that reveals E – otherwise known as Richard Fletcher – was born in 1944. This would have made E age 55 in 1999: List of MI6 Officers Worldwide (Asia, Africa, Australia) www.cryptome.org This officers list was originally anonymously released in 1999 to the magazine *Executive Intelligence Review*.

Whether the jury realised the significance of this passing comment could be a matter of debate, but what it meant was E was a senior member of MI6, present during the assassination plots of Gaddafi, Saddam and Princess Diana.[a]

This evidence appears to add weight to the possibility – raised above – that E could have lied when he answered with "Categorically no", to Burnett's "Are you aware of ... any proposal that there be an assassination?"

- Burnett asked H: "When did you join SIS?" H replied more vaguely: "In the 1970s." Then Burnett: "And in that time, since you joined in the 1970s...."

Again Burnett fails to even attempt to establish how long H was at MI6. As with E, the general evidence shows that H was at MI6 in 1992. And again, there is also evidence of an MI6 document signed by H in January 1994.[b]

Burnett asked H about the 1998 event, but there is no indication from H about whether he was still at MI6 at that stage.[c]

On the available evidence, it is not possible to know if H is still in MI6, or if and when he left (see preceding footnote).

Effectively the Diana inquest jury were not given enough information to know whether Mr I or Mr H[d] were present at MI6 in 1996 and 1997, when three critical assassination plots took place – Gaddafi, Saddam and Diana and Dodi.

Richard Tomlinson, Ex-MI6 Officer: 2001 Book: **Jury Didn't Hear**: "[My] thoughts were interrupted by the PAX[e] ringing on my desk. 'Hello Richard ... I'm afraid that CX of yours has been spiked. And H/SECT[f] wants to see you about it – go up and see him right now.' I dropped the phone and urgently made for the lift to take me up to the 18th floor...."

---

[a] At this stage, I am not suggesting MI6 were involved in the Diana plot, but the evidence shows that E was still in MI6 when that assassination occurred.

[b] This came up during MI6 lawyer, Robin Tam's questioning of X, two days previously: 27 Feb 08: 164.17.

[c] An MI6 officers list reveals that H – otherwise known as Maurice Kendwrick-Piercey – was born in 1948 and was posted to Athens in 1994: List of MI6 Officers Worldwide (Asia, Africa, Australia) www.cryptome.org According to this list, if H had retired at age 65, he would have left MI6 around 2003.

[d] In the case of E a passing reference the following day would have indicated to an astute jury member that he was still in MI6 in 1997 – see above. Mr A was never asked about his knowledge of assassination plots. The inquest evidence was clear that both X and Dearlove were at MI6 in 1997 – X was there for the Paget investigation in 2004, Dearlove retired in 2004 – see earlier.

[e] Internal phone system.

[f] MI6 Chief Colin McColl's personal secretary.

"[Alan] Judd [H/SECT] addressed me ... 'That CX report you wrote about Tory party[a] funding[b].... I'm afraid we can't possibly issue it. If it leaked out, it could bring down the government.... The [MI6] Chief[c] has decided to issue it as a "hot potato", meaning that it will go only to the Prime Minister[d]. I want that CX report destroyed.' Judd handed over the paperwork that I was required to sign to have the report officially struck off the records. There was no choice but to sign, though I knew it was wrong. 'And you are to talk to nobody about this report or this incident,' Judd threatened ominously as I was getting up to leave." [111]

Peter Wright, ex-MI5 Officer: 1987 Book *Spycatcher*: **Jury Didn't Hear**: "Years later, when I was coming up for retirement, I tried to find the details of this operation in the MI6 files. I arranged with Sir Maurice Oldfield, the then Chief of MI6 to spend the day in their Registry looking for the papers. But I could find nothing; the MI6 weeders had routinely destroyed all the records years before." [112]

Comment: There are two major obstacles when it comes to the seeking of evidence regarding the activities of MI6.

First, MI6 witnesses have an allegiance to the Queen and to the national interest that supersedes any legal requirement to tell the truth under oath in a court of law.

Second, there are MI6 "weeders" who have gone through the files long before any outside investigators – the MPS[e] – are allowed to have access.[f]

On the one hand we have Richard Dearlove assuring the inquest jury that the MPS "were given full access[gh], full cooperation" during their investigation into the Gaddafi plot, while Peter Wright – who the jury didn't hear – tells us "the MI6 weeders had routinely destroyed all the records" of an operation he knew had taken place.[i]

---

[a] This was in 1993 and the Conservatives were in power in the UK, with John Major as Prime Minister.

[b] This was intelligence Tomlinson had received that the Bosnian Serb leader, Radovan Karadzic, had supplied money to the British Conservative party.

[c] Colin McColl.

[d] John Major.

[e] There is no evidence of anyone else ever being allowed access to MI6 files.

[f] Nigel West states in his 1990 book: "The ever-vigilant [MI6] 'weeders' ... scrutinise everything before it is shipped to the Public Records Office at Kew.": *The Friends*, p2.

[g] To MI6 files.

[h] X provided evidence that a similar full access was accorded Operation Paget during their investigation into the deaths of Princess Diana and Dodi Fayed.

[i] Wright – who retired in 1976 – was referring to a secret operation his father had been involved in during WWI. There is no reason to suggest that this same process of weeding files doesn't occur today. In 2011 Keith Jeffrey completed an officially authorised book on the history of MI6 from 1909 to 1949 – entitled *The Secret*

X alluded to a culture of removal of information when Richard Keen, representing the Pauls, asked if ideas were sometimes "tippexed out of the record". In a possibly inadvertent response, X replied that tippexing out of the record "was a normal way of treating correspondence".[a]

Richard Tomlinson also confirms that in certain circumstances MI6 documents are "destroyed" and "struck off the records".[b]

Mr I – private secretary to the MI6 Chief – was asked by Michael Mansfield: "Do you remember any occasions when documents were shredded?" Mr I replied: "Oh, well, documents are very frequently shredded if they are ephemeral."[cd]

The question is: What is the point in giving the police full access if the records have been removed?

This superficial openness creates a false facade of "nothing to hide".

These problems in obtaining MI6 evidence – dishonest witness testimony and destruction of records – means that we are forced to look elsewhere for the evidence. This is a key reason why the bulk of the evidence presented in this chapter has been derived from the testimonies of former MI6 and MI5

History of MI6. Jeffrey has stated that he was provided "uniquely privileged access to the ... [MI6] archives". But what Jeffrey either doesn't realise, or doesn't state, is that those archives had been weeded before he was allowed near them.

[a] H also stated at the inquest: A's proposal document "was destroyed, we would not accept it on the archive because it was completely against the ethos of the service [MI6]. We don't keep documents which are against the ethos of the service, we don't have documents like this.": 28 Feb 08: 131.19.

[b] Martin Ingram alluded to the attitude towards treatment of paperwork surrounding the Irish intelligence agent Stakeknife (codename for Freddie Scappaticci), who carried out many assassinations in the 1980s and 90s: "I became friendly with one of Stakeknife's primary handlers, a man that I will call 'Andy'.... I believe Andy knew as early as the mid-1980s that this case could come back to haunt not only him but the FRU as a unit. On occasions when I suggested he be careful, he intimated that the paperwork generated would not accurately reflect much of [Stakeknife's] activities, certainly not the aspects which were clearly illegal."; *Stakeknife*, pp63-64. On page 221 of the same book, Ingram's co-author Greg Harkin writes about British intelligence involvement in the assassination of Francisco Notorantonio in October 1987: "Charlotte Notorantonio ... is demanding an inquiry into her father's murder. It has been suggested to me, however, that the FRU destroyed all references to that murder after the *People* story of August 2000. That should come as no surprise."

[c] Ephemeral means "lasting or living for a very short time" – Oxford. I suggest that the very act of shredding a document could ensure that it is short-lived.

[d] At the inquest X referred to a document which should be seen as significant – a later "write-up" by A regarding the assassination proposal – as "ephemeral": 26 Feb 08: 112.25.

officers, the works of intelligence experts and media reports at the time of the events – mostly not heard by the inquest jury.[a]

Richard Tomlinson's evidence was that a proposal was put forward by A to assassinate Slobodan Milosevic. Other MI6 witnesses – primarily A and H[b] – have stated that the named target on the proposal was not Milosevic.

At the inquest Richard Keen asked X: "Has that other person since been assassinated, Miss X?" X refused to answer this: "I think that is probably edging closer to the area –" and MI6 lawyer, Robin Tam, broke in: "Sir, I have thought about that for a moment because the 'neither confirm nor deny' principle would apply there as well.... The name itself is sensitive. I think everyone here recognises that. If questions are asked about what has happened to that individual since, it could tend to identify him."

When seen in the light of the general MI6 evidence that they never contemplate assassinations, this question from Keen would seem rather innocuous.

So why then did MI6 – both X and Tam – immediately refuse to answer it?

There would appear to be just three possible reasons:

1) the named target was actually Milosevic and MI6 have lied when they say it was someone else, but they refuse to give further information to avoid complicating the lie

2) the named target was not Milosevic, but the person has since been assassinated. This possibility would automatically raise the question: Was the target person assassinated by MI6?

3) the named target was not Milosevic, and the person has not been assassinated.

If either of options 1 or 2 are correct, then MI6 comes out looking bad – option 1 would show that they had lied repeatedly under oath in declaring that Milosevic was not the target; option 2 would automatically lead to an assumption that MI6 may have been involved in the assassination, when they have consistently stated that is not something they would consider.

That leaves option 3 – that the person, who is not Milosevic, has not been assassinated.

That is the only option that leaves MI6 untarnished – so if option 3 was true, why didn't Tam let X answer the question?

Tam stated that if X was allowed to say "what has happened to that individual since, it could tend to identify him".

Yet in 1998 – about three years after the conclusion of the Yugoslav war[a] – A wrote: "It seems to me ... that [Tomlinson] is being mischievous as there

---

[a] Another reason for this is because Baker failed to address the Saddam and Gaddafi assassination plots – see earlier.

[b] A: 26 Feb 08: from 191.6 and from 221.24; H: 28 Feb 08: 112.25.

is far more mileage in an SIS plot to kill a president[b] than in a possible contingency plan to kill someone who might become more powerful but in 1993 was, and <u>remains, unknown to the public at large</u>." [cd]

---

[a] The war concluded in November 1995 with the signing of the Dayton Peace Accords.

[b] Slobodan Milosevic, president of Serbia.

[c] This was quoted at the inquest from a four page 1998 memorandum (not shown to the jury) written up by A – it is his official "recollections of events ... after matters went into the public domain through newspaper articles": 26 Feb 08: 174.21 & 190.25. Earlier in A's inquest evidence he had referred to the intended target as a "nationalist leader" – at 185.13 – and confirmed to Burnett that the person was an "extreme nationalist politician" – 180.6. The 2006 Paget Report failed to report on individual MI6 officer testimony, instead producing a "summary of the interviews". In that summary, the proposed target is described as "a named extremist leader" – Paget Report, p762. This evidence – the Paget Report and A's inquest testimony – appears to conflict with A's 1998 memorandum that the target "in 1993 was, and remains, unknown to the public at large". I suggest that it is common sense that if this individual was an "extreme nationalist politician" that MI6 were considering assassinating, then the target would not have been "unknown to the public at large" in both 1993 and 1998, as A has stated in the 1998 memorandum. There is a possibility that MI6 have changed their story between 1998 – A's memorandum – and 2004-6 – the Paget inquiry. Then in 2008 at the inquest they have maintained the line given to Paget. But both the Paget Report and the inquest evidence appear to differ significantly from A's statement in 1998. As the time got closer to an official scrutiny of the evidence, it is possible that MI6 decided that a low level person who "in 1993 was, and remains, unknown to the public at large" may not be seen by anyone investigating as a likely proposition for assassination. There is a possibility that this part of A's 1998 memorandum was read out inadvertently by inquest lawyer, Ian Burnett.

[d] Richard Tomlinson provides a graphic account of his conversations with Mr A in his 2001 book – not heard by the jury: "Nick Fish [Mr A] ... called me into his office. 'How'd you like to work on my plan to assassinate Slobodan Milosevic then?' he asked casually as if asking my views on the weekend cricket scores. 'Oh come off it, I'm not falling for your little games', I replied dismissively, believing that Fish was just trying to wind me up. 'Why not?' continued Fish indignantly. 'We colluded with the Yanks to knock off Saddam in the Gulf War, and the SOE tried to take out Hitler in the Second World War.' 'Yes, but they were legitimate military targets in wartime,' I replied. 'We are not at war with Serbia, and Milosevic is a civilian leader. You can't top him.' Fish was undaunted. 'Yes we can, and we've done it before. I checked with Santa Claus [John Bidde, Operational Security officer] upstairs..... We tried to slot Lenin back in 1911 but some pinko coughed at the last minute, and the Prime Minister, it was Asquith then, binned the plan.' Fish's disappointment was plain. 'Santa Claus has got the papers in his locker, but he wouldn't show them to me. They're still more secret than the Pope's Y-fronts, apparently'.... I did not take

The plot to assassinate this person – either Milosevic or someone else – was contrived in the context of the Yugoslav war. According to A, after the war had long concluded, this unnamed person was still "unknown to the public at large".

This evidence appears to indicate that if X had stated at the inquest that the unnamed person had not since been assassinated – option 3 above – then it would be most unlikely that the figure, who after the war was still "unknown to the public", could have been identified from that information.

An earlier footnote indicates that MI6 may have changed their description of this assassination target – between 1998 (six years after the proposal) and the inquest (another ten years later). In 1998 the person was described as "unknown to the public at large", but by 2008 the same witness, A from MI6, has confirmed that the target was an "extreme nationalist politician" [ab]

This latter description – the account put forward to the inquest – fits more comfortably with X and Tam's refusal to answer Keen's question. But the 1998 account – someone "unknown to the public at large" – does not.[c]

This evidence appears to raise questions about the validity of the MI6 evidence on the Milosevic assassination plot.[d]

Fish's proposal too seriously but a few days later ... he casually threw over a couple of sheets of A4. 'Here, take a butcher's at this.' It was a two-page minute entitled 'A proposal to assassinate Serbian President Slobodan Milosevic'." Tomlinson then proceeds to describe the document and his reaction, most of which is described in the Tomlinson affidavit – shown earlier – or in the inquest transcripts (transcript references to the Milosevic plot have been shown in an earlier footnote). In the book, Tomlinson concludes his comments on the subject: "I never heard anything more about the plan, but then I would not have expected to. An indoctrination list would have been formed, probably consisting only of the Chief [McColl], C/CEE [Fletcher, Mr E], P4 [the desk officer in charge of Balkan operations] and MODA/SO [SAS liaison officer]. Even Fish himself would probably have been excluded from detailed planning at an early stage. A submission would have been put up to the Foreign Secretary to seek political clearance, then MODA/SO and the [SAS] increment would have taken over the detail of the operational planning. If the plan was developed further, it clearly did not come to fruition, as Milosevic remained very much alive and in power for many years.": The Big Breach, pp141-2.

[a] And a person that was also allegedly the subject of an MI6 assassination proposal.

[b] See the earlier footnote for the detail on this.

[c] There are two issues here: a) the change in the MI6 account from 1998 to 2008; b) the refusal of MI6 to answer what seems an innocuous question from Keen: "Has that other person since been assassinated....?"

[d] As stated, this book has not focused on the Milosevic assassination plot and references to the inquest transcripts have been listed earlier. To be frank, the change in the MI6 account indicates that A could be lying in his descriptions of the proposed assassination target. If A is lying, this in turn could indicate that Tomlinson's

There are serious inconsistencies in Miss X's inquest evidence on her search in the MI6 database regarding the Milosevic assassination plot:

Mansfield asked X: "When you typed in 'Milosevic' and you got a fair amount of material, did any of the material relate to assassination?" X replied: "I honestly – I hope this is not a difficult answer here – I honestly don't remember."

Five minutes later, Mansfield tried again: "Did you look, within the material headed 'Milosevic', for anything that could be associated with the word 'assassination'?" This time X answered: "I do not believe I did, no."

Initially X cannot remember if anything related to assassination, then five minutes later she admits she didn't actually look for the word "assassination" – this is despite the fact that the issue X was dealing with was an alleged assassination plot against Milosevic.

Then Baker asks X: "Did you look at the material that was thrown up by the request 'Milosevic'?" X: "I looked at it as far as the carding of the name went and any hits that brought up, but I did not ... carry out a file search, sir."

So we then find out that X did not actually "carry out a file search" on Milosevic.

Next, Baker: "What were you actually looking for?" X: "In that instance, yes, I was looking for anything which might associate Milosevic with assassination".

So, to Mansfield: "I do not believe I did, no" to: "Did you look, within the material headed 'Milosevic', for anything that could be associated with the word 'assassination'?"

Then to Baker: "I was looking for anything which might associate Milosevic with assassination".

These are completely opposite responses: "I do not believe I did" look for Milosevic and assassination. Then: "I was looking for ... Milosevic [and] assassination".

Mansfield, who by now appears to be understandably confused, seeks clarification of X's position – X: "the papers related to the card that I searched, they had no reference to assassination."

There are two issues here: 1) What was X looking for? Did she look for Milosevic and assassination? and 2) What did X find? Did she find anything on assassination under Milosevic?

1) What was X looking for?

X's first answer on this was: "I do not believe I did" look for "anything ... associated with ... 'assassination'"

---

testimony that the target was Milosevic is correct. That would then lead to option 1 above – that the named target was Milosevic – being the true option.

Her second answer was: "I was looking for anything which might associate Milosevic with assassination".

As stated before, these are opposite answers – only one could be right.

2) What did X find?

X's first answer on this was: "I honestly don't remember" if "any of the material [related] to assassination".

Her second answer was: "the papers ... had no reference to assassination".

So again a major conflict: "I honestly don't remember" to a definite statement: "no reference to assassination".

On both issues X has provided conflicting evidence under oath.

If X's initial response – "I do not believe I did" look for "anything ... associated with ... 'assassination'" was true, then her later account – "the papers ... had no reference to assassination" – must be a lie.[a]

What is the significance of this?

Miss X was relied on at the inquest to provide critical evidence on MI6's systems of records, particularly in connection with the Milosevic plot.

The above issues raise serious questions over the veracity of X's evidence under cross-examination – she appears to have lied under oath. This should be viewed in the light of earlier evidence that X lied about her knowledge of MI6 assassination proposals.[b]

As has been stated, the Milosevic plot has not been addressed in detail, but the analysis of areas that have cropped up during this investigation has cast serious doubts on the veracity of the MI6 evidence – in turn, this indicates that Richard Tomlinson's account has substance.[c]

The general evidence from the MI6 witnesses was that MI6 did not contemplate assassinating people – it was not part of the organisation's ethos.

This appears to be a lie – there is a huge amount of evidence pointing to MI6 involvement in assassination plots. It could be argued that assassination is a part of MI6's ethos.

Independent Operations[d]

Is it possible that Princess Diana and Dodi Fayed were assassinated by an independent group of MI6 officers acting without the service's approval? **Richard Tomlinson**, Ex-MI6 Officer: 13 Feb 08: 22.8:

---

[a] Because if X couldn't remember if she looked for assassination, then she is not in a position to comment on whether there was anything about assassination in the papers.

[b] See earlier in this Conclusions section.

[c] This also should be viewed in the light of the repeated lying on other issues by MI6 witnesses at the inquest.

[d] This section should be viewed in conjunction with the material in the following section, Allegations Against MI6.

Hilliard: Q. What you said to the French magistrate, Mr Tomlinson, August of 1998.... You are recorded as having said this: "I have never heard any mention, either during or subsequent to my service, of any plan to assassinate a member of the Al Fayed family, Princess Diana or anyone else for that matter, other than President Milosevic. It is impossible, given the structure of MI6, for an assassination plot of this type to have been hatched by the department. It could have been done independently by members of MI6, but not by the service itself. This is only my assessment, however, as I have never heard any mention of such a plot." Was that accurate at that time?

A. Yes, I believe so. I certainly never saw any plan to assassinate the subject of this inquisition – this inquest. As I said there, at the time it would be institutionally quite – very difficult to carry out an assassination. It is not completely impossible, I do not believe, but it would be institutionally quite difficult.

Q. I do not want to split hairs, Mr Tomlinson. We have here, "It is impossible, given the structure of MI6, for an assassination plot of this type to have been hatched by the department". Are you happy about that or not?

A. Well, you know, nothing is impossible, but it would be very difficult, I would say. You know, to get the necessary – it would depend who the – it would depend also who the subject of the assassination was to quite a substantial degree. Certainly to assassinate someone who was universally very unpopular around the world and amongst MI6 officers themselves would be easier, institutionally, to carry out than it would be to assassinate someone who was not unpopular. So, for example, if MI6 had wanted at some point to assassinate Saddam Hussein, institutionally I think that would have been feasible and possible, and I have subsequently heard, since leaving MI6, that there is a credible account that they did actually plot to assassinate Muammar Gaddafi of Libya –

Q. That is after you have left the service, is it?

A. I read that in the newspapers after I left the service.

Q. I am trying to stick, do you follow, because if we go into – not just you, but what other people have read in newspapers and so on, you appreciate we will be here a long time.

A. Yes. What I was saying is it would be very, very difficult for MI6 to assassinate a – the popularity of the subject would make a difference. So a target who was very, very unpopular would be easier to assassinate within MI6 than someone who was not.

At 93.10: Mansfield: Q. What did you mean when you said ... that it[a] could be done independently?

---

[a] The Paris crash.

A. I think nowadays that would not be the case, but I think in the olden days
... the intelligence services were not as tightly controlled as I have no doubt
they are nowadays. I think that that has been controlled a lot more deeply....
There was, at the time of the Harold Wilson Government – I think it was
quite well established now – there was a cabal of MI5 officers who were
interested in – or were talking loosely about a plot[a] and there have been other
incidences where MI5 and MI6 officers have done things independently well
outside of the control of the organisation. I don't think it is something that
happens regularly and I don't think it could ever happen nowadays.
Q. In relation to those days – and we are talking about the 1990s as opposed
to since 2000 – if an MI5 officer – and if there is an objection, please say – if
a MI5 officer or an MI6 officer felt that what was happening in the United
Kingdom or elsewhere was in the interests of the United Kingdom and was
subversive, undermining the state or the Monarchy, that might generate
discussion about what to do about it, mightn't it, then?
A. I think that is possibly the case, yes. I think that is the case, yes.
Q. Once again it might range across a number of options. It might not be a
car crash in order to murder; it could be a car crash in order to frighten. That
is another possibility, another option, isn't it?
A. Well, I think that we are getting into speculation. It is a possibility but,
you know, it is speculation. At the time in MI6 I think there was not as strict
control over their activities as there is now and that is all I can really say on
that matter.
Richard Dearlove, MI6 Director of Operations, 1994 to 1999, UK: 20 Feb
08: 31.13:
Burnett: Q. What would your comment be to a suggestion that rogue
elements within SIS, if such existed, could mount an operation of any sort
without authority, let alone an assassination...?
A. I would have regarded that as an impossibility.
At 36.7: Q. Are your stations authorised to act independently of head office
in London?
A. No, they are not. In any significant matter, they are controlled from
London.
At 57.25: Q. What about a suggestion that the Paris station or perhaps
someone in the Paris station was freelancing at the end of August 1997?
A. Out of the question. It is just not conceivable within the structures that I
have described, and I should add that any and every part of the service was
under my control in terms of operations.
At 119.9: Mansfield: This is what [Tomlinson] said in relation to being
carried out independently and not by the service as a whole.... "I think
nowadays", would you please listen to the answer if you haven't heard it,

---

[a] This is addressed by Peter Wright in *Spycatcher*, pp368-372.

"that would not be the case ... but I think in the olden days ... the intelligence services were not as tightly controlled.... I don't think [an independent operation] is something that happens regularly and I don't think it could ever happen nowadays."[a] Now, that is what he said last week. Do you disagree with that?

A. I fundamentally disagree with that.

Mr 6 aka Richard Spearman, MI6 Officer. British Embassy, Paris: 29 Feb 08: 63.2:

Mansfield: Q. I want to ask you about people who would not necessarily be working, as it were, according to the rule book. Was that possible in this period in the 1990s, that there might be people not working to the rule book?

A. I can only speak to my experience. My experience is that we work very hard – and of course, we are always improving our processes, but my experience, including during that period, was that our processes were broad, were deep and were adhered to. In that context, I cannot imagine circumstances in which someone within the organisation would be working beyond the rule book, no.

At 81.24: Q. [Tomlinson] was aware – you don't agree with it – that officers did operate independently from time to time....

A. That is not my experience. It is not the way we work.

Coroner: Summing Up: 31 Mar 08: 70.13:

"Freelancing was inconceivable. Tomlinson's was a mischievous and fanciful allegation."

Coroner: Summing Up: 31 Mar 08: 71.9:

"It is only after the allegation against the Duke of Edinburgh was shown to be fanciful that the claim shifted to a rogue element within SIS being responsible."

Comment: There are problems with Baker's Summing Up comments to the jury:

1) Baker says: "the allegation against the Duke of Edinburgh was shown to be fanciful". This never actually occurred because Baker refused to allow Philip to be cross-examined and the jury heard no evidence from him.[b]

2) Baker says: "the claim shifted to a rogue element within SIS being responsible". In all the evidence in the police investigations and the Baker inquest, there are only two people who have ever used the term "rogue element" – they are Scott Baker and his inquest lawyer, Ian Burnett.

---

[a] Mansfield read out the full text – it is already shown in Tomlinson's cross-examination, see above.

[b] The allegation against Philip is addressed later in this book.

It was never used by Richard Tomlinson or Mohamed Al Fayed, or anyone else.

Burnett was the first person to bring in "rogue elements" during his cross-examination of Richard Dearlove. Burnett is not quoting anyone – he asks: "What would your comment be to a suggestion that rogue elements within SIS....?" Burnett calls it "a suggestion", but the only person making the suggestion is himself.

That then is the only mention during the entire six months of the inquest, until Baker latches onto it on the first day of his Summing Up: "the claim shifted to a rogue element within SIS being responsible".[a]

Baker calls it "the claim". Who is making the claim? Baker must be referring to Burnett, but he fails to tell the jury that.

Tomlinson made a claim: "it could have been done independently by members of MI6".

Tomlinson consistently uses the term "independent". Burnett and Baker use the term "rogue".[b]

There is a big difference:

- "independent" means "free from outside control or influence" or "separate"
- "rogue" means "behaving in a faulty, unpredictable or dangerous way".[113]

3) Baker wrongly links "the allegation against the Duke of Edinburgh" with "the claim ... [of] a rogue element". He says that "the claim shifted to a rogue element" only "after the allegation against the Duke of Edinburgh was shown to be fanciful".

Inquest lawyer, Nicholas Hilliard, was the first person to introduce into the inquest Richard Tomlinson's allegation: "It [the crash] could have been

---

[a] Baker takes this fabrication a step further when, towards the end of his Summing Up, he uses it in his final summary of the allegations made for the jury's benefit: "I remind you, without comment, of some, not all, of the features of how staged accident is put [in the allegations]. It includes the following: .... Are there features of the crash itself which point towards a staged accident, in other words.... Was a flashing light of this kind a technique used by MI6 – see the evidence of Tomlinson – and could rogue MI6 officers have decided to use it here?" 2 Apr 08: 31.9. When Baker tells the jury he is summarising the allegations "without comment", I suggest the jury would have presumed the words he would be using would be the same ones used by the persons making the allegations. The use by Baker of the word "rogue" shows that he used the word of his own inquest lawyer, Ian Burnett – a person who has never alleged this was a staged crash.

[b] To be fair to Baker he did also use the word "independently" twice on the first morning of his Summing Up – at 31 Mar 08: 50.24 and 72.7 – but the previous footnote reveals that he placed emphasis on the word "rogue" when he included it in his final summary to the jury, made just 30 minutes before he sent them out for their deliberations. The context of this is that Baker's Summing Up went on for 2½ days.

done independently by members of MI6" – that was on 12 February 2008. As Hilliard pointed out, he was quoting from Tomlinson's evidence "to the French magistrate ... [in] August of 1998".

Mohamed Al Fayed was the main witness making the allegation that "my son and Princess Diana were murdered ... on the orders of Prince Philip, Duke of Edinburgh" – see below. Mohamed was cross-examined on 18 February 2008 – six days after Tomlinson's allegation was heard by the jury.

This then means that Baker has lied in his Summing Up – not only was "the allegation against the Duke of Edinburgh" not "shown to be fanciful" (see point 1 above) but the chief proponent of it, Mohamed, was not heard from until well after the Tomlinson allegation of an independent MI6 operation had been put forward and subjected to questioning from Hilliard and Mansfield.[a]

In his Summing Up Baker presented the jury a picture of a changing and faltering case being proposed: "It is only after the allegation against the Duke of Edinburgh was shown to be fanciful that the claim shifted to a rogue element within SIS being responsible."

In doing this, Baker appears to have deliberately misled his own jury.

Allegations Against MI6

Four witnesses have claimed that MI6 could have been involved in the Paris crash.

Mohamed Al Fayed, Dodi's Father, UK: 18 Feb 08: 55.23:

Burnett: Q. I think it is clear already that you would adhere to this view [from 5 July 2005 statement]: "I am in no doubt whatsoever that my son and Princess Diana were murdered by the British security services on the orders of Prince Philip, Duke of Edinburgh." That remains your view and you have expanded upon it.

A. Definitely.

At 43.5: Q. What you say is that Prince Philip and Prince Charles, both at Balmoral, organised an assassination using MI6 in Paris?

A. Yes, definitely.

At 127.12: Horwell: Q. A letter that you wrote to the Right Honourable Paul Murphy of the Intelligence and Security Committee. It is dated 14th February 2006. You mention that the security services were acting on the orders of the Royal Family and these are your words "the Prime Minister and his senior henchmen", and you went on to say this: "There is equally no doubt in my mind that such a momentous and horrific action would have been directly sanctioned by the Prime Minister." .... Mr Al Fayed, the list of conspirators;

---

[a] See above excerpt from Tomlinson cross-examination.

those who are involved in ... this murderous plot.... We can add Tony Blair to that list, can we?

A. You can, because I am sure he knows what they are going to do, definitely.

Q. And you say in that letter: "Not only is Tony Blair involved, but also his senior henchmen." Now, who did you mean by "his senior henchmen"?

A. Maybe his chief of staff.

....Q. And the Foreign Secretary of the day, Robin Cook, he must have been involved?

A. It is a possibility.

Mohamed Al Fayed: 15 Feb 06 Letter to John Stevens[a]: **Jury Heard Part Only**:

"There is no doubt that Messrs Langman, Spearman and Spedding have all been directly implicated, acting, I am sure, directly to the orders of the Royal Family, the Prime Minister and his senior henchmen." [114]

John Macnamara, Al Fayed Director of Security: 14 Feb 08: 134.6:

Horwell: Q. You go on to say in this statement[b] that: "I have become convinced that [Diana and Dodi] were murdered and that the British and French security services were complicit in their deaths."

A. Yes.

Q. Yet another assumption that you are prepared to put into a witness statement?

A. That was my belief, yes.

Q. Without any evidence? [c]

A. Well, there was evidence of people like Richard Tomlinson, for example.

David Shayler, Ex-MI5 Officer: Quoted in 2005 book: **Jury Didn't Hear**:

"Having looked at the available evidence I am personally inclined to think that MI6 paid to have Diana and Dodi involved in an accident, in the same way they paid to have Gaddafi assassinated, using a 'surrogate'." [115]

---

[a] According to the Paget Report (p747) this letter included this extract from the letter sent the previous day to the Intelligence Security Committee, quoted in Horwell's question – see above.

[b] 3 July 2006 statement to the British police.

[c] Horwell's questioning is misleading – he was very selective in the part of the statement he quoted. Macnamara had spent years on an investigation of the crash on behalf of Mohamed Al Fayed. The full paragraph from Macnamara's statement reads: "From the investigations I have made and the people I have spoken to through a period of almost nine years I am led to the inescapable conclusion that the deaths of Diana Princess of Wales, Dodi Al Fayed and Henri Paul were not as a result of a simple traffic accident. In consequence I have become convinced that [Diana and Dodi] were murdered and that the British and French security services were complicit in their deaths.": John Macnamara, MPS Witness Statement, 3 July 2006, reproduced in *The Documents* book, p532.

Comment: There are four witnesses who have claimed the involvement of MI6 or British security services in the deaths of Princess Diana and Dodi Fayed – Richard Tomlinson, David Shayler, Mohamed Al Fayed and John Macnamara.[a]

Outside of Tomlinson, four other MI6 employees – former and current – were cross-examined on this.

Richard Dearlove, MI6 Director of Operations, 1994 to 1999, UK: 20 Feb 08: 45.20:

Burnett: Q. Are you able to confirm from your own knowledge – it follows from what you have said – that no authorisation was sought in respect of any activities concerning Princess Diana?

A. I can absolutely confirm that.

Q. It would plainly have been outside the functions of SIS to do so?

A. Had it been done, it would have been outside the functions of the service.

At 174.2: Horwell: Q. A plan to murder a group of people because the Duke of Edinburgh did not like the man whom the Princess of Wales was having a relationship with, a relationship of four to five weeks' standing, that plan goes all of the way to murder; a plan that was executed either within days or possibly within an hour, Sir Richard, on one analysis of the evidence.... Is it your evidence that it is impossible that [this proposal] could have been executed in the manner suggested?

A. It is quite impossible. It is completely fanciful.

....Q. The idea that the Duke of Edinburgh had a hotline to SIS to order murder, equally absurd?

A. Completely absurd.

Q. You have been asked about another potential motive, landmines, and you have been asked about a dossier. I believe there are only two people in the world that call these documents a "dossier"; one is Simone Simmons and the other is Mr Mansfield. The dossier, as those two people describe it, is a collection of documents and information that Diana compiled. No one knows from where, but Simone Simmons accepted the suggestions that it was likely to come from the British Landmines Trust and the Red Cross and they were kept in an envelope. There is no evidence that that evidence contained highly secret or confidential information. The suggestion appears to be that because Princess Diana was compiling information of that nature, that she would have been a target for assassination. Again I do not know why I am asking the question, but I will do so: what is your response, Sir Richard?

A. I am outraged that it should even be suggested. It is just again –

---

[a] Their evidence is assessed later in this section.

"ridiculous" is the only word that I can use, and, you know, personally to me and to my senior staff in SIS, you know, really deeply offensive.

Miss X, MI6 Administrator, UK: 26 Feb 08: 60.9:

Burnett: Q. If, for the sake of argument, there had been any plan at all involving Diana, Princess of Wales, and Dodi Al Fayed, would that have been thrown up by your searches?

A. Yes, it would.

Q. Do you thus conclude that there was none?

A. There was absolutely no plan whatsoever.

.... Q. Had there been any MI6 interest in the relationship between Dodi and Diana, would that have shown up in the records?

A. Yes, it would.

Q. And there was nothing?

A. It is not that I am trying to be rude in any way, there was just no interest. It is not our sort of thing.

Q. Therefore, the records, do they or do they not confirm Sir Richard Dearlove's evidence that SIS simply had no interest whatsoever in Dodi or in Diana or in them jointly?

A. No, we had no interest whatsoever.

At 169.8: Tam: Q. Do you have any doubt yourself about whether there is information lurking in SIS's systems that you have just overlooked despite the fact that you have done all of these searches?

A. I am sure I am able to say this: I am absolutely 100% certain that there is nothing, absolutely nothing.

Mr A, MI6 Head of Balkan Target Team: 26 Feb 08: 238.2:

Horwell: Q. What is suggested here is that, because the Duke of Edinburgh did not like the Princess of Wales' partner of some four to five weeks, the Duke ordered the assassination of the Princess and that order was put into operation almost instantly. In your 25 years of experience now of SIS and the way it operates, what in your opinion are the prospects of such a plan being put into operation?

A. It is absolutely unthinkable.

Mr E, MI6 Controller of Central and Eastern Europe: 29 Feb 08: 27.7:

Horwell: Q. The suggestion now is that the Duke of Edinburgh takes against the partner of the Princess of Wales, of just some four or five weeks standing, no more than that, and he orders that MI6 scares the occupants of a car in Paris that night and MI6 takes the order and carries it out within a very short period of time. What, in your opinion, are the prospects of MI6 getting involved in any such operation?

A. Nil.

Comment: The MPS lawyer, Richard Horwell, should have been asking Dearlove a simple question: What was his response to the suggestion that

"Princess Diana was compiling information" about landmines and that made her "a target for assassination"?

But in Horwell's build-up to the question he made several comments that raise serious concerns:

1) Horwell says: "I believe there are only two people in the world that call these documents a 'dossier'; one is Simone Simmons and the other is Mr Mansfield".

Yet just the previous month Paul Burrell had stated to the inquest: "I knew that the Princess did compile a dossier on every fact of the landmine mission. She took it very seriously." [116a]

2) Horwell said: "No one knows from where [the dossier information came from] but Simone Simmons accepted the suggestions that it was likely to come from the British Landmines Trust and the Red Cross".

The closest Simone Simmons got to saying what Horwell is suggesting was during Horwell's cross-examination of Simmons on January 10.

This is what was said:

Horwell: "[Diana] obviously had access to a number of people and organisations who would be able to give her relevant information?"
Simmons: "Information, yeah."
Horwell: "And obviously one source of information on this topic would have been The Red Cross?"
Simmons: "Possibly, yes." [117]

But Horwell didn't remind the jury that on the same day Simmons had also said to Mansfield: "Most of [the dossier] was information that she had got from other sources. They were her notes as well and she always had her notes on the ... top of it all." [118]

The only mention of the British Landmines Trust in the entire inquest is this from Horwell. Neither Simmons, nor anyone else, has ever mentioned the British Landmines Trust in any of their evidence.

The reason for this is that there is no organisation called the British Landmines Trust – and there never has been. And no organisation with a name even like the British Landmines Trust.[b]

---

[a] This was Burrell's response to a question from Mansfield, but it should be noted that Mansfield never used the word "dossier" during his entire cross-examination of Burrell.

[b] Princess Diana had contacts with Mike Whitlam, the Head of the International Red Cross at the time. In Angola in January 1997 she was working with the Halo Trust. Later in August Diana travelled to Bosnia with the Landmine Survivors Network, a US based organisation. Also in 1997, the UK Working Group on Landmines – later renamed Landmine Action – was the British arm of the International Campaign to Ban Landmines (ICBL). Sources: Paul Burrell, *A Royal Duty*, p280; Simone

Horwell has made this up – he has told the inquest that Diana got her information from the British Landmines Trust, even though he knows that this organisation does not exist.

All Simmons did was confirm to Horwell that the Red Cross would possibly have been "one source of information on" landmines and Horwell has deliberately turned this into: "Simone Simmons accepted the suggestions that [the landmine dossier information] was likely to come from the British Landmines Trust and the Red Cross".[a]

3) Horwell states: The dossier was "kept in an envelope".

Although this is technically true, Horwell misleads the inquest by failing to state the size of the envelope. Simmons indicated at the inquest that the dossier was about five inches thick[119] – so it is obvious the envelope would have been very large.[b]

4) Horwell then says: "There is no evidence that that evidence [in the dossier] contained highly secret or confidential information."

The context of Horwell's comments is the issue of whether Diana's dossier on landmines could constitute a motive for assassination – he asks Dearlove to respond to the suggestion "that because Princess Diana was compiling information of that nature" she was assassinated. Horwell indicates this suggestion is so ridiculous that he states: "I do not know why I am asking the question, but I will do so".

So Horwell's point appears to be that there is no evidence that the dossier contained anything that could have provided a motive for Diana's assassination.

Is that true? What is the evidence?

There are several points that indicate there was sensitive material in the dossier:[c]

- Diana saw the need to give copies of the dossier to two friends – Simone Simmons and Elsa Bowker – for safe-keeping
- Diana told Simmons, referring to the information in the dossier: "I'm going to go public with this and name names"
- Diana claimed to Simmons that the dossier "would prove that the British Government and many high-ranking public figures were profiting

---

Simmons, *Diana: The Last Word*, p186; Halo Trust website – www.halotrust.org; Landmine Action website – www.landmineaction.org; Electronic Mine Information Network – www.mineaction.org

[a] Although Baker failed to intervene at the time, he did not support Horwell's lie on this point in his Summing Up – he said: "Simone Simmons did not know where [Diana] got [the dossier information] from.": 1 Apr 08: 11.16.

[b] Simmons also said: The dossier "was very big".: 10 Jan 08: 74.17.

[c] This should be viewed in the light of the chapter on the Anti-Landmines Campaign in Part 2 – this is a summary of points already addressed in detail in that volume.

from" the proliferation of landmines – Simmons said: "[Diana] intended to call her report 'Profiting Out Of Misery'"

- Diana appeared to refer to her increasing knowledge about landmines in a 1996 Christmas card to Simmons: "The knowledge is expanding at alarming speed. Watch out world." [a]

- Simmons stated that she didn't read the dossier, so "there is nothing anyone can get out of me"

- Simmons destroyed the dossier – "straight after [Diana] died I burnt it" and "that's why I burnt it, I was more than nervous" [b]

- when the inquest lawyer, Nicholas Hilliard, told Simmons: "It would be easier [for people to believe you] if you [still] had the [dossier] material...." Simmons replied: "If I had the material, would I have been bumped off as well?" [c]

The above seven points reveal that Horwell's assertion to Dearlove – "there is <u>no evidence</u> that ... [the dossier] contained highly secret or confidential information" – is a lie.

In the previous question to Dearlove, Horwell addressed another alleged motive for the assassination of Princess Diana. In his build-up to this question – regarding the motive being Diana's relationship with Dodi – Horwell again included misleading comments that should cause concern:

1) Horwell says the allegation is that it was "a plan to murder a group of people".

Part 2 has revealed that the evidence indicates the plan was primarily to murder Princess Diana. Trevor Rees-Jones survived the crash and there is no evidence of any plan to murder him, even though he was a central player in the events of that night – see Part 3.

2) Horwell indicates the suggested reason for the assassination: "the Duke of Edinburgh did not like the man whom the Princess of Wales was having a relationship with".

Horwell appears to have deliberately put this at its lowest. Although there is evidence that Philip disliked Dodi, there are significant factors – omitted by Horwell – that could point to Philip's involvement in the assassination.

Philip's relationship with Diana may be more significant than his dislike of Dodi. There is also the impact of a potential pregnancy of Diana to Dodi.

---

[a] This was just a few weeks before Diana's visit to the minefields of Angola in January 1997.

[b] In her book Simmons said: "Two days [after the crash] I took the big brown envelope [Diana] had given me containing the Profiting out of Misery dossier and ... set fire to it.... It was not something I wanted to hang onto for a moment longer.": *Diana: The Last Word*, p189.

[c] See the Anti-Landmines chapter of Part 2 for the detail on all these points.

Evidence in Part 2 shows that Diana feared Philip and made suggestions that Philip wanted to kill her long before her involvement with Dodi Fayed.

The evidence pointing to Philip's possible involvement is addressed later in this book.

3) Horwell says it is alleged the "plan that was executed either within days or possibly within an hour".

The evidence in the Prior Knowledge section of Part 1[120] shows that the perpetrators of the assassination would have had at least a week to plan and organise the detail of the crash. For Horwell to suggest that it was "executed ... possibly within an hour" is absurd, but also misleading.

In summary, Horwell appears to have deliberately made the two possible motives – the relationship with Dodi, the anti-landmine campaign – look as ridiculous and outrageous as possible, even lying to the inquest to achieve this.

In what comes across as a stage-managed production, Dearlove has responded on cue and to order – "it is quite impossible", "it is completely fanciful", "completely absurd", "I am outraged", "'ridiculous' is the only word that I can use", "personally to me and to my senior staff in SIS, you know, really deeply offensive".

Horwell has based the questions on such false and fictitious scenarios that I suggest Dearlove was able to honestly disown involvement.

Whether MI6 were involved in the assassinations though is a different matter to what Horwell has put – Horwell never straight out asked Dearlove if MI6 was involved.

By the time Horwell got to the cross-examination of Mr A, he had modified his questioning. This time landmines has not been addressed at all and Horwell states: "the Duke ordered the assassination of the Princess and that order was put into operation almost instantly".

So "a plan that was executed either within days or possibly within an hour" has morphed into "that order was put into operation almost instantly".

Not satisfied with "possibly within an hour", we now have "almost instantly".

A is confronted with a ridiculously impossible scenario – an order is given for an assassination and it is carried out by organising a complex, orchestrated car crash "almost instantly".

Horwell gets the answer he wants: "it is absolutely unthinkable".

I would answer the same, and what A has said is not a denial that Princess Diana could have been assassinated by MI6 as a result of an order from Prince Philip.

Three days later Horwell, cross-examining E, changed the scenario again – minus the landmines, and it becomes an order to scare, not assassinate.[a] Horwell says: "the Duke of Edinburgh ... orders that MI6 scares the occupants of a car in Paris that night and MI6 ... carries it out within a very short period of time".

This scenario appears to presume that Philip is somehow monitoring the movements of Diana and Dodi in real time and is aware that they are "the occupants of a car in Paris" on the night of 30-31 August 1997. MI6 then takes the order to scare the car's occupants and "carries ... out" the organisation of a complex, orchestrated car crash "within a very short period of time".

So this time Horwell has illustrated a situation where Philip has determined the method to be used – he "orders that MI6 scares the occupants of a car" – whereas with the previous witnesses, Horwell has Philip making the order, but leaving the method up to MI6.

But again, Horwell has outlined an impossible scenario – a complex car crash organised in "a very short period of time" – and E confirms there is "nil ... prospects of MI6 getting involved".

Burnett asked Dearlove: "Are you able to confirm ... that no authorisation was sought in respect of any activities concerning Princess Diana?" Dearlove: "I can absolutely confirm that."

But, I suggest, if an order came from a senior royal or from within the UK government, then MI6 would not need to seek authorisation.[b]

Robin Tam, the MI6 lawyer, asked Miss X: "Do you have any doubt yourself about whether there is information lurking in SIS's systems that you have just overlooked despite the fact that you have done all of these searches?" X confidently responded: "I am sure I am able to say this: I am absolutely 100% certain that there is nothing, absolutely nothing."

The question is: What is the point of X saying this if prior to her searches the MI6 weeders – mentioned earlier by Wright and West – have cleared the records of any operation MI6 does not want to be seen to be associated with?

In summary at this point, there were several factors that would have prevented the inquest jury from arriving at an informed decision on the degree of MI6 involvement in the deaths of Princess Diana and Dodi Fayed:

---

[a] The background to this change has been addressed in the earlier section on Does MI6 Frighten People? In short, Horwell changed from assassination to scare even though Mansfield had only introduced frightening the target as "one of the possibilities".
[b] Such a situation had already occurred in 1956 when Prime Minister Anthony Eden ordered the assassination of Gamal Abdel Nasser – all MI6 were doing was following orders and no authorisation was sought from the FCO: see earlier.

- the lawyers – primarily Richard Horwell, to a lesser degree Ian Burnett – were either including lies in their question build-ups or were asking their questions in a devious way
- the MI6 weeders could have cleared the MI6 files – opened up to Operation Paget – of all records of their involvement in the crash
- there is evidence that lying is endemic within MI6 and officers are expected to put national security or the national interest ahead of telling the truth – in other words, if MI6 were involved in the deaths of Diana and Dodi, their officers would have been expected to lie under oath at the inquest
- the inquest was run by a corrupt judge – Scott Baker – who seemed to quickly shut down avenues that could have caused embarrassment to the British Establishment.

Back to the four witnesses who have claimed MI6 involvement in the crash – Tomlinson, Shayler, Mohamed and Macnamara.

There is some conflict in their evidence:

- Tomlinson: "it is impossible, given the structure of MI6, for an assassination plot of this type to have been hatched by the department. It could have been done independently by members of MI6, but not by the service itself. This is only my assessment" – French statement[a], August 1998
- Tomlinson: "I am absolutely certain that there is substantial evidence in [the MI6] files that would provide crucial evidence in establishing the exact causes of this tragedy"[b] – affidavit, May 1999
- Tomlinson: "either or both of these [MI6] officers[c] will have knowledge that will be of crucial importance in establishing the sequence of events leading up to the deaths" – affidavit, May 1999
- Tomlinson: "a target who was very, very unpopular would be easier to assassinate within MI6 than someone who was not" – at inquest, February 2008
- Tomlinson: "if ... an MI6 officer felt that what was happening in the United Kingdom or elsewhere ... was subversive, undermining the state or the Monarchy, that might generate discussion about what to do about it" – confirmed at inquest, February 2008
- Tomlinson: "there have been other incidences where MI5 and MI6 officers have done things independently well outside of the control of the organisation" – at inquest, February 2008

---

[a] This is part of an excerpt read out by Nicholas Hilliard, inquest lawyer (see earlier) – this document has never been made public, has not been viewed by the author of this book and was not made available to the inquest jury.
[b] Some may think that information in MI6 files could indicate their involvement, but it would be possible for MI6 to hold information or "intelligence" without necessarily being directly involved in the crash.
[c] Spearman and Langman – see earlier.

- Shayler: "I am personally inclined to think that MI6 paid to have Diana and Dodi involved in an accident" – in 2005 book
- Mohamed: "my son and Princess Diana were murdered by the British security services on the orders of Prince Philip" – statement, July 2005
- Mohamed: "Prince Philip and Prince Charles, both at Balmoral, organised an assassination using MI6 in Paris" – confirmed at inquest, February 2008
- Mohamed: "Messrs Langman, Spearman and Spedding[a] have all been directly implicated, acting ... directly to the orders of the Royal Family, the Prime Minister and his senior henchmen" – letter, February 2006 [b]
- Macnamara: "[Diana and Dodi] were murdered and ... the British and French security services were complicit in their deaths" – statement, July 2006.

If MI6 were involved in assassinating Princess Diana and Dodi Fayed, there are three main possibilities:

1) an authorised operation: authorisation by the Prime Minister, Tony Blair, the Foreign Secretary of the day, Robin Cook, or the Queen

2) an unauthorised operation: MI6 carried out the assassinations without the government or Queen's approval

3) an independent operation: an MI6 officer or group of officers conducted the operation independently without the approval of MI6 or the government.

Mohamed has consistently described the first option – a government or royal authorised operation involving MI6.

Macnamara appears to describe the second option – "the British and French security services were complicit". Macnamara has never suggested government or royal authorisation. At the inquest he was asked by Horwell if Philip was involved – his answer: "Not to my knowledge. I have never mentioned the Duke of Edinburgh".[121]

Shayler may also believe it is the second option – he makes no mention of anyone other than MI6, who he suggests "paid to have Diana and Dodi involved in an accident".

Tomlinson supports the third option – "it could have been done independently by members of MI6, but not by the service itself".

So from the four witnesses, we see all three options being canvassed.

There are several points from Tomlinson's evidence to consider:

- When Tomlinson gave his strongest support for the third option, in 1998, he qualified it with: "This is only my assessment".

---

[a] All three are MI6 officers – their roles are discussed later in this book.

[b] Read out by Richard Horwell at inquest – see earlier.

- At the inquest Tomlinson appeared to back off a little from his 1998 assessment.

In 1998 Tomlinson had said: "It is impossible, given the structure of MI6, for an assassination plot of this type to have been hatched by the department".

Ten years later, in 2008, he said: "It is not completely impossible ... but it would be institutionally quite difficult".

"Impossible" had been changed to "not completely impossible" and "quite difficult".

- Tomlinson states: "a target who was very, very unpopular would be easier to assassinate within MI6 than someone who was not".

Princess Diana was very, very popular – Tomlinson therefore appears to be suggesting she would be more difficult "to assassinate within MI6 than someone who was not". I suggest that is common sense.

However countering this, Tomlinson did confirm to Al Fayed lawyer, Michael Mansfield: "if ... an MI6 officer felt that what was happening in the United Kingdom or elsewhere ... was subversive, undermining the state or the Monarchy, that might generate discussion about what to do about it".

- Tomlinson said at the inquest: "There have been other incidences[a] where MI5 and MI6 officers have done things independently well outside of the control of the organisation".

There is a critical missing aspect to this: what sort of "things" – were there any assassination plots?

- In 1999 Tomlinson stated: Richard Spearman "had been, prior to his appointment in Paris, the personal secretary to the Chief of MI6 Mr David Spedding. As such, he would have been privy to even the most confidential of MI6 operations. I believe that there may well be significance in the fact that Mr Spearman was posted to Paris in the month immediately before the deaths."

Spearman is obviously a senior MI6 officer with ties to the Chief at the time, David Spedding. Tomlinson is suggesting it could be significant that Spearman was posted to Paris just before the crash.

This position would seem to conflict with Tomlinson's "impossible ... for an assassination plot of this type to have been hatched by the department" assessment, made just a year before.

Tomlinson's general position is that "it would be institutionally quite difficult" for MI6 as an organisation to have carried out the Paris assassinations. But there are conflicts from that – "it is impossible ... for an assassination plot of this type to have been hatched by the department" but then: "There may well be significance in the fact that Mr Spearman was posted to Paris in the month immediately before the deaths".

---

[a] Other than the plot against Harold Wilson.

There are several factors that raise serious questions over Tomlinson's original assertion that "it is impossible, given the structure of MI6, for an assassination plot of this type to have been hatched by the department":

- the earlier evidence indicates that all the previous known assassination plots involving MI6 against VIPs occurred on the orders of or with the knowledge of the MI6 Chief – Nasser, Grivas, Milosevic[a], Gaddafi, Saddam
- there is no known evidence of any assassination plots hatched or carried out by an independent element within MI6
- Parts 1, 2, 3 and 4 show that the assassination of Princess Diana and Dodi Fayed and the ensuing cover-up was an extremely complex operation that would have required inter-governmental cooperation between France and the UK[b] and the resources of a major organisation
- Tomlinson provides no support for this evidence – he just says "given the structure" without explaining what that means.[c]

In summary, the suggestion that the Paris crash operation could have been carried out by independent MI6 officers is not logical and does not stack up.

Why then has Tomlinson consistently suggested that it is more likely the Paris crash operation could have been independently conducted, rather than by the organisation?

I suggest that Richard Tomlinson, who is a highly educated person[d], is possibly aware that the opposite is true – that it was more likely carried out by the MI6 organisation, rather than a group of independents.[e]

---

[a] Tomlinson stated that "Alan Petty, the personal secretary to the then Chief of MI6, Colin McColl" was on the distribution list for the proposal document. Mr A, the MI6 officer who drew up the document, did not support that. There is no reason to disbelieve Tomlinson on this – it would be logical that if the document was going to be seen by E, Head of Central and Eastern Europe Operations (agreed by A), then it could also have been listed to go to the Chief's department. At the inquest A showed some uncertainty over who was on the distribution list – see 26 Feb 08: 230.25.

[b] This is also alluded to in Macnamara's allegation – "the British and French security services were complicit".

[c] Tomlinson also failed to explain this at the inquest.

[d] Tomlinson obtained "a scholarship to study engineering at Cambridge University" and after graduating went on to win a "scholarship to study at the Massachusetts Institute of Technology", where he earned a masters degree. The Rotary Foundation then offered Tomlinson a year of additional study in any country of his choice.: *The Big Breach*, pp20-22.

[e] This is also supported by his rather diffident answers when first confronted by this at the inquest: "institutionally quite – very difficult"; "it is not completely impossible, I do not believe, but it would be institutionally quite difficult"; "very difficult, I would say. You know, to get the necessary – " – this is an unfinished

There is a real possibility that from the time of his original French statement in 1998, right through to the inquest and possibly beyond that, Tomlinson has felt under threat from MI6. Tomlinson's 2001 book *The Big Breach* reveals that he has been subjected to massive mistreatment by the MI6 organisation, including several arrests and stints in jail, since his firing in April 1995.[a]

I suggest that the pressure Tomlinson has been put under over a sustained period has led to him feeling he needed to temper his evidence and not directly implicate his former employers, MI6, in the assassinations of Diana and Dodi – an allegation which he would be unable to prove, but which could potentially subject him to further harassment by MI6.

In short, there is an understandable possibility Tomlinson is intimidated by MI6's power and ability to destroy his life.

Use of Powerful Flash Equipment[b]

Part 1 revealed that key witnesses saw a single powerful flash in the Alma Tunnel just prior to the crash.

The question here is: Is this something that could have been caused by equipment used by or on behalf of MI6?

Richard Tomlinson., Ex-MI6 Officer: 13 Feb 08: 52.3:

Mansfield: Q. A strobe or flashlight. Now, were you, during training, ever shown such an item?

A. I believe that I was when I went to Poole, to a visit to the SBS, and they had a number of special weapons which they used.... One piece of equipment there that I remember was a very bright – a piece of equipment that could give a very bright flashing light. I was told at the time that this was used for – in the case of if they wished to disorient, for example a helicopter pilot, on landing for example. Because clearly at night or suchlike, a helicopter pilot might have been landing with night vision goggles or even, at night, just using the naked eye and a very, very bright flashing light would lead to disorientation and being unable even to see outside references and to likely being unable to control the helicopter.

Q.... Can you describe the light in any way at all that you saw in your training, which would be obviously near the beginning of the period of your employment?

A. No, I cannot remember with any clarity that anymore. It was just a piece

---

sentence: we never get told what it is necessary to get; "it would depend who the – it would depend also who the subject".

[a] Tomlinson's treatment would appear to be worse than that accorded to David Shayler – see earlier footnote in Gaddafi section.

[b] Evidence in this section should be viewed in the light of the Powerful Flash section in Chapter 4B of Part 1.

of equipment amongst several.

Q. But is there any doubt in your mind that you saw such a thing?

A. I am sure I saw it, yes.

Q.... Was it something that was portable?

A. Yes, I believe it was portable, yes. It was small enough – if it was not portable, I am sure I would remember that it was not portable. It must have been small enough to be carried quite easily.

Q. All right. This may be a bridge too far, but the sort of size, can you remember even that, now?

A. There was a large table and there were several items on it, so it must have been small enough to fit within a small portion of the table.

At 161.22: Tam: Q. The flashing light or the device for a flagging[a] light that you say that you saw when you were training. Now, it is right, isn't it, that as a piece of equipment – I think you gave this answer before – it would need to be portable and that in fact it should be really ideally small as well, should it not?

A. Yes.

Q. Do you now remember anything about this device that you were shown when you were training?

A. I remember being in a military hall, as it were. There was a large table at the end of the room, and on that they placed the whole series of gadgets which they used in their operations. There were several rather interesting, you know, hand-guns and hand-arms and underwater breathing apparatus, and I remember there being something along those lines. There was a corporal from the SBS who was explaining what each did, and he just went through and said, "This is what we use this for", et cetera, and explained what they were all for. I do not particularly remember what it looked like, but I remember being explained that this is what various items did.

....Q. Can you remember what sort of size it was?

A. The size – no, I cannot remember specifically what size it was, but there were several items on the table and they were all portable – the sort of size of something that would be portable.

Q. Now, if you could just answer this question "yes" or "no": were you told whether or not it had a name?

A. I cannot remember. Sorry.

Q. Do you think you would now recognise it if you saw it again?

A. No.

Richard Dearlove, MI6 Director of Operations, 1994 to 1999, UK: 20 Feb 08: 121.20:

---

[a] This probably should read: "flashing".

Mansfield: Q. What do you know about strobe lights?

A. No more than the average, I believe.

Q. Training in MI6 – SIS at that time – was there training which involved them seeing and watching the use of strobe lights for disorientating –

A. I can say, I think with confidence, that no there were not. I was pretty familiar with the service's training programmes and I think that that also is a Tomlinson construction. Under oath, I think I am very confident in saying that, although I am judging from my knowledge of the training. This is not part of SIS's training.

Q. Yes. What I wanted to ask you is: have any inquiries that you are aware of been made in relation to those charged with training at that time? I can give you roughly the date and roughly the place where he says he was trained and saw something of this nature. Have any inquiries been made in relation to that?

A. I do not know the reply to that because I think, as I have said to you, it was believed in the services that it is not part of SIS's training.

Q. Believed –

A. Mr Tomlinson made many, many allegations and statements. He used bits of knowledge on which he elaborated with a very clear intention, of causing mischief for the service and the greatest possible difficulty. I think that the strobe light allegation is, in my view, spurious. It does not apply to SIS.

Miss X, MI6 Administrator, UK: 26 Feb 08: 70.2:

Burnett: Q. You are aware, I am sure, that one of Mr Tomlinson's suggestions is that he saw a strobe light or bright light of some sort when he was undergoing SIS training.

A. Yes, that is correct.

Q. Were you able to identify when Mr Tomlinson did his training?....

A. That is a matter of record. His course ran from September to February.

Q. September 1991 to February 1992?

A. Yes.

Q. Was it then part of the training that those undergoing it would spend a day with the Special Boat Service?

A. They would have various briefings, yes.

Q. And that would be one of them?

A. That would be one of them, yes.

Q. You have checked the records and they don't show anything more detailed of what occurred?

A. No, I am afraid they don't, no.

Q. Had you undergone similar training or been involved in training at about that time or just before?

A. I have been involved in training, yes.

Q. When were you involved in training?

A. Sort of intermittently over the years.

Q. But were you involved in training at the end of the 1980s, so just before Mr Tomlinson joined the service?

A. Yes, I was.

Q. Did you work on that initial training course?

A. I was involved with that, yes.

Q. In that capacity, did you attend the SBS briefing?

A. Yes, I did.

Q. On how many occasions?

A. Over the next two or three years, probably about three or four times, something like that, at that stage, and then also on other occasions.

Q. What you say in your statement, if I can remind you, is that you went on two occasions in the late 1980s, which we will come on to a bit later. Were any strobe lights used or shown to you?

A. No, they were not.

Q. Was there anything of a bright flashing loud nature shown?

A. Yes, the only thing that I could recall, when trying to think "I wonder what Mr Tomlinson might have meant", was that they do use sort of those pyrotechnic kind of – I only know them as "flash bangs". You sort of chuck them in a room to disorientate people and so on. They are little fireworky things.

Q. You attended again later in the 1990s, did you?

A. Yes, I did.

Q. And were you shown strobe lights or flashing lights?

A. No, I was not, no.

Mr A., MI6 Head of Balkan Target Team: 26 Feb 08: 172.11:

[In an undated MI6 document]: "For the record, I had never heard of blinding strobe lights until I saw some conspiracy theory television programme this year about the death of the Princess of Wales."

At 195.20: Burnett: Q. You add for good measure there that you have never heard of blinding strobe lights "... until I saw some conspiracy theory television programme after the crash in Paris".

A. That is correct, sir.

Q. Can we take it from that that during such training as you received for SIS, you were not trained in the use of strobe lights or blinding lights?

A. Absolutely not, sir.

Comment: Does MI6 use portable equipment that could have been used in the Alma Tunnel on 31 August 1997 to produce the huge, bright flash that was described by witnesses? [a]

As with everything else, the evidence is conflicting:

---

[a] For the witness accounts, see Part 1.

- Tomlinson: "I remember ... a piece of equipment that could give a very bright flashing light ... that ... was used ,,, to disorient"
- Dearlove: "no there were not" to Mansfield's: "was there training which involved them seeing and watching the use of strobe lights?"
- X: "no, they were not" to Burnett's: "were any strobe lights used or shown to you?"
- A: "I had never heard of blinding strobe lights until ... this year" – in an undated document written some time after the Paris crash
- A: "absolutely not" to Burnett's: "you were not trained in the use of strobe lights or blinding lights?"

There are several points to note from Dearlove's cross-examination:

1) Dearlove doesn't let Mansfield finish his initial question[a] on what occurred in training. Mansfield's last word is "disorientating", but Dearlove doesn't give him a chance to say or ask who might be disorientated or the potential uses of the strobe lights.

2) Dearlove appears to be in two minds about the integrity of his evidence – "I can say, I think with confidence"; "under oath, I think I am very confident"; "I am judging from my knowledge"; "I think ... in my view".

3) When Mansfield asks if "any inquiries [have] been made in relation to" Tomlinson's recollection, Dearlove appears dismissive – "it was believed in the services that it is not part of SIS's training". In other words, the account was dismissed by Dearlove, or MI6, as "a Tomlinson construction" and apparently not investigated.

4) Just as Mansfield starts his next question about that, he gets one word out – "believed" before Dearlove interrupts again, this time with an attack against Tomlinson – "Tomlinson made many, many allegations"; "a very clear intention, of causing mischief for the service" then, "the strobe light allegation is, in my view, spurious[b]".[c]

X was evasive at times.

Burnett asked X: "Had you undergone similar training [to Tomlinson] or been involved in training at about that time [of Tomlinson] or just before?" X didn't answer this – she said: "I have been involved in training,[d] yes."

---

[a] There is a "–" at the end of the question which indicates the witness interrupted before Mansfield had finished talking.
[b] Oxford lists two meanings for "spurious": 1. "not being what it seems to be; false"; 2. "(of reasoning) apparently but not actually correct".
[c] Mansfield then moved on to the next subject.
[d] When X says she was "involved in training" she appears to mean in a role other than as a trainee. For example, she could have been a helper in some way. When Burnett asked: "Did you work on that initial training course?" X replied: "I was involved with that, yes." X fails to explain what she means by "involved" and Burnett fails to ask her.

Burnett: "When were you involved in training?" X is again evasive: "Sort of intermittently over the years."

X states she was "involved" – see previous footnote – with "that initial training course"[a]. Without finding out what "involved" means, Burnett then asks X: "In that capacity, did you attend the SBS briefing?"

What "capacity"?

The jury is hearing X's answers without being privy to what her role was at the SBS briefings.[b] For example, X may have had a role that wouldn't have brought her in contact with a strobe light, whether such lights were there or not.

So when Burnett finally asks: "Were any strobe lights used or shown to you?" X is not evasive: "No, they were not."

But the questions are: What was X's role at the SBS briefings? Why did Burnett not even try to find out what her role was? Would X's role have brought her in contact with strobe lights had any been there?

Mr A stated[c]: "I had never heard of blinding strobe lights until ... this year[d]" – this is an interesting statement from an experienced MI6 officer, who was Head of the MI6 Balkan Target Team during the Yugoslav war. A gave the strongest denial[e] evidence from any of the MI6 witnesses – he is not just saying that blinding strobe lights weren't shown or heard about during training, but he is denying that he had ever heard of them in his life up to when he "saw some conspiracy theory television programme after the crash in Paris".

This is particularly significant because Tomlinson stated in his affidavit: "Dr Fishwick[f] suggested that one way to cause the crash might be to disorientate the chauffeur using a strobe flash gun...."

It may not be a coincidence that the MI6 officer who provides the strongest denial – complete ignorance of the existence of strobe lights – is the very one who is alleged to have put forward the proposal to use a strobe light in an assassination plot.

---

[a] There is also no explanation from Burnett or X as to what is meant by "that initial training course".

[b] When finally Burnett establishes X attended the SBS briefing at around the same time as Tomlinson, there appears to be a conflict on how often – at the inquest: "probably about three or four times"; in her statement – (not shown to the jury and not seen by the author): "two occasions in the late 1980s".

[c] In a statement not seen by the jury or the author.

[d] Sometime after 1997.

[e] A emphasises this by using the term: "for the record".

[f] Mr A is Dr Simon Fishwick – see Tomlinson affidavit.

Tomlinson has never suggested that MI6 keeps stocks of strobe lights. His evidence is that SBS uses them, or something similar, in their work and he saw one during his training at an SBS display in Poole. By inference, the lights could be used on behalf of MI6 – see earlier evidence of MI6 using SBS and SAS to conduct field operations.[a]

The official SAS website includes a "Strobe Light Pouch MkIII[b]" in its list of equipment products.[122cd] This appears to provide independent supporting evidence for Tomlinson's sworn affidavit account – see earlier – that "a strobe flash gun [is] a device which is occasionally deployed by special forces".[f]

Tomlinson has provided a logical reason why the SBS had the "piece of equipment that could give a very bright flashing light" – it was: "this was used ... to disorient ... a helicopter pilot, on landing for example".

One could argue that since strobe lights exist, and apparently they have since 1931[123], why wouldn't they be used by special forces and be known to intelligence agencies?

The question is: If the SAS and SBS do not use strobe lights in their line of work, then one could ask, why? Why wouldn't SAS and SBS include strobe lights as part of their useful equipment?

I suggest that the attempts by MI6 to distance themselves from knowledge of or use of strobe lights would tend to arouse suspicion, rather than be seen as credible evidence.

Involvement With Landmines[g]

The introduction of this issue struck a sensitive chord with MI6.

Richard Tomlinson., Ex-MI6 Officer: 13 Feb 08: 54.7:

Mansfield: Q. Were you at any time aware, whilst you were working in this period of the early to mid-1990s, of any SIS or MI6 involvement in the war that was being waged within Angola?

A. Yes, I can say – yes, there was –

---

[a] This would fit with Tomlinson's 1999 affidavit: "a strobe flash gun ... is occasionally deployed by special forces". Special forces being SAS and SBS.

[b] "MkIII" could indicate there were earlier versions of this product – MkI and MkII.

[c] Product Code P19.

[d] There is also another listed product called "AW Modular Minimi Pouch" (Product No. 9000502) which includes "2 molle strips on top of pouch to attach smaller pouches such as micro accessory, strobe or multi tool".

[e] SAS and SBS.

[f] If SAS and SBS have strobe lights in their equipment – and this evidence indicates they have – it is not logical to suggest they wouldn't be used on missions carried out on behalf of MI6.

[g] This should be viewed in the light of the Landmines chapter in Part 2.

Q. Don't give me the detail for the moment –

A. Yes.

Q. – because there may be objection. I do not know.

A. That is what I am hesitating for, yes.

Q. I am not asking for the detail from you, but you remember.

A. Mm.

.... Coroner: Is the relevance of this landmines?

Q, It is....

Coroner: Is that going to get into the detail?

Q. Well, there is a risk of it....

Coroner: We will see what Mr Tam says about this.

Tam: Sir, I was listening to see what the next question was going to be, but if there is a risk of detail being given, then that detail may well be detail which should not be given.

Coroner: The trouble is, once the detail is given, it is then too late. That is the problem.

Tam: That is why I was listening to the question to see exactly sort of answer might be –

Coroner: Mr Mansfield is content to leave this until next week, anyway, so that may be the way out of this.

Q. I think there may be time today to consider how to deal with this because, obviously, as you have rightly pointed out, it bears absolutely on what Princess Diana was doing in 1997. I would want to ask this witness, so that everyone knows what the question is, what the role of MI6 was in Angola – when he was obviously part of MI6, what he learned to be that role. That is all.

Tam: Can we take instructions on that and return to it?

Coroner: Yes.

At 123.6: Q. This concerns the possibility of a role of MI6 in Angola, and you were about to say something and then stopped. Is your recollection in relation to this issue based on any document or conversation that you had while you were employed at MI6?

....A. Well, MI6 would have several roles in Angola. It would not just be one.

Tam: Stop, stop, stop. This is the road that I did not want the witness to be going down without some care being taken. My learned friend asked the question that he very kindly agreed to start with, which is simply to try to ascertain from the witness the basis for him talking about the subject matter. Only once that we have that established can we then go on to see what of that it is possible safely to talk about in future.

Coroner: Did you hear that, Mr Tomlinson?

A. Yes, I did. I am not sure I entirely understand how far I am allowed to go.

Q. Can I put the question again? The preparatory question is this: what is the basis for your recollection about any role that MI6 may have had in Angola in the 1990s? Can I illustrate it, so that it is very clear? Is it the result of a document you saw at the time or conversations or training? What is the source?

A. I think I can answer that. There was a possibility of a posting to Angola and I was interested in going myself because I thought it would be an interesting posting and challenging. I do not know whether that is still the case, but in the 1990s we had postings there.

Tam: Stop, stop. Sir, so that I am not beating about the bush, I understand that my learned friend wants to explore with this witness an allegation that has been made that SIS were in some way involved in the supply of landmines to factions in Angola and I have said that that is an aspect that he can properly ask questions about. Our sensitivities and proper sensitivities, as you will appreciate, lie in protecting the questions of whether there were any requirements from the Government for intelligence relating to Angola, that is to say whether or not there were; whether or not there were any intelligence operations in Angola, and if there were, how they were carried out. It is that area that we are seeking to protect for sensitivity.

Coroner: So you have no objection to the narrow question on landmines?

Tam[a]: The narrow question on landmines is fine. We have no wish to stand in the way of a proper question. What we are concerned about is that the witness does not stray into other areas which do not concern that, but which might adversely affect –

Coroner: He has been showing some signs of wanting to stray. Can you ask the narrow question on landmines?

Q. May I make it clear? The suggestion is not that MI6 supplied landmines because they would not do that. The question I want to explore with this witness is the role that MI6 played in the war between two factions and on which side were they playing it and, of course, the indirect connections that may then arise in relation to weaponry and landmines going into Angola.

Coroner: Unless that is public knowledge, which I suspect. it is not, I cannot see that that would be allowed.

Tam: Sir, that is all going into operational matters –

Coroner: Indeed.

Tam: – in great specificity.

A. If I can say something here please?

Coroner: Well, I think it is rather dangerous for you to say things without a question because you might be trespassing the wrong side of the line.

A. No, but what I do wish to say does not trespass on anything. I am being

---

[a] The inquest website shows this as "A" (for "Answer") indicating it is an answer from Tomlinson. That is not correct.

perfectly responsible. I do not actually know any of the answers to the potential questions on landmines that may be put to me. I just don't know. So perhaps that will answer the question. I just don't know what – except in broad terms, I do not know – what MI6 were potentially doing there, I don't know. I can tell you on landmines, I do not know anything about it at all.
Richard Dearlove., MI6 Director of Operations, 1994 to 1999, UK: 20 Feb 08: 127.9:

Mansfield: Q. In 1997, in January, Princess Diana went to Angola. Did you know that?

A. Yes, I did.

Q. Were there MI6 agents in Angola at the time?

A. I am not prepared to divulge details of SIS's involvement or positioning in Angola, but what I can say, because we might as well push forward, is that SIS – and I state this categorically – was not involved in the supply of weapons to either side in the Angolan civil war in 1997 and had no involvement in specifically the supply of landmines to either side.

Coroner: I think what Mr Mansfield is ultimately getting at, if we can try to shorten this, is that Princess Diana expressed a very considerable interest in landmines and their elimination and the elimination of their supply. We know that the Government changed in May 1997, and the incoming Government's policy, which I think may be part of the ethical foreign policy, if I remember rightly at the time, was different from the Conservative Party's previous policy when they were in Government. Can you throw any light at all on the suggestion that the security services may have killed Diana and Dodi because of her interest in landmines?

A. None whatsoever. SIS had no involvement in the manufacturing or supply of landmines. I might also point out that the job of SIS is to support the Government policy. The Prime Minister announced the end of manufacture and use of landmines, as my Lord has mentioned –

Coroner: Then at some point we signed up to the Ottawa Convention, but I cannot remember the date –

A. In May 1997.[a] I can make no attachment between these two issues whatsoever – none.

Q. Perhaps I can just prepare the ground so you can see what the suggested link is. There had been, in Angola, a civil war going on for a number of years.

A. Correct.

---

[a] This is not correct. The convention was signed in December 1997. The false date Dearlove has proffered – May 1997 – is three months <u>before</u> the crash, whereas the true date of the Ottawa signing was over three months <u>after</u> the crash.

Q. The best part of 20 years by 1997.

A. Correct.

Q. Is it also right that the war basically was fought between two factions, UNITA and MPLA?

A. That is correct.

Q. And that MPLA was basically an organisation backed by the Soviet Russians at that point and UNITA was another organisation that was given support by the United States and the United Kingdom; correct?

A. You have to be very careful. You are throwing around dates here and I am not sure. I cannot recall now. I do not think the British Government were ever particularly supportive of UNITA.

Q. No, not officially, but unofficially.

A. Well, that is your statement.

Q. What is the answer?

A. I am not going to speculate on British policy towards UNITA of that period because, frankly, I just cannot remember.

Q. I can obviously just put the bold statement and I know the answer. I want, if I may, just to put the bricks in the wall to you. So you know why I am asking these questions, it is because there was some evidence that Diana was compiling a dossier and that the dossier was capable of exposing historically British involvement in Angola because of who manufactured the weaponry, how it was got in there. Please understand that there is no suggestion that the SIS themselves would manufacture anything or would themselves, as it were, take weaponry into Angola, but that MI6, along with parish[a] companies and British mercenaries, were playing a role in that war. Can you answer that?

A. I do not recall, as I said, that the SIS was involved in the supply of weaponry to either side.

Q. Yes. That was not the suggestion, that MI6 was involved in the supply, but that British companies were involved.

.... Q. The reason I was asking you about Angola is, through one source or another, did you become aware that she was asking a lot of questions?

A. Frankly, we did not take any interest –

Q. Really.

A. – in what she was doing. It is not a national security issue. My job was to contribute to national security.

Q. But, of course, if it was thought that Diana was going to expose a great deal of what was going on and had been going on in Angola and was teaming up – I am going to put it so that it is clear – with a family[b] who were certainly persona non grata in the plural and, worse than that, actually by some loathed, that might become an issue of security, mightn't it?

---

[a] This probably should read "pariah".

[b] The Al Fayed family.

A. That is your speculation. I do not think this was an issue of any security concern whatsoever. I think that is very – it is fanciful.

Q. You think it is fanciful?

A. Yes, it was entirely fanciful. It was of no concern to my service whatsoever.

.... Q. Going back to the Angolan situation for a moment – that is why I want to ask you this question or is it a question of deniability – MI6 had a role in Angola during the war between UNITA and MPLA, did they not?

A. We mentioned the JIC[a] earlier. There would have been intelligence requirements on the situation in Angola.

Q. Did it go beyond that?

A. No.

Q. Nothing more –

A. Not that I can recall and I really don't think it went beyond that.

Comment: MI6 was notably sensitive about their involvement in Angola:

-   Tam: "if there is a risk of detail being given, then that detail may well be detail which should not be given"
-   Tam: "can we take instructions on that and return to it?"
-   Tam: "Stop, stop, stop. This is the road that I did not want the witness to be going down without some care being taken."
-   Tam: "Stop, stop.... Our sensitivities ... lie in ... whether or not there were any intelligence operations in Angola, and if there were, how they were carried out."
-   Tam: "we are concerned ... that the witness does not stray into other areas which ... might adversely affect – " – interrupted at this point by Baker
-   Tam: "that is all going into operational matters ... in great specificity" – in support of Baker's: "I cannot see that that would be allowed"
-   Baker: "you might be trespassing the wrong side of the line" – speaking to Tomlinson.

Tam said: "The narrow question on landmines is fine." This appears to be because MI6 – who had employed Tomlinson – must have known that he had no specific knowledge about their involvement with landmines in Angola. And Tomlinson confirms this with: "I do not actually know any of the answers to the potential questions on landmines that may be put to me."

Mansfield clearly stated during the cross-examination of Tomlinson: "May I make it clear? The suggestion is not that MI6 supplied landmines because they would not do that." [ba]

---

[a] Joint Intelligence Committee.

[b] This is also common sense – that MI6 are not involved in carrying stocks of or supplying weapons into war zones. Weapons like landmines are purchased by nations or organisations from arms dealers and manufacturers.

In spite of this, just a week later, Dearlove – the witness – avoided answering questions by focusing on exactly that subject:

- "SIS – and I state this categorically – was not involved in the supply of weapons ... in the Angolan civil war in 1997" – the question was: "Were there MI6 agents in Angola [in 1997]?"
- MI6 "had no involvement in ... the supply of landmines to either side" – the question was: "Were there MI6 agents in Angola [in 1997]?"
- "SIS had no involvement in the manufacturing or supply of landmines" – the question was[b]: "Can you throw any light ... on the suggestion that the security services may have killed Diana and Dodi because of her interest in landmines?"

Even after Mansfield directly told Dearlove: "Please understand that there is no suggestion that the SIS themselves would manufacture ... or ... take weaponry into Angola", Dearlove immediately continues with his mantra: "I do not recall ... that the SIS was involved in the supply of weaponry to either side".[c]

Mansfield again had to state: "That was not the suggestion, that MI6 was involved in the supply" – then finally Dearlove shifted from that line.

Dearlove evaded answering most of Mansfield's questions on Angola:[d]

- "I am not prepared to divulge details of SIS's involvement or positioning in Angola"
- "you are throwing around dates here and I am not sure"
- "I am not going to speculate on British policy towards UNITA of that period"
- "not that I can recall and I really don't think it went beyond that ... there would have been intelligence requirements".

In a courtroom situation it is normal for a lawyer to build up his cross-examination with a series of questions probing various aspects of an issue. Michael Mansfield had in the stand Richard Dearlove – the main MI6 witness on potential knowledge within the organisation regarding motives for the

---

[a] Instead Mansfield said: "The question I want to explore ... is the role that MI6 played in the war ... and ... the indirect connections that may then arise in relation to weaponry and landmines going into Angola."

[b] This time from Baker.

[c] The question there was: The suggestion is "that MI6, along with [pariah] companies and British mercenaries were playing a role in that [Angolan] war. Can you answer that?"

[d] Dearlove answered the first few questions confidently, indicating a knowledge of the situation in Angola in the late 20th century, before clamming up, becoming evasive and losing his memory of events: "frankly, I just cannot remember"; "I do not recall".

deaths.[ab] It had been alleged that Diana's anti-landmine campaign was a key possible motive.[c]

Mansfield got to ask just two questions on this critical subject – "Did you know that ... Princess Diana went to Angola?"; "Were there MI6 agents in Angola at the time?" – before Baker intervened.

Mansfield hadn't even used the word "landmines" – that was first used by Dearlove in his answer.[d] Dearlove – who was supposed to be a witness in the stand answering questions – included in his "answer", "we might as well push forward". In other words, let's finish with the "landmines" issue as soon as we can.

Baker then intervened, latching onto this, and apparently decided to attempt to completely circumvent Mansfield's line of questioning: "I think what Mr Mansfield is ultimately getting at, if we can try to shorten this.... Can you throw any light at all on the suggestion that the security services may have killed Diana and Dodi because of her interest in landmines?" To which Dearlove included his earlier mantra: "SIS had no involvement in the manufacturing or supply of landmines."

Mansfield managed to ignore this and continued with his original questioning:[e] "There had been, in Angola, a civil war going on for a number of years?"

In the end, though, between Tam's sensitivities[f], Dearlove's mantra and evasiveness and Baker's attempted circumvention, Mansfield was able to gain very little understanding of MI6's role in Angola.

The most climactic points appeared to be from Tomlinson before he was shut down each time[g]: "in the 1990s we had postings there [in Angola]" and "MI6 would have several roles in Angola".[h]

Dearlove's biggest admission was: "There would have been intelligence requirements on the situation in Angola."

---

[a] If MI6 was involved.

[b] Dearlove was the MI6 Director of Operations during the period being examined.

[c] This is supported by the evidence in Part 2.

[d] Dearlove answered with: MI6 "had no involvement in specifically the supply of landmines to either side" even though neither "landmines" nor "supply" had been mentioned by Mansfield.

[e] Michael Mansfield is a lawyer with 40 years experience: Michael Mansfield, *Memoirs of a Radical Lawyer*, p22.

[f] On behalf of MI6.

[g] By Tam.

[h] Tomlinson also said: "What MI6 were potentially doing there [in Angola], I don't know."

However, it may be that more relevant than the dearth of MI6 evidence was the reaction of the lawyer, Tam, the witness, Dearlove and the judge, Baker, when this subject of landmines was raised by Mansfield.

The question is: Why was there such a concerted effort by Baker, Dearlove and Tam to shut down the inquest evidence on the MI6 involvement with landmines?

The following excerpt from Tomlinson's book highlights the level of MI6 interest in the arms industry.

Richard Tomlinson., Ex-MI6 Officer: 2001 Book: **Jury Didn't Hear**:
"'Battle' was one of the arms dealers that MI6 had on its books. Arms dealers are useful sources of intelligence on international arms deals and can be influential in swinging the deals to British companies. 'Battle', a multi-millionaire Anglo-Iranian, earned a salary of around £100,000 per year from MI6.

"In late 1991, the United Arab Emirates (UAE) asked Battle to buy them a consignment of new [Russian-made] BMP-3 armoured personnel carriers.... The MOD[a] heard rumours that [the BMP-3's] performance was better than Western equivalents and asked MI6 for intelligence.

"Battle set to work on the deal, flying regularly between the BMP design bureau in Kurgan and Abu Dhabi, and he eventually sealed a deal for the Russians to sell a batch of the lower specification export variant BMP-3s to the Gulf state. He did not omit to see his MI6 handler every time he passed through London, however, and on one visit mentioned that he had been shown around the advanced variant of the BMP-3 on his last trip to Kurgan. MI6 persuaded him to try and acquire one. On his next trip, with a £500,000 backhander and forged end-user certificate provided by MI6, Battle persuaded his Russian contact to hide one of the advanced specification BMP-3s amongst the first batch of 20 export variants which were shipped to the UAE.

"The consignment of BMP-3s went by train from Kurgan to the Polish port of Gdansk. There the 20 UAE vehicles were offloaded into a container ship and sent on their way to Abu Dhabi. The remaining vehicle, under the cover of darkness and with the assistance of Polish liaison, was loaded into a specially chartered tramp steamer and shipped to the army port of Marchwood in Southampton." [124]

---

[a] Ministry of Defence.

1B   MI6 in Paris: 30-31 August 1997

Miss X, MI6 Administrator, UK: 26 Feb 08: 64.7:
Burnett: Q. You arranged for interviews to be carried out by Paget of [MI6] staff who were serving in Paris at the time. That is right, isn't it?
A. Yes, correct.

Sightings In and Around the Ritz Hotel

If MI6 was involved, it is quite possible they would have had officers or agents present around the Ritz Hotel prior to the departure of the Mercedes S280.

Bar Vendôme

The presence of two men who spent over two hours in the Bar Vendôme drew the attention of witnesses.
François Tendil, Night Security Manager, Ritz Hotel: 3 Dec 07: 79.9:
Horwell: Q. You have been asked[a] about two men that you saw in the Bar Vendôme. You have said in your witness statements or your depositions that they were dressed like journalists. Is that right?
A. Yes, indeed. Pictures were taken.
Q. I am sorry, you say "pictures were taken". What did you mean by that?
A. With the cameras, with the video cameras, you can have print-outs and I state that in my deposition. These people arrived at the same time as the paparazzi and they left when Diana left, so I thought it was strange.
Q. Right. You believed that they were linked to the paparazzi, did you?
A. No.
Q. Or were journalists?
A. I do not know.
Q. You described them as each having a plastic bag that they carried; yes?
A. Yes. It is what I said at that time.
Q. Mr Tendil, thank you.

---

[a] Asked in his statements – not during his earlier inquest cross-examination.

Alain Willaumez, Barman, Ritz Hotel, Paris: 20 Dec 07: 75.16:
"The first time [Henri Paul visited the Bar Vendôme], according to me – I remember very well this first time. When I saw him he was speaking with Mr Allidiere, as I say in my deposition, and Mr Allidiere told him that at table 15 there were two people being seated looking like paparazzi with jackets and bags. Mr Paul went to see what was happening without speaking to them."

Jean-Pierre Allidiere, Senior Head Waiter, Ritz Hotel, Paris: 2 Oct 97 Statement read out 12 Mar 08: 176.2:
"I saw these guards[a] again at about 22.00 hours [10 p.m.] accompanied by a security officer, Mr François Tendil or a person with the first name of Vincent[b]. I think I placed them[c] at table number 1, at that point he[d] whispered in my ear that he thought the customers at table number 15 could be paparazzi. I glanced over to this table and I saw men of European appearance aged about 40, of normal height and build. And I remember that one of them was badly shaven, was wearing a light coloured sleeveless jacket with lots of pockets. They were sitting down and there were two plastic bags bearing advertising beneath their chairs, one dark and the other light, with something in them which was not very large and whose shape I could not make out. I cannot say whether it was cameras. These men were drinking Macallan whisky. I took the order and served the bodyguards with toast and lobster[e] and Schweppes. I did not know these men[f], who were in a completely normal state, composed and pleasant.... I returned to my duties as Mr Tendil or Vincent had left the bar. Then I saw Mr Henri Paul go past and I went to see Vincent to ask him if he had told him about the two men who could have been paparazzi. He told me that he was going to do so. Then I saw Mr Paul come back, pretending to be a guest and asking me whether it was possible to get to the terrace through the door and passing in front of table 15 in order to observe its occupants. Then he beckoned to me to come closer and I joined him outside. He told me that Vincent had already pointed out these two people to him and that their bags might contain small cameras. He told me that he found them well behaved and that he would see what happened."

---

[a] The two bodyguards of Diana and Dodi – Trevor Rees-Jones and Kez Wingfield.
[b] It is possible Allidiere is referring to Vincent L'Hottelier, who was Head Barman and has never been interviewed by any police investigation and was also not heard from at the inquest. He is listed in the Witnesses Not Heard in Part 1.
[c] The bodyguards.
[d] Tendil or "Vincent".
[e] Lobster – this could be seen as further evidence contradicting Wingfield's account: "the focus of attention was to get a sandwich down my neck as quickly as I could, and then get back on the job": see Part 1, section on Was Henri Drunk?
[f] Allidiere appears to be referring to the two men at Table 15, but there is a possibility he is describing the two bodyguards.

At 180.25: Burnett: The two people who were described in [Allidiere's] statement, they were followed up and we have heard evidence that they were not paparazzi and that they can safely be excluded from our consideration.
Paul Carpenter, Paget Officer: 3 Dec 07: 143.3:

MacLeod: I think Mr Tendil referred to two persons who he observed in the Bar Vendôme and who he pointed out to Mr Henri Paul. I think he gave a description of those two men in his witness statement both as to their physical appearance and as to the clothing that they were wearing. He identified those two individuals as sitting at either table 15 or table 16 in the Bar Vendôme.[a]

A. Yes.

Q. First of all, have you had an opportunity, if that is the correct word, of scrutinising the CCTV footage of all persons entering and leaving the Ritz Hotel at the relevant time in order to determine whether you could identify those two individuals whom Mr Tendil had observed?

A. Yes. I have looked at the CCTV and based on Mr Tendil's description, I have been able to identify them, although it was quite a while ago now so I am doing this from memory.

Q. I think it is right that the relevant CCTV footage and any photographs available from that are not currently loaded into the court system. Is that right?

A. That is right. Yes.

Q. But if there is any dispute about the matter, they could be produced at a later date?

A. They could be, yes.

Q. Now, first of all, can I ask you whether those two men were in fact traced by the French police?

A. Yes, they were, through their Carte Bleue.

Q. I think the Carte Bleue came from the bill from table 15 at the Bar Vendôme. It is INQ0001694[b] and it is at the right-hand side of the page, the third entry down, table 15, if that could be highlighted. Was it possible, with reference to the computer record bill from the Bar Vendôme, to identify this as the table at which the two gentlemen were sitting?

A. I think from memory it was described as such, yes.

Q. Does that bill show the drinks that the two men consumed and, at the top, the time that the order was placed, 21.29?

A. That is right, yes.

---

[a] MacLeod appears to be referring to information from Tendil's statement which was not read out and was not available to the jury.

[b] Although this was shown on the inquest screen at this point, the jury were not provided with a hard copy and there is also no copy on the inquest website.

Q. And the time that payment was made and the bill closed at the foot of the page, 23.41?

A. Yes, that is correct.

Q. From your recollection of studying the CCTV footage of the movements of those two men, can you recall at what time they entered the Ritz?

A. From memory, it was just after 9 o'clock. It could be quarter past 9. I cannot remember exactly, but I know it was around 9/9.30. Something like that.

Q. Again, from your recollection, can you say at what time those two men left the Ritz?

A. My memory of it is just after midnight.

Q. And if necessary, can those times be checked?

A. They can, yes.

Q. And was the identity of those two men established by the French investigation?

A. Yes, it was.

Q. And who were the two men?

A. I cannot remember if their surname was Klukker, K-L-U-K-K-E-R, or Kukker, K-U-K-K-E-R, but they were both traced through the card, two brothers.

Q. And was the purpose of their visit to the Ritz established?

A. They had bought some expensive cigars and they went to the Ritz to smoke them.

Q. And there was reference made to the two plastic bags that these gentlemen were carrying. Do you know from the French investigation what those bags contained?

A. Yes, sir, expensive cigars.

Q. I have no more questions.

Burnett: I just allow myself the observation that I hope the Perrier water was not poured into the malt whisky....

Sue Reid, Investigations Editor, *Daily Mail*: 4 Dec 04 Article: **Jury Didn't Hear**:

"The hotel's CCTV cameras captured ... the presence of two men who at first mingled with the crowd outside and then entered the lobby bar of the hotel for a drink while they spoke intently and quietly in perfect English.

"This week ... the presence of these two men was raised more than once by our informants. One well-placed source said: 'The rest of the crowds outside the Ritz were either tourists hoping to catch a glimpse of Diana or paparazzi planning to make a fortune from photographs of her. However, these two men – who looked in their late 30s – appear more than once on the hotel film and have never been identified. Were they secret service men from our own side?'

"Another source went further: 'We know that the two men entered the Ritz and sat down at the main lobby bar. They ordered several rounds of drinks and remained, carefully observing events, until shortly before midnight when the Princess was about to leave the hotel. Their conversation was constant but very terse, according to the staff on duty.'

"The film footage is believed to have been seen by Scotland Yard. However, the two men's faces are unclear and their identities have not been confirmed."[125]

Comment: The evidence of three witnesses – Tendil, Willaumez and Allidiere – was heard. Vincent L'Hottelier's evidence is missing – he was the Head Barman and should have been heard, but in fact, he was never interviewed by any investigation – French, British or Baker. Other barmen who were also present – Sébastien Trote and Philippe Doucin – do not seem to have ever been asked about these two men, despite being cross-examined at the inquest.[a]

The most important heard witness appears to be Jean-Pierre Allidiere – he served the two men and the Diana-Dodi bodyguards. Yet he is not cross-examined – the jury only hear his statement. And critically, his statement is not read out until the penultimate week of the inquest evidence, three months after Tendil was cross-examined.[b]

So there are at least eight potential witnesses, all of whom were in the Bar Vendôme during the critical time period – 9.29 to 11.41 p.m.: Tendil, Willaumez, Allidiere, L'Hottelier, Trote, Doucin, Rees-Jones and Wingfield.

Of these eight people, only one – Tendil – was briefly cross-examined about his recollection of the two men; one voluntarily mentioned them in passing – Willaumez – and was not asked any more about it[c]; four were cross-examined but not asked about the men – Trote, Doucin, Rees-Jones, Wingfield; one had his statement, which described the men, read out – Allidiere; and one has never been interviewed at all – L'Hottelier.

There was a comparatively lengthy cross-examination of the Paget officer, Paul Carpenter, but unfortunately he was not present in the Bar Vendôme on 30 August 1997.[d]

Of the two primary sources of heard eye-witness evidence – Tendil and Allidiere – Tendil was heard on 3 December 2007 and Allidiere's statement was held back until 12 March 2008, 3 months and 9 days later.

---

[a] See excerpts from their evidence in Part 1.
[b] The MacLeod-Carpenter cross-examination fails to mention the existence of Allidiere's account, even though they already had his statement.
[c] The full context can be viewed on the inquest website – the lawyer, Jonathon Hough, was asking about Henri Paul's movements.
[d] Carpenter's evidence is analysed below.

Why is this? Why was the jury fed so little information on these two men? And why was there over three months between serves?

Even Tendil – the sole eye-witness cross-examined on this – was asked only a few basic questions by the police lawyer. There was nothing probing.[a]

François Tendil was evidently concerned about the presence of these two men – "I thought it was strange".

Tendil states: "These people arrived at the same time as the paparazzi and they left when Diana left", yet says they were not "linked to the paparazzi".

Instead of making a real attempt to establish what Tendil thought they might have been doing there, Horwell simply asks: "Were [they] journalists?" even though Tendil has already said they weren't "linked to the paparazzi".

Tendil replies: "I do not know". Then that is the end of that line of questioning. In fact, just one more question and that's it from Horwell altogether. It comes across like this was a road that Horwell didn't want to travel down.

Maybe the inquest had decided it was safer to pursue the subject with Paul Carpenter, an MPS officer, because that is what happened later that same day – 3 December 2007. Once again it was the police lawyer, but this time Horwell's colleague, Duncan MacLeod.

MPS lawyer, MacLeod, cross-examining an MPS witness, Carpenter.

There are several important points regarding the MacLeod-Carpenter cross-examination:

1) Carpenter states: "I have looked at the CCTV and ... have been able to identify [the two men] although it was quite a while ago now so <u>I am doing this from memory</u>."

The question is why is Carpenter answering these questions "from memory"? Does Paul Carpenter – an officer who provided extensive MPS input into key inquest evidence[b] – not take notes?

Carpenter says it "was quite a while ago" since he did the research. Yet when he did that research he must have known he could be called on to testify about it. So why wouldn't he have taken notes?

Did he leave them at home? They must have known Tendil was up for cross-examination that day[c], so this is very sloppy work by the inquest or the MPS, or both. Why wasn't Carpenter rescheduled to the next day[d], when it became known that he didn't have his notes with him?

---

[a] The longest cross-examination was of Paul Carpenter – not an eye-witness.
[b] See Part 1.
[c] Each week throughout the inquest, the coming week's witnesses – with the day they were scheduled to appear – would be listed ahead of time on the inquest website.
[d] This was a Monday.

2) Next, Carpenter confirms: "the relevant CCTV footage and any photographs available [regarding the two men] are not currently loaded into the court system".

Well, why not?

Is the possible evidence of the presence of intelligence agents or officers inside the Ritz not an important enough issue for the inquest jury to view what's available?

The point is the inquest watched hours of CCTV footage on other issues[a], yet on a topic that could involve an intelligence agency, the footage – which the inquest had – is suddenly not available for the jury to see.

The jury are not even provided with Tendil's descriptions of the two men, given in his statement – all they hear is:

- Horwell quoting Tendil: "they were dressed like journalists"
- MacLeod to Carpenter: "I think [Tendil] gave a description of those two men in his witness statement both as to their physical appearance and as to the clothing that they were wearing".

3) Then MacLeod suggests: "if there is any dispute about the matter, [the CCTV footage and photographs] could be produced at a later date", to which Carpenter concurs.

How can there be a dispute if there is no evidence provided to have a dispute about?

The only dispute could be that the jury were again kept in the dark – not provided with anything: not Tendil's statement, not the CCTV footage and not the photographs[b].

None of the lawyers present appear to have made any protest.

There is a possibility that MacLeod and Carpenter – both representing the MPS – put their account together quickly during the day.

François Tendil was the final witness heard during the morning session and Horwell asked questions for the police throughout the day. MacLeod makes his first appearance right at the end of the day – solely to cross-examine Carpenter about Tendil's evidence.

Horwell asked Tendil: "You have said ... that [the two men] were dressed like journalists. Is that right?" Tendil confirms this – "yes, indeed" – but then adds: "Pictures were taken." Horwell's response indicates that he wasn't expecting that: "I am sorry, you say 'pictures were taken'. What did you mean by that?"

It is possible that there was no intention by Horwell to reveal to the jury that there was actually CCTV footage of the two men. Once Tendil had

---

[a] See particularly Parts 1 and 2.

[b] No one described what the photos showed or who took them.

volunteered that information, it may have been decided that the police had to now officially address the existence of this CCTV footage and what it revealed.

But not by doing the logical thing, which would have been to show the CCTV to the jury with Tendil present – allowing the eye-witness, Tendil, to point out the two men on the footage.[a]

Instead it appears it was decided to present it as a cross-examination by MacLeod of Carpenter[b], who was not an eye-witness and gave evidence with the caution: "it was quite a while ago now so I am doing this from memory" – and all this without showing the jury an inch of CCTV footage.

I am suggesting that if Tendil hadn't stated that "pictures were taken", then this whole issue may not have been addressed – even though Carpenter reveals in his evidence:[c] "I have looked at the CCTV[d] and ... I have been able to identify [the two men]".[e]

Carpenter confirms: "those two men were in fact traced by the French police".

This is the first time this has ever been suggested – that the French investigated into the evidence relating to these two men.

Outside of this verbal account from Carpenter there is no other known witness or documentary support that the French traced these two men. It also does not fit with what is known about the French investigation into the deaths of Diana and Dodi – that it followed limited avenues, primarily pursuing leads regarding Henri Paul[f] and the paparazzi[g] who pursued the Mercedes, and were later arrested.[h]

---

[a] If logistically it couldn't have been done at the time, then Tendil could have been recalled, as happened with other witnesses. Alternatively, this could have been done with Allidiere, who was never cross-examined – see earlier.

[b] Both representing the MPS, as stated earlier.

[c] On the same day Tendil's account was heard.

[d] "quite a while ago" – see earlier.

[e] This is supported by the fact that the 832 page Paget Report omitted this issue, even though they had Tendil's statements – Tendil said: "I state that in my deposition" – and Carpenter was a part of the Paget team.

[f] See Part 3.

[g] Tendil stated at the inquest that he did not believe "that they were linked to the paparazzi". Willaumez said "Allidiere told [Henri] that at table 15 – there were two people being seated looking like paparazzi with jackets and bags". Allidiere said that either Tendil or Vincent "whispered in my ear that he thought the customers at table number 15 could be paparazzi". There is no suggestion though that either of these men could have been in the paparazzi contingent that followed the Mercedes. The evidence relating to the paparazzi has been covered in Part 1.

[h] See Part 3.

Carpenter said that the French traced the men "through their Carte Bleue".[a] The jury weren't shown that, but "the bill from table 15" was put up on the inquest screen.[b] MacLeod then asked Carpenter: "Was it possible, with reference to the computer record bill[c] ... to identify this as the table at which the two gentlemen were sitting?" Carpenter's answer appears tentative: "I think from memory it was described as such, yes".

The next few questions relate to what is shown on the bill, including the two times: order placement – 9.29 p.m.; payment – 11.41 p.m.

MacLeod then asks: "From your recollection ... can you recall at what time they entered the Ritz?" And next: "what time those two men left the Ritz?"

Now, Carpenter has already said: "it was quite a while ago" that he studied the CCTV of this. So the question is: Can Carpenter – who has already been providing tentative evidence[d] – really be relied on to remember the times these men entered and left the Ritz Hotel?

This time Carpenter answers very tentatively: "From memory, it was just after 9 o'clock. It could be quarter past 9. I cannot remember exactly, but I know it was around 9/9.30. Something like that." And: "My memory of it is just after midnight."

When one bears in mind – see earlier – that it would be a normal police investigation procedure to take notes when studying CCTV footage of this nature, the question should be raised: Was Carpenter really getting this information from his memory, or was he just basing it on the known times – order placement – 9.29 p.m.; payment – 11.41 p.m.?

In other words, it is obvious that if the order was placed at 9.29 p.m. then the men could have entered the building sometime after 9.00 p.m. Likewise, with payment at 11.41 p.m., they would leave the Ritz around midnight.

Then MacLeod asks: "Can those times be checked?"

I ask: Who would be checking the times on behalf of the court? And I suggest it would be the MPS officer, Paul Carpenter.

When it gets to the MacLeod-Carpenter assessment of the results of the French investigation on this, once again there are no documents and Carpenter again has no notes. So, not only does Carpenter have nothing in writing about his CCTV analysis, he also has nothing in writing about the results of the French investigation.

---

[a] Carte Bleue, or "blue card", is a French debit card.
[b] The jury were never provided with a hard copy of this and also there is no copy on the inquest website.
[c] Which was up on the screen.
[d] "it was quite a while ago now so I am doing this from memory"; "they could be"; "I think from memory".

MacLeod asks: "Who were the two men?"

Carpenter: "I cannot remember if their surname was Klukker ... or Kukker ... two brothers."

Carpenter states that the French conclusion was that the Klukkers or Kukkers "had bought some expensive cigars and they went to the Ritz to smoke them" and the bags they carried contained "expensive cigars".[ab]

The jury were shown minimal evidence on this – just one witness out of eight cross-examined, and then only a few passing questions; no CCTV footage; no carte bleu slip; no documents from the French investigation.[c]

Yet it is possible evidence of the presence of intelligence officers or agents inside the Ritz Hotel prior to the crash – Tendil said: "I thought it was strange", but wasn't asked to elaborate.

The available witness evidence is that these two men on Table 15 drew attention:

- Tendil: "these people arrived at the same time as the paparazzi and they left when Diana left, so I thought it was strange"
- Willaumez: "Mr Allidiere told [Henri Paul] that at table 15 there were two people being seated looking like paparazzi with jackets and bags"
- Willaumez: "Mr Paul went to see what was happening without speaking to them"
- Allidiere: "[Tendil or Vincent] whispered in my ear that he thought the customers at table number 15 could be paparazzi"
- Allidiere: "I saw men of European appearance aged about 40, of normal height and build"
- Allidiere: "one of them was badly shaven, was wearing a light coloured sleeveless jacket with lots of pockets"
- Allidiere: "there were two plastic bags bearing advertising beneath their chairs"
- Allidiere: "these men were drinking Macallan whisky"
- Allidiere: "these men ... were in a completely normal state, composed and pleasant"

---

[a] Burnett's joke at the end of Carpenter's questioning – "I hope the Perrier water was not poured into the malt whisky" – confirms that the bill for table 15 was on the screen. This fits with Allidiere's account: "These men were drinking Macallan whisky."

[b] At the conclusion of the MacLeod-Carpenter evidence, other lawyers were not given the opportunity to ask Carpenter questions about what they had just heard. See 3 Dec 07: 146.3.

[c] A search of the White Pages for the whole of France reveals that in early 2012 there are no Kukkers or Klukkers in France. The closest is a Kuker in Belfort and there are several Cluckers, but none in Paris.

- Allidiere: "Mr Paul ... [passed] in front of table 15 in order to observe its occupants.... He told me ... that their bags might contain small cameras ... [and] he found them well behaved and that he would see what happened".

There is an apparent conflict. Allidiere and Willaumez[a] both state that the concern on the night was that the two men could have been paparazzi.[b] Whereas at the inquest Tendil indicated that he did not believe that –

Horwell: "You believed that they were linked to the paparazzi, did you?"

Tendil: "No."

It seems likely that after the men left around midnight without attempting to take any photos, that any fear that they were paparazzi could have been dispelled. So even though there was an initial concern that the men could have been paparazzi – Allidiere, Willaumez – it actually turned out that they probably weren't – Tendil.

It could be significant that Tendil "thought it was strange", even though he didn't believe the men were paparazzi.

In the MacLeod-Carpenter evidence – aimed apparently at establishing the identity of the men – there is no mention of the word "paparazzi", but three months later[c] inquest lawyer, Ian Burnett, states: "The two people ... were followed up and we have heard evidence that they were not paparazzi and that they can safely be excluded from our consideration."

The evidence Burnett is referring to was that provided by MacLeod and Carpenter. This indicates that the purpose of that period of cross-examination was to rule out the two men from the list of known paparazzi – even though that was not mentioned by MacLeod or Carpenter at the time.

The context of the MacLeod-Carpenter evidence seems to reveal otherwise. Carpenter appeared to be cross-examined on this topic for two possible reasons: a) a reaction to Tendil's unexpected revelation: "Pictures were taken"[d], and b) after Tendil's cross-examination there was an element of mystery surrounding the two men – Tendil had said he didn't believe "that they were linked to the paparazzi", but he still "thought it was strange".

The MacLeod-Carpenter evidence appears to have been aimed at removing the mystery – identifying the two men and showing that the fact

---

[a] Willaumez was shown in Part 1 to be an unreliable witness, but there does not appear to be any reason for him to lie about this issue.

[b] Allidiere: "[Tendil or Vincent] whispered in my ear that he thought the customers at table number 15 could be paparazzi"; "I went to see Vincent to ask him if he had told [Henri Paul] about the two men who could have been paparazzi". Willaumez: "Mr Allidiere told [Henri Paul] that at table 15 there were two people being seated looking like paparazzi".

[c] Straight after the Allidiere statement was read out.

[d] This has already been mentioned above.

223

"pictures were taken" is true, but is no cause for concern. The word "paparazzi" is not mentioned because that was not the issue – Tendil, the sole witness heard at that stage[a], had already said that he didn't believe "that they were linked to the paparazzi".

As already seen, the MacLeod-Carpenter evidence has no credible basis – no supporting documents; no CCTV footage shown; no notes taken by Carpenter.

Following Allidiere's account Burnett was able to say: "The two people ... were followed up and ... they were not paparazzi" but three months earlier when the "following up" evidence was heard, that was not the issue.[b]

In all of this, there was no following up of: a) Tendil's concern: "I thought it was strange"[c], and b) the other seven witnesses, who were not cross-examined.[d]

The evidence appears to rule out the two men from being paparazzi.

The unsupported evidence from MacLeod and Carpenter shows them to be cigar-smoking guests.[e]

There are three main possibilities:

1) the MacLeod-Carpenter evidence is correct and they have been very clumsy and incompetent in their presentation of it to the court

2) the MacLeod-Carpenter evidence is false[f] but the two men were innocent bar guests oblivious to the events that were occurring that night in the hotel

3) the MacLeod-Carpenter evidence is false and the two men are in some way involved in or observing events, possibly on behalf of an intelligence agency.

There are several points that could be relevant:
-   the two men placed their order at 9.29 p.m.: this is around the time that Diana and Dodi left Dodi's apartment – they arrived at the Ritz around 9.50 p.m.[g]

The men's order was paid up and closed at 11.41 p.m. – this is just after a key phone call between Claude Roulet and Henri Paul and is just over half an hour before the final departure of Diana and Dodi.[h]

---

[a] Willaumez was heard later in December and Allidiere in March the following year.
[b] It was only possible for Burnett to say this because there was so much time distance between hearing Tendil and Allidiere.
[c] Horwell effectively ignored this comment, focusing instead on the paparazzi – "You believed that they were linked to the paparazzi, did you?"
[d] These witnesses were listed earlier.
[e] Carpenter: "They had bought some expensive cigars and they went to the Ritz to smoke them."
[f] Cobbled together in a rush in order to respond to Tendil's surprise evidence.
[g] See Part 1, chapter 2.
[h] These events are covered in Part 1, chapter 3.

This could fit with the men arriving in time to observe events inside the hotel and then leaving in time to observe events outside the hotel, prior to the couple's departure at 12.18 a.m. on 31 August 1997.

The timings appear to basically fit with the account in the *Daily Mail* article which said: "The ... two men ... at first mingled with the crowd outside and then entered the lobby bar of the hotel for a drink.... They ordered several rounds of drinks and remained ... until shortly before midnight".

-   the 2004 *Daily Mail* article was written three years before the evidence about these two men was heard at the inquest.

Allidiere described "men of European appearance aged about 40". The article described "two men who looked in their late 30s".[a]

-   why wasn't Tendil's concern: "I thought it was strange", followed through by police lawyer, Richard Horwell?

Tendil was the only witness cross-examined on this subject – had any of the other seven witnesses been questioned, it is possible similar concerns could have come to light.

It could also be significant that Tendil voiced concern even though he believed the men were not paparazzi, yet three months later Burnett stated to the jury: "they were not paparazzi and that they can safely be excluded from our consideration".

So, concern – "I thought it was strange" – from the eye-witness, Tendil, but no concern – "they can safely be excluded from our consideration" – from the inquest lawyer, Burnett.

-   Carpenter stated that the French investigation found that the men "had bought some expensive cigars and they went to the Ritz to smoke them" and that the bags they carried contained "expensive cigars".

Allidiere said that "these men were drinking Macallan whisky" but there is no indication from any witness that they were smoking cigars.[b] The

---

[a] This is the only direct point of comparison between Allidiere and the *Daily Mail* account. The article states: "Their conversation was constant but very terse" and "they spoke intently and quietly in perfect English", but the inquest accounts do not describe the nature of their conversation at all. Allidiere says: "these men ... were in a completely normal state, composed and pleasant". The demeanour of the men is not mentioned in the article. The article states: "They ordered several rounds of drinks". Allidiere says: "These men were drinking Macallan whisky", without commenting on the quantity drunk or the number of rounds. It is obvious that more of the eight witnesses present and still alive should have been asked about their recollections of the two men.

[b] Ritz Hotel president, Frank Klein, stated in an email to the author that in 1997 "ashtrays were not automatically [on the tables] but were brought by the waiter". This indicates that if the two men were smoking cigars they would have needed to request

225

contents of the bags were unknown.[a] If the men were smoking cigars and the bags contained cigars, it seems likely they would have had to open the bags to access the cigars.

- Allidiere reveals that on the night it is Henri Paul who makes the decision on whether the two men are paparazzi: "I saw Mr Paul ... pretending to be a guest ... passing in front of table 15 in order to observe its occupants.... He told me that he found them well behaved and that he would see what happened."

Part 1 has shown that the evidence points to Henri Paul working on behalf of a second employer on the night, which could have been an intelligence agency. If these men were intelligence officers or agents they may have been known to Henri Paul.

- why was a police lawyer – MacLeod – able to cross-examine his own witness – Carpenter – without any offer of cross-examination to the lawyers from the interested parties[b]?[126]

- Carpenter indicated the men's surname was "Klukker ... or Kukker ... two brothers".

There are no Kukkers or Klukkers in the White Pages for France – see earlier footnote.

- there have been several occasions where Paul Carpenter and Duncan MacLeod have been caught out misleading the inquest – see footnote.[c] Is this another?

---

ash trays. No witness has suggested they did that. Source: Email from Frank Klein to John Morgan, 21 July 2011.
[a] Allidiere said there was "something in them which was not very large and whose shape I could not make out".
[b] For example, Mansfield or Keen.
[c] Carpenter, who spent years on the Paget and inquest police team investigating the crash: a) wrong positioning of the Rat and Darmon motorbike – Part 1, Hotel Crillon Lights section; b) twisting the French motorbike speed test evidence – Part 1, Were the Motorbikes Paparazzi? section; c) undermining the relevance of Alma Tunnel eye-witness evidence – Part 1, Fleeing Motorbikes section; d) misrepresenting the evidence on the Chauvel and Langevin photos – Part 3, Speed Camera section. MacLeod: a) deliberately misrepresented Atholl Johnston's evidence – Part 3, Chapter 3B, Results Analysis section; b) with Forrest, falsely suggested that Henri Paul's BAC result was supported by the CDT result – Part 3, Chapter 4, Validity of the Result section; c) deliberately misrepresented Dominique Mélo's evidence – Part 3, Chapter 5, Drugs Prescribed section; d) deliberately misrepresented Claude Garrec's evidence – Part 3, Chapter 5, Tolerance to Alcohol section; e) misled John Oliver by suggesting Zentel would be addressed – Part 3, Chapter 6, Zentel section; f) misled Allan Jamieson – Part 3, Chapter 7A, Another Body section; g) deliberately misquoted Robert Forrest's evidence to John Oliver – Part 3, Chapter 7B, Effect of Smoking section; h) misrepresented the evidence on Henri Paul's smoking – Part 3, Chapter 7B, Was Henri Paul a Heavy Smoker? section; i) misrepresented the

- the MacLeod-Carpenter evidence is so lacking in credibility – see earlier analysis – that it is difficult to see how the errors could be put down to incompetence alone.

The reality is that even if the MacLeod-Carpenter evidence is correct – that the French did investigate the two men and found them to be cigar-smoking Kukker or Klukker brothers – that may rule them out from being paparazzi, but it could not rule them out from being intelligence agents.

As we know from earlier, things are not always as they seem in intelligence – two men could be sitting at Table 15 in the Ritz Hotel Bar Vendôme working for an intelligence agency, but using a cover as brothers smoking expensive cigars they had just purchased.

Figure 2 Still from Ritz CCTV showing two unidentified persons (at rear) outside the hotel, just around 43 minutes before the departure of the Mercedes S280 carrying Diana and Dodi.

---

evidence on chain of custody for Henri Paul's first autopsy – Part 3, Chapter 8, First Autopsy section; j) misrepresented the evidence on chain of custody for Henri Paul's second autopsy – Part 3, Chapter 8, Second Autopsy section; k) misrepresented the status of LGC – Part 3, Chapter 9, British Testing section; l) misrepresented blood sample label description evidence – Part 3, Chapter 9, Which Samples Were DNA Tested? section.

[a] Carpenter also spent three years working in Operation Paget – 3 Oct 07: 112.2. The result of that operation was the Paget Report – an 832 page document that has been shown to be severely flawed. See the book: *Cover-Up of a Royal Murder: Hundreds of Errors in the Paget Report.*

Place Vendôme

Serge Benhamou, Paparazzo, Paris: 17 Oct 97 Statement read out 10 Mar 08: 58.12:
"I would point out that when talking very recently with [Laslo] Veres[a], we recalled a car with some people in it on the other side of the Place Vendôme. There were often plain clothes police watching the place and I did not pay any particular attention to this on the day. In any event, it was not a Fiat Uno."

Eric Gigou, Brigade Criminelle Lieutenant, Paris: 10 Mar 08: 93.3:
Croxford: Q. Do you know, did anyone make any inquiries to try to establish who might have been sitting in a car in the Place Vendôme as described there by Mr Benhamou?
A. Well, I am just discovering the matter today because obviously until today, I did not have access to this because it was heard by the magistrate. And to my knowledge, there was no investigation concerning those people, or this car.

Laslo Veres, Paparazzo: 22 Oct 97 Statement read out 11 Mar 08: 195.8:
"On the other side of the Place there were some people in a white Renault 21 which had stopped but I do not know who they were."

Comment: This is possible further evidence that events were being observed, maybe by intelligence officers or agents.[b]

The presence of this car was significant enough to Benhamou and Veres that they both raised it in their evidence.

Nevertheless, Gigou was able to avoid dealing with the issue: "until today, I did not have access to this because it was heard by the magistrate".

Gigou also states: "to my knowledge, there was no investigation".

The person who should be able to answer the questions relating to this car is French magistrate, Hervé Stéphan.

---

[a] Fellow paparazzo.
[b] Harrods' Director of Public Affairs, Michael Cole – who has an extensive background in the media – said in his 2006 Paget statement: "An American journalist ... told me that among the continental paparazzi outside Hotel Ritz, there was an unknown British man (I think he said English) who mingled with the media crowd and had camera equipment that looked 'professional'. The Briton was asked: 'Who are you doing it for?' meaning, which publication has assigned you? The stranger replied: 'The *Daily Mirror*'. I know from my own observation and knowledge that no one from the *Daily Mirror* was in Paris that night. I know Kent Gavin, the paper's veteran Royal photographer. Mr. Gavin was not there and if the *Daily Mirror* had sent someone to cover the story, he would have been the man. So, who was the man? It is my supposition that he was not a professional news photographer but was in fact working for the British security services." There is no evidence of the British police investigating this lead and it was left out of the Paget Report and not addressed at the inquest. Source: Michael Cole, Witness Statement, 6 July 2006, pp13-14.

The question is: Why didn't Stéphan ask further questions and investigate this clear evidence from two eye-witnesses?

The next question is: Why did Scott Baker not ask Hervé Stéphan to testify at the inquest into the deaths of Princess Diana and Dodi Fayed?

Other Possible Sightings

Near Alma Tunnel

Sabine Dauzonne: 17 Jan 98 *Hello!* Magazine Interview: **Jury Didn't Hear**: "I remember thinking that if there hadn't been any railings, the driver of the Fiat seemed so lost and out of it that he could have crashed into the three [pedestrians] there at the corner." When asked about the demeanour of the three pedestrians, who would have just heard the crash, Sabine said: "They looked absolutely calm, like typical bystanders." [127]

Comment: Sabine Dauzonne is the only witness to record the presence of these three bystanders.

Other evidence in Part 1 shows that the crash was at high speed and made a huge noise heard by many witnesses in the area.

It could be significant that these three witnesses, who must have also seen the two speeding cars witnessed post-crash by Gary Hunter (see Part 1):

- didn't react – "they looked absolutely calm"
- have apparently never been sought out or interviewed by any of the investigations
- appear to have never come forward as witnesses.[a]

There is a possibility these people were intelligence officers or agents.

MI6 Internet List

In 1999 a list of MI6 officers mysteriously appeared on the internet.
Richard Tomlinson, Ex-MI6 Officer: 2001 Book: **Jury Didn't Hear**: "On 13 May [1999] another site about MI6 appeared on Lyndon Larouche's website, publishing a list of 115 names purporting to be of serving and former MI6 officers. This news exploded onto the front pages of newspapers worldwide.... I was immediately assumed to be the author." [128]
Richard Norton-Taylor, Intelligence Journalist: 13 May 99 *Guardian* Article: **Jury Didn't Hear**:

---

[a] Sabine Dauzonne's evidence is thoroughly covered in Part 1. Her evidence addressed here should be viewed in the light of that fuller account of the events she witnessed.

"Britain's secret intelligence service, MI6, was thrown into unprecedented disarray last night when a renegade former officer published the names of over 100 agents - some said to be false - on the internet.

"The names on the website were provided by Richard Tomlinson, the former MI6 officer now living in Switzerland. Government lawyers were last night frantically trying to close down the site as senior MI6 officers were mounting a desperate damage-limitation exercise.

"Though Mr Tomlinson had recently warned MI6 he would publish the names of his former colleagues on the internet, the first confirmation that he had carried out the threat came in a message to British editors from Rear Admiral David Pulvertaft, secretary of the Defence, Press and Broadcasting Advisory Committee, which advises the media on issues of national security.

"In a message to the Press Association news agency, whose service is used by all national and provincial newspapers, he said: 'I understand that a US-based website has today published on the internet a list which identifies a large number of SIS (MI6) officers.'

"Publishing such details could put lives at risk, he said, adding that Whitehall was examining how 'the damage of this disclosure can be minimised.'

"A foreign office spokesman said it would be 'inappropriate' to comment further since there were 'obvious legal implications.' Though Whitehall did not name Mr Tomlinson as the source, they made clear that in their view he was the culprit....

"One hundred and fifteen individuals are named on the website. Though Whitehall sources described the list as 'a mixture of fact and fantasy,' there is little doubt that it includes a high proportion of MI6 agents who have been engaged in extremely sensitive work. Some may find their careers in the secret services are now untenable....

"Some of the agents named are overseas, while others are based at MI6's headquarters at Vauxhall Cross on the south bank of the Thames, sources told the *Guardian* last night.

"Though individual MI6 agents have been named in the past, this is the first time whole swaths have been named in a medium which is out of control of government lawyers." [129]

Richard Norton-Taylor[a], Intelligence Journalist: 15 May 99 *Guardian* Article: **Jury Didn't Hear**:

"In a BBC radio interview from Switzerland, Mr Tomlinson last night denied he was responsible for placing the names on the internet.

"'A denial might sound a bit thin because I did indeed threaten to put names [on] the internet but I didn't actually do this.' He offered MI6 an examination of his computer and internet service provider records.... Mr Tomlinson said: 'It is not impossible that M16 may have engineered this to discredit me.' MI6

---

[a] Written with David Pallister.

might have been angered because he gave evidence to the judge examining the death of Princess Diana in Paris....

"The foreign office said last night that despite the denial, their position was that 'the balance of probabilities' pointed to Mr Tomlinson being responsible. 'There is no one else in the frame. Even if he did not physically put the names on the internet, there's no real difference if he provided the names for someone else to do it.... To an extent, the cat is out of the bag.'

"Scotland Yard said a police investigation was under way 'in connection with possible breaches of the official secrets act.'

"By last night the list of MI6 officers which includes the name of a son of a former Tory cabinet minister and a Cambridge don alleged to be a recruiter for MI6 had spread through the internet like a virus with dozens of people joining in chat groups to discuss the publication.

"One site was charging for access to see it but it was still freely available on two New York sites, including one of the most popular on the web. This then linked to a site in Denmark where it was also displayed." [130]

Richard Norton-Taylor, Intelligence Journalist: 19 May 99 *Guardian* Article: **Jury Didn't Hear**:

"Robin Cook, the Foreign Secretary, was in no doubt that the list originated from Mr Tomlinson, who, he said, nursed a 'deep-seated and irrational grievance' against his former employers. 'The release of any such list, however inaccurate it may be, is a deeply irresponsible and dangerous act,' Mr Cook said.

"Mr Tomlinson, who now lives in Switzerland, admits placing his affidavit on the Internet, together with the names of nine MI6 officers, but denies putting the 117 names on the EIR[a] site." [131]

Richard Tomlinson, Ex-MI6 Officer: 2001 Book: **Jury Didn't Hear**:

"To this day[b], I do not know who published the famous list, but it was not me. I have my suspicions, however, that it was MI6 themselves. They had a motive – to incriminate and blacken me. They had the means to make the list and the knowledge to post it onto the internet without leaving a trace. And, despite their protestations to the contrary, the list was not particularly damaging to them. Later I got the chance to study it for myself. I did not recognise most of the names and so cannot comment as to whether they were from MI6 or from the FCO. Of the names that I did recognise, all were retired from the service or were already widely blown. If MI6 had set out to produce a list that caused me the maximum incrimination, but caused them the minimum damage, they could not have done a better job.

---

[a] Executive Intelligence Review – the site where the list was initially placed.
[b] Published in 2001.

"The way the existence of the list was publicised to the world's press was also odd. The first announcement was made when the British government's official censor, Rear-Admiral David Pulvertaft, issued a 'D-notice'[a] to stop UK newspapers publishing the web address of the list or any of the names. There was no better way to generate publicity because immediately every journalist in Britain wanted to know what the D-notice was censoring, and foreign newspapers the world over, to whom the D-notice was irrelevant, published the web address and even the entire list. The next peculiarity was the manner in which the FCO announced the incident. If MI6 really wanted to limit the damage, they would have used a junior spokesperson to dismiss the list as a hoax. Instead, British Foreign Secretary Robin Cook announced at a packed news conference that not only was the list accurate but, without presenting a shred of evidence, named me as the culprit. Both these tactics can only be explained by a plan to incriminate and discredit me.

"They certainly succeeded if it was their intention. Until the list was produced, the press had been fairly sympathetic to me. But after Cook's accusation, the media turned on me with vitriol." [132]

Comment: The MI6 officer list can be viewed at:
http://cryptome.org/mi6-list-276.htm

Additional MI6 officer names were posted to the internet in 2005.[b]

It is impossible to prove where this list originated from, but there are some relevant points:

- no one on the list has put their hand up to say they are not an MI6 officer – this indicates that the list is authentic

- due to the secrecy within MI6 – see earlier – it seems unlikely that anyone but a very senior officer could be certain of the identity of so many other MI6 officers, stationed all over the world

- Robin Cook has been shown to have lied on other issues – see earlier in this volume

- although it was reported in 1999 that "Scotland Yard said a police investigation was under way" into "possible breaches of the Official Secrets Act", nothing appeared to materialise, even though a release of such a large number of MI6 officer names would appear to be a clear breach of the act.

When these points are viewed in the context of Richard Tomlinson's denials, it does seem possible that this MI6 officer list was posted onto the internet by MI6.

---

[a] This is a notice issued by the government that is advisory, but not mandatory.
[b] These are included in the lists on the given website address.

Movements of MI6 Officers

The evidence will show there were a significant number of MI6 officers in Paris at the time of the crash.

The movements of these officers in the days and weeks leading up to the assassination of Princess Diana and Dodi Fayed is of crucial importance in determining the level of involvement by MI6.

Michael Jay, British Ambassador to France, 1996-2001, Paris: 11 Feb 08: 95.25:

Burnett: Q. It is certainly common knowledge for the purposes of these proceedings and more generally that within the Embassy in France there were people from the Secret Intelligence Service. If you forgive me, I will call them "MI6".

A. Yes.

Q. Was there anybody there, as far as you can recollect, also from MI5?

A. As I recollect, there was a member of MI5 who was also in Paris at that time, yes.

Q. On secondment to MI6 or not? Maybe it does not matter.

A. I cannot remember the exact circumstances, but there was a representative of MI5 working in the Embassy, yes.

....Q. Your statement ... where you said this: "There was such a team [that is referring to MI6] at the British Embassy in Paris, staffed by members of the SIS and one member of the security service." So that would seem to have been your recollection in 2005 and something no doubt you checked about before saying?

A. That was my recollection at the time. That I believe to be the case.

At 117.14: Mansfield: Q. At the time, in August 1997, did you know how many personnel were engaged by MI6 in your Embassy?

A. I would know the senior members of the SIS station, not necessarily some others. I do not think I could, at the time, have answered the question "How many are there?"

Q.... The answer therefore is that you did not know how many people were engaged in the security services based in your Embassy in August 1997?

A. I would not have known. I would not have been able to answer that question about that or any of the other sections of the Embassy.

Q. No, I am concentrating not on other sections, just this section, in terms of really getting to grips with how much you would have known and did know.... Were you aware of how many were declared and how many were undeclared?

A. I am, sir, in a position to answer that question[a], but I would prefer not to unless instructed to do so because I think it breaches the terms in which we normally deal with intelligence matters.[b]

At 128.16: Q. The Diplomatic List.... Is it right to say that the [1998] list that we have in front of us does contain names of those who work for the security services?

A. It contains the lists of those who worked in all sections of the Embassy, including the [MI6] station, yes.

Q. But you cannot tell from the list ... which ones they are, can you?

A. No, you cannot. It is extremely important that members of the security services, who carry out very important, often dangerous and very difficult tasks on behalf of this country, are able to do so under the cloak of anonymity and confidentiality, otherwise they would not be able to protect us in the way we need to be protected –

Coroner: It would destroy the whole purpose of the thing.

A. It would destroy the whole purpose of having the security services.

Q. It is built on – and there is no particular secret – it is built on authorised deceit, as it were, isn't it?

A. I would have said it is based on a common-sense approach to ensuring that people who are doing difficult and dangerous tasks on our behalf are able to continue doing so without being compromised.

Q. What was the question, Lord Jay?

A. I am afraid I cannot remember the question, sir.

Coroner: The question was: was it authorised deceit?

Q. Yes. It is a very straightforward question I want to put to you that it has to be authorised deceit; in other words, the person who reads the [diplomatic] list is not given any indication of who is doing what.... That is right?

---

[a] There appears to be a conflict – Jay says: "I do not think I could, at the time, have answered the question 'How many [MI6 officers] are there?'", yet also states that he is "in a position to answer ... how many [MI6 officers] were declared and how many were undeclared".

[b] There is an interesting section of cross-examination between Mansfield, Jay, Tam and Baker regarding disclosure of declared – known to the host country, France – and undeclared – not known – MI6 officers. It can be viewed on the inquest website, starting at 118.10. It is not included here but the subject is covered in testimony from Richard Tomlinson below. It has already been shown in Part 3 that the French authorities were deeply involved in the huge cover-up starting from within a few minutes after the crash. There is evidence pointing to, at the least, prior French knowledge of the crash. It will be shown later that it would have been impossible for MI6 to carry out this operation without French complicity or involvement. In this environment it seems likely that the MI6 officers would have been declared to the French and that is the evidence that the inquest heard.

Coroner: Mr Mansfield, surely there is a difference between deliberately misleading and, on the other hand, supplying limited information.

Q. I think it is called "economic with the truth". I will not argue the difference between the two. You do appreciate the point that I am putting to you?

A. I am not entirely clear I do, to be honest, no.

Q. Let's deal with an agent working in Paris. Is he going to go around using his own name? Is an agent working for MI6 in Paris going to go around using his own name or is he given a false identity to do a certain task that he may have to do, in principle?

A. Sir, I do not think I should get into discussions about the operations of the Secret Intelligence Services.

Coroner: This is getting into the operational mode of MI6, isn't it, Mr Mansfield?

Q. It is, only in principle though.

A. It is always extremely difficult to balance the need for openness and transparency, such as the legitimate public interest in publishing documents of this kind and the need to maintain certain degrees of confidentiality, and this list achieves that balance, it seems to me, in a sensible and proper way.[a]

....Q. One of the functions of MI6 ... was to collect information from informants in France, Paris in particular, wasn't it?

A. I am not going to answer questions – I do not think I should answer questions – about the operations of the MI6 station in Paris. I have answered questions about the structure and the governance and my relationship with the head of the station. I do not think I should go beyond that.

....Q. Lord Jay, the security services in fact are not really responsible to you; they are responsible to headquarters in London, aren't they?

A. The relationship is exactly the same as with other sections of the Embassy. For their ordinary day-to-day work they would report back to their headquarters in London, just as the commercial section would report back to the Department of Trade or the agricultural attaché would report back to the Ministry of Agriculture. But when there were major issues which arose, they would be brought to my attention and I had overall responsibility for the conduct of the Embassy as a whole, all the different sections in it, including

---

[a] Michael Jay was speaking in February 2008. He neglected to tell the inquest that in 2006 the FCO made a decision to stop any further publications of the Diplomatic Service List – a book that had been published annually for the last 155 years. It may not be a coincidence that 2006 was also the year in which the British police investigation into the Paris crash was completed. It will be shown later that a forensic analysis of the Diplomatic Lists reveals key information on MI6 Paris personnel movements.

the MI6 station. But of course, yes, their day-to-day operations were conducted through their headquarters and on the instructions of their headquarters in London.

Coroner: If anything came to your notice that for whatever reason you did not approve of, whether in the MI6 section or any of the other sections for which you were ultimately responsible in Paris, I take it that you would have taken it up with headquarters in London?

A. I would have done. I would have done, and on occasions that did happen and I did.

Coroner: If you could not get satisfaction out of the head of section on the spot.

A. Yes, yes.

Q. That is all premised on the fact that somebody tells you, isn't it?

A. It is premised on the fact that I have a relationship of trust with those working for me and that I trust what they say to me, yes. That is true for the head of that section as for other sections of the Embassy, which is the basis on which I tried to manage the Embassy.

Charles Ritchie, Military Attaché British Embassy, Paris: 12 Feb 08: 148.15:

Mansfield: Q. During that time therefore that you were working based at the Embassy, were you familiar with people who worked for the security services there?

A. I had met one or two people who I knew were in the security services, but this is a subject clearly that I do not feel comfortable to talk about.

Q. I am only asking you – don't worry, you are not going to be asked anything, if you know anything about it – how much did you know about that work there? Did you know a lot or a little?

A. I think a little is the answer.

Richard Tomlinson, Ex-MI6 Officer: 13 Feb 08: 105.17:

Mansfield: Q. In a foreign embassy which houses an MI6 or SIS station, is it right that there are declared and undeclared operatives at that station?

A. That is correct. That is correct. Depending on the station, but that is, in general, correct.

Q. Again I pause. Does that mean that the ones who are undeclared are undeclared to the host nation? That is fine. You can answer that one.

A. That is the case, yes. That is correct.

.... Q. Are those responsible for agent-handling amongst the undeclared?

Tam: That question is okay as it is.

Q.... Would the people or persons responsible for agent-handling be amongst the declared or the undeclared?

A. They could be amongst either.

Q. I will ask a specific question. Do you happen to know in relation to the Paris Embassy?

Coroner: No, I think you have gone too far now.

Michael Jay: 13 Dec 05 Statement: **Jury Didn't Hear**:[a]

"I have been asked whether I had overall responsibility for MI5 and/or Secret Intelligence Service deployments in Paris during my role as the British Ambassador to France. Many of the UK's overseas posts have a number of intelligence officers of the Secret Intelligence Service (SIS) seconded to the post. There may also be officers of the Security Service [MI5] on attachment.

"There was such a team or station at the British Embassy in Paris, staffed by members of the SIS and one member of the Security Service, who were engaged for example in liaison work with the French authorities in relation to such matters as counter-terrorism and in tackling organised/international crime. I was kept informed by means of regular briefings and reporting about the matters in which they were involved. As Ambassador I had overall responsibility for their conduct, so that for example I should expect to be informed of any significant complaint by the French authorities about their work. I should also expect to be briefed by the Head of the SIS station or his representative about any particular operation that was of an unusual and/or sensitive nature so that I should have the opportunity to comment.

I have been asked how the command structure of both MI5 and the SIS linked to me as Ambassador. The Secret Intelligence Service is separate from the FCO but operates under the umbrella of the FCO and is answerable for its activities to the Foreign Secretary. Although members of the SIS stationed abroad with the post receive their instructions from SIS headquarters in London, there are close liaison arrangements between the SIS and the FCO ensuring that the SIS operates in accordance with principles and policies laid down by the FCO. At the same time, as I have already mentioned, the Head of Post[b] is routinely kept aware of the general activities of the SIS personnel stationed with the post, including any member of the Security Service on attachment, so that their activities are monitored at two levels: at FCO and post level. I am entirely satisfied that no significant operation would have been managed from the Paris Embassy, or by the SIS personnel stationed there, without my knowledge. I have already mentioned that I should expect to be informed of any operation of an unusual and/or sensitive nature.

"It was not my role to give the SIS officers stationed at the British Embassy in Paris specific instructions. These instructions they would receive from SIS headquarters in London. I should however expect to be kept broadly

---

[a] Although the jury didn't hear or have Jay's statement, some of the same material was covered in Ian Burnett's cross-examination – excerpts from that are included in the British Embassy chapter, see section on Role of Michael Jay.

[b] The Ambassador.

informed of the nature of their instructions at regular briefing meetings and I would comment as I saw fit.

"I have been asked if I recall whether any MI5 or SIS officers were deployed in Paris during the weekend of 30/08/1997 to 31/08/1997 and if this was the case, who the individual(s) were. I am not aware that any MI5 or MI6 officers, in which description I would include both SIS officers and any persons working with them or on their behalf, had been deployed in Paris during the weekend of 30/31st August 1997." [133]

Comment: Michael Mansfield asked Jay a simple question: "Did you know how many personnel were engaged by MI6 in your Embassy?"

Jay answered: "I would not have known." Then added: "I would not have been able to answer that question about that [MI6] or any of the other sections of the Embassy."

Table 1 – shown later in this chapter – lists and ranks all the department personnel in the Paris embassy around the time of the crash. It reveals that there were about 40 staff listed.

That is not a huge number of staff to be responsible for. I suggest that it seems odd, given that Jay was in charge of the embassy at the time, that he wouldn't know the approximate numbers of staff in each specific department.

It will be shown later – and it has already been seen in Part 4 – that Jay has lied in parts of his evidence proffered in this case.

It is in his interest to be able to distance himself from the activities of MI6 conducted in his embassy. I suggest that part of that is his indicated lack of knowledge of the numbers of personnel.

It will be shown later in this book that the evidence points to MI6 being involved in the crash and it will become increasingly likely that Michael Jay would have been aware.

Richard Spearman and Nicholas Langman

The evidence regarding Richard Spearman and Nicholas Langman is particularly significant because they are the only two named MI6 officers who were alleged to be on the ground in Paris on the night of the crash.

It has been suggested that they could have been involved.

Michael Jay, British Ambassador to France, 1996-2001, Paris: 11 Feb 08: 82.14:

Burnett: Q. There has been public speculation and suggestion that two of your first secretaries had posting dates that were somehow suspicious. Is that something you are aware of?

A. I am aware of that allegation, yes.

Q. And the two first secretaries concerned are Mr Spearman and Mr Langman. Now, we are going to be hearing shortly a statement read from Susan Le Jeune.... She explains that there is simply nothing in that at all, and that is your understanding as well?

A. That is my understanding. That was the case, yes.

Michael Mansfield, QC for Al Fayed: 11 Feb 08: 116.4:

"The published Diplomatic List.... This is for 1998.... 'Mr Spearman, First Secretary, Political', underneath Mr Moss' name. 'First Secretary Economics, Mr Langman'."

Susan Le Jeune d'Allegeershecque, FCO Personnel Dept, UK: 17 Dec 07 Statement read out 11 Feb 08: 158.18:

"There is attached to my statement an annex consisting of a ten-page bundle of documents including, at pages 1 and 6, two documents both entitled 'Overseas posting notification'. An overseas posting notification sets in train the process for posting an officer overseas. All the documents in the bundle were retrieved from the files of the British Embassy in Paris.

"The first document is a copy of the overseas posting notification for Nicholas Langman. It is dated 18th May 1994.... The copy of the document in the bundle has a number of small redactions to remove irrelevant detail such as the name of an official.... There are similar small redactions in the copies of other documents in the bundle.... The date of arrival at the new post of Paris is scheduled to be 1st October 1994 for a period of two plus two years, that is, a total of four years, with mid-tour leave after two years. In fact, Mr Langman departed from Paris on 27th August 1998....

"The document at page 6 is the overseas posting notification for Richard Spearman. This form was produced by a computer and is dated 18th December 1996. The form ... shows the grade DS5[a] and the 'Margin' designation for the period 1st April 1997 to 30th June 1997.[b] (Although the form describes this as 'present posting', the computer system is in fact set up to record the post immediately preceding the overseas posting).[c] The date of arrival at the new post in Paris is scheduled to be 1 July 1997 for a period of two plus two years.... There are several manuscript annotations. The first is dated 23/12/1996 by an official in 'PG1, PMD', which stands for postings group 1, personnel management department. There are also manuscript annotations in the top right-hand corner and what appears to be a date '9/i' which I take to mean 9th January The exhibit bundle also includes a letter dated 23rd March 1997 from Mr Spearman to the management counsellor at the Paris Embassy about accommodation and a reply from the Embassy dated 5th April 1997. There are also documents relating to the transport of heavy

---

[a] Diplomat Service Grade 5.

[b] In another part of the statement Le Jeune says: "Each job in the Foreign and Commonwealth Office has [a] slot code and when an officer is between jobs, for example taking end of tour leave, maternity leave or undergoing language training, the interior designation is 'Margin'."

[c] It is not known what Le Jeune means by this and it was not explained.

baggage and to travel details, showing that these were arranged in the middle of August 1997.

"It was the practice of the Foreign and Commonwealth Office in the relevant period (1994 to 1997) and remains the practice to schedule the posting of officers well in advance and the attached overseas posting notifications are in accordance with this practice. The purpose of arranging postings well in advance is to allow proper business planning for posts overseas as well as to allow officers to make the necessary arrangements for language training , transport of heavy baggage, accommodation, schooling and so forth. This process can be seen in the other documents relating to Mr Langman and Mr Spearman."

Burnett: She goes on to say: "I believe that the facts stated in this witness statement are true", and then signs it.

Coroner: Well, now, Mr Burnett, what are we going to do about the clip of documents, the ten pages? They really add I think nothing of consequence to the statement, do they, except that they support what it says?

Burnett: Sir, I was not proposing to read them out and it would be a laborious and fairly meaningless exercise.

Coroner: It does not seem to me to serve any purpose in either reading them out or putting them into the jury bundle, but they are there if anyone wants them at any stage.

Burnett: Well, all the interested persons have had the documents and, as you say, sir, they support the narrative that one finds in Mrs le Jeune d'Allegeershecque's statement.[a]

---

[a] This is an interesting little discussion between Baker and Burnett, possibly even premeditated. They appear to be convincing themselves – and by extension the court and jury – there is no need for key documents to be read out or put "into the jury bundle". They conclude that "the interested persons have had the documents" and it is unnecessary for the jury to see them. Baker tries to make it sound okay by adding: "they are there if anyone wants them at any stage". In other words, a member of the jury would have had to specifically ask to see them. These are important documents relating to the movements of Spearman and Langman. Spearman's documents are of particular significance because he is an alleged suspect in the orchestration of the crash and it has been shown that he arrived in Paris on 26 August 1997, just 5 days ahead of the assassinations. Baker also states that the 10 pages of documents "really add I think nothing of consequence to the statement, do they". This needs to be viewed in the light of the fact that although Le Jeune's statement was read out by Burnett – as with all statements read out – copies were not provided to the jury. The point here is it is common knowledge that intelligence agencies are masters at creating false documentation, so any document that helps provide an alibi for an MI6 suspect in the deaths would need to be subjected to independent forensic scrutiny. There is no evidence of that occurring in the case of these critical documents – they appear to have been accepted at face value and not even passed on to the jury who were expected to be drawing conclusions regarding the deaths.

Mohamed Al Fayed, Dodi's Father: 18 Feb 08: 42.12:

Coroner: You said a little earlier that you would expose the gangsters who killed Diana and your son. Would you like to explain who you believe that those gangsters were?

A. The gangsters are the members of MI6 which Richard Tomlinson has told me and he mentioned in his witnesses. A person called [Langman][a] and Spearman. Spearman was the person –

Burnett: Wait a minute, Mr Al Fayed. We have had evidence read that was uncontroversial[b] –

A. Yes, fine.

Burnett: You will remember that there was a suggestion made at one stage that there was something suspicious about the posting by the Foreign Office of those two people to the Embassy in Paris, but that point has gone, hasn't it? That evidence was read by agreement –

A. As a team, they worked together. They had –

Burnett: Without naming names, if you would be so kind....[c]

At 150.8: A.... My son being murdered by MI6, and the two officers of MI6 are [Langman] and Spearman. They have been there. Spearman was senior assistant to Spedding, the head of MI6, and the documents – and the proof is lying in MI6.

At 179.1: Coroner: Q. One final matter I want your help about: do you think that there is any possibility, however remote, that your beliefs about a conspiracy might be wrong and that the deaths of Diana and Dodi were in truth no more than a tragic accident; any possibility?

A. No way. 100 per cent. I am certain..... I am fighting unbelievable forces. How can I get to the truth? But with your power as a judge sitting there, you had to force MI6 to open their box and find that result. This is exactly what happened, and the two people who have committed and organised it, [Langman] and Spearman. Right? And Spedding was the number one who was in charge. He was assigned Spearman, who was his own personal chief of staff, and he was in Paris organising/executing the whole plan. This is what happened. If you can help me to find the truth, I still believe in your commitment and your judgment and your firmness as a judge, try to force that.

Coroner: Opening Remarks: 3 Oct 07: 75.3:

---

[a] Throughout his testimony Mohamed incorrectly referred to Nicholas Langman as "Langham".

[b] Burnett appears to be referring to the evidence of Susan Le Jeune. There are issues surrounding that evidence that are addressed later.

[c] Burnett changed the subject here – this is discussed in the next Comment. For context see 18 Feb 08: 43.4.

"The question of the appointment and recall of diplomats accredited to the British Embassy in Paris is something that can be and has been checked. Tomlinson named two such people who were accredited, Richard Spearman and Nicholas Langman, as being people whose arrival at or departure from the embassy was suspicious, given the dates involved and Tomlinson's belief that each was an MI6 officer. He suggested that one had been suddenly recalled to London before the end of his term and the other had been deployed only very shortly before the crash.

"Mr Spearman did indeed arrive in Paris very shortly before the crash, but Tomlinson may have overlooked the fact that diplomatic appointments are usually decided upon many months before they are taken up, and so, it would appear, was the case with Mr Spearman. The evidence suggests that his appointment was made in the autumn in 1996 and from May 1997 he was receiving training, including language training, to prepare for the posting. He arrived on Tuesday 26th August.

"If the detail of his posting and training is correct, then it is very difficult to see that there is anything in this point at all. Evidence will be called on the matter. Similarly, the investigation on behalf of the coroner by the Metropolitan Police has shown that Mr Langman did not leave his posting in Paris suddenly, but stayed on until its completion.

"To be entirely fair to Tomlinson, in recent discussions he has suggested that he did no more than suggest that the movements of these two individuals was 'curious'. It may be that he now accepts that there is nothing in this point at all, but it will, nevertheless, need to be covered in evidence, if only because it has been represented repeatedly as part of the foundation of the MI6 involvement."

Keith Moss, British Consul General, Paris: 22 Nov 07: 48.7:

Mansfield: Q. [1998 Diplomatic List][a] Right after your name is: First Secretary, political, Mr RD Spearman, and then another political one and then another political one; in fact, five or six politicals, several economics and so on.

A. Yes.

Q. Yes?

A. Yes, probably, if it is there.

Q. Did you know Mr Spearman?

A. I do not recall him.

Q. Don't you?

A. No, to be honest. I don't remember him.[b]

---

[a] Reproduced below.

[b] I suggest this would seem to be unlikely, unless Moss is suffering from an unusual case of early-onset memory loss – at the time of cross-examination Moss was age 61. It will be shown later that the fact that Moss and Spearman are shown right next to each other in the Diplomatic List – both 1998 (quoted by Mansfield) and 1999 –

Q. Richard Spearman?

A. No.

Q. Posted a few days before the crash to Paris. Did you know that?

A. No, I didn't.

Q. You didn't.

Nicholas Gargan, British Police Liaison with French Investigation, Paris: 13 Dec 07: 29.7:

Mansfield: Q. Did you have occasion to liaise with various people at the Embassy beside the Ambassador?

A. Yes.

Q. Does a Mr Spearman or that name mean anything to you?

Johnson:[a] Sir, I am sorry to interrupt my learned friend. Sir, as you know, I am Mr Johnson and I represent the interests of the Secret Intelligence Service. I am a little concerned about the direction that the cross-examination is now taking. As you are aware, sir, it is the long-standing and well-established policy of the Government not publicly to reveal the identities of those who work for the Secret Intelligence Service. Mr Mansfield is now seeking to put specific names to this witness to ask whether this witness liaised with individual people and what their role is. I would invite you not to permit that cross-examination.

Coroner: Well, Mr Mansfield, I think the position is that the Secret Intelligence Service will never either confirm or deny whether any particular individual was employed by them and I think you had better be careful in the way that you phrase your questions.

Q. Which I was. If I may say so, it is a premature intervention. I was not going to connect that name with anything. I first of all wanted to know whether you liaised with him –

A. I do not think I can answer that question.

Johnson: The names –

Coroner: Sorry, two people were speaking at once.[b] You said?

A. I do not think I can answer that question.

Johnson: Sir, the point I was going to make is that if it is not my learned friend's aim to connect the name with anything, then the name is irrelevant and the line of questioning should not be developed.

Coroner: Would you like to approach this from another direction, Mr

---

indicates they had a similar ranking within the embassy. Both were first secretaries and both were there between 26 August 1997 and April 2000 – 2 years and 8 months. There are only about 40 diplomatic staff in the embassy at any one time. Source: Diplomatic Service List 1999, p34.

[a] MI6 lawyer – Jeremy Johnson.

[b] Apparently Johnson and Gargan.

Mansfield?

Q. Certainly. The British Embassy contained within its, as it were, parameters – physical, I mean – the security services, did it not?

A. Yes, it contained representation –

Q. You can say that –

A. – from the Secret Intelligence Service, yes.

Q. It is in the public domain that there were MI6 officers based there and Security Service MI5 officer or officers based there.

A. Yes.

Q. Right. Unless there is objection, I merely want to ask you whether you liaised with them.

A. I did, yes.

At 34.12: Q. In the Diplomatic List – you may not know, but I can perhaps check with you – Cowper-Coles is heading the political branch of the Embassy, is he not? He is the senior one.

A. Yes.

Q. Under him, in fact, comes a first secretary, Mr Moss, and a first secretary, Mr Spearman, as listed. You knew that?

A. Again, I am moving into difficult territory, sir, and if you don't mind, I do not think I can answer that question.

Q. Well, it is in the public domain and I am not suggesting anything more than the list contains all of these names. There are more names than these.

A. I have never seen the list. If you show me the list, I can confirm what the list says, but I have not seen the list.

Q. No. I am putting it to you so that it might remind you about what the position was in 1997, at least what you knew about it. This gentleman –

A. My answer is, though, if you are asking me to confirm what is on a list because it is self-evident, then if you show me the list, I will try to help. But if you want me to go beyond what is on the list, I fear that I might move into difficult territory.

Q. It has some writing on, but there is [the] list. It is [a] photocopy.... I think it is at the bottom of the page there.

A. Yes, I can see you have highlighted "Mr KC Moss" and "Mr RD Spearman".

Q. I have not highlighted Mr Cowper-Coles, but if you look further up, he is at the top there.

A. You have and, yes, he is there too.

Ambassador: Sir Michael Jay KCMG
Minister: Mr S F Howarth
Defence/Air Attaché: Air Commodore P H
Eustace, RAF
Naval Attaché: Captain D J Thompson, RN
Military Attaché: Brigadier A C I Gadsby
Counsellor (Political): Mr S L Cowper-Coles, CMG,
LVO
Counsellor (Finance and Economic): Dr V Caton
Counsellor (TPI): Mr R J Codrington
Counsellor (Management): Mr M A Price, LVO
Counsellor (Cultural) (British Council Director):
Ms C Gamble
Counsellor (Technology): Dr M A Darnbrough
First Secretary and Consul-General: Mr K C Moss
First Secretary (Political): Mr R D Spearman
First Secretary (Political): Mr C Roberts
First Secretary (Political/Internal): Mrs C H
Copley
First Secretary (Political): Mr A N S Wightman
First Secretary (Political): Mr G J Hendry, OBE
First Secretary (Economic): Mr P J E Raynes
First Secretary (Commercial): Mr S S Calder
First Secretary (Economic): Mr R D Fitchett
First Secretary (Economic): Mr N J A Langman
First Secretary (Labour): Ms M M L Hartwell
Cultural Attache (British Council Deputy
Director): Mr D H Jackman
First Secretary (Agriculture): Mrs E M Morris
First Secretary: Mr D O Hay-Edie
First Secretary (PPA): Mr T L Livesey
First Secretary/Defence Equipment: Mr J C Palmer
First Secretary /Defence Procurement: Mr R C B
Little
First Secretary (Management): Mr R C Woodward
First Secretary and Consul: Miss A M Cowley
Assistant Air Attaché: Wing Commander S
Gunner, RAF
Second Secretary (Political): Mr H E Powell
Second Secretary (Technical): Mr R M Hardy
Second Secretary (Technology): Mr K Shannon
Private Secretary: Mr P C Johnston
Third Secretary: Miss E M Doherty
Third Secretary (Management): Ms S M Weeks
Third Secretary (Information): Ms C S Rowett
Visits Officer: Mr S P Ferrand
Third Secretary (Commercial): Mr W C Kelly

Figure 3

Excerpt showing the Paris Embassy personnel section of the 1998
Diplomatic List – listing diplomatic staff present in September
1997. Richard Spearman is listed as a "First Secretary (Political)"
directly under Keith Moss, who was also a First Secretary.
Nicholas Langman appears as a "First Secretary (Economics). This
also is shown on the inquest website: INQ0049222.

DIANA INQUEST: WHO KILLED PRINCESS DIANA?

Paget Report, p766: **Jury Didn't Hear**:

"In support of his claim relating to Richard Spearman, Richard Tomlinson wrote to Judge Hervé Stéphan on 19 November 1998 (French Dossier D6951-D6953) stating that: 'The 1998 British 'Diplomatic Service List' shows that Richard David Spearman was posted to the British Embassy in Paris, just before the incident at the Pont d'Alma, as the number two MI6 officer in France. I do not believe it a coincidence that Mr Spearman should arrive in Paris only a few weeks before the incident at the Pont d'Alma. I enclose photocopies of the relevant pages of the 1998 "Diplomatic List.'

"The British Diplomatic Service List 1998 referred to by Richard Tomlinson showed: 'First Secretary (Political): Mr R D Spearman, not as Richard Tomlinson claimed 'the number two MI6 officer in France'. This is an interpretation Richard Tomlinson has put on the list.

"The British Diplomatic Service List 1998 also showed: First Secretary (Economic): Mr N J A Langman."

Paget Report, p767: **Jury Didn't Hear**:

"Richard Spearman applied for, and was successful in obtaining a post in Paris in autumn 1996. From May 1997 he received pre-posting training, including language training, as is common practice (and incidentally as described by Richard Tomlinson). He moved to Paris on Tuesday 26 August 1997 to begin a four-year posting, following a holiday abroad....

"Richard Spearman's eventual arrival in Paris following his pre-posting training (26 August 1997) occurred before it was generally known that Dodi Al Fayed and the Princess of Wales would be in Paris on the weekend of 30 August 1997."

Paget Report, p830: **Jury Didn't Hear**:

"Claim [by Richard Tomlinson]: 'Richard Spearman in particular was an extremely well connected and influential officer because he had been prior to his appointment in Paris the personal secretary to the Chief of MI6 David Spedding. I believe that there may well be significance in the fact that Mr Spearman was posted to Paris in the month immediately before the deaths.'"

Paget's Answer: "Richard Spearman had been posted to the British Embassy in Paris almost a year earlier. After a course of language training and other routine preparation for working in France, he arrived in Paris in the days before the collision. There is no significance in this routine posting arranged in 1996."

Mr 6 aka Richard Spearman, MI6 Officer. British Embassy, Paris: 29 Feb 08: 53.2:

Burnett: Q. It is right, isn't it, that you were in Paris on the weekend of 30th and 31st August 1987[a]?

A. I was.

Q. And you were a member of SIS?

A. Indeed I was.

Q. Prior to your going to Paris, is it right that you had occupied a central position within SIS that put you at the heart of policy making?

A. Yes, indeed. That is exactly right. I occupied a central position, a position of trust, at the centre of the organisation.

Q. Now I would like to ask you first about 30th August 1997. Are you able to tell us what you were doing on the evening of 31st August?

A. My wife and I were out at dinner.

Q. Is it right that the restaurant you were at was the Bistro d'a Côte?

A. Yes, it was the Bistro d'a Côte.

Q. Forgive my appalling pronunciation. You were able to verify that even in 2005 because you had a credit card statement that showed that?

A. I am afraid I am one of those who does not throw away their credit card statements, and so when I was asked for it, I was able to produce it.

Q. Had you left your children at home with a babysitter?

A. I had indeed.

Q. Was it right that this was the first occasion that you had used that particular babysitter and so you did not stay out very late?

A. Indeed, and they were young children so we did not want to leave them for too long.

Q. Are you able to now remember at what time you got back to your home in Paris?

A. I have given it some thought. I think it was somewhere between 10.30 and 11.15, something like that. It was certainly before midnight.

Q. At that stage, had you become aware that the Princess and Dodi Al Fayed were in Paris?

A. No, I had no idea at all.

Q. Did you know, before they came to Paris, that they were coming to Paris?

A. The first time I was aware of it was on the Sunday morning, when I learned of the crash.

Q. What were the circumstances on the Sunday morning in which you learned of the crash?

A. We had been disturbed by our children, who wanted us to get up. I went through to turn the television on, and I was aware, as soon as I turned the television on, of sombre music and coverage of a car crash, and it became clear quickly that it involved the Princess of Wales.

Q. Presumably, given that you turned the television on in the morning, it also

---

[a] This should read "1997".

was immediately apparent that both Dodi Al Fayed and the Princess had died as well as their driver, Henri Paul?

A. Indeed, yes.

Q. On that Sunday, so that is Sunday 31st August 1997, did you make any contact with the British Embassy?

A. I did not, no.

Q. Did you go into work on the Monday morning, so that is 1st September?

A. I did, yes.

Q. Did you take part in a regular meeting with the Ambassador?

A. There was a morning meeting which the Ambassador called for, I think, all UK-based staff to explain what had happened and to make dispositions for the week ahead, yes.

.... Q. Before the crash, had you ever heard of Henri Paul?

A. I had not, no.

Q. Had you any professional dealing with any Ritz Hotel staff in Paris?

A. I had no dealings at all with any Ritz Hotel staff in Paris. In fact, I never visited the hotel during my four years in Paris.

At 57.14: Mansfield: Q. You were asked about the Ritz Hotel. Now, as far as that is concerned, your principal opportunity for that to arise comes after the crash rather than before it, doesn't it? Is that a fair observation?

A. I am sorry, I am not quite sure I understand where you are going with that.

Q. If I spell it out, there will be a problem. So that is why I am putting –

A. I think – maybe I can help. I can confirm that neither before nor after the crash, nor at any time, did I have any dealings with anybody or indeed visit the Ritz Hotel in Paris.

Q. Of course, the prime period might be before the crash.

A. The same is true.

Q. I appreciate that. But so you see why I am asking it, the question is how much time before the crash you would have had. Do you follow?

A. I do. I do follow –

Q. That is why I am treading very carefully.

A. I can see that. From my perspective, the answer I think remains the same, both before I arrived in Paris, when I was in Paris and since. There has been no point at which I had contact with anybody –

Q. I am less interested for obvious reasons – although I can do it retrospectively, in other words, the period afterwards.

Paget Report, pp765, 767, 769: **Jury Didn't Hear**:

"Richard Tomlinson, in his evidence to Judge Stéphan ... claimed that Nicholas Langman had completed half of his three year posting in Paris and was suddenly recalled to England a few weeks after the accident. Richard Tomlinson stated that it was extremely rare for someone to be recalled before the end of their posting as there was a major investment involved; for example they would have undergone an eight-month French course. Although Richard Tomlinson did not name Nicholas Langman in this particular evidence it was clear he was referring to him and not Richard Spearman, as he was very specific about his claim of Richard Spearman's posting dates as described above." [134]

"The British Diplomatic Service List produced in January 1997, which is a publicly available document, showed Nicholas Langman at the British Embassy, Paris as First Secretary, (Economic) since October 1994. He left, as scheduled, after four years to return to London in August 1998....

"Richard Spearman and Nicholas Langman have provided signed statements to Operation Paget. Corroborating statements have been obtained. Official communications and other supporting documents seen by Operation Paget support those statements." [135]

"The statement that Nicholas Langman had completed half of his three year posting and was *'suddenly'* recalled to England a few weeks after the crash is factually incorrect." [136]

Richard Tomlinson, Ex-MI6 Officer: 28 Aug 98 Statement:[a] **Jury Didn't Hear**:

Tomlinson: "At the time of the accident the number two of the Paris outstation of MI6 had just completed half of his three year posting to Paris, but a few weeks after the accident he was suddenly recalled to England."

Paget Comment: "Richard Tomlinson is believed to be referring to either Richard Spearman or Nicholas Langman, the British Embassy staff he has named in other documents. He is wrong about the facts relating to the postings of both men. There is no evidence to support this claim."

Tomlinson: "It is extremely rare for someone to be recalled before the end of their posting as it represents a major investment. The person concerned had for example been on an eight-month French course, as had his wife."

Paget Comment: "All of the evidence available supported Nicholas Langman and Richard Spearman's statements that their postings to the British Embassy were entirely in keeping with normal procedures. Neither person was recalled before the end of their posting." [137]

Coroner: Summing Up: 31 Mar 08: 66.11:

"The last particular matter raised by Tomlinson's evidence was the dates of deployment of two MI6 operatives in Paris. This was, you may think, a particularly mischievous – even unreasonable and malicious – aspect of Tomlinson's various accounts. He casually identified two people as possible murderers, relying upon the dates of their postings to Paris, in support of his account that they could have been posted for a sinister purpose. He must have known very well that diplomatic postings are arranged months before they

---

[a] As quoted in Paget Report.

are taken up. That was such a baseless allegation that it was dealt with by a single statement from the Foreign Office head of personnel, which was read to you as undisputed evidence."

Comment: Richard Spearman and Nicholas Langman are the only two MI6 officers who have been named as potential suspects – and possibly involved on the night, on the ground, in Paris.[a]

Given that allegation – made by both Richard Tomlinson and Mohamed Al Fayed – it is astounding that the jury investigating the deaths never heard any evidence from Langman and also thought they didn't hear from Spearman.

The jury did hear Spearman cross-examined – he was Mr 6 (see below) – but his identity was withheld from them.[b]

There are several factors that indicate Richard Spearman and Mr 6 are one and the same person:

1) Both men have said they went out to dinner with their wives.

Mr 6 confirmed at the inquest: "My wife and I were out at dinner ... on the evening of 31st August".[cd]

---

[a] Officers, as opposed to agents. Officers recruit and "handle" agents. There are other people who have been shown in these volumes to be involved, who could have been working as agents for an intelligence agency, possibly MI6 or French intelligence – Henri Paul, Claude Roulet, Jean-Marc Martino, Arnaud Derossi, Dominique Lecomte, Gilbert Pépin, Jean Monceau.

[b] There is a possibility that Langman also was heard, but there is not enough known about him to show that he was, and if he was, which code he was allocated at the inquest. According to the Paget Report, Langman's alibi was that he "was on leave on the weekend of 30/31 August 1997, staying with relatives in England" (p767). None of the MI6 officers cross-examined at the inquest provided that alibi.

[c] It is possibly significant that Mr 6 confirmed the date of the dinner as "the evening of 31st August" – this is not the critical evening. The crash occurred at 12.23 a.m. on 31 August 1997, therefore the critical evening – just prior to the crash – is Saturday, 30 August 1997. Paget does not specify the exact date of the dinner – it reads "that evening". The Paget Report states on p767: "Richard Spearman was in Paris on the weekend of 30/31 August 1997. That date coincidentally was his birthday (as confirmed in the British Diplomatic Service List) and he was out that evening for a meal with his wife at a named restaurant." Paget says: "That date coincidentally was his birthday" – but "that date" was "30/31 August 1997". People generally are born on a specific day – either 30 or 31 August, but not both. Although the 1998 Service List (p294) does state that Spearman's birthday is August 30, the other evidence appears to indicate he may have gone to the restaurant with his wife, but not on the critical evening before the crash (August 30), and instead on the evening following the crash, Sunday, 31 August 1997.

[d] Mr 5 also had dinner at a restaurant with his wife, but they took their child with them (see point 2 below re babysitter): "During the evening I had a meal with my

The Paget Report – not available to the jury – stated: "Richard Spearman ... was out that evening for a meal with his wife at a named restaurant".[138]

2) Both men employed a babysitter.

Mr 6 confirmed to Burnett: "I had indeed ... left [our] children at home with a babysitter".

The Paget Report stated: "[The Spearman's] children were left at home with a babysitter".[139]

3) Both men were in Paris for four years.

Mr 6 said: "I never visited the hotel during my four years in Paris".

The Paget Report stated: "Richard Spearman ... moved to Paris on Tuesday 26 August 1997 to begin a four-year posting...."

4) Both men had a pre-Paris job at the centre of MI6.

Mr 6 confirmed at the inquest: "Prior to ... going to Paris ... I occupied a central position, a position of trust, at the centre of the [MI6] organisation."

Richard Tomlinson stated in his 1999 affidavit: "Mr Spearman ... had been, prior to his appointment in Paris, the personal secretary to the Chief of MI6 Mr David Spedding."

Mr 6's pre-Paris role was addressed again during Mansfield's cross-examination. Mansfield said he had a question "I am asking you because of your seniority at the time".[a] Spearman replied: "It is less seniority than a position with a wide-ranging vision of what is going on".[140]

I suggest that again fits with Spearman's role of "personal secretary to the Chief of MI6", as described by Tomlinson – that's a position that is not necessarily very senior, but enables a wide vision of activities within MI6.[b]

5) By the time of the inquest, both men had served up to 20 years in MI6.

Mr 6 said to Mansfield: "I have been in the [MI6] organisation nigh on two decades".[141]

The MI6 officer list that was anonymously posted onto the internet includes a reference to Spearman: "Richard David Spearman: 92 Istanbul, 97 Paris; dob[c] 1960."

This entry indicates that Spearman was born in 1960, so at the time of the 2008 inquest would have been age 48. It also appears to show that

---

wife and child at the Thoumieux Restaurant in Rue St Dominique.": 29 Feb 08: 37.18. The only other MI6 witness who has admitted to being in Paris was Ms 1. She said in her statement: "the [30 August 1997] Saturday evening [diary] entry is blank, which indicates to me that I was at home with my husband": 29 Feb 08: 36.5. Of course, being female, Ms 1 couldn't be either Spearman or Langman anyway.

[a] Referring to 6's position prior to his transfer to Paris.

[b] Spearman also transferred to Paris just a few days before the crash – see later. At one stage during Mansfield's cross-examination Mr 6 said: "... the proposition that we were involved in [the crash is] preposterous. I am talking now from my own perspective. So there is the business of timing of folks' arrivals within Paris...."

[c] Date of birth.

Spearman's initial international MI6 posting was to Istanbul in 1992 – 16 years before the inquest.

This then seems to fit with Mr 6's passing reference at the inquest to his time in MI6: "nigh on two decades".

The above points indicate that Mr 6 was none other than Richard Spearman, one of the two[a] prime named MI6 suspects for involvement in the orchestration of the Princess Diana assassination.

The inquest lawyer, Ian Burnett, asked Mr 6: "Had you any professional dealing with any Ritz Hotel staff in Paris?" Mr 6 replied: "I never visited the hotel during my four years in Paris".

The point here is that Burnett, as one of the lawyers, had been made aware of Mr 6's true identity[b] – Spearman – but the jury were not.

Other evidence[c] has shown that Spearman didn't arrive in Paris until 26 August 1997, just five days before the crash. Burnett asked about his dealings with the Ritz, with the full knowledge – withheld from the jury[d] – that out of the four years Spearman was there, only five days were in the critical pre-crash period. The only relevance to the case of dealings with the Ritz was pre-crash, not post-crash.

Michael Mansfield, who followed Burnett, evidently realised the significance of this – he immediately asked: "Your principal opportunity for that[e] to arise comes after the crash rather than before it, doesn't it?"

When Mr 6 replies, "I am not quite sure I understand", Mansfield then says: "If I spell it out, there will be a problem."

I suggest that the "problem" was that the reason the "principal opportunity" for Mr 6 to have dealings with the Ritz staff was "after the crash rather than before" was because out of 6's four years in Paris, only five days of it[f] were before the crash. If Mansfield had spelt that out then Mr 6's cover before the jury could have been blown – the jury would have realised they were listening to Richard Spearman himself giving answers.

---

[a] The other is Nicholas Langman.
[b] Although not expressly stated, this is apparent from the questioning by the lawyers – they were asking questions based on the statements that had been taken from the witnesses by Operation Paget. This will become increasingly clear as this Comment section develops.
[c] Heard by the jury.
[d] The jury were told that Spearman arrived in Paris on 26 August 1997, but they would have had no idea that Mr 6 was Spearman.
[e] Dealings with the Ritz Hotel.
[f] From 26 August to 30 August 1997.

This could have in turn led to an expectation of 6 being subjected to more specific questioning regarding the allegation that he was a suspect in the deaths.

Instead, 6, realising his predicament tries to rescue himself: "maybe I can help" then proceeds to deny any dealings with Ritz staff – "neither before nor after the crash".

Mansfield is not satisfied and states the obvious: "the prime period might be before the crash" – because that's when the significant dealings[a] with the Ritz staff (Henri Paul and Claude Roulet) must have taken place. In other words, dealings after the crash are not relevant to this case.

The reality is that if MI6 orchestrated the crash, the handlers of both Henri Paul and Claude Roulet could have been dealing with them even before Spearman's arrival on 26 August 1997 – just 5 days before the crash. So it is possible that Spearman himself may not have had direct contact with them before the crash.

Not only were Spearman and Langman not knowingly[b] cross-examined, but they have also never been acknowledged by the authorities as MI6 officers – neither by Paget[c] nor at the inquest.[d]

This is despite the fact that: a) both Tomlinson and Mohamed have alleged they were MI6 officers[e]; b) they both appear as MI6 officers on the

---

[a] Related to the case.

[b] To the jury.

[c] Paget may have inadvertently admitted that Spearman and Langman were MI6 officers, when they wrote about a 2004 meeting with MI6: "The SIS offered full co-operation to Lord Stevens and two senior members of the [Paget] team. They agreed to identify those individuals referred to in Richard Tomlinson's claims [Spearman and Langman] only by code, pseudonym or description.": Paget Report, p753.

[d] It was never directly disclosed at the inquest that Richard Spearman was an MI6 officer, but to even a careless observer the reaction by the MI6 lawyer (Jeremy Johnson), when the name "Spearman" cropped up, should have given the game away:

Michael Mansfield to Nicholas Gargan: "Does a Mr Spearman or that name mean anything to you?"

Jeremy Johnson: "Sir, I am sorry to interrupt.... I represent the interests of the Secret Intelligence Service. I am a little concerned about the direction that the cross-examination is now taking.... It is the long-standing and well-established policy of the Government not publicly to reveal the identities of those who work for the Secret Intelligence Service. Mr Mansfield is now seeking to put specific names to this witness to ask whether this witness liaised with individual people and what their role is. I would invite you not to permit that cross-examination."

....Mansfield: "It is a premature intervention. I was not going to connect that name with anything."

[e] When Mohamed tried to make more specific allegations against Spearman and Langman he was twice cut off by inquest lawyer, Ian Burnett:

list anonymously posted on the internet; c) Spearman was cross-examined as an MI6 officer – under the code-name Mr 6 – at the inquest.

It is significant that even though Richard Tomlinson had alleged[a] that "either or both of these officers[b] will have knowledge that will be of crucial importance" to the case, at the inquest Tomlinson was not asked any questions about them.[c]

Why is this?

Richard Tomlinson is an ex-MI6 officer. He had made an allegation that was critical to the case. Scott Baker had told the jury in his Opening Remarks that "Tomlinson named ... Richard Spearman and Nicholas Langman", yet when Tomlinson is on the stand, he is not asked about them. This is despite Baker assuring the jury: "It[d] will, nevertheless, need to be covered in evidence, if only because it has been represented repeatedly as part of the foundation of the MI6 involvement".

So how can this be?

An allegation that Baker sees as "represented repeatedly as part of the foundation of the MI6 involvement[e]", yet the very person who made the original allegation – Richard Tomlinson – is not asked anything at all about it.

It could be significant that Baker completely avoided using the name Richard Spearman[f] – and also failed to address any specific timing of his movements – in his Summing Up to the jury at the conclusion of the inquest.[g]

First instance: Mohamed: "The gangsters are the members of MI6.... A person called [Langman] and Spearman. Spearman was the person –"
Burnett: "Wait a minute, Mr Al Fayed. We have had evidence read that was uncontroversial –"
Second instance: Mohamed: "As a team, they worked together. They had –"
Burnett: "Without naming names, if you would be so kind...."
This is despite the fact that Baker had just moments earlier asked Mohamed: "Would you like to explain who you believe that those gangsters [who killed Diana and Dodi] were?" Mohamed tries to answer and Burnett tells him: "Without naming names". We have Baker asking Mohamed to name the perpetrators, and Burnett telling him not to name them.

[a] In his affidavit.

[b] Spearman and Langman.

[c] Also, at the inquest none of the MI6 witnesses were asked about Spearman or Langman.

[d] Tomlinson's evidence about the movements of Spearman and Langman.

[e] In the crash.

[f] And Nicholas Langman.

[g] Baker's Summing Up comments on this issue are addressed elsewhere in this section.

The jury were told just once that Richard Spearman arrived in Paris on 26 August 1997 – not though during the presentation of the evidence on the subject. Instead it was heard on 3 October 2007 during Scott Baker's Opening Remarks – over four months before Spearman's Paris posting was addressed in the inquest evidence.[a]

Baker said in his Opening Remarks: "[Spearman] arrived on Tuesday 26th August [1997]." He continued: "If the detail of [Spearman's] posting and training[b] is correct, then it is very difficult to see that there is anything in this point[c] at all. Evidence will be called on the matter."

I suggest that it is amazing that when the evidence on this was presented before the jury no one bothered to remind them that Richard Spearman arrived in Paris just five days before the crash.[d] Given that the jury had been flooded with a huge amount of evidence on varying subjects in the intervening four months since Baker's Opening Remarks, I suggest it would have been difficult for them to possibly even remember he said it. After all Opening Remarks are just that, opening remarks, and it would have been reasonable for the jury to have expected points of evidence to be fleshed out through the inquest – not diminished.

Yet this is what occurred. A vital piece of information on a key suspect, Richard Spearman – the date of his arrival in the city of the crime – was not pointed out to the jury during the presentation of evidence.

Instead what the jury heard was the reading of an FCO statement based on "documents ... retrieved from the files of the British Embassy in Paris". The "overseas posting notification for Richard Spearman ... dated 18th December 1996.... The date of arrival at the new post in Paris is scheduled to be 1 July 1997.... There are also documents relating to the transport of heavy baggage and to travel details, showing that these were arranged in the middle of August 1997."

As mentioned in an earlier footnote these documents were not shown to the jury and there is no evidence they were subjected to forensic scrutiny.

In the evidence presented the jury were left with: the "travel details ... were arranged in the middle of August 1997".

Tomlinson – who made the original allegation – was not asked about this. I suggest that is very odd.[e]

---

[a] Most of the evidence on this came out on 11 February 2008.

[b] As presented in the Paget Report, which is where he was quoting from – see earlier and later.

[c] The point that Spearman arrived not long before the crash.

[d] This timing becomes more significant when it is viewed in the context of the Paris arrival times of other senior MI6 figures revealed later in this book.

[e] Baker, in his Opening Remarks, said: Tomlinson "suggested that [Spearman] ... had been deployed only very shortly before the crash.... If the detail of his posting and training is correct, then it is very difficult to see that there is anything in this point at

The only witness evidence heard was ambassador Michael Jay briefly confirming that there had been a "suggestion that two of [the embassy's] first secretaries[a] had posting dates that were somehow suspicious". Burnett then proceeded to tell the inquest that "we are going to be hearing shortly a statement read from [FCO employee] Susan Le Jeune.... She explains that there is simply nothing in that at all". And then Jay confirmed that – "that there is simply nothing in that at all".

That's what the jury heard.

Susan Le Jeune didn't actually explain "that there is simply nothing in that at all". That is a Burnett interpretation. What Le Jeune[b] did is describe the contents of "documents ... retrieved from the files of the British Embassy in Paris" – see above – and added that it is normal "practice to schedule the posting of officers well in advance". She said the documents showed that that is what occurred with Spearman and Langman's postings. Le Jeune outlined what was normal practice and stated that the documentation fitted with that.

These were documents that were not passed on to the jury.

---

all. Evidence will be called on the matter." Yet when the evidence was heard during the inquest, Tomlinson was not asked any questions at all about Richard Spearman. So we have a situation where in his Opening Remarks Baker has already suggested to the jury – without having heard anything from Tomlinson – that "it is very difficult to see that there is anything in this point at all". That is basically prejudging the issue for the jury. Then when evidence is finally heard – four months later – the jury still don't get to hear anything from Tomlinson on it, even though he is the one who made the original allegation regarding the timing of Spearman's arrival in Paris. The closest the jury got to hearing Tomlinson's account of this was from the lips of Scott Baker himself on 3 October 2007 and at that time they are told by Baker that "it is very difficult to see that there is anything in this point at all". Baker then went on to say: "To be entirely fair to Tomlinson, in recent discussions he has suggested that he did no more than suggest that the movements of these two individuals was 'curious'. It may be that he now accepts that there is nothing in this point at all." Baker says "recent discussions" – he is referring to an interview with Operation Paget on 2 May 2005, so 2 years and 5 months before Baker is speaking. Paget has failed to pass on the actual words spoken by Tomlinson on this occasion and has only given a third person account, which can be viewed on page 768 of the Paget Report. It reads: "[Tomlinson] stated that he only ever thought that [Spearman's] movements may have appeared 'curious'. Having been presented with the facts, he now accepts that those suspicions would appear to be unfounded." Paget does not tell us which set of "facts" they presented Tomlinson with. It will be shown in this section of this book that the "facts" appear to vary, depending on whether they come from Paget or Le Jeune. See later Table.

[a] Named as Spearman and Langman.

[b] This is a shortened version of her name – see earlier.

The closest the evidence heard got to Spearman's date of arrival was actually a conflict of evidence. The jury heard:

- "the date of arrival at the new post in Paris is scheduled to be 1 July 1997"
- "the transport of heavy baggage and ... travel details ... were arranged in the middle of August 1997".

This conflict – with no explanation provided – could have helped to confuse the jury.

Given that Le Jeune was describing the contents of documents from the Paris embassy, I suggest it seems very strange that the embassy records don't describe the actual date Spearman arrived or started work.[a]

Baker had the date – see above – and I suggest he got it from the Paget Report[b], which stated: "[Spearman] moved to Paris on Tuesday 26 August 1997 to begin a four-year posting, following a holiday abroad".

Le Jeune didn't mention a holiday. She did say: the "travel details ... were arranged in the middle of August 1997".

One could argue that we are looking at a very short "holiday abroad"[c], or are we looking at a holiday that was cut short?

That is a possibility, but there is simply not enough information provided to progress beyond speculation.

Richard Tomlinson wrote in his 1999 affidavit: "I believe that there may well be significance in the fact that Mr Spearman was posted to Paris in the month immediately before the deaths." [d]

Paget replied: "Richard Spearman had been posted to the British Embassy in Paris almost a year earlier."

That is a major conflict – Tomlinson: "in the month immediately before the deaths"; Paget – "almost a year earlier".

The conflict – raised by Paget – appears to revolve around the meaning of the word "posted".

The Oxford definition of the verb "post" is: "send someone to a place to take up a job". In other words, it is the action of posting someone.

The actual posting of Spearman to Paris evidently took place in late August 1997 and it is difficult to understand why Paget has suggested

---

[a] According to the Paget Report, p767, they do: "Operation Paget has checked the details of ... 'arrival in post' for [Spearman and Langman] at the British Embassy in Paris."

[b] Who say they got it from the Paris embassy – see previous footnote.

[c] If the travel arrangements were made before the holiday started, then it would seem the holiday could have been about a week. Arrangements made say on the 15th or 16th – "middle of August" – and arrival in Paris embassy on the 26th, 11 days later.

[d] At the time he wrote this Tomlinson was evidently unaware of the 26 August 1997 date – had he been, that may have made him even more suspicious.

"Spearman had been posted to ... Paris almost a year earlier". Later in the paragraph Paget refers to Spearman's "routine posting arranged in 1996".

According to the evidence from Le Jeune, "the overseas posting notification for Richard Spearman ... is dated 18th December 1996".

That is just over eight months before the actual posting on 26 August 1997 – so even the notification form is not dated "almost a year earlier".

This raises the question: Who is correct?

Paget's: "almost a year earlier" or Le Jeune's reading of the embassy document: "18th December 1996".

On what did Paget base its "almost a year earlier"? Paget claims to have got its information from the same source as Le Jeune.[a]

Are neither of these – Paget and the Le Jeune embassy document – correct?

Was the embassy documentation manufactured by MI6 after the Paget Report was written, after it became accepted the inquest would occur and that issues regarding MI6 would have to be addressed at it?[b]

Le Jeune states: "It was the practice of the Foreign and Commonwealth Office ... to schedule the posting of officers well in advance". That was certainly not always the experience of ex-MI6 officer Richard Tomlinson, who described in his 2001 book an incident that occurred in 1993[c]. Tomlinson says that he was called to a meeting with Rick Fowlcrooke[d], the second in command in the MI6 Personnel Department. Fowlcrooke told Tomlinson: "We've decided to post you to Bosnia.... You'll be taking over from Kenneth Roberts in two weeks. It's not a lot of time to prepare for the post, but I'm sure you will cope." [142]

This shows that in certain situations MI6 post people to overseas locations after only a very short preparation period.

Evidence in Part 1[e] has already shown that through surveillance MI6 could have been aware that Diana was travelling to Paris as early as 18 August 1997, and at the latest, August 23.

There appear to be three main possibilities:

1) the fact that Richard Spearman arrived in Paris just five days ahead of the crash is purely coincidental

---

[a] Paget Report, p767: "Operation Paget has checked the details of 'posting dates' and 'arrival in post' for both men [Spearman and Langman] <u>at the British Embassy in Paris,</u> viewing written communications between France and the United Kingdom."
[b] Royal coroner John Burton made a concerted effort to delay or abandon altogether the holding of an inquest – see Part 4.
[c] Just four years before the Paris crash.
[d] Codename: PD/1.
[e] See Chapter 2A.

2) the arrangement for Spearman's posting was made in December 1996 (Paris embassy records) or September-October 1996 (Paget Report), but the plans were sped up – possibly his overseas holiday was cut short (see earlier) – so that Spearman could arrive in Paris in time to help orchestrate the crash

3) both the Paris embassy records and the Paget statements are false and Spearman was rushed to Paris in late August 1997 to assist in orchestrating the crash.

In other words, either Richard Spearman was involved in orchestrating the assassination of Princess Diana, or it is a major coincidence that he arrived in Paris soon after telephone surveillance would have made MI6 aware that Diana would be in Paris at the end of August 1997.

These possibilities should be assessed in the light of evidence regarding the timing of movements into Paris of other senior MI6 figures – see later in this chapter.

Richard Spearman Transfer to Paris – Critical Dates		
Item	In Paget Report	Inquest Evidence Heard[ab]
Spearman Request	Autumn 1996	Not Heard
Appointment Notification	September-October 1996[c]	18 December 1996
Language Training	From May 1997	1 April 1997 to 30 June 1997
Travel Arrangements Made	Not Stated	Mid-August 1997
Overseas Holiday	Before 26 August 1997	Not Heard
Scheduled Arrival	Not Stated	1 July 1997
Actual Arrival Date in Paris	26 August 1997	Not Heard

[a] From Susan Le Jeune evidence.
[b] Scott Baker's Opening Remarks, which were based on the Paget Report and were heard four months earlier than the inquest evidence, are not included here. They have been shown earlier.
[c] Paget Report says "Autumn 1996" on p767 and "almost a year" on p830.

The table on the previous page compares the timing details in the Paget Report to the evidence presented by Susan Le Jeune at the inquest, regarding Richard Spearman's transfer to Paris in August 1997. Both Operation Paget and Le Jeune claimed that their information came from the same source – the files in the British Embassy in Paris. There are two main points of concern: 1) most of the information is not comparable: Paget stated that "Spearman applied for" the transfer – the inquest was not told that; Paget stated that Spearman went on "a holiday abroad" before arriving in Paris – the inquest was not told that; the inquest heard Spearman's arrival in Paris was "scheduled to be 1 July 1997" – this was not mentioned in the Paget Report; the Paget Report stated that Spearman "moved to Paris on Tuesday 26 August 1997" – that was not included in the inquest evidence. 2) The information that is able to be compared appears to be conflicting: Paget stated that Spearman "had been posted to ... Paris almost a year earlier" than the crash – the inquest heard that Spearman's "overseas posting notification ... is dated 18th December 1996" – 8½ months before the crash; Paget stated that "from May 1997 [Spearman] received pre-posting training, including language training" – the inquest heard that Spearman's period of training "between jobs" commenced on 1 April 1997.

The question is: Why is the evidence in the Paget Report so different to what the inquest heard? The information in this comparison table indicates that the documents referred to by Le Jeune in her inquest statement appear to be different to the documents accessed by Operation Paget, even though both said they used the same source – the Paris embassy files.

Richard Spearman's late-August 1997 posting should also be viewed in the light of his previous position as personal secretary to MI6 Chief at the time, David Spedding. There is a possibility Spearman was directly sent to Paris by Spedding and assigned a role to fulfil in the assassination of Princess Diana.

If this was the case, it would mean that the Spearman posting documentation quoted from at the inquest was fabricated. I suggest that the conflicts and substantial differences between the information quoted in the Paget Report and the inquest does indicate that documents have been doctored or fabricated.

Events would have had to move quickly for MI6 in the latter part of August 1997. The earliest prior knowledge of the Paris visit by Diana and Dodi would have been 18 August 1997 and the latest August 23.[a]

It would seem logical that if Spedding had received instructions to eliminate Princess Diana – see later in this volume – then he would have needed to pick loyal and trusted staff to oversee the operation. It is also logical that one of those staff members could have been Richard Spearman.

Spearman stayed in Paris for several years, but I suggest it is obvious that if he had been withdrawn from Paris in the aftermath period of the crash, then his posting timing would have looked doubly suspicious. Deniability is an integral part of the MI6 culture – see earlier – and Spearman's role would have been much more deniable if he was left in Paris for a normal posting period.

Evidence and discussion regarding other possible MI6 officers chosen for this special mission appears later in this chapter.

Central to the inquest evidence regarding Spearman and Langman were earlier statements made by Tomlinson about the posting dates of MI6 employees.

Richard Tomlinson said in his 1998 French statement: "At the time of the accident the number two of the Paris outstation of MI6 had just completed half of his three year posting to Paris, but a few weeks after the accident he was suddenly recalled to England."

In his Opening Remarks Scott Baker stated: "Tomlinson named ... Nicholas Langman as [a person] whose ... departure from the embassy was suspicious, given the dates involved.... He suggested that [he][b] had been suddenly recalled to London before the end of his term...."

Tomlinson has never suggested that <u>Langman</u> departed early – he said the person was "the number two of the Paris outstation of MI6".[c]

Inquest lawyer Ian Burnett reinforced this perception (in Baker's Opening Remarks) when he told ambassador, Michael Jay: "There has been ... [a] suggestion that two of your first secretaries had posting dates that were somehow suspicious.... The two first secretaries concerned are Mr Spearman and Mr Langman".[d]

---

[a] See Part 1.

[b] Baker is referring to Langman.

[c] This is addressed in more detail below.

[d] Jay confirmed this and a statement from Susan Le Jeune from the FCO regarding the details of the Langman and Spearman posting dates was read out to the inquest. In fact, Langman's details were read first even though there is no record of Tomlinson ever making any allegation regarding Langman's posting dates – see later. I suggest that the evidence covering Langman's dates was gone through as a red herring, to muddy the waters regarding the truly suspect posting date – that of Richard Spearman. This approach also assisted to undermine the substance of

When Baker got to his Summing Up to the jury he upped the ante: He now describes Tomlinson's suggestion regarding Langman[a] – a suggestion it will be shown that Tomlinson never made – as "particularly mischievous – even unreasonable and malicious". Baker continues: "[Tomlinson] casually identified two people[b] as possible murderers, relying upon the dates of their postings to Paris". Baker finishes up by calling it "a baseless allegation".

This is an amazing attack, when one considers that Tomlinson never even made the allegation in the first place. The statement by Tomlinson – quoted above – referred to "the number two of the Paris outstation of MI6".

So we graduate from Baker's Opening Remarks where he suggests that "it is very difficult to see that there is anything in this point at all" to his Summing Up[c], now it is: "particularly mischievous ... and malicious".

Baker was not original on misquoting Tomlinson on this issue.

In 2006, the authors of the Paget Report had already suggested the same – that Tomlinson was referring to Nicholas Langman when he made this statement.

They wrote: "Although Richard Tomlinson did not name Nicholas Langman in this particular evidence it was clear he was referring to him and not Richard Spearman, as he was very specific about his claim of Richard Spearman's posting dates."

Then 64 pages later:[d] "Richard Tomlinson is believed to be referring to either Richard Spearman or Nicholas Langman, the British Embassy staff he has named in other documents."

Paget has changed its story.

First: "it was clear he was referring to [Nicholas Langman] and not Richard Spearman", but then later on: "Richard Tomlinson is believed to be referring to either Richard Spearman or Nicholas Langman".

Tomlinson said he was "the number two of the Paris outstation of MI6".

We were told by Miss X that Operation Paget was given "God's access" – see earlier. Paget themselves specifically stated: "SIS offered full co-operation.... Details of all SIS officers that had worked in Paris at the relevant time were ... provided." [143]

Tomlinson's evidence, because it is obvious from the Diplomatic Lists and Le Jeune's evidence that Nicholas Langman had been in the Paris Embassy for years – since 1994 – and was clearly not posted just before the crash and also did not apparently leave until a year after the crash.

[a] Baker was also referring to the allegation by Tomlinson about Spearman's posting to Paris – that issue is dealt with separately in this Comment.

[b] Spearman and Langman – see previous footnote.

[c] Just two days before the jury started deliberations.

[d] The first statement is from page 765 and the second from page 829.

This means that Paget were given enough information – "details of all SIS officers" – to be able to establish the identity of "the number two of the Paris outstation of MI6".

So why didn't Paget do that? Why did they speculate on the identity of this person when they had the ability to resolve who it was, at their fingertips?

In fact they speculated twice – first they came up with "[Nicholas Langman] and not Richard Spearman" and second: "either Richard Spearman or Nicholas Langman".

On both occasions Paget has provided reasons for its speculative conclusions:

-    In the first instance: "it was clear he was referring to him and not Richard Spearman, as he was very specific about his claim of Richard Spearman's posting dates".

This is not particularly logical. Paget is saying that the reason Tomlinson is referring to Langman is because "he was very specific about ... Richard Spearman's posting dates".

That is a logical reason why Tomlinson is not referring to Spearman, but it has absolutely nothing to do with whether or not he is referring to Langman.

I suggest that it is quite incredible that the police can come up with flawed reasoning of this nature and expect people to believe it.

-    in the second instance: "Richard Tomlinson is believed to be referring to either Richard Spearman or Nicholas Langman, the British Embassy staff he has named in other documents."

Paget appears to be suggesting that Tomlinson is referring to either Spearman or Langman because they are the "British Embassy staff he has named in other documents".

This also is flawed logic. Just because Tomlinson referred to Spearman and Langman in other documents is no basis to suggest that he is referring to one of them in this document.

Paget doesn't appear to have any problem with converting their flawed and inconsistent[a] speculation into definitive statements:

-    "Richard Tomlinson ... claimed that Nicholas Langman ... was suddenly recalled to England a few weeks after the accident"

-    "the statement that Nicholas Langman had completed half of his three year posting and was *'suddenly'* recalled to England a few weeks after the crash is factually incorrect" [b]

---

[a] "Inconsistent" because two separate speculative conclusions were drawn – first, Langman and second, Spearman or Langman: see above.

[b] The statement is factually incorrect, but the problem is that Tomlinson never made that statement.

- "[Tomlinson] is wrong about the facts relating to the postings of both men.[a] There is no evidence to support this claim".

These statements by Paget – although definitive – are false, as Tomlinson has never made any claims about Langman's posting dates, to or from Paris.

By the time Baker had finished with this – just two days ahead of the jury going out for deliberations – he had escalated it into: "particularly mischievous – even unreasonable and malicious". He went on: "[Tomlinson] casually identified two people as possible murderers, relying upon the dates of their postings to Paris."

All this vitriol, even though Tomlinson was not asked a whisper about Spearman, Langman or MI6 officers' posting dates in and out of Paris, at Baker's "thorough" inquest.

Paget doesn't appear to have considered that Tomlinson may have been referring to a third person – an MI6 officer other than Spearman or Langman. Yet there are several factors that point to this – that Tomlinson was referring to neither Spearman nor Langman:

1) The person Tomlinson was referring to "at the time of the accident ... had just completed half of his three year posting to Paris".

According to the FCO personnel records[b] Nicholas Langman's "overseas posting notification" for Paris "is dated 18th May 1994.... The date of arrival ... is scheduled to be 1st October 1994 for a period of ... four years.... Mr Langman departed from Paris on 27th August 1998."

The details of Langman's posting therefore differ from the person Tomlinson is describing in two critical ways:

a) Tomlinson describes a three year posting, whereas Langman's was four years

b) Tomlinson describes a posting that was just over 18 months through[c] on 31 August 1997.

Langman's posting commenced on 1 October 1994[d], so by the time of the crash on 31 August 1997, he had already been in Paris for around 2 years and 11 months.

Langman had been in Paris for almost twice the amount of time of the person Tomlinson is describing – 2 years 11 months as opposed to one year 6 months.

---

[a] The allegation regarding Spearman is covered separately – see later. Tomlinson made no allegation about Langman's posting – see above.

[b] As described by Susan Le Jeune d'Allegeershecque – see above.

[c] "just completed half of ... three" years.

[d] This is the scheduled date of commencement. The 1996 Diplomatic Service List confirms – in the Biography section – that Langman commenced in Paris in October 1994.: 1996 Diplomatic Service List, p223.

2) Tomlinson describes a person who "a few weeks after the accident ... was suddenly recalled to England".

Langman – according to the personnel records – didn't leave Paris until 27 August 1998, so almost a year after the crash.[a]

3) Tomlinson describes a person who was "the number two of the Paris outstation of MI6".

There is no evidence suggesting that Langman was number two in Paris.[b]

4) Tomlinson stated: "The person concerned had ... been on an eight-month French course, as had his wife."

The context of this is in relation to the investment put into a specific posting. This then indicates that the "eight month course" would have taken place between the posting notification and the person's actual arrival in Paris.

In the case of Nicholas Langman, his posting notification was dated 18 May 1994 and his scheduled arrival date[c] was 1 October 1994. So there is only 4½ months between notification and arrival – this does not allow enough time for the 8 month course Tomlinson is referring to.

Tomlinson said: "The person concerned had ... been on an eight-month French course, as had his wife." The Diplomatic Service Lists reveal that Langman married Sarah Pearcey in 1992.[144] It is reasonable to assume that if Paget – or Baker – had been able to show that Langman and his wife had been on an 8 month course before arriving in Paris, then they would have done so.

The facts from the FCO records indicate otherwise.

5) Although a major effort has been made, by Paget and Baker, to suggest that Tomlinson could only have been referring to Spearman or Langman, other evidence indicates there were actually quite a few MI6 staff based in Paris around the time of the crash.[d]

Later evidence will show that when Burnett cross-examined Mr 4 – who stated he was Head of Station in Paris at the time of the crash[145e] – Burnett confirmed that "Witnesses 1 and 5 ... were in Paris that weekend ... [and]

---

[a] The 2000 Diplomatic Service List confirms that Langman took up a new posting at the FCO in September 1998.: 2000 Diplomatic Service List, p230.

[b] One could suggest that if Langman had been number two then either Paget or Baker would have made that known. That is not necessarily the case though, because there has never been an open admission from the police investigation or the inquest that either Langman or Spearman were MI6 officers. They have only ever conceded that they both worked at the embassy – this is despite Baker having Spearman cross-examined at the inquest as an MI6 officer under a code name, Mr 6 (see earlier).

[c] According to the FCO records.

[d] It will be shown later that there were up to 11 based in Paris. The issue of whether they were actually in Paris on the night of the crash is addressed later.

[e] This would have made Mr 4 the direct boss of the "number two" that Tomlinson was referring to. It will though be shown later that Mr 4 lied about his role.

witness 6 ... was in Paris that weekend". Burnett then goes on to say that "all the others in their statements set out where they were that weekend".

We then end up with MI6 officers 1, 5, 6, 4 and "all the others". I suggest that "all the others" would have to be at least four, so then a minimum total of eight MI6 officers based in Paris around the time of the crash.

Of these eight officers we can identify Spearman – Mr 6 – and we know that Ms 1 was female. We also know that the "number two" was not Langman – see above.

Effectively Langman could have been any one of the five remaining officers. If the official line is correct, then Langman was in the UK for the weekend – that would preclude him from being Mr 5, who stated he was in Paris. That would then mean Langman could be one of at least four officers.

Likewise, the "number two" described by Tomlinson could also be one of at least five officers – Mr 5 or any of the at least four "all the others" mentioned above.

But – as shown already – the "number two" described by Tomlinson cannot be Nicholas Langman.[a]

Michael Jay, British Ambassador to France, 1996-2001, Paris: 11 Feb 08: 93.2:

Burnett: Q. Now you have explained to the jury that also the French authorities did not know[b], and that followed the investigations made by your head of the political section at the Embassy, a Mr Cowper-Coles. Is that right?

A. That is correct, yes.

Q. As it happens, am I right in thinking that Mr Cowper-Coles arrived to take up his posting in Paris only at lunchtime on 31st August?

---

[a] Although I have been able to show that the person Tomlinson described as "the number two of the Paris outstation of MI6" could not be Nicholas Langman – see above – positively determining his identity is a lot more difficult, because of the limited information that is available. Tomlinson makes no reference to the Diplomatic List in this allegation and he appears to be speaking from his inside knowledge as a former MI6 officer. There is a possibility the person is Mr G.J. Hendry, OBE, who was a senior officer in the political department in the 1998 List but was gone from the 1999 List. Hendry also appears in the 1996 and 1997 Lists, meaning he had been in Paris for at least 21 months at the time of the crash. Tomlinson states that the person "had just completed half of his three year posting" – that would be just over 18 months. Virtually nothing else is known about Hendry because he is not included in the biography section of any of the Lists and does not show on the MI6 internet list. He may be an undeclared officer. There is also a possibility that Tomlinson is referring to an MI6 officer who doesn't appear on the official Paris embassy Lists.

[b] That Princess Diana was in France – this has been covered in Part 3.

A. Yes. He was in language training, I think, in the South of France, and when he heard the news, he got into his car and drove straight up.
Q. So he was thrown into the thick of it really?
A. Yes.
Q. You tell us in your statement – and perhaps we can deal with this quickly and you can just confirm it – that Mr Cowper-Coles also asked for investigations or inquiries to be made by Chief Inspector Gargan, who was the Embassy's drug liaison officer.
A. Yes.

Richard Tomlinson, Ex-MI6 Officer: 19 Nov 98 Letter to Stéphan:[a] **Jury Didn't Hear**:
"The 1998 British 'Diplomatic Service List' shows that Richard David Spearman was posted to the British Embassy in Paris, just before the incident at the Pont d'Alma, as the number two MI6 officer in France.
"I do not believe it a coincidence that Mr Spearman should arrive in Paris only a few weeks before the incident at the Pont d'Alma.
"I enclose photocopies of the relevant pages of the 1998 'Diplomatic List.'"
Paget Comment: "The British Diplomatic Service List 1998 referred to by Richard Tomlinson showed: 'First Secretary (Political): Mr R D Spearman', not as Richard Tomlinson claimed 'the number two MI6 officer in France'. This is an interpretation Richard Tomlinson has put on the list." [146]
Comment: Richard Tomlinson stated: "The 1998 British 'Diplomatic Service List' shows that ... Spearman was posted ... as the number two MI6 officer in France." [b]
    Paget stated: "This is an interpretation Richard Tomlinson has put on the list."
    Is there any truth to Tomlinson's statement?
    It is clear that the Diplomatic List does not spell out details of MI6 staff, but it is also known that MI6 officers generally operate from within embassies and this was the case with the British Embassy in Paris in 1997.[c]
    Therefore, because the Diplomatic List shows all the FCO staff in British embassies around the world, it must also include details of MI6 officers – without disclosing they are MI6 personnel. So the list of embassy staff in Paris contains the MI6 officers working within the embassy at that time.

---

[a] As quoted in the Paget Report.
[b] Tomlinson here named Spearman as the number two officer in France. Earlier there was discussion about Tomlinson's comments regarding "the number two of the Paris outstation of MI6". Tomlinson is referring to two separate people – Spearman in his role as number two in France and the unnamed officer in his role as number two in Paris.
[c] This was confirmed by the ambassador, Michael Jay – 11 Feb 08: 96.2 – and MI6 Director of Operations, Richard Dearlove – 20 Feb 08: 35.20.

Given that Tomlinson was writing to Stéphan in 1998 in his role as an ex-MI6 officer, with about four years experience, it is logical that he would have inside knowledge of how MI6 operated within embassies.

The general evidence indicates that MI6 officers in embassies are listed in two main departments, Political and Economic.[a]

A study of the 1998 Diplomatic List for the British Embassy in Paris[b] reveals that the names have been entered in a certain order.

The order is:

1) ambassador

2) minister[c]

3) three military-related attachés

4) six counsellors – political, economic, TPI, management, cultural, technology

5) consul-general

6) 15 first secretaries (and the cultural attaché) – 5 political, 4 economic, agriculture, general[d], PPA[e], 2 defence, management

7) consul

8) assistant air attaché

9) three second secretaries – political, technical, technology

10)   private secretary

11)   four third secretaries (and the visits officer) – general[f], management, information, commercial.

Ambassador, Michael Jay, stated at the inquest that counsellors were the heads of their respective departments.[g]

---

[a] The Paris embassy lists in the Diplomatic Lists show different fax numbers for each department, but the political and economic departments are reached on the same fax number: 44513485.

[b] Reproduced above.

[c] The minister is the ambassador's deputy – Michael Jay: "The Ambassador is ... the head of the Embassy. In Paris, working for me, there was a deputy, who was known as the Minister in the Embassy, and then, underneath him, a series of different departments in the Embassy.": 11 Feb 08: 81.7.

[d] No department allocation shown.

[e] Press and Public Affairs.

[f] No department allocation shown.

[g] Michael Jay: "There was ... a series of different departments in the Embassy; for example, a political section; financial and commercial section; consular section; Visa section. A number of different sections all of which would be headed by a diplomat, a man or a woman, of the rank of counsellor, who, as I say, would then report either to my deputy or, in many cases, directly to me.": 11 Feb 08: 81.8.

It appears that the list is presented in order of seniority – counsellors, or heads of department, come above first secretaries, then second secretaries and finally third secretaries.

But then even within the group of 15 first secretaries, they are not in name alphabetical order – the political are first, then economic and so on. And even in the group of five political first secretaries, they are also not in alphabetical order[a], or order of arrival[b] – that would indicate they too are in order of seniority.

The logical conclusion is that the persons shown on the Diplomatic List of the British Embassy in Paris have been listed in order of seniority.

As stated above, the general evidence appears to show that MI6 officers in embassies show up in either the Political or Economic departments. The Diplomatic List indicates that the Political department is more senior than the Economic – the Political counsellor[c] is shown at the top of the list of counsellors and the Political secretaries are shown first.[d]

It is possible that this could indicate that the Political counsellor would be the Head of MI6 in France and the "number two" could be the top Political first secretary.

In the 1998 Diplomatic List – published in January 1998 – the Political counsellor is Sherard Cowper-Coles and the top Political first secretary is Richard Spearman. Both of these men appear on the list of MI6 officers posted on the internet.[e]

Paget is correct in saying that the Diplomatic List does not state that Spearman was "the number two MI6 officer in France". They also correctly point out: "This is an interpretation Richard Tomlinson has put on the list."

Even though Paget was given "God's access"[f] to the MI6 files, they do not comment on the veracity of Tomlinson's interpretation – they just say "this is an interpretation". I suggest that if Tomlinson's interpretation had been wrong, then Paget would have pointed that out.

---

[a] For example, Spearman comes before Roberts.

[b] Spearman arrived just a few months before the Diplomatic List was published, yet he is shown at the top of the five political first secretaries.

[c] Head of department – see earlier.

[d] Jay also listed the Political department first in his evidence at the inquest: "In Paris, working for me, there was a deputy ... and then, underneath him, a series of different departments in the Embassy; for example, a political section; financial and commercial section; consular section; Visa section.": 11 Feb 08: 81.8.

[e] At the time the list was posted Cowper-Coles had become the UK ambassador to Saudi Arabia. This posting occurred in 2003. It may not be a coincidence that a senior member of MI6 would be posted to Saudi Arabia in the same year as the commencement of UK hostilities – as a part of the coalition – against Iraq.

[f] See earlier.

They didn't.[a]

When this is viewed in the light of the above analysis of the order of entries in the Diplomatic List, it would seem that Tomlinson has correctly interpreted that Spearman was "posted ... as the number two MI6 officer in France".[b]

Would Stéphan have understood how Tomlinson arrived at this interpretation?

On the face of it, one would have to say "no".[c] However, we have never been shown the full letter Tomlinson wrote to Stéphan, where he made this interpretation – it is possible he explained his reasoning in a part of the letter that has not been included in the excerpt provided by Paget.

Mr 4, MI6 Officer. British Embassy, Paris: 29 Feb 08: 40.1:

Burnett: Q. Is it right that you were the head of station in Paris in August 1997?

A. Yes, that is correct.

Q.... Were you in charge of any and all SIS staff in Paris?

A. Yes, and indeed in France.

Q. In France. I am not going to ask you for details of how many such staff there were or may have been, but we have heard read to us the evidence of Witnesses 1 and 5 who were in Paris that weekend. We are also going to be hearing from witness 6, who was in Paris that weekend. Are you able to tell the jury whether there were any other SIS staff in Paris that weekend?

A. I know that – I remember well that Witness 6[d] was in town, and I am clear that we would have made arrangements for duty personnel, a duty officer and duty support staff, but in terms of who specifically was doing what, I cannot clearly remember that.

Q. Have you had an opportunity of reading the witness statements provided by other members of the Paris station to Operation Paget?

A. Yes, I have.

Q. Again, without identifying numbers, it is right, isn't it, that Operation

---

[a] Paget tended to point out errors whenever they could. There was a claim by Mohamed Al Fayed that "Richard Spearman [was] formerly chief of staff to the Head of MI6". Paget correctly pointed out: "The description in the claim of Richard Spearman as a Chief of Staff was incorrect." Richard Tomlinson's claim that Spearman "had been ... the personal secretary to the Chief of MI6" went unchallenged, because it was correct: Paget Report, pp816, 830.

[b] It will be shown later that at that time of the crash there is a possibility that Dr Valerie Caton was no. 2 and Richard Spearman could have been no. 3.

[c] There is no reason to suggest that Stéphan had any special understanding of the inner workings of the British Embassy.

[d] Richard Spearman – see earlier.

Paget took statements from all SIS members of the station?
A. Yes, that is correct.
Q. All the others in their statements set out where they were that weekend and none was in Paris. That is what they say, isn't it?
A. That is right.

Embassy Tables

Ambassador: M H Jay, CMG
Minister: The Hon Michael Pakenham, CMG
Defence and Air Attaché:
Air Commodore P H Eustace
Military Attaché: Brigadier C D M Ritchie CBE, ADC
Naval Attaché: Captain D J Thomson, RN
Counsellor and Head of Chancery: M A Arthur,
CMG
Counsellor (Cultural) (British Council Director):
D T Ricks, OBE
Counsellor (Chancery): T R Ewing
Counsellor (Management): M A Price, LVO
Counsellor (Technology): Dr M A Darnbrough
Counsellor (Information): P N Livesey
Counsellor (Finance and Economic): P F Ricketts
Counsellor (Director of Trade Promotion and
Investment): R J Codrington
First Secretary and Consul-General: K C Moss
First Secretary (Labour): Ms M M Hartwell
First Secretary (Political): E G Curley, OBE
First Secretary (Commercial): S S Calder
First Secretary (Defence Procurement): (vacant)
First Secretary (Political/Military): M J L Kirk
First Secretary (Political/Internal): Mrs A T Kirk
First Secretary (Political): G J Hendry, OBE
First Secretary (Political/Internal): Ms J E Nolan
First Secretary (Economic): R D Fitchett
First Secretary (Political): A N S Wightman
First Secretary and Consul: Miss A M Cowley
First Secretary (Economic): S J Fraser
First Secretary (Defence Equipment): G J Muir
First Secretary: D O Hay-Edie
First Secretary (Management): B A Lane
First Secretary (British Council): D H Jackman
First Secretary (Agriculture): Mrs E M Morris
First Secretary (Economic): N J A Langman
First Secretary (Press/Information): G Livesey
Assistant Air Attaché: Wing Commander S Gunner,
RAF
Second Secretary (Political): H E Powell
Second Secretary (Commercial): S J Green
Second Secretary (Technical): R M Hardy
Second Secretary (Technology): K Shannon
Second Secretary (Private Secretary to
Ambassador): P C Johnston
Third Secretary (Chancery); P D Batson
Third Secretary (Information): Ms C S Rowett
Third Secretary (Management): Ms S M Weeks

Figure 4ᵃᵃ

Excerpt from 1997 Diplomatic
Service List showing staff at
the Paris Embassy in
September 1996. The
equivalent list for 1998
(September 1997) has been
shown earlier.

ᵃ The Embassy Tables are based on information from the annual Diplomatic Service
Lists. The National Archives now states: "The Diplomatic Service List published
annually since 1852, ceased publication in 2006.":
http://yourarchives.nationalarchives.gov.uk Search: "Diplomatic Service List".

[a] Diplomatic lists are published in January but are "based on information available in [the previous] September ... but [include] details of some later changes". For example, the 1997 List was published in January 1997, but was primarily based on information from September 1996. Source: 1997 Diplomatic Service List, Preface. This leads to confusion. To avoid this confusion, from this point on, in the Comment text and the related footnotes the diplomatic lists are referred to by the year in which their information relates (unless otherwise specified) – so the 1998 List (FCO title) is referred to as the 1997 List in the Comment text because the information in it is as at September 1997. In the Bibliography and footnote and endnote sources provided (and also in the inquest transcripts), the List will be described based on the FCO title. So in the note sources and transcripts, the List that is referred to in the Comment text as 1997 is shown as 1998.

Table 1: **British Embassy Staff Comparison Between September 1996 and September 1997**[abc]

Role	September 1996			September 1997		
	Rank	**Person**	**In MI6 List?**	**Rank**	**Person**	**In MI6 List?**
	[d]		[e]			
Ambassador	1	Michael Jay	No	1	Michael Jay	No
Minister	2	Michael Pakenham	No	2	S.F. Howarth	No
Defence/ Air Attaché	3	P.H. Eustace	No	3	P.H. Eustace	No
Military Attaché	4	Charles Ritchie	No	5	A.C.J. Gadsby	No
Naval Attaché	5	D.J. Thomson	No	4	D. J. Thomson[f]	No
Counsellor/ Head of Chancery[g]	6	M.A. Arthur	No		NO POSITION	
Counsellor Political		**NO POSITION**		6	**Sherard Cowper-Coles**	**Yes**
Counsellor Cultural	7	D.T. Ricks	No	10	Ms C. Gamble	No
Counsellor Chancery	8	Timothy Ewing	No		NO POSITION	

[a] New personnel in 1997 have been underlined.
[b] Political and economic department employees have been shown in **bold**.
[c] The timing method used by the FCO – publisher of the Lists – can lead to confusion. The 1998 List reveals the staff list as at September 1997 and the 1997 List reveals the staff list as at September 1996. See earlier footnote.
[d] Based on the Diplomatic List being ordered by seniority, as discussed above.
[e] This is the MI6 list on the internet – it is not complete so it is likely that a person could be an MI6 officer but not be included on the list.
[f] This person is shown in the 1998 list spelt "Thompson". It is not known which is correct.
[g] "Chancery" refers to the office building in which the diplomatic staff work: Wikipedia, under "Diplomatic Mission".

DIANA INQUEST: WHO KILLED PRINCESS DIANA?

Role	September 1996			September 1997		
	Rank	Person	In MI6 List?	Rank	Person	In MI6 List?
Counsellor Management	9	Michael Price	No	9	Michael Price	No
Counsellor Technology	10	Dr M.A. Darnbrough	No	11	Dr M.A. Darnbrough	No
Counsellor Information	11	Timothy Livesey[a]	No		NO POSITION	
Counsellor Finance & Economic	12	**Peter Ricketts**	No	7	**Dr Valerie Caton**	No
Counsellor Trade[b]	13	Richard Codrington	No	8	Richard Codrington	No
Consul General	14	Keith Moss	No	12	Keith Moss	No
1st Secretary Labour	15	Ms M.M. Hartwell	No	22	Ms M.M. Hartwell	No
1st Secretary Political	16	**Eugene Curley**	No	13	**Richard Spearman**	Yes
1st Secretary Commercial	17	Stanley Calder	No	19	Stanley Calder	No
1st Secretary Political/ Military	18	**Matthew Kirk**	No	14	**Colin Roberts[c]**	Yes
1st Secretary Political/ Internal	19	**Mrs Anna Kirk**	No	15	**Mrs Caroline Copley**	No

[a] He shows as P.N. Livesey on the List. His full name is Timothy Peter Nicholas Livesey: The Diplomatic Service List 1997, p235.

[b] Director of Trade Promotion and Investment. Shown as "TPI" on the 1998 List.

[c] Roberts shows only as "First Secretary Political" under Paris in the Diplomatic List, but in the Biography section it reveals that he became "First Secretary Political/Military" in March 1997. Matthew Kirk, who Roberts took over from, became a Counsellor FCO in London in the same month, March 1997.: Diplomatic List 1998, pp228, 279.

Role	September 1996			September 1997		
	Rank	Person	In MI6 List?	Rank	Person	In MI6 List?
1st Secretary Political	20	G.J. Hendry	No	17	G.J. Hendry	No
1st Secretary Political/ Internal	21	Julia Nolan	No		NO POSITION	
1st Secretary Economic	22	Robert Fitchett	Yes	20	Robert Fitchett	Yes
1st Secretary Political	23	Andrew Wightman	No	16	Andrew Wightman	No
1st Secretary & Consul	24	Miss Aileen Cowley	No	30	Miss Aileen Cowley	No
1st Secretary Economic	25	Simon Fraser	No	18	P.J.E. Raynes	No
1st Secretary Defence Equipment	26	David Muir	No	27	J.C. Palmer	No
1st Secretary	27	David Hay-Edie	No	25	David Hay-Edie	No
1st Secretary Management	28	Bari Lane	No	29	Roger Woodward	No
1st Secretary British Council[a]	29	D.H. Jackman	No	23	D.H. Jackman	No
1st Secretary Agriculture	30	Mrs E.M. Morris	No	24	Mrs E.M. Morris	No
1st Secretary Economic	31	Nicholas Langman	Yes	21	Nicholas Langman	Yes

[a] In the 1998 List this position shows as "Cultural Attaché British Council".

DIANA INQUEST: WHO KILLED PRINCESS DIANA?

Role	September 1996			September 1997		
	Rank	Person	In MI6 List?	Rank	Person	In MI6 List?
1st Secretary Press/ Information[a]	32	Geoffrey Livesey	No	26	Timothy Livesey[b]	No
1st Secretary Defence Procurement		NO POSITION		28	R.C.B. Little	No
Assistant Air Attaché	33	S. Gunner	No	31	S. Gunner	No
2nd Secretary Political	**34**	**Hugh Powell**	**No**	**32**	**Hugh Powell**	**No**
2nd Secretary Commercial	35	Steven Green	No		NO POSITION	
2nd Secretary Technical	36	Richard Hardy	No	33	Richard Hardy	No
2nd Secretary Technology	37	Keith Shannon	No	34	Keith Shannon	No
Ambassador's Private Secretary	38	Paul Johnston	No	35	Paul Johnston	No
3rd Secretary Chancery	39	Philip Batson	No		NO POSITION	
3rd Secretary Information	40	Caroline Rowett	No	38	Caroline Rowett	No
3rd Secretary Management	41	Sarah Weeks	No	37	Sarah Weeks	No
3rd Secretary		NO POSITION		36	Emer Doherty	No

[a] Shows as "First Secretary PPA" in the 1998 List. PPA stands for "Press and Public Affairs".

[b] It appears to be a coincidence that both men are Liveseys – Geoffrey and Timothy. Timothy played a role in the post-crash events – see Part 4. It is interesting that neither person is shown as being present at the Paris embassy in the biography sections of the Diplomatic Lists. Geoffrey is stated to be "Deputy Head of Mission Maputo [capital of Mozambique] since August 1996" and before that was in the FCO from 1993. Timothy Livesey (T.L. Livesey on the 1998 list) is omitted from the biography section. There is another Timothy Livesey (showing as P.N. Livesey on the 1997 list) who is stated to be "First Secretary FCO since April 1993".: Diplomatic List 1998, pp234-5.

Role	September 1996			September 1997		
	Rank	Person	In MI6 List?	Rank	Person	In MI6 List?
Visits Officer		NO POSITION		39	Simon Ferrand	No
3rd Secretary Commercial		NO POSITION		40	Willam Kelly	No

The above table comparing the British Embassy staff between September 1996 and September 1997 reveals the following:[a]

1) Overall there was a marginal decrease in the number of staff between the two years – in 1996 there were 41 and in 1997 that had fallen to 40.

2) Within that, there was no change in the number of staff employed in the political and economic departments, shown in **bold** – 11 in both years.[b] Just over a quarter[c] of all Paris embassy staff are employed in the political and economic departments.

3) All the embassy staff that show on the MI6 list on the internet come from within either the political or economic departments.

I suggest that most – probably all – of listed MI6 officers in embassies show up as part of the political or economic departments of their embassy.[d]

4) There were 16 new staff employed during the year – shown underlined in the 1997 column – and of those, 6 were in the political and economic departments, and 10 were in other departments.

That then shows that the number of new staff in the political and economic departments was disproportionate – 6 of 11 people were replaced in 1997[e], so 55%[f], while in the rest of the embassy only 10 out of 30[g], or 33%, were replaced.

---

[a] Some of these points will also be made clearer by referring to Table 2 below.

[b] This is shown more clearly in Table 2 below.

[c] Close to 27% in both years.

[d] In possible support of this, the 1997 List biography for Robert Fitchett – who shows on the MI6 internet list – reads "First Secretary EU Affairs Paris" yet he appears on the 1997 official Embassy list (shown earlier) as "First Secretary Economic".: 1998 Diplomatic Service List, p186.

[e] Between September 1996 and September 1997.

[f] If this were to happen every year then that would mean the average posting would be under two years. My research indicates that the normal embassy posting is around three or four years – as was the case with Nicholas Langman (see earlier).

[g] Total staff is 41 less 11 political and economic employees, leaves 30 in other departments.

When the senior staff – first secretary upwards – are looked at, the difference is even more stark.

There were 32 senior staff in September 1996 and this reduced to 30 a year later. Of the 32, 10 were from the political and economic departments.

There were 12 replacements of senior staff throughout the year and 6 of those were for political or economic staff.

So 6 out of 10, or 60%, of political-economic staff were replaced. The other 6 replacements[a] were from the remaining 22 senior staff[b] in other departments – 6 replacements out of 22, which is only 27%.

5) In September 1996 the political counsellor role was vacant.[c]

By September 1997, not only had that position been filled, but the four most senior political and economic staff had also been replaced – Peter Ricketts, Eugene Curley, Matthew and Anna Kirk were gone; Sherard Cowper-Coles had been installed as the political head and Valerie Caton, Richard Spearman, Colin Roberts and Caroline Copley were now the four most senior-ranked political-economic officers under him.

6) The political-economic staff have been replaced by higher ranked people.

As stated in point 3, 60% of the senior political and economic staff were replaced in 1997. The new staff were more senior than the staff they were replacing:

a) In the official 1996 list there was no political counsellor. A year later Sherard Cowper-Coles had been brought in – he was ranked 6th in the embassy.[d]

b) Peter Ricketts, the economic counsellor in 1997, was ranked 12th. He was replaced by Valerie Caton who was ranked 7th.

c) Eugene Curley, ranked 16, was replaced by Richard Spearman, ranked 13.

d) Matthew and Anna Kirk, who were 18 and 19, were replaced by Colin Roberts, 14, and Caroline Copley, 15.

e) Julia Nolan, ranked 21, left on Special Unpaid Leave in June 1997. She was effectively replaced by Sherard Cowper-Coles, ranked 6th – see a) above.

f) Simon Fraser, ranked 25th, was replaced by P.J.E. Raynes, ranked 18.

This shows that all six political or economic staff who left in 1997 – Ricketts, Curley, the Kirks, Nolan, Fraser – were replaced by people more senior to them in the embassy.

---

[a] 12 in total, less the 6 political-economic replacements.
[b] 32 total senior staff, less 10 in the political-economic departments.
[c] It shows as "no position" in the table.
[d] Cowper-Coles' appointment was effectively offset by the departure of Julia Nolan – ranked 21 – who left on Special Unpaid Leave in June 1997.: Diplomatic Service List 1998, p261.

That is not the case with most of the staff from other departments who were replaced – see footnote.[a] In only one case out of six replacements was the new person more senior within the embassy.

To understand the unusual nature of these staff movements, the reader is encouraged to look at similar comparisons[b] of the political-economic movements in the British embassy in Bonn, Germany over the same period – see Appendix 1 near the end of this book; and the Paris embassy comparison between 1995 and 1996 – see Appendix 2.

---

[a] Pakenham, no. 2, was replaced by Howarth, also no.2; Ritchie, 4 replaced by Gadsby, 5; Ricks, 7 replaced by Gamble, 10; Muir, 26 replaced by Palmer, 27; Lane, 28 replaced by Woodward, 29; Geoffrey Livesey, 32 replaced by Timothy Livesey, 26.

[b] Similar to Table 2.

Table 2: **Political and Economic Departments Comparison Between 1996 and 1997**[a]

Role	September 1996			September 1997		
	Rank	Person	In MI6 List?	Rank	Person	In MI6 List?
	b		c			
Counsellor Political		NO POSITION		6	Sherard Cowper-Coles	Yes
Counsellor Finance & Economic	12	Peter Ricketts	No	7	Dr Valerie Caton	No
1st Secretary Political	16	Eugene Curley[d]	No	13	Richard Spearman	Yes
1st Secretary Political/ Military	18	Matthew Kirk	No	14	Colin Roberts[e]	Yes
1st Secretary Political/ Internal	19	Mrs Anna Kirk	No	15	Mrs Caroline Copley	No
1st Secretary Political	20	G.J. Hendry	No	17	G.J. Hendry	No

---

[a] New personnel in 1997 have been <u>underlined</u>.
[b] Based on the Diplomatic List being ordered by seniority, as discussed above.
[c] Yes/No. This is the MI6 list on the internet – it is not complete so it is likely that a person could be an MI6 officer but not be included on the list.
[d] This is based on the information in the official 1996 list. It will later become apparent that at the time of the crash Curley had been promoted to the role of political counsellor and would therefore have been directly replaced by Cowper-Coles and not Spearman.
[e] Roberts shows only as "First Secretary Political" under Paris in the Diplomatic List, but in the Biography section it reveals that he became "First Secretary Political/Military" in March 1997. Matthew Kirk, who Roberts took over from, became a Counsellor FCO in London in the same month, March 1997.: Diplomatic List 1998, pp228, 279.

Role	September 1996			September 1997		
	Rank	Person	In MI6 List?	Rank	Person	In MI6 List?
1st Secretary Political/ Internal	21	Julia Nolan	No		NO POSITION	
1st Secretary Economic	22	Robert Fitchett	Yes	20	Robert Fitchett	Yes
1st Secretary Political	23	Andrew Wightman	No	16	Andrew Wightman	No
1st Secretary Economic	25	Simon Fraser	No	18	P.J.E. Raynes	No
1st Secretary Economic	31	Nicholas Langman	Yes	21	Nicholas Langman	Yes
2nd Secretary Political	34	Hugh Powell	No	32	Hugh Powell	No

Table 2 reveals that of the 11 political and economic department personnel in September 1996, just two show on the MI6 list – Fitchett and Langman. A year later, although there are still only 11 staff, now five of them are on the MI6 list – Cowper-Coles, Spearman, Roberts, Fitchett and Langman. Three of these are new staff – Cowper-Coles, Spearman and Roberts.

It is also notable that even though only 5 of the 11 1996 staff remained a year later[a], among those five were the two MI6-listed officers – Fitchett and Langman.

---

[a] The five are: Hendry, Fitchett, Wightman, Langman and Powell.

Table 3: **Political/Economic Department Employees in Paris Embassy 31 August 1997**

Name	Role	Inquest ID	Start Date[a]	Rank	On MI6 List?	MI6?	List Biography[b]	Location/Alibi Stated	Checked
Cowper-Coles	Couns Political	Not Heard	Not Given	6	Yes	Yes	FCO London	South of France	No
Caton	Couns Econom	Not Heard	Not Given	7	No	Likely	On Special Leave	None Given	No
Spearman	1st Sec Political	Mr 6	26 Aug 97[c]	13	Yes	Yes	Paris	Paris Restaurant	No
Roberts	1st Sec Polit/Milit	NA	Mar 97	14	Yes	Yes	Paris	NA	No
Copley	1st Sec Polit/Intern	Ms 1	Jun 97	15	No	Yes	Paris	At home	No
Hendry	1st Sec Political	NA	Not known	17	No	Likely	Not Shown	NA	No
Fitchett	1st Sec Econom	NA	Sep 94	20	Yes	Yes	Paris	NA	No
Wightman	1st Sec Political	NA	Apr 94	16	No	Likely	Paris	NA	No
Raynes	1st Sec Econom	NA	Not known	18	No	Likely	Not Shown	NA	No
Langman	1st Sec Econom	NA	Oct 94	21	Yes	Yes	Paris	In UK	No
Powell	2nd Sec Political	NA	Apr 93	32	No	Likely	Paris	NA	No

[a] Dates are from Diplomatic List biographies unless otherwise stated.
[b] This is the person's location according to their official Diplomatic List biography. It refers to their assigned location over the period that includes the night of the crash – it does not specifically state where the person was on the night of the crash.
[c] From general evidence.

Mr 4 aka Eugene Curley[a], MI6 Officer. British Embassy, Paris: 29 Feb 08: 41.13:

Burnett: Q. Were you aware that the Princess and Dodi Al Fayed were in Paris that weekend, before the crash occurred?

A. No, I was not.

Q. Now is it right that on that weekend, 30th and 31st August 1997, you were in fact out of Paris yourself?

A. Yes, I was returning from a two-week holiday in the Dordogne.

Q. So you were elsewhere in France. Are you able to recollect where you were on the Sunday morning, that is to say 31st August?

A. Yes, clearly we were in a hotel in Western France, near La Rochelle.

Q. In what circumstances did you learn of the crash?

A. I remember clearly my wife – I was still in bed with our baby daughter and I remember my wife coming back to the room and telling me that it was on the news that Diana had died, so I suppose that was about 9 o'clock.

Q. What did you do immediately thereafter?

A. Well, I suppose, like everybody else, switched on the television and watched that as the events unfolded and then I rang up the Embassy. I cannot remember who specifically I rang up, but to find if I was required, and I was told that there would be a meeting of senior staff the following day, so I planned and –

Coroner: Could you try to keep your voice up a little bit? I think that you are dropping your voice and I am hoping that everybody in the annex can hear this.

Q. To recap that, you telephoned the Embassy.

A. Yes.

Q. For what purpose?

A. To see if I was required back, as a member of the senior staff in the Embassy, and to find out what arrangements were being made and that sort of thing.

Q. That was to find out if you were required back that day?

A. Yes.

Q. When were you otherwise intending to go back to work?

A. I was intending to go back to work some time the following Monday in any case.

Q. What were you told?

A. I was told that there was no need for me to rush back, obviously it had nothing to do with SIS, but that the Ambassador would be holding a meeting of senior staff the following day.

---

[a] Evidence revealing Mr 4 is Eugene Curley is shown below.

Q. Did you then attend a meeting of the senior staff the following day?

A. Yes. If I am correct, there was a series of meetings and I went to at least one of them.

Q. Why was SIS involved in such meetings at all?

A. It was not so much SIS as me as head of station, as a member of the senior management team in the Embassy.

At 44.22: Mansfield: Q. After the crash and in December 1998, were you still at the Paris station?

A. No, I was not.

Q. So you are not able to help about any communications then between the Embassy and the French investigation?

A. This is in late 1998?

Q. Well, I will be precise. The dates I wanted to ask you about were 1st December and 16th December.

A. No, I was not.

At 50.8: Q. At the time you were there – so I am dealing specifically so that you know the period – between September 1997 and possibly early 1998, were you still there?

A. I was.

Q. Did the name "Andanson" crop up?

A. No.[a]

Michael Jay: 13 Dec 05 Statement: **Jury Didn't Hear**:

"As I recollect, my first step, after returning from my second visit to the Hospital at about 0900 [9 a.m.] in the morning of 31/08/1997, was to have a meeting with the people available at the Embassy in order to allocate responsibilities. There is so far as I am aware no record of the meeting, and I cannot recall in detail who attended....

"The meeting was ... joined by Mr Sherard Cowper-Coles, Political Counsellor at the Embassy, and I tasked him with acting as my assistant in dealing with French officials and also with those in the UK. Mr Cowper-Coles had arrived at about noon on 31/08/1997, to take up his new appointment as Political Counsellor.

"There were probably others at this meeting but I believe I have covered the main areas of responsibility.

"One official who was not at the meeting was the Second Secretary (Political), Mr Paul Johnston, who was not in Paris that weekend. On Monday 01/09/1997 I asked him to act as the point of contact with the judicial side of the French inquiry into the accident, given his responsibilities for Justice and Home affairs issues in the Embassy." [147]

---

[a] 4 appears to give an unequivocal answer. One could ask, recalling events over ten years ago, how could he be so sure? Normally when asked a question this specific a witness would say they could not recall the name "Andanson" coming up.

"I had asked Paul Johnston to make inquiries about the state of knowledge of the French authorities, and I refer to his minute dated 12/09/1997 to Mr Cowper-Coles (Head of Political Section at the Embassy): - '.... Neither the Interior Ministry nor the Prefecture de Police had been aware of the Princess' visit....'

"Mr Cowper-Coles also asked the Embassy's Drug Liaison Officer, Chief Inspector Nick Gargan to make enquiries of the French Police as to whether protection had been requested for the Princess of Wales, and I refer to Chief Inspector Gargan's minute to Mr Cowper-Coles of 15/09/1997: - ".... The first [the French police] heard of the Princess of Wales' visit was when they learned of the accident at the Pont d'Alma." [148]

Comment: To fully understand the significance of the embassy staff changes[a] – which have already been shown to be unusual – one needs to study each one on a case by case basis.

Sherard Cowper-Coles

Sherard Cowper-Coles was the most senior infusion into the political and economic departments of the Paris embassy in 1997. He came in as the political counsellor, which means that he immediately became the head of that department.

On the surface, Cowper-Coles did not directly appear to replace anyone – the official September 1996 list shows no person as the political counsellor.

There is however a possibility that Eugene Curley – First Secretary Political in September 1996 – became political counsellor at some point between January and 31 August 1997.

Curley's biography in the September 1996 List reads: "First Secretary Paris since March 1993".[149] In the following year, 1997, where Curley is removed from the official embassy list – see earlier – his biography has been changed to "First Secretary later Counsellor Paris since March 1993".

There are two aspects missing in the biography entries: a) there is no department shown[b] in either 1996 or 1997; and, b) the 1997 entry gives no month or year for the promotion from first secretary to counsellor.

Given that Curley appears as "First Secretary Political" in the 1996 embassy list, it would seem logical that his promotion to counsellor would have been in the same department and indeed it is the political department where the counsellor vacancy appears to exist on the 1996 List.

---

[a] The changes between September1996 and September 1997, highlighted in the above tables.
[b] Departments are normally shown in the List biography entries.

If Curley was promoted to political counsellor – the head of department – sometime between January and August 1997, then, based on the earlier discussions[a], that could have made Curley the head of MI6 France.

At the inquest, Mr 4 claimed that he was head of MI6 in France at the time of the crash – Burnett asked: "Were you in charge of any and all SIS staff in Paris [in August 1997]?" 4 replied: "Yes, and indeed in France."

Mr 4 also described himself as "a member of the senior staff in the Embassy".

During Mr 4's description of the circumstances in which he learned about the crash, he mentions in passing that he was "in bed with our baby daughter".

So there are three key facts known about Mr 4 in August 1997: a) he was head of "all SIS staff in Paris" and France; b) he was a senior Paris embassy staff member; and, c) he and his wife had a "baby daughter".

In the earlier Tomlinson evidence discussion it was indicated that the head of MI6 in France would also be the head of the political department.

The above evidence showed that Eugene Curley was promoted at some point in 1997 to become political counsellor, or the head of the political department. The biography sections of both the 1996 and 1997 Lists reveal that Curley also was father to a daughter born in 1996.[150b] She appears to be the "baby daughter" described by Mr 4.

This evidence indicates that Mr 4 at the inquest is Eugene Curley.

By September 1997 Cowper-Coles is showing in the official Diplomatic List as the political counsellor of the British Embassy in Paris and Curley no longer appears at all on the Paris list.

Sherard Cowper-Coles also appears on the MI6 list posted on the internet.[c]

---

[a] Regarding Tomlinson's account of embassy movements.

[b] Later evidence will show that Cowper-Coles may have actually been the head of MI6 in Paris at the time of the crash – contradicting the evidence of Mr 4. The List biography reveals that in 1997 Cowper-Coles did have a daughter, but she was born in 1986 and would have been 10 or 11 at the time of the crash – i.e. not a baby. This rules Cowper-Coles out from being Mr 4.

[c] UK journalist, Robert Fisk, wrote in *The Independent* in 2007: "I remember way back in the late 1970s – when I was Middle East correspondent for *The Times* – how a British diplomat in Cairo tried to persuade me to fire my local 'stringer', an Egyptian Coptic woman who also worked as a correspondent for the Associated Press and who provided a competent coverage of the country when I was in Beirut. 'She isn't much good,' he said, and suggested I hire a young Englishwoman whom he knew and who – so I later heard – had close contacts in the Foreign Office. I refused this spooky proposal. Indeed, I told *The Times* that I thought it was outrageous that a British diplomat should have tried to engineer the sacking of our part-timer in Cairo. *The Times's* foreign editor agreed. But it just shows what diplomats can get up to. And the name of that young British diplomat in Cairo back in the late 1970s? Why,

In summary, the points that indicate Mr 4 is Eugene Curley are:
- earlier discussions have indicated that the political counsellor in the Paris embassy would also be the head of MI6 in France
- only Curley and Cowper-Coles were political counsellors – at different times[a] – throughout 1997
- Curley had a daughter born in 1996 – she would have been the "baby daughter" described by Mr 4. Cowper-Coles had an 11 year old daughter
- the inquest evidence, and therefore the official MI6 account, is that Mr 4 was the head of MI6 France at the time of the crash and that Cowper-Coles didn't take up duties as political counsellor until lunchtime on 31 August 1997, after the crash. The 1997 Diplomatic List reveals that Curley was promoted to counsellor – which must have been political – prior to September 1997
- Mr 4 stated that he left the Paris embassy in early 1998[b]. Curley appears to have left sometime up to September 1997 as he is not in the September 1997 List. Cowper-Coles stayed in Paris until 1999. Mr 4 appears to have lied about the timing of his departure from Paris – this issue is addressed below.

At some point in 1997 Sherard Cowper-Coles replaced Eugene Curley as the head of the political department and I suggest also as the head of MI6 in France.

The question is: When did this occur? Was it before or after the Paris crash?

Mr 4 – Eugene Curley – gave sworn evidence at the inquest that he was still in Paris in early 1998[c], but that does not appear to be true as he was removed from the official Paris list published in January 1998, based on information from September 1997.[d]

In fact, the List published in January 1998 states in its Preface: "The List ... is based on information available in September 1997 but includes details of some later changes." [151]

Sherard Cowper-Coles, of course." Robert Fisk, 'Abu Henry' and the Mysterious Silence, *The Independent*, 30 June 2007.

[a] Given that the counsellor is the head of the department – see earlier – it is logical that there would be only one counsellor in a department at any one time. The official diplomatic lists support this – there is only one counsellor listed for each department in the embassy.

[b] This will be shown to be false.

[c] Mansfield asked: "Between September 1997 and possibly early 1998, were you still there?" Apparently without hesitation Curley replied, "I was". Curley did confirm that he had left Paris by December 1998 – see Mansfield questioning above.

[d] See earlier.

This then indicates that Eugene Curley may have been gone from Paris by September 1997 – not during 1998 as he stated at the inquest (see above and previous footnote).

This is supported by Michael Jay's account that Cowper-Coles started in Paris on 31 August 1997 – it is unlikely that two political counsellors would be working at the embassy at the same time, certainly not for any lengthy period.[a]

Why would Curley lie at the inquest about the timing of his departure?

Well, clearly it is not in MI6's interests to be seen bringing in a more senior section head – Sherard Cowper-Coles – just ahead of the assassination of Princess Diana.

It is a much better look to have the person who has been in Paris since 1993[b] – Eugene Curley – still there at the time of the crash and then replaced by Cowper-Coles at some point after the crash.

People could start asking questions if they learned that the head of MI6 in France had changed just before the tragic crash, particularly when it is already known – see earlier and later – that Richard Spearman had also arrived only five days ahead of the deaths.

Ambassador Michael Jay indicated that the transition to Cowper-Coles occurred about 12 hours after the crash, on 31 August 1997, when he rushed to Paris.[c]

But is that actually how it occurred? This requires investigation.

Cowper-Coles was not heard from at the inquest – he was not cross-examined and neither was his statement read out. I suggest this is incredible when one considers the admitted importance of Cowper-Coles' position – "head of the political section at the Embassy"[d] – and the claimed timing of his arrival – "lunchtime on 31st August" 1997.[e]

The fact that the 1997 Diplomatic List is based primarily on information from September 1997 indicates not only that Curley was gone by September, but also that Cowper-Coles was installed as political counsellor by September 1997.

I suggest that this is logical – why would they need two heads of that MI6 section operating from inside the same embassy?

The question is: Did the transition from Curley to Cowper-Coles take place before September 1997 – i.e. before the 31 August 1997 crash?

---

[a] See earlier footnote.

[b] The biography section of the List states that Curley had been in Paris since March 1993: Diplomatic List 1998, p167.

[c] See below and above: Jay: "[Cowper-Coles] was in language training, I think, in the South of France, and when he heard the news, he got into his car and drove straight up."

[d] Confirmed by Jay to Burnett.

[e] Confirmed by Jay to Burnett.

As stated above, there is no evidence from Cowper-Coles, but Curley was cross-examined, under the name Mr 4.

Curley's evidence raises several points to note:[a]

- Curley falsely confirmed to Mansfield that he was working in the Paris embassy "between September 1997 and possibly early 1998" – this has been covered above

- Curley was asked: "What did you do immediately" after hearing "the news that Diana had died". Instead of directly answering, Curley replies: "Well, I suppose, like everybody else, switched on the television".

- Curley then says he called the embassy: "I cannot remember who specifically I rang up"

- Curley was speaking so softly that there were concerns his evidence couldn't be properly heard – the Coroner told him: "I think that you are dropping your voice". This is the only time in the six months of hearings that this occurred

- Curley appears to be uncomfortable – he doesn't apologise for speaking too softly and in fact makes no comment on it at all.

Michael Jay said in his Paget statement: "At about 0900 in the morning of 31/08/1997 ... [I called] a meeting with the people available at the Embassy in order to allocate responsibilities.... The meeting was ... joined by Mr Sherard Cowper-Coles, Political Counsellor at the Embassy, and I tasked him with acting as my assistant in dealing with French officials and also with those in the UK. Mr Cowper-Coles had arrived at about noon on 31/08/1997, to take up his new appointment as Political Counsellor."

Then at the inquest Jay elaborated on this: "[Cowper-Coles] was in language training, I think, in the South of France[b], and when he heard the news, he got into his car and drove straight up."

So according to Jay, Cowper-Coles is in the south of France – that is about 700 km[c] from Paris. He hears the news of the crash, jumps in his car and heads for Paris, arriving at the embassy "at about noon" – in time to join a meeting Jay had commenced at about 9 a.m.

Eugene Curley's reaction to the news was completely different.

Curley says: "I was still in bed ... and I remember my wife ... telling me that it was on the news that Diana had died ... [at] about 9 o'clock.... I ... switched on the television and watched that as the events unfolded and then I

---

[a] These points relate directly to his inquest evidence – they need to be seen in the light of the general context of this Comment. The picture of what has occurred will become clearer as this chapter develops.

[b] In a 2011 interview Cowper-Coles said he did his language training in Lille – this is addressed later in this section.

[c] This is addressed in detail below.

rang up the Embassy. I cannot remember who specifically I rang up ... to see if I was required back, as a member of the senior staff.... I was told that there was no need for me to rush back, obviously it had nothing to do with SIS, but that the Ambassador would be holding a meeting of senior staff the following day.... There was a series of meetings [on 1 September 1997] and I went to at least one of them ... as a member of the senior management team in the Embassy."

If both Curley and Jay are telling the truth[a], then on 31 August 1997 the British Embassy in Paris had two heads of the political department – Eugene Curley and Sherard Cowper-Coles.

The first, Eugene Curley, had been working in the political department of the Paris embassy for 4½ years, since March 1993, part of the time as counsellor[152] – so he presumably would have had extensive recent experience in dealing with French authorities. With that background it would also be logical to presume that Curley spoke fluent French.

The second, Sherard Cowper-Coles, had no experience at all of working or living in Paris[b] and according to Jay appears to have cut short his French language training to rush up to Paris – "he was in language training ... he got into his car and drove straight up". Then when he arrives Jay "tasked him with acting as my assistant in dealing with French officials".

The question is: Why would Jay task a person – Cowper-Coles – who had no Paris experience with "dealing with French officials", when he had a person in the same role[c] – Curley – who was closer to Paris[d] and had 4½ years experience working in Paris?

Bearing in mind that we are looking at the handling of possibly the most significant event in Jay's five year[e] tenure as British ambassador to France.

Is Jay lying? Is Curley lying? Or are they both lying?

Jay said that Cowper-Coles was "in language training, I think, in the South of France". The south of France is a fairly large area – it covers four

---

[a] In the past, both Curley and Jay have been shown to be liars – Curley earlier in this chapter and Jay in Part 4.
[b] Cowper-Coles' 1997 Diplomatic List biography reads: "Counsellor FCO [London] since May 1993; born 8.1.55; [started] FCO 1977; Language student MECAS [Middle-East Centre for Arab Studies] 1978; Third later Second Secretary Cairo 1980; First Secretary FCO [London] 1983; Private Secretary to the Permanent Under-Secretary 1985; First Secretary (Chancery) Washington 1987; First Secretary FCO [London] 1991; on secondment to the International Institute of Strategic Studies 1993.": Diplomatic Service List 1998, p164.
[c] Head of the political department.
[d] See below.
[e] 1996 to 2001.

administrative regions.[a] According to LanguageCourse.net, in the south of France there is a French language school in Bordeaux, another in Toulouse, one also in Marseille, and three each in Montpellier and Nice. These schools were all operating in 1997.

All of these cities are at least 6½ hours by car from Paris – Bordeaux is approximately 6½ hours, Toulouse around 7½ hours, Marseille and Montpellier are both about 8¼ hours and Nice is close to 10 hours.[bc]

We are told by Jay that Cowper-Coles "heard the news ... got into his car and drove straight up" and he "arrived at about noon on 31/08/1997".

Princess Diana officially died at close to 4 a.m.

Given that six out of the eight language schools are in Marseille, Nice or Montpellier it seems likely that when Cowper-Coles left he was embarking on a driving journey of at least eight hours. According to his List biography, in 1997 Cowper-Coles had five children[d], the eldest was 15 and the youngest just 7 years old. I suggest this would make it unlikely for Cowper-Coles to have been accompanied by his wife. This, travelling solo, suggests that Cowper-Coles could have needed to have breaks on a long drive of this nature.

Even if Cowper-Coles had been notified of Diana's death soon after 4 a.m. one would have to add around 1½ hours for trip preparation and breaks. Added to the 8 hours, that makes at least 9½ hours for the trip. This means that the earliest Cowper-Coles could have arrived would have been 1.30 p.m. with limited sleep the previous night. Jay indicates that on arrival Cowper-Coles joined the meeting. This would have been at least 4½ hours after the meeting began at 9 a.m. – see earlier.

This evidence indicates that it would only have been possible for Cowper-Coles to have arrived in Paris by noon if he was learning French at the school in Bordeaux. But to do that, Cowper-Coles, who presumably was asleep, would have needed to have been notified very soon after Diana's 4 a.m. death – within 30 minutes of the announcement.[e]

---

[a] Running west to east: Aquitaine, Midi-Pyrenees, Languedoc-Roussillon and Provence-Alpes-Cote d'Azur.: www.south-of-france.com

[b] The distances by road are: Bordeaux – 583km; Toulouse – 678km; Marseille – 776km; Montpellier – 762km; Nice – 932km.

[c] Distances and times are from Himmera.com Map Distances: http://distancecalculator.himmera.com

[d] Four sons and one daughter.

[e] If Cowper-Coles had been in Bordeaux and had left at 5 a.m. he could have had a half hour break during the 6½ hour drive and arrived in Paris at around 12 noon, as stated by Jay.

Meanwhile according to Eugene Curley, he was "in a hotel ... near La Rochelle". He never received any notification of Diana's death, instead learning about it from his wife at about 9 a.m.[a]

The opposite reaction compared to Cowper-Coles, Curley was in no rush – and was not put into a rush by Jay. Curley says that: a) he "switched on the television and watched that as the events unfolded"; b) "then I rang up the Embassy ... to see if I was required back"; c) "I was told that there was no need for me to rush back, obviously it had nothing to do with SIS"; d) he was told "that the Ambassador would be holding a meeting of senior staff the following day"; e) On 1 September 1997 "I went to at least one of [the meetings] ... not so much SIS as me as head of station [but] as a member of the senior management team in the Embassy".[ba]

---

[a] I suggest that the head of MI6 in France would be contactable at all times.

[b] This appears to conflict with the gist of Jay's evidence – see earlier – that MI6 was effectively run as a separate department within the embassy. Jay said this: "Members of the SIS stationed abroad with the post receive their instructions from SIS headquarters in London". A fuller account of Jay's statement is near the start of this "Movements of MI6 Officers" section. I am suggesting that Curley has painted a picture of a dual role – head of MI6 in France and a member of senior management at the embassy. Jay's evidence indicates that as far as he was concerned those roles were one and the same – Jay just looked on MI6 as a section of the embassy. At the inquest he said things like: "The [reporting] relationship [of MI6] is exactly the same as with other sections of the Embassy."; "I had overall responsibility for the conduct of the Embassy as a whole, all the different sections in it, including the MI6 station."; "That is true for the head of that [MI6] section as for other sections of the Embassy". I suggest that Jay's account is common sense – in other words, MI6 officers working inside the embassy had one job – working for MI6 – and even though their official title might be "Counsellor Political", there was no dual role. As Mansfield suggested, "it is built on authorised deceit" – the title "political" is a name, but the person's sole job was to work as an MI6 officer. Peter Heap, who retired in 1995 after a long career in the British diplomatic service, including a stint as ambassador to Brazil, spoke out in 2003 about the MI6 role in embassies. Heap stated: "As a diplomat who worked in nine overseas posts over 36 years, I saw quite a lot of MI6 at work. They were represented in almost all of those diplomatic missions. They presented themselves as normal career diplomats, but often, indeed usually, they were a breed apart. And it normally only took the local British community a few weeks to spot them.... In one capital, the MI6 officers rarely wore suits to the office while the rest of us did..... The MI6 station within an embassy operates on a budget that is quite separate from and kept secret from the rest of the diplomatic staff, including the ambassador.... Ambassadors and diplomatic staff saw and commented on their intelligence reports that went to their HQ in London, but could not alter nor stop them, nor know the identity of the sources." Heap's comments indicate that other people in the embassy – not just the ambassador – would know who was in the MI6 section; there was a separate budget for the MI6 section and also reports by MI6

There is a huge difference between the situation and accounts of Cowper-Coles compared to Curley:
- Curley has 4½ years experience in Paris – Cowper-Coles had none
- Curley would have been a fluent French speaker – Cowper-Coles had just cut short his French language course
- Curley was in La Rochelle, about 5½ hours from Paris[b] – Cowper-Coles was probably at least 8¼ hours[c] away and at closest 6½ hours[d] from Paris
- Curley was already due to return to Paris on the Monday[e] – Cowper-Coles was apparently undergoing French language training; Jay doesn't say when Cowper-Coles was expected to transfer to Paris
- Curley does not receive any notification from the embassy: his first knowledge of Diana's death is from his wife[f] – Cowper-Coles has somehow learned about the death in the middle of the night.[g] I suggest it would be most unlikely that Cowper-Coles would drive "straight up" without first having communication from the embassy. It is implied that Cowper-Coles was notified very early by the embassy about the death of Diana
- Curley is told by the embassy after 9 a.m. "that there was no need ... to rush back" – Cowper-Coles appears to have been told close to 4 a.m. that he was needed urgently
- Curley attends an embassy meeting on Monday 1 September 1997 – Cowper-Coles attends a meeting at about noon on Sunday 31 August 1997.

At the meeting Cowper-Coles attended, Jay entrusts him "with acting as my assistant in dealing with French officials".

This is despite Curley being an officer who had over four years experience in dealing with French officials and also was located closer to Paris at the time of Diana's death.

---

staffers that could not be altered or stopped. Source: Peter Heap, The Truth Behind the MI6 Facade, *The Guardian*, 2 October 2003.

[a] Ms 1 describes attending a meeting on September 1 – she was an MI6 member, but not a "Head of Station" – see later. Ambassador Michael Jay made no mention of any meetings on 1 September 1997.

[b] Distance 470km.

[c] Marseille, Montpellier, Nice.

[d] Bordeaux.

[e] Curley said: "I was intending to go back to work some time the following Monday in any case."

[f] Curley: "I remember my wife ... telling me that it was on the news that Diana had died".

[g] Jay says, "he heard the news", but to make it to the embassy by noon, Cowper-Coles would have had to have been in Bordeaux and heard about the death very soon after it occurred – see above.

Jay makes no mention of Curley in any of his evidence[a], but does refer to Cowper-Coles several times:
- his attendance at the August 31 meeting – see above
- memo from Paul Johnston "dated 12/09/1997 to Mr Cowper-Coles (Head of Political Section at the Embassy)"
- "Mr Cowper-Coles also asked the Embassy's Drug Liaison Officer, Chief Inspector Nick Gargan to make enquiries of the French Police"
- "I refer to Chief Inspector Gargan's minute to Mr Cowper-Coles of 15/09/1997".

Michael Jay, who had access to reports drawn up at the time of the events[153], did state this: "One official who was not at the [31 August 1997] meeting[b] was the Second Secretary (Political), Mr Paul Johnston, who was not in Paris that weekend. On Monday 01/09/1997 I asked him to act as the point of contact with the judicial side of the French inquiry...."

So Jay specifically mentions the absence of Paul Johnston on 31 August 1997 and then his subsequent presence on the following day, when he assigned Johnston with a responsibility.

The question is: Why would Jay mention Johnston but not Curley, when Johnston ranked far lower in the embassy than Curley[c] – and Curley was a head of department?

Johnston and Curley both missed the August 31 meeting, but both turned up on September 1. Curley is the head of the department, Johnston is a second secretary. Johnston is mentioned by Jay, but Curley is ignored.

Why?

There are now several points that indicate Eugene Curley was no longer employed at the Paris embassy at the time of the crash:
- Curley does not appear on the official list of staff members drawn up from September 1997 information[d]
- Jay makes no mention of Curley in any of his evidence, but he does mention, a) Cowper-Coles, the officer who replaced Curley, and b) Johnston who was much more junior to Curley, but according to Jay, worked in the same political department[e]

---

[a] His diary written at the time, his Paget statement and inquest cross-examination.
[b] Attended by Cowper-Coles.
[c] In the 1996 List Curley was ranked 16 while Johnston was 38.
[d] See earlier list reproduced from the Diplomatic Service List 1998 (September 1997).
[e] There is some conflict over the position of Paul Johnston. Jay said that Johnston was the "Second Secretary (Political)" and this is supported by a letter from Hervé Stéphan to Johnston dated 1 December 1998 – he describes him: "Second Secretary for Political Affairs" (INQ0049253). Johnston is however listed in the official 1996 List as "Second Secretary (Private Secretary to Ambassador)" and in the 1997 List as "Private Secretary". Jay has never described Johnston as his private secretary – in his

- Curley's evidence regarding his movements around the time of the crash came across as diffident, at best – see earlier
- Cowper-Coles shows in the 1997 List as the political counsellor – it is unlikely that there would be two political counsellors at the same time
- at the time of the crash Curley would have had 4½ years of experience in speaking French and dealing with the French, yet Jay said he asked the inexperienced[a] Cowper-Coles to act "as my assistant in dealing with French officials"
- both Curley and Cowper-Coles[b] were heads of the political department yet they present almost opposite scenarios as to the response to the death of Diana
- Curley describes a meeting on 1 September 1997 that is not mentioned in any non-MI6 evidence, particularly Jay, who provided an in depth account of the events based on written reports made at the time.[c]

This evidence reveals that Curley has lied in his account – it has already been shown that Curley lied when he said to Mansfield that he was still at the embassy in early 1998. It now appears that Curley has also fabricated an account that he was returning from holiday and was at La Rochelle on 31 August 1997 and returned to work at the embassy the following day.

Why would Eugene Curley lie about this?

The reason will become clearer as this chapter progresses.

Michael Jay has stated that Sherard Cowper-Coles arrived at the Paris embassy around noon on 31 August 1997. It is significant that Cowper-Coles himself has never been interviewed and was not heard at the inquest.

There is an obvious link between Curley and Cowper-Coles – Curley was made the political counsellor at some point between September 1996 and August 1997 (see earlier), and Cowper-Coles succeeded Curley in that role.

Paget statement when referring to the people who attended the 31 August 1997, 9 a.m. meeting Jay said: "The meeting was I am almost sure attended by my Private Secretary, Mrs Catherine Bouron". Although there appears to be no logical explanation for this conflict, it does not seem to have any bearing on the case. Source: Michael Jay, Witness Statement, 13 December 2005, reproduced in *The Documents* book, 2010, p638 (UK Edition).

[a] In speaking to and dealing with the French.

[b] If both Jay and Curley were speaking the truth – it will be shown later that neither were.

[c] Ms 1 refers to a meeting she attended on September 1 – see later. That meeting is not the "meeting of senior staff" described by Curley, but a staff meeting chaired by Jay to deal with specific details.

The above evidence indicates that Curley vacated the Paris embassy at some point before the crash and it is logical that his successor, Cowper-Coles, would have taken up his new posting around the same time.

There are reasons to believe that Michael Jay has lied in his evidence regarding the circumstances of Sherard Cowper-Coles' arrival at the Paris embassy:

1) The timing of Cowper-Coles' arrival, as stated by Jay, is in itself extremely coincidental at best.

The suggestion by Jay is that the embassy's incoming political counsellor – the head of that department and also effectively the head of MI6 in France[a] – took up his duties just 12 hours after the crash.

This account should be viewed in the light of other factors:

a) that Jay indicated Cowper-Coles "was in language training" – this infers that he cut that training short to rush up to Paris.[b] This also indicates that Cowper-Coles' appointment was made well before the crash

b) that Richard Spearman, an MI6 officer who was also a senior employee in the political department[c], arrived in Paris on 26 August 1997, just 5 days before the crash – see earlier

c) the significance of the crash – it has already been shown to be the orchestrated assassination of Princess Diana and Dodi Fayed[d]

d) that MI6 are prime suspects for involvement in that assassination.

2) Jay appears to suggest that Cowper-Coles – a father to five children at the time[e] – made an instant decision to make the approximately 700km trip: "when he heard the news, he got into his car and drove straight up".

a) Based on the earlier calculations there is a logistical issue. Evidence has shown that distances from Paris to French language schools in the South of France range from 583km to 932km, with the majority being over 750km away.

There was not enough time[f] for Cowper-Coles to have made the trip if he had been located in the places where most of the schools are – Marseille, Montpellier or Nice (see earlier).

Even if he had been in Bordeaux, where the closest school is, there are certain factors – not indicated by the evidence – that would have had to fall into place:[g]

---

[a] See earlier.

[b] This is addressed earlier.

[c] Ranked second in the political department in 1997 – see Table 2 earlier.

[d] See Parts 1 to 4.

[e] See earlier.

[f] Between the death of Diana at 4 a.m. and his alleged arrival at noon.

[g] There are only 8 hours between 4 a.m. and noon and the driving time from Bordeaux to Paris is 6½ hours – see earlier.

- Cowper-Coles would have had to be called in the middle of the night (after 4 a.m.) or otherwise – if he is a light sleeper – have woken up and switched on the news

- Cowper-Coles would have needed to communicate with the embassy before leaving. I suggest that it is very unlikely that Cowper-Coles would have embarked on such a long drive around 5 a.m. in a foreign country without consulting the destination embassy first.[a]

3) Jay's original statement account makes no comment on the circumstances of Cowper-Coles' embassy arrival – "Cowper-Coles had arrived at about noon on 31/08/1997".

I suggest that when it was determined that Jay would be subjected to inquest cross-examination, a decision was made – because of the obvious problem with the timing[b] – that his evidence would have to be fleshed out.

Jay was asked by Burnett: "Am I right in thinking that Mr Cowper-Coles arrived to take up his posting in Paris only at lunchtime on 31st August?" I suggest that this is such an unusual piece of evidence that it had to be explained. This is when Jay replied with: "Yes. He was in language training, I think, in the South of France, and when he heard the news, he got into his car and drove straight up."

There was no challenge to this and no further questions were asked by any of the lawyers present.

The question is: Did Sherard Cowper-Coles arrive before the crash – in a similar way to Richard Spearman – and Jay has come up with, or been told to come up with, evidence indicating he arrived after the crash?

At this stage, I suggest it is logical that Cowper-Coles would have arrived at a time close to the departure of Curley, his predecessor.[c]

This issue will be addressed further after covering the evidence relating to the other political department officer changes, discussed below.

At the inquest Michael Jay said: "I would know the senior members of the SIS station". It has earlier been shown that Sherard Cowper-Coles would have been the most senior amongst the MI6 staff at the time of the crash.

---

[a] There also is a possible argument that the job Jay claims to have given Cowper-Coles after he arrived – "dealing with French officials and also with those in the UK" – doesn't logically justify the "hell for leather" rush trip that Cowper-Coles undertook to get to the embassy. What difference would it have made if Cowper-Coles had not arrived at work until the following day?

[b] That the head of the political department would commence his new position about 12 hours after the crash.

[c] It could be significant that in this evidence alleging Cowper-Coles took over on the day of the crash – 31 August 1997 – there is no mention of any contact between Cowper-Coles and the person he is taking over from, Eugene Curley.

In his 2005 statement Jay said: "I am not aware that any ... MI6 officers ... had been deployed in Paris during the weekend of 30/31st August 1997." Yet later in the same statement Jay says: "At about 0900 in the morning of 31/08/1997 ... [I called] a meeting.... The meeting was ... joined by Mr Sherard Cowper-Coles, Political Counsellor at the Embassy, and I tasked him with acting as my assistant in dealing with French officials and also with those in the UK."

Jay has said "I would know the senior [MI6] members"[a] and he says that he wasn't aware of any MI6 working that weekend, yet he admits meeting with Cowper-Coles on the Sunday and issuing instructions.

At some point in this Jay has lied.

There are different possibilities:[b]

a) Jay doesn't know who the senior MI6 staff are – in this case, the head of MI6 France[c]

b) Jay is aware that MI6 staff were working that weekend

c) Jay didn't meet with Cowper-Coles and didn't issue instructions.

Jay specifically stated: "I tasked [Cowper-Coles] with acting as my assistant in dealing with French officials and also with those in the UK".

Yet earlier in the statement he had said: "It was not my role to give the SIS officers stationed at the British Embassy in Paris specific instructions. These instructions they would receive from SIS headquarters in London."

There is no evidence linking Jay to MI6 and it is therefore illogical that he would be giving instructions to an MI6 officer – Cowper-Coles was the head of the political department and also appears on the MI6 internet list.

There is also no evidence of these "instructions" from Jay to Cowper-Coles being carried out.

---

[a] I suggest that is common sense, that the person in charge of the embassy would know who the senior MI6 personnel were.

[b] The three listed here are not mutually exclusive – more than one could be true.

[c] Richard Tomlinson wrote in his 2001 book: "Andrew Markham ... was selected for the 'Orcada' slot in Bonn. This was a deep-cover job, running MI6's most important agent in Germany, a high-ranking official in the Ministry of Finance. In return for a substantial salary, Orcada provided five-star CX on the German economy and interest rate movements.... The Orcada posting was so sensitive that only the ambassador in Bonn and H/BON were briefed and no one else in the embassy was even aware that Markham was from the 'friends' (FCO-speak for MI6). Markham thus had to learn to become a thoroughly convincing diplomat to fool his FCO colleagues, so he attended the FCO pre-posting training courses in addition to all his MI6 courses.": *The Big Breach*, pp158-9. This excerpt describes Markham being given an unusually sensitive posting – "only the ambassador in Bonn and H/BON were briefed". This indicates that most of the time the general embassy staff were aware of who among them was MI6 – except when it was very sensitive – and the ambassador and the local head of MI6 (in this instance, H/BON) would always be made aware.

The documents referred to by Jay in his statement were not reports from Cowper-Coles to Jay, but instead were minutes addressed to Cowper-Coles:
-   "I refer to [Johnston's] minute dated 12/09/1997 to Mr Cowper-Coles"
-   "I refer to Chief Inspector Gargan's minute to Mr Cowper-Coles of 15/09/1997".

Michael Jay made a very specific and thorough declaration: "I am not aware that any MI5 or MI6 officers, in which description I would include both SIS officers and any persons working with them or on their behalf, had been deployed in Paris during the weekend of 30/31st August 1997".

Mr 4 – Eugene Curley – stated at the inquest: "I am clear that we would have made arrangements for duty personnel, a duty officer and duty support staff" over the weekend.[a]

Mr 4 indicates here that there would always be MI6 staff on duty, even over a weekend – and I suggest that is common sense.

It appears that Jay has again lied – I suggest that it is unbelievable that, as ambassador, Jay would have been unaware that there were MI6 staff members on duty on weekends.

The evidence points to both Eugene Curley and Michael Jay lying in their evidence – Curley lied by stating he was still head of MI6 in France at the time of the crash and was still there in early 1998; Jay lied when he stated that Cowper-Coles had arrived in Paris at noon on 31 August 1997, just 12 hours after the crash.

Why did they do this?

What follows includes some speculation based on the known evidence.

There is a possibility that some of the senior MI6 officers in Paris, after they learned that they were needed to play a role in the assassination of Princess Diana, refused to participate.

This could account for late changes of staff in senior positions in the days or weeks leading up to 31 August 1997. It is possible that junior officers – even if they did play a role – may not have fully understood what they were involved in, because MI6 only provide information on a "need to know" basis.[b]

I suggest that Eugene Curley, who was head of MI6 France, could have refused to be involved in the assassination of the princess.[c]

---

[a] In reply to the question: "Are you able to tell the jury whether there were any other SIS staff in Paris that weekend?"

[b] See earlier.

[c] The 1999 List biography for Curley indicates that he took up a post in London in February 1998 – it reads: "Counsellor FCO since February 1998". It is not known what Curley did between the time he left Paris and took up the London post – he may have been on leave. The 1997 List – published in January 1998 – reveals that

This could have led to a decision to transfer Sherard Cowper-Coles from London to Paris. According to Cowper-Coles' List biography he had been "Counsellor FCO since May 1993"[154] and the 1996 List reveals that he was the head of the Hong Kong Department in September 1996.[155a]

I believe that there is a difference between prior involvement in the crash and later involvement in the cover-up. It is possible that an MI6 officer could refuse to participate in the orchestration of the crash, but agree to play a part in the subsequent cover-up[b], as part of an agreement to stay employed in the intelligence agency.

The evidence indicates that Eugene Curley has left Paris ahead of the crash, but has agreed to testify and provide false evidence at the ensuing inquest into the deaths.

The effect of Curley's evidence has been to protect Cowper-Coles:

- Curley helps distance Cowper-Coles from involvement in the crash.

Curley falsely states that he was head of MI6 France and was in charge – even though he was at La Rochelle – at the time of the crash. There could not be two heads of MI6 France at the same time.

- Curley helps distance Cowper-Coles from being an MI6 officer.

Curley indicates that he was still in France into early 1998. The inquest also heard that Cowper-Coles arrived by lunchtime on 31 August 1997.[c]

If Curley was head of MI6 France at the time of the crash and into 1998, then Cowper-Coles couldn't have been, even though he was head of the political section. This helps to create a false impression that there may not even be a link between MI6 membership and the embassy's political section. In so doing – and seen in the context of Cowper-Coles being openly named at the inquest (see below) – it also could raise the possibility in the minds of the jury that Cowper-Coles may not have had any association with MI6.

Scott Baker went to great lengths to ensure the names of MI6 officers were not used throughout the inquest proceedings. I believe this would have

---

whatever Curley was doing, he was not in Paris, because he is not listed in the Paris embassy staff list for September 1997 – shown earlier. Source: Diplomatic Service List 1999, p167.

[a] Cowper-Coles' biography in the List reveals that he had spent a substantial part of his MI6 career in London – from 1977, 1 year; from 1983 to 1987, 4 years; from 1991 to 1997, 6 years. Altogether, 11 out of 20 years in London.: Diplomatic Service List 1998, p164.

[b] "It's in the national interest."

[c] If the jury had had any idea that Cowper-Coles was an MI6 officer then this could have raised questions for them – the arrival 12 hours after the crash would have appeared more suspicious. Instead the jury were led away from drawing any links between Cowper-Coles and MI6 – see below.

led to a perception amongst the jury members that if a name was used then that person could not have been a member of MI6.[a]

Sherard Cowper-Coles was openly named during Michael Jay's cross-examination. I suggest this could have led the jury to falsely conclude that Cowper-Coles was not an MI6 officer. Other evidence – see earlier – shows that he was.

Cowper-Coles was never himself cross-examined and has never been interviewed by any of the police investigations. Had he been cross-examined it would have been under one of the MI6 codenames, but none of those people fit with what is known about Cowper-Coles.

In summary, what occurred at the inquest was:

- Curley[b] gave a false account that he was head of MI6 France until early 1998, when the truth is he left his Paris post prior to the crash
- Jay gave a false account of Cowper-Coles arriving at the Paris embassy just 12 hours after the crash
- this false evidence from Curley and Jay protected Cowper-Coles, who took Curley's place as head of MI6 France prior to the crash, and would have been in charge of the Paris MI6 staff orchestrating the crash.

Curley's false account that he was head of MI6 France and was on holiday in La Rochelle at the time of the crash had the effect of completely distancing MI6 from orchestrating the crash.

How could MI6 have been involved if their head in France wasn't anywhere near Paris at the critical time of the crash?

This strategy fits with the general cover-up that has occurred – how could the French have been involved if no authorities there even knew that Diana was in France until after the crash? How could anyone in the British embassy Paris be involved if they too had no awareness that Diana was in France?

How could MI6 have been involved if their head in France was 470km from the Alma Tunnel at 12.23 a.m. on 31 August 1997?

How could Cowper-Coles have been orchestrating a crash in Paris if he didn't even arrive in Paris until 12 hours after that crash had occurred?

Some might say – "the perfect alibi". But these are all falsehoods.[c]

Curley wasn't the head of MI6 France at the time of the crash. Curley was no longer employed in Paris[d] – Cowper-Coles had taken Curley's place.

---

[a] The names of Richard Spearman and Nicholas Langman were both used, but there was never any official admission that they were a part of MI6.

[b] Under the codename Mr 4.

[c] The French authorities' knowledge of Diana's whereabouts is covered in Part 3. The knowledge of British embassy members is addressed later in this volume.

[d] It could be significant that even though Curley is completely missing from the official 1997 Paris list (he has been replaced by Cowper-Coles) – based on

Cowper-Coles arrived in Paris well ahead of the crash – not 12 hours after it, as falsely stated by Jay at the inquest.

It was Cowper-Coles who organised the Paris end of the crash orchestration.[a]

And in a damning indictment on Lord Justice Scott Baker, it was Eugene Curley who was heard, whereas Cowper-Coles escaped cross-examination and the jury heard no evidence at all from him.[bc]

Sherard Cowper-Coles, Political Counsellor, Paris Embassy: 2011

Interview: **Jury Didn't Hear**:

"My reward for Hong Kong[d] was to be sent to Paris to be Political Counsellor there from 1997. I did some language training in Lille and I had a very happy just under two years there as head of the Political Section. I lived in the Gate House of the Embassy in Paris, working for Michael Jay who was the nicest of Ambassadors. We did the St Malo Agreement on Franco-British co-operation in defence but it wasn't, frankly, a terribly heavily loaded job.

"At Christmas 1998/Spring 1999 I discovered that Robin Cook was asking about me.... He decided to appoint me as his Principal Private Secretary and I went back to London in April 1999." [156]

Comment: Cowper-Coles was interviewed at his London workplace – at BAE systems – in March 2011.

There are several points about Cowper-Coles' comments regarding his stint in Paris:

September 1997 – his 1997 List biography still reads: "First Secretary later Counsellor Paris since March 1993". Curley's is not the only case where this type of conflict occurred. This is addressed later.

[a] The 1997 List biography reveals that Sherard Cowper-Coles was awarded a CMG – Commander, Order of St Michael and St George – in 1997. It is not known how or exactly when this occurred because Cowper-Coles does not appear on the official Queen's Birthday or New Year's honours lists for that year.: 1998 Diplomatic List, p164.

[b] Cowper Coles' biography states: "Language Student MECAS 1978" for two years. MECAS was the Middle East Centre for Arabic Studies based in Shemlan, Lebanon. It is possible that Cowper-Coles learned the French language during his college education (Hertford College Oxford). There is a further possibility that he acquired practical experience with French during his time in Lebanon where French is the second language.: 1998 Diplomatic List, p164.

[c] It is also notable that Cowper-Coles received no mention in the Paget Report even though the Michael Jay statement – quoted earlier – was taken by Paget officers during their investigation.

[d] Cowper-Coles was Head of the Hong Kong Department in the FCO for the three years preceding the handover to China on 30 June 1997.

1) The interviewer, Malcolm McBain, starts off the interview: "We are here to talk about your Diplomatic Service career." [a]

The shortest topic in the entire interview is Cowper-Coles' 20 months as Head of the Paris Embassy Political department – all-up the interview is over 4,000 words with just 83 words spent describing his time in Paris.

2) The elephant in the room is Princess Diana.

According to Michael Jay – see earlier – Cowper-Coles arrived on the day of Diana's death, 31 August 1997. Jay told the British police: "The death of the Princess of Wales was an event of immense importance.... The death of the Princess of Wales ... was momentous and unprecedented in my experience".

The question is: Why is it that Cowper-Coles does not mention Diana's death in this lengthy interview?

Instead Cowper-Coles suggests the whole job was low-key: "it wasn't, frankly, a terribly heavily loaded job".

Why? [b]

In the entire interview Cowper-Coles makes no such suggestion regarding any other diplomatic job he had – instead providing considerably more detail about his various roles, than he has given regarding the Paris position.

3) Despite Cowper-Coles providing very little information on his role in France – see earlier points – he manages to mention: "I did some language training in Lille".

If this statement was true, then it strengthens the case that Cowper-Coles was not rushed into Paris ahead of Diana's assassination.[c] In other words, the transfer to Paris was planned and language training took place ahead of Cowper-Coles taking up the post.

Although this concurs with Jay's inquest account – "he was in language training" – there is a significant conflict on where Cowper-Coles' training took place: Cowper-Coles says Lille, but Jay stated under oath at the inquest, "I think ... South of France".

---

[a] This interview was part of the British Diplomatic Oral History Program (BDOHP). The full interview can be viewed at: www.chu.cam.ac.uk/archives

[b] Cowper-Coles fails to explain this comment. It appears to be an explanation for why he has provided such little detail on his role in France. I suggest that this lacks common sense, as France is a key state to the UK – it is the next-door neighbour, it is an important nation in the EU.

[c] Lille is much closer to Paris than the South of France – see below and later footnote.

LanguageCourse.net[a] doesn't list any French language schools in Lille, but a general search on the internet reveals there would have been at least one school in Lille in 1997.[b] This account from Cowper-Coles needs to be viewed in the context of the other points mentioned here and bearing in mind that it is odd that Cowper-Coles mentions his language training location, but fails to spend much time explaining his actual role in the Paris embassy.

It was suggested in an earlier footnote that Cowper-Coles could have learned French at college and then later during his two years as a language student at MECAS (1978-80), which was in Lebanon, where French was the second language – see earlier.[c]

4) Cowper-Coles describes the posting to Paris as "my reward for Hong Kong" – he was Head of the FCO department that organised the transfer to China in 1997.

Cowper-Coles fails to explain what he means by this – is he suggesting that Paris was a "plum job"?

Again, this appears to undermine the suggestion that Cowper-Coles could have been rushed to Paris to organise the assassination.

But, is it true?

I suggest that the key points are 1 and 2 – that Cowper-Coles has only spent 83 words out of over 4,000 on his role in Paris; that Cowper-Coles has failed to mention his role in the aftermath of the Paris crash, despite it being one of the most significant events of the 20th century.

Dr Valerie Caton

Valerie Caton, the Paris embassy Finance and Economic counsellor, was one of only two females listed in the political and economic departments on the 1997 List.[d]

Caton replaced Peter Ricketts, who according to his 1997 List biography, was transferred back to London after three years in Paris, in April 1997.[157][e]

It is significant that even though Caton is officially listed as being in the embassy in September 1997, her biography in both the 1997 and 1998 Lists does not reflect that – they both read "SUPL[f] since October 1996".[158] Then in

---

[a] The same site used earlier to analyse the locations of the South of France language schools.

[b] There is the French language centre in the Lille Catholic University – ICL-Clarife.

[c] I suggest that it is likely Cowper-Coles would have read the Jay inquest evidence relating to him. In this interview – which was taken just last year – Cowper-Coles may have introduced Lille because of its proximity to Paris (about 226 km and 2½ hours travel): it makes a lunchtime arrival at the embassy more plausible.

[d] The other female was Caroline Copley – see later.

[e] He became Deputy Political Director to the Permanent Under-Secretary of State and Head of HM Diplomatic Service.: Diplomatic Service List 1998, p4.

[f] Special Unpaid Leave.

the 1999 List the biography reference to SUPL has been removed but there is still no reference to her being in Paris – even though she is still the Paris embassy's Finance and Economic Counsellor in September 1999.[159] In the 2001 List[a], the biography section finally acknowledges Caton's presence in Paris – "Paris since 1997" – but omits giving the month of her arrival.[160b] By this time – September 2001 – it appears Caton had moved on because the Finance and Economic Counsellor for Paris is now listed as David Frost.[161]

Why has Caton's 1997, 1998, 1999 and 2001 List biography not been correctly updated?

I suggest two possible reasons:

1) it is a mistake – this is unlikely because: a) it has been wrongly updated at least four times – 1997, 1998, 1999, 2001; and b) over the four years looked at, there are three different errors – first, in 1997 and 1998 Caton was showing as SUPL – on leave – when in fact she was working in the Paris embassy; second, in 1999 Caton is not showing on leave or in Paris – even though she was in Paris; third, when finally in 2001 the biography shows Caton in Paris since 1997, the month has been omitted.

2) it covers up Caton's date for moving to Paris.

Regarding point 2, it is important to understand that a person's name appearing on the official list gives no indication of the month in which the move was made. In other words, Caton appears on the 1997 list[c] as "Counsellor Finance and Economic: Dr V. Caton".[d] All this shows is that by the end of September 1997 Caton was installed as the Finance and Economic Counsellor in Paris. It does not show what month her move to Paris was made.

The information that reveals the month of the move is shown in the Biography section of the List. Because there is no entry in the 1997, 1998 or 1999 List biography for Caton's Paris move it is not possible to know – from the List – when it occurred. And even when the biography is updated showing Paris, in the 2001 List, the month of arrival is missing – it just reads "1997".

This omission becomes more significant when further research reveals that the very same "error" – omission of mention that he had moved to the Paris embassy – has occurred in both the 1997 and 1998 List biography for

---

[a] The author has not been able to obtain a copy of the 2000 List.
[b] It is standard for the month of arrival to be shown in the biography entry for the latest posting.
[c] And also the 1998 and 1999 Lists.: Diplomatic Service List 1999, p34; Diplomatic Service List 2000, p34.
[d] See 1997 Paris List reproduced earlier.

Sherard Cowper-Coles.[a][b] The first admission in the Biography section of Cowper-Coles' move to Paris comes in the 1999 List – by which time he had already been moved back to the FCO in London and it was no longer required to show the month of the Paris arrival.[c]

I suggest that this is no coincidence – both of these people, Caton and Cowper-Coles, made significant moves into Paris around the time frame of the crash. It is not that the information was not known, even at the time the 1997 List was made – the month of the move must have been known because both Cowper-Coles and Caton were included in the 1997 official Paris List.[d]

So I suggest that both the 1997 and 1998 Paris Lists have been updated but the biography sections for Cowper-Coles and Caton have deliberately not been updated.[e][f][a]

---

[a] The latest entry for Cowper-Coles in both years' biography section reads: "Counsellor FCO since May 1993". There is no reference at all to his transfer to Paris, despite the fact that the 1998 official List reveals that he was still serving as Counsellor Political in Paris.: Diplomatic Service List 1998, p164; Diplomatic Service List 1999, pp34,163.

[b] The 1999 List reveals that Cowper-Coles took up a new post in April 1999 – "Private Secretary to the Secretary of State for Foreign and Commonwealth Affairs".: Diplomatic Service List 2000, p166.

[c] The month of arrival is always only shown for the latest move – which in this case, by 1999, was the move to the FCO.

[d] This is not to do with biographies not being updated. For example, it has been shown earlier that Richard Spearman's 1997 List biography showed an August 1997 transfer to Paris. This is why Richard Tomlinson was able to declare in his November 1998 letter to Judge Stéphan: "I do not believe it a coincidence that Mr Spearman should arrive in Paris only a few weeks before the incident at the Pont d'Alma." It was later revealed that Spearman moved to Paris on 26 August 1997 – see earlier.

[e] The 1997 List biography for Caton shows that she was First Secretary Chancery in Paris from 1988 to 1992-3. Looking through other people's biographies it appears to be unusual for someone to be reposted to the same city after just a few years. Caton left Paris in 1993 but was reposted there in 1997.: Diplomatic Service List 1998, p154. One could argue that if the reposting to Paris was made in a hurry and was connected to the crash, it may have been useful to have someone with recent prior experience in Paris.

[f] As stated in the previous footnote the 1997 List biography for Caton reads "First Secretary Chancery Paris 1988" to 1992-3. In a 2006 press release publicising the appointment of Valerie Caton to the role of ambassador to Finland, Downing Street provided her curriculum vitae – it includes "1988-1992 Paris; First Secretary Political". As shown earlier MI6 officers are generally found in the political and economic sections of embassies. Why is there a conflict between the government press release and the List biography? Has the List biography been doctored? Source: Press Office Downing Street, Change of Her Majesty's Ambassador to the Republic of Finland, 26 January 2006: www.gov-news.org/gov/uk/news

Other MI6 Officers

The inquest heard evidence from other MI6 officers who said they were in Paris on the weekend of the crash.

Ms 1, MI6 Officer. British Embassy, Paris: 12 Jan 05 Statement read out 29 Feb 08: 35.24:

"I worked on the Paris station ... I was in Paris on the weekend, on 30th/31st August 1997 as I was on call and had to be in the city. I had friends staying during the previous week who left I believe on Saturday morning. My diary shows that I had a restaurant reservation on the Friday evening (probably with the friends) and the Saturday evening entry is blank, which indicates to me that I was at home with my husband.

"On Sunday morning, one of the Embassy locally employed staff ... telephoned my home to confirm arrangements for a pre-arranged barbecue at his country home. He spoke to my husband and during that conversation he told my husband of the crash involving Diana. This was the first I knew of the crash or the presence of Diana and Dodi Al Fayed in Paris. I had had no indication that they may be coming to the city. I would not have expected to be informed of any visit by the Princess of Wales unless it was an official visit and required attendance at functions.

"I was not asked to carry out any tasks in relation to the crash as it had no connection to SIS work....

"I do not know where any of the other SIS station staff were that weekend...."

Mr 5, MI6 Officer. British Embassy, Paris: 13 Jan 05 Statement read out 29 Feb 08: 37.14:

"I was part of the SIS station team in Paris. On Saturday 30th August 1997 I was in Paris. I cannot remember specifically, but I believe that during the day I may have gone shopping with my wife and child. I do however recall that during the evening I had a meal with my wife and child at the Thoumieux Restaurant in Rue St Dominique. We were at the restaurant from about 7.30 pm until about 10 pm. It was dark when we left. I believe that we took a taxi home because of the lack of public transport from the restaurant to my home.

"I am a light sleeper and often sleep with the radio on. On that night I recall listening to BBC5 Live and at about 2 or 3 am I first heard reports of the crash involving Princess Diana. I turned on the TV and watched the coverage, some of which was from the Alma Tunnel. I recall the formal statement at about 6 am that Princess Diana was dead. I believe I was the

---

[a] Valerie Caton spoke fluent French and would not have required any language training. Caton was a French tutor at the University of Exeter from 1978 to 1980.: Debrett's People of Today, Biography: Dr Valerie Caton: www.debretts.com/people/biographies

duty officer on call that weekend, but I took no action because I believed the response to the incident was not an SIS responsibility. The Embassy staff would be responsible for any arrangements and action necessary following such an incident. I had the impression that I was the only SIS member of staff around Paris that weekend, but do not know the movements or locations of any of the other staff.[a]

"I went to work at the Embassy on Monday morning and attended a meeting chaired by the Ambassador, Sir Michael Jay. A roster was set up to supervise the book of condolences in the residency and work was planned for a memorial service for Diana the following week, but I did not get involved in any of this.

"I knew from media coverage that Diana had recently been on a boating holiday in the South of France but I had no knowledge of her visit to Paris until I heard it on the radio, as I have already stated...."

Comment: It is more difficult to identify Ms 1 and Mr 5, than Mr 4 (Curley) and Mr 6 (Spearman)[b] – 1 and 5 were never cross-examined, and there is less known information about the other people who were in the political and economic departments at the time of the crash: Cowper-Coles, Caton, Roberts, Copley, Hendry, Fitchett, Wightman, Raynes, Langman and Powell.[c]

In the above list, there are two females – Valerie Caton and Caroline Copley.

Ms 1 states: "the Saturday evening [diary] entry is blank, which indicates to me that I was at home with my husband". There is no mention of any children.

The 1997 List reveals that Caton had a son born in 1994[162], and a British government press release at the time of her 2006 appointment as ambassador to Finland states: "Children: One daughter (1992) & one son (1994)".[163d]

Caroline Copley's 1997 List biography reveals that she was married in 1996 and has no children listed.[164]

This evidence indicates that Ms 1 is very likely to be Caroline Copley.

---

[a] 5's assertion: I had the impression that I was the only SIS member of staff around Paris that weekend" appears to conflict with his very next statement: "but do not know the movements or locations of any of the other staff". The evidence from 6 and 1 was that they were in Paris and 4 (Curley) indicated that on any given weekend there would be at least three staff on duty – see later.
[b] See earlier.
[c] Other personnel have been left off this list because their 1997 biography states they left Paris before the crash: Ricketts – April 1997; the Kirks – March and April 1997; Nolan – June 1997; Fraser – March 1997.
[d] It is not known why there is a conflict between the List and the press release.

We are then left with the remaining eight males – Cowper-Coles, Roberts, Hendry, Fitchett, Wightman, Raynes, Langman, Powell – one of which should be Mr 5.

Mr 5 said in his statement: "during the day I may have gone shopping with <u>my wife and child</u>.... During the evening I had a meal with <u>my wife and child</u> at the Thoumieux Restaurant".

Of the eight men listed above, there are two who are not included in the List biography section, even though they are on the official 1997 embassy list[a] – they are first secretaries G.J. Hendry (political) and P.J.E. Raynes (economic).[b]

Of the remaining six men, only one is described in the 1997 List biography section as married with one child[c] – he is Hugh Powell, who had been second secretary political at the Paris embassy since April 1993. Powell's biography reveals that he was married in 1993 and had one son born in 1996.

I suggest it is likely that Hugh Powell is Mr 5, but one can't be certain because the biographical details of Raynes and Hendry remain unknown (see above).[d]

There appears to be a significant conflict in the MI6 evidence regarding who was on the ground in Paris on the Saturday night, 30 August 1997.

Eugene Curley (Mr 4) was asked: "We have heard read to us the evidence of Witnesses 1 and 5 who were in Paris that weekend. We are also going to be hearing from witness 6, who was in Paris that weekend. Are you able to tell the jury whether there were any ... SIS staff [other than Ms 1, Mr 5 and Mr 6[e]] in Paris that weekend?" Curley replied: "I know that – I remember well that witness 6 was in town, and I am clear that we would have made arrangements for duty personnel, a duty officer and duty support staff, but in terms of who specifically was doing what, I cannot clearly remember that."

Curley has failed to answer the question.

---

[a] Reproduced earlier.

[b] Hendry and Raynes also don't show on the MI6 internet list.

[c] The others are: Sherard Cowper-Coles – married in 1982, 5 children, born in 1982, 1984, 1986, 1987 and 1990; Colin Roberts – single, no children; Robert Fitchett – married in 1985, 3 children, born in 1987, 1988 and 1993; Andrew Wightman – married in 1988, no children; Nicholas Langman – married 1992, 2 children, born in 1994 and 1995.: Diplomatic Service List 1998, pp164, 186, 230, 279, 316.

[d] It is not known why Raynes and Hendry do not have biographical details published. There is a possibility that they were undeclared MI6 officers, but I suggest it is unlikely that undeclared officers would appear on the official list for the Paris embassy.

[e] Richard Spearman.

The question is about "whether there were any other SIS staff in Paris that weekend". Burnett has just told Curley that Ms 1, Mr 5 and Mr 6 have already said they were in Paris – but was there anyone else?

Instead of answering the question, Curley: a) reiterates part of what he has already been told – "witness 6 was in town"; b) makes a general comment[a] – "we would have made arrangements for duty personnel, a duty officer and duty support staff"; c) says he doesn't remember "who specifically was doing what".

Basically Curley's answer, despite being lengthy, completely sidesteps the question.

Why?

All the information Curley has given could have been provided by a former head of MI6 France who by 30-31 August 1997 was no longer involved in what was happening with MI6 in Paris:[b]

- Curley says: "witness 6 was in town" – Burnett has just told him that
- Curley relates general weekend duty arrangements – that is something Curley would have known from his general past experience as political counsellor in Paris
- Curley says he doesn't remember "who specifically was doing what" – this is completely unrelated to the question[c] and adds to the perception that Curley wasn't involved.[d]

All Burnett was trying to ask was: who amongst the MI6 staff was in Paris on the weekend of 30-31 August 1997?

Burnett, who already knows the answer[e], now comes at the same question from a different angle. He asks if Curley has "had an opportunity of reading the [Paris MI6 Paget] witness statements". Curley confirms.

Then Burnett asks if "Paget took statements from all [Paris] SIS members". Again Curley confirms.

Next Burnett tells Curley the answer to his original question about "whether there were any other SIS staff in Paris that weekend". Burnett states to Curley: "All the others in their statements set out where they were that weekend and none was in Paris." Burnett asks Curley to confirm that – Curley: "That is right."

---

[a] It's non-specific – doesn't name anyone who could have been there, by codename or otherwise.

[b] As was Curley's situation – this has been shown earlier.

[c] The question was about "whether there were any other SIS staff in Paris that weekend" – not what they were doing.

[d] Some might argue that Curley was still on holiday in La Rochelle. I suggest that even if he was in La Rochelle but was still in charge in France and wasn't aware of "who specifically was doing what" on the weekend Princess Diana was assassinated, he would have made it his job to find out after he returned to work.

[e] He gives it to Curley below.

In this period of cross-examination one simple question – were MI6 staff in Paris? – was not answered and then turned into a series of four questions.[a] In all of this, Curley provided no information at all from the perspective of a person who was actually in charge of the personnel he was meant to be commenting on.

Instead all the information came from Burnett – "witnesses 1 and 5 ... were in Paris that weekend"; "witness 6 ... was in Paris that weekend"; "Operation Paget took statements from all [Paris] SIS members"; "all the others ... set out where they were that weekend and none was in Paris".

I suggest that when Burnett asked Curley the original question – "Are you able to tell the jury whether there were any other SIS staff in Paris that weekend?" – the true answer would have been "No".[b]

That would not have been a good look for MI6 – Mr 4 was claiming to be the head of MI6 in Paris, so why would be not be able to answer such a simple question?

This was an easy question for someone who knew the official answer[c] – "Yes" and then "There were no other SIS staff in Paris that weekend".

But Curley was not able to answer it. He didn't – and possibly never did – know the answer. The reason being that he had already left his posting in Paris at some point prior to the crash – see earlier.

Instead of answering "No" (see above), Curley had to bungle his way through territory he "should" have known but didn't.[d]

Curley starts off his answer: "I know that – I remember well that witness 6 was in town". Now Curley had just been told by Burnett that "witness 6 ... was in Paris that weekend".

It is possible that Curley started off with "I know that" and then reminded himself that he was supposed to be portraying a person who was a witness recalling events that they were a part of. He then starts again "I remember well", but then he doesn't provide anything more than what Burnett has just told him. For example, why or how does he remember it so well? [e]

---

[a] See the original questions and answers shown just before the Embassy Tables section.

[b] "No, I am not able to tell the jury whether there were any other SIS staff in Paris that weekend."

[c] This is the official answer provided by MI6 – I suggest that the evidence indicates this is not the truth (see earlier and later).

[d] He "should" have known it if he had been in charge, but the earlier evidence indicates that he was no longer in charge – Cowper-Coles, who wasn't cross-examined, had taken over.

[e] Bearing in mind that Curley has said that he was near La Rochelle at the time.

Curley can "remember well" something he has just been told by Burnett, but is unable to remember the answer to the question.

I am not suggesting that Curley – if he had been near La Rochelle – would remember from on location knowledge, because he is not claiming to have been in Paris. But the point is that if Curley was the head of MI6 Paris – as he claims[a] – then when he arrived back at the office he would have been finding out where his staff had been over that weekend. The Diana assassination was so big, and Curley's officers have been labelled as suspects right from early on – it is clear that if MI6 were not involved from the top, then they would be finding out who was involved. They would be asking questions like: "Do we have rogue officers in Paris?" or "Where were all our officers that weekend?"

So, if Curley was still in charge and MI6 were not involved in orchestrating the crash, then I suggest Curley would have made it his business to find out where his officers had been that weekend.

I believe the reality though is: a) that Curley was no longer in charge in Paris – Cowper-Coles was (see earlier); and b) MI6 were involved – from the top on down.[b]

The assertion that Curley was no longer in charge is supported by his failure to provide an answer to Burnett's simple question: "Are you able to tell the jury whether there were any other SIS staff in Paris that weekend?"

Nevertheless, in his initial answer Curley did provide critical evidence regarding MI6 Paris staffing on any given weekend – "I am clear that we would have made arrangements for duty personnel, a duty officer and duty support staff".

"A duty officer and duty support staff" – that's three or more people: one duty officer and two or more duty support staff.

Mr 5 has stated: "I believe I was the duty officer on call that weekend".

Ms 1 has stated: "I was in Paris ... as I was on call and had to be in the city".

It is important at this point to understand that there is a critical difference between being on "duty" and on "call".

The Oxford Dictionary states under "on duty": "doing one's regular work" – so in the current scenario, that would mean an officer working for MI6 Paris during the weekend of 30-31 August 1997.

The Oxford definition for "on call" is: "available to provide a professional service if necessary".

Curley – who had before this been the head of MI6 France – does not say anything about staff being on call, he says: "duty personnel, a duty officer and duty support staff". He then adds: "but in terms of who specifically <u>was doing what</u>, I cannot clearly remember that".

---

[a] See earlier.
[b] This will become clearer as this book progresses.

Curley describes staff "doing" things – this would fit with the above dictionary definition for "on duty".

Mr 5 and Ms 1 describe something quite different – they describe themselves doing nothing workwise, following their normal weekend pursuits, but being "on call".

My understanding of intelligence – from extensive research – is that it does not shut down come the weekend.

Even when a major event does occur right in the middle of their territory, these "on call" MI6 officers do not let it affect their weekend – Ms 1: "I was not asked to carry out any tasks in relation to the crash as it had no connection to SIS work"; Mr 5: "I took no action because I believed the response to the incident was not an SIS responsibility".

The point here is that the primary stated function of an intelligence officer is to gather information – otherwise known as intelligence. I suggest that if MI6 wasn't involved in the assassination of the British princess, then MI6 would have been making it an urgent priority to covertly find out who had eliminated their princess.

And Mr 5 and Ms 1, being on the ground "on call" in Paris, would be where MI6 would start its post-event secret gathering of intelligence regarding this unexpected disaster.

Ms 1 has stated she was "on call", but has never suggested she was on duty – she has instead provided evidence that: "I had friends staying ... who left ... on Saturday morning"; "on Sunday morning, one of the Embassy locally employed staff ... telephoned my home to confirm arrangements for a pre-arranged barbecue at his country home".

Mr 5 has described himself as "the duty officer on call that weekend", but later goes on to say: "I had the impression that I was the only SIS member of staff around Paris that weekend, but do not know the movements or locations of any of the other staff." [a]

Although he has used the same term – "duty officer" – as Curley, 5's evidence does not fit with Curley's. Curley does not say anything about "on call" and Curley also indicates there would be at least two "duty support staff" – by inference the support staff would be supporting the duty officer.

Yet, Mr 5 has claimed to be the "duty officer on call", with apparently no support staff that he knew of – "I was the only SIS member of staff around Paris" and "[I] do not know the movements or locations of any of the other staff".

---

[a] 5 also said he went shopping and to a restaurant with his wife and child.

Evidence has also been heard from Mr 4 and Mr 6.[a] I suggest this is a key part of an MI6 officer's evidence – if they were on duty on the weekend of the crash then that would be one of the first things they would divulge in their account.

Neither of these officers – 4 (Curley) and 6 (Spearman) – have indicated that they were on duty or on call: 4 said he was near La Rochelle; 6 arrived in Paris just five days before the crash and was at a restaurant birthday celebration with his wife.[b]

I suggest it is unlikely that Mr 6 would have been on duty or on call, if he was out on a birthday celebration with his wife, and he has never said that he was on duty.

Eugene Curley confirmed – see above – that "all the others[c] ... set out where they were that weekend and none was in Paris".

This evidence – from the MI6 officer accounts – indicates that <u>no one was on duty</u> and Mr 5 and Ms 1 are the only personnel who were on call in Paris on the weekend of 30-31 August 1997.

This is a major conflict from Curley's evidence – "I am clear that we would have made arrangements for duty personnel, a duty officer and duty support staff".

I suggest that Curley's account is common sense – it is ridiculous to suggest that a key organisation like MI6 would have no staff members on duty in a city the size of Paris on a normal weekend.

Curley has at least three people on duty, whereas the evidence supplied by the MI6 officers in Paris shows no one on duty and just two people on call – Mr 5 and Ms 1.

There are only two possibilities:

1) Curley is wrong and the other MI6 officer statements are all true – this would mean that there were no MI6 officers on duty[d] on the weekend of 30-31 August 1997

2) Curley is right – there are three or more duty staff on a normal weekend.

I suggest – as stated above – that it would be ridiculous to conclude that there would be no MI6 officers in Paris on duty in a normal weekend. This indicates that Curley is correct, which also I believe is common sense.

This then leads to one of two inescapable possibilities:

1) that MI6 officers have lied in their accounts – not just one, but three or more have stated that they were out of Paris or not working, when in fact they

---

[a] There were other MI6 officers who were heard, but they were not part of the Paris MI6 station – they gave evidence in connection with the Milosevic assassination plot (see earlier).

[b] See earlier.

[c] Other than Ms 1, Mr 4, Mr 5 and Mr 6.

[d] And only two on call – Ms 1 and Mr 5.

were on duty in Paris. This is not to say they were involved in orchestrating the crash, but that the officers have lied in their evidence

2) that MI6 was involved in the orchestrated assassinations of Princess Diana and Dodi Fayed and there has been a major cover-up in the statements and inquest evidence of Paris-based MI6 officers.

If point 1 was true, it would mean that these three or more officers have lied in unison for no apparent reason, because they have nothing to cover-up – they were not involved in the assassinations.

I suggest that is very unlikely – why would three or more MI6 officers lie for no reason?

The evidence points to number 2 above and the question again is: Why is there a cover-up if there is nothing to cover up?

This evidence adds to the evidence already seen in this volume – a building dossier that will lead to the conclusion that MI6 were not innocent bystanders, but instead had been involved in previous assassination plots, made sure that the right people were stationed in the Paris embassy before the weekend of the crash, were involved in the orchestration of the assassinations of Princess Diana and Dodi Fayed and have been a major party to the ensuing huge cover-up.

In summary, there are two main issues that indicate the MI6 evidence is not credible:

1) Taken together, all the MI6 witnesses are saying that no one was on duty in the MI6 Paris station on the weekend of 30-31 August 1997 – I suggest this is not credible[ab]

---

[a] This type of evidence fits with the thematic way the general cover-up has been conducted. The French unanimously said they never knew Diana was in France – see Part 3; the British Embassy staff unanimously said they never knew Diana was in France – see later this volume; and here, MI6 staff are unanimously saying they were not working that weekend – most even were out of Paris. How could they possibly have been involved if no one was aware or on duty? In this way, the authorities in both France and the UK have attempted to distance themselves from involvement in the crash.

[b] The British Embassy staff interviewed – which included all the MI6 staff – all (except Ritchie and Gunner – see later) said they weren't aware Diana was in France until after the crash had occurred. The reality is – see Part 2 – that Diana and Dodi arrived in Paris at 3.20 p.m., with paparazzi and police at the airport to welcome them. This means that we have people like Mr 5 – who said "I am a light sleeper.... On that night I recall listening to BBC5 Live and at about 2 or 3 am I first heard reports of the crash" – listening to the news in the early hours, but not during the afternoon or evening, when Diana's arrival would have been reported.

2) Even if one believes that the MI6 accounts that no one was on duty are true, then if MI6 were not involved in the orchestration of the crash, there would have had to have been personnel on duty following the crash.[a]

In other words, MI6 was either involved in the crash, or would have taken a very keen interest following the crash – to establish through intelligence whether it was an accident, or who actually was responsible.

MI6 witnesses in Paris have said that they were not involved in the crash and also took no specific interest following the crash[bc] – I suggest this also is not credible.

We have a situation where there were 11 political and economic department staff[d] working in the British Paris embassy around the time of the crash – see earlier Table 3. Earlier evidence has indicated that these staff are the people that made up the MI6 Paris station.

Of those 11 – Cowper-Coles, Caton, Spearman, Roberts, Copley, Hendry, Fitchett, Wightman, Raynes, Langman, Powell – only one (Spearman, Mr 6) was cross-examined at the "thorough" inquest held by Scott Baker.[efg]

Not one of these 11 people – who are alleged suspects involved in the assassinations – have ever had their alibis for the night of 30-31 August 1997 properly checked.

---

[a] The MI6 evidence – Curley and Ms 1 – indicated that meetings involving MI6 officers didn't take place until Monday, 1 September 1997, the day following the crash. This tends to also have the effect of undermining the significance of the crash regarding MI6 and reinforces their mantra: "We had nothing to do with it".

[b] In addition to the reactions of Ms 1 and Mr 5 shown above, Mr 6 (Richard Spearman) has also admitted to being in Paris at the time of the crash. When he was asked at the inquest: "On that Sunday, so that is Sunday 31st August 1997, did you make any contact with the British Embassy?" He replied: "I did not, no."

[c] One could argue that Sherard Cowper-Coles is the exception – he rushed up to Paris from the South of France (see earlier). Cowper-Coles though has never been interviewed by any of the investigations – that evidence came from Michael Jay who has been shown at times to have lied under oath. At the inquest it was also never admitted that Cowper-Coles was in MI6. Other evidence indicates that he was, and that he was already in Paris at the time of the crash – see earlier.

[d] Excluding Curley, who has been shown to have left ahead of the crash and is not in the official 1997 List.

[e] Others, Ms 1 and Mr 5, had statements read out, but were not subjected to cross-examination.

[f] Eugene Curley, Mr 4, was cross-examined, but he was not part of the Paris embassy staff at the time of the crash – see earlier.

[g] It is significant that while only one Paris-based MI6 officer – Spearman (Mr 6) – was cross-examined, three MI6 officers who were part of the Balkans team – Mr A, Mr E and Mr H – were cross-examined in connection with a 1992 piece of paper (which has since been destroyed) outlining the Milosevic plot. This is despite the fact that Diana was assassinated in Paris and not in the Balkans.

For example, Spearman says he produced his credit card statement –
"when I was asked for it, I was able to produce it" – substantiating he was at
a restaurant, the Bistro d'a Côte. It has been shown in an earlier footnote[a] that
this may have been for a dinner on the night following the crash, not before
it.

The question here is: Why was this credit card statement – which is
crucial to Spearman's alibi – not shown to the inquest jury who were
investigating the deaths?

Spearman does not tell us who "asked for it". It is interesting that Paget
make no comment about Spearman providing a credit card statement or any
corroborating documentary evidence[b], even though they normally appeared
very keen to state they had supporting evidence where they could.[c]

Ms 1's alibi is: "the Saturday evening[d] [diary] entry is blank, which
indicates to me that I was at home with my husband". I suggest that this is
not a particularly convincing alibi – there is no evidence of Ms 1's husband
being questioned on this.

Mr 5 said: "during the evening [of 30 August 1997] I had a meal with my
wife and child at the Thoumieux Restaurant in Rue St Dominique". Again,
there is no evidence this has ever been checked out with: a) the restaurant;
and, b) 5's wife. There was no documentary evidence proffered.

Sherard Cowper-Coles – who it has been shown was the head of MI6
France at the time of the crash – does not appear to have ever been asked for
an alibi. Michael Jay has said that Cowper-Coles was "in the South of
France" and "arrived [in Paris] at about noon on 31/08/1997" – 11½ hours
after the crash.[e]

Why has Cowper-Coles never been interviewed by any police and was not
heard from at the inquest?

The jury was told by inquest lawyer, Ian Burnett:[f] "All the others[a] in their
statements set out where they were that weekend and none was in Paris".

---

[a] In the Richard Spearman and Nicholas Langman section.

[b] Paget only state that the restaurant was named, without supplying the name. See
next footnote.

[c] Paget's account of this is on page 767 of the Paget Report: "Richard Spearman was
in Paris on the weekend of 30/31 August 1997. That date coincidentally was his
birthday (as confirmed in the British Diplomatic Service List) and he was out that
evening for a meal with his wife at a named restaurant. Their children were left at
home with a babysitter (named)."

[d] 30 August 1997.

[e] Earlier evidence in this volume has raised issues regarding the timing of Cowper-
Coles' trip.

[f] Confirmed by Curley, who wasn't in Paris – see earlier.

Why were the jury not shown these statements from "all the others"?

Not only have the alibis from these people not been properly checked, but the jury have not even been told what their specific alibis are.[b]

Why is this? Why this casual disregard of key evidence from suspects to the assassinations of Princess Diana and Dodi Fayed?

---

[a] Paris MI6 employees.

[b] Paget gave an alibi for Nicholas Langman – not heard by the jury: "Nicholas Langman was on leave on the weekend of 30/31 August 1997, staying with relatives in England. Statements corroborating his account have been obtained." (Paget Report, p767). The question though is: Who actually gets to see these corroborating statements Paget talks about? They are not shown in the Paget Report, they have never been made public and the jury were never even told that Langman said he wasn't there, let alone hearing corroborating statements.

Table 4: **Likely List of MI6 Officers in the Paris Station – 30-31 August 1997**[a]

Real Name[b]	Inquest ID	Embassy Position	Start Date	Emby Rank	Stated Location	Alibi Claimed[c]
Sherard Cowper-Coles	Not Heard	Political Counsellor	Not Published	6	South of France	Not in Paris
Dr Valerie Caton	Not Heard	Economic Counsellor	Not Published	7	NA	Not in Paris
Richard Spearman	Mr 6	2nd in Political Section	26 August 1997	13	Paris	At restaurant
Colin Roberts	Not Heard	1st Secretary Political	March 1997	14	NA	Not in Paris
Caroline Copley	Ms 1	1st Secretary Political/Internal	June 1997	15	Paris	At home with husband
Robert Fitchett	Not Heard	2nd in Economic Section[d]	Sep 1994	20	NA	Not in Paris
Nicholas Langman	Not Heard	1st Secretary Economic	Oct 1994	21	UK	Not in Paris
Hugh Powell	Mr 5	2nd Secretary Political	April 1993	32	Paris	At restaurant

[a] This list is based on the available evidence and probably doesn't include all the MI6 officers in the Paris embassy at the time: see above reference to "all the others" – any not on this list cannot be identified at this stage. Other people who were in the political and economic departments – see earlier Table 3: Raynes, Wightman, Hendry – may well be MI6 officers, but there is no available evidence to confirm that.

[b] People with real names showing are all included in the MI6 officers list posted on the internet and are all also in the 1997 Diplomatic Service List.

[c] For the evening of 30 August 1997

[d] Both of Fitchett's 1996 and 1997 List biographies read: "First Secretary (Economic) Paris since September 1994". His 1998 List biography has been inexplicably changed to: "First Secretary (EU Affairs) Paris since September 1994" – this is despite his official position in the 1998 List remaining unchanged: "First Secretary (Economic)" (reproduced earlier). This appears to be a significant alteration when one considers that Fitchett is on the MI6 internet list and MI6 officers show in the Economic section of the embassy – see earlier.: Diplomatic Service List 1996, p175; Diplomatic Service List 1997, p182; Diplomatic Service List 1998, p186.

Conclusion

Out of probably 11 MI6 officers based in Paris at the time of the deaths, only one – Mr 6, Richard Spearman – was cross-examined.[a]

Why only one?

When it came to the evidence regarding a single document – since destroyed – regarding the Milosevic assassination plot, there were three MI6 officers[b] cross-examined.

But this inquest is not about the Milosevic assassination plot – it is the inquest into the deaths of Princess Diana and Dodi Fayed.

So why cross-examine only one out of eleven officers, when three officers were cross-examined over what effectively was used as a red herring.[c]

After all, Diana was assassinated in Paris, not Sarajevo.

The MI6 suspects in this case were primarily officers from the Paris station – not part of the Balkan division.

So if Scott Baker had been genuinely interested in finding out what occurred in Paris on the weekend of 30-31 August 1997, he would have arranged for the cross-examination of Paris MI6 officers – particularly when one considers that Paris-based MI6 officers are alleged suspects in the assassinations that the jury were expected to investigate.

Instead what occurred was just one Paris-based officer was cross-examined – in fact, he was Richard Spearman, brought into Paris on 26 August 1997, just five days before the deaths occurred.

The jury heard Spearman cross-examined, yet, again, they were kept in the dark on two critical facts relating to his cross-examination:

- they were not given the identity of the person being cross-examined, so they never even knew it was Spearman they were listening to[d]

- in evidence, they were not told that Spearman arrived in Paris just five days before the crash.[e]

---

[a] Eugene Curley was cross-examined at the inquest, as Mr 4, but the evidence indicates that he lied when he claimed to be still at the Paris station at the time of the crash, and he instead left at some point before the assassinations were carried out.

[b] Mr A, Mr E and Mr H.

[c] It has earlier been shown that if the inquest was going to delve into other MI6-connected assassination plots, there was far more evidence of the Gaddafi plot than the Milosevic plot. Yet they spent around three days on Milosevic and a few lines of a page on Gaddafi.

[d] They knew him as Witness 6, or Mr 6.

[e] They were told this four months earlier, during Scott Baker's lengthy Opening Remarks – it went on for 1½ days – but not during the evidence or Baker's final Summing Up. The jury were never told that Spearman was an MI6 officer.

In keeping with leaving this jury in the dark, during his cross-examination Spearman was not asked anything about the specific allegations of involvement that had been made against him.

The inquest heard very little about MI6 officer movements in the period leading up to the Paris crash, yet in such an environment of incredible secrecy[a] any evidence pointing to unusual officer movements could be significant.

The evidence in this section points to the real possibility that there were major changes in the senior MI6 personnel in Paris in the weeks and days leading up to the climactic crash in the Alma Tunnel. This evidence particularly related to the three most senior people in the political and economic departments of the Paris embassy in the Diplomatic List for September 1997[b] – Sherard Cowper-Coles, Dr Valerie Caton and Richard Spearman.

The inquest jury heard that Cowper-Coles – who came in as the head of the political department – arrived at the Paris embassy about 12 hours after the crash. But there is evidence – shown earlier in this chapter – that points to Cowper-Coles being in Paris in the days leading up to the crash.

The general evidence indicates that a major coordinated effort was made at the inquest – lies by Eugene Curley and Michael Jay and the failure to hear from Cowper-Coles at all – to place Cowper-Coles in the South of France at the time of the assassinations.

At the very least, there are major questions hanging over the movements of Sherard Cowper-Coles in late August 1997.

The jury were never going to hear the answers – or even the questions – because Cowper-Coles was not on the list of people they would hear from, either by cross-examination or read statement.

In fact there is no specific record of Cowper-Coles ever being interviewed by any investigation.

Why?

The jury heard nothing at all about Valerie Caton – the head of the economic section in September 1997 – yet it is very likely that she too arrived at the Paris embassy in the period leading up to the crash.

She also has no specific record of ever being interviewed.

There are significant omissions to the Biography sections of Diplomatic Lists relating to both Cowper-Coles and Caton – these have been outlined earlier in this chapter.

---

[a] In MI6.
[b] Published in January 1998 – see earlier.

When all of this is viewed in the light of the lies MI6 officer Eugene Curley, Mr 4, told in his inquest testimony – that he was still head of MI6 France at the time of the crash when he wasn't – it appears that a major cover-up of MI6 officer movements has occurred.

Then we have statements from all MI6 officers based in Paris stating that they were not on duty on the weekend of the crash – neither before the 12.23 a.m. Sunday morning crash, nor after it.

MI6 cannot have it both ways.

Either MI6 was:

1) involved in the assassinations of Princess Diana and Dodi Fayed, and therefore Paris-based officers would have had to have been on duty on the Saturday immediately before the crash, or

2) not involved in the assassinations, in which case, as UK's major intelligence agency on the ground in Paris, MI6 would have been attempting to establish the precise nature of what had actually occurred in the Alma Tunnel[a] – and therefore Paris-based officers would have had to be on duty on the Sunday immediately following the crash.

This policy of "unanimous distancing" – "all MI6 officers in Paris were not working that weekend therefore we couldn't have been involved" – simply does not work in this case of Princess Diana's assassination.[b]

A significant point here is that there has never been any proper independent verification of alibis for MI6 officers, and in most cases the jury were not even made aware of what the alibi was, let alone see any evidence of it being checked.

This is standard, basic policing.

These people are suspects in the assassination of the British princess. Get their alibis. Check their alibis with independent verification.

In this special one-off case with such intense public interest, these alibis should have been subjected to expert analysis outside of the police.[c]

Then when the inquest occurs, show that alibi information to the jury who are responsible for establishing cause of death.

Did any of these steps occur with the MI6 officers in Paris?

Well, most of their statements have never been made available so it was impossible for the jury – or anyone else outside of MI6 and Operation Paget – to know.

---

[a] It involved the death of a prominent British citizen who was also mother to the future King of England – Diana, Princess of Wales.

[b] This policy was also tried by the French authorities – see Part 3 – and the British embassy in Paris – see later this volume – and it doesn't work for any of these organisations.

[c] As occurred with parts of the Henri Paul autopsy evidence – see Part 3.

As with pretty much every aspect of this case, there is evidence that a huge cover-up has occurred to prevent knowledge of the level of involvement of Paris-based MI6 officers ever reaching the public.

And as with every other aspect of this case of the assassination of Princess Diana, the question must be asked: If there is nothing to cover up, why has there been a cover-up regarding the activities of Paris-based MI6 officers on the weekend of 30-31 August 1997?

1C   Rosa Monckton

Rosa Monckton – 13 December 2007: 117.3:
"I very deliberately have not read a single book about [Diana]. I might have seen the occasional newspaper article, if it was a headline"

There has been much speculation about the significance of the relationship between Rosa Monckton – who appears to have connections with MI6 – and Princess Diana.

It has already been shown in Part 2 that Rosa and Diana spent five days on a yacht in the Greek islands[a], just two weeks before the Paris crash.

---

[a] Between 15 and 20 August 1997.

Timeline of Events

1991

March	Andrew Morton writes an article in the *Sunday Times*, based on deliberately leaked information from Princess Diana[a], regarding the situation in the Charles-Diana household [165]
April	Diana and Lucia Flecha de Lima travel to Brazil with their husbands – this is the beginning of the Diana-Lucia friendship
July	James Colthurst starts conducting interviews with Princess Diana on behalf of Andrew Morton at Kensington Palace [166]
November	Andrew Morton's central London office is burgled – his files are gone through, and a camera stolen [167]
December	Patrick Jephson warns Diana that the "men in grey suits" know about the Morton book and her involvement in it [168]

1992

January	Diana is warned by Buckingham Palace that they are aware of her co-operation with Morton's book [169]
February	Rosa Monckton's initial meeting with Diana [b]
June	Andrew Morton's book *Diana: Her True Story* is published
August	Squidgygate tapes are published
November	Queen declares 1992 as her "annus horribilus"
	The Way Ahead Group is set up
December	Official separation of Diana and Charles

1993

August	Holiday with Diana, Rosa, Lucia and Beatriz to Bali and Moyo Island, Indonesia – organised by Rosa

1995

November	BBC *Panorama* broadcasts Diana interview by Martin Bashir
December	Queen requests divorce between Diana and Charles

1996

July	Diana commences involvement in the anti-landmine campaign [170]
August	Divorce becomes absolute. Diana is removed from the royal family and is stripped of her HRH title

---

[a] Given to Morton through James Colthurst.

[b] There is conflict over when this first meeting occurred, but this is the most likely date – see later.

1997

January		Diana makes anti-landmine trip to Angola
February		Diana is warned by Tory minister Nicholas Soames to drop her anti-landmine campaign and is threatened with an "accident" [a]
June		Diana provides Simone Simmons with a copy of her "Profiting out of Misery" dossier
	1	Rosa Monckton's daughter, Domenica Lawson's, 2nd birthday
	3	Royal gala performance of Swan Lake at the Royal Albert Hall – Mohamed Al Fayed invites Diana to holiday at his St Tropez residence
	11	Diana writes note to Mohamed saying she and the boys are "greatly looking forward to" the St Tropez holiday
	12	Diana makes major anti-landmine address to Royal Geographic Society stating that she is on a personal anti-landmine crusade
	30	Rosa Monckton arranges to borrow a boat from "friends" to use on a Greek Island holiday cruise with Diana set for mid-August
July		
	11	Diana, William and Harry travel to St Tropez for a 10 day holiday with the Al Fayed family
	20	Diana, William and Harry return to London from St Tropez
August		
	8	Diana travels to Bosnia on a 3 day anti-landmine campaign trip
	10	Diana returns to London from Bosnia
	15	Diana flies to Greece with Rosa Monckton, commencing a 5 day holiday sailing around the Greek Islands
	20	Diana and Rosa return to London
	27	*Le Monde* publishes an interview with Diana – on the royal family she says: "From the first day I joined that family, nothing could be done naturally anymore"
	31	Princess Diana dies following a car crash in the Alma Tunnel, Paris

---

[a] This is detailed in the Landmines chapter of Part 2.

Relationship with MI6

At the inquest Rosa Monckton provided conflicting evidence on her connections with MI6.

Rosa Monckton, Friend of Diana: 13 Dec 07: 111.13:

Burnett: Q. It has been suggested that ... Madam Flecha de Lima invited you to get to know the Princess of Wales, that you in fact did so to pass on information to MI6. Can I just remind you of exactly what was said and then ask you to deal with it? In Mr Al Fayed's statement of 5th July 2005, he said this: "Rosa Monckton was used to discredit my statements about the relationship between my son and Princess Diana. Rosa Monckton established a friendship with Princess Diana simply in order to pass information she had obtained to MI6." What is your comment on that?

A. That is an absolute fantasy on his part.

Q. Now, it is right, isn't it, that you do in fact have someone close to you who you believe to be an MI6 officer?

A. I believe that somebody close to me is connected to the SIS.

Q. But you are unable to say more because of the importance of the need neither to confirm nor deny whether any individual works for SIS?

A. Exactly.

Q. But that is the limit of your connection, if that is the appropriate word?

A. It is.

At 149.11: Mansfield: Q. Were you aware at any time that Diana herself was concerned about her relationship with you?

A. In what way concerned?

Q. Because of your connections.

A. Which connections are you referring to?

Q. Well, there are two main ones. The connection with the editor of the Sunday Telegraph.

A. My husband, absolutely. That is a connection.

Q. I am being careful because the next question is the connection with the security services.

A. I have no connection with the security services.

Q. Well, I am going to suggest that you do and that it is a very close person. I am not going to name anybody.

A. As I said earlier, I believe that someone close to me is connected with the SIS.

Q. MI6?

A. "SIS" is what I know it to be called. I don't know.

Q. MI6 is its correct term, isn't it, or one of the terms?

A. Thank you for correcting me. I did not know that.

Q. Well, it is not the correct term. It is just another term. You did know that SIS was otherwise known as "MI6", didn't you?

A. I suppose it had not occurred to me to think about it very much.

Q. Well I would like you to think about that answer. Are you really suggesting that you had no idea that the SIS was MI6, foreign intelligent[a] agents that work on behalf of the United Kingdom?

A. I thought that is what SIS did.

Q. Yes, quite. This person works for that agency, doesn't that person? I am not even going to disclose obviously the sex of the person either. You knew that, didn't you? Didn't you? You knew it?

A. I have said all I am prepared to say, that somebody close to me is connected with SIS or MI6, as you would rather describe it.

Q. Well, whatever. Diana knew that. Diana, Princess of Wales, knew that you had that connection, did she not?

A. No, she did not.

Q. Because I suggest that the belief that you have – and I will put it like that for the moment – in fact is a very well-publicised belief, isn't it?

A. I do not understand the question.

Q. Yes, it is in the public domain.

A. Belief about what?

Q. The connection that you have. I do not want to spell it out. It is just that there is a lot of information in the public domain suggesting that association.

A. I do not think that information was in the public domain when the Princess of Wales was alive. So she would not have known and could not have known.

Q. I want to suggest to you that the one thing she did not do was tell you about the matters which she thought might be at risk if she did tell you. Do you follow?

A. She told me what she chose to tell me.

Lucia Flecha de Lima, Friend of Diana and Wife of Brazilian Ambassador, UK: 18 Dec 07: 132.2:

Mansfield: Q. Did you know or not whether Rosa Monckton, in 1996 and 1997, had connections with the security services, a relative?

A. Rosa Monckton had connections with Secret Service? I do not believe so.[b]

Simone Simmons, Friend of Diana and Healer: 10 Jan 2008: 72.21:

Mansfield: Q. Was [Diana] aware that Rosa Monckton had a connection with the security services, in particular MI6 or SIS?

A. Yes.

Q. Thank you. Secondly, as a result of that, as far as you could tell, did she

---

[a] This should read "intelligence".

[b] Lucia's answer to this is addressed in detail later in the section on the Diana-Rosa relationship.

trust Rosa Monckton?

A. No, not 100%. She would speak to Rosa about children and family things, but when it came to major issues, no. And I said to her, I was actually very puzzled, I said, "Are you sure about all of this?" and she said "Yes".

At 84.24: A. Most of the time Rosa didn't have time for Diana and Diana made time for Rosa, because it was very much that sort of relationship, where Diana was the strong one and Rosa found it very easy to off-load. They could talk about families and children and household stuff, you know, and just medical bits and pieces which from that point of view they were very close.[a]

Simone Simmons: 2005 Book: **Jury Didn't Hear**:

"[Diana] once wrongly suspected [Rosa] of spying on her for the Government when she was campaigning for a ban on landmines." [171]

"Due to Diana's concern about the Establishment and the Intelligence Services, she was understandably wary of Rosa at times." [172]

Paget Report, p808: **Jury Didn't Hear**:

"Rosa Monckton stated that the claim[b] that she was 'recruited' by MI6 to befriend the Princess of Wales was totally wrong.[c]

"She is married to Dominic Lawson. The only reference to Rosa Monckton's brother allegedly being linked to the SIS came from articles in the media and postings on websites."

MI6 Internet List: 2005 Cryptome Site: **Jury Didn't Hear**:

"Anthony Leopold Colyer Monckton: dob 1960; 90 Geneva, 96 Zagreb, 98 Banja Luka, 01 Belgrade, 04 London".[d]

Diplomatic Service List: 2001 Biographical List: **Jury Didn't Hear**:

"Monckton, The Honourable Anthony Leopold Colyer; Counsellor Belgrade since March 2001; born 25.9.60; HM Forces 1979-87; Second Secretary FCO 1987; Second later First Secretary UKDEL[e] Geneva 1990; First Secretary FCO 1992; First Secretary (Political) Zagreb 1996; British Embassy Banja

---

[a] This was in response to a question relating to why Rosa hadn't seen the later Philip letters (see later section on the Letters): "Can you explain why these letters weren't shown … to Rosa Monckton…?" – at 84.21.

[b] Paget does not say who made this claim. They do quote a claim by Mohamed Al Fayed: "Rosa Monckton established a friendship with Princess Diana simply in order to pass information she obtained to MI6." He does not use the word "recruited" which is showing in quotation marks in the police report.: Paget Report, p746.

[c] There is more on how Rosa befriended Diana in the Meeting Diana section.

[d] Numbers and place names denote year of posting and embassy location. See earlier MI6 Internet Lists section for details.

[e] UKDEL = UK delegation.

Luka[a] Office 1998; First Secretary FCO 1999; Band D6; m 1985 Philippa Susan Wingfield (1s 1988, 1d[b] 1989)." [173]

Sunday Times: 16 Aug 04 Article: **Jury Didn't Hear**:

"A Belgrade newspaper has blown the cover of Britain's most important secret agent in the Balkans, shortly after he left the Serbian capital.

"Anthony Monckton, an MI6 officer ... had his photograph published last week, along with his business card with telephone and e-mail details.

"Diplomats close to Monckton said he had been betrayed by Serbian interior ministry officials close to the paper, the Nedeljni Telegraf....

"One friend described Monckton, who is understood to have overhauled Britain's Balkan intelligence operation, as 'the classic gentleman spy'.

"Monckton['s] brother Christopher was once a policy adviser to Margaret Thatcher.... [c]

"According to Nedeljni Telegraf, Monckton was shocked when his name and photograph were first published in February in a book written by Zoran Mijatovic, the former deputy chief of the Serbian intelligence service, the DB....

"According to the newspaper, a team from MI6 visited Belgrade recently to assess [Monckton's] predicament and decided it would be best for him to leave the city.

"Friends in the diplomatic community insisted he had moved on as part of a normal rotation." [174]

The Guardian: 27 Aug 04 Article: **Jury Didn't Hear**:

"A Croatian newspaper [has] revealed the identities of several alleged British spies....

"The weekly news magazine, Nacional, published the names of four British diplomats it described as important spies. Nacional's claim followed the recent unmasking by a Belgrade tabloid of the chief MI6 officer in Serbia, Anthony Monckton, who has just left the Serbian capital in what was seen as a blow to MI6's activities. Mr Monckton was then named by at least one British newspaper....

"The tabloid published a full front-page picture of Mr Monckton and gave his private phone numbers....

"A Foreign Office spokesman said: 'We never comment on intelligence matters.'...

"The magazine published a picture of a blue Bedford van with Croatian number plates, one of three said to have been brought into Croatia by British intelligence and bristling with monitoring equipment." [175]

The Independent: 17 Dec 98 Article: **Jury Didn't Hear**:

---

[a] City in Bosnia and Herzegovina.

[b] m = married; s = son; d = daughter.

[c] Rosa's grandfather, Walter Monckton, worked as a lawyer for King Edward VIII.

"Is Dominic Lawson, the editor of The Sunday Telegraph, a paid MI6 agent? The question was raised yesterday in the House of Commons under parliamentary privilege.

"It follows reports at the weekend that renegade MI6 officer Richard Tomlinson claimed that a national newspaper editor had been recruited and paid by MI6. Speculation over the identity of the editor has been rife in the media.

"Yesterday, Labour MP Brian Sedgemore (Hackney South and Shoreditch) named Mr Lawson as being at the centre of the allegations. 'That seems a very odd thing,' he said.

'It would be very damaging for the press if it were true. It's an allegation being made by Mr Richard Tomlinson. I have no idea whether it is true but it surely is something we should look at.'

"Mr Lawson yesterday denied he was an agent for anybody.

"A spokesman for the Foreign Office, which oversees MI6, said: 'This comes from a now wearily familiar source to us of sensational inventions.... We can point out very forcefully that [we] would never have an agent who is the editor of a British newspaper.'" [176a]

The Guardian: 26 Jan 01 Article: **Jury Didn't Hear**:

"Dominic Lawson, the editor of the Sunday Telegraph and son of the former Tory chancellor, Nigel Lawson, provided journalistic cover for an MI6 officer on a mission to the Baltic to handle and debrief a young Russian diplomat who was spying for Britain, the renegade MI6 officer, Richard Tomlinson, has alleged.

"He also claimed he was given cover by the Spectator magazine while on a mission to Macedonia to develop contacts with ethnic Albanian politicians.

"In his controversial book being published in Russia, Tomlinson, according to book excerpts leaked to the Moscow press, said that in the early 1990s the editor of the Spectator was on MI6's books and provided cover for an agent named as Spencer who was put on the case of a young Russian diplomat, Platon Obukhov, in Tallin, the capital of Estonia.

"Tomlinson writes that Mr Lawson's MI6 identity was "Smallbrow". Mr Lawson was the editor of the Spectator from 1990-95 before moving to its sister publication, the Sunday Telegraph.

"Mr Lawson yesterday strongly denied both allegations. 'It is complete rubbish that I gave journalistic cover to an MI6 officer who wanted to go to Tallin,' he added....

---

[a] Peter Wright reveals in *Spycatcher*: "The *Daily Mirror* tycoon, Cecil King, who was a long-time [MI5] agent, made it clear that he would publish anything that MI5 might care to leak in his direction.": p369.

"Komsomolskaya Pravda, the bestselling Moscow tabloid ... has obtained a copy of the Tomlinson book and has been publishing excerpts this week....
"Tomlinson ... writes that for his mission to Macedonia he was given a letter of accreditation from the Spectator and told by his superiors that if his Albanian interlocutors phoned the Spectator to check on him, Mr Lawson would vouch that Tomlinson was a Spectator journalist.
"Mr Lawson's Spectator has been at the centre of a row over MI6 and journalism before. Tomlinson has previously alleged that MI6 agents were asked to write media articles under pseudonyms while in Bosnia during the 1992-95 war.
"The Guardian reported in 1998 that the Spectator ran articles by an MI6 officer under a false name during the Bosnian war. The articles were written from Sarajevo by a Kenneth Roberts, though the Spectator noted that the author's name had been changed at his request without revealing his true employer. The MI6 officer has since been publicly identified as Keith Craig.
"Mr Lawson yesterday repeated what he said two years ago. 'I have never been an agent either paid or unpaid of MI6 or any other government agency.'
"A Foreign Office spokesman speaking for MI6 said that Mr Tomlinson's claim 'comes from someone now wearily familiar as a source of sensational inventions'." [177]
Richard Tomlinson, Ex-MI6 Officer: 2001 Book: **Jury Didn't Hear**:
"MI6 likes to recruit from the same family as it simplifies the vetting process." [178]
Comment: When the issue of MI6 arose, Rosa Monckton became particularly evasive.

Burnett asked Rosa if her statement, "somebody close to me is connected to the SIS", was "the limit of your connection". Rosa replied: "It is."

That then is an admission by Rosa that she has a connection to MI6.

Yet later to Mansfield, Rosa says: "I have no connection with the security services".

A clear conflict – Rosa admits a connection to Burnett, but "no connection" to Mansfield.

Then, under Mansfield's questioning, Rosa takes her claimed ignorance a step further. She states: "I did not know that" MI6 is "one of the terms" to describe the SIS.

The evidence – see above and below – shows Rosa's husband, Dominic Lawson, and brother, Anthony Monckton, both working for MI6. Later evidence will also point to Rosa Monckton herself being an MI6 agent.

I suggest that – in light of Rosa's connections – it is unbelievable that she would not be aware that MI6 is the same as SIS.

Yet under oath that is what Rosa has stated: "I did not know that".

Why does Rosa say this?

It appears to be another example of excessive distancing by players in this extremely important case.

The point is – and it will be shown – that Rosa has carried out work as an MI6 agent in connection with Princess Diana.

Rosa's distancing – "I did not know that" MI6 is SIS – appears to be saying that if she is unaware of what MI6 is, then how on earth could her admitted connection – her brother, Anthony – have anything to do with her? [a]

What is not mentioned or disclosed at the inquest is that there is evidence in the public domain that Rosa's husband, Dominic Lawson[b], is an MI6 agent, and other evidence[c] that she herself has operated as an MI6 agent.

This form of false distancing appears to be designed to throw those seeking the truth – primarily the jury – off the scent. They may think something like: "If this poor woman doesn't even know that MI6 is SIS, then it is not possible that she could have involvement in any MI6 operation."

In a similar way, in Part 3, French authorities said they did not even know Princess Diana was in Paris, so it is not then possible that they could have had any prior knowledge of the crash.

In short, the inquest heard of one unnamed MI6 connection that Rosa admitted to – her brother, Anthony[d] – but heard nothing of the evidence pertaining to Rosa's two other connections – her husband, Dominic, and herself.[e]

Three connections in total, of which the inquest heard of only one – and that, unnamed.

This appears to fit with Tomlinson's account that "MI6 likes to recruit from the same family" – three people from the same family: Rosa, Anthony and Dominic.

---

[a] This excessive distancing is similar to the evidence put forward during the inquest that no British Embassy staff or French authorities were aware Diana was in France on 30 August 1997 and that no MI6 officers were on duty in Paris on the weekend of the crash. See Part 3, and earlier and later in this volume.

[b] Dominic Lawson is the cousin of Fiona Shackleton, who was principal lawyer for Prince Charles during his divorce from Princess Diana.

[c] Shown in this chapter.

[d] The inquest transcript does not reveal whether the unnamed connection Rosa admitted to was her brother or husband, but the context – "an MI6 officer" (Burnett) – indicates it was her brother who was being referred to, because her husband is not an officer – he is instead an MI6 agent.

[e] Christopher Monckton, who travels the world speaking out against taking measures to prevent climate change, is Rosa and Anthony's brother. Christopher also makes false claims that he is a member of the House of Lords and in July 2011received a letter from David Beamish, the Clerk of the Parliaments (UK), ordering him to cease and desist from doing that.: www.parliament.uk/business/news/2011/july

Anthony Monckton is listed as an MI6 officer on the internet list. He also, as with other MI6 officers discussed earlier, appears in the official Diplomatic Service Lists – the 2002 entry is shown above. Anthony shows up as the First Secretary Political in Zagreb in 1996 and the sole Counsellor in Belgrade[179] in 2001. Earlier evidence indicated that MI6 officers are found in the Political departments of British Embassies.[a] Anthony's cover was blown in 2004.

As seen above, the evidence pointing to Dominic Lawson being an MI6 agent appears to come solely from Richard Tomlinson.[b] That it doesn't come from other sources may simply be a reflection of the general secrecy regarding anything to do with MI6 – see earlier. Lawson and the FCO have issued repeated denials[c] but, as we have seen earlier, that is standard practice for current MI6 employees and British authorities.

Earlier analyses of the evidence of Richard Tomlinson in this book have shown that, as far as veracity is concerned, his evidence stacks up favourably against the conflicting evidence of other present and past MI6 employees.

There is no apparent reason to doubt the credibility of Tomlinson's account in respect of Dominic Lawson.

Lawson has denied that he is an MI6 agent, but he has failed to address the issue on which the allegation is based – that Lawson published "articles by an MI6 officer under a false name". If this allegation was false, it should have been a simple matter for Lawson to prove that the articles were submitted by a legitimate journalist.[d]

Dominic Lawson has failed to do this.

---

[a] The Paget Report states: "The only reference to Rosa Monckton's brother allegedly being linked to the SIS came from articles in the media and postings on websites." The point of course is that those sources stand alone because of the secrecy of MI6 and that former and present employees are prevented from naming officers under the Official Secrets Act.

[b] Dominic Lawson "graduated from Oxford [University] in politics, philosophy and economics". Peter Wright has stated: "The cords which bind Oxford [University] and British Intelligence together are strong". Sources: John Plunkett, Profile: Dominic Lawson, *The Guardian*, 14 June 2005; *Spycatcher*, p245.

[c] There is a striking similarity between the FCO denials in 1998 and 2001. 1998: "This comes from a now wearily familiar source to us of sensational inventions...";
2001: This "comes from someone now wearily familiar as a source of sensational inventions".

[d] The *Guardian* stated: "The articles were written from Sarajevo by a Kenneth Roberts, though the Spectator noted that the author's name had been changed at his request without revealing his true employer. The MI6 officer has since been publicly identified as Keith Craig." Keith Craig appears on the MI6 internet list and is also listed in the Diplomatic Service List 1996, p151.

It is not the purpose of this book to analyse in detail the evidence relating to Lawson and Anthony Monckton – the focus is on Rosa Monckton, as she was the member of this trio that worked directly with Princess Diana.

The evidence in this chapter will show that the issue is not so much whether Rosa had MI6 connections – the focus at the inquest – but that Rosa herself appears to have been working as an MI6 agent in her dealings with Diana, Princess of Wales.

Meeting Diana

There is significant conflict in the evidence relating to the circumstances of the initial meeting between Princess Diana and Rosa Monckton.

Rosa Monckton, Friend of Diana: 13 Dec 07: 109.10:

Burnett: Q. What were the circumstances in which you first met [Diana] and became a friend and confidante?

A. We met through a mutual friend, somebody called Lucia Flecha de Lima, who's husband was then the Brazilian Ambassador in London. She had met both the Prince and Princess of Wales when they went on an official trip to Brazil. And as is the custom, the Ambassador to the Court of St James accompanied them on this trip and that is when Lucia got to know Diana. Clearly on this trip, Diana confided in her about the unhappiness of her marriage. When they returned from the trip, Lucia rang me and asked me to go and have lunch with her and told me all about this trip and said, "I want to introduce you to Diana because you are English, I am not, I am a foreigner in this country, and I do not really understand how things work and she needs somebody who she can trust".

Q. Did you, before that time, know the Princess of Wales at all?

A. I had met her. I first met her in September 1987, when we were celebrating Tiffany's 150th anniversary and Tiffany London's first anniversary. We had a big ball at Sion House and she was our guest of honour, and so I spent that evening with her.

Q. At this time, did one of Lucia Flecha de Lima's daughters work for Tiffany?

A. Yes. That is exactly how I met Lucia. Her daughter was called Beatrice, and she was introduced to me by another friend of Lucia's called Nina Pillai, who was an Indian who was then living in London. So Beatrice came to work for me at Tiffany's and her mother came in one day to thank me for employing her daughter and we became friends after that.

Q. So your connection with Lucia Flecha de Lima was entirely through that nexus, that connection?

A. Exactly.

Q. What was it that Madam Flecha de Lima thought you could offer the Princess of Wales that she was unable to offer?

A. I think that Lucia did not understand the whole workings of the Royal Family. She did not understand what would be the implications if there was a divorce, whether there could just be a separation. I think she just wanted somebody else to help her because it was an enormous responsibility to have somebody like Diana, you know, talk to her in this way and she just wanted to share it with somebody.

Q. So was it that she understood that you had an insight into the workings of the Royal Family and the part of society from which the Princess of Wales came from that she did not perhaps?

A. Yes, I think that is probably what she felt.

.... Q. When you first got to know the Princess of Wales, can we identify it in time? Can you remember when it was?

A. Yes, it was – we first met with Lucia for lunch in February 1992.

Q. In your statement in July 2004, you mentioned 1989. Is that simply a mistake?

A. That is a mistake.

Q. Was the Princess aware that Lucia Flecha de Lima was introducing you for the purpose of becoming a confidante and assisting her through what must have been a rather difficult period?

A. Absolutely she was and that was made very clear at our first meeting.

At 174.4: Mansfield: Q. [Quoting from *Sunday Telegraph*[a]] "Traditionally, senior Royal Family members are reluctant to issue denials over media reports because it can fuel publicity over false claims." I think the adage is: don't complain and don't explain. That is the way it is normally approached by the Royal Family, isn't it?

A. Sorry, I thought that was a statement. Was that a question?

Q. I am asking you, is that right, since you know the workings of the –

A. I do not know the workings of the Royal Family.

Q. I thought that is what you said a little earlier, that the reason you became a confidante in one regard was that you knew the workings.

A. No. Lucia thought that I would know the workings of the Royal Family because I was English.

Q. You must have told Lucia –

A. No, it was an assumption that Lucia made because I was English.

Q. Did you disavow that?

A. I said I would help if I could.

Q. Did you say, "I do not know the workings"?

A. I cannot recall.

---

[a] Article on 24 November 2002 – quoted extensively later in the section on the Philip-Diana Letters.

Q. Or do you know the workings?

A. I have no idea of the arcane ways of the Royal Family, no.

Lucia Flecha de Lima, Friend of Diana and Wife of Brazilian Ambassador, UK: 18 Dec 07: 85.17:

Burnett: Q. Now, Mrs Flecha de Lima, I hope I can take quite a lot of the background information fairly quickly..... As wife of the Brazilian Ambassador [to the UK], did you first meet Diana, Princess of Wales in about July 1990?

A. Just slightly before that, at a Court function in 1990.

Q. Then in April 1991, did the Princess, along with the Prince of Wales, make an official visit to Brazil?

A. Yes.

Q. And did you and your husband, the Ambassador, accompany them to Brazil?

A. Yes, we did.

Q. And on that visit to Brazil, did you stay in the same hotels as the Prince and Princess and eat with them?

A. Yes.

Q. During that time, you became friendly with the Princess; is that right?

A. Yes.

....Q. Following your return to London, did you receive a bunch of flowers from the Princess and a note saying ... that she would like to see you again?

A. Yes.

Q. Following that, did you and she meet regularly in restaurants or at the Embassy for meals?

A. Yes.

Q. Did you regularly stay for weekends at the home of mutual friends, Lord and Lady Palumbo?

A. Yes.

Q. During this period in 1991, would it be fair to say that you and the Princess became very close friends?

A. Yes.

Q. During this period, did you sometimes meet her every day and, on other occasions, perhaps once a week?

A. Oh yes. It was like all friendships.

Q. Did you regularly speak on the telephone as well?

A. Yes, very much so.

Q. During this period, 1991 and into 1992, we know that the marriage of the Prince and Princess of Wales was in particular difficulty. Did she speak to you about that?

A. Yes, she did.

Q.... Did she confide in you? Did you become someone on whose advice she began to rely?

A. Yes.

....Q. Did you have a daughter who was working in London at the time? [a]

A. Yes.

.... Q. Did you have a daughter who worked at Tiffany's in London?

A. Yes, I did, Beatriz.

Q. At the time, did you know the chief executive of Tiffany's in London, Rosa Monckton?

A. Yes, she went to work for Rosa.

Q. Did you take any steps to introduce Rosa to the Princess of Wales?

A. Yes, I did.

Q. What exactly did you do, Mrs Flecha de Lima?

A. I thought, when I first met the Princess of Wales, she was a very lonely person and I thought it was very sad for a Royal Princess of England to have to find friends amongst foreign people. So I thought it would be proper for her to become friends with Rosa, if she wanted to.

Q. In your statement, you say that you did not understand the monarchy or the aristocracy and you thought Rosa would be better able to assist the Princess because she might understand both. Is that right?

A. Yes, that is right.

Q.... It has been suggested by Mr Al Fayed that Rosa was planted as a friend with the Princess of Wales by the Secret Intelligence Service. Is there any truth in that?

A. I do not believe so because I am the one who introduced her, Rosa, to the Princess.

Lucia Flecha de Lima: 1 Sep 04 Statement: **Jury Didn't Hear**:

"I first met Diana Princess of Wales at a Buckingham Palace ceremony in July 1990 through my husband's diplomatic status. He was the Brazilian Ambassador in London.... I saw her on various occasions in a formal setting but it was not until April 1991 when we became friends.

"Princess Diana and Prince Charles went to Brazil on an official visit and my husband and I accompanied them. The four of us travelled together and stayed in the same hotel, eating meals together. Princess Diana and I clicked. I would say she chose me as a friend rather that the other way round due to the position she held and it was not my place to do so. Princess Diana returned to England first and I returned ten days later to a huge bunch of flowers and a letter from her saying she would like to see me again. I wrote her a thank you letter and then Princess Diana telephoned me. In Brazil our conversations had always remained general as there were always a lot of people around but on my return she invited me to lunch in a London

---

[a] "1991 and into 1992": 88.7.

restaurant. I invited her to the Brazilian Embassy. This would have been May to June 1991. In July she invited me to Wimbledon for the men's finals and then onto Kensington Palace. Our friendship grew stronger and stronger. I met her boys, Prince William and Harry and we met regularly at restaurants or the Embassy or to go shopping or spend weekends at Lady Palumbo's house. Lord and Lady Palumbo were mutual friends of ours. Sometimes we would meet almost every day, sometimes once a week. It depended on our engagements. We spoke on the phone, once, twice, three times a day. We had good times together. I am 20 years her senior but people are wrong to suggest that I took the place of her mother. She trusted and confided in me.

"In the second half of 1991 the relationship between Princess Diana and Prince Charles was very, very bad.... Some time after they got married it seemed to become very bitter.... They split up in 1992....

"I tried not to let them split but it was already too late. I introduced Rosa Monckton. My daughter worked for Tiffany's. It was Rosa who employed her. As a foreigner I didn't know the 'other side'. I didn't understand the monarchy and the aristocracy. To help someone you need to know both sides and it wasn't easy for the wife of a foreign Ambassador to mix with royal problems. I thought of approaching Prince Philip but it wouldn't be right and it was a very private affair. Rosa understood that side of things better. I thought a separation would be as bad as an abdication at the time. I wanted her to have peace of mind and I didn't want the boys to suffer. Knowing the press here I knew her life would be unbearable after the divorce. Rosa is a clever woman and could understand the issues better...." [180]

Paget Report, p808: **Jury Didn't Hear**:

"Rosa Monckton began her friendship with the Princess of Wales around 1989. Lucia Flecha de Lima, a friend of the Princess of Wales, stated that she introduced the two women [Paget Note: Lucia Flecha de Lima believed this was in 1991]. Both stated it was at the time of the Princess of Wales' marriage break-up. Lucia Flecha de Lima's husband was the Brazilian Ambassador in England at the time and she met the Princess of Wales during an official trip to Brazil. After the trip, Lucia Flecha de Lima believed the Princess of Wales needed someone to help her, someone she could talk to, as she was very unhappy and was having troubles in her marriage. Lucia Flecha de Lima felt that although she could offer friendship and strong emotional support herself, she did not understand the English system and so she approached Rosa Monckton because of her background and because she would be discreet and not run to the press.

"Rosa Monckton was introduced as a confidante who understood the monarchy and aristocracy more than Lucia Flecha de Lima and could help the Princess of Wales through this time in her life. Rosa Monckton stated that the claim that she was 'recruited' by MI6 to befriend the Princess of Wales was totally wrong."

Rosa Monckton, Friend of Diana: 25 Oct 98 *Telegraph* Article: **Jury Didn't Hear**:

Responding to allegations in a book[a] that Princess Diana had an affair with her bodyguard, Barry Mannakee, who died in 1987.[b] "Mannakee became a close friend [of Diana's]. He was just a father figure – he was the sort of guy who would hug her and say 'you can cope'. It's very convenient that this is coming out when Mannakee and Diana are dead. How on earth would these so called friends of Charles know? True friends would realise that this campaign would do harm to him and his sons and the memory of Diana. At the time that this was supposed to have happened, she had both William and Harry and she was trying to make the marriage work. At that time [Diana] was still in love with Charles. The family[c] disapproved of her friendship with Mannakee, but that was because of who he was. She did have a keepsake from him – a teddy bear. It was something to hug, but it was not because of any sexual relationship. It was close but platonic." [181]

Comment: The account from Rosa Monckton and Lucia Flecha de Lima is that Rosa first met Diana through Lucia.

Despite there being just two living witnesses – Rosa and Lucia – there are several dates that have been given for when Rosa was introduced by Lucia to Diana:

- "Rosa Monckton began her friendship with the Princess of Wales around 1989" [d] – Rosa's statement, in Paget Report and confirmed at inquest
- "we first met with Lucia for lunch in February 1992" – Rosa at inquest
- "[Diana and Charles] split up in 1992.... I tried not to let them split but it was already too late. I introduced Rosa Monckton" – Lucia statement
- "when I first met the Princess of Wales, she was a very lonely person and I thought it was very sad for a Royal Princess of England to have to find friends amongst foreign people. So I thought it would be proper for her to become friends with Rosa" – Lucia at inquest
- "Lucia ... believed this [introduction] was in 1991"[e] – Paget Report
- Rosa's 1998 interview with the *Telegraph* appears to indicate that she was a witness to the nature of the Diana-Mannakee relationship – this ended in July 1986.

---

[a] *Charles: Victim or Villain?* by Penny Junor.
[b] The circumstances around the death of Barry Mannakee have been addressed in Part 2.
[c] This appears to refer to the royal family – Mannakee was removed from his post as Diana's bodyguard in July 1986. He died in May 1987.
[d] Third person account in the Paget Report – the statement of Rosa Monckton has never been made available and was also not given or read out to the inquest jury.
[e] Probably stated during a 2006 phone call with police – see later footnote.

So the timing of the commencement of Rosa Monckton's relationship with Diana varies, with dates extending from 1986 through to 1992 – and conflicting evidence from Rosa and Lucia.

Rosa's 1998 media interview – July 1986 or earlier; Rosa to Paget – 1989;[a] Rosa at inquest – February 1992.

Lucia to Paget – 1991; Lucia statement – 1992; Lucia at inquest – after "I first met" Diana: after July 1990.

Rosa said in her statement that she "first got to know the Princess of Wales" in 1989, but at the inquest she changed this to "February 1992", saying that the statement account "is a mistake". Considering that sworn police statements are generally thought through and reread, it is surprising that Rosa was not asked to explain how this "mistake" arose.

Is it also a mistake that Rosa was able to provide the *Telegraph* with a detailed account of the nature of the 1986 Mannakee-Diana relationship – "how on earth would these so-called friends of Charles know?" – even though the earliest she has put the start of her own relationship with Diana is 1989? [bcd]

Lucia has also provided conflicting timing evidence.

---

[a] In the preamble to an interview with Rosa Monckton on 5 September 1997 – just five days after the crash – US TV journalist, Barbara Walters, referring to Diana and Rosa, stated: "The two had known each other for seven years." That would be 1990, but it is not known whether Walters had arrived at that from research or had asked Rosa.: Barbara Walters, Princess Diana's Best Friend, ABC 20/20, 5 September 1997.

[b] Two years after Mannakee had died.

[c] I am not suggesting that Penny Junor is correct and that there was an affair between Diana and Mannakee. The issue here is whether Rosa Monckton had first-hand evidence of the nature of the relationship. Part 4 has already indicated that Junor's account – in the same 1998 book – about Charles' involvement in the Diana repatriation decisions was incorrect.

[d] At the inquest Rosa's timing was surprisingly specific – February 1992. Burnett asked her: "Can we identify it in time? Can you remember when it was?". Rosa replies: "Yes, it was – we first met with Lucia for lunch in February 1992." Rosa appears to hesitate – "Yes, it was", then checks herself. Then the answer is: "we first met with Lucia for lunch in February 1992". Now, "we" here is Rosa and Diana. Rosa has been asked for the timing of "when you first got to know the Princess of Wales". Yet the way she has answered it indicates that it is her and Diana – "we" – who "first met with Lucia".

According to the Paget Report, Lucia "believed this [introduction] was in 1991".[a] But in her statement to Paget, Lucia said that Diana and Charles "split up in 1992[b].... I tried not to let them split but it was already too late. I introduced Rosa Monckton."

At the inquest Lucia makes no specific comment on the timing, but indicates that it was after she "first met" Diana – an event that Lucia said occurred in July 1990.

There is not only conflict between the timing accounts of the two witnesses – Rosa and Lucia – but also each of these witnesses has provided a different year for the initial meeting[c] each time they have been asked.[d] Why?

It could be significant that on two occasions Rosa has indicated a relationship with Diana prior to July 1990 – the date at which Lucia says was her initial meeting with Diana. These were during the media interview about Mannakee – before July 1986 – and in her Paget statement – around 1989.

The point here is that if Rosa knew Diana prior to July 1990, then it would be false to suggest Rosa had been first introduced by Lucia – who didn't meet Diana until July 1990.

Why did Lucia introduce Diana to Rosa?

Again, there is conflict in the evidence.

There are three accounts of Lucia's evidence:

- in Lucia's Paget statement: "I tried not to let [Diana and Charles] split but it was already too late. I introduced Rosa Monckton.... As a foreigner I didn't know the 'other side'. I didn't understand the monarchy and the aristocracy.... Rosa understood that side of things better.... Rosa is a clever woman and could understand the issues better"

- a third person account from Paget: "Lucia ... believed [Diana] needed someone to help her, someone she could talk to, as she was very unhappy and was having troubles in her marriage.... She approached Rosa Monckton because of her [English] background and because she would be discreet and not run to the press"

- Lucia's inquest evidence: "[Diana] was a very lonely person and I thought it was very sad for a Royal Princess of England to have to find friends amongst foreign people. So I thought it would be proper for her to become friends with Rosa".

---

[a] At the inquest it was mentioned that there were "two notes recording telephone discussions [Lucia] had with the police in 2006": 18 Dec 07: 85.5. It is possible that the "1991" evidence came from one of those phone calls.

[b] The official separation was announced in parliament on 9 December 1992.

[c] Between Diana and Rosa.

[d] Lucia was not specifically asked about the timing at the inquest. It could be argued that Lucia's comment that the introduction occurred after she herself had first met Diana – July 1990 – could mean later in 1990, 1991 or even 1992.

Lucia's inquest account of her reasons for introducing Diana to Rosa is completely different to what she stated three years earlier in her Paget statement.

In September 2004 to Paget the reasons were around the Diana-Charles "split" – "Rosa understood that side of things [the monarchy and aristocracy] better" than Lucia.[a]

With the 2006 Paget Report account[b] the reasons became: "[Diana] was very unhappy and was having troubles in her marriage"; Rosa's English background; Rosa "would be discreet and not run to the press".

By December 2007 the reasons had now completely changed from Lucia's 2004 statement: "[Diana] was a very lonely person"; "it was very sad for [Diana] to have to find friends amongst foreign people".

The two key reasons in 2004 were help with the Diana-Charles separation and Rosa's understanding of the monarchy-aristocracy.[c]

By 2007 those two reasons have gone and have been replaced by two other reasons – Diana was lonely and needed English friends.[d]

This is despite the fact that inquest lawyer, Ian Burnett, was basing his questions on Lucia's 2004 statement and had already reminded Lucia of the marriage problems: "During this period, 1991 and into 1992, we know that the marriage of the Prince and Princess of Wales was in particular difficulty."

---

[a] Princess Diana was born into aristocracy and already was friends with other members of the aristocracy – people like the Palumbos and Annabel Goldsmith. At that time Diana was also close to her sister, Sarah McCorquodale. Diana's family had a long association with the royal family – when she was growing up her family had holidayed with the royals at Sandringham. Other books have recounted how Diana's father had been an equerry to the Queen and her mother had been a lady in waiting to the Queen Mother. Diana also was friends with the *Daily Mail* royal reporter, Richard Kay.

[b] Which may have included input from two 2006 phone calls between Lucia and the police – see earlier footnote.

[c] Lucia had said earlier in her 2004 police statement: "we ... [would] spend weekends at Lady Palumbo's house. Lord and Lady Palumbo were mutual friends of ours". This was also confirmed at the inquest: Lucia replied "Yes" to: "Did you regularly stay for weekends at the home of mutual friends, Lord and Lady Palumbo?" Diana also spent time with her sister, Sarah, and Annabel Goldsmith – see Part 2. This issue of relationships with the aristocracy is addressed later.

[d] I suggest Rosa's inquest account also comes across as a bit odd, if you put yourself in Diana's shoes. Burnett, who was working from Rosa's statement: "Was the Princess aware that Lucia Flecha de Lima was introducing you for the purpose of becoming a confidante and assisting her through what must have been a rather difficult period?" Rosa: "Absolutely she was and that was made very clear at our first meeting."

Burnett was apparently not comfortable with Lucia's answer, so he next reminded her about one of her 2004 reasons: "In your statement, you say that ... you thought Rosa would be better able to assist the Princess because she might understand both" the monarchy and aristocracy.[a] Lucia confirmed that, but her significant inquest account had already been given in her initial response.

There are other conflicts between the Rosa and Lucia accounts of what occurred.

At the inquest Rosa referred to the Diana-Lucia Brazil trip: "Clearly on this trip, Diana confided in [Lucia] about the unhappiness of her marriage. When they returned from the trip, Lucia rang me and asked me to go and have lunch with her and told me all about this trip and said, 'I want to introduce you to Diana'."

There are problems with this account:
- communication on the Brazil trip

Rosa: "clearly on this trip, Diana confided in [Lucia] about the unhappiness of her marriage".

Lucia stated the opposite: "in Brazil our conversations had always remained general as there were always a lot of people around".[b]

So according to Lucia, Diana didn't confide in her until after the Brazil trip. Rosa though has stated under oath that "clearly on this trip, Diana confided in" Lucia.

- post-trip timing issues

Rosa: "when they returned from the trip, Lucia ... said, 'I want to introduce you to Diana'"

The Brazil trip occurred during April 1991.[c] Rosa's own inquest account is that her first meeting with Diana was "for lunch in February 1992" – that is about 10 months after the Brazil trip.

Lucia has also indicated that there was a significant time gap between the Brazil trip and the introduction of Rosa to Diana – she describes her developing relationship: "This would have been May to June 1991. In July she invited me to Wimbledon ... and then onto Kensington Palace. Our

---

[a] It is interesting that Burnett doesn't remind Lucia about the Diana-Charles separation reason here. Is that because to do so would have alerted the jury to a major conflict in Lucia's evidence, bearing in mind the jury were never shown Lucia's statement? Instead he brings up the aristocracy- monarchy reason, almost as though it is just a clarification of what Lucia had already said: "it was very sad for a Royal Princess of England to have to find friends amongst foreign people".
[b] In a possible conflict with this, Lucia told Daphne Barak in November 2003: "We met them both [Diana and Charles] when they visited Brazil together, we joined them. That's when we really got close.": Daphne Barak, Building Up Confidantes, *Sunday Times*, 19 March 1995.
[c] That is consistent evidence from Lucia in her statement and at the inquest.

friendship grew stronger and stronger." According to Lucia, it was some stage later, before Rosa was introduced to Diana.

  - the content of the Rosa-Lucia conversation

Rosa said under oath at the inquest: "when [Diana and Lucia] returned from the [Brazil] trip, Lucia ... told me all about this trip".

That is only likely to be true if the timing put forward by Lucia and Rosa herself – see above[a] – is false.

Rosa Monckton's police statement has never been leaked and was not seen or heard at the inquest. The closest we get to it is the Paget Report third person description of the Rosa-Lucia accounts – see earlier.[b]

It may be significant that there is no specific mention in the Paget description of Rosa suggesting she met Diana through Lucia. The description instead reads: "Rosa Monckton began her friendship with [Diana] around 1989. Lucia Flecha de Lima ... stated that she introduced the two women. Both stated it was at the time of the Princess of Wales' marriage break-up." [c]

Paget has specifically written that "Lucia ... stated that she introduced the two women" – if Rosa's account had concurred with that, then I suggest Paget would have stated that.[d]

––––––––––––––––––––

[a] That the timing of the introduction to Diana took place up to 10 months after the trip.

[b] As outlined in an earlier footnote, in addition to Lucia's statement there were notes from phone calls between the British police and her. There is no evidence of any phone calls between Rosa and the police and it is fair to presume that Paget descriptions of Rosa's evidence come from her statement only.

[c] Some may argue that the "marriage break-up" occurred well after 1989, but a study of the Diana-Charles marriage reveals that the break-up cannot be pinned down to one specific event or year. The break-up occurred over a long period, possibly starting in 1984 and culminating in the divorce in 1996. In 1992 Diana talked about the marriage relationship following Harry's birth in September 1984: "As Harry was born it just went bang, our marriage, the whole thing went down the drain.... Harry arrived, Harry had red hair, Harry was a boy. First comment [by Charles] was 'Oh God, it's a boy', second comment 'and he's even got red hair'. Something inside me closed off. By then I knew [Charles] had gone back to his lady [Camilla] but somehow we'd managed to have Harry." Andrew Morton later wrote: "Charles's reaction finally closed the door on any love Diana may have felt for him.... [After his] dismissive remarks he left for Kensington Palace. The following day he played polo. From that moment, as Diana told friends: 'Something inside me died.' It was a reaction that marked the beginning of the end of their marriage.": Andrew Morton, *Diana: Her True Story – In Her Own Words*, 1997, pp 54-55, 155. In early 1987 Diana embarked on the well-known five year affair with army captain, James Hewitt.

[d] Paget does then say: "Both [Rosa and Lucia] stated it was at the time of the Princess of Wales' marriage break-up." "it" appears to refer to the first meeting

347

There are three relationships involved here – Diana and Rosa; Diana and Lucia; Lucia and Rosa.

The Lucia-Rosa inquest evidence points to: a) the friendship between Diana and Lucia, starting around April 1991; b) Lucia meeting Rosa, through Lucia's daughter, Beatriz[a]; and finally, c) Diana meets Rosa through Lucia's introduction.

In a 2003 interview with Richard Kay, Lucia said: "The first thing Diana said to me was: 'You are Lucia. I've been told we should become good friends.' It was all on her initiative...."[182] The jury did not hear that.

We are not told who suggested to Diana that she "should become good friends" with Lucia. And we don't know why Diana was told that.

This apparently occurred at a time when Lucia and Rosa were already friends – Rosa said: "[Lucia] came in one day to thank me for employing her daughter and we became friends after that".[b]

Rosa explains how this came about: "That is exactly how I met Lucia. Her daughter ... was introduced to me by another friend of Lucia's called Nina Pillai, who was an Indian who was then living in London. So Beatrice[c] came to work for me at Tiffany's".

It is obvious that if the police were going to thoroughly investigate the Rosa-Lucia accounts[d] then both Beatriz Flecha de Lima and Nina Pillai[e] would have been interviewed. That never occurred and they were also not heard from at the inquest.

---

between Diana and Rosa. It could be argued that "it" refers to the introduction of Rosa to Diana by Lucia. Most of the remainder of the Paget description though appears to come from Lucia's statement. The only other comment that clearly comes from Rosa is when Paget says: "Rosa Monckton stated that the claim that she was 'recruited' by MI6 to befriend the Princess of Wales was totally wrong." If Paget had wanted the evidence to be clear, they should have provided verbatim excerpts from both statements, but that never occurred. That raises the question: Why? Was it because there were irreconcilable conflicts in these witness accounts?

[a] It is interesting that whenever Rosa Monckton said the name of Lucia's daughter at the inquest it was transcribed as "Beatrice", but when Lucia, her mother, gave it, it was correctly transcribed as "Beatriz". There is a possibility that Rosa was pronouncing the name incorrectly.

[b] There is no precise timing on this, but if it is true then it obviously had to occur before Lucia contacted Rosa about helping Diana – if that is how it occurred.

[c] Lucia's daughter – should be "Beatriz", see earlier.

[d] Which have been shown earlier to be extensively conflicted.

[e] Nina Pillai was the wife of Rajan Pillai, a controversial businessman who died aged 48 in a Delhi jail in suspicious circumstances, on 7 July 1995.: Kuldip Singh, Obituary: Rajan Pillai, *The Independent*, 10 July 1995; K.S. Narayahan, 10 Questions: Nina Pillai, *Outlook India Magazine*, 11 June 1997.

Rosa does not explain how she knew Nina Pillai – "another friend of Lucia's" – and Lucia makes no mention of her in her statement or inquest evidence.

There appear to be three main possibilities:

1) the Lucia-Rosa account is all true – Rosa first met Diana through Lucia and it is all innocent, and Rosa is not an MI6 agent and did not spy on Diana

2) Rosa was an intelligence agent and Lucia was used as a way for Rosa to meet Diana

3) Rosa met Diana without any help from Lucia – and the Lucia-Rosa account of Diana meeting Rosa through Lucia is a complete fabrication.[a]

At this stage I would suggest that possibility 1 is extremely unlikely – if the Lucia-Rosa evidence was completely true we would not see the extensive conflicts, between each other and within each person's own accounts – see earlier.[b]

According to Lucia, Diana told her at their first meeting in April 1991: "I've been told we should become good friends." And after interviewing Lucia in 2003, Richard Kay wrote: "A mutual friend suggested to Lucia that she would be a 'good help' to Diana".

At that time the Charles-Diana marriage was already in serious trouble and in March Diana had deliberately leaked information to Andrew Morton about the Diana-Charles household, which was published in the *Sunday Times*.[183]

It is significant that the Lucia-Rosa evidence provides timings for the start of the Lucia-Diana and the Diana-Rosa[c] relationships – but there is nothing from them on the timing of the first meeting between Lucia and Rosa.

Why is this?

There is a possibility that Rosa already knew Lucia before the April 1991 Brazil trip took place.[d] The trip to Brazil could have been seen, by certain

---

[a] This would also point to Rosa being an intelligence agent, otherwise, why would the evidence be made up?

[b] If a person suggests that the Rosa-Lucia account is true, then the question must be asked: Which account – Rosa's statement; Rosa at the inquest; Lucia's statement; Lucia at the inquest? Because they all differ markedly in key aspects. The reality is that there are only two known witnesses who have given their accounts and are still alive – Lucia and Rosa. Why then is there so much conflict in their evidence?

[c] Albeit very conflicting.

[d] Lucia's husband, Paulo Tarso Flecha de Lima, was posted to London in 1990. It is possible that Lucia's daughter, Beatriz, looked for work and secured the job at Tiffany's soon after arriving.

members of the Establishment, as a chance for a Diana-Rosa connection to be made through Lucia.[a]

It will be shown later that in her evidence Lucia has lied to protect Rosa. There is a possibility that Lucia and Rosa have lied about the reasons for Lucia introducing Diana to Rosa.[b] It may be that the introduction occurred as a result of a request from Rosa to Lucia – not the other way around, as both Lucia and Rosa have testified.

These possibilities need to be considered in the light of the evidence in the remainder of this chapter.

Bali-Moyo Island Holiday: August 1993[c]

On 14 August 1993 Diana travelled to Bali and onto Moyo Island for a holiday, accompanied by Lucia Flecha de Lima and Rosa Monckton.

Lucia Flecha de Lima, Friend of Diana and Wife of Brazilian Ambassador, UK : 1 Sep 04 Statement: **Jury Didn't Hear**:

"In August 1993 Princess Diana, Rosa and I went on holiday with my daughter, Beatriz to Bali and the Island of Mowy. We had been scheduled to go for ten days but Princess Diana came back early. She was feeling very insecure at the time and had become very nervous about the press, Prince Charles and his courtiers. Princess Diana and I did argue and this was one such occasion. Rosa had gone to a lot of trouble to organise the trip and Princess Diana returned after three or four days. She would say, 'I'm not Beatriz. You can't treat me like that.' I would say, 'You're acting worse than Beatriz'....

"Princess Diana and I had been to Paris together in May 1993 but that was completely different. She had been there as the Princess of Wales and she still had her Scotland Yard protection officers with her." [184]

Ken Wharfe, 2002 Book: **Jury Didn't Hear**:

"[Diana] was determined to go ... [to Paris] incognito.... 'I just want to go shopping with a couple of girlfriends. I just want to be normal. Please fix it for me, Ken,' she pleaded.... Her travelling companions were Lady [Hyatt] Palumbo and Lucia Flecha de Lima.... We had use of a private jet and we flew undetected to Paris on a beautiful May[d] afternoon." [185]

Richard Kay, 2003 Interview with Lucia: **Jury Didn't Hear**:

"[Diana and Lucia] would go on holiday together. But travelling with Diana was not always easy. Once Diana, Lucia, her daughter Beatriz and Rosa

---

[a] This is supported by the comment Diana made to Lucia: "I've been told we should become good friends."

[b] There is a huge amount of conflict in that area of their evidence – see earlier.

[c] The evidence regarding this holiday should not be viewed on its own, but is part of the bigger picture of the relationship between Princess Diana and Rosa Monckton and the actions of the latter.

[d] 1993.

Monckton travelled to the remote Indonesian island of Mojo. [Lucia said] 'After 12 hours, [Diana] wanted to come home. In the end, she came home alone.'" [186]

Lucia Flecha de Lima: 18 Dec 07: 93.21:
Burnett: Q. Had you in fact been on holiday with the Princess, with your daughter, Beatriz, and Rosa Monckton to the Far East in August 1993?
A. Yes, we had.

Rosa Monckton, Friend of Diana: 13 Dec 07: 135.2:
Burnett: Q. During that period, did you go on holiday with the Princess and Lucia Flecha de Lima to the Far East?
A. Yes, we did. We went to Bali and I think that must have been in about 1993. I can't remember exactly, but I think it was around that time.

Michelle Green, Journalist: 6 Sep 93 *People* Article: **Jury Didn't Hear**:
"Unhappy about losing her sons to Charles for an 18-day vacation, the stressed-out Princess flew to Bali on Aug. 14 for a five-day idyll – hiding away at two luxury Aman resorts....

"Slipping out of London without attracting the attention of a single reporter, Diana was accompanied by Rosa Monckton, 39, managing director of Tiffany & Co. in London, Lucia Flecha de Lima, 52, wife of Brazil's ambassador to Great Britain, and bodyguard Det. Sgt. Carol Quirk. Her stay in Bali – said to have been planned with the aid of millionaire Adrian [Zecha], head of the company that owns the resorts – was remarkably private: Not one picture of her was snapped at either hideaway. Di was a 'guest of the hotel', first at Amanusa, a deluxe thatched-roof refuge ... and later at Amanwana, a retreat in the tropical forest on the island of Moyo. Her presence caused barely a ripple...." [187]

Ken Wharfe, 2002 Book: **Jury Didn't Hear**:
"[Diana's] sons, instead of being at Balmoral with their father, as they usually were in August, were free; free to do what other children did on holiday. My reconnaissance some weeks earlier had proved invaluable. I advised Diana in my [2 August 1993] briefing memo that ... Disney, unlike any other theme park, has a VIP package which uses reserved routes [to avoid the media].... As well as the two-day stopover at Disney's Florida complex in Orlando, she proposed to spend the rest of the week at the holiday home of her friend Kate Menzies at Lyford Cay in the Bahamas.... Diana would be accompanied by her girlfriends Kate Menzies and Catherine Soames and ... the boys' nanny, Olga Powell.... My team consisted of Trevor Bettles, 'Jack' Tarr, Dave Sharp and night-duty officer PC Knights.... [After arriving in Lyford Cay] I had been on duty for fourteen days without a break...." [188]

Michelle Green: 6 Sep 93 *People* Article: **Jury Didn't Hear**:

"On Aug. 24 [Diana] swept Prince William, 11, and Prince Harry, 8, off to Florida to begin a 10-day vacation.... With Fleet Street camped out in Orlando, she would have the opportunity not only to take her sons on an unforgettable outing to Disney World but also to demonstrate that she – and not Prince Charles – was the boys' more dedicated parent....

"Accompanied by close friends Kate Menzies, 32, and Catherine Soames, 35, plus Soames' son Harry, 9, and three detectives, Diana and the boys hit Big Thunder Mountain Railroad....

"Why was the trip so important? For one thing, Di's estranged husband had scored his own coup just the week before. On holiday with his sons at Balmoral, Charles, who normally shuns photo ops, made a valiant attempt to counteract his image as a distant father by allowing an ITV documentary crew to shoot him fishing with his sons....

"Nine months after their parents' separation, princes William and Harry are in the midst of a royal public relations tug-of-war. On one side is their mother – a needy soul with a genius for manipulating the press. On the other is Prince Charles – scandal-plagued but apparently bent on revamping his image. Ricocheting between two very different worlds, William and Harry live one week with hugs, kisses and trips to McDonald's, and the next with pomp, circumstance and a carefully nurtured sense of duty." [189]

Paul Burrell, Diana's Butler: 2006 Book: **Jury Didn't Hear**:

"[Diana's] friends came from all walks of life.... It was only after the princess's death that all those friends met for the first time.... It was the first time that mother-figure Lucia [Flecha de Lima] met sister-figures Susie Kassem and Rosa Monckton. I looked around Westminster Abbey on the day of her funeral ... and realised it was the only time those friends had gathered under the same roof.... In life, she had kept them deliberately apart.... She compartmentalised [her friends].... I was at the centre of her world ... so I had an overview of the entire jigsaw. As Rosa Monckton said, in a [2002] article[a] ... 'Diana chose to live her life in compartments.... Only Paul [Burrell] had the key to all the doors.'" [190]

Roberto Devorik, Friend of Diana and Fashion Executive: 17 Jan 08: 160.21:

Hough: Q. You knew Lady Bowker, but you didn't know very many of [Diana's] other confidants?

A. Well, I knew some of them, but it was on the character of the Princess to protect us one from each other and to take advice from each of us in different cubbyholes.... I have to say I know Lucia Flecha de Lima and I know Lady Rosa Monckton and I knew Lord Palumbo, but we had never been put in a room all together at the same time.

---

[a] Published in the *Sunday Telegraph* on 3 November 2002.

Comment: The evidence of the trip to Bali and Moyo Island[a] in Indonesia comes from Lucia, Rosa and the *People* magazine.[b]

Paul Burrell, Diana's butler for her final ten years[c], has stated: "After the princess's death ... was the first time that ... Lucia [Flecha de Lima] met ... Rosa Monckton".

Both cannot be true. If Lucia and Rosa had never met before September 1997 then it is not possible that they holidayed together with Diana on Moyo Island in August 1993.

All three of these witnesses – Lucia, Rosa, Burrell – have been shown to have lied on aspects of this case.[d]

Burrell's account appears to be supported by widespread evidence that Diana compartmentalised her friendships[e] – as described at the inquest by Roberto Devorik.[f]

Part 2 has revealed that the compartmentalising evidence is true, however, I suggest that the contemporary account written by Michelle Green in early September 1993 is overwhelming evidence showing the trip did occur – that on 14 August 1993 Diana, Lucia and Rosa left London to holiday together on Moyo Island in Indonesia.

There are I believe two possibilities.

a) Burrell has again lied. It may be that a possible reason for doing so was to promote his image as "the centre of [Diana's] world" and the one person with "the key to all the doors".

b) Burrell was unaware that all three – Diana, Lucia, Rosa – went on the trip. For example, he may have thought it was only Lucia and Diana.

If Burrell lied and it was his intention to promote himself – and he knew that Lucia and Rosa had been on holiday with Diana – it really begs the question: Why didn't Burrell just name another friend combination instead of Lucia, Rosa and Susan Kassem – e.g. Annabel Goldsmith, Rosa, Susan Kassem? Or Goldsmith, Lucia and Kassem?

---

[a] In Lucia's police statement she has incorrectly written "Island of Mowy". Richard Kay, in his article, calls it the "island of Mojo" – this is apparently an old spelling. The correct spelling is "Moyo".

[b] There is also mention that Princess Diana had visited the island in internet-based promotional material for tourism to Moyo. For example: www.indonesia.travel

[c] From 1987 to 1997.

[d] See Part 2.

[e] This is covered in more detail in Part 2 in the section on Sharing of Information.

[f] The trip to Moyo Island is also not covered in Ken Wharfe's book, but that may not be significant because that book does not cover every event that occurred.

This trip is significant, because it provides credence to the earlier accounts – from Lucia and Rosa – that Diana met Rosa through Lucia, who had earlier met Rosa through her daughter, Beatriz.[a]

There are though some points that require consideration relating to the Moyo Island evidence.

Lucia has made false claims in her police statement.

In her statement – not heard by the jury – Lucia says: "Princess Diana and I had been to Paris together in May 1993 but that was completely different [to the Moyo Island holiday]. She had been there as the Princess of Wales and she still had her Scotland Yard protection officers with her."

Lucia has pointed out two differences between the May 1993 Paris visit with the August 1993 Moyo Island trip. Lucia said that in Paris:

a) "[Diana] had been there as the Princess of Wales"

b) "[Diana] still had her Scotland Yard protection officers with her".

Lucia used these two points to show that the Paris trip was "completely different" to the Moyo Island trip.

Ken Wharfe, who went as police protection on the Paris trip, has stated: "[Diana] was determined to go ... [to Paris] incognito.... We had use of a private jet and we flew undetected to Paris on a beautiful May afternoon."

Michelle Green wrote about the Moyo Island trip: "[Diana] flew to Bali ... for a five-day idyll – hiding away at two luxury Aman resorts.... Slipping out of London without attracting the attention of a single reporter".

This reveals that there is no difference between the two trips – they were both low-key, "incognito" and didn't draw media attention. Neither visit was made official with Diana as "Princess of Wales" – as Lucia wrongly describes the Paris trip.[b]

Was there police protection on both the Paris and Moyo Island trips?

Diana's police protection wasn't removed until December 1993[c] – the Moyo Island holiday took place in August 1993, four months earlier.

Michelle Green's September 1993 article stated: "Diana was accompanied by ... [her] bodyguard Det. Sgt. Carol Quirk".

---

[a] One could also argue that if Rosa and Lucia already knew each other before Rosa met Diana, then there is less reason for Diana to keep their relationships separate.

[b] Wharfe points out in his book, regarding the Paris trip: "No one had any idea we were there, and I had taken the decision not to ask for any help from local police this time for fear of leaks to the press.": *Closely Guarded Secret*, p214.

[c] The evidence in the Surveillance chapter of Part 2 shows this. Figure 10 reproduces the police record of a meeting with Diana on 18 October 1994, where Diana says that "some 10 months have elapsed since she had requested the withdrawal of her [police] protection". Ken Wharfe, who was employed by the MPS, states in his book that he worked as Diana's personal protection officer from 1987, until he resigned from that position in November 1993.: *Diana: Closely Guarded Secret*, pp230-5.

Up until the removal of police protection Diana had to be accompanied by at least one officer on any holiday and Green's article confirms that.

Ken Wharfe went on the Paris trip – both trips had police protection for Diana.

Lucia has falsely indicated that Diana "still had her Scotland Yard protection officers with her" in May in Paris, but not in August at Moyo Island.

In short, Lucia has supported her statement that the Paris trip "was completely different" to Moyo Island by citing only two differences – "Scotland Yard protection" and going as "the Princess of Wales".

Both are completely false.

Lucia also said: "Princess Diana and I had been to Paris together". I suggest the use of the word "together" indicates that Lucia and Diana went unaccompanied to Paris.[a]

This is also false – Wharfe states that Hyatt Palumbo went. In fact, not only was she there, but Wharfe says: "Through Hyatt Palumbo ... we had use of [the] private jet" the group travelled in.[191]

So present on the Paris trip were Diana, Lucia, Hyatt and Ken Wharfe.

There is some conflicting evidence on whether Beatriz was present on the Bali-Moyo trip:
- Lucia: "Diana, Rosa and I went on holiday with my daughter, Beatriz" – 2004 statement
- Kay: "Diana, Lucia, her daughter Beatriz and Rosa Monckton travelled to ... Mojo" – 2003 interview with Lucia
- Lucia: "we had ... been on holiday with the Princess ... Beatriz, and Rosa Monckton" – 2007 confirmed at inquest
- Rosa: I went "on holiday with the Princess and Lucia" – 2007 confirmed at inquest
- Green: "Diana was accompanied by Rosa Monckton ... Lucia Flecha de Lima ... and bodyguard Det. Sgt. Carol Quirk".

In a 1996 *Daily Mail* article, journalist Nigel Dempster made a passing comment on Beatriz's relationship with Princess Diana: "[Beatriz and Diana] holidayed together in Bali and the island of Moyo in the Indian Ocean".[192] There is no reference in the article to the timing.

---

[a] It is interesting that Nigel Dempster also used the same misleading word in connection with Lucia's daughter, Beatriz and Diana, possibly based on information from Beatriz: "[Beatriz and Diana] holidayed together in Bali" – when clearly Lucia and Rosa were also there. But neither Dempster nor Beatriz were completing a signed, sworn police statement in the case of the assassination of a British princess.

At the inquest both Lucia and Rosa were cross-examined by the same inquest lawyer, Ian Burnett, who was asking questions based on their respective police statements. As mentioned earlier, Rosa's statement has never been made available and was not given to the jury.

Burnett's question to Lucia was: "Had you ... been on holiday with the Princess, with your daughter, Beatriz, and Rosa Monckton....?"

His question to Rosa was: "Did you go on holiday with the Princess and Lucia Flecha de Lima....?"

Beatriz is there in the Lucia question, but not in the question to Rosa. This indicates that Rosa did not include Beatriz in her statement, which Burnett was using as the basis for his questions.

The most thorough account appears to be Michelle Green's. She writes: "Diana was accompanied by Rosa Monckton, 39, managing director of Tiffany & Co. in London, Lucia Flecha de Lima, 52, wife of Brazil's ambassador to Great Britain, and bodyguard Det. Sgt. Carol Quirk."

Green even names the police accompaniment – Carol Quirk, who had been assigned to Diana's protection just four months earlier, in April 1993.[193]

In the same article Green applies similar detail to her description of the people on the holiday to Florida, that took place just 10 days later: "Accompanied by close friends Kate Menzies, 32, and Catherine Soames, 35, plus Soames' son Harry, 9, and three detectives, Diana and the boys...."

It is notable that Green includes "Catherine Soames' son Harry, 9".

If Green is thorough enough to include the presence of the nine year old Harry Soames, why wouldn't she also have included Lucia's much older daughter, Beatriz Flecha de Lima?

I suggest that on balance, it would appear that Beatriz, who would have been 24 at the time, was on the holiday, but it may be that she travelled separately to the others.[a] This would account for why Beatriz is missing from the Green article. It is possible that Rosa didn't consider Beatriz's presence relevant to her evidence.

Lucia said to the police: "Diana returned after three or four days". This is basically supported by Green who described the holiday as "a five-day idyll".

Kay wrote – based on his interview with Lucia – "after 12 hours, [Diana] wanted to come home".

This is not necessarily a conflict – Diana might have "wanted to come home" after 12 hours, but didn't actually leave until about four days later.

The question though is: Why would Diana have wanted to leave after just 12 hours?

There is no clue in the Kay article – just, apparently from Lucia: "Travelling with Diana was not always easy".

---

[a] The 1996 article – written 10 months before the deaths – from Dempster confirms Lucia's account. There is no apparent reason at that time for Beatriz to lie about this.

In her statement – which does not mention about the 12 hours – Lucia says: "[Diana] was feeling very insecure at the time and had become very nervous about the press, Prince Charles and his courtiers." Lucia also makes it very clear that she didn't approve of Diana's premature departure: "Princess Diana and I did argue and this was one such occasion. Rosa had gone to a lot of trouble to organise the trip". Lucia apparently told Diana: "You're acting worse than Beatriz".

So Lucia has given two reasons for Diana leaving early: a) "the press", and b) "Prince Charles and his courtiers".

The Green article says that the group slipped "out of London without attracting the attention of a single reporter"; "was remarkably private"; "not one picture of her was snapped at either hideaway"[a]; "[Diana's] presence caused barely a ripple".

There are absolutely no press reports of this holiday at the time, and as Green says: "not one picture". Green's article was published retrospectively, on 6 September 1993[b] – about 19 days after Diana had returned to London.

There were no press snooping around Bali or Moyo Island.

It appears that Lucia has lied when she stated to the police that Diana "had become very nervous about the press" as a reason why "Diana came back early".

In contrast, Green describes the press reaction to the Florida trip Diana embarked on just five days after her return from Bali – "Fleet Street [were] camped out in Orlando".

And that was no accident.

Ken Wharfe, who organised that trip, describes what happened during his reconnaissance mission to Florida, well ahead of the holiday: "I ... asked one of Disney's senior security chiefs if it would be possible to run a name check through the company's computer. Within seconds the name 'Richard Kay' flashed up on the screen. The *Daily Mail* journalist was booked to arrive at the Grand Floridian on exactly the same day as Diana; even more significantly, the booking had been made on the very day that Diana had told me of her wish to go to Florida.... It was clear that [Diana] had personally tipped Kay off, and I was reasonably certain that he would have passed on the information, at her behest, to the rest of the royal rat pack." [194]

This behaviour by Diana – revealed by Wharfe and confirmed by Green – does not suggest a person that "had become very nervous about the press", as described by Lucia Flecha de Lima.

---

[a] Amanusa in Bali and Amanwana on Moyo Island.
[b] The article was published simultaneously in *Time* magazine and *People*.

Lucia also says that Diana "had become very nervous about ... Prince Charles and his courtiers".

Ken Wharfe, who by 1993 had spent six years with the princess, says of that period: "For Diana, her sons always came first, and as the far-reaching implications of the dissolution of her marriage became clearer she began to focus on preparing them both, and William in particular, for what lay ahead."[195] And regarding Diana's own state of mind: "At last liberated from the shackles of her marriage[a], [Diana] was a woman determined to enjoy herself after the years of frustration." [196]

Diana's concern with Charles at this time appears to focus on the battle over time spent with William and Harry – as Green points out: Diana was "unhappy about losing her sons to Charles for an 18-day vacation". But there is clear evidence from Wharfe that well before the Moyo Island holiday occurred, the Florida-Bahamas trip with the boys – starting on August 24 – had been planned.

In her signed police statement Lucia said: "We had been scheduled to go for ten days". The holiday started on August 14, so that would mean it would conclude on August 24.

Yet on August 24, Diana jets off with William, Harry and others on a holiday to Florida that was planned weeks earlier – see Wharfe above.[b]

This indicates that the original schedule for the Bali holiday must have been less than 10 days – another factual error in Lucia's sworn statement. It is evident that if Diana had stayed in Indonesia for 10 days, then she would have been too late to leave for the earlier scheduled Florida-Bahamas holiday.

Did Diana return after five days to make sure she was back home well ahead of the upcoming holiday with William and Harry? Even if she did, that still would not explain Kay's: "after 12 hours, [Diana] wanted to come home".[c]

Lucia – see above – appears to have provided dubious signed evidence regarding the reasons Diana left early: the press and Charles.[d] There is no other support for what Lucia has said.

This raises the possibility that Lucia may be covering up for the real reason why Diana wanted to leave after 12 hours.

---

[a] The formal separation had been announced in December 1992.

[b] Wharfe wrote a briefing memo for Diana after his reconnaissance trip to Florida and the Bahamas. The memo was "dated 2 August 1993". This indicates the decision for the trip was made in July or earlier. It is normal practice for overseas trips made by royals to be organised well in advance. Source: Ken Wharfe, *Diana: Closely Guarded Secret*, p222.

[c] Based on an interview with Lucia.

[d] One could argue that if Diana was concerned about Charles, it would be a good reason to go on a holiday, not return back to London.

It is notable that Lucia apparently didn't consider the reason, whatever it was, as valid – "you're acting worse than Beatriz": see above.

There are three important questions that need to be answered:

1) Why has Lucia apparently covered up the real reason Diana wanted to leave early?

2) Lucia says: "Rosa had gone to a lot of trouble to organise the trip". Why did Rosa organise this holiday? [a]

3) This Bali-Moyo break occurred four years ahead of the Paris crash. Why is detail about it included in Lucia and Rosa's police statements[b], which were made as part of the investigation into the circumstances of the crash?

There is some speculation in what follows.

I suggest that the inclusion of the Moyo holiday in both Lucia and Rosa's 2004 police statements is significant. In March 1995, Lucia was interviewed extensively about her relationship with Diana, by Daphne Barak. Yet, even though this interview was conducted just 19 months after the Bali holiday, there was no mention of it at all in Barak's lengthy article.[197] There was a brief mention in the 2003 Kay article, but the police statement account is quite detailed.

It is possible that Lucia and Rosa have included the Moyo Island holiday in their statement evidence, because it lends credibility to their accounts of the way in which Diana met Rosa – via Lucia (see earlier). As has been shown, that Lucia introduction evidence was littered with contradictions and conflict, enough to consider the possibility that parts, or all, of it may have been fabricated.[c]

There is substantial evidence – see Part 2[d] and Devorik above – showing that Diana tended to not mix her friends with each other. Although, not always – clearly on the Florida-Bahamas holiday, just three months earlier, Diana had holidayed with both Kate Menzies and Catherine Soames.

The balance of the earlier evidence is that – even though it was massively under-reported in the media, and not mentioned in the books of Wharfe or Burrell – the Bali trip did occur. And both Lucia and Rosa were there.

So were Rosa and Lucia there because they already knew each other pre-Diana, or is there another reason?

The evidence suggested that the Diana introduction to Rosa didn't necessarily occur in the way Lucia and Rosa have said – see earlier. Having

---

[a] This is a question that also arises in connection with the final Rosa-Diana holiday which took place just two weeks before Diana died – see later.

[b] We do not have Rosa's statement, but Burnett's questioning indicates that Rosa included this holiday in her statement.

[c] This has been addressed earlier.

[d] Section called "Sharing of Information".

said that, it is still possible that Lucia and Rosa knew each other outside of Diana[a] – probably through the Tiffany's-Beatriz connection they have both cited.

The general evidence from both is that they were critical of Diana on similar issues – the way she was handling her marriage to Charles, the arrangement to holiday with Mohamed Al Fayed.

During this 1993 period, the big issue was the Diana-Charles marriage – the separation had occurred the previous year, but there were still issues over the children, and no doubt whether this was going to stay as a separation, or end in divorce. The prior year had seen the publication of Diana's view of her marriage in a book by Andrew Morton, the publishing of the Squidgygate transcripts, the separation and the Queen announcing her "annus horribilus".[b]

If the Establishment wanted pressure put on Diana to prevent a final termination of her marriage, then the ideally placed people to influence her were Rosa Monckton –who had MI6 connections – and the conservative-thinking Lucia Flecha de Lima – who was a close confidante.

Lucia has stated: "Rosa had gone to a lot of trouble to organise the trip". Was the trip also initiated by Rosa?

A possible scenario is that Rosa was asked by Establishment figures to either influence Diana or find out what she was thinking or planning. Rosa may have organised the trip[c], but worked through Lucia to approach Diana with the idea. At that point Diana may have been more likely to go on a holiday with Lucia present, than with Rosa on her own.

Lucia told Kay: "After 12 hours, [Diana] wanted to come home". Why?

There is then a possibility that Rosa was working to an agenda[d] during this Bali holiday that she had organised.

Was Diana feeling pressure as a result of that? Such a scenario could have led to Diana wanting to leave after just 12 hours.

Maybe Rosa then backed off. Diana stayed for the five days before leaving early in order to be home ahead of the pre-planned trip with William and Harry to Florida.

Some of the above is speculation, but it is based on what is known from the available evidence.[a]

---

[a] Although Devorik is not explicit, he appears to raise the possibility that he knew some of the others outside of his relationship with Diana: "I know Lucia Flecha de Lima and I know Lady Rosa Monckton and I knew Lord Palumbo, but we had never been put in a room all together at the same time."

[b] These events are addressed in Part 2.

[c] Apparently with the help of Adrian Zecha – see Green article.

[d] Lucia stated earlier, regarding the Diana-Rosa relationship: "Princess Diana thought maybe Rosa did have a hidden agenda".

Nature of the Diana-Rosa Relationship

Rosa Monckton, Friend of Diana: 13 Dec 07: 113.4:

Burnett: Q. Did you in fact become regular friends and meet regularly in 1992?

A. Yes, we did, very often.

Q. Now we have heard from others already about the very difficult state of the Princess's marriage at that stage and I am sure everyone here understands that. In general terms, when you first met her properly in February 1992 and in the weeks that followed, how did you judge the way in which she was dealing with the breakdown of her marriage?

A. She was not dealing with it very well. She was very upset. She felt very isolated from her husband and she was very upset because of her children.

Q. The breakdown of a marriage is always a traumatic event or one supposes it must be. Was she coping well with it or not? [b]

A. At that time she was not coping with it very well, no. She was very emotional about it and could sometimes be a little bit irrational. She found it difficult to see things clearly, which is understandable when you are in a marriage that is beginning to go wrong and in such a public way. I think that was very, very difficult.

Q. What did you and Lucia Flecha de Lima seek to do to assist [Diana] at that stage?

A. In the beginning, certainly in the first weeks, we both advised her very strongly to try to make it work. We felt that that would be best for both of them and certainly for the boys.

Q. Was that advice to which she was receptive at that time?

A. She was not particularly receptive to it because she was convinced that her husband was seeing Camilla Parker-Bowles and she did not see that there was any way that she could get him back.

Q. During this period – in the early months after you met the Princess of Wales properly – did you progress from being a confidante who had a particular purpose[c] to somebody who became a friend?

A. Absolutely and very quickly. I think when you meet somebody who is in such an emotional state and you click, you become friends very quickly. There was a lot of pressure on her and so we did spend a lot of time together.

---

[a] It will be shown later that Lucia has lied to protect Rosa – part of that could have included coming up with a false reason for Diana's early departure from Indonesia (see above).

[b] This was the second time Burnett asked this question – see previous question.

[c] The purpose being: "we both advised her very strongly to try to make [her marriage] work".

She used to come to my flat or I would go round to Kensington Palace or we would meet in the Brazilian Ambassador's residence.

Q. At that stage, how often roughly were you meeting Princess Diana?

A. Certainly from February/March 1992, it was at least once a week.

Lucia Flecha de Lima, Friend of Diana and Wife of Brazilian Ambassador, UK: 18 Dec 2007: 130.19:

Mansfield: Q. Is it right from what Diana told you that she had reservations about trusting Rosa Monckton?

A. Nothing to do with the case.

Q. Well, I want to read to you what you have put in your statement –

A. I will not comment about a friend whose daughter is my god-daughter.

Q. But you have commented in this statement. With your permission, I am going to quote what you told the police.

A. Please. Go ahead.

Q.... "Rosa is a clever woman and could understand the issues better, but I do not think Princess Diana trusted her as much as she trusted me. I had no hidden agenda, I was foreign and would move on. Princess Diana thought maybe Rosa did have a hidden agenda as any friend of hers would have a special position, even as the estranged wife of Prince Charles."

Do you remember telling the British police that?

A. Of course I do.

Q. Is it true, what you have said to the British police?

A. I would not lie to the British police.

Q. So is it true, therefore, that Princess Diana, in speaking to you, conveyed to you that she thought that Rosa might have a hidden agenda?

A. My opinion.

Comment: The witness evidence on the Rosa-Diana relationship is:

- Rosa: "we did ... become regular friends and [met] regularly" – confirmed at inquest

- Rosa: "you click, you become friends very quickly" – at inquest describing what happened

- Rosa: "[Diana] did not" know that Rosa had [MI6] connections – confirmed at inquest [a]

- Rosa: "she told me what she chose to tell me" – at inquest

- Lucia: "I do not think ... Diana trusted [Rosa] as much as she trusted me" – statement

- Lucia: "Diana thought maybe Rosa did have a hidden agenda as any friend of hers would have a special position" – statement, confirmed at inquest

- Simmons: Diana was "aware that Rosa ... had a connection with ... MI6" – confirmed at inquest

---

[a] Rosa repeated this at 181.20: "She did not know of my [MI6] connection."

- Simmons: "No, not 100%" – reply to "Did [Diana] trust Rosa Monckton?" at inquest
- Simmons: "Rosa didn't have time for Diana and Diana made time for Rosa" – at inquest
- Simmons: "Diana was the strong one and Rosa found it very easy to off-load" – at inquest
- Simmons: "[Diana] would speak to Rosa about children and family things, but when it came to major issues, no"
- Simmons: "[Diana] once wrongly suspected [Rosa] of spying on her" – 2005 book
- Simmons: "[Diana] was understandably wary of Rosa at times" – 2005 book.

There are three different witnesses, with three different accounts.

There are two issues – first, the overall nature of the friendship, and second and more important, whether Rosa's MI6 connections[a] influenced the friendship. This is where the key evidence conflicts occur.

Simmons confirmed that Diana was "aware that Rosa ... had a connection with ... MI6" and also has stated: "Due to Diana's concern about the ... Intelligence Services, she was understandably wary of Rosa at times." [b]

Lucia said: "Princess Diana thought maybe Rosa did have a hidden agenda as any friend of [Diana's] would have a special position".

Rosa stated that Diana did not know that she had MI6 connections.

The statements of Simmons and Rosa are directly opposite – Simmons says Diana was aware of an MI6 connection and Rosa says Diana wasn't aware.

If Diana wasn't aware of Rosa's MI6 connection, then clearly it couldn't influence the relationship.

But was Diana aware?

Lucia says Diana had a problem with trusting Rosa, but it was nothing to do with an MI6 connection – instead it was "a hidden agenda as any friend of [Diana's] would have a special position". In other words, any friend – including Rosa – couldn't be trusted because they could manipulate the relationship to their own ends. That is, except Lucia: "I had no hidden agenda, I was foreign and would move on."

Lucia appears to be suggesting that Diana could trust no friends unless they were foreigners or had connections to foreign diplomats and therefore

---

[a] It is not in dispute that Rosa has connections to MI6 and she admits that herself – see earlier in this chapter.
[b] Not heard by the jury.

would be leaving the country. So, because Rosa did not fall into that category, "Diana thought maybe Rosa did have a hidden agenda".

I suggest that Lucia's argument could be flawed, as Diana had several British-based friends who she appeared to share trusting relationships over long periods of time – Carolyn Bartholomew, Annabel Goldsmith, Elsa Bowker and Elton John are a few examples.

Lucia has, however, raised the issue of Rosa's "hidden agenda" in her police statement – this does indicate that at some stage Diana voiced concerns about Rosa to Lucia.

This raises the possibility that Lucia correctly detected that "Diana thought maybe Rosa did have a hidden agenda", but deduced incorrectly the reason – that it was because Rosa "would have a special position".

It could be significant that when Lucia was first asked by Mansfield about this[a], she refused to answer: "Nothing to do with the case". Then when Mansfield said he wanted "to read to you what you have put in your statement", Lucia interrupted: "I will not comment about a friend whose daughter is my god-daughter".

I suggest that if this was just about "a hidden agenda <u>as any friend of [Diana's]</u> would have a special position", Lucia may not have been so resistant under oath.[b]

Was the "hidden agenda" Lucia spoke of instead because of Rosa's MI6 connection?

Lucia should have been asked about this at the inquest – but she wasn't.

Mansfield did ask Lucia – see earlier: "Did you know ... whether Rosa Monckton ... had connections with the security services, a relative?" Lucia replied: "Rosa Monckton had connections with Secret Service? I do not believe so."

Mansfield's question was in connection with the "security services" – that is a general term, which covers British Intelligence, including both MI5 (Security Service[c]) and MI6 (Secret Intelligence Service). Lucia has restated Mansfield's question, before she answers – but she has changed "security services" to "Secret Service", which appears to be short for "Secret Intelligence Service", SIS or MI6.

So Lucia has changed Mansfield's general "security services" to the more specific "Secret Service".[d]

---

[a] The question was: "Is it right from what Diana told you that she had reservations about trusting Rosa Monckton?"

[b] Another question is: Why was Lucia attempting to suppress evidence? Was it just that the evidence was unpalatable, or had she been told not to talk about this subject at the inquest?

[c] Singular with first letter capitals.

[d] The inquest transcriber correctly picked up that "Secret Service" had first letter capitals, whereas "security services" did not.

It does not seem to be a coincidence that it was the Secret Intelligence Service that the "relative" – Anthony – Mansfield was referring to, worked for. I suggest that this is an indication that Lucia was aware of Anthony's employment in MI6, and therefore she was aware – contrary to what she has stated – that "Rosa Monckton had connections with [the] Secret Service".

Lucia may have lied on this issue to support Rosa's assertion – see below – that Diana wasn't aware of her MI6 connection.

Rosa was asked: "Diana ... knew that you had that connection, did she not?" She categorically replied: "No, she did not."

Rosa's answer is completely bereft of logic.

Rosa says Diana didn't know that she had a connection with MI6. The point here is that if Diana had known, she would not necessarily tell Rosa.

So how then is it possible for Rosa to insist, "No, she did not" know.

Obviously it's not possible[a][b] – yet that is what Rosa asserted under oath at Diana's inquest.

In contrast, Simmons said that Diana was "aware that Rosa ... had a connection with ... MI6". That was supported by what Simmons wrote in her earlier book: "Due to Diana's concern about the ... intelligence services, she was understandably wary of Rosa at times".

As much as it is illogical for Rosa to insist that Diana didn't know about her MI6 connection[c], I suggest that it is logical that if Diana did have intelligence concerns about Rosa, she could have shared that with one or two close friends.

Simone Simmons recounts a conversation about the subject – "I said, 'Are you sure about all of this?' and [Diana] said 'Yes'."

I suggest it is also common sense that, as Princess of Wales, Diana had connections in high places. All it would take is for one friend – or even acquaintance – who was aware of both Rosa's friendship with Diana and her MI6 connection, to warn Diana.[d] It is not a big stretch to suggest that Diana may have been warned.

In summary, Rosa's insistence that Diana didn't know seems illogical; Lucia's evidence that Rosa's hidden agenda was having "a special position" appears flawed; Simmons' account that Diana knew about Rosa's MI6 connection seems credible and is I suggest supported by common sense.

Later evidence will indicate that the Diana-Rosa relationship was not as close as it has been made out to be.

---

[a] The normal way for someone to find out would be to ask the person if they knew or not – but if Rosa had done that, then Diana would have then known.

[b] Rosa could have said, "I think she did not know", but Rosa's answer was categoric.

[c] See above.

[d] This is over a period of 5½ years, if Rosa first met Diana in February 1992.

Period of "Radio Silence"

Rosa Monckton has said that Princess Diana cut off communication with her for a month or two in June-July 1997 – just two or three months before her death in Paris.

Rosa Monckton, Friend of Diana: 13 Dec 07: 130.9:

Burnett: Q. Now there were some times where you gave advice or expressed views to the Princess with which she was not very happy, I think.

A. Yes, on a few occasions.

Q. What would happen when that event had occurred?

A. Typically, there would be radio silence. I would not hear from her for some time, until she had worked through it, and then she would pick up the telephone again.

Q. So, in those circumstances, as you put it, radio silence, you waited for her to get back in touch with you?

A. Yes, I did, always.

Q. You have identified one particular event which led to that to do with an official visit – I infer an official visit – that the Princess made with Prince Charles to Korea. Is that right?

A. Yes, that is right.

Q. Can you explain what happened?

....A. There were lots of television images of her and front-page newspapers of them sitting – the Prince and Princess of Wales sitting next to each other, but Diana absolutely turned away from him and looking down, and there was a lot of adverse comment at the time. So I rang her up in Korea and I said, "You have just got to pull yourself together and get on with it. This is not doing any of you any favours".

Q. What was her reaction to that?

A. She was very quiet and silent and I did not hear from her probably for about two months after that.

Q. Then did the relationship pick up again?

A. Straightaway. She would pick up the telephone and say "Come and have lunch" and off we went again.

Q. Did something similar happen when the Princess was considering an invitation from Mr Al Fayed to join him on holiday in St Tropez in July 1997?

A. Yes, it did.

Q. Now could you explain how you came to discuss that matter with the Princess at all?

A. She came round to our house in London on 1st June for my daughter and her God-daughter's second birthday party. At the end of the birthday party she said to me, "Can I stay because I want to discuss something with you?" She then said that she had been offered this invitation to go on holiday with the Al Fayeds to the South of France and she was considering accepting it because it would be fun for the boys and she would not have any worries about security. What did I think? I said that she should not even consider going on holiday with Mr Al Fayed, that it was an inappropriate thing for her to do, and at about that time, my husband came home from work and he sat down and told her the same thing.

....Q. After giving that advice, was there then some radio silence?

A. There was definitely radio silence after that.

Q. In what circumstances did you learn that the Princess had indeed accepted the invitation from Mr Al Fayed?

A. Because at the time my husband was editing the *Sunday Telegraph*, and he rang me on a Saturday evening to say that there were pictures coming down the wire of Diana on Mr Al Fayed's yacht. So I said to him, "Well that explains why I haven't heard from her because she has gone on holiday".

Q. So if your recollection of dates is correct, it would indicate that for the whole of June and the first ten days of July at least, you did not hear from the Princess?

A. That is correct.

At 152.16: Mansfield: Q. When you saw her, after you had given very strong advice that she should not go in the first place, what did you say? Did you say, "I am amazed that you went on that holiday with a person who is connected with Mohamed Al Fayed"?[a] Did you?

A. I cannot remember exactly what I said to her.

Dominic Lawson, Rosa Monckton's Husband: 4 Jun 06 Article: **Jury Didn't Hear**:

"On June 1, 1997, Diana, Princess of Wales, was taking part in the second birthday celebrations of our daughter Domenica, who was born with Down's syndrome.... After the other guests had left and we were sitting down together, she told us that she'd had an invitation from Mohamed Al Fayed to spend a few days in the South of France on his newly acquired yacht, the Jonikal. She was very tempted and wanted to know whether we thought it was a good idea. My wife Rosa asked her why she was keen on taking up the invitation from the deeply controversial owner of Harrods. Diana replied that she wanted to take 'the boys' and that she knew that Fayed had a very big security operation, which would remove one of her biggest headaches - how to keep her sons protected from the Press and other intruders.

"I acknowledged that, but strongly urged her not to accept. I said it didn't seem right that she - and especially her sons - should be closely associated with a man who successive British Governments, both Conservative and

---

[a] Referring to the first cruise with Dodi.

Labour, had decided was not fit to be given a passport (ever since a 1989 Department of Trade investigation into his takeover of Harrods condemned him as a serial liar with 'a capacity for fantasy'). I believe that I added: 'The man is nothing but trouble.'

"Diana looked steadily at us with those big doe eyes, and then said: 'Thank you so much, I'm very glad I asked you.'

"Six weeks later I was in the newsroom of the paper I then edited when the picture editor came marching towards me with a look of satisfaction on his face. 'There's our front page,' he said, and slapped down on the table in front of me a long-range photograph from a French news agency of a man and a woman on a big boat. 'That's Princess Diana and Mohamed Al Fayed,' he exclaimed.

"'Yes,' I sighed, 'I know who they are.' After he wandered off, probably thinking what an ungrateful editor he was working for, I called my wife and told her what I had just been shown. She laughed. 'Well, that explains why I haven't heard a peep from Diana recently.'

"That was so typical of Diana: she often asked my wife for advice, but seldom took it. And when she did something that she knew Rosa disapproved of, she found it impossible to own up." [198]

Michael Cole, Director of Public Affairs, Harrods: 10 Jan 08: 104.5:

Hilliard: Q. On 9th June 1997 you had a telephone call from [Diana], and ... she was calling to discuss an invitation which had been extended to her and her sons to join Mr and Mrs Al Fayed and their five children at their residence in St Tropez the following month, the holiday we have heard about?

A. Yes.... On this night, I think it was 3rd June, and that's what my diary says and that's what his[a] diary says, although Ms Monckton said that she spoke to Diana about the invitation on 1st June and she knew that because it was one of her children's birthdays, but my recollection is on 3rd June Mohamed went to this gala presentation of Swan Lake and afterwards there was a dinner at the Churchill International Hotel in Portman Square and he and Heini were sitting next to Diana, Princess of Wales, and they got to talking about what was going to happen in the summer.... She volunteered the fact that she was at a little bit of a loose end, she didn't know quite where to go, this was after [all her] first year as a divorced mother of two young boys and he said in a very nice way, "You are most welcome to come" and as a result of that invitation, which of course Heini endorsed and said, "We are there, if you want to come, come", she telephoned me on 9th June, I know it was that day because I was moving into a house and I was actually pushing my sofa through the door when the phone rang.... She said, "Mohamed has asked me to come down" and she really wanted to know what was there, essentially.

---

[a] Mohamed Al Fayed.

Now, I was able to tell her about the wonderful facilities that were there....
Subsequent to that conversation, I wrote her a letter, which I am sure a copy
could be provided, just listing what there was there and also providing all the
phone numbers for the house in St Tropez.... Subsequently when she decided
to go, I telephoned her just to confirm that the helicopter would come and
pick the family up in Kensington Gardens....

Michael Cole: 6 Jul 06 Statement: **Jury Didn't Hear**:

"The Princess had known Mr. and Mrs. Al Fayed for many years. The
invitation to stay with the Fayed family in St. Tropez was extended to the
Princess on 2 June during a gala dinner following a performance by the
English National Ballet[a] at the Royal Albert Hall. The Princess was the
patron of the ENB. Mr. Al Fayed was a supporter of the ballet and had
sponsored a notable production of 'The Nutcracker'.... Following the Royal
Albert Hall performance of 'Swan Lake', Mr. Al Fayed was seated next to
the Princess at a dinner in the Churchill Hotel in Portman Square. The
Princess told Mr. Al Fayed that she was concerned because she did not know
where she could take her sons during their summer holidays. She said that
she had asked her brother if they could use a house on the estate at Althorp....
Her brother had at first agreed but then rescinded the invitation because he
considered her presence would attract the sort of media attention that would
spoil the holidays for his own children....

"Mr. Al Fayed said that she and the Princes William and Harry were most
welcome to join his family in St. Tropez. Mr. Al Fayed had extended this
invitation in previous years and though the Princess had wanted to go, her
schedule had ruled out an acceptance." [199]

Lucia Flecha de Lima, Friend of Diana and Wife of Brazilian Ambassador,
UK: 18 Dec 07: 98.9:

Burnett: Q. Did the Princess speak to you about whether she should go on
holiday to Mohamed Al Fayed's house in France?

A. Yes, she did.

Q. What was your reaction to that?

A. I did not think it was a proper thing to do.

Q. Why was that?

A. Because she is a Royal Princess of England. She could be among her
peers.

Q. Was there anything in particular that worried you about her going on
holiday with Mr Al Fayed?

A. He is a bit of a controversial person.

---

[a] ENB.

Q. Well, I do not think I need to ask you more about that. We have heard a bit from Rosa Monckton.

Lucia Flecha de Lima: 1 Sep 04 Statement: **Jury Didn't Hear**:

"When Princess Diana told me she was going on holiday with Mohamed Al Fayed to the South of France, neither Rosa, Richard Kay nor I were very happy about it knowing of Mr Al Fayed's bad reputation as a business man and the problem over his passport being refused. However Princess Diana was fond of Mr Al Fayed's wife and she said, 'I have nowhere else to go.' This was true. She needed a country home. She had two boys who needed space, a place where they could invite their friends. Mr Al Fayed had tried to be friends with Princess Diana in the past. Raine, her stepmother was public relations at Harrods. I don't know if she was involved in planning the trip but there was a lot to organise, the security etc. The Royal family didn't interfere. I told her I was not happy. Princess Diana said that Mohamed Al Fayed could give her protection against the press." [200]

Comment: There is a key conflict in the evidence:

Rosa Monckton has stated: "[Diana] came round to our house in London on 1st June [1997] for my daughter and her god-daughter's second birthday party[a].... [Diana] then said that she had been offered this invitation to go on holiday with the Al Fayeds...."

Rosa is supported by her husband, Dominic Lawson's, 2006 account.

Michael Cole said: "I think it was 3rd June, and that's what my diary says and that's what [Mohamed's] diary says.... Mohamed went to this gala presentation of Swan Lake and afterwards there was a dinner.... [Mohamed] said ... 'You are most welcome to come',"

Both witnesses have tied Diana's Mohamed holiday offer to an event – Rosa to her daughter's 1st birthday and Cole to the special Swan Lake production.

Both cannot be true. It is not possible that Rosa and Lawson could have heard about Mohamed's offer on June 1, if the offer was not proffered until June 3.[b]

The full significance of this "radio silence" evidence is addressed in the Comment parts of the Greek Holiday section.

---

[a] Domenica Lawson, who has Down's Syndrome, was born on 1 June 1995. This was confirmed in a *Daily Mail* interview with Rosa Monckton in 2007.: Helen Weathers, My Down's Daughter Changed My Life, *Daily Mail*, 14 November 2007.

[b] There is an additional conflict in Michael Cole's accounts. In his 2006 statement he says that the Swan Lake concert was on June 2, but at the inquest – apparently after checking his diary – he has said it was on June 3. The Royal Albert Hall website states: "On 3 June 1997 the Princess of Wales paid her last visit to the [Royal Albert] Hall, as patron of English National Ballet, to see Swan Lake." This confirms Cole's inquest account that the performance was on June 3. Source: Royal Albert Hall website: www.royalalberthall.com/about/history-and-archives Click on "Timeline".

Greek Islands Holiday: 15 to 20 August 1997

Princess Diana holidayed with Rosa Monckton for five days, just two weeks before the Paris crash that took Diana's life.

Rosa Monckton, Friend of Diana: 13 Dec 07: 138.21:

Burnett: Q. As far as the holiday to Greece is concerned, was it organised in the period after she came back from St Tropez or was it organised long before?

A. It was organised before and it was organised – I do not know when the Hong Kong handover was, but I was in Hong Kong for that, and we organised it on the telephone then, whenever that was. I cannot remember what month that was of 1997.

Q. That is something we can easily find out.... Now this was, I think, a sailing holiday –

A. Yes, it was.... It was a very small 20-metre motorboat.

Q. With three crew?

A. With three crew.

Q. Other than you and the Princess, were there any other guests on board?

A. No, it was just the two of us.

Q. This was a boat that had been lent to you by friends?

A. Exactly.

At 144.3: Q. Just reverting to the timings between June and your going away, you mentioned that the arrangement to go away in Greece was made whilst you were in Hong Kong for the handover. Now the handover was on 30th June 1997, so it is about that time that you had a telephone conversation with her to arrange the holiday later.

A. Yes.

Q. But are we right to understand that in that conversation she did not tell you that she was in fact going to St Tropez in the interval?

A. No, she did not.

Q. Because you have told us that you were alerted when you became aware of press coverage a little bit later.[a]

At 182.5: Mansfield: Q. Just as a matter of interest, how did you get to this holiday? It is a simple question in one sense.

A. We had booked scheduled flights and paid for them and a few days before we left, Diana rang me and said that Mr Al Fayed had offered her his plane and that she was inclined to do that, because then we could get away without the press seeing us.

Q. You must have been a bit shocked about that, mustn't you?

---

[a] At this point Burnett changed the subject, without waiting for a response.

A. We discussed it and she said that that is what she wanted to do and she very strongly wanted to avoid the press and she felt that this was the way to do it.

Q. Perhaps you regard it as rather small beer really, but this was accepting Mohamed Al Fayed's facilities, wasn't it?

A. It was.

Q. Did that trouble you?

A. It did, and I discussed it with my husband. But Diana wanted to get away. We wanted to get away and that was the way that she wanted to do it. You can say to your friends what you believe to be true. You can say what you think, but there comes a point when, if they don't accept it, you don't want to put your friendship on the line.

Dominic Lawson, Rosa Monckton's Husband: 4 Jun 06 Article: **Jury Didn't Hear**:

"A month [after Diana's St Tropez holiday] ... Diana took up Rosa's invitation to join her on a boat trip around the Greek Islands.... The boat Rosa had chosen was tiny - barely room enough for the two of them and three crew. The world's Press had got wind of the fact that Diana was touring the Greek Islands, but it never occurred to them that it would be on such a small boat....

"A fortnight later, both Diana and Dodi were dead." [201]

Comment: Rosa Monckton's evidence regarding the "radio silence" and the Greek holiday raises several concerns.

There is a conflict between Rosa's account and that of her husband, Dominic Lawson.

Rosa says: "At the end of the birthday party she said to me ... that she had been offered this invitation to go on holiday with the Al Fayeds.... I said that she should not even consider going on holiday with Mr Al Fayed.... at about that time, my husband came home from work and he sat down and told her the same thing".

Lawson says: "After the other guests had left and we were sitting down together, [Diana] told us that she'd had an invitation from Mohamed Al Fayed... My wife Rosa asked her why she was keen on taking up the invitation.... Diana replied that she wanted to take 'the boys' and that she knew that Fayed had a very big security operation.... I ... strongly urged her not to accept."

In Rosa's account Lawson is not there for the birthday party and Diana asks Rosa for the advice. Then Lawson "came home from work" and gave his advice.

In Lawson's article he is there before the guests left – "after the other guests had left and we were sitting down together" – and he fully describes the initial question from Diana and then a return question from Rosa.

One, or both, of these accounts has to be false.

Rosa has stated that the radio silence started straight after advice[a] she and her husband gave Diana on 1 June 1997 – "there was definitely radio silence after that" advice – but has never made a clear statement about when and how the silence ended.

Under oath at the inquest Rosa indicated that she hadn't heard from Diana between June 1 and July 12.[b] In the context of the radio silence, Rosa was asked: "In what circumstances did you learn that the Princess had indeed accepted the invitation from Mr Al Fayed?" Rosa replied: "My husband ... rang me on a Saturday evening to say that there were pictures ... of Diana on Mr Al Fayed's yacht. So I said to him, 'Well that explains why I haven't heard from her because she has gone on holiday'." Burnett then asked for confirmation: "For the whole of June and the first ten days[c] of July at least, you did not hear from the Princess?" Rosa confirmed: "That is correct."

Yet just 10 minutes later, still talking under oath to the same lawyer, but about a different topic – the Greek Islands holiday – Rosa contradicts this account.

Burnett asks Rosa: "The holiday to Greece ... was it organised in the period after she came back from St Tropez or was it organised long before?"

The question appears to be based on Rosa's earlier radio silence evidence – if there was a radio silence that lasted from June 1 until the St Tropez holiday[d], then it is logical that the Rosa-Diana Greek holiday would have to have been organised before the radio silence ("long before") or "after [Diana] came back from St Tropez".

Rosa replies: "I was in Hong Kong for [the handover], and we organised it on the telephone then.... I cannot remember what month that was of 1997."

Rosa may have been hoping no one would check it out, but Burnett said, "That is something we can easily find out". He later came back: "The handover was on 30th June 1997". Burnett then asked Rosa to reconfirm her assertion: "so it is about that time that you had a telephone conversation with her to arrange the holiday". Rosa confirms.

So Rosa has now confirmed: a) "For the whole of June and the first ten days of July at least, you did not hear from [Diana]", and b) "so it is about [June 30] that you had a telephone conversation with [Diana] to arrange the [Greek] holiday".

One of these assertions made under oath – or both – has to be false.

---

[a] Advice "that [Diana] should not even consider going on holiday with Mr [Mohamed] Al Fayed".
[b] The St Tropez holiday started on Friday July 11 and Rosa says she found out about it "on a Saturday evening".
[c] It is actually 12 days – see previous footnote.
[d] That holiday started on July 11 and finished on July 20.

There can't have both been a Rosa-Diana radio silence that lasted from June 1 to July 10 and a phone call between Rosa and Diana on or about 30 June 1997.

What does Burnett do with this?

Burnett appears to try and ease the minds of jury members, who may have been starting to doubt Rosa's evidence, while at the same time fails to challenge Rosa on an obvious conflict.

Burnett deftly ignores Rosa's confirmation of: "For the whole of June and the first ten days of July at least, you did not hear from [Diana]". He instead reverts back to: "[Diana] did not tell you that she was in fact going to St Tropez in the interval?" Rosa confirms: "No, she did not." Burnett then reinforces this, probably for the "benefit" of the jury[a]: "Because you have told us that you were alerted [about the St Tropez holiday] when you became aware of press coverage a little bit later." And Burnett quickly moves onto a new subject.[202]

Burnett moved the focus away from Rosa's categorical but conflicting evidence of a radio silence lasting well into July, instead directing focus to whether Diana had told Rosa that she was going on the St Tropez holiday.

In doing this the inquest lawyer, Ian Burnett QC, has corruptly protected a false witness, Rosa Monckton.

Why has Rosa provided such conflicting evidence on her communications with Diana?

This question will be readdressed and answered later in this section.

Rosa said that after her husband alerted her to the fact Diana was in St Tropez with Mohamed, she told him: "Well that explains why I haven't heard from her because she has gone on holiday." [b]

There is overwhelming evidence in Part 2 that phone conversations between Diana and her friends didn't stop when she was on holiday.[c]

Lucia said in her statement: "The last fax [Diana] sent me was giving me the telephone number of the house in the South of France[d].... I remember that she left in July 1997. We talked on the phone but less than normal as she was in the South of France, I was in Brazil and sometimes the reception did not work. We used the house phones rather than the mobile." [203]

Lucia is referring to the same July 1997 St Tropez holiday that Rosa spoke of, but their evidence is completely different:

- Rosa: "I haven't heard from her because she has gone on holiday"

---

[a] I am suggesting that Burnett is actually intending to deceive the jury and protect Rosa Monckton – see below.

[b] Supported by Lawson: "Well, that explains why I haven't heard a peep from Diana recently."

[c] This is also addressed in the next section on Rosa's final phone call to Diana.

[d] Confirmed at the inquest: "Princess Diana sent me a fax giving ... her phone numbers in St Tropez.": 18 Dec 07: 99.1.

- Lucia: "we talked on the phone but less than normal".[abc]

This is despite the fact that Lucia had also conveyed her disapproval of the holiday – "neither Rosa, Richard Kay[d] nor I were very happy about it knowing of Mr Al Fayed's bad reputation.... I told [Diana] I was not happy".

So Rosa and Lucia both expressed their disapproval of Diana joining Mohamed on holiday, but according to their evidence, Diana's reaction to each is quite different.

Diana keeps up contact with Lucia but shuts off communication with Rosa – she enters a period of radio silence. There is no mention by Lucia of any radio silence or similar.

Is this plausible?

There appear to be four main possibilities:

a) Lucia is lying, possibly by omitting to mention that Diana shut off communication with her after her criticism of the holiday

b) Rosa is lying – Diana did not react in the way Rosa has described – see Radio Silence section

c) Rosa is lying – she has made up her evidence about Diana telling her in advance about the holiday: the 1 June 1997 conversation never happened in the way described

d) Diana viewed her relationship with Rosa quite differently to Lucia's – Lucia could get away with criticising Diana, but Rosa couldn't.

The main support amongst Diana's friends[e] for Rosa's radio silence evidence comes from Simone Simmons. Simmons has described periods of falling out between her and Diana, although not exactly in the way Rosa has suggested.

---

[a] The reason they talked "less than normal" was nothing to do with Lucia's criticism of Diana going – it was because "[Diana] was in the South of France, I was in Brazil and sometimes the reception did not work".

[b] Also confirmed at inquest: Burnett: "Did you and she speak while she was in St Tropez?" Lucia: "Yes, we did, but obviously not on a daily basis.": 18 Dec 07: 99.10.

[c] Lucia was in Brazil, which made communication more difficult, but presumably Rosa was in the UK – so communication for her should have been simpler.

[d] This cannot be checked – Kay was not asked about this at the inquest and his statement was not shown to the jury and has never been made available.

[e] There is also support for the radio silence in Paul Burrell's descriptions of Diana's relationship with her staff. In his book *A Royal Duty* Burrell describes it as a "no speaking spell". He states that several staff encountered this, including his wife, Diana's dresser, Maria Burrell – one month; chef, Mervyn Wycherley – nine months; butler, Harold Brown; Paul Burrell, butler – two weeks.: *A Royal Duty*, pp199-200.

Rosa's account was that when she "gave advice or expressed views ... with which [Diana] was not very happy ... typically, there would be radio silence. I would not hear from her for some time".

In her 2005 book Simmons does mention two instances where Diana reacted to criticism by cancelling her appointments, but they appear to have been very short-lived and also occurred early in the relationship.[204a]

Simmons wrote that Diana asked her opinion after the 1995 *Panorama* program. She says she told Diana: "You made a real prat of yourself.... It was completely unprofessional." Simmons states that "[Diana] accepted it." She says that "by then our friendship was based on telling each other what we really thought, not what the other person wanted to hear." [205]

Simmons relates that their most serious falling out occurred in June 1997, around two months before the Paris crash. It lasted until Diana's death, but it had nothing to do with giving advice or expressing views.[b]

There is very little support for the radio silence evidence from Diana's other friends: Annabel Goldsmith, Lucia Flecha de Lima, Richard Kay, Susan Kassem, Roberto Devorik[c], Rita Rogers, Elsa Bowker, the Palumbos.[d] The closest we come to it is an incident with Richard Kay recounted in Simmons' book – see footnote.[e]

---

[a] Simmons first met Diana in early 1993, so overall knew her for a shorter period than Rosa – see earlier.

[b] Simmons relates it in her book – it appears to have resulted from a misunderstanding in a communication between Simmons and Paul Burrell, which, according to Simmons, Burrell passed on in an exaggerated form to Diana.: *Diana: The Last Word*, p216. This falling out was referred to at the inquest – 10 Jan 08: 42.21.

[c] Devorik, whose relationship with Diana commenced in 1981, had a falling out with her in 1996, but the evidence indicates that Devorik was upset with something Diana did – it was not a cutting off contact over views as described by Rosa: "At that time [Diana] decided to do something else without telling us and I looked like a fool to the other [auction] house".: 17 Jan 08: 165.7. It's interesting that the inquest lawyer, Jonathon Hough, tried to paint this differently – and then said "we don't need to go into the details" – but was later corrected by Devorik. See 164.13. Devorik did confirm that he said in his statement, narrated by Hough: "the Princess's friends sometimes fell out of grace – these are your words – with her and then were sometimes, after a period of time out in the cold, welcomed back" (163.19). This is stated in the context of his own falling out, recounted above, and Devorik apparently does not relate which friends he is referring to here – it could simply be Rosa Monckton, who was known to Devorik (161.2). Devorik's statement has never been made available and was not heard or seen by the inquest jury.

[d] Elsa Bowker and the Palumbos have only spoken on documentaries – there is no official police or inquest evidence. Bowker died in 2000.

[e] Simmons writes: "On one occasion the opening paragraph of a story [Kay] had written didn't meet with [Diana's] approval, she stopped speaking to him and

The general evidence[a] seems to point to Diana's relationship with Rosa being less trusting[b] – and therefore less close and forgiving – than she had with her other known friends.

The following can be derived from the evidence:

-   Rosa's timing of the Diana conversation about the Mohamed holiday offer is June 1, two days before the offer was proffered, according to Cole
-   Rosa has two conflicting accounts about when the radio silence could have ended – June 30 with the Greek holiday organisation, or sometime after July 12
-   Rosa has never directly explained how the radio silence ended – just how it started
-   Burnett protected Rosa at the inquest, even though it was clear she had unreconciled conflicts in her evidence
-   Diana appears to have had less trust of Rosa than other friends
-   Rosa stated: "I haven't heard from [Diana] because she has gone on holiday", when there is overwhelming evidence that Diana still communicated with her friends whilst on holiday
-   Diana kept up contact with Lucia even though she had criticised Diana for going on holiday with Mohamed
-   although radio silence was an issue with Diana's staff, and there are instances of it occurring at times with some friends, there is little support for Rosa's inquest account that "typically there would be radio silence" when she "gave advice or expressed views ... with which [Diana] was not very happy".

Two factors stand out:

1) that the relationship between Diana and Rosa was not particularly close or trusting [c]

2) that there are substantial areas of conflict in Rosa's evidence – both with comparison to other people's and also within her own accounts.[d]

I suggest that these factors are linked to the reality that Rosa had MI6 connections, and appears to have been working as an MI6 agent herself – see later.[a]

---

slammed the phone down when he called.... After leaving him to stew for a couple of days [she] called him as if nothing had happened.": *Diana: The Last Word*, p199.

[a] Particularly Lucia – see earlier – but also apparently other close friends could say to Diana things she didn't want to hear without it leading to radio silence.

[b] Lucia stated: "I do not think Princess Diana trusted [Rosa] as much as she trusted me" – see earlier.

[c] This also fits with earlier witness evidence – Lucia and Simmons – in the Nature of the Relationship section.

[d] There were also conflicts in Rosa's earlier evidence on how and when she met Diana.

As part of the police investigations Rosa Monckton's phone records and bank accounts should have been checked. This never occurred.

The general evidence shows that the Rosa-Diana holiday definitely took place between 15 and 20 August 1997.

The question is: If the Diana-Rosa relationship was not that trusting or close, why did Diana agree to a holiday alone with Rosa?

Rosa has said that "we organised [the Greek holiday] on the telephone" around 30 June 1997.

Michael Cole stated that the Mohamed holiday invitation was made on June 3 and he received an enquiry call from Diana six days later, on June 9: "she really wanted to know what was there". Cole then said: "I wrote her a letter ... listing what ... was there.... Subsequently ... she decided to go."

A letter – shown below – reveals that Diana had made her decision, to join Mohamed on the holiday, as early as 11 June 1997. I suggest there would have been phone calls to do with this.[b]

Evidence in Part 2 showed that Diana's phones were being monitored by intelligence – this would then indicate that sometime between 10 and 15 June 1997 British intelligence would have become aware that Diana was going to be holidaying with Mohamed at St Tropez in mid-July.

There is a possibility that parts of the British Establishment were taken by surprise at this knowledge – that Princess Diana, the mother of the future King of England, was going to be taking her sons on a holiday with Mohamed Al Fayed.

David Davies, Head of Royalty Protection, MPS: 31 Jan 08: 183.21:

A. I phoned Sir Robert [Fellowes] at I think about 7.30/7.45 in the morning.[c]

Hilliard: Q. Right. What did he say? You tell us what you said to him first, perhaps.

A. Well, I told him that the Commissioner[d] had directed me to inform him that Her Royal Highness or Princess was going on holiday with the two Princes, and that, in our conclusion, the matter gave us cause for concern, and that, was he aware. I think we weren't sure or I wasn't sure at that stage whether Sir Robert, as the principal private secretary, was aware. There was a silence as I recall – and I remember that specifically – and I was not sure whether he had heard me – and this I recall very well – so I repeated it, and I said words to the effect, "It is the Commissioner's opinion that the visit or the

---

[a] This will be addressed later in this chapter.

[b] This is discussed further in the next Comment.

[c] Davies was not sure of exactly which day this occurred, but it was prior to the St Tropez holiday that started on 11 July 1997. Evidence from Davies and Robert Fellowes – who denies this phone call took place – and Fellowes' diary, indicated that it could have been on July 9 or 10, when the Queen was at Holyrood Palace in Edinburgh. See 41.16 to 42.19.

[d] Paul Condon.

holiday shouldn't go ahead in our humble opinion". He said "Her Majesty is aware", or at least that's my recollection, or "We are aware". That's my recollection.

Q. Sorry, aware of what? Aware of your opinion or aware –

A. He was aware of the circumstances; in other words, he was already aware that the holiday/visit was going to go ahead.

Paul Condon, MPS Commissioner: 17 Jan 08: 39.3:

Mansfield: Q. [Regarding Davies' evidence] You don't remember the events at all.

A. Not in the way that that is described. I don't remember having conversations with David Davies in the way that he describes.

Q. Well, in what way did you have – you see, I do not want there to be any error about this, that, "Oh, well, there might have been a conversation which led to advice but I don't remember it". Did you participate in an exercise to provide the Queen with advice that Diana should not visit the Al Fayed family because the police took a view of the Al Fayed family?

A. I honestly believe I did not.

David Veness, MPS Asst Commissioner Specialist Operations, UK: 15 Jan 08: 87.14:

Mansfield: Q. A telephone conversation with [the Queen's] private secretary, Sir Robert Fellowes, who is fairly short with Mr Davies but indicates clearly that the Queen already knew. That's the import of all of this. In fact, in the midst of it all, this is how he puts it: "I should clarify that the collective wisdom of the Commissioner [Sir Paul Condon] and myself that the advice that should be given to the Queen that it was unwise for the intended holiday to take place at all." Did you know that advice was being given?

....A. I must admit I was not aware of it in those terms. That was not something I can recall.

Robert Fellowes, Brother-In-Law of Diana and Queen's Private Secretary, 1990-99: 12 Feb 08: 43.3:

Burnett: Q. Presumably, you and Her Majesty, other members of the Royal Family, your family, knew well that the boys were going on holiday. Would that be right?

A. It is hard to remember. I am sure I was aware, but I cannot remember when I was made aware.

Q. What would the normal protocol, if that is the right word, have been for members of the Royal Family, and in particular the Princes, going abroad?

A. Patrick Jephson, the Princess's Private Secretary, would have written a note to me.

Q. Why was that?

A. Because it was a rule that the Queen always knew where members of her family were at any given time. Not within this country, but overseas.

....Coroner: Presumably there would have been some form of communication, would there, between Patrick Jephson and the Prince of Wales' office?

A. Certainly, sir.

....Q. Was the visit, as far as you can recollect, the subject of anxious discussion in Buckingham Palace, centring on Mr Al Fayed's suitability as a host?

A. I do not remember any discussion of it.

Q. Is that the sort of thing that would even be likely to be discussed?

A. No.

At 98.10: Mansfield: Q. Information about Mr Al Fayed [from Davies was] being put and, at the same time, the Commissioner's view that the holiday should not take place at all. He called it the "collective wisdom" – he did not use that word to you – was communicated to you.

A. I do not remember it.

Q. And that you said – he had to say it twice. You did not say "I know about the arrangements but I do not know about Al Fayed" or anything of that kind. According to him, you said – and he is clear about this – "Her Majesty is aware, thank you, Mr Davies", and that is it. Were you aware that Mr Al Fayed was under investigation?

A. No.

Q. Not at all, nothing?

A. No.

Q. No view about Mohamed Al Fayed at all?

A. No.

....Q. You see the 8th is just at the time that the signing off of this holiday is taking place, as we have seen on the other document, isn't it?

A. Yes.

Q. You were aware of the holiday?

A. I cannot say now, but I suppose I was, yes. I would think very likely I was.

Miles Hunt-Davis, Private Secretary to Prince Philip: 13 Dec 07: 79.11: Mansfield: Q. Now, I want to ask you to think back to ... July 1997. They left on 11th July. Do you remember any discussion before they left, in other words, about the very fact of an invitation to the mother of an heir to the throne being invited to stay with Mohamed Al Fayed?

A. I do not recollect anything about it.

Q. No. So if, in fact, again, the Duke of Edinburgh had views about it, you are not in a position to tell us what they were?

A. That is correct.

.... Q. As the summer wore on in 1997, there was an increasing amount of hostile publicity about Diana and the Al Fayeds, wasn't there?

A. I cannot recollect anything specifically, but I imagine you may be right.

You presumably have researched it. I will not gainsay that. But I do not recall the detail.

Q. I really don't want it to be a memory test for you.

A. Thank you.

Q. But I want to suggest to you that it was of extreme concern to the Royal Family, in other words, Her Majesty the Queen and His Royal Highness, that the Princess of Wales was cavorting on a yacht in the Mediterranean with the son of somebody who was regarded as undesirable. That was something that concerned everybody at the Palace, wasn't it?

A. Specifically what dates are you talking about?

Q. I can give you the specific dates, but I will deal with it generally. It starts in July, mid-July, and it goes all the way through to the crash.

A. The divorce was in August 1996.

Q. Yes.

A. The lady concerned ceased to be a member of the Royal Family.[a]

Q. Yes.

A. That is all I am going to say.

Nicholas Soames, Minister for Armed Forces to 1997: 12 Dec 07: 51.19:

Mansfield: Q. Did you have any involvement at all in questions concerning the Princess's holiday arrangements and, in particular, any dealings with anybody about her visit to Mr Al Fayed's villa in St Tropez?

A. No, never, at any stage.

Richard Dearlove, MI6 Director of Operations, 1994 to 1999, UK: 20 Feb 08: 134.11:

Mansfield: Q. Were you aware, at least on some of the evidence, that a phone call was being made to stop the initial holiday in the first place, in other words, Diana going to the South of France because Al Fayed was under investigation? Did you know anything about that?

A. Of course not. You are taking me into areas about which I know absolutely nothing.

Princess Diana: 11 June 97 Letter to Mohamed Al Fayed read out 18 Feb 08: 189.1:

"Dear Mohamed, A very special thank you indeed for inviting the boys and I to stay in France next month. Needless to say we are greatly looking forward to it all and we are so grateful to you for giving us this opportunity.... I know we will speak soon, but until then, my love to you all, Diana."

Comment: There was a lot of Establishment denial whenever the issue of the St Tropez holiday came up:

---

[a] This sentiment has been addressed in Part 4, in the section on the Post-Divorce Status of Princess Diana.

- Fellowes: "it is hard to remember. I am sure I was aware, but I cannot remember when I was made aware"
- Fellowes: "I do not remember any discussion of it"
- Fellowes: "I cannot say now, but I suppose I was, yes. I would think very likely I was"
- Hunt-Davis: "I do not recollect anything about it"
- Soames: "no, never, at any stage"
- Fellowes: "no.... no.... no" – regarding issues relating to Mohamed Al Fayed
- Hunt-Davis: "I cannot recollect anything specifically, but I imagine you may be right" – regarding "hostile publicity about Diana and the Al Fayeds"

And on the Davies evidence:[a]

---

[a] The Davies evidence is not covered in detail in this series of books, primarily because it strays too far from the central issues of this case. Having said that, it was addressed in some detail at the Diana inquest – the transcript references for those interested are shown below. As can be seen from the above excerpts, David Davies' account was denied by Fellowes, Condon and Veness – even though it was fully supported in detail by Davies' wife, Della. There is no evidence to suggest that Davies had any reason to make up his account, whereas, on the other hand, there is a significant reason why Fellowes, Condon and Veness could have colluded to deny Davies' account. That reason is that it was not in the Establishment interest to – before the Paris crash – appear in any way to have been anti-Al Fayed. And that is what Davies' evidence indicates – that MPS Commissioner, Paul Condon, was supportive of suggesting to the Queen that Princess Diana should be discouraged from taking William and Harry on a holiday with Mohamed Al Fayed. Davies also states that Fellowes said the Queen was aware of the holiday. There is nothing particularly significant in that, because the phone call to Fellowes was just a few days before the holiday started, and it is logical the Queen would have been aware because William and Harry were involved. The relevant inquest transcripts are: David Davies – 31 Jan 08: from 109.15; Della Davies (statement read out) – 13 Mar 08: from 56.3; Robert Fellowes – 12 Feb 08: 39.20 to 45.4, 87.3 to 104.3, 125.10 to 129.15; Paul Condon – 16 Jan 08: 169.11 to 172.24; 17 Jan 08: 31.5 to 45.12, 95.13 to 98.19; David Veness – 15 Jan 08: 81.14 to 89.11. The main relevance of these accounts is that it is further evidence of the willingness of senior Establishment figures to cover up material that could be damaging to their position.
That the police would have taken a stance that was anti-Al Fayed – Davies: "a gentleman who, at that time, I had some concerns about" (115.18) – is supported by the sentiments expressed by Lucia Flecha de Lima and Rosa Monckton in connection with the July holiday: Lucia (statement) – "Mr [Mohamed] Al Fayed's bad reputation as a business man and the problem over his passport being refused"; Rosa: "Mr [Mohamed] Al Fayed is the man who put lots of cash in brown envelopes and bribed MPs; there was an official Board of Trade inquiry into his taking over the House of Fraser, where he was called a fantasist and a compulsive liar; and he was refused British citizenship because of his bad character" (13 Dec 07: 132.24). The validity or

- Fellowes: "I do not remember it"
- Condon: "I don't remember having conversations with David Davies in the way that he describes"
- Veness: "that was not something I can recall"
- Dearlove: "you are taking me into areas about which I know absolutely nothing".

The questions here are: Who would have had prior knowledge of the Diana-Mohamed St Tropez holiday? And, when would they have known?

David Davies stated: "I was simply told verbally by one of the Prince of Wales' security team."[206] He says he heard about it "a day or two before" the holiday commenced.[207]

Others attempted to distance themselves from prior knowledge of the holiday – Hunt-Davis: "I do not recollect anything about it".

Fellowes was initially asked by Burnett: "Presumably, you and Her Majesty, other members of the Royal Family, your family, knew well that the boys were going on holiday. Would that be right?"

That should have brought about a straightforward, "Yes". But it doesn't.

Instead, Robert Fellowes – who was the Queen's private secretary and Diana's brother-in-law – tries to distance himself. He starts off: "It is hard to remember", then appears to realise what he is saying, and continues: "I am sure I was aware, but I cannot remember when I was made aware".

The question wasn't about "when I was made aware" – Fellowes appears to have come up with that in an attempt to rescue himself from his initial, "It is hard to remember".

The question was about whether they "knew ... that the boys were going on holiday". The answer was, "I am sure I was aware"[a], but that's not Fellowes' initial response – "It is hard to remember".

Then later Fellowes is asked much the same question again, but more directly, by Mansfield this time: "You were aware of the holiday?" [b]

---

otherwise of these comments by Rosa and Lucia is not the issue here. The remarks are shown because they appear to support David Davies' evidence of his view in 1997. Lucia appeared to tone down her comments at the inquest – she initially avoided describing Mohamed: "[Diana] could be among her peers", then when asked more specifically said: "[Mohamed] is a bit of a controversial person".

[a] Even the "I am sure I was aware" doesn't fully answer the question because Burnett was asking about the prior knowledge of "Her Majesty, other members of the Royal Family, your family".

[b] More directly because this time Fellowes is asked specifically about his own knowledge, whereas previously Burnett had asked about his recollection of the knowledge of "Her Majesty, other members of the Royal Family, your family". So this is a simpler question for Fellowes to answer.

Again a simple "Yes" should have been forthcoming.

But no, Fellowes stalls again: "I cannot say now", then again appears to change his answer mid-sentence: "but I suppose I was, yes. I would think very likely I was".

Why this obfuscation and denial over such simple questions by the two key representatives of the royal family at the inquest – Fellowes and Hunt-Davis?

I suggest that it is common sense that members of the royal family and household – and particularly Robert Fellowes[a] – would have been aware ahead of time that William and Harry were being taken on holiday to France by Princess Diana. And it is a natural extension that they also would have known their destination – Mohamed Al Fayed's St Tropez residence.

So why does Hunt-Davis deny it and why does Fellowes obfuscate?

It has already been established in Part 2 that Diana's phone calls were being monitored. Diana's letter to Mohamed Al Fayed – transcript shown above – reveals that she had decided to join Mohamed for the St Tropez holiday by 11 June 1997.

It is very likely that Diana would have been discussing her plans over the phone[b] – and therefore the St Tropez holiday could have become known to British intelligence by, at the latest, say the middle of June.

Later evidence in this volume will show that there are links between senior royals and British intelligence.[c] I suggest that intelligence that Diana was planning a holiday with William and Harry in France at Mohamed's would be quickly passed onto the royal family.

This indicates that there would have been prior knowledge of this holiday in senior royal circles around three or four weeks before it took place.[d]

I suggest that the reason Hunt-Davis and Fellowes have not given straight answers is because they are aware that the royal family had early prior knowledge of the holiday[e] – as early as mid-June 1997, and much earlier than

---

[a] Being also Diana's brother-in-law.

[b] The way Diana has written the note to Mohamed indicates that she had already communicated her decision to go, to him – probably by phone – before it was written. The letter does not include the word "accept", but rather says: "we are greatly looking forward to it all", as though Diana's acceptance of the holiday offer had already been conveyed. The note appears to be a confirmation.

[c] See the chapter on The Royals.

[d] Some may wonder why David Davies, the Head of Royalty Protection, says he found out only a couple of days before the holiday. Other evidence – primarily in this volume and Part 2 – shows that the MPS (who employed Davies) is not necessarily in the intelligence loop. Davies was notified by a protection officer of Charles – that is a normal official channel.

[e] Passed on from intelligence.

they would have been notified through the formal channels.[a] Hunt-Davis and Fellowes may have been instructed not to admit at the inquest to the early knowledge – Hunt-Davis denied any recollection; Fellowes equivocated and appeared to answer nervously.

As suggested above, there is a possibility that the British Establishment may have been surprised by this development – Princess Diana and their future king holidaying with Mohamed Al Fayed in France.

Further to this though, on 12 June 1997[b] Diana made a keynote address to the Royal Geographic Society stating that she was on a personal anti-landmine crusade.[cd]

This is a double whammy.

Diana has accepted an offer of a holiday by Mohamed – June 11 – then the very next day – June 12 – she ramps up her public involvement in the anti-landmine campaign.

(We are again entering an area of speculation based on the limited evidence that is available.)

These two events could have triggered a mild panic in some echelons of the British Establishment.

I suggest this led to some high-level discussions and finally triggered an order to British intelligence – from someone in the Establishment[e] – to find out more about what Diana had in mind and possibly asking the question: Where is all this heading?

Enter, Rosa Monckton – a person who, it has been shown earlier, had MI6 connections <u>and</u> had a relationship with Princess Diana.

---

[a] The formal channel was explained by Fellowes: "Patrick Jephson, the Princess's Private Secretary, would have written a note to me".

[b] The day after Diana confirmed with Mohamed her decision to join him on the St Tropez holiday.

[c] Excerpts from the transcript of this speech appear later. At the inquest Michael Mansfield said that Diana stated she "was not about to be put off by 'ghastly Conservatives'" – 12 Dec 07: 82.14. There is no record of Diana saying that in the speech transcript which is reproduced in full at http://thespeechsite.com in English – Famous Speeches By Famous People. Jon King and John Beveridge state: "Diana referred to the British Establishment as 'those ghastly Conservatives'". They indicate that Diana said this at some point before the May 1997 election that brought Tony Blair to power.: Jon King and John Beveridge, *Princess Diana: The Hidden Evidence*, p349.

[d] This is included in the Landmines chapter of Part 2.

[e] Precisely who could have been panicking and who may have given such an order will be addressed in the latter part of this volume.

I now suggest that Rosa was asked to find out what she could and this led to the arrangement for the Greek islands boating holiday, 15 to 20 August 1997 – just Rosa and Diana.

Rosa provided the inquest with some details about the holiday:
- "we organised it on the telephone" around 30 June 1997 [a]
- it was a "sailing holiday" – confirmed to Burnett
- the "boat that had been lent to [Rosa] by friends" – confirmed to Burnett
- they were in "a very small 20-metre motorboat"
- there were "three crew"
- "it was just the two of us". [b]

Rosa confirmed to Ian Burnett – who was basing questions on Rosa's police statement[c] – that the "boat that had been lent to her by friends".

No one asked who the "friends" were. It is interesting that the term "The Friends" is used to mean MI6, in certain circles.[d]

It could be significant that Paul Burrell states in his book that the vessel was "hired".[208e] This could fit with the boat being supplied by MI6. If Rosa had told Diana that it came from "friends", Rosa may have been expected to identify them. So it is logical that she could have told Diana the boat was hired – that would not be so likely to attract questions.[f]

That then is a conflict of evidence: Rosa confirmed at the inquest – the "boat that had been lent to [her] by friends"; Burrell, whose information probably came from Rosa via Diana – "[Diana's] friend Rosa Monckton had hired a yacht with a crew of four".[209]

The main point appears to be that if anyone wanted complete surveillance and monitoring of an entire holiday, there is actually no better way to do it than confine that holiday to a limited space – I suggest that a 20 metre boat is ideal.

---

[a] Rosa confirmed to Burnett that she "had a telephone conversation with [Diana] to arrange the holiday".

[b] Rosa failed to provide a name for this boat – normally when people holiday on a boat, they identify it by its name. A later footnote indicates it was named *Della Grazia*.

[c] A document we – and the jury – have never had access to.

[d] Intelligence historian, Nigel West, wrote in his 1990 book *The Friends*: "In more recent years initiated outsiders, mostly Foreign Office regulars and business contacts, have referred to the [MI6] organisation simply as 'the Friends'." *The Friends*, p1.

[e] Lawson said: "the boat Rosa had chosen was tiny". That indicates that there was more than one boat to choose from. It raises the question: If Rosa was lent the boat "by friends" then why would she choose a "tiny" boat if a larger one was being offered? There is no suggestion in Rosa's evidence of a choice of boat being on offer.

[f] Later evidence will indicate that the boat was chartered.

Where a holiday is say at a resort, only part of the time is in the room. But on a small boat, possibly the entire holiday is confined to the space of the boat. This allows bugs to be planted[a] all over the vessel[b] and it also enables MI6 to possibly plant their own agents on board – the three crew members.

Somehow Rosa was able to convince the princess that she needed to go on a secluded holiday alone with her – "just the two of us". On the available evidence, it is impossible to know how Rosa achieved this. At face value, it certainly appears odd that Diana would allow a one-on-one holiday with a person she: a) had trust issues with – Lucia; b) thought had "a hidden agenda" – Lucia; and c) knew had MI6 connections – Simmons.

It may be that Rosa applied some sort of emotional pressure to lure Diana into agreeing to this holiday.[c]

Nick Buckley, Journalist: 17 Aug 97 Article: **Jury Didn't Hear**:
"Diana, Princess of Wales, lapped up the Greek sunshine yesterday as she took her third cruise in a month. On this trip, however, the Princess was accompanied by her close friend, Rosa Monckton....

"The two were staying on the remote island of Inousses, home to the Lemos family of Greek shipping magnates.... At Athens airport she was met by a convoy of limousines, arranged for her security by the Onassis Foundation. They delivered Diana to a waiting Lemos family yacht, which took her on the final eight-hour journey by sea to Inousses, a group of seven islets off Chios.... And she seemed quite at ease as she plunged off the deck of Panagiotis Lemos's white three-masted yacht, *Sunrise*, for a swim in the warm waters of the Aegean.

"Locals on Inousses ... were delighted at their surprise visitor." [210]

Lawrence Van Gelder, Journalist: 19 Aug 97 Article: **Jury Didn't Hear**:

---

[a] Timothy Maier has written that "intelligence sources" say the 1993 APEC (Asia-Pacific Economic Cooperation) meeting in Seattle was extensively bugged by the US. "The operation was huge – more than 300 locations were bugged, including a chartered boat [Bill] Clinton and other national leaders used to visit Blake Island....": Timothy Maier, The Bugging of the APEC in Seattle, *Insight Magazine*, 29 September 1997.

[b] Mansfield asked a question about conversations Rosa may have had with Diana during the holiday regarding landmines: "So even when she does talk to you about that sort of thing [landmines], she certainly does not go into that kind of detail, does she?" Rosa replied: "It would depend upon the subject, it would depend on what else we were doing, it would depend where we were on the boat. You know, we were on holiday.": 13 Dec 07: 181.1. It is interesting that Rosa connects conversations on landmines to "where we were on the boat".

[c] It will be shown later that the Rosa-Diana relationship was not particularly close.

387

"Greece's television networks agreed that Diana, who arrived in Athens aboard a private jet on Friday night, had sailed along the eastern coast of the Peloponnesus, calling at the islands of Spetsai and Kythera. Athens newspapers featured eyewitness reports that placed her on the islands of Mykonos and Andros. Reporters flocked to the little island of Oinousa, off Chios, in the belief that she might visit her friends in the London family of the shipowner Panayotis Lemos. 'We don't know where Princess Diana is,' Mr. Lemos told Greek television. 'We don't know whether she will come here.'" [211]

Richard Kay & Ian Cobain, Journalists: 20 Aug 97 Article **Jury Didn't Hear**:

"For four days [Princess Diana] and Rosa [Monckton] … have drifted unseen around the Greek islands. They have ventured ashore, but always remained one step ahead of the paparazzi…. The two friends came ashore [at Hydra] aboard the motor cruiser *Della Grazia*…. Diana has had an impressive armada available for her island hopping – the *Della Grazia*, the *Sea Sedan*, complete with heli-pad, and the *Malrala* – so it is no surprise she has remained so tantalisingly out of sight." [212]

The News Letter: 21 Aug 97 Article: **Jury Didn't Hear**:

"The Princess of Wales left Greece last night after a quiet cruise around islands near Athens. Princess Diana and her friend Rosa Monckton returned to the capital after their Saronic Gulf cruise and immediately left aboard a private jet allegedly owned by Harrods. Scores of reporters had swept the Aegean to find the princess, who reportedly jetted to Greece last Friday, again allegedly aboard a Harrods plane. According to the crew of the charter yacht *Della Grazia*, the princess's friend Dodi Al Fayed did not join Diana on the cruise." [213]

Stephen White, Journalist: 8 Sep 97 Article **Jury Didn't Hear**:

"The friends' August holiday began on the Greek island of Mikynos, flying out on Dodi's private jet…. They then flew to Naxos and travelled to the small island of Hydra. As photographers searched for Diana, the two women boarded a motor-cruiser, the *Della Grazzia*. The princess dubbed it their 'cottage' as she relaxed for five days." [214]

Daily Record: 1998 Article: **Jury Didn't Hear**:

"Diana stepped into [the Harrods Gulfstream] to fly out to Athens with close friend Rosa Monckton…. She and Rosa drifted round the Greek islands, flitting from island to island using yachts lent by friends….

"The two women made a trip from Inousses to Spetses … and on to Hydra. They used various different types of vessel – a yacht called *Sunrise*, the ocean-going cruiser *Sea Sedan* and a smaller boat, the *Malrala*…. They had moored off the Peloponnese resort of Kiparissi.... They travelled to Hydra on the *Della Grazie*, a motor vessel belonging to Greek tycoons[a]...."[215]

Comment: There is a considerable amount of conflict in the media accounts of what occurred on this Greek cruise.

We effectively end up with several different accounts:

- Rosa: it was a "sailing holiday" for "just the two of us" on a "a very small 20-metre motorboat" with "three crew" – the "boat ... had been lent to [Rosa] by friends"
- Buckley: a trip hosted by the Lemos family on a Lemos yacht – the *Sunrise* – including a journey to Inousses, where they "were staying on the remote island"
- Van Gelder: a sailing trip visiting islands in the Aegean – but not including Inousses[b]
- Kay and Cobain: "four days" where they "drifted unseen around the Greek islands" with an "armada" of boats – "the *Della Grazia*, the *Sea Sedan* ... and the *Malrala*"
- *The News Letter*: "a quiet cruise around islands near Athens" on "the charter yacht *Della Grazia*"
- White: "the two women boarded a motor-cruiser, the *Della Grazzia* ... [and Diana] relaxed for five days"
- *Daily Record*: they "drifted round the Greek islands ... using yachts lent by friends" – "a yacht called *Sunrise*, the ocean-going cruiser *Sea Sedan* and a smaller boat, the *Malrala* ... [and] the *Della Grazie*".

The *Della Grazia* is a boat listed as available for charter on several websites – it was built in 1987, is 22 metres and comes with three crew.[216]

The other named boats are all described in promotional material as superyachts and the three vessels are[c], or have been, available for charter.

The *Malrala* appears to be the *Marala* – it was originally launched in 1931 and is 59 metres with 18 crew. The *Sunrise* was launched in 1991 and is 90 metres with 70 crew, and the *Sea Sedan*, which was built in 1997, is 55 metres with 14 crew.[217]

The *Della Grazia* is the only named boat that comes close to matching the description put forward by Rosa Monckton at the inquest – 20 metres with three crew.

---

[a] This article – written the year following the crash – states that the unnamed Greek tycoons were "friends of Mohammed al Fayed". The only evidence of a connection between Mohamed Al Fayed and the Diana-Rosa Greek cruise is that the two women flew to Greece and back on an Al Fayed plane.

[b] Inousses is across the other side of the Aegean from Athens, where Diana and Rosa apparently landed.

[c] In 2012.

In summary, there appear to be three conflicting accounts:

1) a single small boat in which Rosa and Diana cruise for the five days – Rosa, White, *The News Letter* [a]

2) a five day cruise involving several boats – one is small, but the others are superyachts – Kay and Cobain, *Daily Record*

3) a lengthy boat journey[b] to a fixed island locale where Diana and Rosa stay – Buckley.

There are three other points to consider:

- Buckley's account was published on 17 August 1997, the third day of the holiday, and van Gelder's is on the day before it finished – the other accounts were written around the conclusion of the cruise, except for the *Daily Record*, which was published the following year

- Van Gelder's account conflicts directly with Buckley's – Buckley states they went straight to Inousses, whereas van Gelder says that they hadn't been there by the 19th and instead lists other locations visited

- Richard Kay was a personal friend of Diana's and may have been provided personal knowledge of the holiday from her.

Bearing in mind that Rosa Monckton, the only living direct witness[c], has lied in other evidence – see earlier and later – and there is also a considerable amount of conflict in the various media accounts, it is really very difficult to determine precisely what occurred on this Greek holiday.

It has been stated earlier that MI6 could have been involved in organising this trip and I suggest that possible misinformation to the media could be a further indication of that.[d] What is certain is that there is a considerable amount of conflict in the available accounts.

If MI6 were involved, it is unlikely they would have wanted accurate media involvement. In that regard, only one photo of the entire trip has ever surfaced – reproduced below – and some sections of the media admitted at the time that they couldn't locate Diana:

- "dozens of reporters have been sweeping the Aegean Sea since Friday, trying to find the princess, who jetted to Greece for a cruise" [218]

- "the Princess of Wales eluded dozens of paparazzi for a third day Monday as they scoured the Greek islands for the world's most photographed woman, believed to be vacationing incognito in the Aegean" [219]

- "the hunt for Diana is on" under the headline: "The Media Swarm Greek Isles, In Search Of Diana"[220].

---

[a] Van Gelder's account could also be included in this, but he does not have a name or size for the yacht.

[b] Buckley said the journey was from near Athens to Inousses – this is around 330 km.

[c] The only witness heard at the inquest – there were other witnesses, such as the *Della Grazia* crew.

[d] Misinformation fits with the MI6 culture – see earlier Chapter 1A.

So we have: a) sections of the media who had no information and were therefore unable to describe the trip or locate Diana; and b) major conflicts between those media reports that do claim to either describe the trip or locate Diana.

Why is this?

It appears that after the Buckley article – which stated Diana was on Inousses as guest of the Lemos family – was published on 17 August 1997, media converged on that remote island which lies over 300 km east of Athens. But they found no sign of Diana and also no sign that she had been there.[a][b]

The general evidence – Rosa, White, *The News Letter*, van Gelder, Kay and Cobain, *Daily Record* – is that Diana and Rosa cruised for the full five days, dropping ashore at various islands, but not staying at any particular location as anyone's guest.

The evidence also indicates that the two women were cruising in the small yacht[c] – even the articles (other than Buckley) that mention the presence of superyachts[d] appear to only claim sightings of Diana on the smaller *Della Grazia*.

The evidence raises questions about the veracity of the Buckley account:

- no other media – including Greek media – was able to confirm that Diana was at or had visited Inousses: see earlier footnotes
- Buckley claimed to be on the island[e] at the same time as Diana, yet he does not have any supporting photos – the only published photo from the entire trip was taken on Hydra[f]
- the Buckley account places Diana about 330 km from Athens, whereas the general evidence from the time indicates this was a relaxing cruise spent

---

[a] Van Gelder reported: "Reporters flocked to the little island of Oinousa, off Chios, in the belief that she might visit her friends in the London family of the shipowner Panayotis Lemos. 'We don't know where Princess Diana is,' Mr. Lemos told Greek television. 'We don't know whether she will come here.'"

[b] Buckley stated: "Locals on Inousses … were delighted at their surprise visitor". He continued: "Taxi driver Vassily Chryssopaido said: 'Diana is someone we would not expect to see here normally so it is a real pleasure for us.'" This would then indicate that locals were not trying to hide the presence of Diana, which makes it increasingly strange that other media – including Greek journalists – were apparently not able to confirm that Diana was there, or had been there. Source: Nick Buckley, Diana and, in the Aegean, Diana is Cruising Again, *Mail on Sunday*, 17 August 1997.

[c] Not a superyacht.

[d] Kay and Cobain, *Daily Record*.

[e] He signed off: "From Nick Buckley on Inousses".: Nick Buckley, Diana and, in the Aegean, Diana is Cruising Again, *Mail on Sunday*, 17 August 1997.

[f] It is referred to in the Kay-Cobain article and is reproduced below.

around islands closer to the Greek mainland – van Gelder: Spetsai, Kythera, Mykonos, Andros; Kay-Cobain: Hydra; White: Mikynos, Naxos, Hydra; *The News Letter*: "islands near Athens", Saronic Gulf [a]

- Richard Kay, who writes for the *Daily Mail* – a paper very closely connected to the *Mail on Sunday* that Buckley wrote for – completely ignores the information in the Buckley article, even though it was written just three days earlier.[b]

The following includes some speculation, but is based on the limited available evidence.

Although Buckley states he was on Inousses, his account does not appear to reflect that. There is a possibility that MI6 may have supplied Buckley with false information.

The effect of the Buckley article is that it removes the possibility of MI6 involvement in the Greek island cruise. In fact the trip is no longer a cruise on a small boat – it is a 330 km trip on a superyacht to a remote island where Diana and Rosa stay with friends. The event is organised and financed by Greek participants – the Lemos family and the Onassis Foundation[c].

This changes the whole nature of the holiday and removes the possibility of MI6 control – a small boat that could have been bugged to record conversations throughout the five days of the cruise.[d]

Richard Kay and the *Daily Record* reported that the *Della Grazia* was accompanied by superyachts – see earlier. It is possible that MI6 could have used these boats as security or decoys to mislead the media. The newspaper reports indicate journalists were searching the Aegean and it is likely they

---

[a] *The Daily Record* – the account written the following year – is the only report outside of Buckley's that mentions Inousses: "The two women made a trip from Inousses to Spetses ... and on to Hydra". Looking at this on the map, the "trip from Inousses to Spetses" is about 370 km. The article makes no mention of how they got to Inousses, which is about 330 km from Athens. There is a possibility that the reference to Inousses in this 1998 article is based on the Buckley account.

[b] Kay also doesn't mention the *Sunrise*, which is the only vessel referred to in the Buckley article. The only other report that includes the *Sunrise* is the 1998 *Daily Record* account, which appears to have based some information on the Buckley article – see earlier.

[c] The Onassis Foundation was set up in 1975 following the death of its founder Aristotle Onassis. According to its website, "culture, education, the environment, health, and social solidarity come first on [its] agenda". It states: "All projects ... relate to Greece or Greek culture and civilisation.... According to both the Foundation's regulations and the wishes of Aristotle Onassis, individual charity is not allowed.": Onassis Foundation website – www.onassis.gr/en/ It is debatable whether organising "a convoy of limousines ... [to deliver] Diana to a waiting Lemos family yacht" – as described by Buckley – would be an activity entered into by the Onassis Foundation.

[d] See earlier.

were looking for a superyacht. The presence of three superyachts in the area could certainly have distracted the media from checking out the much smaller *Della Grazia*.

Buckley's account is the only one from the time that suggests a boat provided by friends[a] – the Lemos family – but it is not primarily for a cruise, instead a journey across the Aegean to Inousses.

The *News Letter* – who apparently interviewed the crew – described the *Della Grazia* as a "charter yacht".

The other 1997 articles give no indication of any involvement from friends.

In summary, the evidence points to a five day relaxing cruise, with stop-offs at various islands, using the chartered boat, *Della Grazia*, but with about three superyachts – acting as decoy vessels – in the vicinity.

Rosa Monckton's inquest evidence appears to be deliberately non-specific – no mention of the name of the boat and no mention of the names of the friends she borrowed the boat from.

---

[a] The *Daily Record* account – published 1n 1998 – says "using yachts lent by friends" – but as indicated in an earlier footnote, that article may have been influenced by Buckley's.

Figure 5

Della Grazia – the boat Diana and Rosa cruised
the Aegean Sea in, from 15 to 20 August 1997.
11 days later Princess Diana was dead.

Figure 6

Photo of Rosa Monckton and Princess Diana walking
on Hydra Island during the August Greek cruise. This
was the only published photo from the holiday.

It has already been pointed out that there is a major conflict in Rosa's
evidence – she claimed that there was radio silence and there had been no
contact between her and Diana from June 1 to at least July 12, 1997. Yet ten
minutes later Rosa gives an account of organising by phone with Diana the
Greek Island holiday around June 30.

There is a possibility that Rosa has fabricated the radio silence evidence to
protect her role as an MI6 agent.[a]

Rosa was asked by Burnett: "In that [June 30] conversation she did not
tell you that she was in fact going to St Tropez in the interval?[b]" Rosa
replied: "No, she did not."

This is likely to be true – why would Diana tell Rosa about the Mohamed
holiday if she knew she would not approve?

---

[a] Lawson provided support for it, but he also is an MI6 agent – see earlier.
[b] The interval between June 30 and the August 15 boat holiday.

395

But I suggest that by June 30 Rosa already knew about the St Tropez holiday – not from Diana, but from British intelligence[a] who had asked her to organise the boat holiday – see above.

The key effect of the radio silence account is that it distances Rosa from prior knowledge that the St Tropez holiday was going ahead – if she wasn't communicating with Diana, how could she know about it? – and therefore also distances her from having an ulterior motive in organising the Greek Island holiday.

If Rosa didn't know Diana was going on the Mohamed holiday then how could she be accused of organising the boat holiday to try and learn more about or counter Diana's involvement with the Al Fayeds?

In turn, the radio silence protects Rosa's role in working for MI6 in her dealings with Diana – yet I suggest that the evidence indicates that Rosa did perform such a role.

The general evidence on this points to Rosa Monckton being faced with a quandary when she came to give her Paget and inquest evidence:

-    Rosa needed to be shown to have organised the Greek Island holiday prior to her knowledge of Diana going on the Mohamed holiday – otherwise her organising of the holiday could be seen as trying to counter the Al Fayed relationship with Diana

-    Rosa had to position herself as a close friend of Diana right up to the crash, yet come up with a reason why she was unaware that Diana had decided to go on holiday with Mohamed.

I suggest that this is the reason Rosa has fabricated both the June 1 approach by Diana asking for advice on the St Tropez holiday and the ensuing radio silence.[b]

This also explains why Rosa came up with the major conflict of evidence about her June-July contact with Diana within 10 minutes at the inquest – one minute she hasn't spoken with Diana between June 1 and at least July 12, 10 minutes later she is organising a boat trip with Diana on June 30.

In doing this, as noted earlier, Rosa avoided providing evidence on precisely how the radio silence finished. She did though support her 1997 radio silence allegation with a detailed account of an earlier instance at the time of Charles and Diana's 1992 trip to Korea. Rosa provided information about how it started – "I said, 'You have just got to pull yourself together and get on with it'" – and finished – "[Diana] would pick up the telephone and say 'Come and have lunch' and off we went again".

---

[a] Or someone else in the Establishment.

[b] As noted earlier, there was no evidence of a radio silence from Lucia, who was consulted by Diana regarding the St Tropez holiday.

The question is: Why does Rosa provide clear evidence of how the Korea radio silence finished – when that has nothing to do with the case – and is unable to do so for the 1997 instance, which is relevant to the case?

It is significant that Rosa brings up the Korea incident as support for her radio silence evidence, yet is not able to provide proper unconflicting evidence on the detail of the radio silence that she claims occurred in the months leading up to the crash.

Final Phone Call

Rosa Monckton phoned Diana on 27 August 1997, just four days before the crash.

Rosa Monckton, Friend of Diana: 13 Dec 07: 146.2:
Burnett: Q. After the trip to Greece which, as we know, finished on 20th August, I understand you spoke once further to the Princess of Wales.
A. Yes, that is right.
Q. When did that happen?
A. That was on the Wednesday of the following week, I think.
Q. So that would be Wednesday 27th August?
A. Right.
Q. Did you ring the Princess or did the Princess ring you?
A. I rang her.
Q. At that time, she was on the Jonikal. Did you get in touch with her through the communications centre on the boat or – how did you do it?
A. No, I rang her mobile telephone.
.... Q. Can you remember the nature of the discussion that you had with her on 27th August?
A. It was a very brief discussion because she was getting from one boat to another. I think she was just starting the trip back. So it was very brief. She said it was lovely, it was bliss, but she wanted to come home, see the boys, get back to the gym and looked forward to seeing me as soon as she was back.
Comment: Rosa Monckton was among several people who spoke to Diana by telephone in the final week of her life.

The others were: Frank Gelli, Annabel Goldsmith, Sarah McCorquodale, Rita Rogers, Richard Kay, Susan Kassem, Lucia Flecha de Lima, Elsa Bowker, Richard Attenborough, Roberto Devorik and Paul Burrell.[a]

There could be significance in how these calls occurred.

The evidence is:
-   Rosa: "I rang [Diana's] mobile telephone"

---

[a] The witness evidence is all in Section 1 of Part 2, unless specified in endnotes.

- Gelli: "Diana called ... from the ... yacht" [221]
- Goldsmith: "Diana rang me"
- McCorquodale: "[Diana] rang me" [222]
- Rogers: "[Diana] called me"
- Kay: "[Diana] rang me"
- Bowker: "[Diana] called me ... five days before she died" [223]
- Attenborough: "[Diana] rang me on a mobile ... on the Wednesday evening prior to her death" [224]
- Devorik: "on the Thursday or the Wednesday ... Diana called from a mobile" [225]
- Kassem: Paget Report: "the Princess of Wales contacted [Kassem]" [a]
- Lucia: "the last conversation we had was the Wednesday before her death"
- Burrell: "I did make several telephone calls via her mobile phone" [226]
- Burrell: "[Diana] ... phoned [me at] my brother-in-law's home" on the Friday[227].

All up there are twelve witnesses who have stated they talked directly with Diana by phone during the final week of her life.[bc] Of these, only one has not made clear who made the call – that is, Lucia Flecha de Lima.

Out of the remaining eleven people, only two made phone calls to Diana – Rosa Monckton and Paul Burrell[d] – and the other nine[e] were all called by Diana.

Even Burrell – who clearly was a member of Diana's staff and made calls – was also himself called by Diana on the Friday, August 29.

And Richard Kay – who was a journalist and friend – did not call Diana, but instead left it for her to call him.

So we have the evidence of 12 people – only two called Diana, Burrell, the butler, and Rosa; one, Lucia, we are not sure; 9 friends were called by Diana.

Rosa does not appear to be on Diana's call list.[a]

---

[a] The fuller Paget quote is: "[Susan Kassem] ... spoke to the Princess of Wales on three occasions by telephone on Saturday 30 August 1997.... The first telephone call was when the Princess of Wales contacted her around 11a.m., at which time they were unable to speak, so Susan Kassem called back a short while later".

[b] According to Andrew Morton there was also a call to Diana from Prince William on 30 August 1997 – at the time he was 15 years old.: *Diana: Her True Story In Her Own Words*, p283.

[c] Mohamed Al Fayed and Melissa Henning also both spoke on the phone to Diana, but only after speaking to Dodi first – see Part 2, Chapter 2.

[d] Susan Kassem also rang Diana, but she was returning a call – the initial contact was made by Diana: see earlier footnote.

[e] Gelli, Goldsmith, McCorquodale, Rogers, Kay, Bowker, Attenborough, Devorik, Kassem.

It is possible that this says something – when viewed in the light of earlier evidence – about the nature of the Rosa-Diana relationship.

I suggest that the work in the friendship appears to be done by Rosa Monckton, not Princess Diana. It is Rosa who organised the boat trip[b] and it appears to be Rosa making whatever calls that occur – around June 30 and August 27.

Why is this?

Once again, the evidence points to this appearing to be a relationship lacking in mutual trust and not particularly close.

Is this because Rosa Monckton's allegiance was first to the Establishment and second to Diana?

Was Rosa simply calling Diana to seek intelligence on how the relationship with Dodi was going?

That's possible. A credible account of this final Rosa-Diana conversation published soon after the event reads: "'Just tell me, is it bliss?' asked Rosa Monckton when she phoned Diana on her mobile phone on 27 August, just days before her death. Her reply said it all: 'Yes bliss. Bye bye.'" [228c]

Rosa described the 27 August 1997 call: "It was a very brief discussion because she was getting from one boat to another".

Did Diana offer to call her back at a better time?

Apparently not.

Rosa says: "I think she was just starting the trip back".

The *Jonikal* cruise did not finish until the morning of Saturday, August 30 – three days later.

---

[a] Simone Simmons was also not called – by her own admission she had a falling out with Diana: see earlier.

[b] And the 1993 holiday – see earlier.

[c] This account – from Andrew Morton's 1997 book – raises the possibility that the conversation was very, very brief and Rosa has added comments in her sworn evidence that were not actually said by Diana: e.g. "she wanted to come home".

Philip-Diana Letters[a]

Between June and September 1992 Prince Philip and Princess Diana corresponded regarding the issues involved in the crumbling Diana-Charles marriage.

Rosa Monckton, Friend of Diana: 13 Dec 07: 115.11:

Burnett: Q. How did you become aware that the Duke of Edinburgh was being supportive of her?

A. Because he wrote a letter to Diana – and I think it was in April of that year, of 1992 – really offering to help; you know, having witnessed them together, seeing that the marriage was not going well and offering her advice.

Q. Now we will come on and look at some letters in a moment. As far as the date is concerned, are you confident it was April or might it more likely have been June?

A. I would have to look. I honestly cannot remember.

Q. Don't worry. We will come to those in a moment. Now, in your statement to the police in July 2004, if I might just remind you of what you said: "He was entirely supportive of Diana and was trying to help her leading up to her separation from Prince Charles. He told her how difficult it had been for him to get used to Royal life, having to give up a career and to always be one step behind." Now, you did not, at that stage, mention to the police that you had seen correspondence between the Duke and Diana and, indeed, had copies of some of it, did you?

A. I did not because I did not think it had any relevance at all to the case.

Q. Were you aware of the fact that publicly there had been suggestions that letters between Diana and the Duke had gone astray?

A. No, I was not aware of that at all, and it was only when this case started – and I think in the opening remarks[b] there was some reference to these letters. I was at a dinner party that night and somebody said to me, "Oh, this is what has happened and there are these letters", and it suddenly occurred to me that these might be the letters that I had copies.

Q. We having now been here for 10 or 11 weeks, we have seen a torrent of information on all sorts of matters, but does it mean, therefore, that you did not read books and article[c] about the Princess and the myriad people who

---

[a] This section should be viewed in conjunction with the Part 2 section Letters: June to September 1992. The issue being addressed here is the connection with Rosa Monckton – it is not the nature of the letters or their timing. Those issues were dealt with in Part 2 and it was shown that there were two sets of letters – one set in 1992, which several people (including Rosa Monckton) have seen, and a second later set that were hostile in content, but not widely viewed by others or talked about by Diana.

[b] By Scott Baker.

[c] Probably should read "articles", plural.

have published accounts of their relationships? All of this you did not bother with?

A. I very deliberately have not read a single book about her. I might have seen the occasional newspaper article if it was a headline, but apart from that, no.

Q. So you have never hunted out that sort of press coverage?

A. No, never.

Q. You have mentioned that you heard at the time that the inquest started that remarks had been made by the Coroner about missing correspondence. Did you have a look at the Coroner's website to see what had been said?

A. No, I did not, no.

Q. But instead you got in touch with the inquests?

A. Exactly.

Q. You showed the correspondence as you had it to the Secretary to the Inquests; is that right?

A. Exactly. That is right.

Q. Dealing with the correspondence in general terms first, you have copies of letters that were written by the Duke of Edinburgh to the Princess in the summer of 1992, I think.

A. Yes, I do.

Q. How did you receive those letters?

A. Well, when Diana received the first one, she rang me and she was very, very upset, very tearful, and she said, "Can I come and see you because I have received a letter and it has made me very upset?" So she came round to our flat in Cambridge Street and we looked at it together, and I was able to calm her down and point out that actually this was an offer of help, a very genuine offer of help from her father-in-law, and that rather than being hysterical about it, that we should read it very carefully, go through it and reply, and that to have a dialogue going with him might help all sorts of things get better.

Q. So the first letter the Princess showed you in London?

A. Yes, all of them were in London, either in my flat or in Kensington Palace, or if, for some reason, we could not meet up, she would fax them to me and then we would talk about it on the telephone and I would draft the replies and get them back to her.

Q. We will take that stage by stage, if we can. First of all, you are aware, I know, that it has been suggested that the Duke wrote nasty letters to Diana, that they were unkind and vituperative. All sorts of words have been used. Is that true of any of the correspondence that you saw?

A. Absolutely not at all. On the contrary. They were very – sorry, I am finding it difficult to concentrate with that. They were very thoughtful, kind, intelligent, considered letters.

Q. Why was it that the Princess of Wales was upset when she received the first of them?

A. She was upset when she received each of them, and I think it just was a reflection of her emotional state at that time.

Q. So you looked at the letters and sometimes the Princess faxed you a copy and then you mentioned that you drafted replies. Before we come to drafting of the replies, did you show anyone else the letters at that time?

A. I only showed them to my husband after having consulted Diana and he helped draft a lot of the replies with me.

Q. So you and he drafted replies. Were they typed up by you and given to the Princess and discussed with her?

A. Yes, that is right. I would have a long conversation with her, then I would go away and think about it and then get them back to her and then we would discuss them again.

Q. So far as you are aware, did the Princess use the guts of your draft replies or do you just not know?

A. I am sure that she did. She told me that she did.

Q. Was her practice to write the replies in longhand?

A. She wrote them in longhand, and I remember her saying to me, "It is all very well for you, you have typed them. This is taking me a very long time", because they were quite lengthy, some of the replies.

Q. As indeed were some of the letters themselves from the Duke.

A. Indeed.

Q.... What I am going to show you now is one or two of the letters.[a] It may be helpful if you had open in front of you the second page of your November statement[b] because, in that statement, you helpfully set out the dates of the letters that you saw from the Duke of Edinburgh. Are you with me? Now, just running through them in order, the first letter that you have is an undated draft reply to a letter from Prince Philip, which you don't in fact have. So that is a draft which you, with the help of your husband, put together for the Princess and which she then copied by hand.

A. Exactly.

Q.... We see the beginning, just the opening section of a letter from the Princess, June 21st. "Dearest Pa ...", that is how she referred to him?

A. Yes, always.

Q. How did he sign off his letters?

A. "Pa".

---

[a] Burnett says "one or two letters", but actually goes through all of the available Philip-Diana letters – four from Philip and five from Diana.

[b] This is referring to Rosa Monckton's pre-inquest statement, completed on 29 November 2007 – not to be confused with her police statement, completed on 7 July 2004.: see 13 Dec 07: 108.22.

Q. "... I was so pleased to receive your letter and particularly so to read that you are desperately anxious to help." Was that the Princess's genuine sentiment about the letter?

A. Absolutely it was. Yes, it was.

Q.... "Once again, Pa, I am very grateful to you for sending me such a heartfelt and honest letter and I hope you will read mine in the same spirit. With fondest love, from Diana." Was that a true reflection of her sentiments?

A. Yes.

Q. Did you put in your drafts the references to "Pa" or did she introduce those herself?

A. Well, a lot of the time, you know, we did them together.

Q. I see.

A. Do you see what I mean?

Q. Yes.

A. I mean sometimes I was not with her, but a lot of the time I was, so ...

Q.... This is the opening paragraph of a letter from Prince Philip dated 25th June 1992. If I can just explain this because I do not suppose you have seen this version before. This is what, in the old days, would have been called a "carbon copy", so it comes without the headed notepaper part and without the topping and tailing.[a] But is it right that one of the letters that you have is the letter of 25th June?

A. Yes, it is.

Q. Is that on headed paper?

A. Yes, it is.

Q. Are you able to remember from where?

A. I would have to look. Some were from Balmoral and some were from Windsor Castle, but I cannot remember which came from where.

Q. And that was sent to you by fax?

A. Yes.

Q. Then you identify an undated draft reply to that letter.... "Thank you for responding to my long letter so speedily. I agree that this form of communication does seem to be the only effective one in this situation, but that is at least a start and I am grateful for it." Again, did that reflect the Princess's sentiments?

A. Yes, it did.

Q. And then [the ending]: "I hope you do not find this letter overlong, but I was so immensely relieved to receive such a thoughtful letter as the one you sent me, showing such obvious willingness to help. "With my fondest love,

---

[a] Topping and tailing is handwritten additions to a letter after it has been typed – e.g. the signature.

from Diana." Similarly those were her sentiments?

A. Yes.

Q. You saw the correspondence. Was that obvious from what you read in the Duke's letter?

A. Yes, it was.

Q. The next one we have ... you describe as a letter from Prince Philip from July 1992. The date is otherwise indecipherable. You had a fax copy. But we think it is this one, 7th July. Even on this copy, the date is not that easy to read. Do you recognise the opening sentence –

A. Yes.

Q. – of the letter.[a]

A. Yes, I do.

Q. So that identifies that. Similarly ... the end of the same letter: "I can only repeat what I have said before. If invited, I will always do my utmost to help you and Charles to the best of my ability, but I am quite ready to concede that I have no talents as a marriage counsellor!!!"

A. Absolutely. I remember that.

Q. Quite a memorable phrase?

A. Yes.

Q. Then you helped the Princess draft a reply to that one.... A letter of 12th July: "I was particularly touched by your most recent letter which proved to me, if I did not already know it, that you really do care."

A. Yes.

Q. And you recognise that?

A. Yes.

Q. Again it is a sentiment that the Princess expressed?

A. Yes, it is.

Q. That was a very long letter, at least when handwritten, nine-odd pages. If I can take you to the end of it ... maybe you can read the Princess's writing rather more easily than I can because you have had a lot of experience of it over the years. Would you read this part?

A. Yes: "You are very modest about your marriage guidance skills and I disagree with both! This last letter of yours showed great understanding and tact and I hope to be able to draw on your advice in the months ahead, whatever they may bring. With my fondest love, yours, Diana."

Q. Then the next letter that you identify in your statement is one from Prince Philip dated July 1992, which again was faxed to you.... "Phew! For the last few days I have had the feeling that I might have overdone things in my last letter. It was good of you to be so understanding and to reply." Do you recognise that as the opening part of the letter that you have?

A. Yes.

---

[a] It reads: "Thanx for your very interesting letter.": Inquest evidence: INQ0058929.

Q. The Princess's draft reply ... "Dearest Pa, thank you once again for such a thoughtful and revealing letter ..." That coincides with the draft that you and the Princess did?

A. Yes, it does.

Q. And the end of that letter ... "... but even if you are unable to succeed in this, I still would like you to know how much I admire you for the marvellous way in which you have tried to come to terms with this intensely difficult family problem." Then the signature is lost, at least in this version. That too you recognise?

A. Yes, I do.

Q. The next letter that you identify in your statement is a letter which you can date to 28th September ... "You will be relieved to see that this letter is rather shorter than usual." That you recognise as coming from that one?

A. Yes, I do.

Q. These copies have all come from the Duke of Edinburgh via his private secretary.

A. I see.

Q. If the date was there, it certainly has not come out in the copying, but yours shows 28th September, does it?

A. Yes, it does.

Q. Then 30th September 1992, a reply from the Princess of Wales ... "Thank you so much for your letter ..." And then, at the end ... but the jury have seen this this morning, so I will just read it if I may. "Thank you again for taking the trouble to write and keep up our dialogue. It is good that our letters are getting shorter. Perhaps it means that you and I are getting to understand each other. With much love from Diana." That series of correspondence, was that the totality of the exchanges between the Duke and Diana?

A. Yes, it was.

Q. In your statement, you mention one other document that you have, a sort of bread-and-butter letter, a short thank-you letter from Diana for the boys' trips to Balmoral, but not in response to any letter from Prince Philip. So that is a thank-you note of some sort. Now all of that correspondence takes place over the summer of 1992 and is at a time when we know that there were particular difficulties that had to be confronted. Then, in December 1992, it is right, isn't it, that there was an official announcement of separation?

A. Yes, that is right.

Q. Now, you have mentioned that Diana was upset, emotional, when she received the letters. Have you thought about how somebody might inadvertently, as it were, have got the impression from the Princess that the letters were unpleasant?

A. Yes, I can very easily see how that would have happened because, even

405

when we were halfway through this correspondence, even then receiving the letters, her first reaction was generally tearful and not really understanding. If she was like that with me, who was helping her with them, helping her reply to them, I imagine that she could have said – expressed similar sentiments to other people in her circle.

Q. After the correspondence that we have seen, did the Princess ever show you any other correspondence from the Duke of Edinburgh?

A. No, she did not.

Q. Did she ever mention to you that there was other correspondence from the Duke of Edinburgh?

A. No, she did not.

Q. Would she have done?

A. I am absolutely 100 per cent certain that she would have done had there been any other letters.

Q. Why is that?

A. Because of the help I gave her with this correspondence.

Q. There has been a suggestion that there may have been correspondence all the way through the mid-1990s from the Duke. Is that, in your view, even a possibility?

A. I do not think it is a possibility at all.

Q. In particular, it appears to be suggested that the interview that the Princess gave to Panorama, which was broadcast, if I might remind you, in November 1995, may have sparked vitriolic correspondence from the Duke of Edinburgh. That is what is being suggested.

A. I am sure, if that had been the case, she would have showed it to me because she would have wanted help replying to it.

Q. During the intervening period – so this correspondence comes to its conclusion at the end of September 1992 – until the Bashir programme, then the divorce, did you continue to be close to the Princess of Wales?

A. Yes. We were, by then, very firm friends.

Q. During that period, did you continue to see her frequently?

A. Yes, I did.

Q. With what sort of frequency?

A. Well, it would depend on her schedule and mine because I was running Tiffany's and she was very busy too. But we met when we could, which was very often.

Q. And spoke on the telephone?

A. Spoke a lot on the telephone, yes.

Q. And that was a consistent pattern?

A. Yes, it was.

At 157.9: Mansfield: Q. I want to take it in stages. First of all, when Princess Diana first showed you letters – and I am going to ask a bit later for some time to – you see, we have not seen the copies that you have provided. You have provided copies of letters, is that right, to the learned Coroner?

A. To the Coroner, yes, I have.

Q. You don't have more copies yourself?

A. I have the copies – I copied them and gave them to the Coroner.

....Q. Just in relation to these letters, when she showed them to you, first of all, as far as Princess Diana is concerned, did you tell her that you had shown them to your husband?

A. Yes, I did.

Q. And that he was helping draft as well?

A. He sat down with myself and Diana on two or three occasions to do this.

Q. Did you tell Diana that you were keeping copies?

A. She asked me to keep copies.

Q. Right. As far as you were aware, did she keep copies?

A. Yes, she did.

Q. Where did she keep them?

A. I have no idea, but she told me that she was going to keep them very safe because, for her, this was a very important correspondence and she wanted history to know that she tried.

Q. Yes, right. So you don't know where she kept this very important correspondence?

A. No, I do not.

Q. Of course the correspondence that she kept would have been first of all the original letters sent by the Duke of Edinburgh because she would have them.

A. Yes.

Q. You sometimes only got a fax?

A. Yes.

Q. That is just in this period. Plainly she would be asking for a copy of the letter that she was sending. How was that copied? I am sorry to ask you the particular, but was it just a photocopier that did it or what?

A. It depended where I was. Either I passed it to her or I would fax it. Those were the two ways, as far as I can recall.

Q. But if she wanted her future to know that she had tried, you had a copy but she had a copy of the letters that she was sending?

A. Yes.

Q. Plainly you are not in a position to help us today as to where at least that section of letters, that is the 1992 June to September letters, that Diana kept are?

A. No, I have no idea.

At 155.11: Q. Let's talk about very private letters between the Duke of Edinburgh and Diana.

A. I have never talked about those letters.

Q. Haven't you?

A. Except to my husband.

Q. Really? Please think. Are you saying that you have never talked about those letters other than to your husband?

A. I think there was a newspaper article, somebody was talking about these letters some years ago, but that is – I cannot recall any more. But I did not reveal the content of them. I think that somebody had been saying that the Duke of Edinburgh was not being nice to Diana and had written her some letters that were not nice and I went on record as saying that they were, that he was being kind to her. I did not discuss the letters with anybody, I have never showed them to anybody except my husband and I was merely going on record to set it straight, which is all I have ever done with anything concerning Diana.

Q. Well, we will come to this because I am going to suggest that what you did, at the time you did it, for whatever good reason, was a breach of confidence, wasn't it?

A. I do not think so at all.

Q. You were entitled to go to the press, were you?

A. I did not go to the press. The press came to me because – I cannot even remember because it was such a long time ago. There was something in the public domain about these letters and I think I might have even been in touch with the Duke of Edinburgh's office at the time because I think they also had a quote about them.

Q.... Do you remember the newspaper that particularly led on all of this?

A. It was the Sunday Telegraph.

Q. Yes, your husband's newspaper.

A. My husband was the editor, but it was not him who was discussing this.

Q. How did it come about, this article in the Sunday Telegraph? Did your husband, Dominic, say to you one night, Would you mind being interviewed by a columnist in the Sunday Telegraph?"

A. No, I got – I cannot even remember, but I think I would have got a call from whoever it was – I really cannot remember, but I think that somehow the fact of these letters had got into the public domain and I thought that I had to put the record straight about the content of these letters.

At 159.21: Q. When it came to 2002 – and so that it is clear, in November 2002 – and you went public about these letters, first of all, before you did it, did you contact the Palace?

A. I honestly cannot remember the sequence of events.

Q. I would like you to think very carefully because what I am suggesting to you is that there is a possibility here, at the very least, that you have broken trust by discussing in public these letters. Now by 2002, of course, Diana is no longer with us, but the Duke of Edinburgh is and so is his private secretary[a], as we have heard today. Did you contact the Brigadier and say, "Look, I hope he does not mind, but I am going to go public on these letters?" A. I honestly cannot remember. I do not think I did. I cannot remember the sequence of events that led to this newspaper article. As I have said before and I reiterate, I have only ever gone on record to put a fact right that was wrong.

Q. Yes. That depends in whose interest it is, you see. The question I am on about here is not so much putting something on record, it is doing it when it is in a breach of a confidence. Do you follow? That is the point.

A. I do not see that I have breached any confidence. I never have with Diana.

Q. Well then I think it will be necessary, I am afraid, for you to see the extent of this article.... There is a hard copy for you. It is up on screen. Just before we go through it, I am afraid I am going to ask you because this is an article that is fundamentally really based around you, you see. This is the Sunday Telegraph. Although it is not written by Dominic, he obviously knew about it, didn't he? [b]

Coroner: Do we have a date for this, Mr Mansfield?

Q. We do. I am sorry, it is very faint. It is 24th November 2002.

Coroner: The reason I asked that was because I wanted to see whether it matched the date of the statement of correction from the Palace.

Q. Yes, it does. It is the day after.

....Q. Let me just go through this particular article please.... :"According to Rosa Monckton, one of the Princess's closest friends, the tone of Prince Philip's letters was far from being aggressive and abusive towards his daughter-in-law, as Simone Simmons, a faith-healer, claimed in a Sunday newspaper a fortnight ago." May I just pause there? Were you aware of what Simone Simmons was saying...?

A. I must have been, which was why I agreed to do this interview, because as I have said – and this is the third time now I shall say it – I have only gone on record when I think something is wrong. Simone Simmons was wrong and I did not think it was fair to leave that uncorrected.

Q. But that is on the assumption that you have seen all the letters, isn't it?

A. It is, and ... I am convinced that I have seen all of the letters.

Q. You see, we will come to the fact that I suggest to you – and I think in part you have agreed – Diana is not going to tell you everything, is she?

A. The help that I gave her with these letters, I know absolutely that had she had any more letters from Prince Philip, she would have rung me straightaway and asked me.

---

[a] Brigadier Miles Hunt-Davis.

[b] This question doesn't get answered due to the Coroner's interruption.

Q. Unless she decided that since things had gone a little sour after the Martin Bashir interview[a], that actually she would not seek your advice?
A. Who can know? All I can say is what I believe and I believe she would.
Q. Yes. I understand your belief entirely, but you do understand that your belief may be wrong, may it not?
A. As far as these letters are concerned, I do not accept that.
Q. These letters, yes. Other letters, you really don't know, do you?
A. I am as sure as I can be.
....Q. Did she ever show you any letters from the Queen?
A. No, she did not.
Q. Can you explain, given your belief in your relationship with her, why she did not show you? There was a very particular letter that she received in December of 1995, after the Martin Bashir interview, concerning divorce. Did she ever show you that?
A. She did not show it to me but she told me about it.
Q. Yes. Didn't show, didn't want your help about replying to it?
A. No. We discussed – the divorce at that stage was inevitable.
Q.... You said that: "... Prince Philip had written four or five times to Diana and that the Princess had shown her all the correspondence. Although [you] declined to discuss the contents of the letters, her version of events supports the account given by Prince Philip in a Buckingham Palace statement yesterday.... 'I saw every single one of these letters and helped Diana to reply. I was struck by how kind and compassionate and understanding he was of her circumstances. They had an interesting dialogue and there was a lot of understanding on both sides. I was very impressed by the tone of Prince Philip's letters. They were thoughtful and wise.' It was in the aftermath of the collapsed trial of Paul Burrell, the Princess's former butler, that the Mail on Sunday ran an interview with Miss Simmons."
....Q. Did you tell anybody, as the [Burrell] trial was going along and as you were going to be a witness, at the time – the trial in fact ended shortly before all of this. So we have the dates and so that there will be hopefully no errors here, it began in October the 16th, restarted on the 17th, ended on 1st November. So it is the beginning of this month where these matters are discussed. Now did you tell anybody during the trial, "Oh, actually, I have some letters"?
A. No, I did not.
Q. Is there any reason why you did not?
A. Because I would not have thought that they were in any way relevant to the trial.
Q. Well, we will just come on to the next part of this.... "The letters were alleged to have been part of the so-called 'Crown Jewels' – confidential

---

[a] The *Panorama* interview in November 1995 – see Part 2.

letters, documents and other belongings that the police had been searching for in January last year [that is the year before, so it is 2001] when they raided Mr Burrell's house in Cheshire and arrested him."... So this part of the article – did you read this, by the way, once it was published on 24th November?

A. Yes, I must have done.

Q. Well, did that part of it strike you in any way, that here were the police and here you are with letters at home that the police had actually been looking for, something called the "Crown Jewels"?

A. I would not have made the association.

....Q. The letters that you were talking about, as you have indicated today, appeared to upset Diana. That is what you said.

A. What I said was she was in a very emotional state at the time of this correspondence, that every time she picked up one of these letters she started crying before she had even got through the first paragraph.

Q. Did she say why?

A. Because she could not work out what it was that he wanted, to begin with.

Q. This was a letter from the Duke of Edinburgh. Why would a letter from the Duke of Edinburgh cause her so much anguish before she even opened it?

A. It is just her emotional state at that time. I think a letter from anybody would have made her cry. But when we sat down and we read through them and she understood them, then she realised that this was an offer of help.

.... Q. "The Sunday Telegraph can ... however reveal that Prince Philip consulted Farrer & Co, the Royal Family's solicitors, and considered a claim for defamation. He also considered complaining formally to the Press Complaints Commission (PCC) and the press watchdog." Do you know how the Sunday Telegraph got hold of that information?

A. No, I have no idea.

Q. Is there a particularly close relationship between the Sunday Telegraph and the Royal Family?

A. My husband was the editor, not me.

Q. Yes, I know. I do appreciate that, but you don't have a Chinese wall at home, do you, when you just don't discuss with each other what you have been doing that day?

A. Strangely, there were lots of things that we did not discuss at that time.

Q. I am sure. But at that time the Burrell trial and the fall-out from the Burrell trial was capturing the interest and imagination of a large number of newspapers, wasn't it?

A. Yes, I think it was.

Q. Are you saying it was not discussed in your household?

A. What, the Burrell trial?

Q. That is right.

A. No, we did discuss it, as I was going to be a witness.

Q. But you cannot help how the Sunday Telegraph got hold of that particular information in that paragraph?

A. No, I cannot.

.... Q. Was it your husband who suggested that you should be interviewed about these matters?

A. I cannot recall. It could have been or it could have been me having heard about the Mail on Sunday article and wanting to put the record straight. I honestly cannot remember which of those two it was.

At 14 Dec 07: 33.14: Croxford: Q. I would just like to know from your perspective: did Mr Alderson[a] come to you some days before that Saturday and ask you about having, in some way, identified that you knew about correspondence between the Princess and the Duke and that you were willing to discuss the confidential dealings you had had with the Princess? Did he come a few days before or did he coincidentally manage to identify you as the person who had had that involvement and was willing to talk in the few hours after the release of the press release[b] on that Saturday?

A. I do not remember. I do not remember how this happened. As I said, when I was speaking yesterday, it could have been one of two things. I could have seen Miss Simmons' comments in The Mail and decided that I needed to put the record straight or he could have approached me. I cannot remember which way round. But as I have said on so many occasions, I have only done things when there has been something that has been incorrect and that was incorrect. But I cannot remember timing, I am sorry.

Q. Just to press you gently on this a little further. To go public in the way that you did would have been a decision which you would have taken some time to consider, presumably?

A. Not if I knew what the truth was, no. It would not have taken me any time.

Q. Your dealings with the Princess had been confidential as far as you and she were concerned?

A. Yes, they were.

Q. And –

A. If you notice in this article, I did not reveal any of the content of these letters. I just revealed their existence and the tone of them.

Q. Did you not regard that as being confidential?

A. Not at all.

Q. Was it just coincidence, do you think, that you had been asked about these letters at the same time as the Duke released his press release or were you in some way coordinating?

A. I have no idea.

---

[a] Author of the *Sunday Telegraph* article.
[b] From Buckingham Palace.

Lucia Flecha de Lima, Friend of Diana and Wife of Brazilian Ambassador, UK: 18 Dec 07: 89.21:

Burnett: Q. Now during this period, so we are now into 1992, did the Princess show to you any letters that she had received from Prince Philip?

A. Yes, she did.

Q. When she showed them to you, what were the circumstances?

A. When she received the first one, she was quite upset about it, because although she liked and respected very much the Queen and the Duke of Edinburgh, she did not know exactly what to expect from them at this moment.

Q. Was this at the time when the marriage was in particular difficulty, in 1992?

A. Yes. It was around June 1992, and the Duke of Edinburgh was trying to help to solve the problems of the marriage.

....Q. [In your statement] you said this: "[Diana] never feared Charles. Prince Philip tried to help her during the difficult period of her marriage, in his own way. He was sometimes a bit brutal. I have read the letters. They were not unkind. He is a clever man. He would not hurt her." Then you go on to deal with the divorce and finances.

A. Yes.

....Q. The letters you have referred to, can you remember over what period they continued?

A. I think the first one was on 18th June and the last one was towards the end of September.

Q. Are those dates that you have in mind or dates that you have managed to remind yourself of as a result of evidence given here?

A. No, no, because I cannot follow the evidence given in England. We don't have British newspapers here as easily as in another place.

Q. It is just that you have a very clear recollection of 18th June 1992. It is a very long time ago and I wonder how you have such a good recollection.

A. Oh, because I went through my statement and I just remember.

Q. I see....

....Q. Did Diana ever show you her replies to the letters that she had received from the Duke?

A. Yes, Princess Diana did show me some replies.

Q. Were you aware that Rosa was assisting Diana in drafting those replies?

A. Yes, I was.

Andrew Alderson, 24 Nov 02 Interview with Rosa Monckton:

"According to Rosa Monckton, one of the Princess's closest friends, the tone of Prince Philip's letters was far from being aggressive and abusive towards his daughter-in-law, as Simone Simmons, a faith healer, claimed in a Sunday newspaper a fortnight ago....

"The Telegraph understands that the letters were written at the time that the Princess wanted advice from Prince Philip[a] on how she could come to terms with her husband's rekindled relationship with Camilla Parker Bowles....

"Ms Monckton said that Prince Philip had written four or five times to Diana and that the Princess had shown her all the correspondence.

"Although Ms Monckton declined to discuss the contents of the letters, her version of events supports the account given by Prince Philip in a Buckingham Palace statement yesterday. He denied 'insulting' his daughter-in-law or writing to her in a 'derogatory' way.

"'These letters were written between June and September 1992,' said Ms Monckton, who shared a holiday with the Princess two weeks before her death in 1997.

"'There was an extensive correspondence between the two of them. I saw every single one of these letters and helped Diana to reply. I was struck by how kind and compassionate and understanding he was of her circumstances....'

"It was in the aftermath of the collapsed trial of Paul Burrell, the Princess's former butler, that the Mail on Sunday ran an interview with Miss Simmons.

"The letters were alleged to have been part of the so-called 'Crown Jewels' - confidential letters, documents and other belongings that the police had been searching for in January last year when they raided Mr Burrell's house in Cheshire and arrested him." [229]

Richard Kay, 29 Nov 03 Interview with Lucia Flecha de Lima: **Jury Didn't Hear**:

"At the height of the recriminations that swirled around Diana, the de Limas allowed her to use their home as a sanctuary.... It was there that she took the now infamous letters from Prince Philip (in which he tried to help patch up her marriage), and there that [Diana] and Lucia would pour [sic] over her responses.

"It is also, I can reveal, the place where these letters - which Lucia described as 'warm, courteous and helpful' - were hidden for years....

"It was during the dying days of the royal marriage that Prince Philip began his correspondence with his daughter-in-law.

"Lucia recalls how the Princess kept the letters, together with copies of her responses (written with the help of Lucia and another of Diana's close friends, Rosa Monckton, the wife of *Sunday Telegraph* editor Dominic Lawson) in a safe at the embassy.

"'She was afraid that someone might find them at Kensington Palace,' she says. 'At that time, she and Charles were not separated and all sorts of people

---

[a] The first letter was from Philip to Diana – not the other way around.

could come and go in her apartment.' There were about half a dozen letters from Philip. 'He was trying to be helpful. They were warm and kind, and were like a father writing to a daughter. He referred to himself as "Pa" and the Queen as "Ma", and always signed off with love.

"'He drew on his own experiences: in one letter he wrote about how, when he and the Queen married, they thought they would have some years together living their own lives. But it was not to be, and "Ma" was called to her duty and he had to give up the career he loved.

"'Philip felt Diana and Charles could live separate lives, with separate apartments at Kensington Palace, but they should remain together. Diana thought Philip wanted her to be submissive towards the royals.

"'I wish I had spoken to Prince Philip because I am sure if he had known my side of the story, he could have helped Diana more effectively. But I thought he would refuse to see me or, worse, ask why an ambassador's wife was interfering in a private family matter.

"'In retrospect, knowing what I do, I wish I'd taken that risk and perhaps I could have helped.' Later, Lucia attempted to return the Philip letters to Diana. 'My husband said they were an important part of British history and should remain in Britain,' she says.

"'But Diana wanted me to keep them so, in the end, we compromised. I had copies made, which I kept in the diplomatic pouch.'" [230]

Paget Report, p128: **Jury Didn't Hear**:
"The Princess of Wales did receive letters from HRH Prince Philip. No one claims to have possession of any of these letters any longer."

Coroner: Opening Remarks: 3 Oct 07: 59.19:
"It seems probable that ... there were such letters [from Philip to Diana], but where they went and whether they still exist remains a mystery. We shall have to see whether the mystery unfolds in the coming weeks...."

Coroner: Summing Up: 31 Mar 08: 112.12:
"When the first letter arrived from the Duke in June 1992, Diana got in touch with Rosa Monckton and sought her help in drafting a reply. Rosa Monckton explained that she drafted replies to a number of letters from the Duke over that summer. She could see how people might have got the wrong impression about the content of the letters because Diana's first reaction on receipt of a letter was generally to be upset, but they were in fact very supportive and trying to help, she said. Diana had faxed a number of letters to Rosa Monckton and she, in turn, provided me with copies of those faxes. She also provided copies of drafts she had compiled for Diana to use in answer and these she produced before you. Following receipt of what Rosa Monckton had in her possession, inquiries of the Palace revealed that the Duke of Edinburgh had copies of the letters he had written to Diana and also the

original responses from Diana.... My office asked for a complete set of correspondence and Hunt-Davis in turn asked the Duke."

Philip-Diana Letters: June to September 1992				
Date	From	To	Inquest Shown[ab]	Faxed to Rosa[c]
June 18	Philip	Diana	No	Not Stated
June 21	Diana	Philip	Yes	NA
June 25	Philip	Diana	Opening Only	Yes
June 29	Diana	Philip	Yes	NA
July 7	Philip	Diana	Yes	Yes
July 12	Diana	Philip	Yes	NA
July 20	Philip	Diana	Opening Only	Yes
July 26	Diana	Philip	Yes	NA
September 28	Philip	Diana	Opening Only	Not Stated
September 30	Diana	Philip	Yes	NA

Comment: We are looking at the role of Rosa Monckton in respect of the 1992 Philip-Diana letters.

Did Princess Diana seek help from others in answering the Philip letters, and if so, who did she look to?

There are only two key witnesses who have provided evidence: Lucia Flecha de Lima and Rosa Monckton.

Lucia's accounts:

- "it was [at Lucia's home] that ... [Diana] and Lucia would [pore] over her responses" to Philip's letters – Richard Kay based on interview 2003

- "[Diana's] responses [were] written with the help of Lucia and ... Rosa Monckton" – Richard Kay based on interview 2003[d]

- "[Diana] kept the letters, together with copies of her responses ... in a safe at the embassy" – Richard Kay based on interview 2003

---

[a] Letters shown were very heavily redacted – at the most, only opening and closing remarks were revealed.

[b] The letters shown to the inquest – both from Philip and Diana – were provided by Buckingham Palace.

[c] Applies only to letters from Philip.

[d] The evidence will indicate that Kay has included Monckton here as a result of her November 2002 media account – i.e. it is unlikely that Lucia, during this interview, said Rosa helped with the responses.

- "later ... Diana wanted me to keep [the letters and reply copies] so ... I had copies made, which I kept in the diplomatic pouch" – to Richard Kay in 2003
- "I have read the letters" – Paget statement 2004
- "[Diana] did ... show [me] ... letters that she had received from Prince Philip" – confirmed at inquest 2007
- "Princess Diana did show me some [of her] replies" – inquest 2007
- "I was ... aware that Rosa was assisting Diana in drafting [the] replies" – confirmed at inquest 2007.

Rosa's accounts:
- "I saw every single one of these letters and helped Diana to reply" – Telegraph interview 2002
- "all of [the letter showings] were in London, either in my flat or in Kensington Palace, or if ... we could not meet up, she would fax them to me and then we would talk about it on the telephone and I would draft the replies and get them back to her" – to Burnett at inquest
- "I ... showed [the letters] to my husband after having consulted Diana and he helped draft a lot of the replies with me" – to Burnett at inquest
- after giving the draft replies to Diana "I would have a long conversation with her, then I would go away and think about it and then get them back to her and then we would discuss [the replies] again" – to Burnett at inquest
- "I am sure that she did – she told me that she did" – reply to Burnett's: "Did [Diana] use the guts of your draft replies?" at inquest
- "a lot of the time ... we did [the replies] together" – to Burnett at inquest
- "sometimes I was not with her, but a lot of the time I was" – to Burnett at inquest
- "[my husband] sat down with myself and Diana on two or three occasions to" help draft the replies – to Mansfield at inquest
- "[Diana] asked me to keep copies" – to Mansfield at inquest
- "[Diana] told me that she was going to keep [the correspondence] very safe" – to Mansfield at inquest
- "I passed it to [Diana] or I would fax" the draft replies – to Mansfield at inquest.

There are two striking factors that jump out when initially assessing the evidence of these two women: a) Lucia's evidence has changed considerably between her Kay interview in 2003 and her sworn account at the 2007 inquest; and b) after stating her case to the *Telegraph* in late 2002, Rosa then said absolutely nothing about seeing or helping with the letters in her Paget statement in 2004.

In November 2003[a] Lucia Flecha de Lima is openly telling Richard Kay that at her home she and Diana pored over the responses and that Diana kept the letters and the responses "in a safe at the [Brazilian] embassy".

Just nine months later – in a much more important document, her police statement regarding the deaths – Lucia has pulled her head in. Now, all we see is a short description of the nature of the letters' content and this: "I have read the letters".

At the inquest three years later, Lucia's statement account is read out to her. Lucia confirms that, but there is now a huge conflict with her 2003 Kay interview:

- Lucia now completely distances herself from any involvement in formulating the responses: "Princess Diana did show me some [of her] replies"

- instead, she says Rosa was doing that: "I was ... aware that Rosa was assisting Diana in drafting [the] replies"

- makes no claim of the letters being kept at the Brazilian embassy.

In 2003 Lucia said that she helped Diana reply: "[Diana] and Lucia would [pore] over [Diana's] responses". By 2007 she is saying: "I was ... aware that Rosa was assisting Diana in drafting [the] replies".

So Lucia helping with the responses in 2003, but four years later it is Rosa helping with the responses.[b]

Why has Lucia changed her evidence? [c]

In 2002 Rosa Monckton told the British public: "I saw every single one of these letters and helped Diana to reply". But when it came to Rosa's police statement to the inquiry[d] into the deaths, she is even quieter than Lucia – there is no mention at all that Rosa has seen any letters, let alone helped with replies. Instead we see a brief description of what Philip said in the letters but, because Rosa does not mention reading the letters, the implication is that she could have been told this from Diana.

Rosa is asked by Burnett about this – "you did not ... mention to the police that you had seen correspondence ... and, indeed, had copies" – and she replied: "I did not think it had any relevance at all to the case".

There are several points:

---

[a] Published 29 November 2003.

[b] In the 2003 article Kay also wrote: "[Diana's] responses [were] written with the help of Lucia and ... Rosa Monckton". But this does not appear to be a quote from Lucia – Kay's knowledge of Rosa helping with the responses appears to come from Rosa's November 2002 *Telegraph* coverage. This is addressed later.

[c] This question will be answered later.

[d] Less than two years after the *Telegraph* article – the article was November 2002 and the statement was July 2004.

1) Philip had been named as a suspect – so therefore the sighting and possession of correspondence between him and the victim, Diana, is obviously relevant

2) Rosa had already publicly recounted her version of the letters just 20 months earlier – that indicates that she saw it as relevant at that time

3) Rosa included a summary of her version of the letters in the statement – it is ridiculous to suggest that the content of the letters is relevant, but not how she obtained her knowledge of that content.[a]

I suggest that it is no coincidence that both Rosa and Lucia reduced their accounts for the British police – Rosa had no claims of viewing, possessing or helping write the letters; Lucia had no claims of possessing or helping write the letters and simply stated: "I have read the letters". This is revisited later.

Then at the inquest we see a major merging of their accounts[b] – Lucia lessens her role to "[Diana] did ... show [me] ... letters" and "some [of her] replies" and acknowledges Rosa's helping role: "I was ... aware that Rosa was assisting".

Rosa, though, at the inquest now increases her role to full involvement – "I would draft the replies and get them back to her"; "[Diana] asked me to keep copies".

So whereas Rosa made no claims regarding the letters in her police statement, three years later, she is claiming all three actions: viewing, possessing copies and helping write the letters.

Are Rosa's 2002 and 2007 accounts true? Why has Lucia's account changed so radically between 2003 and 2007?[c]

An analysis of the evidence is difficult because there are just the two witnesses – Lucia and Rosa – and both have been shown to have lied on other issues.

There are three important questions that must be asked:

1) Would Diana share these Philip letters – and seek help with replies – from someone, Rosa, she had just met four months earlier?[da]

---

[a] There is a huge difference between a witness providing second-hand knowledge – verbally from Diana or Lucia – and first-hand knowledge – from reading the letters herself.

[b] Merging, particularly as far as Rosa's role is concerned.

[c] It is almost as though there has been a role switch. In 2003 Lucia said through Kay: "[Diana] and Lucia would [pore] over her responses". That is gone from Lucia's 2007 account and is replaced by Rosa saying: "we did [the replies] together".

[d] Rosa's inquest account was their initial meeting was in February 1992 and the first Philip letter was June 1992.

2) Would Diana share and seek help with these letters from someone with whom she had issues of trust? [b]

3) Would Diana allow a Sunday newspaper editor – Dominic Lawson[c] – to have access to these letters? [d]

The answer to these questions would need to be "yes" for Rosa Monckton's inquest evidence to be credible.

There are a number of significant concerns surrounding the Philip letters' evidence:[e]

1) Rosa was often evasive in her inquest testimony, but when it came to her role in the Philip letters her initial answers could be described as effusive – there are large amounts of volunteered information.

Rosa acknowledged having copies of the letters from Philip, then Burnett asked a simple question: "How did you receive those letters?" Instead of answering this question, Rosa goes into a detailed account of what happened "when Diana received the first" letter.[f]

Based on that response, Burnett then asked the next question: "So the first letter the Princess showed you in London?" That is really a "yes/no" question, and Rosa does answer "yes", but then proceeds to volunteer information on much more: "Yes, all of them were in London, either in my flat or in Kensington Palace, or if, for some reason, we could not meet up, [Diana] would fax them to me and then we would talk about it on the telephone and I would draft the replies and get them back to her."

All Burnett was seeking was a confirmation that Diana showed Rosa the first letter in London.

Rosa has given much more:
- stated that "all of [the letters] were [shown] in London"
- the specific locations: "either in my flat or in Kensington Palace"
- "if ... we could not meet up, [Diana] would fax" the Philip letters
- "we would talk about it on the telephone"
- "I would draft the replies and get them back to [Diana]".

These responses led to Burnett next saying: "We will take that stage by stage, if we can."

---

[a] Rosa says: "When Diana received the first [letter], she rang me and she was very, very upset, very tearful, and she said, 'Can I come and see you because I have received a letter and it has made me very upset?'" Why wouldn't Diana have called Annabel Goldsmith or Lucia Flecha de Lima, both of whom she had known much longer?

[b] Simmons and Lucia – see earlier.

[c] Identified as an MI6 agent – see earlier.

[d] As stated by Rosa.

[e] The concerns listed here need to be viewed together – each on its own may not be particularly significant, but the evidence builds up as this progresses.

[f] For the full text of her response, see earlier.

I suggest there is a possibility that Rosa had pre-prepared her testimony on her role in the Philip letters and as soon as Burnett brought the subject up[a], Rosa basically launched into what she had prepared – rather than just answering the questions put to her.

The reason why Rosa might have done this should become clearer as this subject develops.

2) Lucia was asked: "When [Diana] showed [the letters] to you, what were the circumstances?" She replied: "When she received the first one, she was quite upset about it".

Rosa stated: "She was upset when she received each of" the letters.[b]

Burnett's question to Lucia was regarding all the letters and her response was that Diana was upset with the first one – that indicates she was not upset with the later ones, and that is supported by the reason Lucia gives: "[Diana] did not know exactly what to expect from [the Queen and Philip] at this moment". In other words, it appears that receiving the first letter was a shock that upset Diana, but after that she was okay.

In contrast, Rosa was asked only about the first letter but replied that Diana "was upset when she received each of" the letters, and then provided a completely different reason for it: "I think it just was a reflection of her emotional state at that time".

I suggest that Lucia's account is more common sense – a process of written communication had been set up after the first of Philip's letters was received and answered by Diana, so why would Diana be upset each time she received a letter after that?

So there is conflict here between Rosa and Lucia on two points: a) her level of upset – Lucia says Diana was upset once; Rosa says five times[cd]; b) the reason for the upset – Lucia says Diana "did not know exactly what to expect from" her in-laws; Rosa says it was "just ... her emotional state".[e]

---

[a] The subject being, Rosa's role in the Philip letters – not the letters themselves.
[b] This was another possible case of Rosa over-answering – the question was: "Why was it that the Princess of Wales was upset when she received the first of them?"
[c] Rosa says each time and there were five letters.
[d] There is also an apparent conflict between Rosa's: "She was upset when she received each of [the Philip letters]" and Rosa's repeated confirmations to Burnett's: "Was that the Princess's genuine sentiment?" For example: Diana wrote to Philip: "I was so pleased to receive your letter". Burnett asked: "Was that the Princess's genuine sentiment about the letter?" Rosa replies: "Absolutely it was. Yes, it was." But how could Diana have genuinely written, "I was so pleased to receive your letter", if "[Diana] was upset when she received each of" the Philip letters?
[e] During a later period of cross-examination – from Mansfield – after reiterating that "[Diana] was in a very emotional state at the time of this correspondence", Rosa then

At the inquest Rosa repeatedly pushed her evidence about Diana's emotional condition:
- "she was very upset"
- "she was very emotional about" the marriage breakdown
- "she ... could sometimes be a little bit irrational"
- "somebody who is in such an emotional state" – referring to Diana
- "she was upset when she received each of" the Philip letters
- "it just was a reflection of her emotional state"
- "receiving the letters, her first reaction was generally tearful"
- "she was in a very emotional state at the time of this correspondence"
- "every time she picked up one of these letters she started crying before she had even got through the first paragraph"
- "it is just her emotional state at that time"
- "a letter from anybody would have made her cry".

In doing this, Rosa appeared to have a dual purpose:

a) to explain her claimed rapid development of her relationship with Diana – "when you meet somebody who is in such an emotional state and you click, you become friends very quickly"

b) to counter the other evidence that there were later letters from Philip describing Diana as a "harlot" and a "trollop" – these letters really did upset Diana[a]: this has been addressed in Part 2. Rosa appears to have deftly attempted to shift the upset from those later letters to the 1992 letters.[b]

There is no support from other witnesses for Rosa's vivid descriptions of Diana's emotional condition.

3) Lucia said in 2003: "the Princess kept the letters, together with copies of her responses ... in a safe at the embassy". Then Lucia said: "Later ... I had copies made, which I kept in the diplomatic pouch".

---

said the reason was "because [Diana] could not work out what it was that [Philip] wanted, to begin with", but then, when further questioned, again reverted to: "It is just her emotional state at that time" – which was her main evidence on this. It will be shown later that it is unlikely that Diana sought Rosa's help with the letters and she may have been told from Lucia that Diana wasn't sure what was expected. Lucia has never provided support for Rosa's account that the reason for Diana's upset was her emotional state.

[a] Simone Simmons has said: "[Diana] had death threats which were worded nicer than [Philip's] letters".: Louise Pritchard, A Harlot, a Trollop and a Whore...., *Mail on Sunday*, 10 November 2002.

[b] The fact that there were two sets of letters – as shown in detail in Part 2 – has been allowed to cause a great deal of confusion in the Philip Letters evidence. This was one of the central issues in the *Telegraph* article – Rosa talks about 1992 letters, whereas the letters seen by Simone Simmons were later and much more vitriolic.

Rosa said she has copies of the letters from Philip, minus the first one – Burnett: "a letter from Prince Philip, which you don't in fact have" – and the draft replies.[a]

Yet in 2007 Lucia fails to disclose that she has copies of any letters – from Philip or Diana – and it is Rosa who confirms to Burnett that she "showed the correspondence as you had it to the Secretary to the Inquests".

Instead of disclosing what she had, Lucia has indicated that she was just shown letters and has confirmed this by also failing to disclose that she helped with the replies.[b]

Why didn't Lucia disclose to the inquest that she had copies of the Philip-Diana correspondence?

The answer will emerge.

4) Under cross-examination by the Al Fayed lawyer, Michael Mansfield, Rosa Monckton appeared at times to go on the offensive:

a) Mansfield asked Rosa: "Did you tell [Diana] that ... [your husband] was helping draft" the replies. Rosa responded: "[My husband] sat down <u>with myself and Diana</u> on two or three occasions to" help with the replies.

Rosa's earlier account to the inquest lawyer, Ian Burnett, was: "I only showed them to my husband after having consulted Diana and he helped draft a lot of the replies <u>with me</u>".

So, to Burnett we have: Lawson[c] "helped draft a lot of the replies with me", but later to Mansfield, it is: Lawson "sat down with myself and Diana on two or three occasions" to draft replies.[d]

b) Mansfield asked: "Did you tell Diana that you were keeping copies?" Rosa replied: "[Diana] asked me to keep copies".

If Diana was relying on Rosa to keep copies then I suggest one could expect Rosa to have a full set of the correspondence – as apparently Lucia has, according to the 2003 interview.

---

[a] Rosa is not claiming to have copies of Diana's actual final replies: Burnett asked: "Did the Princess use the guts of your draft replies or do you just not know?" Rosa answered: "I am sure that she did. She told me that she did."

[b] In failing to disclose to the police or the inquest that she had correspondence between a suspect – Philip – and a victim – Diana – Lucia has placed herself in a position where she could be guilty of withholding evidence relevant to the investigation into the deaths of Princess Diana and Dodi Fayed.

[c] Rosa's husband, Dominic Lawson.

[d] Rosa's husband was the *Sunday Telegraph* editor, Dominic Lawson. The question put earlier was: Would Diana allow a Sunday newspaper editor to have access to these letters?

The evidence indicates that Rosa was only able to furnish copies of four of Philip's letters and none of Diana's handwritten replies to the inquest – see earlier.

Both of the above appear to be instances of Rosa challenging Mansfield with surprising evidence that is independently unverifiable – that Diana asked her to keep copies; that Lawson sat down with Diana and her to formulate replies.[a] In describing the role of her husband to Mansfield, Rosa appears to have given conflicting evidence – see a above.[b]

Later analysis will indicate that there has been a huge effort to try and falsely establish the Diana-Rosa relationship as very close. It may be that Rosa's above two claims are an attempt to show that Diana trusted her implicitly – when the general verifiable evidence indicates that was not the case.

5) Rosa has consistently insisted she saw all Philip's letters to Diana:

- "I am absolutely 100 per cent certain that she would have [told me] had there been any other letters" from Philip – to Burnett

- "I am convinced that I have seen all of the letters" from Philip – to Mansfield

- "I know absolutely that had she had any more letters from Prince Philip, she would have rung me straightaway" – to Mansfield

- "I saw every single one of these letters" from Philip – to the *Telegraph* in 2002.

Burnett asked why. Rosa replied: "Because of the help I gave her with this correspondence". Rosa volunteered something similar to Mansfield, without him asking.[c]

Mansfield rightly challenged Rosa on this: "I understand your belief entirely, but you do understand that your belief may be wrong". Rosa tried to stick to her argument: "As far as these letters are concerned, I do not accept that." [d]

The point here is that Rosa's insistent and repetitive argument – "I saw every single one of these [Philip] letters" – is fundamentally flawed and illogical.

---

[a] I suggest that Lawson – being unindependent and an MI6 agent – would verify Rosa's evidence, whether it was true or not. Nevertheless, Lawson should have been asked for his account, even if it was just a statement. This never occurred.

[b] This surprising evidence is similar to Rosa's earlier unbelievable statement, "I did not know that" MI6 is SIS. It also has similarities with the excessive distancing addressed earlier. Rosa is saying that Diana not only approved of Lawson's role in the replies, he was right there with her doing it; and Diana not only approved of Rosa having copies, she actually asked her to take them.

[c] "The help that I gave her with these letters...."

[d] The full transcript on this is shown earlier.

It is impossible for Rosa Monckton – or any witness – to speak accurately about things they can't know about.

One of the things Rosa can't know is whether there are any other letters from Philip to Diana.[a] For example, letters may have arrived during one of Rosa's "radio silences"; or letters may have arrived with content Diana didn't want Rosa to see.

Rosa can speak about the four, possibly five[b], Philip letters that she has seen, but she cannot speak about any letters from Philip that she hasn't seen.

If Rosa hasn't seen other letters, it does not – and cannot – mean they don't exist. They may exist, they may not exist. The evidence of anyone who may have seen them – in this case, Simone Simmons, Miles Hunt-Davis and Paul Burrell – is instead taken into consideration.[c]

The fact that Rosa is so repeatedly adamant about this, raises the question: What is Rosa's motivation?

This will be addressed in the Conclusion section of this chapter.

6) Rosa volunteered to Burnett: "When Diana received the first [Philip letter] ... we [Diana and Rosa] looked at it together, and I was able to ... point out that ... we should read it very carefully, go through it and reply".

Yet, later regarding this same first draft reply from Diana to Philip, Rosa confirmed to Burnett: "The first letter that you have is an undated ... draft which you, with the help of your husband, put together for the Princess and which she then copied by hand". Rosa replied: "Exactly."

Burnett put it to Rosa that Lawson and her had put together the first reply – and Rosa didn't correct him, in fact her reply is: "Exactly". But earlier, her unsolicited account seems to be just Rosa and Diana putting together the first reply – there is no mention of any contact with Lawson.

This appears to be an unexplained conflict in Rosa's inquest evidence.

7) Burnett asks: "Did you put in your drafts the references to 'Pa' or did she introduce those herself?"

Rosa appears to be caught off guard with this. She doesn't directly answer the question, but replies: "Well, a lot of the time, you know, we did them together."

Even Burnett seems surprised: "I see". Then Rosa: "Do you see what I mean?" Burnett: "Yes."[d] Then Rosa again: "I mean sometimes I was not with her, but a lot of the time I was, so ..."

---

[a] The evidence shown in Part 2 indicates that there were letters from a later period than 1992.

[b] There were five 1992 letters from Philip to Diana, but Rosa only produced copies of four at the inquest – see earlier.

[c] This is done in the Letters Post-1992 section of Part 2.

[d] Possibly hoping Rosa won't try and explain it.

The three dots – "..." – are a part of the original transcript[a], and they indicate that the witness has tapered off, without finishing the sentence. It may be that Rosa – and Burnett, who moved on directly after this – thought that she was digging herself into a hole, so she stopped speaking.

Rosa asks: "Do you see what I mean?"

Well, just what <u>does</u> Rosa mean?

The question was simple enough: Did Rosa put "Pa" in the draft replies, or did Diana "introduce those herself" when she handwrote the final reply?

When Rosa says: "sometimes I was not with [Diana], but a lot of the time I was", she appears to be referring to the making of the draft replies.[b]

Rosa appears to be diverting attention away from Burnett's question – who put the "Pas" in? – by focusing instead on whether Diana was present during the compiling of the draft replies.

The question should have been simple to answer. The gist of Rosa's evidence is that she controlled the draft replies: "I would draft the replies and get them back to her"; "[Lawson] helped draft a lot of the replies with me"; "I remember [Diana] saying to me, ' ... you have typed [the drafts]'".

This essentially means that if the "Pas" were not in the draft replies, then they must have come from Diana. If they were in the draft replies – which weren't shown to the jury – then it appears the "Pas" would have come from Rosa.[c]

I believe that Rosa prepared her inquest testimony on the Philip letters and was taken by surprise by this question from Burnett. This will become clearer later.

8) Burnett asked Lucia: "Can you remember over what period [the Philip letters] continued?" Lucia – who was speaking on video-link from Brazil – gave a stunning reply: "I think the first one was <u>on 18th June</u> [1992] and the last one was towards the end of September."

The question then became: How could Lucia correctly put such a specific date – 18 June 1992 – on a letter written over 15 years earlier?

Burnett provided Lucia with an out: "Are those dates ... that you have managed to remind yourself of as a result of evidence given here?" Lucia replied: "No, no, because I cannot follow the evidence given in England."

---

[a] See 13 Dec 07: 122.9.

[b] As opposed to the writing of the final handwritten replies. At another point, Burnett asked about the handwritten replies: "Did the Princess use the guts of your draft replies?" Rosa said: "She told me that she did." By her own admission, Rosa was not aware of their content and therefore not present when Diana wrote the final replies. That is also supported by what Rosa told Mansfield: "I passed it to [Diana] or I would fax" the draft replies.

[c] This assessment is based on Rosa's evidence. It will be shown later that large parts of Rosa's evidence are false and it is more likely that the draft replies were compiled after the deaths – typed from the handwritten copies.

Burnett had to then state: "I wonder how you have such a good recollection."

Lucia then says: "Oh, because I went through my statement and I just remember."

The reality is that Lucia could not have got the letter date from her statement – as shown earlier, she only briefly mentions her role regarding the letters in the statement: "I have read the letters".[a]

Lucia's knowledge of the exact date of the first Philip letter supports her 2003 article account: "I had copies made, which I kept in the diplomatic pouch".

This also shows that Lucia has a copy of the first 18 June 1992 letter – this is the only Philip letter that was not shown[b] to the inquest, and also was not in the copies Rosa Monckton supplied.[c]

9) Rosa has presented different accounts on how the 2002 *Sunday Telegraph* article came about:

- "I did not go to the press – the press came to me"
- "I might have even been in touch with the Duke of Edinburgh's office at the time"
- "it was not [my husband] who was discussing this"
- "I think I would have got a call from whoever it was ... and I thought that I had to put the record straight about the content of these letters"
- "I honestly cannot remember the sequence of events" – reply to: "before you [went public], did you contact the Palace?"
- "I honestly cannot remember. I do not think I did [contact Hunt-Davis before going public]. I cannot remember the sequence of events that led to this newspaper article"
- "it could have been [my husband's suggestion] or it could have been me having heard about the *Mail on Sunday* article" and suggesting an interview
- "I could have seen Miss Simmons' comments in *The Mail* and decided that I needed to put the record straight or [Andrew Alderson] could have approached me"
- "I have no idea" – reply to: "Were you in some way coordinating" with the Duke of Edinburgh?

---

[a] Lucia's full statement is shown in *The Documents* book, pp29-36.
[b] The letters that were "shown" were very heavily redacted. The letters are reproduced on the inquest website: INQ0058912 to INQ0058961.
[c] Referred to by Burnett, speaking to Rosa: "a letter from Prince Philip, which you don't in fact have".

There are three key parties involved: the *Sunday Telegraph*, whose editor was an MI6 agent[a] and husband to Rosa Monckton, Dominic Lawson; Rosa Monckton; and Prince Philip, the author of the letters to Diana.

There are several points regarding Rosa's evidence:

a) Rosa said at the inquest:

- "the press came to me"
- "it was not [my husband] who was discussing this"
- "I think I would have got a call from whoever it was" – referring to a *Sunday Telegraph* columnist
- "it could have been [my husband's suggestion] or it could have been me" [b]
- "I could have seen Miss Simmons' comments ... and decided that I needed to put the record straight or [Andrew Alderson] could have approached me".

There is a clear conflict here: Rosa's first two responses were that she was approached from the press – "the press came to me"; "I would have got a call".

Later Rosa changes this to the first move being either from her or the press. But again, there is even more conflict in these last two accounts – to Mansfield, Rosa indicates that an approach from the press would have come from her husband, Dominic Lawson, but the next day, to Ian Croxford[c], she indicates it would have come from the reporter, Andrew Alderson.

So, Rosa has three positions – when there should only be one: i) she was approached by the press; ii) she could have approached the press or her husband could have asked her[d]; iii) she could have approached the press or Alderson could have approached her.

b) Rosa said at the inquest:

- "I might have even been in touch with [Philip's] office"
- "I honestly cannot remember the sequence of events" – regarding going public or contacting the palace first
- "I do not think I did [contact Hunt-Davis before going public]. I cannot remember the sequence of events"
- "I have no idea" – regarding coordination between Rosa and Philip.

Again Rosa has three positions on contact between her and Philip: i) "I might have even been in touch"; ii) "I do not think I did [contact Hunt-Davis]"; iii) "I have no idea".

---

[a] See earlier.

[b] Response to question: "Was it your husband who suggested that you should be interviewed about these matters?"

[c] Representing the Ritz Hotel.

[d] This is after denying Lawson's involvement: "it was not [my husband] who was discussing this".

Rosa appears to have made an effort to shift the focus away from her communication with Buckingham Palace onto the "sequence of events". I suggest this was a deliberate distraction – it is obvious that if there was meaningful communication with Philip about her going public, then it had to occur before she went public, not after the event.

The first three of the above four quotes – given by Rosa on 13 December 2007 – all indicate that there was communication between Rosa and Philip's office, even if she is claiming uncertainty over the "sequence of events".

It is only on the following day – December 14 – that Rosa comes up with: "I have no idea".

The timing on this is critical.

The interview with Simone Simmons was published in the *Mail on Sunday* on 10 November 2002.[231] By the following day, November 11, Buckingham Palace had publicly responded, saying there was no comment and "letters between members of the royal family [are] a private matter".[232]

At that stage, that was apparently the end of the matter in the public arena.[a]

However according to the *Sunday Telegraph* Philip was investigating other actions, behind the scenes: "Prince Philip consulted Farrer & Co, the Royal Family's solicitors and ... the Press Complaints Commission (PCC), the press watchdog. In the week after the publication of the story, senior representatives from Farrer and the PCC met Prince Philip at Buckingham Palace for informal discussions about how to resolve the issue.... Eventually, it was decided that a [press] statement, released yesterday, was the 'simplest and quickest way' of putting the matter straight." [233]

The balance of the evidence from Rosa Monckton is that there was communication between her and Philip's office.

This is supported by: a) the timing – the Palace press release and Rosa's interview are only a day apart; b) the two week delay in the publication of Rosa's interview – this matches the two week delay before Philip spoke out.

The evidence indicates that during that two week delay, it was Philip who was initiating the actions – he called in the solicitors and the PCC; he was first to go to the press.

I suggest that is because the letters described by Simmons came from him and it was his reputation that had been called into question – not Rosa Monckton's.

There is some speculation included in what follows, nevertheless based on the available evidence.

---

[a] There is no record of any news articles on the subject between November 11 and 23, when Philip published his press release.

The reason Rosa did an interview was nothing to do with her perceived close relationship with Diana[a] – it was about defending Philip.

I suggest that the above points to the contact between Philip and Rosa being initiated by Philip. It could be that Philip planned to put out his press release on the Saturday – November 23 – with the knowledge that the following day there would be "independent" support coming from Diana's side – in the form of her friend, Rosa Monckton. It is of course no surprise that the paper supporting Philip's account was edited by an MI6 agent, Dominic Lawson, who is also Rosa Monckton's husband.

It will be shown later that it is most unlikely Rosa had seen the letters, or helped Diana with them. It is possible that after Philip contacted Rosa[b], she in turn contacted Lucia – who I suggest had earlier[c] told Rosa that she had helped Diana with the replies, and indeed had copies. It may be that at that stage[d] Rosa was provided copies of the Philip letters – possibly from Philip, but more likely from Lucia.[ef]

I suggest that in the *Telegraph* interview Rosa falsely claimed that "the Princess had shown her all the correspondence" and she had "helped Diana to reply".[g]

What those two false statements do, though, is provide Rosa Monckton with the credibility she required to be able to give solid support to Philip's denial that he sent "insulting letters".[h]

Rosa Monckton is perceived by the public to have been a very close friend of Princess Diana[i] and it is not generally known that she operated as an MI6 agent. Her statement that Diana showed her the letters and she helped with

---

[a] It will be shown later that the Rosa-Diana relationship has been overstated in the public arena.

[b] After reading the 10 November 2002 *Mail* article.

[c] Possibly even at the time, in 1992.

[d] During the two week gap between the *Mail on Sunday* article – November 10 – and the Philip press release – November 23.

[e] The copy that Rosa had at the inquest was apparently of better quality than the copies – taken from Philip's carbon copy – that the inquest was given. Burnett to Rosa: "If the date was there, it certainly has not come out in the copying, but yours shows 28th September, does it?" Rosa: "Yes, it does."

[f] Lucia also would have been supportive of protecting Philip. In her statement Lucia said: "I thought of approaching Prince Philip" regarding Diana's marriage difficulties; "Philip did a good job towards Princess Diana"; and "Prince Philip tried to help" regarding the Charles-Diana marriage.: Lucia Flecha de Lima, Witness Statement, 1 September 2004, reproduced in *The Documents* book, pp30-31, 35.

[g] This will be addressed later.

[h] Philip's 23 November 2002 press release can be viewed on the inquest website: INQ0058969.

[i] This perception is addressed in the Conclusion section of this chapter.

the replies would have been widely accepted as the truth – and would give Philip the support he required.[a]

Rosa-Lucia Evidence on the Philip Letters[bc]							
Evidence Source	**Read Letters**		**Helped Reply**			**Had Possession**	
	Lucia	**Rosa**	**Lucia**	**Rosa**	**Lawson**	**Lucia**	**Rosa**
Lucia's Evidence							
2003 Kay Article	Yes	No[d]	Yes	No[e]	No	Yes	No
Lucia Police Statement	Yes	No	No	No	No	No	No
Lucia At Inquest	Yes	Yes	No	Yes	No	No	No
Rosa's Evidence							
2002 Telegraph Article	No	Yes	No	Yes	No	No	No
Rosa Police Statement	No	No	No	No	No	No	No
Rosa At Inquest	No	Yes	No	Yes	Yes	No	Yes

10)   The above table shows:
-    that the evidence of both Lucia and Rosa is very inconsistent
-    that the role of helping with the replies was claimed by Rosa in 2002 and Lucia in 2003 – by 2007, Lucia was no longer claiming that role

---

[a] The above is a scenario relating to the actions of Rosa around the 2002 article. A fuller scenario of what occurred regarding the Philip letters appears later.
[b] A "Yes" or "No" in a box relates to whether it is mentioned or not. For example, the "No" in "Lucia Read Letters" in the "2002 Telegraph Article" reflects that it is not mentioned.
[c] If evidence included the person helping to reply, it has been automatically assumed they would have read the letters.
[d] See following footnote.
[e] Kay did write that Rosa had helped with the replies, but that appears to be based on the 2002 *Telegraph* article – it is not shown as a quote from Lucia.

- Lucia claimed possession of copies of the letters in 2003, but never repeated the claim
- Rosa has claimed possession of copies of the letters just once, in 2007
- neither Rosa nor Lucia has ever conceded that the other has copies of the letters
- Rosa has never once mentioned that Lucia had any involvement at all with the Philip letters
- Lucia has never mentioned that Rosa's husband, Dominic Lawson, had any involvement with the letters
- Rosa only introduced the role of her husband helping with the replies, at the inquest in 2007.

11)   At one stage during Rosa's cross-examination, Burnett asked her to read a part of one of Diana's letters to Philip. Burnett said: "Maybe you can read the Princess's writing rather more easily than I can because you have had a lot of experience of it over the years".

Rosa, who – according to herself under oath – was "very firm friends"[a] with Diana, actually made two significant mistakes during her reading of the short excerpt from Diana's letter.

| Figure 7 | Closing excerpt from Princess Diana's letter to Prince Philip, dated 12 July 1992. When Rosa was asked to read this at the inquest, she made two key mistakes – she read "both" instead of "you" and "yours, Diana" instead of "from, Diana". |

[a] It will be shown later that Rosa has been portrayed as Diana's "best friend".

Rosa read: "You are very modest about your marriage guidance skills and I disagree with <u>both</u>! This last letter of yours showed great understanding and tact and I hope to be able to draw on your advice in the months ahead, whatever they may bring. With my fondest love, <u>yours</u>, Diana."

Rosa read: "I disagree with <u>both</u>" instead of "I disagree with <u>you</u>". Then also she reads: "<u>yours</u>, Diana", instead of "<u>from</u>, Diana".

Needless to say, from that point on Burnett protected the witness by not asking her to read any more of the letters. But it was too late – the mistakes had been made.[a]

The second mistake – "yours" instead of "from" – is particularly significant, because Diana closed all 9 letters[b] reproduced for the inquest[c] with the words "from Diana".[d]

This was the third letter Diana wrote to Philip – it was dated 12 July 1992. Up to this point Burnett[e] had been reading the letters without making any mistakes. In fact earlier the same day Burnett had correctly read out the identical letter that Rosa got wrong, to Miles Hunt-Davis.[234]

Burnett made the presumption that Rosa "had a lot of experience of [reading Diana's writing] over the years", but her obvious unfamiliarity with the way Diana signed off all her letters puts that in serious doubt.

---

[a] Despite failing the reading test, Rosa was very quick to confirm that she recognised sections of each letter – at one point she confirmed this before Burnett had completed the question: Burnett: "Do you recognise the opening sentence – " Rosa: "Yes." Burnett: " – of the letter." Rosa: "Yes, I do."

[b] To various people, including Philip, Dodi Fayed and Paul Burrell.

[c] There were four letters to Philip – INQ0058917, INQ0058927, INQ0058942, INQ0058961 – another letter to Philip was missing the signature line: 13 Dec 07: 126.13; four letters to Dodi – dd6 (27 July 1997), dd8 (5 August 1997), INQ0058899, INQ0058906; one letter to Paul Burrell – "lastletter" Page 4 (undated). In addition, three letters to Mohamed were read out but not reproduced – 17 December 1996 read out starting 18 Feb 08: 188.7; 21 May 1997 read out starting 18 Feb 08: 188.18; 21 July 1997 read out starting 18 Feb 08: 191.9. There is one other letter of 11 June 1997 read out starting 18 Feb 08: 189.1 that appears to omit the word "from", but it was only read out (not reproduced) and the lawyer (Michael Mansfield) reading it out was hurrying through several letters – "I will do it quickly" at 187:18; "I am going through them fairly quickly" at 188.17. Excerpts of several other letters to Mohamed Al Fayed from Diana were read out, without including the closing lines.

[d] The first mistake – "both" instead of "you" – could also be significant, in that Rosa has claimed that she was the primary author of the letters. Rosa was asked repeatedly by Burnett if she recognised sentences and sentiments in what was in Diana's letters to Philip, and always answered in the affirmative.

[e] Who presumably had never received any letters from Diana.

At the inquest Diana's close friends commented on her prodigious written communications:
- "Oh God, I have stacks of" letters from Diana[235] – Annabel Goldsmith
- "I have a lot of letters from her"[236] – Annabel Goldsmith
- "[I] received a large number of letters from" Diana[237] – Susan Kassem, confirmed to Hilliard.

Lucia Flecha de Lima and Rosa Monckton were not asked about the level of written communications they received from Diana, but the general evidence is that her close friends received lots of letters. Paul Burrell wrote in his book that Diana religiously sent thankyou notes for dinners or gifts.[a]

Rosa's failure to recognise that Diana always signed her letters "from Diana" raises the question: Just how many letters or notes did Rosa receive from Diana?

I suggest that this adds to the growing evidence indicating that Rosa Monckton was not as close to Princess Diana as has been generally perceived.

12)   Michael Mansfield asked Rosa Monckton: "Did you tell anybody during the [Burrell] trial[b], "Oh, actually, I have some letters"? Rosa: "No, I did not." Mansfield asked why. Rosa: "Because I would not have thought that they were in any way relevant to the trial."

This led Mansfield to quote from the 2002 *Telegraph* article that included Rosa's account of the letters: Mansfield: "'The [Philip] letters were alleged to have been part of the so-called "Crown Jewels" ... that the police had been searching for ... when they raided Mr Burrell's house ... and arrested him.'... Did that part of [the article] strike you in any way, that ... here you are with letters at home that the police had actually been looking for...?"

Rosa replied: "I would not have made the association."

Rosa Monckton has stated under oath at the inquest that in 2002 she thought that copies of letters – which she claims she had possession of in 2002[c], and which were believed to be part of the subject of a trial she had agreed to be a witness in – "were [not] in any way relevant to the trial".

---

[a] Burrell wrote: "[On] her birthday, from late afternoon until she went to bed, she wrote letter after letter to say thankyou to relatives, friends, associates and organisations.... She sat there ... as if it were a correspondence production line: write, fold, envelope, seal.... 'If people take the time and trouble to send a gift, the least I can do is thank them,' she said. Before she went out for dinner [on other days] she prepared her thank-you letter for her host or dining companion.... On her return she would write the letter, regardless of the hour....": Paul Burrell, *A Royal Duty*, pp192-3.

[b] This concluded on 1 November 2002, just 23 days before the *Telegraph* article.

[c] Rosa didn't make the claim in 2002, but in 2007 she made the claim that she had copies of the letters from 1992 onwards.

Then less than a month after the Burrell trial was disbanded, an article is written – which Rosa admits to have read[a] – stating that "the police had been searching for" the letters which she claims (in 2007) she had copies of at the time.

Then in 2007, Rosa claims under oath that she "would not have made the association" between the search by the police for the letters[b] and her claim that she at the time had copies of those letters.

I suggest that Rosa Monckton has lied under oath twice within a couple of minutes.

It is simply not credible that Rosa could not see the relevance of copies of the Philip letters to the Burrell trial – a trial where Burrell was accused of stealing letters from Philip among other items.

And it is also not credible that Rosa would not make an association between a police search for the Philip letters and copies of Philip letters that she claims were in her possession.[c]

13)   When Mansfield introduced the topic of the Philip letters to Rosa, he said: "Let's talk about very private letters between the Duke of Edinburgh and Diana."

That is a statement – not a question.

Yet, Rosa immediately volunteers: "I have never talked about those letters".

That is a lie: Rosa gave an interview to the *Telegraph* in 2002 – she had not only talked about the letters, she had talked to the British public about them.

Mansfield: "Haven't you?" Rosa: "Except to my husband."
Another lie.

Then Mansfield asks Rosa to: "Please think."

It is only then that she comes up with: "I think there was a newspaper article, somebody was talking" but then adds: "I cannot recall any more".

That is another lie – as it turns out, Rosa recalls quite a lot more, which is slowly dragged out of her: see earlier.

The question is: Why has Rosa repeatedly lied about this?

It becomes evident that Rosa was very reticent to see the subject of the 2002 *Telegraph* article come up, and may have been hoping that Mansfield –

---

[a] The article contained information from an interview with Rosa Monckton. Mansfield asked: "Did you read this ... [article] once it was published on 24th November?" Rosa: "Yes, I must have done."

[b] Mentioned in the 2002 article.

[c] Other evidence indicates that at the time of the Burrell trial the Philip letter copies would have been in the possession of Lucia – Rosa may have obtained copies from Lucia after the 10 November 2002 *Mail* article. See earlier and later.

or anyone else at the inquest – was not aware of it, as it was published just over five years earlier.

But why was Rosa fearful of this being addressed?

Rosa has described her reason for speaking to the press about the Philip letters in November 2002:

- "I was merely going on record to set it straight, which is all I have ever done with anything concerning Diana"
- "I thought that I had to put the record straight about the content of these letters"
- "I have only ever gone on record to put a fact right that was wrong"
- "I have only gone on record when I think something is wrong – Simone Simmons was wrong and I did not think it was fair to leave that uncorrected"
- "it could have been me [who suggested the interview] ... wanting to put the record straight"
- "I could have ... decided that I needed to put the record straight"
- "I have only done things when there has been something that has been incorrect and that was incorrect".

This is evidently a point Rosa wanted to drive home – that all she was doing was setting the record straight.

That position doesn't fit with the lies Rosa told to try and avoid mention of the article at the inquest – "I have never talked about those letters"; "except to my husband" (see above). If Rosa's motive in doing the 2002 article was simply to set the record straight, then she should have had no concerns about having the record set straight at the inquest.

Rosa's account in the *Telegraph* article has two main effects: a) it defends Philip; and b) it undermines and attacks the evidence of Simone Simmons.

Evidence in Part 2 shows that Simmons' account – that Philip wrote later nasty letters to Diana – is credible and is supported by witness accounts that prior to 1997 Diana feared Philip: in the words of her friend, Roberto Devorik, quoting Diana: "[Philip] really hates me and would like to see me disappear".[ab]

Bearing in mind that Diana was assassinated, one could argue that it is in her[c] interests for the true nature of the later deterioration in the Philip-Diana relationship to be made known to the public – it could help people to further understand the abuse Diana suffered at the hands of senior members of the royal family.

---

[a] See Part 2 – Prince Philip, Nature of the Relationship.

[b] The general evidence indicates that there was a significant decline in the Philip-Diana relationship at some point after 1992 – the 1992 letters show that they communicated cordially at that stage, but later events, such as the 1995 *Panorama* interview, could have led to a deterioration in their relationship.

[c] Diana's.

Rosa then, I suggest, has not just defended Philip, in this 2002 article, but has attempted to undermine evidence that is in Diana's interest – that she was subjected to abuse from Philip in the form of letters describing her as a harlot and trollop. It may be in Diana's interest that these later vitriolic letters – which really have gone missing[a] – are found and made public. These letters may help explain the witness evidence that Diana feared Philip.

It will be shown in the Conclusion[b] that since 1997, Rosa – with the help of the British media – has set herself up as Diana's "best friend" and "most loyal ally".

This article appears to reveal that this perception is false. When Simmons went to the press with a genuine account – she has no apparent reason to lie on this – Rosa is the first person to stand up publicly to Philip's defence, but not Diana's defence.

Rosa defends a person who Diana feared.[cd]

The introduction of this *Telegraph* article at the inquest also placed Rosa in a situation where she had to then tell additional lies to protect her position on the Philip letters – "I would not have made the association" between the police search and the letter copies; "I would not have thought that [the letter copies] were in any way relevant to the [Burrell] trial".

Earlier Rosa had handed over copies of the Philip letters to the inquest. In doing that, she had to falsely claim possession since 1992 – when Diana gave them to her. Other evidence shows that Lucia – not Rosa – had copies of the letters from 1992 and at some stage, possibly in the fortnight between the November 2002 *Mail on Sunday* and *Telegraph* articles, copies had been passed onto Rosa.

This appears to be why Rosa never admitted to having copies at a point earlier than the inquest[e] and therefore was forced into lying to Mansfield, by

---

[a] The issue of the missing box – which contained letters – is addressed in Part 6.

[b] Of this chapter.

[c] One would think that if Rosa was a true friend of Diana, she could have made an effort to find out more about these later vitriolic letters – instead of blindly declaring that they didn't exist.

[d] It is interesting that during the inquest into the death of Diana, it is a perceived attack on Philip that appeared to make Rosa Monckton emotional: Burnett: "You are aware, I know, that it has been suggested that the Duke wrote nasty letters to Diana, that they were unkind and vituperative. All sorts of words have been used...." Rosa: "[The letters] were very – sorry, I am finding it difficult to concentrate with that. They were very thoughtful...." Rosa also appears to make it sound as though this was the first she had heard of it – even though she has just been told that Burnett knows she is aware – but it comes out later that she had already done a media interview in 2002 dedicated to the nature of the letters.

[e] Because she could have had to lie about how they came into her possession.

claiming she couldn't see any connection between the police search for letters, the Burrell trial and the copies of the letters that she handed into the inquest.

14)   Mansfield asked Rosa about where Diana kept the Philip letters. Rosa: "I have no idea, but she told me that she was going to keep them very safe...." Mansfield tried again: "So you don't know where she kept this very important correspondence?" Rosa: "No, I do not."

In the 2003 article Lucia told Kay that "the Princess kept the letters, together with copies of her responses ... in a safe at the [Brazilian] embassy".

It may not be a coincidence that Rosa described "a very safe place" and Lucia revealed that the letters were kept "in a safe".

Other evidence – see earlier and later – indicates that it is likely Rosa would have known Lucia had the letters, but has withheld that information from Mansfield.

Rosa's claimed ignorance of the location of Diana's copies of the letters – Lucia's embassy safe – distances Rosa from the source from which she appears to have later received her copies: Lucia.

I suggest Lucia was also the source from which Rosa learned of the Philip letters. This is addressed in the scenario below.

15)   In his Opening Remarks Baker said: "Where [the Philip letters] went and whether they still exist remains a mystery. We shall have to see whether the mystery unfolds in the coming weeks...."

In his Summing Up, at the conclusion of the inquest, he explained what had transpired: "Diana had faxed a number of letters to Rosa Monckton and she, in turn, provided me with copies of those faxes. She also provided copies of drafts she had compiled for Diana to use in answer and these she produced before you. Following receipt of what Rosa Monckton had in her possession, inquiries of the Palace revealed that the Duke of Edinburgh had copies of the letters he had written to Diana and also the original responses from Diana.... My office asked for a complete set of correspondence and Hunt-Davis in turn asked the Duke."

This account from Scott Baker raises serious concerns:

a) Baker has said that Rosa "provided me with copies of ... faxes" of the Philip letters.

Rosa's evidence is that the Philip letters were passed on from Diana "either in my flat or in Kensington Palace, or if, for some reason, we could not meet up, she would fax them to me".[a]

The earlier table on the Philip letters – which is mostly taken from the Burnett cross-examination of Rosa, based on her inquest statement – reveals

---

[a] When Rosa was first asked, "How did you receive those letters?" she made no mention of faxes, but instead described Diana coming around to her flat with the first letter – see earlier.

that there were five letters, three of which Rosa had stated were faxed. We are not told how she received the other two letters – which are the first and fifth – but Rosa said at the inquest that Diana brought the first letter "round to our flat in Cambridge Street". Based on Rosa's account – "my flat or in Kensington Palace" or faxed – that would leave the fifth letter being passed to Rosa at Kensington Palace.

There are two main problems with this:

i) Rosa's inquest account – and that is all we have[a] – indicates that faxing was only a last resort: "if, for some reason, we could not meet up". Faxing is mentioned as the third option – not the first – yet in her statement, it appears that at least three[b] of the five letters were received by fax.

ii) Baker indicates that all the Philip letters he received from Rosa were copies of faxes – "Diana had faxed a number of letters to Rosa Monckton and she, in turn, provided me with copies of those faxes".

The evidence – see earlier and later – points to Rosa receiving the Philip letters, not from Diana in 1992, but from Lucia in November 2002. And at that time, Lucia was no longer living in London, but had returned to Brazil.[c]

I suggest that Rosa received all the letters by fax – from Lucia in Brazil in 2002.

This could help explain why Rosa's copies of the letters – which were apparently clearer than the photocopies of Philip's carbon copy used by Burnett[d] – were not allowed to be shown to the inquest jury. The fax headers should have been made available, but they weren't. I believe they would show the letters originating from a Brazilian number – not Kensington Palace as was inferred at the inquest.

b) This is an investigation into the death of the ex-daughter-in-law of the Queen and Philip – Princess Diana. Letters were sent from Philip to Diana.

One would think that the Queen and Philip would have been showing an interest in the investigations, as they took place, after 1997.

Bearing in mind that the Philip to Diana letters had already been the subject of contention in the press in November 2002, we see the Paget Report, published in 2006, stating: "No one claims to have possession of any

---

[a] Rosa's police statement was withheld from the jury and has never been made public. Her inquest statement was also withheld.

[b] According to Burnett – who was basing his cross-examination on Rosa's statement. We are not told how Rosa received the other two Philip letters.

[c] Lucia's husband, Paulo Tarso Flecha de Lima, was Brazilian Ambassador to Italy before retiring in 2001 and returning to Brazil.: Wikipedia, http://pt.wikipedia.org/wiki

[d] Burnett: "even on this copy, the date is not that easy to read"; "the signature is lost, at least in this version".

of these [Philip to Diana] letters any longer." Then the following year, on 3 October 2007, the coroner of the inquest said, "whether [the Philip letters] still exist remains a mystery".

All through this, Philip was harbouring carbon copies of the letters in his office at Buckingham Palace. But did Philip offer copies of these letters to Paget or the inquest?

No.

Baker states: "Following receipt of what Rosa Monckton had in her possession, inquiries of [Buckingham] Palace revealed that the Duke of Edinburgh had copies of the letters".

There are two questions:

i) Why did Philip wait for an approach from the inquest before he furnished copies of evidence critical to an investigation into the death of his ex-daughter-in-law?

ii) Why did Scott Baker, coroner for the inquest, wait for Rosa Monckton to produce copies of the letters, before he approached Philip requesting his copies?

I suggest that the answer to these questions is that both Philip and Baker are complicit in withholding, covering up or not seeking evidence until they are placed in a situation where they are forced to act.[a]

c) Baker says he "asked for a complete set of [the Philip-Diana] correspondence" from Philip's office.

It could be significant that the first letter from Philip to Diana – dated 18 June 1992 – is missing from the heavily redacted copies the jury were allowed to see.

The existence of this letter was acknowledged when Burnett cross-examined Miles Hunt-Davis, Philip's private secretary: Burnett – "Perhaps we can first simply identify that the first letter from [Philip] is dated 18th June 1992.... That was a two-page typed letter." That is confirmed by Hunt-Davis, but Burnett continues: "As you indicated earlier, the copy you have is not topped and tailed, as one might call it, so we cannot see that." [238]

Burnett has just stated that the reason the jury "cannot see" that first letter is because it "is not topped and tailed".[b]

Yet just 10 minutes earlier Burnett had told the inquest – confirmed by Hunt-Davis – referring to the full batch of five Philip letters: "The copies of [Philip's] letters ... not on headed notepaper and were not topped and tailed, which would have been done in hand by the Duke himself." [239]

---

[a] In a similar way, the British police held onto and hid evidence from a critical meeting between Victor Mishcon and Princess Diana. This was mentioned in Part 2 and is covered in Part 6.

[b] Someone could argue that Burnett is referring to not being able to see the topping and tailing, but that could only be the case if the letter was being shown to the inquest – it wasn't.

So all the letter copies from Philip "were not topped and tailed".

Later that day, during the cross-examination of Rosa Monckton, Burnett said: "The first letter that you have is [a] ... draft reply to a letter from ... Philip, which you don't in fact have".

This means that the first 18 June 1992 letter was: i) not shown at all to the jury; and ii) was not brought along by Rosa to the inquest.

I suggest that there is a connection.

Why is it that the very same letter that the inquest – which obtained its copies from Philip – didn't show to the jury, was also not brought along to the inquest by Rosa Monckton? [a]

Burnett has evidently lied when he suggests the reason the letter wasn't shown was because it "is not topped and tailed" – all of Philip's copies were not topped or tailed.

Lucia Flecha de Lima's evidence was: "When [Diana] received the first [Philip letter], she was quite upset about it". Lucia also said in her police statement: "[Philip] was sometimes a bit brutal" in the letters.

Towards the end of Diana's reply to that first letter, she wrote: "I am very grateful to you for sending me such a heartfelt and honest letter and I hope you will read mine in the same spirit."

This could be interpreted to mean that Diana read that first letter in a positive spirit – "I hope you will read mine in the same spirit". She appears to suggest that if she hadn't chosen to read the letter in that spirit, it could have been taken quite differently – in which case her sentiment may not have been "grateful", but something else.

There is a possibility that the first letter contained – even if it had been heavily redacted as all the other letters were[b] – material that Philip, or Baker, or both, didn't want the jury to see. In other words, there may have been no sentences in this first letter deemed viewable by the jury. It may not have contained the niceties at the beginning and end that some of the later letters had – written after the receipt of Diana's initial generous reply.[ca]

---

[a] This raises the possibility of another instance of collaboration between Rosa and Philip – as occurred in the fortnight before the 23 November 2002 Buckingham Palace press release and following *Telegraph* article – see earlier.

[b] The other letters are shown on the inquest website – reference numbers have been given in an earlier footnote.

[c] In 2004 Andrew Morton wrote about Diana's reaction to the first Philip letter: "[Diana] was so alarmed when the first letter was delivered that she telephoned a friend and asked him to recommend a solicitor to help draft a suitable reply. He in turn contacted me, but in the time that it took me to produce a couple of names, the Princess had already found her own lawyer.": *Diana: In Pursuit of Love*, p76. The context here is that the first excerpts of Morton's 1992 book *Diana: Her True Story*,

d) Baker said: "[Rosa] ... provided copies of drafts she had compiled for Diana to use in answer and <u>these she produced before you</u>."

This appears to be a bald-faced lie. The only copies shown to the jury were the four letters from Philip[b] – produced by Buckingham Palace – and the five replies from Diana – also produced by Buckingham Palace.

The reason why the jury were never shown the typed-up[c] draft replies should become apparent as this progresses.

The following scenario includes some speculation but is based on the available evidence.

When Princess Diana received the first 18 June 1992 letter from Prince Philip, the evidence indicates that she called Lucia Flecha de Lima – who at that time was living in London – for assistance.

It appears that Diana continued looking to Lucia for help with replying to Philip's letters during the three months that the correspondence continued – June to September 1992.

At Diana's request, Lucia kept copies of Philip's letters and Diana's replies.

On 1 November 2002 the Queen triggered the collapse of the Burrell trial, by suddenly remembering details of a post-Paris crash conversation with Paul Burrell.[d] This intervention had the effect of preventing witnesses – including Simone Simmons – from recounting evidence that could have been damaging to the royal family.

Nine days later, on 10 November 2002, the *Mail on Sunday* published an interview with Simmons, who stated that she had seen nasty letters from

---

which was written in collaboration with Diana, appeared in the *Sunday Times* from 7 June 1992, just 11 days before Philip's first letter. This timing raises the possibility that Philip's first letter to Diana was in direct response to the revelations from the Morton book – it may have been nothing to do with helping with the Diana-Charles marriage problems.

[a] In this light, it should be noted that the redactions on the letters from Philip to Diana were significantly heavier than those on the letters from Diana to Philip: a) the first letter (June 18) from Philip was completely withheld – all Diana's letters were shown; b) the beginning and end of all Diana's letters were shown. When it came to Philip's, only the beginning and end of one letter was shown – the July 7 one – and the beginning only, of the letters written on June 25, July 20 and September 28. Inquest website reference numbers to the letters have been shown earlier.

[b] The first (June 18) letter from Philip was not shown – see above.

[c] By Rosa.

[d] It is not the purpose of this book to provide detail on the Burrell trial – it was fully covered in press reports from the period. It also came up at various times throughout the inquest – during the cross-examination of Rosa Monckton, Michael Mansfield introduced it at 13 Dec 07: 161.16.

Philip describing Diana as a harlot and a trollop. Simmons later told the police that these letters would have been written post-1992.[a]

Two weeks later – on Saturday, 23 November 2002 – Philip put out a press release stating that he never wrote letters of the nature described by Simmons, to Diana.

The next day, November 24, the *Sunday Telegraph* published an article quoting Rosa Monckton supporting Philip's account – she said she had read the letters and had helped Diana reply to them.

The evidence indicates that Rosa had collaborated with Philip – probably at his request – to provide a united front to undermine the Simmons account.

In the fortnight between the *Mail on Sunday* and *Telegraph* articles Rosa appears to have made contact with Lucia Flecha de Lima in Brazil. Lucia has faxed her copies of the Philip letters to Rosa, who was then able to read them.[b] Rosa appears to have told Lucia that she would tell the press that she had helped Diana with the replies to the Philip letters.

In November 2003 Lucia Flecha de Lima was interviewed by Richard Kay of the *Daily Mail* – he writes that Rosa also helped Diana reply to the Philip letters. Lucia may have told Kay this, but it seems more likely that he added this himself, basing it on Rosa's *Telegraph* account of the previous year, 2002.[c]

Operation Paget officers interviewed Rosa on 7 July and Lucia on 1 September 2004. The pair appear to have collaborated to minimise mention of their role in the Philip letters. Rosa did not claim any role – this was true, but it was contrary to Rosa's 2002 *Telegraph* article account. Lucia now minimised her role to reading the Philip letters, with no mention at all that she helped Diana reply to them.[d]

---

[a] This is addressed in Part 2.

[b] Rosa would have sourced the letters from Lucia – and not from Philip – to avoid a trail connecting her to Buckingham Palace and to have copies of what Diana received. The Palace copies were carbon copies – see earlier.

[c] It is not shown as a direct quote from Lucia. Also, in that article, when Lucia is quoted regarding the letters, she makes no mention of Rosa Monckton, but talks as though she is helping Diana on her own: "I wish I had spoken to Prince Philip because I am sure if he had known my side of the story, he could have helped Diana more effectively. But I thought he would refuse to see me or, worse, ask why an ambassador's wife was interfering in a private family matter. In retrospect, knowing what I do, I wish I'd taken that risk and perhaps I could have helped."

[d] There is a possibility that Paget officers told Lucia and Rosa to minimise their accounts regarding the Philip letters, maybe telling them that it wasn't central to the case. Simone Simmons' evidence regarding the later letters receives very brief coverage in the Paget Report: "[Simmons] stated that HRH Prince Philip wrote '…nasty letters to Diana and also to Sarah Ferguson' around 1993/1994, but these

It was a different story from Rosa when these two women prepared to give their evidence to the Diana inquest – the high profile public forum that was set to investigate the cause of the deaths of Princess Diana and Dodi Fayed.

It appears Rosa and Lucia again collaborated. Lucia again downplayed her role – read the letters, but no mention of helping. Instead Lucia, who gave her evidence after Rosa[a], confirmed Rosa helped with the replies.

Rosa pieced together an elaborate but fictional story of how she was phoned – just four months after she claims she first met Diana – by a distraught Diana who visited her with the first 18 June 1992 Philip letter.

Rosa's fictional testimony included a detailed – but at times conflicting – account of Rosa and her MI6 agent husband, Dominic Lawson, helping Diana furnish replies to all five of the Philip letters.

The evidence indicates that at the inquest Rosa fully usurped Lucia's role as the helper to Diana's replies – with the apparent complete acquiescence of Lucia.[b]

In doing this, Rosa created a graphic picture of a helpless and emotionally befuddled Princess Diana – "she was very, very upset, very tearful"; "a letter from anybody would have made her cry" – not supported by any other witness.

Why did Rosa orchestrate this false evidence?

Rosa's sworn evidence of selflessly rescuing and helping the emotionally distraught Princess Diana in an hour of great need has provided Rosa with much credibility in her endeavour to be viewed by the public as Diana's best friend.[c]

Why would Rosa need to be seen as Diana's best friend?

Because then Rosa becomes automatically distanced from her true role as an MI6 agent who was actually working against Diana – see earlier.

Prior to the inquest, as part of this role reversal between Lucia and Rosa, Rosa must have sought Lucia's help to be prepared to downplay her own role regarding the Philip letters.

I suggest that Rosa arranged to receive[d] from Lucia copies of Diana's replies to Philip's letters, and that Rosa used these as a basis for typing up the

---

stopped at the time of the divorce. She read some of these letters and explained how the content of the letters was nasty in a personal sense, not a threatening one.": Paget Report, p127.

[a] Rosa was cross-examined on 13 and 14 December and Lucia, a few days later, on 18 December 2007.

[b] Lucia may have been happy to comply in order to help protect Rosa's image. She could have been talked into this by Rosa.

[c] This public perception of Rosa as best friend will be addressed further in the Conclusion section.

[d] Or, borrow.

"draft replies" – not typed in 1992, but at some point prior to the 2007 inquest.[a] These typed draft replies were never viewed by anyone other than Rosa and Baker[b] – Baker lying in his Summing Up to the jury, when referring to the draft replies: "these she produced before you".

Rosa then falsely claimed at the inquest that the draft replies had been typed back in 1992 and were used by Diana in submitting her replies to Philip.[cd]

In what seems to be an amazing piece of excessive distancing[e], Rosa Monckton claimed at the inquest that she didn't know anything about publicity regarding Diana's copies of the Philip letters going missing.[f] She supported her ignorance by claiming: "I very deliberately have not read a single book about [Diana]. I might have seen the occasional newspaper article if it was a headline".[g]

This claim to be ignorant of the missing letters – and even anything to do with publicity regarding Diana post-crash – could have been a crude ploy by Rosa to distance herself from involvement in suspect actions regarding the letters. In other words, Rosa is saying: "If I am that uninterested and unaware of news regarding the Philip letters, then how could I possibly be involved in any illegal activity or fabrication of evidence connected to them?"

---

[a] Had the draft replies needed to have been aged back to 1992, MI6 are known to be experts in that type of procedure.

[b] They were not included in the inquest evidence dossier.

[c] It was the draft replies that provided the "proof" that Rosa helped Diana – if Rosa had only been able to supply the inquest with copies of the Philip letters, that would not be documentary proof that she helped Diana. Likewise, Lucia's copies of Diana's actual replies – not divulged to the inquest – would also not be proof of helping. It had to be draft replies.

[d] At the inquest Lucia withheld her evidence that she in fact had copies of Diana's actual replies – this effectively removed knowledge of the critical link that enabled Rosa to be able to type up the draft replies. Without Lucia's letter copies of Diana's replies – which the jury were unaware of – it makes Rosa's draft reply evidence more plausible.

[e] Excessive distancing has been discussed earlier – a person distances themselves from knowledge or involvement by making an incredible claim that is unlikely to be true.

[f] Even Ian Burnett, the inquest lawyer, seemed to find this strange, and he asked two more questions to get clarification: "Does it mean, therefore, that you did not read books and article about the Princess and the myriad people who have published accounts of their relationships? All of this you did not bother with?" And then: "So you have never hunted out that sort of press coverage?"

[g] This, even though her husband was the editor of one of the newspapers.

But later Rosa was to claim that she had copies of the Philip letters, and not only that, she also had draft replies.

In short, I believe it was decided that the Diana inquest would be the public forum where it would become set in concrete, through witness and documentary evidence, that Rosa Monckton was a very close, possibly the closest, friend of Princess Diana. When Diana received upsetting letters from Philip, the first person she consulted was not Lucia Flecha de Lima, not Susan Kassem, not Annabel Goldsmith – it was Rosa Monckton.

This strategy, based completely on false evidence, was devised to officially distance Rosa from her true role as an MI6 agent, working against Princess Diana. If Rosa was a close friend, then she couldn't have been working for MI6 against Diana.

The evidence the inquest heard regarding the Philip letters played a huge part in creating this false perception.

Conclusion

The question is: Did Diana's friend, Rosa Monckton, play a role in the events leading to the Paris crash that took the lives of Princess Diana and Dodi Fayed?

In determining the answer, an additional key question is: What was the true nature of the relationship between Princess Diana and Rosa Monckton?

The public perception – which is generally moulded by the media – could be that Rosa was Diana's best friend, or at the least, a very close friend. This is the image that the British newspapers and magazines have consistently portrayed:

- "Rosa Monckton: long-time friend in whom Diana confided" – BBC News, 31 August 1997 [240]
- "Rosa Monckton, one of the Princess's closest friends" – Sunday Telegraph, 24 November 2002
- "[Rosa Monckton] was a rock to her friend Princess Diana" – ES[a] Magazine, 10 November 2006 [241]
- "Diana's best friend, Rosa Monckton" – The Telegraph, 27 August 2007 [242]
- "Rosa Monckton: Diana's most loyal ally" – The Times, 28 August 2007 [243]
- "Rosa Monckton is ... famous for being best friends with ... Princess Diana" – You Magazine[b], 21 October 2007 [244]
- "Diana was a true friend, weeps [Diana's] closest confidante Rosa [Monckton]"[a] – Daily Mail, 14 December 2007 [245]

---

[a] Evening Standard.
[b] Daily Mail magazine.

- "one of [Diana's] closest friends, Rosa Monckton" – The Telegraph, 16 December 2007 [246]
- Rosa Monckton, best friend of ... Diana" – Daily Mail, 29 April 2011.[247]

Is this media and public perception – that Rosa and Diana were best friends – true?

It was strongly supported at the 2007 inquest by Rosa's account that she was the one Diana rushed to after she received upsetting letters from Prince Philip.

This has been shown to be a false account.

There is now a significant amount of evidence that points to this "best friend" perception not only being untrue, but being the opposite of the truth:[b]

- Rosa's brother Anthony is a known MI6 officer
- Rosa's husband Dominic Lawson is a known MI6 agent
- the timing of Rosa's initial meeting with Diana fits with a period when Buckingham Palace was concerned that Diana was cooperating with Andrew Morton on the compilation of a book that could have been damaging to the royal family
- there is a significant degree of conflicting evidence on the circumstances that led to the initial meeting between Diana and Rosa
- Rosa has provided a false account of Diana seeking her advice on an upcoming holiday with Mohamed Al Fayed, before the offer of the holiday was even made
- Rosa organised to borrow a boat[c] from "friends" to go on a cruise with Diana[d] less than 18 days after British intelligence would have become aware of Diana accepting the Mohamed holiday offer and also making a very public address stating she was on a personal crusade against landmines
- Diana was assassinated in Paris just 11 days after the conclusion of her boating holiday with Rosa
- there is credible evidence indicating Diana was aware of Rosa's MI6 connections and didn't trust her

---

[a] This was a headline referring to a statement made by Rosa during her cross-examination by Michael Mansfield – "we were proper true friends": 14 Dec 07: 6.15.
[b] The evidence covered here should be viewed with the knowledge that MI6 is an extremely secretive organisation – see earlier – and information about the status and activities of agents and officers is hidden from public knowledge.
[c] Rosa has never supplied a name for this boat and wasn't asked for it at the inquest.
[d] It may not be a coincidence that MI6 officer, Sherard Cowper-Coles – who was the Head of the Hong Kong Department at the time (see earlier) – would have been in Hong Kong at the same time as Rosa Monckton, for the handover.

- there are substantial areas of conflict in most of the key points of Rosa Monckton's evidence at the inquest – including: a) conflict with the accounts of other witnesses; b) conflict with other accounts Rosa has given; and c) conflict within her own inquest evidence[a]

- Rosa is the only "friend" who rang Diana during her final week – all nine others, who have related how the call occurred, say that Diana rang them

- at the inquest, with Lucia Flecha de Lima's help, Rosa provided false evidence claiming that she assisted Diana with the replies to Philip's 1992 letters – when the truth is that Lucia fulfilled that role[bc]

- when Rosa was asked to read the closing excerpt of a letter from Diana to Philip, she misread "from, Diana" with "yours, Diana" – all nine letters, to various people, reproduced at the inquest closed with "from, Diana"

- there is evidence of Rosa colluding with Philip – a person who Diana feared – to protect his reputation, at the expense of Diana's interests.[de]

Rosa said to Mansfield at the inquest: "We were proper true friends"[248], but the evidence indicates otherwise.

And the question is then raised: Why has Rosa promoted her friendship with Diana to a level that was never achieved?

There has to be a reason.

The evidence points to Rosa being connected to MI6, and – although the evidence is primarily circumstantial because of the secrecy of MI6 – it also points to Rosa working for MI6 against Princess Diana.

This is not to suggest that Rosa was directly involved in Diana's assassination – it is possible that Rosa was as shocked as the next person when she first heard about the crash in the Alma Tunnel.[f] Rosa's role against

---

[a] Meaning, at one point during the inquest cross-examination she may have said something which she contradicts at another point in her inquest testimony.

[b] At the inquest Lucia appears to have provided a supporting role to Rosa in the manipulation of evidence regarding the Philip letters – see earlier.

[c] Rosa also provided copies of the Philip letters to the coroner. Earlier Lucia had stated she had copies of the letters, but did not produce anything for the coroner. The significance of this has been discussed earlier.

[d] When Rosa was asked by Burnett about the frequency of her meetings with Diana, post-1992, she appeared to be evasive: Burnett: "During that period [1992 to 1996], did you continue to see [Diana] frequently?" Rosa: "Yes, I did." Burnett: "With what sort of frequency?" Rosa: "Well, it would depend on her schedule and mine because I was running Tiffany's and she was very busy too. But we met when we could, which was very often."

[e] Rosa Monckton doesn't receive a mention in Diana's bodyguard, Ken Wharfe's book, even though he didn't resign until late 1993, over 18 months after Rosa and Diana met.

[f] I suggest that there are several MI6 agents who were involved, but who would have been unaware of the intention to assassinate – e.g. Henri Paul and Claude Roulet (Part 1).

Diana would have been to seek information and intelligence on her intentions – regarding moving overseas, her anti-landmine campaign, her feelings about the Establishment and the royal family and by August 1997, her relationship with Dodi Fayed.

MI6 operates on a "need to know" basis[a] – and it is unlikely that Rosa would have needed to know that Diana was going to be eliminated.

Rosa went to great lengths at the inquest – particularly regarding the Philip letters evidence – to claim that she was very close to Diana. The automatic effect of that belief is that it discounts the relevance of other evidence that came out, that she had a connection to MI6. And it makes it very unlikely that any jury member would have been taking the MI6 connection any further – to asking themselves if Rosa was actually employed as an MI6 agent.

The establishing of Rosa Monckton being the best friend of Princess Diana is one of the major myths that have emerged since the 1997 Paris crash, with the main witness who could either confirm or deny it – Diana herself – dead and buried.

There is no question that there was some sort of a friendship – Diana was godmother to Rosa's daughter, Diana arranged for the burial of Rosa's stillborn baby in her Kensington Palace yard[b] – but the evidence shows the level of it has been grossly exaggerated.

The fact that there was a relationship between Rosa Monckton and Princess Diana does not mean that Rosa was not an MI6 agent. It is standard procedure for an MI6 agent to come across as normal as possible[c] and it would have been essential for Rosa to befriend Diana in order to obtain useful intelligence from her. The Rosa-Diana friendship has been made to look very close and completely normal – but the evidence in this chapter has revealed otherwise.

On top of lying at the inquest, Rosa Monckton was generally an evasive witness – an analysis of her cross-examinations reveals she replied to questions with "I have no idea" 7 times, she couldn't remember something 40 times and couldn't recall information or events on 11 occasions. That makes 58 times all up that Rosa Monckton failed to provide information that was requested of her at the inquest.

Evidently Rosa Monckton had something to hide from the inquest – I believe this chapter has helped shed light on what that might have been.

---

[a] See earlier.

[b] Since her death, Rosa has been involved in Diana's memorial fund – this appears to have helped promote her standing as an ally of Diana.

[c] That is part of the culture of secrecy and deceit – see earlier.

The evidence indicates that there has been a massive effort to cover up the true nature of the relationship between Princess Diana and Rosa Monckton. The now generally accepted view is that Rosa was Diana's "best friend" – the build-up of evidence reveals something quite different: that Rosa Monckton acted against Princess Diana as an agent working on behalf of MI6.

1D   Other Intelligence Issues

Threats to Other People[a]

Trevor Rees-Jones

Trevor Rees-Jones and his Paris lawyer, Christian Curtil, both received threats prior to the first anniversary of the crash, in August 1998.

Trevor Rees-Jones, Dodi's Bodyguard: 23 Jan 08: 106.10:

Burnett: Q. Was there a time after the events that we have been talking about when you were working for a sports shop in Oswestry, close to where you come from?

A. Yes, sir. That was whilst I was recovering from the accident.

Q. Did you receive some anonymous letters and telephone calls?

A. Yes, sir, I did, yes.

Q. Can you tell us how many of each, roughly, and over what period?

A. I can't remember over what period of time it was, but there was probably two or three letters and a number of telephone calls on one day.

Q. On one day?

A. On one day only, yes.

Q. Were there telephone calls to the shop?

A. To the shop, sir, yes.

Q. And the letters to the shop as well?

A. I believe they were either to myself or through the solicitors' office.

Q. I see. What was the nature of the anonymous communication or communications that you were getting?

A. I don't remember the specifics of the letters. They were generally slightly

---

[a] Evidence in this section should be viewed in the light of the earlier section in Part 2: Fears of and Threats to Other People.

threatening in nature. I didn't take them seriously and I believe I just threw them away. The telephone calls were stating that they know who I am, they know where I work, where I live and to keep quiet. That was the sort of general nature of the telephone call.

Q. No indication of who it was who was talking to you?

A. They said "You know who we are".

Q. Did you?

A. No, I didn't.

Q. But at all events you didn't take it seriously?

A. No, I told them to – if they knew where I was, to come to the shop and see me.

Q. And did they?

A. No.

Trevor Rees-Jones, Dodi's Bodyguard: 2000 Book: **Jury Didn't Hear**:
On 26 August 1998 Trevor Rees-Jones "was working ... when a call came in for him. A man asked for Trevor Rees-Jones, and ... said 'You keep your mouth shut.' The man went on about being from MI6.... Seconds later he called again...."You know who we are".... Next time he called [he said] 'Keep your mouth shut or we'll come round and sort you out. We'll do you.'" [249]

Trevor Rees-Jones, Dodi's Bodyguard: 2000 Book: **Jury Didn't Hear**:
"Christian [Curtil][a] had been receiving threatening calls and letters for several months. At 8.30 a.m., a week before the [crash] anniversary [in August 1998], his secretary took a call from a male voice, saying, 'I'm a new client. I want to speak to M. Curtil.' 'He'll be arriving at any moment,' she responded. A few minutes after nine, Christian ... was approaching the elevator when a tall, rather fat man in a white turban stepped out of the shadows and punched him in the face, striking a blow to the cheek that made Christian faint momentarily, and stumble off balance. The attacker said nothing, made no attempt to steal his wallet, and then vanished.... Shortly, the man called again, and Christian took his call. 'I'll get you another time' was all he said." [250]

Comment: The timing of these incidents – to both Trevor Rees-Jones and Christian Curtil – appears to be significant.

Curtil was assaulted a week before the crash anniversary – so, around 24 August 1998. Two days later, Rees-Jones received threatening calls – "keep your mouth shut".

The anniversary is a significant period – it is just the time when there would be a natural expectation of renewed media interest in the crash and fresh interviews would be sought after.

---

[a] Trevor Rees-Jones' Paris lawyer.

These incidents may have been a warning – or reminder – from MI6 for Rees-Jones and his lawyer not to speak out on the details of the crash.

This evidence should be viewed in the context of Trevor Rees-Jones' loss of memory of the circumstances of the crash – that issue is addressed in Part 6.

It could be significant that at the inquest:

a) the issue of Curtil's assault was missed out altogether – Curtil obviously should have been interviewed for a statement, or cross-examined

b) Rees-Jones was expected to rely on his nine year old memory of the threats. Instead the jury should have been read the excerpt from Rees-Jones' book, shown above. The fact that in 2008 – 9½ years later – Rees-Jones still appeared to recall some of the detail of the conversations indicates that at the time they had a major impact on him.

Hasnat Khan

Hasnat Khan, Diana's boyfriend from 1995 to 1997, described receiving threats, and said in his police statement: "I would be very naive to think that MI5 or MI6 did not have an interest in me because of my relationship with the Princess of Wales.... I never asked too many questions and Diana was careful not to tell me too much as she wanted to protect me. On the odd occasion when she did try to tell me things, I used to stop her because it was none of my business, it did not interfere with my life and I did not want to be put in a position where I knew too much."

The evidence regarding the threats to Hasnat Khan has already been addressed in Part 2[a] – also included in that volume are the fears of Simone Simmons, threats to James Hewitt and the death of Diana's bodyguard, Barry Mannakee.

Interference With Witnesses

Bernard Lefort

There is credible evidence from Bernard Lefort – head waiter at Le Bourgogne Bar in Paris – that there was a post-crash attempt to bribe him into altering his evidence. This occurred on 4 September 1997.

This has already been covered in Part 1, in the section on the Roulet Meeting, Chapter 2C.

---

[a] See section on Fears Of and Threats To Other People.

Clifford Gooroovadoo

Clifford Gooroovadoo: 31 Aug 97 6.00 a.m. Statement[a] read out 12 Mar 08: 102.5:
"I would point out that on the way to your [Brigade Criminelle] offices I was followed by a motorcyclist who asked me my name and address because according to him I was the main witness of this incident. I sent this journalist packing and I will inform you if I am approached in the future."
Comment: Gooroovadoo describes this person as "a motorcyclist", but then appears to presume he was a journalist. He doesn't comment on how he drew that conclusion.

There have been instances during this case – see Part 1 – where possible intelligence agents have masqueraded as journalists or paparazzi.

The person who followed Gooroovadoo could have been a journalist, but he also could have been an intelligence agent.

Role of Other Agencies

French and US intelligence agencies provided statements that were read out at the inquest.
Joann Grube, NSA Deputy Director Policy, USA: 5 Nov 98 Letter read out 13 Mar 08: 79.20:
"This is the final response to your Freedom of Information Act request of 9th June 1998 for any and all records, including but not limited to photographs, recordings, e-mail, memos, graphs and video in connection with Lady Diana Frances Spencer.... After subtracting the foreign press articles from the original total of documents, reported to you in our 10th July 1998 letter, 1,349 documents, we processed 182 documents, for possible release. Of these 182 documents, 143 documents have been forwarded to the originating agencies for their direct response to you.
"The remaining 39 NSA originated and controlled documents responsive to your request have been reviewed by this agency as required by the Act, and have been found to be currently and properly classified in accordance with an executive order. These documents meet the criteria for classification as set forth in that order and remain classified 'top secret' as provided. The documents are classified because their disclosure could reasonably be expected to cause exceptionally grave damage to national security."
Robert Tyrer, US Secretary of State for Defence: 13 Oct 99 Letter read out 13 Mar 08: 82.15:
"My review of the documents located by NSA and CIA in response to Freedom of Information Act requests filed on behalf of Mr Al Fayed did not uncover any information pertaining to the deaths of Princess Diana and Dodi Fayed. The materials that I reviewed were identified through electronic

---

[a] This was Gooroovadoo's second statement – his first was taken at 2.30 a.m.

searches of the NSA and CIA databases for documents containing references to Princess Diana and the other individuals mentioned in the Freedom of Information Act requests."

Scott Muller, CIA General Counsel: 19 Nov 03 Description of Letter read out 13 Mar 08: 83.16:

"This letter referred to an independent review conducted by the CIA Inspector General.... The Inspector General concluded 'the review of agency files yielded no information shedding any light on the automobile accident or deaths of Lady Diana and Dodi Fayed and also this office found no information that would lend credibility to the media reports'.

"Mr Muller's letter also referred to a CIA Directorate of Operations response stating that it's records searches had not located 'any cables concerning information about an alleged involvement of the British Royal Family, Government or intelligence services in the deaths of Princess Diana or Dodi Fayed', or any records indicating that 'the CIA in any way might have been supportive of such a conspiracy'. Mr Muller referred to a public statement by the CIA Office of Public Affairs, stating that 'any allegations of CIA involvement in the death of the Princess were ludicrous and absurd'. At the end of this letter, Mr Muller noted that documents to which he had referred had been provided to Mr Al Fayed in November 2002."

Lewis Giles, NSA Director of Policy: 20 Mar 06 Letter read out 13 Mar 08: 85.9:

"I have personally reviewed the 39 NSA originated and NSA controlled documents referenced by Joann Grube.... I can state that these documents contain no information shedding any light on the circumstances surrounding the death of Princess Diana and Dodi Fayed in the 1997 Paris car accident. Furthermore, I can categorically confirm that NSA did not target Princess Diana nor collect any of her communications.

"The NSA documents acquired from intelligence gathering of international communications contain only short references to Princess Diana in contexts unrelated to the allegations being made by Mr Mohamed Al Fayed. The documents, however, must remain classified as their disclosure could reasonably be expected to cause exceptionally grave damage to the national security of the United States by revealing intelligence sources and methods."

Mark Hodges, Senior Paget Investigator: 10 Mar 08 Statement read out 13 Mar 08: 84.20:

"In the course of the Operation Paget investigation, a formal request was made to the legal attaché at the US Embassy in London, asking that the US authorities either give Paget officers access to the documents which had previously been withheld from disclosure, or that the records be reviewed again in the light of detailed information about the allegations which Paget were investigating. For that purpose, Paget provided a summary of the conspiracy allegations to the US Embassy. The NSA chose to perform a further review of records rather than to release to Paget officers the classified documents."

Jean-François Clair, Deputy Head of DST: 23 Jun 05 Letter read out 13 Mar 08: 76.20:

"Henri Paul, born 3rd July 1956 in Lorient, is known to our department as a former head of security at the Ritz Hotel, 15 Place Vendôme, Paris. As such, Henri Paul has been in touch with members of the DST specifically tasked with inquiries in hotel circles."

M. Henry, Brigade Criminelle Commandant: 16 Jun 05 Verbal Statement Description read out 13 Mar 08: 78.15:

"Commandant Henry of the Brigade Criminelle informed Detective Sergeant Easton[a] that neither Henri Paul nor James Andanson[b] was known to the DGSE and that neither was an informant of that organisation nor had been employed by them. Commandant Henry said that the DGSE was unwilling to record the information in a statement as it would set a precedent, and they would require an exemption from the French Official Secrets Act. This conversation is recorded in a message."

Coroner: Summing Up: 31 Mar 08: 75.21:

"There have been various suggestions made over the years that other countries' intelligence agencies were involved in some way in the murder of Diana and Dodi. There really is no evidence of that. Nonetheless, for completeness, I remind you that both the French and American intelligence agencies were contacted and you heard their denials." [c]

Comment: Scott Baker refers to "suggestions ... that other countries' intelligence agencies were involved in ... the murder of Diana and Dodi". He states that "there ... is no evidence of that' and then reminds the jury: "Both the French and American intelligence agencies were contacted and you heard their denials".

In saying this, Baker has drawn a connection between intelligence involvement in "the murder of Diana and Dodi" and the denials from the "French and American intelligence agencies".

In other words, Baker is indicating that the French and US intelligence agencies – DST, DGSE, CIA, NSA – have denied involvement in the Paris crash.

---

[a] British police officer.

[b] Driver of the white Fiat Uno – see Part 1.

[c] The denials from the NSA and CIA have been addressed in the Intelligence Agencies section of the Surveillance chapter in Part 2. The statements from the French agencies, DGSE and DST, are also included in the section on Links to Intelligence Agencies in the first chapter of Part 1. This section should be viewed in the light of the material included in those other volumes.

But is that true?

This is what the agencies have said:

- CIA: "any allegations of CIA involvement in the death of the Princess were ludicrous and absurd"
- NSA: "NSA did not target Princess Diana nor collect any of her communications"
- DST: "Henri Paul has been in touch with members of the DST specifically tasked with inquiries in hotel circles"
- DGSE: "neither Henri Paul nor James Andanson was known to the DGSE".

The results are mixed.

The CIA statement could be read as a denial of "involvement in the death of the Princess" and the NSA, the communication arm of US intelligence, has said it "did not target Princess Diana".

The NSA may not have targeted Diana themselves, but there is a possibility – that is left open – that they carried out surveillance at the request of another organisation, such as the CIA or MI6. There is certainly a major unresolved question mark over the contents of held material the NSA has that they say must remain "classified because ... disclosure could reasonably be expected to cause exceptionally grave damage to national security".

The information coming from the French agencies – DST and DGSE – is quite different.

DST has confirmed that "Henri Paul has been in touch with members of the DST", whilst DGSE has denied knowledge of him and James Andanson.

The French agencies have not even come close to a denial of involvement in the crash and it appears to be yet another lie on the part of Scott Baker to suggest they have.

In the final analysis, I suggest that the earlier evidence regarding MI6 – that unwanted records get destroyed and lies are told if it's in the national interest – is likely to also apply to agencies from other countries, including the CIA and NSA. If that is the case, then the denials from those organisations become worthless.

Baker has also stated: "There really is no evidence of" overseas intelligence agency involvement in the deaths.

The question though is: How much effort did the inquest put into seeking out evidence of involvement by the CIA, NSA, DST, DGSE or Mossad?

I suggest the answer is: None.

There were no statements or cross-examinations of any officers or agents from any of those organisations who were present in Paris during the weekend of 30-31 August 1997.

So, we find Baker making a categorical closing statement to the jury – "there really is no evidence of that" – on something he appears to know nothing about.

British-French Intelligence Relationship

The evidence from Part 3 has shown that the French authorities were deeply involved in the massive post-crash cover-up. There was also evidence of French prior knowledge of the Diana-Dodi visit, despite later denials.

The general evidence of the case[a] indicates that it would have been extremely difficult to have carried out the orchestrated Alma Tunnel crash without support from inside France.

If MI6 carried out the assassinations, it is likely they would have required support or cooperation from the French intelligence services, DST and DGSE.

Richard Tomlinson, Ex-MI6 Officer: 5 Apr 09 Interview: **Jury Didn't Hear**:

"It's perfectly normal for different intelligence services to work together in close cooperation.... When I was in MI6 I worked quite often with the French intelligence service. I speak French, so I would go off to Paris and talk to the French intelligence services and then we would carry out a joint ... operation....

"There was a protocol that if you were carrying out an operation on a friendly country's soil, you always approach them first and ask for permission, and they are obviously allowed to ask 'why are you doing this?' and they obviously want all the intelligence that might come from it....

"There's a very friendly relationship between all the western intelligence services, some more so than others.... [For example] the New Zealand intelligence service ... is almost regarded as part of the British intelligence service. Most of the Europeans now, especially the northern Europeans, are very, very strongly allied [with the UK]. The French have obviously a much more powerful security apparatus [compared to New Zealand] and they're an ally but ... they're not in the same closeness of alliance as ... New Zealand....

"[The French intelligence] are probably not as powerful as the British, but they're more powerful than most of the other European intelligence services.... Clearly the Americans are just head and shoulders above anyone, with their huge budgets and their huge numbers of personnel.... If you were to look at the European countries, Britain probably has the most global reach.... Germany is quite a well-funded and powerful intelligence service and then the French as well ... are a bit like Britain and have a certain amount of commonwealth around the world.... They're ... not quite as powerful probably as the British, but close."

---

[a] See Parts 1 to 4.

Question: Would the [intelligence] services of one country ever ask another country to look into the activities of the first country's citizens...?
Answer: Yes, absolutely.... For an example, when I was living in France after I had been released from prison and MI6 were wanting to put me under surveillance, they got the French to put me under surveillance and I was under surveillance by the French.... When I was in Switzerland the British asked the Swiss to put me under surveillance.... It's perfectly normal to ask another country." [251a]
Richard Tomlinson, Ex-MI6 Officer: 13 Feb 08: 60.5:
Mansfield: Q. On Friday 31st July, do you see, 1998, shortly before – well, your appointment [with Stéphan] was in September, I believe – you were arrested by the DST – what were the DST?
A. That is the Direction Surveillance Territoire, which is – I would guess the nearest equivalent in Britain is the Special Branch.
Q. – in your Paris hotel room.... What were they asking about, can you remember?
A. No. Principally they wanted to take my computers off me and my PDA, the Psion organiser....
Q. Where did these computers end up, do you know?
A. They took them back to the UK.
Q. They took them back to UK. In this you indicate: "Despite my repeated requests, I was never given any justification for the arrest, was not shown the arrest warrant. Even though I was released without charge, the DST confiscated from me my laptop computer and my organiser. They illegally gave these to MI6 who took them back to the UK. They were not returned for six months...." At that time, were you interviewed by anyone from MI6 in Paris while you were detained?
A. Not by MI6, but by Special Branch officers, police Special Branch officers, who were in Paris, and they interviewed me.... It was them that had requested that the French arrest me, so it was the Special Branch officers who were questioning me via the French officers because the Special Branch could not make questions to me directly on French territory. So the Special

---

[a] In his book Tomlinson relates a situation where DST did work in the 1980s on behalf of MI6: Nahoum Manbar, Nice-based chemical weapons suspect, "was denied entry to Britain [and] put on the first plane back to Nice and MI6 asked the DST ... to keep an eye on him. Through telephone intercepts on Manbar's home and information from other sources the DST established that in 1988 Manbar obtained the plans for a mustard gas plant which he sold at handsome profit to ... a senior Iranian intelligence officer.... The DST picked up Manbar's increasingly frequent telephone conversations with [Joyce] Kiddie [a British businesswoman] and tipped off MI6.": *The Big Breach*, pp180-1.

Branch officers would make questions to the French officers and then the French officers would make the questions to me. So both French and British officers were present at the interviews.

At 65.16: Q. [In January 1999] you booked a chalet in the village of Samoens in the French Alps for ten days snow-boarding and so forth. You picked up your parents from Geneva Airport in a hire car on the evening of January 8th and set off for the French border. At the French Customs post, your car was stopped and you were detained. Four officers from the DST held you for four hours. I am going to pause there. Did they interview you?

A. Yes.

Q. What was it about this time?

A. I cannot remember. They wanted to know what I was doing going to France. They did not say anything specific. It was more like – oh yes, they asked is it true that I work for MI6, so I answered truthfully, and then they asked me what did I do at MI6 and they asked me a lot of questions about my activities in MI6, but I think that was more for their personal curiosity than anything. They asked me some really quite banal questions about guns and weapons. But I think that the impression I had was that they were – the objective of stopping me was to stop me going to France, that they were buying time for someone else to come down from – that is right, because we had to wait for another officer to come down, a more senior officer. So when the more senior officer came down, I was served with papers telling me to get out of the country and not come back again – in fact there was no time limit. I was just told I would have to leave France.

Q.... Was it your belief at the time that this resulted from MI6 activity or advice to the DST?

A. I am absolutely sure even now that that is the only mechanism by which that would happen because I have never broken any law in France, and there is no reason why the French authorities would have ever intervened in that nature if they had not been asked specifically by a foreign intelligence service, and the only foreign intelligence service that could be is MI6.

Coroner: But does it surprise you, Mr Tomlinson, that a foreign country, France or America, should be nervous about your coming to their country, bearing in mind that you were convicted under the Official Secrets Act in this country?

A. It does strike me as strange because why would France be worried about me breaking the Official Secrets Act of Britain? I would have no access to any French secrets. So that does not at all translate into any possibility of me breaking a French law because, even if I had the position to do so, which I do not, I do not know any French secrets, so it is of no interest at all to France to – in fact I have certainly been told by the French authorities on many occasions that they don't give a damn about me breaking the Official Secrets Act in Britain. It is an irrelevance to them. So it is quite clear that both the

French and the Americans were – and indeed the Australians, because I have been refused visas to visit Australia on numerous occasions too – have all been acting at the request or suggestion of Britain. My belief is that that request or suggestion would have come from MI6 because that is the only organisation in Britain which would have been motivated to do that.

Comment: Earlier evidence[a] revealed that ex-MI5 officer, David Shayler, was also arrested by the DST on behalf of the British authorities.[b]

Mr 6 aka Richard Spearman, MI6 Officer. British Embassy, Paris: 29 Feb 08: 62.3:

A. I know there has been some mention of the role of the station in Paris, and our primary role, if you like, as I saw it, was to work closely with our French colleagues in liaison and I think others have spoken to that a bit. Quite clearly, if you are working very closely with your liaison colleagues, you use them and work with them on things, and certainly I am aware of other examples in which we would have asked – we would have asked for assistance and we would not need to have our own, as it were, recourse to our own sources because we would be working with our French colleagues jointly.

Mansfield: Q. The French colleagues are DGSE; yes?

A. We worked with the whole range of French services.

Q. It includes DGSE?

A. It included DGSE, yes.

Comment: The evidence reveals a working relationship between MI6 and French intelligence:

- Tomlinson: "I worked quite often with the French intelligence service"[c]

- Spearman: "our primary role ... was to work closely with our French colleagues in liaison".

Given that the assassinations of Princess Diana and Dodi Fayed occurred on French soil, I suggest that it is common sense that if MI6 were involved they would have been coordinating the action with the assistance of French intelligence.

CIA-MI6 Relationship

The evidence indicates that there is generally a close relationship between MI6 and the CIA.

---

[a] In the section on the Gaddafi assassination plot.

[b] This actually occurred a day after Tomlinson's first DST arrest – Tomlinson was on July 31 and Shayler on August 1, 1998.

[c] Tomlinson was never posted to the Paris embassy. This appears to be evidence of cooperation between MI6 officers based outside France and French intelligence.

Richard Tomlinson, Ex-MI6 Officer: 2001 Book: **Jury Didn't Hear**:
"MI6 were always warm and cordial with CIA liaison because the Americans had such fabulous resources." [252]

Comment: In his extensive book on MI6 special operations, Stephen Dorril describes a long history – despite ups and downs – of close cooperation between MI6 and CIA:

-    1950s: "relations between MI6 and the CIA ... became particularly close, with joint planning on a number of special operations" [253a]

-    1950: "one of the MI6/CIA cooperative operations ... was the Congress for Cultural Freedom" [254]

-    1960s: "Britain's secret intelligence-gathering had come to depend substantially on the cooperation of the US 'cousins'" [255]

-    mid-1970s: Chapman Pincher[b]: between MI6 and CIA "dependence is so great and cooperation so close that I am convinced that the security and intelligence chiefs would go to any lengths to protect the link-up" [256]

-    1970: "the planned uprising to bring down Gaddafi had originally been a joint MI6/CIA affair" [257c]

-    1991: "there was close cooperation between Britain and America over the invasion of Kuwait by Iraq, but the episode served only to emphasise the gulf between the capabilities of the two nations' intelligence services and the subservience of MI6 to its Atlantic partner [CIA]".

The question becomes: Would the CIA have involved itself in the operation to assassinate Princess Diana and Dodi Fayed?

Was the CIA Involved?

Daily Mail: 19 Aug 97 Article: **Jury Didn't Hear**:
"Princess Diana scored her biggest political victory last night when President Clinton said he would support an international ban on landmines by the end of the year. As recently as three months ago, Mr Clinton said it would not be possible to stop the use of landmines until the next century. Since then the

---

[a] Bearing in mind the CIA was only officially created in September 1947, the post-war period of intelligence sharing between the UK and US appeared to provide a strong base for later cooperation. Dorril describes the nature of various MI6/CIA joint operations and intelligence sharing during the 1950s: telephone tapping in Vienna (p131); atomic intelligence (p155); the set-up of a centre in Frankfurt to exploit the assets of the Russian National Labour Council, the NTS (p422); establishment of the Congress for Cultural Freedom (CCF) in Europe (p475). : *MI6: Fifty Years of Special Operations*.

[b] British intelligence writer.

[c] This operation is not to be confused with the 1996 assassination attempt – see earlier – that did not directly involve the CIA. This 1970 plot took place soon after Gaddafi came to power in September 1969 – it was a planned overthrow, not an assassination plot.

anti-mine publicity largely generated by Princess Diana ... has persuaded the White House to change course.

"White House insiders say Diana's campaign has struck a chord with First Lady Hillary Clinton and her daughter Chelsea. 'They have made the President very much aware of Diana's work,' said one aide. He insisted however that in the end Mr Clinton made up his own mind without being 'overly influenced' by his wife and daughter.

"Jerry White, cofounder of the Washington-based Land Mine Survivors Network, said last night: 'Princess Di can be very proud. She was central to pushing Clinton off the fence.' Mr Clinton will send a senior team of officials to Geneva this week to negotiate America's role in what has become known as the 'Canadian Initiative' to ban mines by the end of this year." [258]

CNN: 15 Sep 97 Report: **Jury Didn't Hear**:

"US government sources told CNN the Pentagon became resigned to the possibility of signing the [anti-landmine] treaty when Diana became an active supporter of a ban." [259]

CNN: 17 Sep 97 Report: **Jury Didn't Hear**:

"President Bill Clinton said the United States would not sign the [anti-landmine] treaty. 'There is a line I simply cannot cross' Clinton said." [260]

Mail on Sunday: 30 Nov 97 Article: **Jury Didn't Hear**:

"President Bill Clinton has finally decided not to sign a treaty banning landmines.

"Military leaders from 100 countries gather in Canada on Wednesday to sign the treaty which gained enormous momentum following the death of Princess Diana who campaigned vigorously for its acceptance.

"Up to the last minute there has been intense diplomatic and human rights pressure on Mr Clinton to sign – even his wife Hillary is in favour – but he shares the Pentagon's view that the US still needs landmines. The US has a million antipersonnel devices buried in South Korea and refuses to clear them in case there is an invasion from the North.

"The Ottawa treaty requires nations to destroy all stockpiles within four years and all minefields in a decade. Mr Clinton says the US has destroyed 1.5 million mines and plans to destroy a further 1.5 million more than any other nation. He is also increasing the American de-mining budget by 25 per cent. He said: 'It's a question of how the treaty is worded and the unwillingness of some people to entertain change in the wording.'" [261]

Jon King, Investigative Writer: 2001 Book: **Jury Didn't Hear**:

On Saturday 23 August 1997, 8 days before the crash, Jon King met with an anonymous US Special Forces veteran and CIA contract agent, who told him: "[This information] came into my possession some short while ago, and it concerns a plot to eliminate one of the most prominent figures on the world stage, someone like Martin Luther King and John Lennon – someone with the ability to undermine the social and political control mechanisms currently in place.... I do not know precisely where or when the hit will take place. I do not know the precise schedule.... It has been planned for a good many months and it will take place within days from now ... very soon.... This one will be bigger than Kennedy ... even my own sources are extremely nervous about this one.... This person has become a loose cannon on a world stage.... This person has upset an awful lot of very influential, very powerful people....." [262] Jon King stated: "I now suspect that [my contact] was ... perhaps part of a more liberal faction within British and US intelligence who evidently opposed the assassination, but were powerless to prevent it. And who thus decided to spotlight it instead." [263]

OTHER INTELLIGENCE ISSUES

U.S. Government Assassination Plots

The U.S. bombing of Iraq, June 26, 1993, in retaliation for an alleged Iraqi plot to assassinate former president George Bush, "was essential," said President Clinton, "to send a message to those who engage in state-sponsored terrorism ... and to affirm the expectation of civilized behavior among nations."

Following is a list of prominent foreign individuals whose assassination (or planning for same) the United States has been involved in since the end of the Second World War. The list does not include several assassinations in various parts of the world carried out by anti-Castro Cubans employed by the CIA and head-quartered in the United States.

1949 - Kim Koo, Korean opposition leader

1950s - CIA/Neo-Nazi hit list of numerous political figures in West Germany

1950s - Chou En-lai, Prime minister of China, several attempts on his life

1950s, 1962 - Sukarno, President of Indonesia

1951 - Kim Il Sung, Premier of North Korea

1953 - Mohammad Mossadegh, Prime Minister of Iran

1950s (mid) - Claro M. Recto, Philippines opposition leader

1955 - Jawaharlal Nehru, Prime Minister of India

1957 - Gamal Abdul Nasser, President of Egypt

1959, 1963, 1969 - Norodom Sihanouk, leader of Cambodia

1960 - Brig. Gen. Abdul Karim Kassem, leader of Iraq

1950s-70s - José Figueres, President of Costa Rica, two attempts on his life

1961 - Francois "Papa Doc" Duvalier, leader of Haiti

1961 - Patrice Lumumba, Prime Minister of the Congo (Zaire)

1961 - Gen. Rafael Trujillo, leader of Dominican Republic

1963 - Ngo Dinh Diem, President of South Vietnam

1960s - Fidel Castro, President of Cuba, many attempts on his life

1960s - Raúl Castro, high official in government of Cuba

1965 - Francisco Caamaño, Dominican Republic opposition leader

1965-6 - Charles de Gaulle, President of France

1967 - Che Guevara, Cuban leader

1970 - Salvador Allende, President of Chile

1970 - Gen. Rene Schneider, Commander-in-Chief of Army, Chile

1970s, 1981 - General Omar Torrijos, leader of Panama

1972 - General Manuel Noriega, Chief of Panama Intelligence

1975 - Mobutu Sese Seko, President of Zaire

1976 - Michael Manley, Prime Minister of Jamaica

1980-1986 - Muammar Qaddafi, leader of Libya, several plots and attempts upon his life

1982 - Ayatollah Khomeini, leader of Iran

1983 - Gen. Ahmed Dlimi, Moroccan Army commander

1983 - Miguel d'Escoto, Foreign Minister of Nicaragua

1984 - The nine *comandantes* of the Sandinista National Directorate

1985 - Sheikh Mohammed Hussein Fadlallah, Lebanese Shiite leader (80 people killed in the attempt)

1991 - Saddam Hussein, leader of Iraq

1998 - Osama bin Laden, leading Islamic militant

1999 - Slobodan Milosevic, President of Yugoslavia

Figure 8

264

> The above list has been reproduced from William Blum's 1995 book *Killing Hope*.

Comment: The above assassination list put together by highly-respected US investigative journalist, William Blum, reveals the huge involvement by the CIA around the world in assassination plots – right from the beginning of its operations in the late 1940s.

So, clearly the CIA had the resources to assist with the assassination of Princess Diana – they may even be the experts in the assassination business.

Richard Tomlinson also said – referring to the early 1990s period – "the Americans had such fabulous resources".

There are several points that indicate the US intelligence organisation, the CIA, could have been involved in the Paris assassinations:

1) The assassination of Princess Diana by car crash in Paris was an extremely complex and heavily orchestrated operation – see Parts 1 to 4. It is common sense that it could only have been carried out by a very well-resourced organisation.

According to Tomlinson the CIA was the most resourced intelligence organisation in the western world: "Clearly the Americans are just head and shoulders above anyone, with their huge budgets and their huge numbers of personnel".

Stephen Dorril stated – in connection with the 1991 Gulf war – "the episode served only to emphasise the gulf between the capabilities of the [UK and US] intelligence services and the subservience of MI6 to its Atlantic partner [CIA]".

There is a possibility that MI6 would have sought out CIA resources in carrying out the Paris assassinations.

2) There is a long history of cooperation and the conduct of joint operations, between the CIA and MI6 – see Dorril and Tomlinson, above.

Tomlinson's description of "warm and cordial" contact between MI6 and the CIA liaison in the 1990s is supported by Dorril's accounts of cooperation throughout the life of the CIA, from 1950 onwards.[a]

Earlier evidence pointed to the 1996 plot to assassinate Saddam Hussein being a joint CIA/MI6 operation – this occurred the year before the assassination of Princess Diana.

3) The CIA has extensive experience with assassinations – see the Blum list above.

It is the CIA that published, in the 1950s, an assassination manual called "A Study of Assassination".[b] The manual reads: "A further [assassination]

---

[a] The CIA was set up in 1947.

[b] The 19 page document was declassified and approved for release in July 1995. An ebook version by sokol can be viewed at www.whale.to/b/ciaass1.html *A Study of Assassination* states: "No assassination instructions should ever be written or recorded.... No report may be made, but usually the act will be properly covered by normal news services, whose output is available to all concerned.... Killing a political leader whose burgeoning career is a clear and present danger to the cause of freedom

type ... is caused by the need to conceal the fact that the subject was actually the victim of assassination, rather than an accident or natural causes. If such concealment is desirable the operation will be called 'secret'.... Successful secret assassinations are not recorded as assassination at all."

This is what occurred in Paris in 1997 – this "secret" assassination of Diana has been passed off by two police investigations[a] as an "accident".

Under "Planning", the document reads: "All planning must be mental; no papers should ever contain evidence of the operation."

Operation Paget reported that they found no documentary evidence of MI6 involvement in the Paris crash – see earlier.

The manual: "For secret assassination ... the contrived accident is the most effective technique. When successfully executed, it causes little excitement and is only casually investigated."

As has been stated in these volumes, when a person dies by car accident – no matter who they are – it is generally assumed to be an accident.

Under Techniques: "Falls into the sea or swiftly flowing rivers may suffice if the subject cannot swim. It will be more reliable if the assassin can arrange to attempt rescue, as he can thus be sure of the subject's death and at the same time establish a workable alibi."

Although this is not referring to death by a car crash – and car accidents were not recommended[b] – there is a striking similarity to the death of Diana. The SAMU ambulance team, who were the very people expected to assist in saving Diana, actually ensured that the assassination was successfully executed – see Part 2.

The general evidence indicates that both the CIA and MI6 – see earlier – are very much in the assassination business.

---

may be held necessary.... The essential point of assassination is the death of the subject.... Death must be absolutely certain. The attempt on Hitler's life failed because the conspiracy did not give this matter proper attention.... Arson can cause accidental death if the subject is drugged and left in a burning building. Reliability is not satisfactory unless the building is isolated and highly combustible."

[a] In France and the UK.

[b] "Automobile accidents are a less satisfactory means of assassination."

PLANNING

When the decision to assassinate has been reached, the tactics of
the operation must be planned, based upon an estimate of the situation
similar to that used in military operations. The preliminary estimate
will reveal gaps in information and possibly indicate a need for special
equipment which must be procured or constructed. When all necessary data
has been collected, an effective tactical plan can be prepared. All
planning must be mental; no papers should ever contain evidence of the
operation.

In resistance situations, assassination may be used as a counter-
reprisal. Since this requires advertising to be effective, the resistance
organization must be in a position to warn high officials publicly that
their lives will be the price of reprisal action against innocent people.
Such a threat is of no value unless it can be carried out, so it may be
necessary to plan the assassination of various responsible officers of
the oppressive regime and hold such plans in readiness to be used only
if provoked by excessive brutality. Such plans must be modified
frequently to meet changes in the tactical situation.

TECHNIQUES

The essential point of assassination is the death of the subject. A
human being may be killed in many ways but sureness is often overlooked
by those who may be emotionally unstrung by the seriousness of this act
they intend to commit. The specific technique employed will depend upon
a large number of variables, but should be constant in one point: death
must be absolutely certain. The attempt on Hitler's life failed because
the conspiracy did not give this matter proper attention.

Techniques may be considered as follows:

Figure 9

Page 4 of the 19 page undated CIA assassination manual, entitled "A Study
of Assassination". A copy of this document was "found" in the training files
for CIA staff involved in the 1954 Guatemala coup. There are similarities
between the procedures outlined in this document and the methods used in
the conduct of the 1997 assassination of Princess Diana – see point 3 above.
The full document, which was declassified and released on 23 May 1997,
can be viewed at the US National Security Archive – George Washington
University: www.gwu.edu/~nsarchiv/NSAEBB/NSAEBB4/index.html

4) The CNN reports from September 1997[a] reveal that "the Pentagon became resigned to the possibility of signing the [anti-landmine] treaty when Diana became an active supporter of a ban".

On 17 September 1997, just 17 days after the death of Diana, the treaty was agreed by 90 nations in Oslo, Norway[b] – but the US was not one of them. Instead US President Bill Clinton said: "There is a line I simply cannot cross".

Why was Clinton apparently willing to sign the anti-landmine treaty while Diana was alive, but not willing to, just 2½ weeks after she had died?

Diana's anti-landmine campaign appears to be a very real motive for the US – CIA – to have become involved in her assassination.

5) The evidence from Jon King indicates the CIA had prior knowledge of the crash – King received his information from a "CIA contract agent".

Given that information on intelligence operations tends to flow on a "need to know" basis – see earlier – it seems likely that prior knowledge equates with involvement. In other words, if the CIA knew in advance about the assassination of Princess Diana, then it is also likely they were involved in some way.

---

[a] Supported by other media articles shown above.
[b] The treaty was concluded in Oslo in September and signed in Ottawa in December 1997.

1E   Conclusion

Coroner: Summing Up: 31 Mar 08: 10.15:
"There is no evidence that the Secret Intelligence Service or any other Government agency organised it."

Was MI6 involved in the assassinations of Princess Diana and Dodi Fayed?

Quite different to the other four volumes in this series so far, most (but not all) of the evidence in this chapter has been circumstantial – not conclusive or specific documentary or witness evidence[a].

There is a very good reason for that. It lies in the early evidence that showed the central culture of MI6 is based on secrecy and deceit. We have read the witness evidence of many people, but we have also seen that a lot of it is unreliable – primarily because MI6 officers and their agents have a closer allegiance to their perception of the national interest than to the truth, even when speaking under oath in a UK courtroom.

The essence of the problem is that it is possible Princess Diana was perceived by the Establishment to be a threat to the UK national security – this has been covered in the Motives and Surveillance sections of Part 2.

If Diana was deemed a threat to national security that could be seen to provide an MI6 officer or agent with the moral "right" to lie to the inquest, if necessary, to protect the national interest.

We have already seen in earlier volumes, both French and British witnesses appearing to have been provided a "green light" to say whatever

---

[a] Although it has been shown time and again that witnesses have lied – they appear to be covering something up.

they deemed suitable. In other words, many of the witnesses seem to have been promised that they will never be held accountable for anything they have said at the Diana inquest, irregardless of the level of truth or lies they have spoken.

I believe the MI6 witnesses shared that green light and when you add their loyalty to the national interest[a], we end up with a situation where the general MI6 evidence appears to be unreliable.

These issues muddy the waters and make the search for truth extremely difficult.

The question is: Is there enough evidence in these pages for a person to be confident of MI6 involvement in the assassinations of Diana and Dodi?

In summary, the evidence is:

- the nature of the MI6 culture reveals that MI6 witness evidence cannot be relied on in a court of law – in other words, claims by MI6 personnel that they had no involvement in the Paris crash are worthless
- MI6 withheld crucial evidence from the 2007-8 Diana inquest
- British intelligence – MI6, MI5, SAS, SB – have been involved in a long list of assassination plots between 1942 and 1997: MI6 officers lied about this at the inquest
- MI6 was directly involved in two high-level assassination plots – Saddam Hussein and Muammar Gaddafi – in the 18 months leading up to the Paris crash
- there was a concerted effort at the inquest to shut down discussion on MI6 involvement in landmines
- out of an estimated 11 MI6 officers based in Paris at the time of the crash, only one was cross-examined, and his identity was withheld from the inquest jury
- a mix of strong circumstantial and documentary evidence points to the three most senior MI6 Paris-based officers being replaced by Sherard Cowper-Coles, Dr Valerie Caton and Richard Spearman, in the days preceding the crash[b]
- Caton and Cowper-Coles were not heard from at the inquest and Spearman was heard from, but was not identified, not asked about his pre-crash transfer to Paris and wasn't asked about allegations that he was involved in the assassinations

---

[a] Mentioned above.
[b] I suggest it is bizarre that Richard Spearman was the prime named suspect on the ground in Paris and was cross-examined, but the jury were never told it was Spearman they were hearing evidence from. None of the MI6 witnesses – including Tomlinson and Dearlove – were asked about Spearman and Baker also failed to mention Spearman's name in his Summing Up.

- there are significant irregularities in the Diplomatic List entries relating to the postings of Cowper-Coles and Caton to Paris
- MI6 witnesses testified that no officers were on duty in Paris on the weekend of the crash – yet; a) none of their alibis have ever been independently verified and b) the former Head of MI6 France said there would have been working duty officers that weekend
- a major effort has been made since the Paris crash to turn Rosa Monckton into Princess Diana's "best friend"
- Rosa Monckton's brother is an MI6 officer and her husband is an MI6 agent
- Rosa's inquest evidence was littered with conflicts – both with others and herself
- Rosa lied repeatedly in her inquest evidence
- Rosa appeared to initially meet with Diana at a time when the Establishment had reason to want intelligence on Diana's thinking and plans
- Rosa organised a boating holiday with Diana in the period just after Diana's first and only major anti-landmines address and agreement to join Mohamed Al Fayed on a holiday
- 11 days after the Rosa-Diana boating holiday concluded, Diana lay dead in a Paris hospital.

The key evidence basically revolves around five major areas – the culture of MI6; its huge record of involvement in assassination plots; the movement of senior MI6 personnel into the Paris embassy in the latter part of August 1997 and the cover up of those movements; the universal – but not credible – Paris MI6 testimony that no one was on duty on the weekend of the crash; the role of Rosa Monckton.

There was a huge effort at the Diana inquest to focus the MI6-related evidence on the varying accounts of the Slobodan Milosevic assassination plot – this moved the focus away from where it should have been: Was MI6 involved in the assassination of Princess Diana?

So the jury heard volumes of conflicting evidence on events in the Balkans in the early 1990s, when they should have been hearing about events that took place in London and Paris in 1997.

This shifting of the focus appeared to have two possible aims: a) to divert the jury's attention away from evidence pointing to MI6 involvement in the Paris crash; b) an attempt to undermine ex-MI6 officer, Richard Tomlinson's evidence, and destroy his credibility.

At the inquest Richard Tomlinson came across as a lone voice, with all other MI6 witnesses arrayed against him and effectively undermining his account of MI6-related evidence. In reality there was a substantial amount of other evidence – not heard by the jury – shown as "Jury Didn't Hear" in this book, that supports Tomlinson's accounts.

When the MI6-related evidence was subjected to scrutiny – as occurred earlier in this book – it is Tomlinson's alone that stacks up. All other MI6 witnesses appear to have at times lied under oath.

Richard Dearlove – the most senior MI6 officer heard[a] – seemed to particularly seek to undermine Tomlinson's evidence:

- "I really don't see why I should speculate on things that Tomlinson has written which I personally believe to be invented by him"[265]
- "I think [Tomlinson] made this up after the event"[266]
- "let's be quite clear about this – [Tomlinson] almost certainly made this up"[267]
- "[Tomlinson] made it up on the basis of knowledge he had gained as an officer in SIS, but my belief is he made this up"[268]
- "this is a Tomlinson construct that we are talking about"[269]
- "I think that that also is a Tomlinson construction"[270]
- "Tomlinson made many, many allegations and statements"[271]
- "[Tomlinson] used bits of knowledge on which he elaborated with a very clear intention, of causing mischief for [MI6] and the greatest possible difficulty"[272]
- "that is, I am afraid, Tomlinson again elaborating"[273]
- "that is an invention" from Tomlinson[274]
- "this is Mr Tomlinson again causing mischief"[275]
- Tomlinson is "very, very embittered"[276]
- Tomlinson's motives and integrity "are highly questionable"[277] – confirmed to Horwell.

Any investigation into the activities of MI6 – or probably any intelligence agency – is fraught with difficulty because of the pervasive culture of secrecy and deceit.[b] With that in mind, I suggest that the evidence uncovered in this chapter is significant – and that it points to MI6 involvement in the assassinations of Princess Diana and Dodi Fayed.

The evidence also brings out – and I believe this is common sense – that MI6 would not have been able to bring about this orchestrated crash in Paris without a great deal of help from the local French intelligence agencies, DGSE and DST.[c]

Other evidence points to the involvement of the CIA – their incredible record in high-level assassinations; their long-time close cooperation and

---

[a] Dearlove was a former head of MI6 – see earlier.
[b] In this particular case, added to this were the lies and deceit of the coroner of the inquest, Lord Justice Scott Baker.
[c] There has already been a significant amount of evidence in Part 3 indicating the involvement of French police in the post-crash cover-up.

conduct of joint MI6 operations; the sudden change of mind regarding signing the anti-landmine treaty by President Bill Clinton; the CIA's extensive resources.

The earlier British Intelligence Assassination table showed that in the known cases of MI6 involvement in assassination plots there is a very low success rate. Of course, we don't know what the success rate is in the operations that have remained secret, but this evidence gives additional support for the argument that the CIA was involved in the Diana-Dodi assassination.

Part 2 indicated that Diana's campaign against landmines would have been a significant motive – but not alone[a] – for her assassination. It is logical that once Diana had achieved success on the landmine front, she may have been expected to move on to other weapons, e.g. cluster bombs. There is no question that both the USA and France have a very strong commitment to the worldwide arms industry and their operations could have been severely impacted, had Princess Diana been allowed to continue living.

I believe that the evidence we have seen in this chapter, although mostly circumstantial, is enough to indicate the involvement of MI6 in the orchestration of the Paris crash and the subsequent deaths of Princess Diana and Dodi Fayed. I suggest that the evidence – seen in the light of landlines as a motive[b] – also points to the assassination of Princess Diana being a joint effort from the intelligence agencies of three major powers: UK, France and USA.

When this is put together with the extensive evidence in the earlier volumes, one can begin to formulate a view on how such a massive complex undertaking could have been pulled together. The evidence indicates a huge operation conducted by MI6, but in conjunction with the CIA, DST and DGSE, and enlisting the services of quite a few agents on the ground – some identifiable and some not.

Intelligence agents who provided their services on the weekend of 30-31 August 1997 included Henri Paul, Claude Roulet, the several unidentified motorbike riders that pursued the Mercedes S280, Jean-Marc Martino, Arnaud Derossi, Dominique Lecomte, Gilbert Pépin and Jean Monceau.

The assassination of Princess Diana took place under the watch of David Spedding[c] – as head of MI6 – and Richard Dearlove – as Director of Operations. By virtue of their positions, both these men are implicated in the events.

---

[a] Other possible motives are addressed later in this volume and in Part 2.

[b] See Part 2.

[c] Richard Spearman, who was a part of Spedding's immediate circle, was transferred to Paris five days before the crash.

As a part of the police investigations the phone records of all of the agents listed above and Spedding, Dearlove, Richard Spearman, Sherard Cowper-Coles and Valerie Caton should have been subjected to scrutiny. As it turned out, only the phone records of Henri Paul were obtained[a] – and that by the French police, not the British.

The question now is: Was MI6 – in concert with the other agencies – authorised to assassinate Princess Diana?

The known evidence in high-level assassination plots – particularly in the Gaddafi plot, where there is a lot of information available[b] – points to MI6 not acting independently of the British government of the day. In the Gaddafi case, it appears an attempt was made to pin the assassination plot on MI6 alone, but when the evidence is closely analysed it is revealed that MI6 was acting with government authorisation.

Can the same be said about the Diana assassination that took place the following year? Was it authorised or was it ordered?

If someone gave the order for Diana to be killed, who was it? Was it the British government? Was it the royal family?

These questions should be answered in the remainder of this volume.

---

[a] See Part 1. Henri Paul's records were obtained but even they weren't shown to the jury.
[b] See earlier.

2 British Embassy in Paris[a][b]

Embassy-Consulate Relationship

Keith Moss, British Consul General, Paris: 22 Nov 07: 6.2:
"In Paris, because that is where the Embassy is located, the Consulate General was, if you like, a department of the Embassy and was solely responsible – and therefore me as Consul General – was solely responsible for consular and entry clearance activities."
At 7.23: Hough: Q. Turning to the links between the Embassy and the Consulate, I think certainly in August 1997 the Consulate was in a building physically separate from the Embassy, but close to it. Is that right?
A. That is correct, yes.
Q. I think that you had a line manager who was Mr Pakenham.
A. Correct.
Q. What was his role?

---

[a] Evidence in this chapter needs to be viewed in the light of British Embassy involvement in the Embalming, Royal Control and Repatriation – Chapters 2, 3 and 4 – in Part 4.
[b] Coroner, Scott Baker, only used the word "embassy" four times in his 2½ days of Summing Up for the jury: twice in connection with allegations of Robert Fellowes' presence there on the night of the crash – 31 Mar 08: 45.23 and 45.25; twice when describing Consul-General Keith Moss as being "from the embassy" – 31 Mar 08: 85.15 and 86.1. Ambassador, Michael Jay, also receives just four mentions: three in connection with the allegation that Jay was involved in the decision to embalm (addressed in Part 4) – 31 Mar 08: 47.13, 50.3 and 86.15; once regarding the claim that Jay was part of the murder conspiracy – 31 Mar 08: 71.5.
In contrast, during Baker's Opening Remarks, at the beginning of the inquest, he used "embassy" 20 times and referred to Jay 14 times.

A. Michael Pakenham was the – his title was "Minister" but in effect he was the Deputy Ambassador.

Q. I think in August 1997, at the time we are dealing with, he was actually away on holiday and you were reporting directly to the Ambassador.

A. Yes.

Q. That was Sir Michael Jay, now Lord Jay?

A. Yes.

Embassy Reports

Three post-crash reports drawn up by Ambassador, Michael Jay, and Consul-General, Keith Moss, have been suppressed.

Keith Moss: 22 Oct 04 Statement: **Jury Didn't Hear**:

"When there is an incident involving the death of a British citizen abroad, it is normal Consular procedure to write a Consular Report at the earliest opportunity, so that the FCO in London can liaise with the relevant authorities involved and the family. As a result of this incident, I compiled my report on Monday 1st September 1997. This was submitted to Sir Michael Jay, the Ambassador, who forwarded it to the Foreign Office on the 2nd September 1997. This report was made whilst the events were fresh in my mind and using contemporaneous notes I had made in a notebook that I disposed of once my report was written. The report was as comprehensive as possible.

"To enable me to complete this statement, I am using a copy of this report in order to refresh my memory of the events that took place in Paris. However, although I was its author, it is not my property, and belongs to the FCO where it lies on file." [278]

Michael Jay: 13 Dec 05 Statement: **Jury Didn't Hear**:

"The death of the Princess of Wales was an event of immense importance, and as I shall explain required the concentrated efforts of an experienced team from the Embassy staff. The first comprehensive report of the events of 31/08/1997 was compiled by my Consul General, Mr Keith Moss, who had been with me at the Pitié Salpêtrière hospital on the night in question. The consular officers of an Embassy would normally prepare a report for the FCO on any death of a British subject abroad that required consular support, and I asked Mr Moss to prepare such a report. Mr Moss' report was sent to Mr Francis Richards, Director – Europe, at the FCO in London. This report went under cover of a letter signed by me. I was of course heavily involved in some aspects of the events described by Mr Moss and I contributed from my own knowledge to his report.

"I subsequently sent my own two-part report to the FCO in two telegrams on 23/09/1997 (Serial number 934), the first part containing a narrative of the events of 31/08/1997, the second discussing the reaction of the French Government and people and the consequences for the relations between France and the UK. Both these telegrams reflected heavily my own input as well as that of members of the Embassy staff.

"I have no objection to any of these reports or records being provided to the Paget inquiry to assist them with their investigation.[a]

"Thirdly, on 30/09/1997 I wrote a personal letter to the then Permanent Under Secretary of State, Sir John Coles, enclosing a private record that covered the same course of events from a more personal point of view. This contained personal detail about my interaction with members of the French Government on 31/08/1997, and also my meeting with the Prince of Wales and my conversation with him. Because of its personal nature, I regarded this record as being 'In confidence'. Sir John Coles replied that he would add it to the archives but in view of its confidential nature would not give it wider circulation. I understand that this record has been made available to police officers from the Operation Paget enquiry, but I should once again prefer it if the record were given no wider circulation. In my view it does not add substantially to the other records mentioned above.

"In paragraph 22 of my record of 30/09/1997 I describe how, after the aircraft carrying the Princess of Wales had departed and we had returned to the Embassy, several of the Embassy staff that had been involved 'met in my office and agreed a telegram reporting the day's events, principally the support we had had from the French authorities.' I draw attention to this telegram, serial number 848, both because it illustrates the manner in which we had handled the emergency and because it reflects the manner in which some telegrams were composed." [279]

Comment: Michael Jay describes three important reports:
-   "the first comprehensive report of the events of 31/08/1997 was compiled by my Consul General, Mr Keith Moss ... sent to Mr Francis Richards, Director – Europe, at the FCO in London.... I contributed from my own knowledge to his report." [b]
-   "my own two-part report to the FCO in two telegrams on 23/09/1997 ... the first part containing a narrative of the events of 31/08/1997, the second discussing the reaction of the French Government and people and the consequences for the relations between France and the UK"
-   "on 30/09/1997 I wrote a personal letter to the then Permanent Under Secretary of State, Sir John Coles, enclosing a private record that covered the same course of events.... This contained personal detail about my interaction

---

[a] These reports and the letter and telegram referred to below were not available to the jury and were not published in the Paget Report.
[b] Evidence of this report is supported by Keith Moss – see above.

with members of the French Government on 31/08/1997, and also my meeting with the Prince of Wales and my conversation with him".

These three reports – one from Moss, two from Jay – contain critical information on the British Embassy view of the events that had occurred. The third includes details of a conversation between Jay and Prince Charles – one of the prime named suspects in the case.

The British Embassy staff were closely involved with the post-crash events[a] – but even more significant, it has already been shown that MI6, whose staff were based in the Political and Economic departments of the embassy, were involved in the orchestration of the crash.

Yet none of these important reports were shown to the inquest jury. And since the jury were also not shown Moss' and Jay's statements, they would not have even been aware of these reports.

Why?

If there is nothing to hide in these key embassy reports, why were they not shown to the jury investigating the events that these reports are talking about?

Jay states that all three were given to Paget – why did Paget not mention the existence of these documents in its report?

Keith Moss stated: "This report was made whilst the events were fresh in my mind and using contemporaneous notes I had made in a notebook that I disposed of once my report was written."

When one considers that the death of Diana on his territory could have been the most important case of Moss' career, the question is raised: Why did Moss dispose of his "contemporaneous notes ... made in a notebook"?[b]

Again, the jury wouldn't have been asking this because they were prevented from seeing Moss' statement.

These issues are significant because: a) Paris MI6 was based in the embassy; b) it is possible that if an order to assassinate Princess Diana came from the UK, it may have been relayed through the Paris embassy; c) it will be shown that some embassy staff have lied in their evidence; and d) as will be seen, the British embassy staff played a critical role in events that occurred in Paris on the weekend of 30-31 August 1997.

---

[a] See Part 4.

[b] Vice-Consul, Stephen Donnelly, said: "the normal procedure would be that [the original notes] would be put into the registration office for filing into the consular file" – see later in Missing Notes section.

Phone Calls and Missing Records[a]

There are conflicts in the witness accounts of key post-crash phone calls.[b]
George Younes, British Embassy Security Officer, Paris: 15 Aug 05
Statement read out 17 Dec 07: 110.21:
"I first became aware of this news when I received a telephone call between
12.50 a.m. and 1.00 a.m. from the then Prefet de Police, Mr Massoni. My
telephone rang and I answered that it was the British Embassy. Mr Massoni
spoke to me in French and introduced himself as the Prefet de Police. He told
me that he was calling as a result of the accident and that there was already
one dead involved in this accident. He was under the impression that I was
aware of an accident having taken place. I informed him that I was not aware
of any accident and this is when he informed me that Diana, Princess of
Wales had been involved in a crash in the Alma Tunnel in Paris. He told me
that he was currently at the scene of the crash and that a Mr Al Fayed had
died in the accident, but I didn't know who he was. He did not tell me
anything about the condition of the Princess of Wales, he simply told me that
Mr Al Fayed was dead. I took all the details from him, including his contact
number. He did not direct me to do anything. Once I had recorded all the
information, it is my responsibility to pass it on. I immediately made an entry
in the Chancery daily occurrence log."
Philippe Massoni, Prefect of Police, Paris: 14 Nov 06 Statement read out 21
Nov 07: 55.25:
"I should point out that as comprehensive as possible a log of the events at
the time was made in 1997. I produce this chronology to you in order that it
can be attached to this statement.[c]
"At 0040 hours [12.40 a.m.], the headquarters of Public Safety informed me
of the accident. As I live at the Prefecture, I was able to inform my staff
officer and my driver in a matter of a few minutes and to attend the scene,
where I arrived at 0050 hours. During the journey, I alerted the Minister of
the Interior, M Chevènement. When I got to the scene, I gave him a situation
report...."
"Question: Did you inform the British Embassy in Paris of the accident? Do
you remember who you informed and when?"
"Answer: This accident was of major international significance. At the same

---

[a] This section should be viewed in conjunction with the Prior Knowledge section of
chapter 9D in Part 2.
[b] The following items of evidence relate the accounts of the phone calls in the
chronological order in which the phone calls are claimed to have occurred.
[c] This chronology – "as comprehensive as possible a log of the events at the time was
made in 1997" – is obviously a very significant document, yet it was not included in
the Paget Report and was not shown to the jury at Baker's "thorough" inquest.

time as the Minister of the Interior was making his way to [the hospital[a]], I notified the British Ambassador, as well as the office of the President, the office of the Prime Minister and the Foreign Minister in person. These notifications were done on my behalf by Nicola Basselier, my assistant private secretary, as my principal private secretary was on holiday at the time. There was frequent contact between my assistant private secretary and these high-level authorities. They were kept informed on a regular basis.

"Reply to a question: I believe that the British Ambassador to France was informed at the same time as the other high-level authorities that I just mentioned, as soon as we knew that the Princess of Wales was one of the victims of the accident. I can say that it was a night the like of which, fortunately, we rarely experience and in the course of which one has to take very quick decisions and to share roles effectively. It was therefore necessary to inform senior officials, including the British Ambassador, without delay. Nine years after the event, I cannot tell you if it was me personally or ...[b] my private secretary who did this.

"I should like at this juncture to pay tribute to his excellency the Ambassador of Great Britain, Sir Michael Jay and his wife who, throughout the events, were present in the command post that we set up in the command post ... of the Pitié-Salpêtrière Hospital. Thanks to their calmness under pressure and their efficiency, both proved to be of great assistance to us."

Paget Report, p613: **Jury Didn't Hear**:

"[Paget Note: Préfet Philippe Massoni, interviewed by Operation Paget, stated that he attended the scene around 12.50 a.m. His assistant, Nicola Basselier, was tasked on behalf of the Préfet to inform key people. This included the British Embassy. Philippe Massoni cannot recall after this length of time when this was done or indeed if he made that call himself.]

George Younes: 15 Aug 05 Statement read out 17 Dec 07: 112.10:

"After the receipt of the telephone call from Mr Massoni, I received a telephone call from a duty officer at the Elysée Palace. I have been shown by DS Grater a copy of the Chancery daily occurrence log relating to this call and subsequent entries. I understand that DS Grater obtained this copy of the log from the Foreign and Commonwealth Office in London. I have had an opportunity of reading this document, which I can now produce as my

---

[a] The words "the hospital" were inserted by Ian Burnett, the lawyer. Without seeing Massoni's statement – which has never been made available and wasn't seen by the jury – it is not possible to know precisely what Massoni said. If the name of the hospital – La Pitié Salpêtrière – was written there then that could be evidence of prior knowledge of Diana's hospital destination well before it was officially decided on (see Part 2).

[b] These dots are in the inquest transcript.

exhibit. The time of the call from the Elysée Palace is logged at 1.10 am on Sunday 31st August 1997 and this is entry number 3 for the day. That entry reads 'Telephone call from Mr [and the name is unreadable] permanence de Palais Elysée to inform the Embassy that Lady Diana had a serious accident, car, at tunnel, Pont de l'Alma, Paris. There is a death in her car. She's being taken away to a hospital, Paris,[a] that is still kept secret for instant take all details from here'.

"To the best of my recollection, this was the second incoming telephone call in relation to this incident, approximately ten minutes after the initial call from Mr Massoni. As a result of this telephone call, I thanked him and I told him that we were already aware of the accident and that someone had died. The caller asked me if we had a crisis unit to liaise with the Elysée Palace for more details. I informed him that at that time it was only me, but that additional people would be informed and deal with the situation."

Paget Report, p612: Jury Didn't Hear:
"Documentation held by the FCO, viewed by Operation Paget shows a copy of George Younes's log entry number '3' on the night in question:
'T/C from Mr (unreadable) Permanence de Palais Elysée to inform the Embassy that Lady Diana had a serious accident car at tunnel Pont de l'Alma Paris. There is death in her car, she is being taken away to a hospital (unreadable) Paris that still kept secret for instant take all details from here.'"

George Younes: 15 Aug 05 Statement read out 17 Dec 07: 111.18:
"Without checking the original Chancery daily occurrence log for that weekend[b] and to the best of my recollection, the telephone call from Mr Massoni would have been either entry number 1 or number 2 of the Chancery daily occurrence log on Sunday 31st August 1997. This entry would have been made at the time of the telephone call from Mr Massoni, which I confirm was taken before any telephone call from the Elysée Palace. It may also be the case that my routine security check log entry could have been entry number 1 for Sunday 31st August 1997 or could have been one of the last entries of Saturday 30th August 1997, but I cannot be sure. What I can say is that my routine security check would not have taken place after the telephone call from Mr Massoni and therefore the security check log entry is unlikely to be entry number 2 for Sunday 31st August."

George Younes: 15 Aug 05 Statement read out 17 Dec 07: 113.13:
"I can confirm that the handwriting and subsequent entries, up to entry 88 in the Chancery daily occurrence log[c], are definitely mine.

"The purpose of this occurrence log is to record all information for any future

---

[a] It has been shown in Part 2 that the hospital was named in the original transcript of the telephone log – see Prior Knowledge section of chapter 9D, Part 2.
[b] This was stated before the police showed Younes a copy of the log – see above.
[c] For 31 August 1997.

use. As an example, I would record information such as a British citizen who called to inform that they had lost their passport ... et cetera.

"I have been asked where the original Chancery daily occurrence log is for 30th and 31st August 1997. I do not know where the original is. I do not know how long the logs are kept. To my knowledge, the security manager would have been responsible for retaining these logs, although I do not know where or for how long. Normally the occurrence logs are filed at the end of each month, but I was not responsible for this and I do not know how the filing takes place. I should explain that the occurrence log is not a book but is in fact loose-leafed and held in a ring-binder. In 1997, Phil Whiteman was the security manager for the British Embassy in Paris. I believe he is now a British police officer but I do not know where. Phil Whiteman was replaced by the current security manager, Mr Andrew Bishop. I would also like to explain that during a night duty shift, it is normal procedure for separate logs to be kept by the Chancery desk and the Residence desk."

Paget Report, pp612-3: **Jury Didn't Hear**:

"The copy log entries '1' and '2' [for 31 August 1997] are missing. George Younes believes number '1' was the routine security check entry after midnight and that number '2' referred to the call from Philippe Massoni. It is not known why logs '1' and '2' were not copied when subsequently the other logs relating to the night were. Christopher Whomersley, the Deputy Legal Adviser to the FCO, has indicated that to the best of his knowledge the original logs would probably have been destroyed in 2001 in line with standard policy. The FCO is unable to identify who copied the original log entries while they were in existence, and consequently who missed logs '1' and '2' and how. The log entries were made on detachable sheets running consecutively.

"While unfortunate in terms of providing a complete picture, the effect of copy logs '1' and '2' being missing is that George Younes believed the Embassy were informed by the police at 12.50am, while other Embassy officials have understood the first call to be from the Elysée Palace at 1.10am, around twenty minutes later. The evidence of George Younes is that both calls were straightforward communications of the relevant information."

Paget Report, p612: **Jury Didn't Hear**:

"George Younes ... took the first telephone calls informing the British Embassy of the crash. George Younes believed this to be at 12.50 a.m., but records indicate it may have been at 1.10 a.m." [a]

---

[a] This is a summary statement by Paget that indicates that the variation in evidence relates to the timing – i.e. 12.50 as opposed to 1.10 a.m. Other evidence – also included in the Paget Report – shows that Younes said the 12.50 (actually 12.50 to 1.00 a.m.) call was from Massoni and the 1.10 a.m. call was from the Elysée Palace.

Michael Jay, British Ambassador to France, 1996-2001, Paris: 11 Feb 08: 114.15:

Mansfield: Q. Are you aware that some log sheets for this night are missing?

A. Those I think are the – as I understand it, those are log sheets which were kept by the security guard who was on duty and who logged calls coming in to the Embassy out of hours.

Q. Have you been asked about this in order to assist locate them?

A. No, I have not been asked about it in order to assist locate them.

Q. But you know, do you, that some of them are missing?

A. I was told that when I was reading some papers in order to prepare for this appearance for today.

Q. Can you help or not?

A. No, I cannot help.

Q.... There is no policy of destruction within the Embassy that you are aware of?

A. There was a policy of destroying documents after a certain period of time in order just to keep down the volume of paperwork. I do not know what the arrangements would have been for those records.

Q. Well, clearly in the context of what happened that night, obviously records for that night would be considered to be of paramount importance at the time, wouldn't they?

A. Of course.

George Younes: 15 Aug 05 Statement read out 17 Dec 07: 114.18:

"As a result of receiving the telephone call from the Elysée Palace and making the relevant entry in the log at 1.10 a.m., I then immediately contacted the duty Chancery officer, Mr Keith Shannon at 1.15 a.m. Keith Shannon did not reply and I left a message on his answerphone at home. I then called his mobile telephone and left another message. I continued to call his home number and eventually managed to wake him at home.

"Although the log might show a five- or ten-minute gap between entries number 3 and number 4, this is because I have to ensure that everything is recorded correctly and locate the details of the appropriate on-call duty officer. Additionally, this night was far from normal and due to the high volume of calls received, I subsequently only recorded what I felt was important and related to this incident in the occurrence log.

"When I spoke with Keith Shannon, I informed [him] of what I had been told by Mr Massoni and the Elysée Palace."

Keith Shannon: Paget Description of Statement: **Jury Didn't Hear**:

"Keith Shannon stated that he first became aware of the crash at just after 1 a.m. on 31 August 1997 when he was woken by a telephone call from George Younes, the Security Officer at the Embassy. This call was followed by a second call from Philippe Massoni, the Préfet de Police of Paris ... who Keith

Shannon understood to be at the scene of the crash. These calls were his first knowledge of the Princess of Wales' presence in Paris." [280]

Keith Moss, British Consul General, Paris: 22 Nov 07: 8.18:

Hough: Q. How did you first become aware that they were in Paris and they were involved in this accident, this crash?

A. I first became aware when I received a telephone call from the Embassy's duty officer.

Q. Is that Mr Keith Shannon?

A. Yes.

Q. Where were you when you received that call?

A. In bed.

Q. At home?

A. Asleep.

Q. Was that at around 10 past 1 in the morning?

A. My statement says 10 past 1, but I think it was a little bit after that.

Q. How long after?

A. I cannot really remember, but I guess it was 10 or 15 minutes probably.

Q. Did Mr Shannon tell you where he had got his information from?

A. If I remember correctly, he told me that the Embassy security guard had received a message or a telephone call from the – it is called the "permanence", which is the duty officer, at the Elysée Palace. I think I recall him saying that he had double-checked to make sure that what he had been told was correct, and then he phoned me because of my consular responsibilities.

Q. What was your first action on hearing the news?

A. I asked him to repeat it.

Q. What did he tell you? What precise information did he give you?

A. He told me – he repeated what he had said before, which was that there had been an accident in which the Princess of Wales was involved. I think he said that Mr Al Fayed was also involved, and I think he said that he had succumbed to the accident –

Q. That he had died?

A. That he had died, and that the Princess had been transferred to the Pitié-Salpêtrière Hospital.[a]

Q. Did he tell you anything about the bodyguard or the driver?

A. I think in my statement I said that he did, but on reflection I cannot be certain.

Q. After you had got that information, got him to repeat it, what did you do

---

[a] This was before a decision on the choice of hospital is supposed to have been made – this has been covered in Part 2.

first?

A. First of all, I tried to collect my senses. I then sat down and worked out the immediate things that I needed to do; for example, who did I need to inform? Well, consistent with what I said earlier, we clearly needed to ensure that the next of kin were informed[a], but I also obviously needed to ensure that the Ambassador was in the picture in view of who was involved.

Q. So to whom were your first calls?

A. Again, I cannot be precise on the actual order, but I am fairly certain that my first telephone call was to the so-called resident clerk in the Foreign Office, who again is a duty officer there on permanent call, to explain to him what I had heard and ask him if, through his channels, a range of contacts could be put in the picture, namely the Royal Household, bearing in mind this was August, it was Buckingham Palace, it was Balmoral Castle, it could have been other places as well; that the Foreign Secretary should be informed, Robin Cook, as was, who at the time was in the Philippines on a journey, and probably a number of other contacts as well. I cannot remember the precise detail, but there would have been a range of people like that who I – oh and the news department in the Foreign Office, that would have been another one – and left it for the duty officer, the resident clerk, to conduct that activity. I then telephoned the Ambassador, got him out of bed and told him what had happened and I also telephoned the Embassy's press attaché, Tim Livesey.

Keith Moss: 22 Oct 04 Statement: **Jury Didn't Hear**:

"On 31st August 1997, at around 0110hrs, I was sound asleep at my home in Paris when I received a telephone call from the Embassy Duty Officer, Keith Shannon, a UK based member of the Embassy staff. He informed me that reports were coming out of [a] vehicular accident involving the Princess of Wales in the tunnel by the 'Pont d'Alma' in Paris, and that she had been transferred to the Pitié Salpêtrière Hospital. He also informed me that the driver was reported dead, along with Dodi Al Fayed, and that their bodyguard Trevor Rees-Jones was injured and had been taken to hospital. In order to make sure I had understood everything correctly, I asked Keith Shannon to repeat what he had just told me. He informed me that he had received this information from George Younes, a British Embassy Security Officer, who in turn had been told via a telephone call from the Duty Officer at the Elysée Palace.

"I immediately telephoned the Resident Clerk / Duty Officer at the FCO. I asked him to inform Buckingham Palace, number 10 Downing Street, and

---

[a] Although Moss specifically mentions the need to contact the next of kin here, in his next answer he details the people who needed to know and the adult next of kin – Diana's mother, stepmother, siblings – are left off it. This issue has been covered in Part 4.

others, including the FCO News Department, and the Foreign Secretary who was at that time in Manila. These calls would have taken some time. "I then telephoned Sir Michael Jay and Tim Livesey, the British Embassy Press Attaché." [281]

George Younes: 15 Aug 05 Statement read out 17 Dec 07: 114.18:

"I also called and informed the duty consulate officer, but I do not recall who this was on this night and this is not recorded in the log. It is normal procedure when an incident such as this takes place for the duty consulate officer and the duty Chancery officer from the on-call list to be informed by the security officer.

"I have been asked if I notified anybody else following my conversation with Mr Shannon. According to the log and to the best of my recollection, I telephoned Simon Jackson to inform him of a busy night ahead. I also recall talking to the Ambassador, Sir Michael Jay, by telephone and informing him of what I had been told, but I do not remember at what time.[a] I informed Tim Livesey, the press officer, at 1.50 am.

"At 1.55 am I received a telephone call from 'Hotel Matignon Permanence', the duty officer from the French Prime Minister's office. By that point Keith Shannon had joined me at the Chancery desk and I handed this call to him. "At 2 am I telephoned the Consul General and put him through to the Ambassador." [b]

Michael Jay, British Ambassador to France, 1996-2001, Paris: 11 Feb 08: 89.18:

Burnett: Q. First, when did you first become aware of the presence in Paris of the Princess of Wales and Dodi Al Fayed?

A. When I was telephoned by Keith Moss, the Consul General, to tell me

---

[a] This communication with Jay almost comes in as an afterthought from Younes – it is in response to the question: "I have been asked if I notified anybody else following my conversation with Mr Shannon." Younes included in the occurrence log calls to Shannon – 1.15 a.m. – and Livesey – 1.50 a.m. But when it comes to this notification to Jay he says: "I do not remember at what time". Jay was the head of the embassy, so from Younes' point of view, that could be a significant conversation. Younes though does not appear to be claiming that he was the one who first notified Jay – he says: "I also recall talking to ... Jay, by telephone and informing him of what I had been told". So Younes doesn't say who initiated the call – it could have been Jay who called Younes. A little further on Younes says: "At 2 a.m. I telephoned [Moss] and put him through to [Jay]." That could have been at Jay's request and Younes could have talked to Jay at that point. The significance of the timing of Jay's notification will become apparent later.

[b] Moss arrived at the hospital and set up an incident room at 2.15 a.m. – see Part 4. It is possible that Jay was trying to contact Moss but couldn't reach him at home and asked Younes to contact Moss and put him through.

about the accident, which I think was at about quarter to two or thereabouts on the morning of the 31st.

Q. Can we take it from that that you and your wife were in Paris at the time?

A. Yes, we were. We were asleep.

Q. That is in the Ambassador's residence which is next door, I think, to the Embassy; is that right?

A. It is next door to the Embassy. They are linked by a door which goes through from one to the other.

....Q. So you received a telephone call telling you there had been an accident. Were you told immediately that the chauffeur and Dodi Al Fayed had died as a result of the accident?

A. Yes. I was told that Dodi Al Fayed had died, that the chauffeur had died and that the Princess of Wales had been badly hurt, and then I had another call immediately afterwards from the press counsellor at the Embassy, Tim Livesey, relaying the same message.

At 102.17: 31 Aug 97 Diary read out: "The phone rang about 1.45 am. First Keith Moss, then Tim Livesey, to tell me that there had been a car accident, that Dodi Al Fayed and a chauffeur had been killed and that the Princess of Wales had been seriously injured and was in hospital."

Michael Jay: 13 Dec 05 Statement: **Jury Didn't Hear**:

"I had no knowledge that the Princess of Wales and Dodi Al Fayed were in Paris until I was woken at my residence which adjoins the Embassy at about 1.45 a.m. in the morning of Sunday 31/08/1997. I received two telephone calls in quick succession. The first was from Keith Moss my Consul General and the second was from Tim Livesey the Embassy's Press Officer. They told me that there had been a car accident in Paris, that Dodi Al Fayed and the chauffeur were dead, and that the Princess of Wales was injured and had been taken to the Pitié Salpêtrière hospital in Paris....

"I have been asked, when to the best of my knowledge was the first time anybody at the British Embassy became aware that the Princess of Wales had been involved in a car crash. I have already referred to the consular report prepared by my then Consul General Mr Keith Moss on 01/09/1997, which I forwarded to the FCO the following day. This opens with the following passage: - 'At approximately 01.10 on Sunday 31 August, the security officer, George Younes, on duty at the Embassy received a telephone call from the duty officer at the Elysée Palace. The Princess of Wales had been involved in a traffic accident in the tunnel by the Pont d'Alma and had been transferred to l'Hopital La Pitié Salpêtrière.' As far as I was aware at the time, this was the first occasion that anybody at the Embassy was made aware that the Princess had been involved in a car crash.

"So far as I was concerned, I first learned of the crash when I was awoken by telephone calls from Keith Moss and Tim Livesey at about 01.45 on Sunday

31/08/1997. I have already described the circumstances of this earlier in the statement." [282]

Timothy Livesey, Embassy Press Attaché: Paget Description of Statement: **Jury Didn't Hear**:

"Timothy Livesey stated he was informed of the crash at about 1.20am on 31 August 1997 in a telephone call from the Security Officer at the British Embassy, who himself had been informed by the Duty Officer at the Elysée Palace." [283]

Table: Phone Calls Involving British Embassy Personnel – Early 31 August 1997[ab]

Time (a.m.)	From		To	
	Name	In Evidence?	Name	In Evidence?
[c]				
12.55	Massoni[d]	Yes	Jay	No
12.55[e]	Massoni	No	Younes	Yes
1.10	Permanence[f], Elysée Palace	No evidence taken	Younes	Yes
1.15 to 1.20[g]	Younes	Yes	Shannon	Yes
1.25[h]	Shannon	No[a]	Moss	Yes

---

[a] Not all phone calls mentioned in the evidence are in this table, but all the important calls are.

[b] This table lists the phone calls claimed to have been made in the evidence. It will be shown later that not all of these phone calls actually took place.

[c] Most times are approximate.

[d] Massoni stated that the call was made "on my behalf by Nicola Basselier, my assistant private secretary".

[e] This call probably never took place – see later.

[f] Duty officer.

[g] Younes said: "I then ... contacted ... Shannon at 1.15 a.m. Keith Shannon did not reply and I left a message on his answerphone at home. I then called his mobile telephone and left another message. I continued to call his home number and eventually managed to wake him at home." Shannon's statement has never been made available.

[h] Moss originally timed this at 1.10 a.m. That is before Shannon had been woken up. It will later be shown that it is unlikely this phone call occurred in the way Moss described, if at all.

DIANA INQUEST: WHO KILLED PRINCESS DIANA?

Time (a.m.)	From		To	
	Name	**In Evidence?**	**Name**	**In Evidence?**
1.30[b]	Massoni	No	Shannon	Yes
1.35	Moss	Yes	Residence Clerk, FCO	No evidence taken
1.45[c]	Moss	Yes	Jay	Yes
1.50[d]	Younes	Yes	Livesey	Yes
1.55	Moss	Yes	Livesey	NA[e]
1.55	Duty Officer, French PM's Office	No evidence taken	Younes[f]	Yes
1.55	Livesey	NA	Jay	Yes
2.00	Younes	Yes	Moss	No
2.00[g]	Moss	No	Jay	No

Comment: There is a major conflict over the early call from Paris Prefect of Police, Philippe Massoni.

The evidence is:

- Massoni – "at the same time as the Minister of the Interior was making his way to [the hospital], I notified the British Ambassador"

- Massoni: "the British Ambassador to France was informed at the same time as the other high-level authorities"

- Massoni: "it was ... necessary to inform ... the British Ambassador, without delay.... I cannot tell you if it was me personally or ... my private secretary who did this"

- Younes: "I received a telephone call between 12.50 a.m. and 1.00 a.m. from the then Prefet de Police, Mr Massoni"

---

[a] Shannon's statement is not available and wasn't shown to the jury. Paget has summarised the information in the statements about phone calls made – Shannon doesn't appear to have mentioned this call. See later.

[b] It is unlikely this phone call took place – see later.

[c] It is unlikely this call occurred – at least, not in the manner described (see later).

[d] Livesey timed this at 1.20 a.m. but Younes appeared to get the timing of 1.50 a.m. from the copy of the log provided by Paget. The log – written up at the time – is likely to give the most accurate information.

[e] Livesey made a police statement which was not shown to the jury and is not available. Paget made no mention of this call in its evidence from Livesey.

[f] Younes passed this call onto Shannon, who by that stage had come into the embassy.

[g] This call is mentioned in Younes' statement.

- Shannon: "just after 1 a.m. on 31 August 1997 ... he was woken by a telephone call from George Younes.... This call was followed by a second call[a] from Philippe Massoni, the Préfet de Police of Paris"
- Jay: "I was woken ... at about 1.45 a.m.... I received two telephone calls in quick succession. The first was from Keith Moss ... and the second was from Tim Livesey".

Massoni states: "I notified the British Ambassador".

Younes says: "I received a telephone call ... from ... Massoni"

Shannon received a "call from ... Massoni"

Jay: "I was woken ... [by] Moss".

Massoni recalls phoning the Ambassador – Michael Jay. Jay says he was called by Moss.

The question is: Is it plausible that Massoni would recall calling Jay, but instead what occurred was, he called Younes at the embassy and Shannon at home?

Younes has provided a detailed account of a very early phone call – "between 12.50 a.m. and 1.00 a.m.":

- "Mr Massoni spoke to me in French and introduced himself"
- "there was already one dead involved in this accident"
- "[Massoni] was under the impression that I was aware of an accident having taken place"
- "I informed him that I was not aware"
- "he informed me that Diana ... had been involved in a crash in the Alma Tunnel"
- "he was currently at the scene of the crash"
- "a Mr Al Fayed had died in the accident"
- "I took all the details from him, including his contact number"
- "[Massoni] did not direct me to do anything".[b]

Younes then says: "Once I had recorded all the information, it is my responsibility to pass it on. I immediately made an entry in the Chancery daily occurrence log."

There are several problems with the phone call evidence from the British embassy employees:

1) Younes states that during the 12.55 a.m. conversation Massoni said: "there was already one dead".

---

[a] This appears to mean a second phone call – the call from Younes being the first. It is unlikely that Shannon said he received two calls from Massoni. Shannon's statement has never been made available.

[b] One could suggest that if Massoni had intended to call Jay, but instead got Younes, that he would have asked Younes to tell Jay. Later evidence will indicate that this call to Younes never occurred.

Younes also says: "[Massoni] was currently at the scene of the crash".

The evidence from the witnesses who were early at the scene reveals they were easily able to tell that there were two dead bodies in the crashed Mercedes S280.[a]

I suggest that would particularly be the case for a senior police officer, as Philippe Massoni was.

2) After detailing what Massoni said, Younes stated: "Once I had recorded all the information, it is my responsibility to pass it on."

There is no evidence that Younes passed anything on to anyone until after the 1.10 a.m. call from the Elysée Palace – that call came in approximately 15 minutes after Younes says he received the Massoni call.[b]

The witnesses said:

- Younes: "as a result of receiving the telephone call from the Elysée Palace ... at 1.10 a.m, I then immediately contacted ... Shannon at 1.15 a.m."

- Moss – "[Shannon] informed me that he had received this information from George Younes ... who in turn had been told via a telephone call from the Duty Officer at the Elysée Palace".

Younes had earlier provided a detailed account of a Massoni call telling him of a crash involving Princess Diana, and had even said: "it is my responsibility to pass it on". The first person Younes notified was Shannon – but not after the Massoni call, instead it was "as a result of receiving the telephone call from the Elysée Palace".

In support of this, Moss makes no mention of being told about a Massoni-Younes call, only the call from Elysée Palace.

Younes makes no comment on why he didn't contact anyone after the Massoni call.[c]

Younes states: "Although the log might show a five- or ten-minute gap between entries number 3 and number 4, this is because I have to ensure that

---

[a] There was an attempt at the scene to revive Dodi Fayed, but according to Younes, Massoni had said, "Mr Al Fayed had died in the accident". Henri Paul died instantly as well and there was no attempt to revive him.

[b] Younes timed the Massoni call as "between 12.50 a.m. and 1.00 a.m." and the Elysée Palace call "is logged at 1.10 a.m." – so that makes a maximum time difference between the two calls of 20 minutes (12.50 to 1.10) and a minimum of 10 minutes (1.00 to 1.10).

[c] Some may argue that there was not enough information on Diana's condition in the Massoni call for Younes to act. Both calls stated that there was one fatality or more in the car. The Elysée call included that Diana was going to hospital. Neither of the calls commented on Diana's condition. I suggest that if Younes received a call from Massoni – and the evidence will indicate that he didn't – stating Princess Diana was involved in a Paris car crash with one dead in her car and the Paris Prefect of Police being at the scene, that would have been enough information for Younes to pass it on immediately, as he did after the Elysée call.

everything is recorded correctly and locate the details of the appropriate on-call duty officer."

Entry 3 is the call from the Elysée Palace and entry 4 is Younes notifying Shannon. Younes says, "five- or ten-minute gap", but the gap is just five minutes: 1.10 to 1.15 a.m.

The question is: Why does Younes feel he needs to explain the <u>five minute delay</u> in notifying Shannon, when he fails to explain the approximately <u>20 minute notification gap</u> between the 12.55 a.m. call from Massoni and the 1.15 a.m. call to Shannon? [a]

3) When Younes recounted the detail of the 1.10 a.m. Elysée Palace call, he read most of it from the entry in the occurrence log.

But that was not the case with the earlier Massoni call, because the log that included that call is missing – see below.

That means that the nine details of that Massoni-Younes phone call – listed above – are Younes' memory of a conversation that took place eight years earlier[b], unless his evidence of the call has been fabricated.[c]

4) The FCO copies of the occurrence log for entries 1 and 2 on 31 August 1997 "are missing".[d]

There are several points about this:

a) Although the jury were informed[e] that "some log sheets for [30-31 August 1997] are missing", they were not told which ones – and therefore could not have realised the full significance of this documentary disappearance.[f]

---

[a] Put another way: What was Younes doing between the 12.55 a.m. Massoni call – after which he knew about the crash – and the 1.10 a.m. Elysée Palace call?

[b] Younes' statement was taken in August 2005, eight years after the crash.

[c] It will be shown that it is unlikely this call ever occurred and that Massoni was in communication with Jay, not Younes.

[d] It is important to understand – and this will be explained – that it is the FCO copies of the log sheets that are missing, not the embassy originals. Paget says: "<u>The copy log entries</u> '1' and '2' [for 31 August 1997] are missing." The jury did not hear this.

[e] During Mansfield's cross-examination of Jay.

[f] Younes' statement does not mention that documents are missing, but a person listening carefully may have deduced that Younes was only presented with FCO copies of entry 3 onwards. Younes was also "asked where the original Chancery daily occurrence log is for 30th and 31st August 1997". It would have been difficult for a jury member to link the information in Younes statement to what was said during the Jay cross-examination – the Younes statement was read out on 17 December 2007, whereas Jay wasn't heard until 11 February 2008, nearly two months later.

b) Both Jay and Younes were asked[a] about what happens with the original log sheets:

- Jay: "I do not know what the arrangements would have been for those records" – referring to whether they had been destroyed

- Younes: "I do not know where the original is. I do not know how long the logs are kept.... The security manager would have been responsible for retaining these logs".

Both Jay and Younes claimed they didn't know what happened to the original log sheets.

Jay went further – he described how he found out the log sheets were missing: "I was told that [the log sheets were missing] when I was reading some papers in order to prepare for this appearance for today".

I suggest this could be another case of excessive distancing.[b] If Jay had only heard about the missing log sheets just before he gave his inquest testimony, then I suggest that indicates to the jury that these missing log sheets can't be that important. Then that perception is consolidated by Jay's: "I do not know what the arrangements would have been for those [log sheet] records".

So Jay doesn't know – until February 2008[c] – that the log sheets are missing and he has no idea how long log sheets are kept. This then indicates – I suggest falsely – that this issue of the log sheets has no importance to Jay and he can't provide evidence on it. In fact, he said just that to Mansfield: "I cannot help".[d]

Michael Jay was ambassador – in charge of the Paris embassy – for around 5 years, from 1996 to 2001. Younes was employed as security officer in December 1993 and was still in that position when interviewed by Paget in August 2005 – so, over 11½ years.[284]

Between Jay and Younes, over 16 years of experience working in the embassy.

---

[a] Jay was asked by Mansfield in 2008; Younes was asked by the British police in 2005.

[b] There have been occurrences of this in Establishment evidence – it has been discussed earlier.

[c] When he gave his inquest evidence.

[d] In his statement Jay had said: "The death of the Princess of Wales was an event of immense importance" and later: "The death of the Princess of Wales ... was momentous and unprecedented in my experience": Michael Jay, Witness Statement, reproduced in *The Documents* book, pp630, 637. Jay also confirmed to Mansfield: "Obviously records for that night would be considered to be of paramount importance at the time".

I suggest it is unlikely that neither of them know what happens with key embassy records like these daily occurrence logs.[a]

c) Younes stated to Paget: "Without checking the original Chancery daily occurrence log for that weekend and to the best of my recollection, the telephone call from Mr Massoni would have been either entry number 1 or number 2".

The use by Younes of the term, "without checking the original", I suggest indicates that the original can be checked – in other words, the original does exist and could be located if really needed.

This is possibly an inadvertent admission from Younes.

d) Jay stated: "There was a policy of destroying documents after a certain period of time.... I do not know what the arrangements would have been for those records."

The Paget Report says: "Christopher Whomersley, the Deputy Legal Adviser to the FCO, has indicated that ... the original logs would probably have been destroyed in 2001 in line with standard policy."

Jay indicates that these records for 31 August 1997 could have been treated differently to normal records, i.e. not necessarily destroyed.[b] In contrast, the FCO officer told Paget: "the original logs would probably have been destroyed in 2001 in line with standard policy", i.e. no special treatment for these records.

e) There are two key points on which there are no explanations in the evidence:

i) Are the log sheets – which are "loose-leafed" – copied at the embassy or the FCO?

ii) What is the purpose of taking copies and then destroying the originals?

Younes said: "I understand that DS Grater obtained this copy of the log from the Foreign and Commonwealth Office in London".

This indicates that copies of the occurrence logs are made for the FCO.[c] There is a possibility that the originals are kept at the embassy – see next point. That would help explain Younes' comment quoted above: "without checking the original Chancery daily occurrence log".[d]

---

[a] Even if Jay didn't know the answer himself, he would have known who did and could have consulted them – if he had wanted to.

[b] This was also supported when Jay confirmed to Mansfield that "records for that night [of the crash] would be considered to be of paramount importance at the time".

[c] That the FCO keeps copies of these logs in London indicates the importance and significance of these documents to the organisation.

[d] I suggest that it is possible copies are made at the embassy close to the time they are written up, before being despatched to the FCO for checking and subsequent storage.

f) Given that Jay said, "I cannot help", why is it that the coroner, Scott Baker, didn't seek evidence from others, within the FCO or British embassy Paris, who could help?

Younes said: "The security manager would have been responsible for retaining these logs.... In 1997, Phil Whiteman was the security manager.... I believe he is now a British police officer.... Phil Whiteman was replaced by the current security manager, Mr Andrew Bishop."

In saying this, Younes has indicated that the original occurrence logs were kept at the Paris embassy, under the care of the security manager.

Why didn't Baker request statements from Phil Whiteman and Andrew Bishop?

g) The focus of the Younes statement and the Paget Report excerpts is the occurrence log sheets for 31 August 1997.

It is obvious that if there was any will on the part of Operation Paget or Scott Baker to establish whether the British Embassy had any involvement in the assassinations, the log sheets to examine would be the ones written up in the days leading up to the crash, particularly 30 August 1997.

Those log sheets do not appear to have ever been subjected to scrutiny. Instead what happened is the official investigations have focused on the phone calls after the crash – i.e. the log sheets after 12.23 a.m. on 31 August 1997. It is possible this misplaced focus is deliberate – concentrating the examination onto post-crash phone calls, when the real significant calls may be in the records that have not been looked at.

Entries 1 and 2 on 31 August 1997 must have been for calls that occurred after midnight and before 1.10 a.m.[a] – that means that one or both could have taken place before 12.23 a.m.

This knowledge places increased significance on the fact that the copy records for entries 1 and 2 have gone missing – and there appears to have been little or no effort to seek out the originals. It also helps one to understand why Younes may have been asked to provide a witness account of a phone call from Massoni – thus accounting for one of the missing log entries – without any documentary record to back up his testimony.

h) There are serious problems with the way the Paget Report addressed this issue:

i) The report stated: "George Younes believes number '1' was the routine security check entry after midnight".

Younes said: "My routine security check log entry could have been entry number 1 for Sunday 31st August 1997 <u>or could have been one of the last entries of Saturday 30th August</u> 1997, but I cannot be sure. What I can say is

---

[a] That is the time given for Entry 3, the Elysée Palace call.

that my routine security check ... is unlikely to be entry number 2 for Sunday 31st August." [a]

Paget has misrepresented Younes' sworn statement.

All Younes would say for sure was that "my routine security check ... is unlikely to be entry number 2 for Sunday 31st August". He expressly left open the possibility that the security check "could have been one of the last entries of Saturday 30th August 1997". [b]

Doing this enabled Paget to put Younes' security check together with his false[c] account of the Massoni call, thus neatly accounting for the two missing entries – 1 and 2 – for the 31 August 1997 occurrence log.

But it quickly unravels because it is based on two lies – one from Younes, his false evidence of the Massoni call; second from Paget, because the security check may have been carried out on either August 30 or 31. [d]

ii) Paget states: "It is not known why logs '1' and '2' were not copied when subsequently the other logs relating to the night were.... The FCO is unable to identify who copied the original log entries while they were in existence, and consequently who missed logs '1' and '2' and how."

In saying this, Paget is – without any reason given – indicating that the blame for the missing log sheets falls on the person who copied them.

There appear to be several possible ways these log sheet copies have gone missing:[e]

- they weren't copied because the originals had already been innocently mislaid
- they weren't copied because the originals had already been deliberately "lost"
- they weren't copied because the person copying missed those two log entries
- they were copied but the copies have been innocently mislaid since
- they were copied but the copies have been deliberately "lost" since.

---

[a] The full quote appeared earlier.

[b] Younes' statement was not made public until it was read out to the inquest on 17 December 2007. This meant that readers of the Paget Report – when it was published a year earlier, on 14 December 2006 – were unaware that they were being misled by Paget's false interpretation of Younes' statement.

[c] It will be shown to be false.

[d] Paget should have shown Younes the log entries for 30 August 1997 – that would have then determined whether the security check occurred before or after midnight.

[e] Bearing in mind, Younes' statement evidence: "the occurrence log is not a book but is in fact loose-leafed".

So there are five ways the copy sheets could have gone missing. This raises the question: Why has Paget focused the blame on the person doing the copying?

Paget says that "the FCO is unable to identify who copied the original log entries", but this may be because the copying is not done at the FCO, but at the embassy – see earlier.

I suggest that if Paget had really wanted to find out who did the copying, they could have simply asked one of their colleagues, Phil Whiteman, who George Younes had already told them "was the [embassy] security manager" at the time and "is now a British police officer".[a]

There is a real possibility that the log sheet originals – or the copies, or both – for entries 1 and 2 have been deliberately "lost", because they may contain information on phone calls that the authorities did not want the jury or public to be privy to.

I suggest that it is not a coincidence that the log entries for 30 August 1997 and the first two log entries for 31 August 1997 were not available for the jury to analyse at the inquest into the deaths of Princess Diana and Dodi Fayed.

The attempt by Paget to blame the copier for the missing log sheets could be an endeavour to make the focus of the missing sheets something inadvertent, rather than something sinister.

　　　iii)　Paget wrote: "The [only] effect of copy logs '1' and '2' being missing is that ... Embassy officials have understood the first call [about the crash] to be from the Elysée Palace at 1.10 a.m."

There are problems with this statement.

Paget has ignored the fact that having two log sheets missing, makes it impossible to know what their content is, and who made the two phone calls. Paget has presumed that they were the security and Massoni calls, but that may not be correct – see earlier and later.

Saying that "Embassy officials have understood the first call to be ... at 1.10 a.m." because the two log sheets are missing, indicates that the officials – presumably Moss and Shannon – are getting their evidence from the FCO copy log sheets.

Moss' account – and we don't have Shannon's[b] – was: "[Shannon] informed me that ... Younes ... had been told via a telephone call from the Duty Officer at the Elysée Palace".[c]

---

[a] Baker should have sought evidence from Whiteman for the inquest.

[b] See earlier.

[c] This is part of the evidence indicating that the Massoni-Younes call never occurred – if it had, then Moss would be quoting Younes saying he had been first alerted to the crash by Massoni, not the Elysée Palace. Paget moves the focus away from that, when they falsely imply that the witnesses were using the occurrence log copies to formulate their testimony.

So Moss' information is based on what Shannon told him – "he informed me". It is Moss' recollection of the phone call from Shannon – it is not based on the FCO copy log sheets as Paget is suggesting.[a]

iv) Paget has gone to "Christopher Whomersley, the Deputy Legal Adviser to the FCO" for information on what happened to the originals of the Paris embassy log sheets. They should have contacted the security manager of the Paris embassy, who – Younes had told them – was "responsible for retaining these logs".[bc]

5) Keith Moss says in his statement that Keith Shannon is "a UK based member of the Embassy staff".

Yet Younes describes phoning Shannon at around 1.15 a.m. "and eventually managed to wake him at home". Then later in his statement Younes says: "At 1.55 a.m. I received a telephone call from ... the duty officer from the French Prime Minister's office. By that point Keith Shannon had joined me at the Chancery desk and I handed this call to him."

So Shannon is woken at some point after 1.15 a.m. and is in the embassy before 1.55 a.m.[d]

This evidence indicates that Shannon is not UK-based.

It seems strange that Keith Moss – who was in Paris for five years – would think that Shannon was UK-based, when he wasn't.

It is not known why Moss said this.

6) Younes made additional comments – that weren't in the occurrence log record – regarding the Elysée Palace call:

- Younes says: "To the best of my recollection, this was the second incoming telephone call in relation to this incident", yet just a bit further on he says: "I told him[e] that we were already aware of the accident and that someone had died".

---

[a] Even if embassy officials did base their evidence on the log sheets – and I am not suggesting they have – they would presumably not be using the FCO copy, but instead the original held at the embassy.

[b] Younes even had told them the identity of the security manager – Phil Whiteman – and who he worked for – the British police.

[c] Whomersley gave the police an answer "to the best of his knowledge". Why didn't Whomersley point them in the direction of the people who would be able to answer their questions? Maybe he did and Paget hasn't said.

[d] This is also a factor that could add to the evidence indicating the Shannon-Moss call may not have occurred. Shannon was woken at home at around 1.20 a.m. and was already in at the embassy before 1.55 a.m. It is not however known where Shannon lived – but this evidence points to a rush into work that may not have left time for making other phone calls. It is possible Younes rang Shannon to primarily ask him to come in to the embassy to help out.

[e] The Elysée Palace caller.

- Younes: The Elysée Palace call was "approximately ten minutes after the initial call from Mr Massoni".

Younes timed the Massoni call at "between 12.50 a.m. and 1.00 a.m." and the Elysée Palace call was documented as occurring at 1.10 a.m. This means that the two calls were between 10 and 20 minutes apart – not "approximately ten minutes".

This gap is significant because there is no record of Younes notifying anyone until after the Elysée Palace call, even though there was a gap of approximately 15 minutes after the Massoni call.

Younes adds the additional unrecorded information about the content of the Elysée Palace call, yet later in his statement says: "The purpose of this occurrence log is to record all information for any future use."

This raises the question: Why didn't Younes record the full details of this extremely significant call?

Or, did he record it fully – and Younes has been asked to add information that infers an earlier call from Massoni was received, when it actually wasn't?

7) The Paget Report included a third person description of excerpts of Massoni's statement. It reads: "[Massoni's] assistant, Nicola Basselier, was tasked ... to inform key people. This included the British Embassy."

Paget has falsely stated that Massoni said the British Embassy was called even though Massoni had repeatedly told them that he called the British ambassador.[a]

The official general witness evidence – Younes, Moss[b] – is that Younes took the call from the Elysée Palace (1.10 a.m.), wrote it up in the log, and notified Shannon (1.15 to 1.20 a.m.). Shannon then passed on the information from the Elysée Palace call to Moss, who then in turn called Jay with that news of the crash.

Younes said: "As a result of receiving the telephone call from the Elysée Palace and making the relevant entry in the log at 1.10 a.m, I then immediately contacted ... Shannon at 1.15 a.m.... I ... eventually managed to wake him at home."

Moss said: "[Shannon] informed me that he had received this information from George Younes ... who in turn had been told via a telephone call from ... the Elysée Palace.... I then telephoned Sir Michael Jay and Tim Livesey".

Younes recorded the information received from the Elysée Palace in the log: "Lady Diana had a serious accident car at tunnel Pont de l'Alma Paris.

---

[a] This Paget lie only became known when the Massoni statement was read to the inquest in 2007.
[b] Possibly Shannon as well, but we don't have his statement.

There is death in her car[a], she is being taken away to a hospital (unreadable) Paris that still kept secret for instant take all details from here." [285]

Moss described what Shannon passed onto him – at around 1.25 a.m. – from the Elysée Palace-Younes call:[b] "[A] vehicular accident involving the Princess of Wales in the tunnel by the 'Pont d'Alma' in Paris, and that she had been transferred to the Pitié Salpêtrière Hospital.... The driver was reported dead, along with Dodi Al Fayed, and that their bodyguard Trevor Rees-Jones was injured and had been taken to hospital."

That was quoted from Moss' statement, which was compiled with the help of his 1 September 1997[c] report.[d] Moss backtracked on a part of this at the inquest: Hough: "Did [Shannon] tell you anything about the bodyguard or the driver?" Moss: "I think in my statement I said that he did, but on reflection I cannot be certain."

---

[a] This quote is taken from the Paget Report – see endnote. When this was read out, during Younes' statement, it was transcribed as "there is a death in her car". Paget directly recorded their version from the occurrence log entry 3. "Death" could refer to one or more bodies, whereas "a death" means just one. Evidence shows there were two dead – Dodi Fayed and Henri Paul. It is not known whether Younes changed it to "a death" or the lawyer who read his statement out changed it. Younes' actual statement has never been made available. A change at the inquest in the reading out of the information regarding the hospital name has already been addressed in Part 2.
[b] In his statement Moss starts by saying Shannon told him "reports were coming out", but then when Moss asked Shannon to repeat the information he says: "[Shannon] informed me that he had received this information from George Younes". These calls occurred too early for accurate information to be coming from media reports. This call was timed by Moss at the inquest as "10 or 15 minutes" after 1.10 a.m. – so, 1.20 to 1.25 a.m. Diana's ambulance didn't leave the Alma Tunnel until 1.41 a.m., but the destination was of course known to the authorities earlier than that – but not to the media. The timings are thoroughly gone through in Part 2. The general evidence is that Shannon would have called Moss straight after hearing from Younes, but Shannon's statement has not been made available. There is a query over whether this Shannon-Moss call occurred in the way it has been described by Moss, or even at all – see earlier and later.
[c] The day after the crash.
[d] Keith Moss, in his police statement: "I compiled my report on Monday 1st September 1997.... [It] was made whilst the events were fresh in my mind and using contemporaneous notes I had made in a notebook.... The report was as comprehensive as possible. To enable me to complete this statement, I am using a copy of this report in order to refresh my memory of the events that took place in Paris.": Keith Moss, Witness Statement, 22 Oct 04, reproduced in *The Documents* book, p648 (UK edition).

Jay has provided two accounts of what he was told by Moss and Livesey[a]:

- 31 August 1997 diary: "there had been a car accident, that Dodi Al Fayed and a chauffeur had been killed and ... the Princess of Wales had been seriously injured and was in hospital"

- 2005 statement: "there had been a car accident in Paris, that Dodi Al Fayed and the chauffeur were dead, and that the Princess of Wales was injured and had been taken to the Pitié Salpêtrière hospital in Paris".

---

[a] According to Younes – apparently from the log: "I informed Tim Livesey, the press officer, at 1.50 a.m." Livesey timed it at 1.20 a.m., but the written record in the log would carry more weight. This means that Jay was called by both Moss and Livesey, both receiving their information from Younes – Livesey directly, and Moss, via Shannon.

Table: Accounts of Information in Call from Elysée Palace[a] to British Embassy

Item	Embassy Log[b]	Keith Moss		Michael Jay[c]		
		Statement	Inquest	Diary Entry	Statement	Inquest
Car accident	Yes	Yes	Yes	Yes	Yes	Yes
Diana involved	Yes	Yes	Yes	Yes	Yes	Yes
Crash Location	Alma Tunnel	Alma Tunnel	None given	None given	Paris	None given
Death[d] in the car	Yes	Yes	Yes	Yes	Yes	Yes
Diana's condition	No	No	No	Seriously injured	Injured	Badly hurt
Diana taken to hospital	Yes	Yes	Yes	Yes	Yes	No
La Pitié Hospital named[e]	Yes	Yes	Yes	No	Yes	No
Driver dead	No	Yes	Not "certain"	Yes	Yes	Yes
Dodi dead	No	Yes	Yes	Yes	Yes	Yes
Bodyguard injured	No	Yes	Not "certain"	No	No	No
Bodyguard taken to hospital	No	Yes	Not "certain"	No	No	No

---

[a] In phone call to George Younes at 1.10 a.m. on 31 August 1997.
[b] Reproduced by George Younes in his police statement and also in the Paget Report, p612.
[c] It is difficult to explain the significant variations between Moss and Jay's accounts. There has to be a possibility that their first notifications were from different undisclosed sources. This is briefly addressed later in this Comment.
[d] "Death" is the word Younes wrote in the log – this could mean one or more dead.
[e] How the Elysée Palace knew that Diana was going to La Pitié at 1.10 a.m., when the ambulance didn't leave the tunnel until 1.41 a.m., has been addressed in Part 2.

The British Embassy staff were asleep on the night of 30-31 August 1997. Younes woke up Shannon. Shannon woke up Moss. Moss woke up Jay.

This is Michael Jay's alibi for the crash: he was asleep until woken by Moss' call – with the news from Younes via Shannon – at around 1.45 a.m., 1 hour and 22 minutes after the crash.

Therefore Jay couldn't have been involved in the orchestration of the crash.

If the evidence from Younes, Jay and Moss was truthful, then the columns in the above table should all be broadly similar – because both Jay and Moss claim they got their earliest information from the same source: the 1.10 a.m. Elysée Palace-Younes conversation.[a]

There are two factors that the table highlights:

a) Far from being broadly similar, the columns actually extensively differ. Out of 11 items of information there is broad agreement on only four points: that there was a car accident, Diana was involved and was taken to hospital, and that at least one person in the car had died.

b) That there was information that Moss and Jay reported receiving straight after they woke up, that was not included in the Elysée Palace-Younes phone call.

The extra information that Moss and/or Jay were privy to – and Younes wasn't – was:

- Jay wrote in his diary that he had been told Diana was "seriously injured"
- Moss and Jay both stated they were told that the driver was dead – Moss backtracked on this at the inquest
- Moss and Jay both stated they were told that Dodi had died
- Moss said he was told "that ... Rees-Jones was injured and had been taken to hospital" – he backtracked on this at the inquest.

A key point is that the additional information from Moss and Jay was all accurate – Diana was seriously injured, the driver and Dodi did both die and Rees-Jones was injured and taken to hospital.

Given that Younes was recording the Elysée Palace information straight into the occurrence log, we should be able to have confidence the log entry 3 is an accurate record of the conversation.[b]

So, why is it that Jay and Moss have provided accounts that conflict with Younes?

There appear to be two main possibilities:

---

[a] Jay doesn't specifically state that, but he does say he was woken by Moss and then Livesey – and their information came from Younes.
[b] It is also likely that when Younes phoned Shannon he would have used his occurrence log notes to ensure he passed on the correct information.

a) Moss and Jay have both lied – they received their information from a source other than Younes and Shannon

b) Moss and Jay are both mixed up about their evidence – they have both made innocent mistakes in their recall of the phone calls that took place after they woke up on 31 August 1997.

I suggest that point b is very unlikely – it is possible that one witness could make mistakes in their recall, but for two independent witnesses to make very similar mistakes is rare. It also needs to be considered that we are not talking about a long period of recall – Jay's diary was written up later that night[a] and Moss says he wrote up his report, which he used in making his statement, the following day.[b]

There really is only one logical conclusion that can be drawn: Moss and Jay received their earliest information from a source other than Younes and Shannon.

This is certainly not the first instance of lying or cover-up from Jay and Moss – see Part 4, particularly.

The question then is: If Moss and Jay did not receive their early information from the Elysée Palace, Younes or Shannon, where did it come from?

I suggest there is a real possibility that Michael Jay was called by Philippe Massoni at around 12.50 a.m.

When Scotland Yard interviewed Philippe Massoni in November 2006, they already had the statements of Jay and Younes, and probably Shannon (see footnote).[c]

Already knowing that Younes and Shannon had stated that Massoni had called them, the police asked Massoni: "Did you inform the British Embassy in Paris of the accident? Do you remember who you informed and when?" In other words, Paget was asking Massoni who he informed at the embassy, and at what time that happened.

The police appear to have asked this because they already had two embassy statements – from Younes and Shannon – both claiming they had received early calls from Massoni.[a]

---

[a] The night of 31 August 1997. See 11 Feb 08: 102.8.

[b] Moss said: "The report was as comprehensive as possible.": Keith Moss, Witness Statement, 22 Oct 04, reproduced in *The Documents* book, p648 (UK edition)

[c] Moss was interviewed first, in October 2004. Younes was interviewed in August 2005 and Jay was four months later in December. The police also probably had Shannon's statement, although the date of his interview is not known. Massoni wasn't interviewed until 14 November 2006, exactly a month before the Paget Report was made public.

There are three key aspects to Massoni's answer: a) he gives much more than the required answer to the question – he volunteers a list of high-ranking personnel who were called: "the British Ambassador, as well as the office of the President, the office of the Prime Minister and the Foreign Minister in person"; b) Massoni states that the calls were "done on my behalf by Nicola Basselier my assistant private secretary" and c) he doesn't confirm what the police may have been expecting – a call to either Younes or Shannon, or both – but instead says: "I notified the British Ambassador" – Michael Jay.[b]

Massoni confirms that he is referring to Jay when he says "British Ambassador" – later he volunteers: "I should like ... to pay tribute to his Excellency the Ambassador of Great Britain, Sir Michael Jay...."

The British police were probably surprised by Massoni's answer – given their knowledge of Younes and Shannon's accounts – and they asked a follow-up question. The nature of that question is withheld from us[c] and we are only told the answer – Massoni reconfirms that the call was to Jay: "I believe that the <u>British Ambassador to France</u> was informed ... as soon as we knew that the Princess of Wales was one of the victims.... It was ... necessary to inform ... the British Ambassador, without delay.... I cannot tell you if it was me personally or ... my private secretary who did this."

In this second answer Massoni opens up the possibility that he could have made the call – backing away from his earlier statement that the call was made by his "assistant private secretary": "I cannot tell you if it was me personally or ... my private secretary".

In summary, Massoni's account is that Jay was called – either by "me personally or ... my private secretary" – "as soon as [he] knew that the Princess of Wales was one of the victims".

It is significant that Philippe Massoni, Paris Prefect of Police, was not cross-examined at the inquest, and neither was George Younes nor Keith Shannon.[d]

---

[a] Although we know Shannon claimed he received an early call from Massoni – he was "at the scene of the crash" – we can't know the precise words Shannon used because Paget only gave a third person description.

[b] Someone could argue that a call to the British Embassy could have been considered by Massoni as the equivalent to a call to the Ambassador. There are two points: a) the police specifically asked if Massoni informed "the British Embassy in Paris". Massoni changed this in his answer to "the British Ambassador" and later in his second answer spoke of "his Excellency the Ambassador of Great Britain, Sir Michael Jay"; b) in the same sentence Massoni detailed communications to "the <u>office of</u> the President [and] the <u>office of</u> the Prime Minister" – apparently meaning he spoke to duty personnel instead of the leaders themselves.

[c] Based on the answer, the question appears to have been related to the precise timing of the call, who made it and who it was to.

[d] Shannon's statement was also not read out to the jury.

I suggest that Michael Jay has distanced himself by being placed, in his and Moss' evidence, down the bottom of the line of notification: Elysée Palace – Younes – Shannon –Moss – Jay: "I was woken at my residence ... at about 1.45 a.m." [a]

I believe that Massoni's account is closer to the truth: "the British Ambassador to France was informed ... as soon as we knew that the Princess of Wales was one of the victims" – at around 12.50 a.m.

In his statement Younes said: "During a night duty shift, it is normal procedure for separate logs to be kept by the Chancery desk and the Residence desk."

Why wasn't the Residence desk log shown to the inquest jury? I suggest that it could have revealed that a very early call was made by Philippe Massoni to Michael Jay.

Why didn't Massoni give the police a straight answer to the straight question about calling the embassy? [b]

There could be an element of cover-up in Massoni's answer – see footnote.[c] It has been shown in Part 3 that the French police were heavily involved in the cover-up. The evidence in the earlier part of this volume also indicates that this operation – the assassination of Diana – couldn't have succeeded without collusion between the British and the French.

---

[a] Moss appears to add to the distancing of Michael Jay in the events. In his statement, after describing his 2.15 a.m. arrival at La Pitié hospital, Moss says: "I hadn't been directed to go to the hospital, but I was aware that the Princess of Wales had been taken there." This is after he briefly mentioned calling Jay. I suggest it is inconceivable that during the Moss-Jay conversation the subject of Moss' role didn't come up. Jay was Moss' boss and I believe it is very likely that, at the least, Moss would have sought Jay's approval for going to the hospital, and quite possibly had been instructed by Jay to set up the embassy operation at the hospital. Jay says in his statement that he gave Moss instructions regarding his role at the hospital: "I left Keith Moss at the Hospital with instructions to ensure that no one entered the room where the Princess' body lay without his agreement and without being accompanied by him or by another member of the Embassy staff." Michael Jay, Witness Statement, reproduced in *The Documents* book, pp635-6 (UK edition). See also the Role of the British Embassy section of Chapter 2 in Part 4 for more on the Jay-Moss relationship regarding the Embalming in Paris.
[b] The question: "Did you inform the British Embassy in Paris of the accident? Do you remember who you informed and when?"
[c] In Massoni's answer – although the question was specifically about a call to the British Embassy – he appears to give a list of high-level calls to remove the focus from his call to Jay. In other words, Massoni is saying something like, "I did call Jay, but I also called these other people or their offices – so there is nothing special about the fact I called Jay".

Michael Jay was in charge of the embassy, which was the base for the Paris MI6 operation that was heavily involved in the mission to eliminate Princess Diana.

It appears possible that Jay could have had some involvement, particularly along the lines of maintaining critical contacts with high-level French authorities[a] – people like the Prefect of Paris, Philippe Massoni. It is quite conceivable that there could have been an early call from the crash scene – Massoni to Jay, maybe just to confirm that the crash had occurred and a report on the status of the occupants of the crashed Mercedes S280.

Massoni's evidence indicates a call was made – "I notified the British Ambassador".

Younes' and Shannon's unsupported earlier evidence – "I received a telephone call ... from ... Massoni"; "[Shannon received] a ... call from Philippe Massoni" – indicates that there has been an attempt to cover up the identity of the recipient of the early Massoni call: Michael Jay.

Younes and Shannon have claimed they both received calls from Massoni, but the evidence strongly indicates that Younes' call never occurred – see earlier. There is also no evidence – outside of the earlier third person Paget account – to support a call from Massoni to Shannon, and it is significant that none of Shannon's evidence was heard at the inquest.

The following scenario includes some speculation, but is nevertheless based on the available evidence.

There is a possibility that Michael Jay was in charge of handling British communication with high-level French contacts – including Massoni – in the lead up to the crash.[b] There may have been a series of calls between Massoni and Jay in the period preceding the deaths of Diana and Dodi.[cd]

---

[a] In Jay's role as the chief British diplomat in France at the time.

[b] This is an aspect Jay says he had to deal with post-crash: "I tasked [Cowper-Coles] with acting as my assistant in dealing with French officials and also with those in the UK" – see earlier.

[c] In this light, it is significant that the inquest heard evidence on the contents of the Chancery occurrence log post-crash, but nothing was said about the pre-crash phone records in both the Chancery and the Residence logs.

[d] In his police statement, Michael Jay related a phone call he made to Philippe Massoni on the night of 31 August 1997 – he quoted from a telegram he sent to the FCO: "I telephoned Massoni, the Paris Prefect de Police. Massoni said that the investigation was now out of the hands of the police and with the judicial authorities." Jay's full account of this is reproduced in *The Documents* book, pp642-3 (UK edition). Jay also appears to refer to this Massoni phone call in a late entry of his diary for 31 August 1997, read out at the inquest: "We regroup in my office until about 9 [p.m.], and I send off a telegram praising the French authorities' reaction and another on the telephone conversation with the Prefet de Police about the accident.": 11 Feb 08: 108.25.

When British police asked Philippe Massoni specifically about a post-crash notification call to the British embassy, he might have been surprised. Whatever is the case, it is clear that he did not directly answer and instead listed a series of high-level people contacted, beginning with "the British Ambassador", who he later identifies more specifically as "his excellency the Ambassador of Great Britain, Sir Michael Jay".

Michael Jay has never been asked about this account from Massoni – he should have been.[a]

The known evidence does indicate that there has been a concerted effort by embassy staff to suggest that instead of Massoni calling Jay, he called Younes and then possibly Shannon:

a) Younes claimed he was called by Massoni

b) Shannon apparently claimed he was called by Massoni – according to Paget

c) Moss claimed that he woke up Jay – i.e. Moss, not Massoni

d) Jay claimed that he was asleep before being woken up by Moss at about 1.45 a.m. – 1 hour and 22 minutes after the crash.

The documentary evidence that could substantiate Massoni's account of a call to Jay – the Residence occurrence log – was withheld from the inquest.

Although Younes gave evidence of receiving a 12.55 a.m.[b] call from Massoni, that is not supported by other evidence.[c]

Taken together, the embassy staff evidence says that the Elysée Palace called Younes, Younes called and woke up Shannon, Shannon called and woke up Moss, Moss called and woke up Jay.

Jay says he wrote in his diary late on 31 August 1997: "The phone rang about 1.45 a.m. First Keith Moss, then Tim Livesey[d], to tell me that there had been a car accident".

I suggest that Jay was fully aware – even on 31 August 1997 – that he was going to need a strong alibi for the night of the crash. Being asleep next to his wife was good enough.[e]

---

[a] There is no excuse for why Jay wasn't asked at the inquest – Massoni's statement was read out in November 2007 and Jay was cross-examined in February 2008. It is also obvious that Massoni should have been cross-examined, but that too never happened.

[b] Approximate.

[c] Paul Johnston – who says he was in Normandy at the time – told Hervé Stéphan in 1998 about a call from "the police" to the "duty officer" – this is addressed later.

[d] Livesey's statement has also never been released.

[e] Jay's wife has never been questioned by any of the investigations and was not heard from at the inquest.

Over the years the police took three embassy statements that have now been released[a] – Moss, interviewed on 22 October 2004; Younes, interviewed on 15 August 2005; Jay, interviewed on 13 December 2005.[b]

Moss' was the first – in 2004 – and his account basically supported Jay's diary. He says: "I ... telephoned Sir Michael Jay". It's interesting that neither Jay in his diary, nor Moss in his statement, mention that Jay was woken up by this call. Moss also makes no comment on the content of this call to Jay – it is inferred that it was to notify him, but that is not stated.

Moss describes the chain of calls: "[Shannon] informed me that he had received this information from George Younes ... who in turn had been told via a telephone call from ... the Elysée Palace." No mention here of any Massoni-Younes call.

The next statement made was from Younes, 10 months later in August 2005. Younes introduces the Massoni call, but he puts it in as though it's an add-on. Younes says: "As a result of receiving the telephone call from the Elysée Palace ... I then immediately contacted the duty Chancery officer, Mr Keith Shannon".

So Younes says he contacted Shannon "as a result of" the Elysée Palace call – not the Massoni call, even though he said that had come 15 minutes earlier.

I suggest that Younes has been told to put the Massoni-Younes call into his evidence and I also suggest he has followed that order reluctantly.[c] Younes' account of the call is quite detailed – see earlier – in fact, surprisingly so, since he was going from an eight year old memory of it. I suggest the detail is in there to give it credibility.

But the reality is that there is no supporting evidence that this call ever occurred – and in fact other evidence indicates the first Younes knew of the crash was from the Elysée Palace.[d]

The last of the embassy statements was made by Jay, four months after Younes, in December 2005. He maintained his diary account of calls from Moss and Livesey and this time introduced the words: "I was woken at my residence ... at about 1.45 a.m." [e]

---

[a] They took statements from Shannon and Livesey that have never been released.

[b] The only public release of the Moss and Jay statements was in *The Documents* book, published in 2010.

[c] Younes provided helpful information on the identities of the security officers – see earlier.

[d] Younes said in his statement: "As a result of this telephone call, I thanked him and I told him that we were already aware of the accident", referring to the Massoni call – but that part is not in the occurrence log and was added by Younes in his statement.

[e] That was in turn supported by Moss' later inquest account: "I ... got [Jay] out of bed".

No mention of a Massoni call[a] – in keeping with the Younes statement.

Then Massoni wasn't interviewed until November 2006. As it turned out, Paget officers asked Massoni who he called at the embassy. And that's when Massoni gave his account of a call to the ambassador, Jay.

The balance of the evidence – gone through earlier – indicates that the Massoni account is correct.[b]

Why was Younes asked to include the Massoni call in his evidence?

I suggest it was because at the time he gave his statement – August 2005 – it was known that Jay and Massoni still had to give their statements to the British police.

Jay, I suggest, was particularly keen to distance himself as far away from the crash as possible[c] – that is why he has been put to the bottom of the notification pile, after Younes, Shannon and Moss. Yet Jay – who by 2005 had left his position in France four years earlier – knew that Massoni might provide an account of a phone call that did take place at around 12.50 a.m.

Jay may have asked Younes to include the account of the Massoni call – so that if Massoni's evidence was to be studied in the future, then there would be testimony from the British side that there was a Massoni call to the embassy. It would look a lot worse if there was no evidence from anyone in the British embassy of a call from Massoni.

I suggest it is logical that French authorities would officially notify the British after the crash – and that did occur when the Elysée Palace called Younes at 1.10 a.m.

Moss altered his account at the inquest, without explanation.

a) His timing of the notification call from Shannon:

- statement: "at around 0110hrs [1.10 a.m.] ... I received a telephone call from ... Shannon"

- inquest: "my statement says 10 past 1, but I think it was a little bit after that".

At the inquest Hough then asked Moss: "How long after?" And Moss replied: "I cannot really remember, but I guess it was 10 or 15 minutes probably."

---

[a] To Jay.

[b] According to Paget, Massoni called Keith Shannon, who was Second Secretary Technology. I suggest it is common sense that Massoni would call the ambassador, rather than a much lower ranked official.

[c] In his evidence Moss appears to help Jay with that – he shows no urgency in contacting him: "First of all, I tried to collect my senses. I then sat down and worked out the immediate things that I needed to do; for example, who did I need to inform?... My first telephone call was to the so-called resident clerk in the Foreign Office.... I then telephoned the Ambassador...."

The statement account of "around 0110hrs" is reasonably specific. Earlier evidence has indicated that Jay was notified of the crash around 12.50 a.m. by Massoni. It is possible that Moss – as Consul-General – may be one of the first people Jay would have contacted. Therefore, 1.10 a.m. is a possible time – if Moss had been notified by Jay.

1.10 a.m. certainly doesn't fit with a notification from Shannon, who was reached by Younes at some point after 1.15 a.m.[a]

I suggest that Moss' statement account that he was woken by Shannon at 1.10 a.m. is false. Moss may have inadvertently left the 1.10 a.m. – the correct time he could have been notified by Jay – in this account, not realising that it didn't fit with entry 3 posted by Younes in the occurrence log.

By the time Moss was cross-examined at the inquest – three years after his statement – he appears to have become aware of the inconsistency between his and Younes' statement and the occurrence log. When asked, Moss admits the statement timing of 1.10 a.m. is wrong – adding on "10 or 15 minutes" solves the problem, but I suggest it is not the truth.

The overall evidence indicates that it was more likely Keith Moss was contacted by Michael Jay[b] – not Keith Shannon – at around 1.10 a.m. – not 1.20 to 1.25 a.m., as Moss stated at the inquest.[ca]

---

[a] Younes called Shannon at 1.15 a.m., but didn't reach him straightaway – see earlier.

[b] The conflict between the initial information received by Jay and Moss – see earlier table – raises the possibility Moss was initially notified by someone other than Jay, but not Shannon. See later footnote.

[c] 1.10 a.m. for the notification of Keith Moss also fits closer with the timing he provided for his arrival at the hospital – 2.15 a.m. Moss told the inquest that after receiving the notification call, "I tried to collect my senses. I then sat down and worked out the immediate things that I needed to do". Later he described his actions up to arriving at the hospital: "Once I had made my calls and there was a series of them – I cannot remember now how long it took, certainly 15 or so minutes – I then washed, brushed my teeth, dressed and I walked to my motor car which, because of where we were living in Paris, it was not parked in the building that we were in, it was in a separate building in an underground lock-up, which would have taken me about ten minutes, I suppose. Then I drove from my residence where I lived to the Pitié Salpêtrière Hospital, which was not very far from where I was living. It must have taken me no more than 15 minutes maximum, I would have thought, to reach the hospital, where I arrived at I think something in the region of 2.15 in the morning." 22 Nov 07: 12.4. If you allow Moss 10 minutes for the notification call and thinking time – working out "the immediate things that I needed to do"; phone calls – 15 minutes; washing, teeth and dressing – 10 minutes; walk to car – 10 minutes; drive to hospital – 15 minutes. All up, that's 60 minutes, or one hour of activities. That means, with a notification call at 1.10 a.m. he could have arrived at the hospital at 2.10 a.m., and Moss said it was "in the region of 2.15 [a.m.]". These calculations of course are based on a call from Jay at around 1.10 a.m. If the call

b)   Information about the bodyguard and the driver.

Hough – who evidently was putting questions based on Moss' statement – asked Moss: "Did [Shannon] tell you anything about the bodyguard or the driver?" Moss replied: "I think in my statement I said that he did, but on reflection I cannot be certain."

Moss had said in his statement: "[Shannon] also informed me that the driver was reported dead ... and that their bodyguard Trevor Rees-Jones was injured and had been taken to hospital."

That is a straight statement – there is no "I think" or "possibly" or "probably" or "to the best of my recall".

Moss should have been asked for an explanation for his change of position on this and the timing (above). That didn't happen.

Why would Moss change his evidence?

There is a possibility that Moss has been given access to the content of Younes' statement – taken 10 months after Moss' – before he gave his inquest testimony.

If you look back at the table that shows the various accounts of the information in the first notification call,[b] Moss' inquest account – once he withdraws information on the driver and bodyguard – lines up with the

---

came from Shannon – as Moss has maintained – then it would have been at around 1.25 a.m. Add on the 60 minutes of activities and we end up with a hospital arrival time of 2.25 a.m. – about 10 minutes later than Moss has stated.

In Moss' police statement he said the walk from his home to the car was 5 minutes – "I took the five-minute walk to the secure underground garage where I kept my car". But in that account he has not provided detailed timings for his other activities, so I suggest the inquest evidence (of 10 minutes) could be more accurate. Source: Keith Moss, Witness Statement, reproduced in *The Documents* book, p649 (UK edition).

[a] Jay has said that Moss phoned him at 1.45 a.m. The timings in the previous footnote indicate that Moss didn't wash and get dressed until after that phone call. If the call – after waking Jay up – lasted say, 5 minutes, then that is 1.50 a.m., then add 10 minutes for washing and dressing, 10 minutes walk to the car and 15 minutes for the drive to the hospital. That would mean that Moss wouldn't have arrived at the hospital until 2.25 a.m. – 10 minutes later than Moss said. Other evidence has shown that Jay was called by Massoni around 12.50 a.m. and his evidence that Moss woke him at 1.45 a.m. is fictional.

[b] Even a quick look at the earlier table regarding the notification call accounts reveals variations between Moss' and Jay's account of what they were told. Although I believe that Moss and Jay got their first notification from the same source, Massoni – Massoni to Jay to Moss – I am not able to explain why their accounts differ. There has to be a possibility that Moss received his information from another source, particularly in relation to his claimed knowledge of information regarding the bodyguard.

occurrence log on all but two points. One is the location of the crash, the Alma Tunnel, which Moss simply doesn't mention at the inquest – that is an omission. The only other variation from the occurrence log is Moss' diffident inclusion at the inquest of Dodi's death: "I think [Shannon] said that Mr Al Fayed was also involved, and I think he said that he had succumbed to the accident".

Now, Younes never mentioned Dodi's death in the occurrence log, but he did have it in his statement – not as part of the Elysée Palace call, but instead he said it was in the Massoni call:[a] "[Massoni] told me that ... a Mr Al Fayed had died in the accident".

It's possible then that Moss has lined his inquest account up with Younes' statement[b] – a document that didn't exist when Moss had put together his 2004 statement.

To summarise the factors indicating that there has been a cover-up regarding an early call to Michael Jay, and that he has lied when he claimed he was woken by Keith Moss at 1.45 a.m. on 31 August 1997:[c]

-   Massoni has stated that he called Jay at around 12.50 a.m.
-   Younes said Massoni told him there was "one dead", when it should have been obvious to a police officer that there were two dead
-   Younes failed to advise anyone about the crash until after the Elysée Palace call, which occurred 15 minutes after the alleged Massoni call
-   Moss said he received a call from Shannon passing on information from an Elysée Palace-Younes call – no mention of a Massoni call to Younes
-   even though it occurred 8 years earlier, Younes recalled from memory a lot of detail about the Massoni call
-   FCO copies of occurrence log entries 1 and 2 for 31 August 1997 – which are claimed to include the Massoni-Younes call – have mysteriously disappeared
-   the inquest jury weren't told which log entries were missing
-   no attempt appears to have been made to locate the original occurrence log sheets and Jay said he couldn't help[d]

---

[a] A call which I suggest never occurred – see earlier.

[b] Bearing in mind that Moss didn't mention the location of the crash – the Alma Tunnel. Moss wasn't asked about this – had he been asked, I suggest he probably would have agreed that the location was mentioned in the call.

[c] There is a build-up of evidence – these factors need to be viewed together as a whole, not individually.

[d] It could be significant that when Mansfield initially asked Jay about the nature of the occurrence log, he failed to mention that phone calls were included in it: Mansfield: "Is a log kept at the Embassy of incoming communications and outgoing communications and other occurrences, rather like an occurrence book in fact?" Jay: "Certainly as far as telegrams and electronic communications, yes, there would be records kept of those telegrams going in and going out.": 11 Feb 08: 114.3.

- Paget investigators lied in their description of Younes' evidence relating to early phone calls on 31 August 1997
- without giving any logical reason, Paget blamed the person who did the copying of the log entries for the missing entries – and then declared that person couldn't be identified
- Paget lied by severely misrepresenting the effect of the missing log entries
- in his statement Younes added unrecorded comments regarding the content of the Elysée Palace call – these remarks appear to be aimed at providing credibility for his account of the Massoni call
- Paget falsely stated that Massoni had said he had his assistant call the embassy, when he actually said the call was to Jay
- Jay and Moss – despite claiming their information was received from Younes after the Elysée Palace call – provided evidence of receiving information[a] that was not included in the Elysée Palace-Younes call
- Massoni voluntarily describes additional calls to high-level people in an apparent effort to undervalue the significance of his call to Jay
- the official embassy witness evidence – Moss, Younes, Jay – places Jay at the bottom of the crash notification list[b], whereas common sense and Massoni places him near the top
- the ambassador's residence occurrence log has never been looked at by any of the police investigations and was not shown to the inquest jury
- key witness statements were withheld from the inquest – Michael Jay, Keith Moss, Keith Shannon, Tim Livesey. Also, Massoni, Younes, Shannon and Livesey should have been subjected to cross-examination
- Michael Jay was not asked about the Massoni call, even though the inquest lawyers had Massoni's statement
- Michael Jay's wife – his main alibi – has never been interviewed by the police
- according to Paget, Shannon claimed he was called by Massoni – no evidence of this has ever been made available
- Moss' original 1.10 a.m. timing for being woken up fits with an early call after the 12.50 a.m. Massoni-Jay call, but doesn't fit with occurring after the 1.10 a.m. Elysée Palace-Younes call
- at the inquest Moss appears to have changed his evidence on the content of his notification call to fit with the account in Younes' police statement.

---

[a] Information that was later shown to be accurate.
[b] After Younes, Shannon and Moss.

Paul Johnston, private secretary to Michael Jay, has stated that he was in Normandy at the time. Although not directly involved in these events, he has, however, provided three accounts of what occurred:

Paul Johnston: 16 Dec 98 Letter to Hervé Stéphan and Marie-Christine Devidal:

"Nobody in the British Embassy in Paris was aware of the Princess of Wales' trip to France.... The first person to have any knowledge of it was the duty officer, who received the call from the police just after the accident." [286]

Paul Johnston: 12 Jan 99 Letter to Hervé Stéphan: **Jury Didn't Hear**:

"As I told you in my letter of 16 December, the Embassy was only advised of the presence in Paris of the Princess of Wales on learning of the accident in which she had been involved in the early hours of 31 August." [287]

Paul Johnston: Paget Description of Statement: **Jury Didn't Hear**:

"[Johnston] stated that the British Embassy in Paris first became aware of the presence of the Princess of Wales at about 1.10am on receipt of a telephone call from the Elysée Palace." [288]

Comment: This is a further case of conflicting accounts in the British Embassy evidence – two of these directly conflict:

-   "the first person to have any knowledge of it was the duty officer, who received the call from the police just after the accident" – to Stéphan, 16 Dec 98[a]

-   "the British Embassy ... first became aware of the presence of [Diana] at about 1.10am on receipt of a telephone call from the Elysée Palace" – to Paget, undated.

So the 1998 account to the French investigation is a "call from the police just after the accident", but the much later account to the British investigation is the 1.10 a.m. Elysée Palace call.

There are a few points:

-   Johnston's 1998 description is very vague: "the police" – no name or position given[b]; the timing – "just after the accident"

-   Johnston's second letter to Stéphan is even more vague: "the Embassy" – no specific person; no explanation of how "advised" or who the advice came from; timing – "in the early hours"

-   we are not given Stéphan's questions to the British embassy – the first Stéphan letter, dated 1 December 1998, appears to be redacted in the critical area[c] and Stéphan's second letter was not provided to the jury [a]

---

[a] This also conflicts with the evidence of Charles Ritchie who says he became aware of Diana's presence in Paris at around 11.55 p.m. on 30 August 1997 – see later.

[b] The Younes evidence was that the call came from Prefect of police, Philippe Massoni – that is a person who could have been well known to Stéphan.

[c] It is viewable on the inquest website – INQ0049253 and INQ0049254.

- the weight of evidence – see earlier – is that the initial call was from Massoni to Jay

- Paget makes no comment on the obvious conflict between Johnston's 1998 letter to Stéphan and his Paget account, even though they appear next to each other in the Paget Report.[b]

Johnston's 1998 account is the earliest evidence of a call from the police, so it is significant, even if Johnston was in Normandy at the time. His information comes from either what he has been told – presumably by Jay or Younes – or from a document, like the occurrence log.

I suggest that if it had come from the occurrence log – and considering that it is a reply to a question from the chief French investigator – then we could expect to see more specific information, particularly the time and the name of the caller.[c]

It appears more likely that Johnston has been provided his information from Jay – who I suggest would have been taking a direct interest in communications with the French investigation. Earlier evidence has shown that Jay was called early by Massoni, but he may not have been willing to pass on that information to Stéphan.

It may be significant that the 1998 Johnston letter is the only one of the three accounts where he specifically identifies the receiver of the call – "the duty officer", unnamed.[d]

It is possible that this is when Jay first decided to shift the initial call from himself to Younes, but at this stage withholding the specific identity of the caller[e] – "the police".

Johnston's Paget account appears to fit with what was submitted by Jay, Moss, Shannon – see earlier.

The elephant in the room in this section is the failure of Baker to ensure that the jury had access to the Residence log[f] – calls to Jay's residence – and the Chancery occurrence log for 30 August 1997.

---

[a] There is a possibility that these Johnston letters are responding to allegations (most likely from Richard Tomlinson) of British embassy – maybe via MI6 – involvement in the orchestration of the crash.

[b] See Paget Report, p611.

[c] The specific information in Johnston's Paget evidence – 1.10 a.m. and Elysée Palace – indicates it has been taken from the occurrence log, entry 3 (see earlier).

[d] This was the only specific information in that 1998 account, and it could have been aimed at deflecting attention away from Jay.

[e] Philippe Massoni.

[f] This log could show an early call from Massoni on it.

If the embassy had prior knowledge of the Alma Tunnel crash, it is possible the records of phone calls received prior to 12.23 a.m. on 31 August 1997 could have shed light on it.

The fact that these records have never been seen by any investigation – and particularly the inquest – raises serious questions about the will of the investigators, including Scott Baker, to get to the bottom of what happened in Paris on the weekend of 30-31 August 1997.

Missing Notes

Stephen Donnelly, British Vice Consul, Paris: 22 Sep 2005 Statement read out 17 Dec 07: 126.25:
"I have been asked whether I made notes that day and whether I still have them. I made some notes at the time of who I spoke to, when and the conversation. These notes were made at the time on some scrap paper and at the end of the day I wrote them up cleanly. I remember taking my notes into the office on the following Monday [September 1], but I do not know where they are now. I certainly don't remember seeing them in the consular case file. I gave them to Keith Moss at the time as he was going to do a report of everything that happened. I am sure that he gave the notes back to me and the normal procedure would be that they would be put into the registration office for filing into the consular file.[a] I do not know what has happened to them, but I definitely did not destroy them."
Comment: Where are Stephen Donnelly's notes?
No one has said.

Communication with the UK

FCO

Michael Jay: 13 Dec 05 Statement: **Jury Didn't Hear**:
"All telegrams from the British Embassy in Paris went out under my name, unless I was absent from the country or on holiday in which case they went out under the name of my Deputy, who was Stephen Howarth. I would have seen all telegrams of importance before they were sent, and I would have drafted some of them, though my degree of input would vary. The more routine telegrams, although issued under my name, may well have been sent out under the authority of another officer in the Embassy." [289]

Scotland Yard

Nicholas Gargan, British Police Liaison with French Investigation, Paris: 13 Dec 07: 14.1:

---

[a] This indicates that Keith Moss did not follow normal procedure when he "disposed of" his original notes – see earlier.

Mansfield: Q. You kept something called the "day book", didn't you?

A. Yes.

Q. And the day book, what did that record? Just that something happened or more detail than that?

A. My day book did not record a great deal of detail because our standard practice in the Embassy would be that we would conduct our correspondence back to the UK in the form of intelligence logs and messages. There is no point putting something in a day book and just immediately then to put it into a log. So the record would be the log.

Role of Michael Jay

How involved was the British ambassador to France, Michael Jay, in the assassination of Princess Diana?

Michael Jay, British Ambassador to France, 1996-2001, Paris: 11 Feb 08: 96.13:

Burnett: Q. Do you, as Ambassador, have overall responsibility for [MI6 and MI5] and their actions and activities?

A. Yes, as Ambassador I have overall responsibility for the conduct and activities of all sections, all departments of the Embassy, including the members of MI6, yes.

.... Q. How, as Ambassador, were you kept informed of the activities of the SIS/MI6 section in the Embassy?

A. I would hold regular meetings with the head of the [MI6] section, as I would do with the heads of other sections of the Embassy. He would keep me informed about the main work that they were doing and he would tell me of any particular operations that might be difficult or sensitive or raise in particular press interest. So I would have a general oversight of the operations.

Q. Would you expect, as ambassador, to be kept informed of particular significant activities of the MI6 section or station, whatever one calls it?

A. I would if there was something which the head of the section, the head of the MI6 section, believed was important enough to bring to my attention. I would not expect him to be telling me everything he got up to, that would be wrong, but I would expect him to tell me about a major activity or a major operation, in particular one that was likely to lead or might lead to some kind of public interest.

At 99.13: Q. You have told us that you and Lady Jay were in Paris that weekend.

A. Yes.

Q. In a way that made you quite rare birds, we infer, because Paris seems to be pretty much deserted in August by senior officials of any sort.

A. They come back in the last week of August and we had come back in the last week of August in order to prepare for what seemed likely to be a busy autumn.

Q. Did you have any guests staying with you that weekend?

A. Yes, we did. We had my wife's father and his partner staying with us.

Q. Now on 30th August itself, the Saturday, are you able to tell us what you were doing during the day and particularly in the evening?

A. I believe that I was working on papers that morning, either in the residence or in the Embassy next door. In the afternoon we took my wife's father and her[a] partner to the bateau-mouche, which are those boats which go along the Seine, where they went on a river trip, and then we picked them up when they came back. As I recall, we had supper together in the residence that evening.

Q. Just the four of you?

A. Just the four of us.

Q. Then can you remember when you went to bed? You have told us that the call you received in the early hours of the morning, that you were in bed.

A. No, I remember when we woke up. I do not remember when we went to bed.

Q. During the course of the day, that is to say the Saturday, had you had any official engagements of any sort?

A. No, not as far as I remember.

Q. With your father-in-law and his partner staying, would you have expected to organise official engagements?

A. No, this was at the very end of the holiday season. This was a weekend. This was a weekend that we would have hoped to have been able to spend with them, showing them something of Paris, before the work really started the following week.

Q. Similarly, for the Sunday, Sunday the 31st, before anyone knew the crash had happened, had you any official engagements planned for that day?

A. No, we had no official engagements, no.

Comment: Michael Jay's role is a significant issue, because he has been named as a possible suspect in the post-crash cover-up.

As we have come to expect in this case, there is no alibi checking, and witness evidence – if the witness is part of the Establishment – is taken as gospel truth.

Jay states: "This was a weekend that we would have hoped to have been able to spend with them[b], showing them something of Paris".

Burnett had earlier asked: "Now on 30th August itself, the Saturday, are you able to tell us what you were doing...?" Jay had replied: "I believe that I

---

[a] This probably should be "his".

[b] The Jays' visitors – Jay's father-in-law and his partner.

was working on papers that morning.... In the afternoon we took my wife's father and [his] partner to the bateau-mouche ... and then we picked them up when they came back. As I recall, we had supper together in the residence that evening."

One could argue there is a conflict there. The Jays have visitors and he said: "we would have hoped to have been able to spend [time] with them, showing them something of Paris".

But instead, on the full day of the weekend before the crash[a] – after being asked to describe his activities – Jay has related "working on papers", dropping the visitors off and later picking them up, and sharing "supper together in the residence".

So it turns out that none of the day's activities – as described by Jay – included "[spending time] with them, showing them something of Paris".

Why is this?

Did Jay have embassy-related engagements preventing him from spending time with his visiting relatives?

Burnett asked Jay: "During the course of the ... Saturday, had you had any official engagements of any sort?" Jay: "No, not as far as I remember."

So what was Jay doing on that Saturday?

This evidence certainly opens the window to the possibility Jay had deliberately kept his time free to deal with issues relating to a planned Paris assassination.

Jay also stated that he "had no official engagements" on the Sunday.

The question has to be asked: Did Michael Jay deliberately ensure ahead of time that the weekend of 30-31 August 1997 was clear?

At the inquest Michael Jay's diary for 31 August 1997 was read out[290b], but the question is: Why wasn't his diary for the previous day – August 30 – also read out? [c]

I suggest that it would be difficult to comprehend that MI6 could plan and conduct an operation of this size and complexity – the assassination of Princess Diana by orchestrated car crash – from inside the embassy, under the nose of Michael Jay, without him being aware or possibly involved.

---

[a] Saturday, 30 August 1997.

[b] There is an issue with the way this was done. Burnett requested Jay to read the diary entry out, which seems appropriate – Jay was the author of the document. What happens though is that when a lengthy document like this is read through by the witness, it doesn't give the lawyer the opportunity to ask questions during the reading – it would be rude for the lawyer to interrupt the witness. The upshot of this is the diary entry was read to the inquest without the scrutiny it deserved.

[c] This also should be viewed in the light of earlier evidence showing the early Massoni-Jay phone call was covered up.

Part 4 has already shown that Jay was involved in the cover-up and was shown to have lied in his evidence to protect the Queen.[a]

There is a possibility Jay was also involved in pre-crash activities – possibly in a diplomatic role involving contacts between high-level French figures and the UK. Earlier volumes (and this one) have shown that this assassination – and the ensuing cover-up – could not have been successful without collusion between British and French authorities.

Michael Jay: 13 Dec 05 Statement: **Jury Didn't Hear**:

"I have been asked whether I received any instructions on 31/08/1997 to carry out a particular course of action and if so, from whom and what exactly it was I was requested to do. The decisions which were taken on 31/08/1997 with regard to the death of the Princess of Wales and my part in the events that followed, including the courses of action that I took and why, are set out in the Reports and Records to which I have already referred. I do not believe that there was any significant course of action that I took on 31/08/1997 that is not described and explained in those Reports and Records." [291]

Comment: Michael Jay was asked a specific question: Did he receive "any instructions on 31/08/1997 to carry out a particular course of action and if so, from whom and what exactly it was [he] was requested to do?"

He did not answer this question.

Instead Jay pointed to "reports and records" that were withheld from the jury investigating the deaths of the people to whom the "decisions" and "courses of action" relate to.[bc]

Why were they withheld?

The failure to provide key evidence – Jay's August 30 diary, the above "reports and records", the residence occurrence log for August 30-31 – raises troubling concerns about the pre and post-crash activities of the British ambassador to France, Michael Jay.

---

[a] See section on Repatriation by Charles.

[b] They were also not included in the Paget Report.

[c] These reports and records were mentioned in Jay's statement, which means that the jury – who had no access to his statement – were not even allowed to know that they existed.

Location of Robert Fellowes[ab]

There is conflicting evidence over where Robert Fellowes, Diana's brother-in-law, was on the night of the crash. Allegations have been made that he was present at the British embassy in Paris.

Mohamed Al Fayed, Dodi's Father, UK: 18 Feb 08: 73.12:

Burnett: Q. Now, in a letter[c] to Lord Stevens, you said this: "At a meeting [your] officers were told of information which I believed to be authentic concerning Lord Fellowes. It is said that he was present at the British Embassy in Paris at 11 pm on 30th August 1997.... Robert Fellowes commandeered the communications centre at the British Embassy and sent messages to GCHQ. I hope that firm evidence of his involvement can be provided, but in the meantime I hope that you will see fit to question him as to this important break-through." Right?

A. That is right.

....Q. Is that still your belief, that Lord Fellowes was in Paris that night?

A. Yes. How can I prove? The Embassy must have documents. Can you discover the documents in the Embassy? I am certain there is some proofs.

Q. My question, Mr Al Fayed, was whether it was still your belief, and I think from the answer you have given, the answer is in fact yes, it is still your belief?

A. I have been told that. I have been told that by a very, very responsible person who knows exactly what happened.

Sue Reid, Investigations Editor, *Daily Mail*: 17 Jun 06 Article: **Jury Didn't Hear**:

"Mr X, was based at the British Embassy in Paris and formerly worked for the Foreign Office in London.... Mr X is said to be a middle-aged, English wireless operator at the [British] Embassy. He came on duty in the early evening of August 30, expecting his night shift to be routine. From his office in the communications room, encrypted phone calls and messages were sent from the embassy via UK listening stations to Downing Street, the heads of Whitehall departments and, if necessary, senior aides of the Royal Family. "Mr X was proud of his job and is an ardent royalist. However, something unexpected happened that night which he found deeply troubling. He says that just before midnight ... two well-spoken men burst through the door of

---

[a] The general evidence in Part 4 shows that Robert Fellowes wasn't in Balmoral with the Queen. Robin Janvrin, Fellowes' deputy, was shown to be on location there and dealt with issues as they arose.

[b] The evidence in this section should be viewed in the light of the next chapter on The Royals.

[c] Dated 21 February 2006 – see Paget excerpt below.

the communications room. Described as 'public school', they brusquely ordered Mr X to leave his post and not to return until [he is] told. Mr X kept silent about this ... until 2000 because he had signed the Official Secrets Act. But then, apparently, he named one of the men to a third party.... He explained: 'It was that bastard Fellowes. He turfed me out of my own office. He was in Paris the night Diana died.'

"[Mr X's] story ... is being actively investigated by Lord Stevens and his [Paget] team.

"The Mail understands that in an initial conversation with the Diana squad, Lord Fellowes has said he was enjoying a break at his Norfolk estate with his wife, Diana's sister, Lady Jane Fellowes. He has dismissed the claim he was in Paris that weekend or any part of the night Diana died." [292]

Robert Fellowes, Queen's Private Secretary, 1990-99, UK: 12 Feb 08: 2.21:
Burnett: Q. It had been suggested, particularly in a letter from Mr Al Fayed, that it was said that you had been present in the British Embassy at 11 o'clock in the evening on 30th August 1997 and commandeered the communications centre to send messages to GCHQ. In other words, it was being suggested that you were intimately concerned in the murder of your sister-in-law. You understand that that was the allegation?
A. Yes.
Q. Were you in Paris on that evening?
A. No.
Q. Both you and your family provided considerable detail to the police of your precise whereabouts in Norfolk, I think, and descriptions of what you were doing.
A. We were in Norfolk that evening. We had people to stay. We went to an entertainment by Mr John Mortimer in Burnham Market Church.

Michael Jay, British Ambassador to France, 1996-2001, Paris: 11 Feb 08: 112.24:
Burnett: Q. It has also been suggested that Lord Fellowes, who was, at the time, the Queen's private secretary and also the brother-in-law of the Princess of Wales, was in Paris on the night of 30th August and had commandeered an operations room in the Embassy essentially to oversee and organise the murder of his sister-in-law. Was Lord Fellowes in Paris?
A. No, he was not.

Paget Report, p606:
"Mohamed Al Fayed in a letter to Lord Stevens, February 21 2006: "It is said that Robert Fellowes was present at the British Embassy in Paris at 11 p.m. on 30 August 1997.... Robert Fellowes commandeered the communications centre at the British Embassy and sent messages to GCHQ."

Paget Report, p622: **Jury Didn't Hear**:
Paget reply to Mohamed Al Fayed's claim: "There is no evidence to support this claim. All of the evidence shows that Lord Robert Fellowes was at home

in England with his family, including his wife, Lady Jane Fellowes, on Saturday night and Sunday morning. Lady Jane Fellowes was the sister of the Princess of Wales. Lord Fellowes was with friends in his local village in England on the night of Saturday 30 August 1997. This information has been confirmed to Operation Paget officers. The two Security Officers on duty at the British Embassy in Paris on the night of Saturday 30 August 1997 have provided statements confirming that nothing like this could happen or did happen at the Embassy. There is no supporting evidence at all to substantiate anything to do with this claim."

George Younes, British Embassy Security Officer, Paris: 15 Aug 05 Statement read out 17 Dec 07: 110.9:

"On Saturday 30th August 1997, Simon Jackson and I were the only two people to be working at the British Embassy. Prior to the incident at the Alma Tunnel I had walked around the Chancery for one of the routine security checks, but I do not recall the time. I can however confirm that there was no one else present in the Chancery offices. Furthermore, if there had been anyone working in the offices, they would have been registered at the security desk."

Comment: This comes across as an incredible allegation – that Robert Fellowes was present in the communications room of the British embassy late at night on 30 August 1997.

It also should have been a simple allegation for either Operation Paget or Scott Baker to dispel – if it is untrue.

All Baker had to do was ensure that two simple things occurred:

1) give the jury access to or a copy of the pre-crash occurrence log for the British embassy chancery

2) give the jury proper alibi details for Robert Fellowes' movements on the night of 30 August 1997.

The fact that neither of these actions were taken – by either Paget or Baker – raises serious concerns about what Fellowes, the British authorities, or both, have to hide.

The most detailed allegation is made in a June 2006 *Daily Mail* article based on witness evidence provided to the newspaper's respected investigations editor, Sue Reid. It is amazing that neither Sue Reid nor the *Daily Mail* are mentioned in either the Paget account or the details provided by lawyer, Ian Burnett, at the inquest.[a]

---

[a] In an article in September 2007, just a week before the inquest commenced, Sue Reid wrote: "A tape recording of one unnamed informant claims that ... Robert Fellowes ... was in the French capital an hour before the crash and was seen in the telecommunications room of the British Embassy." This was also never mentioned

The focus in the Paget Report and at the inquest was on a claim made four months earlier[a] to Operation Paget by Mohamed Al Fayed. Mohamed told the inquest: "I have been told that by a very, very responsible person who knows exactly what happened."

Why wasn't Mohamed asked about the source of the information? [b]

It appears that neither Paget nor Burnett asked him – even though both were presumed to be carrying out thorough investigations into the circumstances of the deaths.[c]

Mohamed stated: "The Embassy must have documents". And I suggest that is correct – see earlier.[d] Next Mohamed asks the inquest lawyer, Ian Burnett: "Can you discover the documents in the Embassy?"

Burnett ignores this, and reiterates his question, even though he was aware Mohamed had already answered it.[e]

The embassy occurrence log for 30 August 1997 is a key part of this and until those records are made public, significant questions will remain about what went on in the embassy on the night of 30-31 August 1997.

Paget – which only provides a third person description of evidence – appears to give two different alibis for Robert Fellowes for the night of 30-31 August 1997:

1) "All of the evidence shows that Lord Robert Fellowes was <u>at home</u> in England <u>with his family</u> ... on Saturday night and Sunday morning"

2) "Lord Fellowes was <u>with friends in his local village</u> in England on the night of Saturday 30 August 1997".

Paget's first alibi is "at home ... with his family" and the second is "with friends in his local village".

So, one with his family, then another one, with his friends.

---

during the inquest. Source: Sue Reid, Diana: The Unseen Evidence Which Has Been Mysteriously Ignored Until Now, *Daily Mail*, 25 September 2007.

[a] Earlier than the first *Mail* article.

[b] The term used in Mohamed Al Fayed's letter to Paget is "communications centre". It may be significant that the identical term is used twice by Michael Jay during his inquest questioning – see above. The description in the *Mail* article is "communications room" which, although not identical, has a similar meaning.

[c] When Paget quoted Mohamed's February 2006 letter, they missed out: "At a meeting [our] officers were told of information which I believed to be authentic concerning Lord Fellowes." Instead they just started with Mohamed saying "it is said", while leaving readers to speculate about what that could mean.

[d] The occurrence logs for 30 August 1997 have never been disclosed.

[e] Mohamed had already answered "yes" to Burnett's question: "Is that still your belief, that Lord Fellowes was in Paris that night?" Then after that, Burnett ignored Mohamed's concern about the embassy documents, and asked the question again: "My question, Mr Al Fayed, was whether it was still your belief, and I think from the answer you have given, the answer is in fact yes, it is still your belief?"

Fellowes also gave an alibi at the inquest: "We were in Norfolk that evening. We had people to stay. We went to an entertainment by Mr John Mortimer in Burnham Market Church."

Fellowes doesn't explain who "we" are. The jury have not been told who the "people to stay" were. The timing of the Mortimer performance is not provided.

At the time, Fellowes – when he wasn't in London – was based at his home in Snettisham. So his "local village" was Snettisham, not Burnham Market, which was about a 23 km drive away.

This indicates that Fellowes has provided conflicting alibis – his local village, Snettisham, to Paget, and Burnham Market to the inquest.

There is absolutely no witness support provided for anything Fellowes has said to either Paget or the inquest.

This person, Robert Fellowes, is a named suspect in the murder of his sister-in-law. An independent witness has described this suspect as a person the sister-in-law "feared".[a]

Yet this is the best that the suspect and the investigators can come up with for an alibi – in fact, three different alibis, only one of which is heard by the jury.

Why is this?

Why is Fellowes – or the British police – not able to come straight out and say precisely where Fellowes was, with the timings, and back it up with sworn witness statements?

Burnett said to Fellowes – not a question – "Both you and your family provided <u>considerable detail</u> to the police of your <u>precise whereabouts</u> in Norfolk, I think, and <u>descriptions of what you were doing</u>."

Where is this "considerable detail"?

Who has seen it?[b] The Operation Paget officers? [c]

If so, why have they kept it to themselves? What is so secretive about the activities and movements of Robert Fellowes on the night his sister-in-law died? [d]

---

[a] Roberto Devorik said: "[Diana] told me three names that she feared – Nicholas Soames, Robert Fellowes, her brother-in-law, and Prince Philip. She said of Robert Fellowes 'He hates me. He will do anything to get me out of the Royals. He cost me the friendship with my sister'." See Part 2, section on Nicholas Soames in Chapter 7.

[b] Even Burnett indicates he's not completely sure – he says "I think".

[c] The Paget investigation was shown to lack credibility in the 2007 book *Cover-Up of a Royal Murder: Hundreds of Errors in the Paget Report* – a copy of which Scott Baker had several months before Fellowes was cross-examined.

[d] The secrecy that has been shown here has similarities to a person who works for MI6 – in those cases Paget kept the statements to themselves and no supporting

If Fellowes is innocent, then there should be no reason for any secrecy.

In summary, there are two main problems with Robert Fellowes' alibis: a) they come across as indefinite, confusing and conflicting; b) nothing he or Paget says is supported by any witness or documentary evidence – no supporting evidence at all.

Michael Jay, British Ambassador to France, 1996-2001, Paris: 11 Feb 08:

113.14: Mansfield: Q. That particular night and day – that is the Saturday and the Sunday – particularly on the Saturday, was there a communications room or centre operative in the Embassy? Can you help?

A. The normal arrangements were that the Embassy's communications centre would be open on the Saturday morning when traffic used to come in from the Foreign Office, and then it would not open again normally – I think I am right in saying – until Monday morning, unless there was a particular reason to expect traffic to come in, in which case there would be a telephone call and then the communications centre would be opened to receive whatever traffic was expected. I think that is the position.

Q. Is a log kept at the Embassy of incoming communications and outgoing communications and other occurrences, rather like an occurrence book in fact?

A. Certainly as far as telegrams and electronic communications, yes, there would be records kept of those telegrams going in and going out.

Comment: Mansfield asked Jay a specific question: "That particular night and day ... particularly on the Saturday, was there a communications ... centre operative in the Embassy?"

This question followed straight after the above question from Burnett to Jay about Robert Fellowes.[a]

The question was about "that particular night and day", but Jay ignored that and answered it generally – "the normal arrangements were...."

The point is of course that this was hardly a "normal" weekend – and one of the key issues is whether this was treated as a normal weekend in the British embassy pre-crash, i.e. on the Saturday. Or was the embassy in a state of alert?

Did Jay shift his answer away from "that particular night and day" to "the normal arrangements" because the real answer would not have been in the interests of the Establishment?

---

evidence has been supplied for their alibis (see earlier). Fellowes' statement was withheld from the jury and has never been made available. There is a possibility that Fellowes – because of his unique position as Diana's brother-in-law – may have been solicited to provide information to British intelligence.

[a] This was Mansfield's first question to Jay – and the above question from Burnett about Fellowes was Burnett's last question to Jay. Mansfield followed straight after Burnett, so there was only a matter of seconds between Burnett's question on Fellowes and this question on the communications operative from Mansfield.

Jay says: "the Embassy's communications centre would be open on the Saturday morning ... and then it would not open again normally ... until Monday morning, unless there was a particular reason".

This appears to conflict with George Younes: "I was on duty that night [of the crash] with another colleague whose name is Mr Simon Jackson. I was on the Chancery desk ... where all the Embassy offices are situated, whereas Simon Jackson was working in the Residence Lodge next door, where the Ambassador lives.... Out of hours incoming calls are all routed to the Chancery and Residence desk simultaneously on the same phone line, but it is the responsibility of the Chancery desk to answer all incoming calls." [293a]

Given that Jay worked in the Chancery and lived in the Residence for five years, it seems unbelievable that he would be unaware that there were people employed overnight who dealt with out-of-hours embassy communications.

Next Mansfield asked: "Is a log kept at the Embassy of ... communications ... rather like an occurrence book in fact?"

We have already seen the Younes account of an occurrence log recording phone calls, and it appears that Mansfield – who would have had a copy of Younes' statement[b] – may have been basing his question on that.

It's interesting that when Jay answers he avoids mentioning that phone calls – which played a very significant role on the night of the crash[c] – were recorded in the occurrence log. In fact, Jay limits the keeping of records to "telegrams and electronic communications" – "certainly as far as telegrams and electronic communications, yes, there would be records kept of those telegrams going in and going out".[de]

The question is: Why is Jay so evasive and dishonest in his answering?

---

[a] Philippe Massoni and Keith Moss both said they called Michael Jay. It has not been explained but those calls could have been on direct lines or mobiles. It is also evident that if the Chancery officer was away from the desk – Younes describes other duties he had to perform (see 17 Dec 07: 109.23) – then the call would be answered by the Residence officer.

[b] Younes' statement had been read out nearly two months earlier, on 17 December 2007.

[c] See earlier – a part of the log detailing a telephone call was read out as part of the Younes statement.

[d] Just after this, Mansfield asked about the missing log entries – covered earlier – and Jay at that stage admitted that there were records kept for phone calls.

[e] Even Patrick Launay, who worked for the French funeral director, PFG, understood that there should have been an embassy log for phone calls: "You ask me if I remember speaking to anyone else from the British Consulate or Embassy that day. I do not recall, but I know that there is a duty system at the [British] embassy/consulate and there would possibly have been a duty log.": Patrick Launay, Witness Statement, reproduced in *The Documents* book, p512.

Burnett asked Jay: "Was Lord Fellowes in Paris?" Jay was very definite: "No, he was not."

Jay tells us nothing about how he knows this – and he is not asked. Is this knowledge Jay has acquired from other witnesses who were at the embassy, or was Jay there at the embassy himself?

The earlier evidence from Jay is that he was asleep – "I was woken at my residence which adjoins the Embassy at about 1.45 a.m."

George Younes has stated: "Simon Jackson and I were the only two people to be working at the British Embassy". Although I believe Younes was generally a helpful witness, he has already been shown to have lied – possibly following instructions – regarding the Massoni phone call. It is possible Younes has been asked to declare there were no other witnesses.

Simon Jackson has never been interviewed by any investigation and was not heard from at the inquest.

Although the concept of Robert Fellowes in the British embassy on the night of the crash initially sounds incredible, there are some factors that give it some credibility:

- the allegation appears to come from two separate sources, only one of which was addressed by Operation Paget and the Baker inquest – the most detailed account[a] has been ignored
- the failure by Fellowes to provide a clear alibi – in fact, he has given conflicting alibis
- the failure to provide even the most basic witness support for any of Fellowes' alibis
- Fellowes was shown in Part 4 to have lied about his location and activities during the week following the crash[b]
- the withholding by the British embassy or the investigators of documentary evidence of embassy communications for 30 August and pre-crash on 31 August 1997
- the failure of the inquest to show any interest in a source that Mohamed Al Fayed had said was "a very, very responsible person"
- the evasiveness of Michael Jay when it came to discussing issues regarding embassy communications on the night of the crash
- the failure by the inquest to cross-examine key witnesses who were known to be at the embassy on the evening of 30 August 1997 – George Younes and Simon Jackson.

---

[a] In the *Mail*.
[b] See section on Robert Fellowes in the chapter on Early Royal Control, in Part 4.

Knowledge of Diana's Presence in France[a]

It has been claimed that all except one of the staff in the British embassy had no knowledge of Princess Diana's presence in the French capital, until after the crash had occurred.

Charles Ritchie, Military Attaché British Embassy, Paris: 12 Feb 08: 142.10:

Burnett: Q. Did your wife approach one of the motorcyclists to inquire, to find out what was going on [outside the Ritz Hotel]?

A. That is correct. My wife went up to one of the paparazzi on a motor bicycle and asked who it was who was in the hotel and she was informed, "It is your Lady Di and Mr Fayed".

Q. By now it was five to midnight?

A. It was almost exactly five to midnight.

Q. And this was information that your wife passed on to you?

A. That is correct.

Q. What was your reaction to being told that the Princess of Wales was in Paris?

A. One of great surprise. I had no idea that the Princess was in Paris.

....Q. And so you would not, as military attaché, expect to be informed of an unofficial visit?

A. No, sir. We would not be informed of an unofficial visit....

Q. So, having discovered, in the way that you have described, that the Princess of Wales was in the Ritz and in Paris, did you linger in the Place Vendôme, or what did you do?

A. For a short while I did. I had no idea that the Princess was in Paris. For all I knew, it might have been that the Embassy had been told....

....Q. So did you judge that there was anything for you to do at five to midnight on that Saturday night?

A. There was nothing much I could do at five to midnight on Saturday night, but I took a good look at what was there and it appeared to me that there was – I said there was a black UK-registered Range Rover at the front, a couple of very professional-looking people standing beside it, another vehicle behind. It all looked to be perfectly in order as far as I could see.

Q. Was it your intention to mention it to the Ambassador the following morning?

A. I actually said my intention was to ring the Ambassador at half past eight in the morning and tell him, "Sir, I happened to be passing and were we aware that Princess Diana and Mr Al Fayed are in Paris, and if not, they are".

---

[a] It may be significant that Scott Baker made no reference to this issue in his Summing Up for the jury.

Michael Jay, British Ambassador to France, 1996-2001, Paris: 11 Feb 08: 89.18:

Burnett: Q. First, when did you first become aware of the presence in Paris of the Princess of Wales and Dodi Al Fayed?

A. When I was telephoned by Keith Moss, the Consul General, to tell me about the accident, which I think was at about quarter to two or thereabouts on the morning of the 31st.

Q. Can we take it from that that you and your wife were in Paris at the time?

A. Yes, we were. We were asleep.

.... Q. Did you cause inquiries to be made within the Embassy as to whether anyone was aware that Dodi Al Fayed and the Princess of Wales were in Paris on 30th August?

A. Yes, I did. I had been told by the French authorities that on that day, on the day of the accident or the day following it, they were unaware of the Princess's presence, but I then read reports in the newspapers that some people – claiming that some of the French authorities were aware. So I then asked my staff to check with all the French authorities concerned to check that nobody was aware and I received assurances from them that nobody among the French authorities was aware of her presence.[a]

Q. And neither was anyone in the Embassy?

A. And nor was anyone in the Embassy.

Michael Jay: 31 Aug 97 Diary read out 11 Feb 08: 105.20:

"None of us here knew the Princess was in Paris and nor did the French authorities."

Michael Jay: 11 Feb 08: 153.9:

"I certainly remember, by the end of that day, as I said in the diary entry that I read out a little while ago, I was aware that the French were not aware of the visit...."

Michael Jay: 13 Dec 05 Statement: **Jury Didn't Hear**:

"I have been asked when I was first aware of the presence of the Princess of Wales and Dodi Al Fayed in Paris on 30/08/1997. I had no knowledge that the Princess of Wales and Dodi Al Fayed were in Paris until I was woken at

---

[a] Jay has failed to answer the question. The question was: "Did you cause inquiries to be made within the Embassy...?" Burnett is asking about the embassy staff – Was "anyone [in the embassy] ... aware that Dodi Al Fayed and the Princess of Wales were in Paris on 30th August?" Even though Jay was the head of the embassy Burnett was inquiring about, Jay has instead given a lengthy answer regarding the awareness of "the French authorities" of Diana's presence in Paris. This has led to Burnett reasking the question: "And neither was anyone in the Embassy?" I suggest that Jay's apparent misunderstanding of Burnett's original question could be an indication that he was nervous around this issue of awareness of Diana's presence. The reason for Jay's apparent nervousness should emerge in the Comment area of this section.

my residence which adjoins the Embassy at about 1.45am in the morning of Sunday 31/08/1997. I received two telephone calls....

"The Embassy's lack of advance knowledge was confirmed to the French Inquiry. In January 1999, Mr Paul Johnston, at the time Second Secretary (Political) at the Embassy, wrote to M Hervé Stéphan, the Juge d'Instruction investigating the case for the French authorities, and told him that: - 'The Embassy was not aware that the Princess of Wales was in Paris until we were notified of the accident early on 31st August. The Princess arrived in Paris from Italy on the afternoon of 30th August. She was travelling as a private citizen. In that capacity, she was not obliged to inform the British Government about her travel plans. Nor would she normally have received protection unless she asked for it. Following her divorce, the Princess had not wanted to have protection except for high profile public engagements. On this occasion, a private visit, she did not ask for protection. The Al Fayeds had their own security arrangements.'

"I am satisfied that this sets out the true position....

"At a later stage the Military Attaché to the Embassy, Brigadier Charles Ritchie, told me that he had learnt that the Princess of Wales was in Paris when he observed a crowd outside the Ritz Hotel in the Place Vendôme shortly before midnight on Saturday 30/08/1997. I do not recollect at what point he told me this." [a]

---

[a] The following is an excerpt from Michael Jay's statement regarding efforts by the British embassy to establish whether French authorities had knowledge of Diana's presence in France. This is relevant to chapter 11 of Part 3, but was not available at the time Part 3 was written: "In response to French media speculation soon after the accident, I had asked Paul Johnston to make inquiries about the state of knowledge of the French authorities, and I refer to his minute dated 12/09/1997 to Mr Cowper-Coles (Head of Political Section at the Embassy): - 'I spoke to Gouyette (Diplomatic Advisor) who rang back today, having checked with the relevant departments, to confirm that neither the Interior Ministry nor the Prefecture de Police had been aware of the Princess' visit. The first they had known was when the accident was reported around 0300 [3 a.m.] the following morning. (Comment: this conflicts with the report earlier this week that Dodi Al Fayed had rung the police from le Bourget when they landed to ask for a police escort given the presence there of paparazzi).'...

"Chief Inspector Gargan's minute to Mr Cowper-Coles of 15/09/1997: - "I spoke to Vianney Dyevres of the Brigade Criminelle this afternoon. He has spoken to the Chef d'Etat Major of the French Police VIP Protection Unit. They have assured him that the first they heard of the Princess of Wales' visit was when they learned of the accident at the Pont d'Alma.": Michael Jay, Witness Statement, reproduced in *The Documents* book, pp632-3. There is no evidence from anyone who was on the plane – Rene Delorm, Trevor Rees-Jones, Myriah Daniels, Debbie Gribble – to support the

Keith Moss, British Consul General, Paris: 22 Nov 07: 8.15:

Hough: Q. Before the crash occurred, were you aware that the Princess of Wales and Mr Al Fayed were in Paris?

A. No, not at all.

Keith Moss: 22 Oct 04 Statement: **Jury Didn't Hear**:

"Prior to the incident that led to the deaths of Dodi Al Fayed and the Princess of Wales, I had not been aware that they were in France. I only became aware of their presence in Paris, when I received a telephone call from the Embassy Duty Officer." [294a]

Nicholas Gargan, British Police Liaison with French Investigation, Paris: 13 Dec 07: 4.18:

Hilliard: Q. 31st August of 1997. On the Sunday, I think you were telephoned by your brother at about 9 o'clock in the morning. Is that right?

A. That is right.

Q. Did he tell you that the Princess of Wales had died in an incident in Paris overnight?

A. He did indeed. That was why he rang me.

.... Q. Prior to hearing what you did from your brother on the 31st, had you had any knowledge before that that the Princess of Wales was in Paris?

A. No.

George Younes, British Embassy Security Officer, Paris: 15 Aug 05 Statement read out 17 Dec 07: 116.23:

"I have been asked if I was aware that Diana, Princess of Wales and Dodi Al Fayed were in Paris prior to receiving the call from Mr Massoni. I was not aware that she was in Paris and I was surprised."

Stephen Donnelly, British Vice Consul, Paris: 22 Sep 05 Statement read out 17 Dec 07: 120.17:

"On the morning of Sunday 31st August at about 8.15 am to 8.20 am, I received a telephone call at my home ... from the Consul General, Keith Moss. I was in bed when I got the call. Keith Moss said, 'Stephen, it's Keith'. I said 'Hello Keith', to which he said 'Diana is dead', to which my response was 'Diana who?' He then told me it was Princess Diana and I was very shocked.... It was not until I received the telephone call from Keith Moss that

---

report cited that "Dodi Al Fayed had rung the police from le Bourget when they landed to ask for a police escort".

[a] Moss also said in his statement: "The French Head of the Brigade Criminelle and Protection ... spoke to me. He said that, if he had been informed that the Princess of Wales had been in France, he would have insured that surveillance, however discrete, would have been applied and this incident would possibly not have happened. I told him that the Embassy had not been informed and did not know of her presence in France." The issue of overall pre-crash embassy knowledge of Diana's presence in France is addressed in the Comment. Source: Keith Moss, Witness Statement, reproduced in *The Documents* book, p656 (UK edition).

morning that I became aware that Diana, Princess of Wales and Dodi Al Fayed were in Paris, let alone France."

Mr 4 aka Eugene Curley, MI6 Head in France. British Embassy, Paris: 29 Feb 08: 41.13:

Burnett: Q. Were you aware that the Princess and Dodi Al Fayed were in Paris that weekend, before the crash occurred?

A. No, I was not.

Mr 6 aka Richard Spearman, MI6 Officer. British Embassy, Paris: 29 Feb 08: 54.17:

Burnett: Q. Did you know, before they came to Paris, that they were coming to Paris?

A. The first time I was aware of it was on the Sunday morning, when I learned of the crash.

Ms 1, MI6 Officer. British Embassy, Paris: 12 Jan 05 Statement read out 29 Feb 08: 36.8:

"On Sunday morning, one of the Embassy locally employed staff ... telephoned my home to confirm arrangements for a pre-arranged barbecue at his country home. He spoke to my husband and during that conversation he told my husband of the crash involving Diana. This was the first I knew of the crash or the presence of Diana and Dodi Al Fayed in Paris. I had had no indication that they may be coming to the city."

Mr 5, MI6 Officer. British Embassy, Paris: 13 Jan 05 Statement read out 29 Feb 08: 37.25:

"I am a light sleeper and often sleep with the radio on. On that night I recall listening to BBC5 Live and at about 2 or 3 am I first heard reports of the crash involving Princess Diana. ... I had no knowledge of her visit to Paris until I heard it on the radio, as I have already stated."

Paul Johnston, Second Secretary, British Embassy: Paget Description of Statement: **Jury Didn't Hear**:

"Paul Johnston stated he first became aware that the Princess of Wales was in Paris, when he heard news of the crash on the *Today* radio programme whilst staying at a friend's house in Normandy." [295]

Paul Johnston: 16 Dec 98 Letter to Hervé Stéphan and Marie-Christine Devidal:

"Nobody in the British Embassy in Paris was aware of the Princess of Wales' trip to France, as it was a strictly private visit. The first person to have any knowledge of it was the duty officer, who received the call from the police just after the accident." [296a]

---

[a] This conflicts with the evidence of Charles Ritchie who says he became aware of Diana's presence in Paris at around 11.55 p.m. on 30 August 1997.

Steven Gunner, Assistant Air Attaché, British Embassy:
"The first I heard of the death of Princess Diana was on the BBC Radio News early on Sunday morning." [297]

Keith Shannon: Paget Description of Statement: **Jury Didn't Hear**:
"Keith Shannon stated that he first became aware of the crash at just after 1 a.m. on 31 August 1997 when he was woken by a telephone call from George Younes, the Security Officer at the Embassy. This call was followed by a second call from Philippe Massoni, the Préfet de Police of Paris ... who Keith Shannon understood to be at the scene of the crash. These calls were his first knowledge of the Princess of Wales' presence in Paris." [298]

Timothy Livesey, Embassy Press Attaché: Paget Description of Statement: **Jury Didn't Hear**:
"Timothy Livesey stated he was not aware of the Princess of Wales' presence in Paris before the crash." [299]

Paget Report, p804: **Jury Didn't Hear**:
"Staff at the British Embassy, Paris were not informed of the visit of the Princess of Wales. They all stated that they personally had no prior knowledge of the Princess of Wales' visit and also believed that the British Embassy had no prior knowledge."

Paget Report, p620: **Jury Didn't Hear**:
"Neither the FCO in London, nor the British Embassy or Consulate in Paris, with the exception of Brigadier Charles Ritchie, were aware of the presence of the Princess of Wales and Dodi Al Fayed in Paris until the Embassy Security Officer was notified at somewhere between around 12.50 a.m. and 1.10 a.m. on Sunday 31 August 1997."

Frank Klein, President, Ritz Hotel, Paris: 29 Nov 07: 99.24:
Mansfield: Q. Because of the press, because we are now into a situation where there is another visit to the South of France by Princess Diana and Dodi and the yacht Jonikal, the second visit, do you remember, was also in the press every day?
A. That is right.
Q. So there would not have been anybody in France, unless they had their eyes shut, that would not have known that he was there with Princess Diana.
A. Absolutely.

Claude Roulet, Assistant President, Ritz Hotel, Paris: 5 Dec 07: 110.23:
Mansfield: Q. Would it be fair to say that the relationship by this stage, that is the last week of August – the relationship between Dodi and the Princess of Wales was extremely well known, was it not?
A. Yes. All the newspapers spoke about it.
Q. Virtually every day?
A. Yes.

Comment: The general witness evidence is that all embassy employees – bar two, Charles Ritchie and Steven Gunner[a] – first learned that Princess Diana was in France when they heard about the crash on Sunday, 31 August 1997.

Ritchie has stated that he became aware of Diana and Dodi's presence in Paris at "almost exactly five [minutes] to midnight" on 30 August 1997 – see above.

Paget has claimed that "the British Embassy [and] Consulate in Paris, with the exception of Brigadier Charles Ritchie, were [not] aware of the presence of the Princess of Wales and Dodi Al Fayed in Paris [until] ... around 12.50 a.m. and 1.10 a.m. on Sunday".

There are about 40 diplomatic staff in the British embassy[b], not including security and other service staff like Younes.

How many of these staff did Paget interview?

Paget states: "Operation Paget has interviewed staff at the British Embassy <u>who had a role in the events after the crash</u>." [300c]

I suggest this strategy is fundamentally flawed ... or very lazy investigation.

I believe it is common sense that there is no connection between pre-crash knowledge of Diana's presence in Paris and an employee having "a role in the events after the crash".

So we effectively have a situation where Paget has – by its own admission – not interviewed all embassy employees who could have known Diana was in Paris on 30 August 1997.

Regarding the knowledge of Diana's presence, the Paget Report includes the statement accounts of nine embassy staff – Jay, Moss, Ritchie, Shannon, Donnelly, Livesey, Gunner, Johnston and Younes.[301]

Of those nine, Paget only provides the first person evidence of one – Steven Gunner. The other accounts are all Paget descriptions of excerpts of their statements with Scotland Yard.[d]

Gunner told Paget: "The first I heard of the <u>death of Princess Diana</u> was ... early on Sunday morning." That is not saying that he was unaware of the

---

[a] See below.

[b] See earlier Diplomatic Service lists.

[c] The police indicate that they have been thorough in doing this – in the case of Steven Gunner, Paget says: "Wing Commander Gunner is posted abroad. Operation Paget officers have spoken to him, and [have received] correspondence".: Paget Report, p611.

[d] Paget did include excerpts from Johnston's letters – see earlier – but when it came to his statement, only provided a description of Johnston's evidence.

presence of Diana in Paris – it is confirmation of when he found out about Diana's death.

The only embassy employee witness whose original words Paget published[a] is Steven Gunner. But Gunner has not said what Paget has claimed he said.

Gunner said he first heard of Diana's death on Sunday morning – not her presence in Paris. This then leaves open the possibility that Gunner could have been aware of Diana's presence in Paris at some point prior to the crash.

Although Paget did not provide the original words of any other witness statements, some of those have since been published, either through the inquest or *The Documents* book: Michael Jay, Keith Moss, Stephen Donnelly and George Younes.[b]

Those four people have all stated that the first they heard of Diana's presence in Paris was when they heard about the Alma Tunnel crash – see above.

The statements of Ritchie, Shannon, Livesey and Johnston have never been published – and of those, only Ritchie was heard at the inquest. Ritchie admitted that he became aware of Diana's presence in Paris about half an hour before the crash – see above.

Paget expects us to rely on them providing a truthful description of evidence for the accounts of Keith Shannon, Tim Livesey and Paul Johnston. Those accounts suggest that Shannon, Livesey and Johnston were all unaware of Diana's presence before the crash.

Nicholas Gargan was also cross-examined at the inquest and he said the same.

Paget says that the police took statements from all MI6 staff in the Paris embassy. The statements of Ms 1 and Mr 5 were read out at the inquest and Mr 6 and Mr 4 were both cross-examined.

Those four MI6 employees claim that pre-crash they were also unaware of Diana's presence in Paris.[c]

Out of the approximately 40 diplomatic staff in the embassy at the time of the crash, Paget has obtained and allowed to be declared evidence on this issue from just 12 – Jay, Moss, Ritchie, Shannon, Donnelly, Livesey, Gunner, Johnston, Spearman, Ms 1, Mr 5 and Mr 4.

This means that there are up to 28 embassy diplomatic staff that Paget apparently never interviewed or took statements from.[d]

---

[a] Rather than a Paget description of their evidence.

[b] Jay and Moss' statements were published in *The Documents* book; Donnelly and Younes' statements were heard at the inquest.

[c] There were more than four MI6 employees in the embassy that weekend, but the exact number is not known – see earlier MI6 chapter.

[d] It is difficult to be precise about the degree of Paget's failure to interview staff because a) Paget said it had taken statements from all MI6 staff but failed to declare

In turn, this leads to the inescapable conclusion that Paget has dishonestly claimed:

- "staff at the British Embassy ... all stated that they personally had no prior knowledge of the Princess of Wales' visit"
- "neither the ... British Embassy or Consulate in Paris, with the exception of ... Ritchie, were aware of the presence of [Diana and Dodi] in Paris until ... somewhere between around 12.50 a.m. and 1.10 a.m. on Sunday 31 August 1997".

The reality is that Paget cannot honestly make these claims because:

- Scotland Yard interviewed well under a third of the embassy staff
- at least one of the employees interviewed by the police – Steven Gunner – did not say they were unaware pre-crash of Diana's presence in Paris, as claimed by Paget.

The general thrust of this evidence appears to be an attempt to distance the British embassy staff from involvement in the orchestration of the Alma crash. If the Paris embassy staff had no awareness that Diana and Dodi were even in France, then how could they possibly have been involved in an assassination plot to remove them in a Paris car crash?

The evidence from embassy employees is very similar to that claimed by the French authorities (see Part 3) – they had no knowledge that Princess Diana was in France.

Is this possible?

The question is: When Princess Diana's plane touched down in Paris at 3.20 p.m. on that warm Saturday afternoon, was there suddenly a media blackout?

We know the paparazzi were present – see Part 1 – and there is famous video footage of that arrival.

Are we seriously expected to believe that the video footage and paparazzi photos of Diana and Dodi arriving in Paris didn't make the television evening news on 30 August 1997? Did the French media carry daily reports of Diana's movements, but as soon as she arrived in the capital, they suddenly stopped reporting it?

Was the "sea of people"[a] present outside the Ritz Hotel at 10 p.m. – described in Part 1 – aware that Diana was in town, but none of the 40 plus British embassy employees were? [a]

---

the number; and b) we are not privy to the numbers of non-diplomatic staff at the embassy. Examples of non-diplomatic staff are George Younes and Nicholas Gargan. Younes was interviewed by Paget, but Gargan was not.
[a] Philippe Dourneau: 3 Sep 97 Statement – see Part 1, p214.

I suggest that the general British embassy employee evidence that was taken – and the Paget claims[b] – don't really add up.

On Sunday 31 August 1997 Michael Jay wrote in his diary: "None of us here knew the Princess was in Paris and nor did the French authorities." [cd]

One question that should be asked is: Why did Michael Jay write this?

Is there a connection between knowledge within the British embassy of Diana's Paris visit and the ensuing crash?

There would appear to be two major reasons why this information could have – at that time – seemed important enough to record:

1) Security concerns.

One could argue that Jay put this in because there may have been an expectation for the British or French to provide security for Princess Diana after her arrival in Paris. The claim that no one knew Diana was there would then release the authorities from any security responsibility.

Paul Johnston wrote to Stéphan in January 1999: "Following her divorce[e], the Princess had not wanted to have protection except for high profile public engagements. On this occasion, a private visit, she did not ask for protection." [f]

---

[a] The Roulet and Klein testimony doesn't make specific reference to Diana's presence in Paris, but they do recall the atmosphere of the time:

- Klein confirmed to Mansfield: "there would not have been anybody in France, unless they had their eyes shut, that would not have known that [Dodi] was there [on the *Jonikal* in the south of France] with Princess Diana"

- Roulet confirmed to Mansfield: "all the newspapers spoke about it ... virtually every day".

[b] Bearing in mind that Paget failed to interview most of the embassy staff – see above.

[c] The issues around the actions and knowledge of the French authorities have been dealt with in Part 3.

[d] It's possibly significant that when Jay did his Paget statement he addressed the issue of embassy knowledge of Diana's presence, yet he made no mention of this diary entry. Jay actually said nothing at all in his statement about his diary, but he did list embassy reports and other evidence. There is a possibility that Jay's 31 August 1997 diary could have been altered or updated well after the event. The evidence has been addressed in this section based on the presumption that has not occurred – in other words, it has been presumed that the diary entry Jay read out at the inquest was how it was written up on 31 August 1997. It is interesting that when Jay was asked by Burnett: "Do you keep a personal diary?" he answered: "I did when I was in Paris." The implication then is that Jay didn't necessarily keep a diary at other times. That leads to the question: Why did Jay keep a diary in Paris, but not at other times in his life?

[e] In late-August 1996. Diana requested reduced protection in 1994 – see Part 2.

[f] This excerpt was included in Jay statement – see earlier.

This indicates that there was an awareness in the embassy that Diana "had not wanted to have protection" – at least not provided by the UK authorities.

Even if Diana had sought official UK security protection for this trip to France, I suggest it wouldn't have been provided by the embassy, but by the UK police, possibly the Royalty Protection division.[ab]

So there does not appear to be any logical basis for Michael Jay, or his Paris embassy staff, to have had concerns about providing security protection for Princess Diana in France.

2) Knowledge of an orchestrated crash or assassination.

If Michael Jay knew that Diana and Dodi had been deliberately eliminated, then I suggest that could have led him to leave documentary evidence that the embassy was not involved.

A diary entry along the lines of: "None of us here knew the Princess was in Paris", could suffice.[c]

As discussed earlier, this appears to be a case of excessive distancing. It should have been enough for the British embassy not to have received any

---

[a] Diana's security protection issues have been covered in the Surveillance chapter of Part 2.

[b] Ritchie detailed the extent of the embassy's role whenever an official visit – which this was not – took place: "We would not be informed of an unofficial visit; official visits, yes, because we often had to look after the Royal Air Force flight coming in, look after the crew and the bill would come to the defence section.": 12 Feb 08: 143.14.

[c] The full quote – shown earlier – includes a reference to the French: "None of us here knew the Princess was in Paris and nor did the French authorities." This indicates that during the first 12 hours after Diana's death Jay went to the trouble of finding out whether the French knew about Diana's presence in Paris. It has been shown in Part 3 – Chapter 11 – that any claims of this nature by the French were lies. These volumes have revealed that there had to be a close coordination between the British and the French, to both, succeed with the assassinations, and then also the huge cover-up. Jay's diary comment that the French didn't know about Diana's presence in their capital – and his continued enquiries in the following days to that effect, described in his statement (see earlier) – appear to be a part of the post-crash cover-up. Jay has effectively, in just a few words in his diary, provided a same day alibi for all French authorities – if they had no idea that Diana was in Paris, then they too could have had no part in orchestrating the crash. At the inquest Jay stated: "I received assurances from [my staff] that nobody among the French authorities was aware of her presence". An "assurance" is "a statement ... intended to give someone confidence" (Oxford). The question is: Why did Jay need confidence that the French weren't aware of Diana's presence in Paris? If the Alma crash was just an accident then it would not have mattered whether the French knew Diana was there, or didn't know. This issue of knowledge only becomes significant if there is already evidence the crash was orchestrated.

notification of the visit.[a] But Jay – and subsequently other embassy officials – took it an incredible step further, by claiming no knowledge of Diana's presence, even though she had been in Paris for around nine hours by midnight on 30 August 1997.

I suggest that if the deaths of Diana and Dodi had been accidental then it would not have mattered whether the embassy staff knew Diana was present in Paris pre-crash. This issue of awareness of Diana's presence only becomes significant if there is already evidence the crash was orchestrated. It has the effect of distancing anyone who was ignorant pre-crash of Diana's presence, of involvement in the assassination.

Michael Jay has indicated that he spent time and embassy resources on the first day trying to establish people's – both British and French – pre-crash levels of awareness of Diana's presence. According to his evidence, Jay appears to have done this, while neglecting to spend time ensuring the protection of Princess Diana from an invasive French embalming, while she lay lifeless in the Paris hospital.[b]

This indicates that Jay was more interested in distancing himself, the embassy and the French authorities from involvement in the crash, than in protecting the body of the dead princess.

Evidence of Stephen Donnelly

Stephen Donnelly, British Vice Consul, Paris: 22 Sep 05 Statement read out 17 Dec 07: 129.7:
"It is only recently when seeing Keith Moss' statement to DS Grater that I understood that the Princess of Wales had been embalmed."
Comment: Why has Donnelly been given Moss' statement to read before completing his account to Scotland Yard officers?

Operation Paget was the British police investigation intended to establish the truth regarding the circumstances of the deaths of Princess Diana and Dodi Fayed.

How can the police establish the truth if they let witnesses read other witnesses' statements? The whole idea of a police investigation is to get the accounts of the various witnesses and compare what each one says in an effort to establish the truth.

This is corrupt behaviour by the police, to allow witnesses to read other people's statements. It is further evidence of a cover-up, in this case involving apparent collusion between embassy staff and the police.
Stephen Donnelly: 22 Sep 05 Statement read out 17 Dec 07: 121.6:

---

[a] I am not suggesting that the embassy didn't know in advance – the evidence shows they would have – but "no notification" would be more believable than claiming no knowledge of Diana's presence until after the crash had occurred.
[b] This issue has been addressed in Part 4.

"I had not been on call at home that weekend. The on-call consular officer had been Gillian Storey, who normally worked in the visa section, but because I dealt with deaths of British citizens in France on a day-to-day basis, I had been informed. My first telephone call after I had finished speaking with Keith Moss was to Gillian Storey in order to inform her of these developments and to take her out of the loop and ask for all calls to be channelled through me, in order to keep her free to deal with all other consular matters. I have been shown a copy of a document marked 'Telephone report of death by DS Grater'. This document appears to have been completed by Gillian Storey and records that I had called her at 8.30 am that morning. This is a standard form completed for the death of a British citizen in Paris."

Comment: Why wasn't the inquest jury provided with a copy of Gillian Storey's report? Why wasn't a statement taken from Storey?

This is another example of a sloppy investigation of these deaths – by both Paget and Scott Baker.

Conclusion

Once one realises that MI6 were heavily involved in the plot to assassinate Princess Diana[a], then it becomes logical – given that MI6 staff are based in embassies – that there had to be some involvement by staff in the British embassy in Paris.

The general claim by embassy and MI6 staff employed in Paris was that they were not involved – and indeed they could not have been, because they were completely unaware that Princess Diana and Dodi Fayed were in Paris, until they were notified after the crash.

This claim has been shown to lack credibility:

-   Diana and Dodi had been in Paris for nearly nine hours by midnight on 30 August 1997

-   their arrival in Paris at 3.20 p.m. was recorded by paparazzi and video footage – it is not credible to suggest there was no coverage on radio and in the TV evening news bulletins

-   the French authorities also claimed they had no knowledge of Diana's presence, yet there were French police present at the airport arrival and they escorted the couple's Mercedes – see Part 3

-   there were well over 40 staff[b] employed at the British embassy, but Operation Paget officers only interviewed well under a third of those, then

---

[a] This has been shown in Chapter 1.

[b] About 40 diplomatic staff and an unknown number of support and services staff.

falsely claimed that all embassy staff said they had no pre-crash awareness of Diana's visit

- during the critical hours following the crash, Michael Jay appears to have spent embassy time and resources establishing how many people – among the embassy staff and French authorities – had been aware of Diana's presence in Paris. The only logical reason for this would seem to be as an attempt to distance personnel from involvement in the assassination.[a]

There is also an accumulation of evidence that indicates British embassy staff were involved in the assassination of Princess Diana:

- Part 4 revealed embassy involvement in the ensuing cover-up – the French embalming, the early royal control and the repatriation

- all the critical embassy reports raised in the hours and days following the crash or during that first month were withheld from the inquest jury

- the inquest jury were not given the embassy occurrence logs for 30-31 August 1997 for both the chancery and the residence

- critical embassy occurrence log entries – numbers 1 and 2 for 31 August 1997 – have mysteriously gone missing

- embassy staff have given false evidence: a) George Younes described receiving a call from Paris Prefect of police, Philippe Massoni, which never occurred; b) Keith Moss and Michael Jay stated Jay was woken up by Moss about 1½ hours after the crash, when other evidence indicates he was awake much earlier

- Stephen Donnelly's notes from 31 August 1997 have gone missing

- Michael Jay has provided confusing evidence on his movements on 30 August 1997 and there has been no attempt by investigators to check his alibis

- it has been alleged that Robert Fellowes was in the Paris embassy on 30 August 1997 – he has failed to provide a consistent and convincing alibi.

As with MI6, a lot of the embassy evidence is circumstantial. There is however a substantial build-up, when all of the points are viewed together.

It becomes very clear that there is a major cover-up involving the evidence surrounding the British embassy in Paris. Embassy staff have lied on certain key issues. All the crucial documentation relating to the weekend of 30-31 August 1997 – including phone call logs and embassy reports – was withheld from the jury investigating the deaths of Diana and Dodi.

Most of the embassy statements taken by the police were not shown to the jury. People who should have been cross-examined – George Younes, Stephen Donnelly, Philippe Massoni, Keith Shannon, Timothy Livesey, Paul Johnston – were not.

---

[a] This conclusion is based on other evidence – shown in this book and Part 3 – that indicates both British embassy staff and the French authorities were involved in the plot to assassinate Princess Diana. See below as well.

Why?

Again the question is asked: Why do we see a cover-up if there is nothing to cover up?

3   The Royals

Timeline of Events

1992

January	Diana is warned by Buckingham Palace that they are aware of her co-operation with Morton's book [302]
June	Andrew Morton's book *Diana: Her True Story* is published
August	Squidgygate tapes are published
November	Way Ahead Group (WAG) is set up and holds first meeting
24	Queen declares 1992 as her "annus horribilus"
27	Announcement that Queen is prepared to start paying tax[a]
December	
9	Official separation of Diana and Charles announced in Parliament

1995

November	
20	BBC *Panorama* broadcasts Diana interview by Martin Bashir
December	
10	Queen requests divorce between Diana and Charles

1996

July	Diana commences involvement in the anti-landmine campaign[303]
August	
28	Divorce becomes absolute. Diana is removed from the royal family and is stripped of her HRH title
September	
16	WAG meeting held

1997

January	
12	Diana starts anti-landmine trip to Angola
16	Diana's Angolan anti-landmine trip finishes
20	WAG meeting held

---

[a] Article by Eugene Robinson in *Washington Post* on 27 November 1992 titled: "Elizabeth II Offers to Pay Taxes: Queen Trimming Family's Costs".

February   Diana is warned by Tory minister Nicholas Soames to drop her anti-landmine campaign and is threatened with an "accident" [a]

June

11   Diana writes note to Mohamed saying she and the boys are "greatly looking forward to" the St Tropez holiday

12   Diana makes major anti-landmine address to Royal Geographic Society stating that she is on a personal anti-landmine crusade

25   Diana is forced to withdraw from attending a Landmines Eradication Group meeting in parliament

30   Rosa Monckton arranges to borrow a boat from "friends" to use on a Greek Island holiday cruise with Diana set for mid-August

July

7   Diana's final meeting with Tony Blair at Chequers

8   Preparatory meeting for July 23 WAG meeting

9   David Davies[b] phones Fellowes warning of police concerns about Diana's upcoming holiday to St Tropez

11   Diana, William and Harry travel to St Tropez for a 10 day holiday with the Al Fayed family

18   Camilla's 50th birthday party is held at Highgrove

20   Diana, William and Harry return to London from St Tropez *Mirror* article states that "Diana" is top of the agenda at the next WAG meeting

21 to 23   Diana and Dodi share significant periods of time including visits to Dodi's apartment and a private movie viewing [c]

23   WAG meeting held

26   Diana visits Paris for two days with Dodi

31   Diana and Dodi commence 7 day holiday cruise in the Mediterranean on the *Jonikal*

August

8   Diana travels to Bosnia on a 3 day anti-landmine trip

15   Start of 5 day Diana-Rosa Greek cruise

20   Diana and Rosa return to London

22   Diana and Dodi commence a 9 day Mediterranean holiday

---

[a] This is detailed in the Landmines chapter of Part 2.
[b] Head of Royalty Protection.
[c] The detail of this is in Part 2.

>   aboard the *Jonikal*
> 27   *Le Monde* publishes an interview with Diana – on the royal
>   family she says: "From the first day I joined that family,
>   nothing could be done naturally anymore"
> 31   Princess Diana and Dodi Fayed die after a car crash in the
>   Alma Tunnel, Paris
>   *Mirror* article states that next week's WAG meeting will
>   table an MI6 report on the Fayeds and will discuss the
>   Harrods royal warrants.

The issue is: Is it possible that a senior member of the royal family or household could have issued an instruction or order to British intelligence to assassinate Princess Diana?

Anti-Landmine Speech: June 1997

Princess Diana: 12 Jun 97 Speech: **Jury Didn't Hear**:
"The world is too little aware of the waste of life, limb and land which anti-personnel landmines are causing among some of the poorest people on earth....

"For the mine is a stealthy killer. Long after conflict is ended, its innocent victims die or are wounded singly, in countries of which we hear little. Their lonely fate is never reported. The world, with its many other preoccupations, remains largely unmoved by a death roll of something like 800 people every month – many of them women and children. Those who are not killed outright – and they number another 1,200 a month – suffer terrible injuries and are handicapped for life.

"I was in Angola in January with the British Red Cross.... Some people chose to interpret my visit as a political statement. But it was not. I am not a political figure. As I said at the time, and I'd like to reiterate now, my interests are humanitarian. That is why I felt drawn to this human tragedy. This is why I wanted to play down my part in working towards a world-wide ban on these weapons....

"The human pain that has to be borne is often beyond imagining.... That is something to which the world should urgently turn its conscience.

"In Angola, one in every 334 members of the population is an amputee. Angola has the highest rate of amputees in the world. How can countries which manufacture and trade in these weapons square their conscience with such human devastation? ...

"Much ingenuity has gone into making some of these mines. Many are designed to trap an unwary de-miner..., I reflected, after my visit to Angola, if some of the technical skills used in making mines had been applied to better methods of removing them....

"These mines inflict most of their casualties on people who are trying to meet the elementary needs of life. They strike the wife, or the grandmother, gathering firewood for cooking. They ambush the child sent to collect water for the family....

"One of the main conclusions I reached after this experience: Even if the world decided tomorrow to ban these weapons, this terrible legacy of mines already in the earth would continue to plague the poor nations of the globe. 'The evil that men do, lives after them.'

"And so, it seems to me, there rests a certain obligation upon the rest of us.

"One of my objectives in visiting Angola was to forward the cause of those, like the Red Cross, striving in the name of humanity to secure an international ban on these weapons. Since then, we are glad to see, some real progress has been made. There are signs of a change of heart – at least in some parts of the world. For that we should be cautiously grateful. If an international ban on mines can be secured it means, looking far ahead, that the world may be a safer place for this generation's grandchildren.

"But for this generation in much of the developing world, there will be no relief, no relaxation. The toll of deaths and injuries caused by mines already there, will continue....

"I would like to see more done for those living in this 'no man's land', which lies between the wrongs of yesterday and the urgent needs of today.

"I think we owe it. I also think it would be of benefit to us, as well as to them. The more expeditiously we can end this plague on earth caused by the landmine, the more readily can we set about the constructive tasks to which so many give their hand in the cause of humanity." [304]

Links to Intelligence Agencies

The general evidence revealed that there are lines of contact between the royals and intelligence agencies, primarily through the FCO.

Richard Tomlinson, Ex-MI6 Officer: 13 Feb 08: 44.13:

Hilliard: Q. I am looking at an affidavit that you made I think in 1999.... It says this: "During my service in MI6, I also learned unofficially and secondhand something of the links between MI6 and the Royal Household. MI6 are frequently and routinely asked by the Royal Household, usually via the Foreign Office, to provide intelligence on potential threats to members of the Royal Family whilst on overseas trips." Presumably there is nothing surprising about that, being asked to provide intelligence on potential threats to members of the Royal Family whilst they were abroad.

A. Well, I would not have thought so. It is a perfectly normal –

Q. No, I just wanted to understand. There is nothing that is surprising about that on the face of it, is there?

A. No.

Q. Then you go on: "This service would frequently extend to asking friendly intelligence services such as the CIA to place members of the Royal Family under discreet surveillance, ostensibly for their own protection." Yes?

A. Well, when members of the Royal Family travel overseas, I believe they have their own security, although clearly the host country is going to be very closely involved in their security, looking after their security as well.

Q. But presumably nothing surprising about that either?

A. No, it is normal.

Q. You said: "This was particularly the case for the Princess of Wales, who often insisted on doing without overt personal protection, even on overseas trips." Yes?

A. Well, I think that is probably something that I learned after I left MI6. I don't think I knew that in MI6 because – that was something that came out after I was in MI6, yes.

At 107.15: Mansfield: Q. [Your 1999 affidavit]: Then you have this part in this paragraph: "Although contact between MI6 and the Royal Household was officially only via the Foreign Office, I learned while in MI6 that there was unofficial direct contact between certain senior and influential MI6 officers and senior members of the Royal Household. I did not see any official papers on this subject, but I am confident that the information is correct. I firmly believe that MI6 documents would yield substantial leads on the nature of their links with the Royal Household and would yield vital information about MI6 surveillance on the Princess of Wales in the days leading to her death." Now I do want to ask you some questions on this. So, first of all, when you say, "I learned while in MI6 ...", what was the source of your information, can you remember?

A. No, I cannot remember that at all now. We were constantly talking amongst ourselves. It could be anything.

Q. Can you now remember which certain "senior and influential MI6 officers" you were thinking of then, that is in 1999, and of course which senior members of the Royal Household were you meaning?

A. I cannot remember names now at this stage. It is too long ago.

Q. Very well. Would you have known names then or was it broached to you in the terms that you put in the statement?

A. At the time obviously there would have been lots of names that I would have known at the time, people that I was currently working with. I guess that is what I was referring to then. But I have no recollection of names of people at this late stage. I can only remember a tiny number of officers there now.

Richard Dearlove, MI6 Director of Operations, 1994 to 1999, UK: 20 Feb 08: 59.1:

Burnett: Q. What was Prince Philip's relationship with the Secret Intelligence Service in the mid-1990s, but please cover the whole period if there is any difference?

A. Absolutely nothing of substance. I say "nothing of substance" because I think there were one or two occasions when he visited the service as Her Majesty's consort.

Q. Now, we have heard – again, it would come as no surprise to anybody – that the service would be involved in providing security advice for foreign visits of the Royal Family.

A. Occasionally.

Q. But to the suggestion that –

A. But I might say not directly. The security assessments would be gathered through the embassy to which the service might make a contribution.

Q. So to the suggestion that Prince Philip was an active operational member of MI6, what do you say? [a]

A. I can say nothing other than it is utterly ridiculous.

Q. Is the same true of Prince Charles?

A. The same is true of Prince Charles.

Miss X, MI6 Administrator, UK: 26 Feb 08: 63.8:

Burnett: Q. Did you also do a similar search[b] in respect of His Royal Highness, the Duke of Edinburgh?

A. I did.

Q. With what result?

A. No, result at all.

Q. So, similarly, he does not have a card nor does he have a P file?

A. I would like to say at this stage, sir, that we don't hold either cards or files on the Royal Family. I could do a search on all of them.

Q. You have nothing?

A. No.

Q. So as far as the Duke of Edinburgh is concerned, you say in your statement that you are aware that he occasionally made official visits to the service –

A. Yes.

Q. – but that that would not generate a card.

A. No, it would not, no.

At 136.25: Mansfield: Q. You have said there is no file or card – I do not know what the right word is – in relation to any member of the Royal Family.

A. That is correct.

Q. I want to ask you this: threat assessments, even on that level, are provided

---

[a] Burnett does not say where this suggestion comes from – I don't think anyone, other than him, has ever suggested this.

[b] Similar to a search X carried out on James Andanson, driver of the white Fiat Uno – see Part 1.

on members of the Royal Family when required by MI6, are they not?

A. No, usually threat assessments are carried out by the Security Service[a], but certainly – and it has been my experience through being overseas – in a more informal way, somebody might say in the Embassy or the High Commission, "Oh, there is going to be a forthcoming visit. Is there anything ..." –

Coroner: "... is there anything about this particular place that we ought to be aware of?"

A. Yes.

Q. I appreciate that it may be done on a very informal basis, but nevertheless there may be important information. Are you aware that members of MI6 attend Cabinet Office meetings from time to time in relation to foreign visits by members of the Royal Family?

A. I am sorry, I do not know anything about that. It is out of my area of expertise, I am afraid.

Q. So as far as you are concerned, there are no records of any such meetings or the provision of advice, even on an informal basis?

A. No more than what I have already said in connection with being overseas and things like that.

Richard Tomlinson, Ex-MI6 Officer: 5 Apr 09 Interview: **Jury Didn't Hear**:

Question: "Did you ever get the impression that there were both official and unofficial contacts between MI6 and the royal family? Do you know anything about any of those?"

Answer: "Of course there's going to be unofficial contacts. The main contact between the royal family and MI6 is via the foreign office. It's inevitable that that gets bypassed at times – just by virtue of personal relationships between people in the government, but I don't know of anything specific. If you've worked in senior levels in government, you know how these things in official channels sometimes get bypassed." [305]

Comment: There are some conflicts in the evidence.

Inquest lawyer, Ian Burnett, said to Richard Dearlove: "We have heard – again, it would come as no surprise to anybody – that the service would be involved in providing security advice for foreign visits of the Royal Family." Dearlove replied: "Occasionally." Burnett let this go[bc] and started on his next question, but Dearlove interrupted him midstream: "But I might say not directly. The security assessments would be gathered through the embassy to which the service might make a contribution." Burnett still didn't see any

---

[a] MI5.

[b] This indicates an unwillingness on the part of Burnett to question Dearlove on a comment that really needed an explanation – see the next footnote.

[c] I suggest what Burnett said – based on evidence from Tomlinson – is common sense. The question is: Who else is going to provide security advice on foreign royal visits, if it is not MI6?

need for Dearlove to explain this and relaunched himself into his next question.

Dearlove's comments appear to conflict with the Paris embassy's military attaché, Charles Ritchie, who said: "We would not be informed of an unofficial visit; official visits, yes, because we often had to look after the Royal Air Force flight coming in, look after the crew and the bill would come to the defence section." [306]

Ritchie makes no mention of embassy involvement in the security for visiting royals. And I suggest that is common sense – that pre-trip intelligence would come from the MI6 officers inside the embassy, not normal embassy staff, and the security itself would be provided by Royalty Protection staff from the UK.

Who is going to provide the royals with security advice, if it is not the MI6 officers in the destination country?

Why would Dearlove make comments like this?

It may simply have been an effort to downplay the connections between royals and MI6, and also further undermine the evidence of Richard Tomlinson.[a]

Burnett had evidently seen no problem with Tomlinson's account on this – "it would come as no surprise to anybody" – which makes it interesting that he quietly accepted Dearlove's comments, with no questions.

X also downplayed the role of MI6 in "threat assessments"[bc], but the question was not asked in the context of "foreign visits".[d]

Mansfield asked X: "Threat assessments ... are provided on members of the Royal Family when required by MI6, are they not?" X replied: "No, usually threat assessments are carried out by the Security Service". That is MI5. I suggest it is common sense that MI5 would be carrying out threat assessments for the royal family on British soil.

On foreign soil, X appears to line up with Dearlove's "the service [MI6] might make a contribution". X said: "Somebody might say in the Embassy or the High Commission, 'Oh, there is going to be a forthcoming visit. Is there anything ...' –"

Then, X came to an abrupt halt, midsentence. Why?

One can speculate, but X never finished that sentence – instead the "impartial" judge intervened and completed it for her: "... is there anything

---

[a] It was Tomlinson's evidence that provided the basis for Burnett's statement.
[b] This has a similar meaning to "security advice", which was the term put to Dearlove.
[c] X was cross-examined six days after Dearlove and it may be that she was told to try and align her evidence to Dearlove's on this issue.
[d] That was the context of Dearlove's questioning from Burnett – see above.

about this particular place that we ought to be aware of?" Which X then confirmed, and Mansfield moved on.

We'll never know what X was going to say, but for some reason she pulled herself up, or perhaps got a disapproving glance from one of the MI6 lawyers.

The inquest evidence tended to focus on the royal family's requirements for security threat assessments to be made by MI5 or MI6 ahead of foreign trips.

That has nothing to do with what occurred in Paris – the deaths of Princess Diana and Dodi Fayed, which was the subject of the inquest.

Regarding the royal-intelligence relationship, the issue is whether senior members of the royal family or household would ever give directions or orders to a British intelligence agency.

Outside of Michael Mansfield's quoting of Richard Tomlinson's affidavit – see below – that issue was not really addressed at Baker's "thorough" inquest.

Tomlinson stated in 1999: "I learned while in MI6 that there was unofficial direct contact between certain senior and influential MI6 officers and senior members of the Royal Household."

This was supported in his 2009 interview: "It's inevitable that [the FCO] gets bypassed at times".

Peter Wright, ex-MI5 Officer: 1987 Book *Spycatcher*: **Jury Didn't Hear**:
"Before I began meeting [Anthony] Blunt[a] I had to attend a briefing by Michael Adeane, the Queen's Private Secretary.[b] We met at his office in the Palace. He was punctilious and correct, and assured me that the Palace was willing to cooperate in any inquiries the Service thought fit. He spoke in the detached manner of someone who wishes not to know very much more about the matter.

"'The Queen', he said, 'has been fully informed about Sir Anthony, and is quite content for him to be dealt with in any way which gets at the truth.'

"There was only one caveat.

"'From time to time,' said Adeane, 'you may find Blunt referring to an assignment he undertook on behalf of the Palace – a visit to Germany at the end of the war. Please do not pursue this matter. Strictly speaking, it is not relevant to concerns of national security.'

"Adeane carefully ushered me to the door....

"Although I spent hundreds of hours with Blunt, I never did learn the secret of his mission to Germany. But then, the Palace had had several centuries to learn the difficult art of scandal burying. MI5 have only been in the business since 1909!" [307]

---

[a] MI5 officer who was later exposed as a Soviet spy.
[b] This occurred around 1964.

Comment: Peter Wright's account is significant for three main reasons:
- it provides a specific case of direct royal-MI5 interaction[a] and therefore is support for Tomlinson's account
- it is evidence of an order being given from a senior royal household member – working on behalf of the Queen – to a senior MI5 officer, Peter Wright
- it is evidence of the royals giving "an assignment" to a senior MI5 officer – Anthony Blunt.[b] This was an assignment that was so secret – or incriminating to the royal family – that the Queen intervened to prevent knowledge of it getting out, nearly two decades[c] after it had been carried out.

Wright's account relates to the period of the 1940s through to the 1960s. But Tomlinson's evidence indicates that unofficial direct contacts between royals and intelligence continued into the 1990s.

Charles Higham, Author: 1989 Book *Wallis*: **Jury Didn't Hear**:[d]
"King George VI personally saw to it that certain damaging Windsor documents were retrieved from Germany and suppressed. The King sent Anthony Blunt, Surveyor of the King's Pictures[e], to the Schloss Kronberg, family home of the princes of Hesse near Frankfurt. The Hesses had retained certain documents relating to the Duke of Windsor and his alleged associations with the Nazis. One of the documents was a complete account of the Duke's conversation with the Führer. Blunt travelled with Owen Morshead, the librarian at Windsor Castle. If questioned by reporters, the two men were to say that they were retrieving works of art stolen by the Nazis from the galleries of western Europe and that they were seeking letters sent by Queen Victoria to her eldest daughter, the Empress Frederick of Prussia. When they arrived ... they discovered ... that the Hesses had moved out of the castle and were staying in a villa. The Schloss Kronberg had been commandeered as a US army club and dormitory. An American woman captain was in charge.

"Blunt and Morshead visited the Hesses. The Princess of Hesse ... authorised the handing over of the documents. But when the two secret agents arrived at the castle, the American captain said she was under instructions not to permit them to take anything. They stayed. At [one] stage the [American] officer made a telephone call. Having been advised by the Princess as to the location

---

[a] Not via the FCO or Home Office.
[b] Blunt was knighted by the Queen in 1956.
[c] The interviewing of Blunt occurred in 1963-4.
[d] Higham sourced this information from an Insight article in the *Sunday Times*, 25 November 1979, authored by Colin Simpson, David Leitch and Phillip Knightley.
[e] Blunt was made Surveyor of the King's Pictures in 1945, the same year as his initial mission.

of the papers, the agents managed to somehow extract them from their hiding place and carry them bodily down a back staircase into their pick-up truck....

"The incriminating documents were conveyed to Windsor Castle. When the Prince of Hesse asked for the return of the documents, they were sent back with certain crucial items missing. To this day the material has not surfaced."[308]

Lynn Picknett, Clive Prince & Stephen Prior, Authors: 2003 Book *War of the Windsors*: **Jury Didn't Hear**:

"[In] the 1980s ... a reference to [the Blunt German mission] was found in a Foreign Office file relating to captured German documents. It appears that Blunt had been sent to recover letters from Prince Philip of Hesse-Cassel's twin brother, Wolfgang, at the Schloss Friedrichshof, the Hesse-Cassels' family seat at Kronberg.... Friedrichshof was the home of Philip of Hesse-Cassel – the Duke of Kent's contact with the Nazi (and Italian) leadership during the time of the 'Willi plot'[a]. Moreover in 1979, Prince Wolfgang of Hesse-Cassel revealed in an interview for the *Sunday Times* that Philip had conducted 'unofficial' mediation between the Duke of Windsor and Hitler – 'discussions conducted with King Edward VIII through his youngest brother, George, Duke of Kent'....

"Since the story of the Blunt mission leaked out, the Royal Archive has allowed historians and biographers to see some of the documents relating to the affair that – they claim – reveal it to be all quite innocent....

"The story that emerges from the official records is that the then Archivist, Owen Morshead, and Blunt, sometimes together and sometimes singly, made several trips to Europe to recover property belonging to the British royal family, in case it should disappear in the confusion of the Allied occupation of Germany. The first trip took place in August 1945, when both men travelled to Friedrichshof, then a US Army rest and recuperation centre, with the aim of retrieving some 4,000 letters[b] written by Queen Victoria to her eldest daughter (Victoria, the Princess Royal), Emperor Frederick III's wife and the mother of Kaiser Wilhelm II. Morshead returned with the letters the following day, while Blunt remained on what Morshead described as 'military business'....

"Over the next two years Blunt undertook three more assignments on the King's behalf.... In December 1945 and March 1946, two trips – both using George VI's private plane – took him to Westphalia to meet with the Duke of Brunswick (the heir to the Kingdom of Hanover) and bring back what are described as 'historic Royal Family possessions'....

---

[a] Operation Willi was a wartime attempt by the Nazis to kidnap the Duke of Windsor. There is a book on this: *Operation Willi: Plot to Capture the Duke of Windsor, July 1940* by Michael Bloch, published by Littlehampton Book Services, 1986.

[b] Known as the Vicky letters.

"His last secret mission, in August 1947, took him to the Kaiser's former home, Haus Doorn in the Netherlands, to examine ... anything relevant to 'relations between the Courts of England and Germany during the past hundred years'[a]....

"Shortly after the publication of *Double Standards*[b] in ... 2001, we were contacted by an individual who claimed to have accompanied Blunt on one of his German trips – and to have read some of the letters he collected.... [He requested] us not to reveal his identity.... We will refer to him by the ... code-name he adopted of "Phoenix'....

"After the war ... [Phoenix] was recruited by MI5. While serving in Berlin, he was called in for a special assignment[c] – to accompany someone named Colonel Blunt on a trip to the south 'to recover properties of the Crown'....

"Dressed in the uniform of a staff officer, Blunt left the next morning with Phoenix and a driver on the long journey to ... Schloss Friedrichshof.

"Phoenix writes: 'Except for a few American officers on R & R, the place seemed somewhat deserted. Blunt, showing his written authority to the custodian of the private apartments, was allowed in, with myself in tow. I quickly realised that [Blunt] either knew the place or he had good directions. He went directly to the exact room, to the exact writing bureau and began emptying the bureau drawers and cubbyholes into a box he brought with him, superficially examining the papers as he did so. After this, he retrieved other knickknacks from the room, which I could not see, and placed them into a cloth bag and put that into his pocket. The whole enterprise took less than an hour from arrival to departure.'

"On the return journey to Berlin, they stopped overnight at a hotel where ... Blunt ... handed [Phoenix] the box with the order to keep it safe until the next morning. (Blunt wanted to go out for the evening). Phoenix was ... astounded to find that the [cardboard] box ... was unsealed. Bearing his secret orders in mind [Phoenix] then spent the night examining the letters. Astounded by their revelations, he wrote the detail on the only material that was to hand – one of his pillowcases, which he handed to his superior on his return to Berlin.

"Nearly 20 years later, Phoenix ... was one of the [MI5] officers present when Blunt was brought in for interrogation. Initially Blunt failed to recognise him, but eventually when Phoenix reminded him about their mission, his jaw

---

[a] Quoted from a letter from Morshead to Alan Lascelles, private secretary to King George VI.

[b] An earlier book by the same authors: *Double Standards: The Rudolf Hess Cover-Up* by Lynn Picknett, Clive Prince, Stephen Prior, published by Time Warner, 2002.

[c] Phoenix says this occurred in September 1945: *War of the Windsors*, p198.

dropped. And when asked why he had left the box unsealed, he replied simply: 'I was tired from the trip, I just forgot'....

"Phoenix can still recall the letters.... Dating from both the immediate pre-war period and the early stages of the war, there was correspondence between the Duke of Windsor and Franz von Papen, Hitler's original Vice Chancellor ... discussing possible peaceful solutions to the impending conflict. There was also correspondence between Windsor and Rudolf Hess relating to the possibility that – in the event of George VI and the royal family fleeing to Canada – the Duke would return as King. There were other letters, covering the same subjects, from the Duke of Kent and Göring.... The documents ... included a letter on Reichs Chancellery notepaper from Hitler to Windsor offering season's greetings for Christmas 1938....

"Phoenix also told us that Blunt remained in Berlin for a day or two after their excursion....

"Phoenix [said that] ... when Blunt was brought in to MI5 in 1964, he repeatedly asked to be allowed to telephone Lord Mountbatten...." [309]

Comment: Both of these books support Peter Wright's 1987 account.

There are however a couple of potential conflicts between the account in the *Wallis* and *Windsors* books and Phoenix's account:

-    the two books describe a Morshead-Blunt visit, whereas Phoenix makes no mention of Morshead

-    Higham describes difficulties accessing the letters, whereas Phoenix says it was straightforward

-    the *Windsors* book times the trip in August 1945, whereas Phoenix says it was in September.

The *Windsors* book quotes Morshead saying that Blunt remained in Germany on "military business".

One possible scenario is that the Morshead-Blunt trip occurred in late August, after which Blunt stayed in Germany, while Morshead returned with a batch of letters. Blunt then organises the "written authority" to make retrieval of further letters much easier, dresses in uniform, and returns with Phoenix for the second visit to Kronberg in early September. It is possible Blunt – who was a double agent working for the Soviets – didn't seal the box straightaway so he could pass on information from the letters to his Russian masters following his return to Berlin.

Putting the accounts from these two books together with Peter Wright reveals a clear case of direct interaction between the royals and Anthony Blunt and Peter Wright, both MI5 officers.

The evidence also reveals that the senior royals directly used British intelligence – not through the government of the day – to carry out a secret mission to fulfil royal requirements, and have since actively sought to cover up what occurred.[ab]

Way Ahead Group

There was a major conflict over the nature of the topics discussed at meetings held by the royal Way Ahead Group (WAG).

Paul Condon, MPS Commissioner: 17 Jan 08: 30.18:

Mansfield: Q. 1997. Did you have in that year or had you had, while you were Commissioner, any liaison, contact with, a group called the "Way Ahead Group"?

A. No.

Q. You are aware of its existence?

A. Only through – I am not sure if I was at the time. I am only aware of it through media speculation.

Q. Oh, I see. So as part of your role as Commissioner, at no stage do you discover that there was a group chaired by the Duke of Edinburgh? [c]

A. No.

Miles Hunt-Davis, Private Secretary to Prince Philip: 13 Dec 07: 58.21:

Burnett: Q. There has been mention, both in public and these inquests, of a body within the household called the "Way Ahead Group". Are you aware of its existence?

A. I am aware of its existence, yes.

Q. Could you explain to the jury what the Way Ahead Group was in 1997?

A. The Way Ahead Group was formed – and to be honest, I do not remember when it was formed, but it was formed sometime in the 1990s – to draw together the senior members of the Royal Family and their close advisers to discuss literally the way forward, to produce a degree of coordination between their programmes. I think it is quite important to realise that although everybody in the Royal Family is there to help the Queen to do her job, by the essence of the family, they all have separate lifestyles because they have separate patronages and they therefore have a wide variety of interests. So the Way Ahead Group was there to make sure that whilst they were carrying out their own life's work, as they perceived it, the central core

---

[a] The cover-up around this mission has continued to this day, over 65 years later. Despite this being a matter of public interest, not one of the secret letters retrieved has been released to the public.

[b] It may be no coincidence that in 1943, when MI6 needed to employ a funeral director to carry out a clandestine activity, they used Levertons – who later became the royal undertakers (see Part 4).: Ben Macintyre, *Operation Mincemeat*, pp169-170.

[c] Later evidence will show the WAG is chaired by the Queen.

of what the Royal Family was doing was properly coordinated. That was done by obviously liaison at a working level between people like myself and other private secretaries, but at the Royal Family's level at probably two meetings per year.

Q. You mentioned that it comprised senior members of the Royal Family and their senior officials. Are we to infer, then, that as the Duke of Edinburgh's private secretary you attended the Way Ahead Group meetings?

A. That is correct.

At 61.15: Mansfield: Q. The Way Ahead Group.... I do not have, as you don't appear to have either, access to any of the documentation relating to this group, so I apologise for asking you questions in the dark a little bit.... The membership of the group, do you remember who actually attended?

A. I think normally it would have been the Queen and Prince Philip, the Prince of Wales, the Duke of York, the Princess Royal and Prince Edward. Whether they all attended all of the meetings, I quite honestly cannot say. And that would have been it as far as the Royal Family was concerned.

Q. But then they would have assistants such as yourself, for example?

A. Yes.

Q. So the group would be swelled by – what, each of them would have an assistant or just some of them?

A. No, certainly not. I would have thought it would have been the Queen's private secretary, myself and possibly the Prince of Wales' private secretary.

Q. So Robert Fellowes would be there?

A. If he was the private secretary at the time, then he would have been there.

Q. Were there any outside advisers present?

A. Never.

Q. Was there somebody who liaised with outside advice?

A. Not in any formal sense that I am aware of. In fact, not in any sense that I am aware of. I mean it was really just to coordinate their programmes.

Q. But it was also discussing, was it not, problems about image of the monarchy or the Royal Family outside; in other words, the concerns that they all may have about how things may appear to the public?

A. To be honest, I cannot remember, but it is quite likely, I should think.

Robert Fellowes, Queen's Private Secretary, 1990-99, UK: 12 Feb 08: 4.8:

Burnett: Q. Who attended the Way Ahead Group meetings?

A. The Queen, the Duke of Edinburgh, their children, the Private Secretaries to the members of the Royal Family concerned, the Lord Chamberlain, who chaired it with the Queen, and the financial department, represented by the Keeper of the Privy Purse.

Q. What in broad terms was the function of the Way Ahead Group?

A. It was brought together as a coordinating group so that the activities, public activities, of the core members of the Royal Family, if I may call them that, were as purposeful and effective as possible.

At 101.3: Mansfield: Q. Now that we have established the date, in November 1992, was it set up in the wake of the speech that the Queen made about –
A. It had no connection with that. I think it was – there was a feeling that there was a lack of coordination in programming for senior members of the Royal Family, and it was an attempt to render more pointful – terrible word – the public appearances of the Royal Family, to make sure that specialisations were kept to and that three members of the Royal Family did not appear in one county in one week and that sort of thing. It was really – it was strategic, but strategic at a pretty lowish level, frankly.
Q. Worried about image, wasn't it?
A. Yes, sure, but all public figures are.
Q. Yes. Don't go down that road. It is just that there had been a series of events – well, you know what they are – that could be perceived as extremely damaging.
A. Yes, the Way Ahead Group was formed in the wake of those or some of those.
Miles Hunt-Davis, Private Secretary to Prince Philip: 13 Dec 07: 59.22:
Burnett: Q. You mentioned that the group met twice a year. Are you able to confirm that, in 1997, it met on 20th January and then again on 20th July?
A. From my personal knowledge, no, but if it is recorded, I am quite sure that that would be right. But I cannot recall the dates specifically.
Q. Now there are two particular allegations that have been made in public concerning what happened at the meeting on 20th July 1997. The first is that – and I quote – "Top of the agenda for the next meeting", that is to say the one on 20th July, "is Diana". Was "Diana" discussed at all at the meeting as an agenda item?
A. I cannot remember. I think it would have been difficult to have done so with the senior officials there, if it was indeed a family discussion, but to be honest, I do not recall the details.
Q. Was the Way Ahead Group considering what might loosely be called an issue arising from the divorce of the Prince and Princess of Wales at that stage?
A. It is quite possible that it might have been. In terms of status, I would have thought that would probably be the meat of it, but I do not recall it at all.
Q. So by way of status, do you mean the title "Her Royal Highness"?
A. Correct.
Q. It is also suggested or it was suggested in the press at the time that the group was going to consider a file on the Al Fayeds prepared by the security services. Is there any truth in that suggestion?
A. I am quite sure that that did not happen. My memory may be bad, but I would have remembered that.

At 69.6: Mansfield: Q. The Way Ahead Group, was there due to be another meeting that year, in fact, in September?

A. I have not the faintest idea.

Q. Were you aware that a newspaper reported on 20th July, the very day that you met in 1997, that there was a meeting of that group? Did you know that?

A. No.

Q. Assuming that that was the date, then the newspaper had particularly accurate information, at least about the existence of the group and the date that it was meeting, didn't it?

A. As I have not seen the article or don't remember seeing the article, I have no way of commenting.

Robert Fellowes, Queen's Private Secretary, 1990-99, UK: 12 Feb 08: 4.20: Burnett: Q. Now the activities or discussions at the Way Ahead Group came into the inquest's purview because of allegations that were made in a newspaper report on 20th July 1997. Is that something of which you are aware?

A. Can you ask me that again? Sorry.

Q. There were allegations made in a newspaper report on 20th July 1997 concerning what was to be discussed at the Way Ahead Group due to take place a few days later.

A. I am afraid I have no recollection.

Q. You don't remember the newspaper article. Well, first of all, how often did the Way Ahead Group meet during the mid-1990s?

A. Twice a year, I think.

Q. Are you able to help the jury with when it met in 1997?

A. We met in late July, having had a preparatory meeting some ten days/fortnight before.

Q. Now, in a letter that was written by the Treasury Solicitor when inquiries were made of the Palace about the Way Ahead Group, it was suggested that the group met twice in 1997, once on 20th January and then, again, on a date which was clarified to be 23rd July. Does that sound right?

A. It does.

At 6.5: Q. In your diary for 1997 – I do not ask anyone to turn it up necessarily, but can I just read you an entry for 8th July? There is a reference to "Way Ahead, 2 o'clock".... Was that a meeting of the Way Ahead Group that involved members of the Royal Family?

A. No.

Q. So what is that a reference to?

A. It was effectively a preparatory meeting chaired by the Lord Chamberlain. It was an agenda meeting really. No more than that.

Q. And the Lord Chamberlain of the day was?

A. Lord Airlie.

At 99.2: Mansfield: Q. The meeting in your diary you have already indicated of the Way Ahead Group, at least part of it – just to go back to your diary, on the 8th. That is in London, is it?

A. The 8th was the preparatory meeting in London, yes.

Q. Well, who would have been at the preparatory meeting?

A. It would have been chaired by the Lord Chamberlain, Lord Airlie, and it would have composed the Private Secretaries concerned and the Keeper of the Privy Purse.

Q. You see the 8th is just at the time that the signing off of [Diana's] holiday is taking place, as we have seen on the other document, isn't it?

A. Yes.

Q. You were aware of the holiday?

A. I cannot say now, but I suppose I was, yes. I would think very likely I was.

Q. Now, on the 8th, would there be a record of that particular agenda meeting?

A. I would think so, yes.

Q. Well, sir, I wonder if we might be provided, if there is a record of that meeting.

At 112.17: Coroner: Was there going to be a meeting of the Way Ahead Group at Balmoral?

A. There – no, the Way Ahead Group met in July, but not – there was no further meeting at Balmoral planned.

Coroner: The suggestion here [Sunday Mirror, 31 Aug 97] is that one was planned for early September.

A. No.

Mansfield: Q. As sometimes happens, do the meetings[a] of a previous meeting indicate when the next – sorry, you are just looking –

A. I am just making sure, sir, that I am right in saying that. No, I can see no reference in my pocket diary anyway to a Way Ahead Group meeting in September.

Q. You see it may be that there was one scheduled, but it was cancelled because of the crash.

A. It would be very unlikely because, as I say, we met twice a year, usually in the first two months, and then in the late summer. That was a regular routine. So it was very unlikely that a third was planned for September, after one in July.

Coroner: Mr Mansfield, I reviewed the minutes and agenda for the July meeting to see whether there was anything relevant in them. Had there been a

---

[a] This probably should read, "minutes".

reference to the next meeting, I would have regarded that as relevant.

Q. That was going to be the next question. Sometimes a date is put for the next.

Coroner: Indeed, I have the minutes and agenda here, but I directed that they should not be disclosed because they contain nothing of relevance.

Burnett: Sir, might I just assist on this? Obviously the relevance that you had in mind was whether there was a meeting identified in the July minutes to occur in September.

Coroner: Yes.

Burnett: Sir, as you will recollect and no doubt you have reminded yourself, there is no such reference, but –

Coroner: Relevance also now includes what they don't contain.

Burnett: Yes, but sir, as to the question of whether the minutes of 23rd July indicate, as so often is the case with minutes, when the next meeting is scheduled, that is something which – I do not know if you have a copy of them available to you.

Coroner: Yes, I have, and I have just said that they don't contain that and I had looked at that originally.

Burnett: Sir, can I just hand something to you to see whether we are looking at –

Coroner: Wait a minute.

Burnett: I think there may be another page there.

Coroner: Ah. Well you show me what you have.

Burnett: I am looking at the last entry on page 5[a], which says "Next meeting".

Coroner: Ah, well, thank you. Well, I was not provided with page 5 in the accompanying letter from the Treasury Solicitor or it may be that this is an error in copying at our end.

Burnett: Sir, given that I have it with page 5, it must have arrived with page 5 but perhaps it has not been copied onto yours. Sir, I wonder, to avoid any confusion, whether Lord Fellowes might just look at the agenda and the minutes and then he no doubt can remind himself of when the next –

Coroner: Yes, thank you. I am sorry, Mr Mansfield, I gave you misleading information because I had not seen the very last page.

A. Shall I read it out? "The next meeting has been arranged for Monday 19th January 1998, Sandringham House."

Adam Chapman, Treasury Solicitor's Department, UK: 17 Mar 08 Letter read out 18 Mar 08: 152.7:

---

[a] Baker had just declared that the minutes "contain nothing of relevance". Burnett then indicates that there could have been other entries on page 5 that Baker hadn't seen, when he says: "I am looking at <u>the last entry</u> on page 5". The question is: Did Baker conclude the minutes were not relevant without actually seeing them all?

"No documents have been located relating to a meeting on 8th July 1997. During a search made for documents ... a memorandum dated 18th July 1997, and relating to the Way Ahead Group meeting on 23rd July 1997, was located. I attach a copy."

Miles Hunt-Davis, Private Secretary to Prince Philip: 13 Dec 07: 74.23: Mansfield: Q. This could not be more serious for the monarchy, could it? Here was a member – in fact she was soon to become not a member – in 1996 she was divested of that, was she not?

A. I believe so.

Q. Well, it was discussed at the Way Ahead Group, was it not, in 1996?

A. I do not think it was discussed in that detail, no.

Q. In some little detail then?

A. I doubt it was even in that detail, a little detail. The Way Ahead Group was to do with coordination. It was not to do with personal affairs of members of the Royal Family. The central theme was coordinating their public life. It was not an inner sanctum where the lives and behaviour of members of the Royal Family was discussed.

Q. So the decision to divest her of membership of the Royal Family would be taken with whom?

A. I imagine Her Majesty the Queen took the decision, having taken advice, I presume. I have no idea.

At 100.13: Burnett: Q. Some questions were asked of the Royal Household about the Way Ahead Group and I just wonder whether you can deal with both the questions and answers insofar as you are able to. The first question that was asked on behalf of the Coroner was for details of whether the group existed at the relevant time, and the answer was "yes" and you have explained what the Way Ahead Group did. If I just read you a response on behalf of the Royal Household: "It was attended by members of the Royal Family and senior officials." That is right, is it?

A. Correct.

Q. "Typical topics considered included the coordination of Royal diaries."

A. Correct.

Q. "Priorities for forthcoming Royal visits."

A. Correct.

Q. "Work with the charitable section"?

A. Correct.

Q. "And the creation of a Royal website"?

A. That, almost certainly, correct.

Q. This was back in 1997. The second question was whether there is any truth in the *Sunday Mirror's* report from 20th July 1997 that the group was making plans for its next meeting and "top of the agenda for the next meeting is Diana". The answer was: "There is no truth in the *Sunday Mirror's* report of 20th July 1997 that 'top of the agenda for the next meeting is Diana'".

A. I am quite sure that that is correct.

Q. The next question concerned the dates which we have dealt with. The question was: "The contents of its discussions [that is the Way Ahead Group's] in relation to Princess Diana at this time". So that is the 1997 meetings and this was the answer: "There were no discussions in relation to Princess Diana at these meetings." Have you any reason to doubt that?

A. I have no reason to doubt it. It was really – as I think I said earlier, the Way Ahead Group was really to coordinate the Royal Family's work and how they went about it, in terms of timing and other matters of common interest. And I would very much doubt that Princess Diana would have come into the discussion in front of officials such as myself, for what was basically by then a family matter.

Robert Fellowes, Queen's Private Secretary, 1990-99, UK: 12 Feb 08: 5.18: Burnett: Q. Indeed, the Coroner received the agenda and minutes for the meeting on 23rd July and considered them. Now one of the reports in the press concerning that July meeting was that – and I quote: "Top of the agenda for the next meeting [that would be the one on 23rd July] is Diana." Is that true?

A. No, I do not think it is.

At 104.12: Mansfield: Q. This is an article that appeared in The *Sunday Mirror* on July 20th 1997, three days before the meeting....: "Speculation about Diana's future, which is as strong at Buckingham Palace as it is in the Princess's camp, comes as plans are made for the next meeting of the Way Ahead Group." How was it that the press had got hold of fact that there was a meeting coming up?

A. An awful lot of people knew about the dates for the Way Ahead Group. It was programmed right round the Royal Household. There was nothing secret about it.

Q. It may not have been secret in the Royal Household. It may have come from somebody in the Royal Household that there was a meeting?

A. Could have been.

Q. "The Queen, Prince Philip, their four children and senior courtiers meet twice a year to discuss new challenges facing the monarchy." Well, that is true, isn't it?

A. Yes.

Q. "Top of the agenda at the forthcoming meeting is Diana."

A. That is not true.

Q. Do you ever have topics that don't actually go down on the agenda?

A. No, I do not think we ever strayed from the agenda. It was pretty structured.

At 105.23: Q. This is August 31st, The Sunday Mirror ... under a headline: "Queen 'to strip Harrods of its Royal Crest'; The Royal Family may withdraw their seal of approval from Harrods."...[a] Firstly, Lord Fellowes, did you ever see that article?

A. Not to my memory.

Q. Secondly, is it right, as it is mentioned in the third paragraph, that the Royal warrants were up for review in February?

A. I do not know when they came up for review, I am afraid.[b]

Q. So you cannot help on that?

A. No. All I know is that the Royal Warrant-Holders Committee met annually and so on.

Miles Hunt-Davis, Private Secretary to Prince Philip: 13 Dec 07: 100.13: Burnett: Q. Some questions were asked of the Royal Household about the Way Ahead Group and I just wonder whether you can deal with both the questions and answers insofar as you are able to.... And then, whether the group considered a file on the Al Fayeds prepared by the security services was the last of the questions, and the answer was: "The group did not consider a file on the Al Fayeds prepared by the security services as suggested in the Sunday Mirror report of 30th August 1997."

A. I can confirm that we did not discuss it.

Robert Fellowes, Queen's Private Secretary, 1990-99, UK: 12 Feb 08: 6.1: Burnett: Q. It was also suggested that the [Way Ahead] group considered a file on the Al Fayeds prepared by the security services. Is that true?

A. No.

....Q. What I wish to ask you is whether you were aware of any animosity directed towards him by the Royal Family in and before 1997.

A. None whatever.

At 44.10: Q. Was the visit[c], as far as you can recollect, the subject of anxious discussion in Buckingham Palace, centring on Mr Al Fayed's suitability as a host?

A. I do not remember any discussion of it.

Q. Is that the sort of thing that would even be likely to be discussed?

A. No.

The Washington Times: 1 Sep 96 Article: **Jury Didn't Hear**:[d]

---

[a] The text of this article, as read out by Mansfield, appears below amongst the various media articles relating to the WAG.

[b] The Harrods royal warrants were removed in 1998. See footnote in later section on MI6 Report on Al Fayeds.

[c] The Diana-Mohamed St Tropez holiday.

[d] The following media articles are in date order.

"The royal family 'committee' that has been discussing issues such as the succession and royal marriages to Catholics was established in the aftermath of the debate concerning royal taxation and is now examining every facet of royal life.

"Known internally as the "Way Ahead Committee," the group comprises Queen Elizabeth, Prince Philip, their children and senior palace officials." [310]

The Spectator:[a] 17 Sep 96 Article: **Jury Didn't Hear:**

Title: "Royal Family Gathers to Chart Its Future: Way Ahead Group Talks About Church Links, Rules for Succession"

"The Queen and her children met in council yesterday in an effort to chart the future of the Royal Family, rocked by two recent divorces and bad press over Prince Charles' relationship with Camilla Parker Bowles.

"Attending were the Queen, Prince Phillip and their four children. Senior courtiers such as the Queen's private secretary, Sir Robert Fellowes, and her financial manager, Michael Peat, were also believed to be present." [311]

Sunday Mirror: 20 Jul 97 Article read out 12 Feb 08: 104.12:

"Speculation about Diana's future, which is as strong at Buckingham Palace as it is in the Princess's camp, comes as plans are made for the next meeting of the Way Ahead Group. The Queen, Prince Philip, their four children and senior courtiers meet twice a year to discuss new challenges facing the monarchy. Top of the agenda at the forthcoming meeting is Diana." [b]

Sunday Mirror: 31 Aug 97 Article read out 12 Feb 08: 105.23:

Title: "Queen 'to strip Harrods of its Royal Crest'; The Royal Family may withdraw their seal of approval from Harrods."

"The Royal Family may withdraw their seal of approval from Harrods ... as a result of Diana's affair with owner's son, Dodi Fayed. The top people's store, with its long and proud tradition of Royal patronage may be about to lose the Prince of Wales Royal crest. Senior Palace courtiers are ready to advise the Queen that she should refuse to renew the prestigious Royal warrants for the Knightsbridge store when they come up for review in February. It would be a huge blow to the ego of store owner Mohamed Al Fayed and would infuriate Diana, who was yesterday understood to be still with Dodi, aboard his yacht, near the Italian island of Sardinia. But the Royal Family are furious about the frolics of Di, 36, and Dodi, 41, which they believe have further undermined the Monarchy. Prince Philip, in particular, has ... made no secret as to how he feels about his daughter-in-law's latest man, referring to Dodi as an 'oily bedhopper'. At Balmoral next week, the Queen will preside over a meeting of the Way Ahead Group, where the Windsors sit down with their senior advisers to discuss policy matters. MI6 has prepared a special report on the

---

[a] Toronto, Canada.
[b] The article was titled: "Is Diana's Baby Clock Ticking?" and was written by Doug Kempster and Fiona Wingett.

Egyptian-born Fayeds, which will be presented to the meeting. The delicate subject of Harrods and its Royal warrants is also expected to be discussed and the Fayeds can expect little sympathy from Philip. A friend of the Royals said yesterday 'Prince Philip has let rip several times recently about the Fayeds – at a dinner party during a country shoot and while on a visit to close friends in Germany. He has been banging on about his contempt for Dodi and how he is undesirable as a future stepfather to William and Harry. Diana has been told in no uncertain terms about the consequences should she continue the relationship with the Fayed boy. Options must include possible exile, although that would be very difficult as, all said and done, she is the mother of the future King of England. She has also been warned about social ostracism. But Diana's attitude is if that means not having to deal with the royals and their kind, then she would be delighted. There are some who believe Diana may be past caring and has decided to look towards those who can afford to keep her in the lifestyle to which she has become accustomed. The Fayed family have all the trappings of vast wealth ... wherever it originated from. Dodi has told Diana what he has told many of his other beautiful girlfriends in the past: 'It is my father's store and you can have what you want. Charge it to my account and I will just sign the bill. But now the Royal Family may decide it is time to settle up." [a]

The Independent: 23 Feb 98 Article: **Jury Didn't Hear**:

"At the Way Ahead Group summit, which happens twice a year to consider long-term issues, members of the Royal Family discussed results of the Mori survey commissioned after the death of Diana, Princess of Wales at a cost of £20,000. A key finding was reportedly that the public considers the royals to be badly advised on a range of issues by their 'numerous courtiers and official royal advisers.' The royals are reportedly regarded as not understanding 'at all' and poor value for money. They are seen as wasteful on account of their 'apparent extravagant lifestyle' and remote because of 'the many physical and invisible barriers thought to have been constructed around them'.

"On the positive side, the royals were seen to be trustworthy, an integral part of British society, respected, and professional in the execution of their duties." [312]

The Economist: 12 Mar 98 Article: **Jury Didn't Hear**:

"The members of the royal family are waging two separate campaigns[b] to reclaim the hearts and minds of the British people, after the disasters of

---

[a] A copy of this article from the paper is reproduced later. The article's author was Andrew Golden – he appears in the list of Witnesses Not Heard in Part 1.

[b] *The Economist* described the second campaign: "The other, private, campaign is being conducted by Prince Charles's staff. It is designed to ensure that he is not

recent years. The best known is one run by the Way Ahead group – a committee of senior members of the royal family and their advisers. This is intended to modernise the monarchy.....

"The Way Ahead group has been considering a mass of changes that could be introduced, after depressing results from focus groups that it secretly commissioned from MORI, an opinion-poll company. People in the groups said that the royals were too distant, and had too many grandiose trappings.

"The Way Ahead group has, for instance, agreed to the government's plan to allow the eldest child, rather than the eldest boy, to inherit the throne. It agreed to cut down on curtseys and bows. It has discussed reducing the number of family members allowed to call themselves 'royal highness'. And, since the royals reckon that reforms introduced so far have gone unnoticed, they have decided to hire a top-flight spin-doctor before implementing any further changes." [313]

BBC News: Aug 98 Article: **Jury Didn't Hear**:

"Several years ago, the Royal Family set up a discussion procedure known as the Way Ahead Group made up of senior members of the family, with the Queen herself in the chair.

"One of the first decisions was that the Queen should pay tax. In 1992, after the fire at Windsor Castle, it was agreed that the taxpayers should not pick up the bill. Buckingham Palace, they decided, would be open to the public in the summer to raise money for the restoration.

"The Way Ahead Group also examined whether the Royal Family was casting its net wide enough in its visits. Were there sections of society being 'left out'?

"There was a brisk spring cleaning of royal finances headed by a hot-shot City accountant, Michael Peat.

"The Civil List was cut. (Today only the Queen, Prince Philip and the Queen Mother are supported by the taxpayer.) Even royal travel was changed. The Royal Yacht Britannia was scrapped. The Queen did not press for a replacement. The budget is now set each year and flights for visits abroad even put out to tender.

"In sum, a great deal was done long before Diana's death. Indeed some at the Palace felt that the worst was over. Then came the events of August 31, 1997.

"The sudden outpouring of public emotion took royal officials by surprise. It quickly became apparent that the changes simply were not enough." [314]

The Guardian: 12 Jun 00 Article: **Jury Didn't Hear**:

"Support for the royal family has fallen to its lowest level in modern times, with only 44% of the public believing that Britain would be worse off

---

passed over for the throne.... Mark Bolland is trying to 'reposition' the prince in the wake of his ex-wife's death. The plan is to make him look friendlier, less controversial and more modern."

without the monarchy, according to a Guardian/ICM opinion poll published today.

"The survey suggests, however, that it is a growing indifference to the royal family rather than a rise in republicanism....

"The survey shows that despite the efforts of Buckingham Palace's "way ahead group" to try to reinvent and modernise the monarchy for the 21st century it is still in deep trouble." [315]

The Mirror: 11 Apr 01 Article: **Jury Didn't Hear**:

"A survey by Mori showed 71 per cent voted for the monarchy. That poll was commissioned by the Way Ahead Group, which is made up of senior royals."[316a]

Daily Mail: 19 Aug 06 Article: **Jury Didn't Hear**:

"The extent to which the Royal Family is governed and run like a business is startling. The future of the family is governed and set by senior family members along with the aid of a clique of key confidants and advisers.

"They meet twice a year and form the powerful group in the Monarchy's inner sanctum known simply as the Way Ahead Group - essentially the twice-yearly general meeting of Windsor plc....

"The Group makes the decisions which have shaped the Royal Family for the past decade or so. Not even the Prime Minister is privy to the details of its discussions.

"Established in the early Nineties by the then Lord Chamberlain, Lord Airlie, the Way Ahead Group is the Royal Family's version of sitting round the kitchen table and thrashing out differences of opinions and plans for the future." [317]

Wall Street Journal: 28 Apr 11 Article: **Jury Didn't Hear**:

"The royal largesse seemed in deep jeopardy in 1997, after Princess Diana, divorced and dating multimillionaire Dodi Fayed, died in a Paris car crash.... The family's popularity was already in decline. In 1992, the public reacted angrily to the family's expectation that the government would pick up the tab for repairs to a fire that gutted a royal residence, Windsor Castle. In 1993, playwright David Hare declared in a speech: 'We shall mock them till they wish they had never been born.'

"To stop the slide, the family turned to the so-called Way Ahead Group, a collection of senior advisers and family members who, from the mid-1990s to the mid-2000s, gathered twice a year to smooth communications between various factions of the sometimes warring family. While many topics were

---

[a] This excerpt is specifically about a poll commissioned by WAG. The article was about a *Mirror* poll which showed – following the "Sophie tapes" scandal – most people wanted the monarchy abolished.

mundane, like the coordination of schedules, at times the group tackled bigger questions like 'palace policy' and 'how they were going to defend themselves,' says Frank Prochashka, a historian and monarchy expert at Oxford University.

"In the wake of Diana's death, the group focused on the question of how to reconnect with the British public. On one occasion, according to a person familiar with the matter, Mr. Lewis, the first public-relations professional at the palace drawn from business, in 1999 introduced a weapon familiar in boardrooms but alien to monarchs: market research. The findings, presented to about a dozen people including the queen in a large room in Buckingham Palace typically used as a movie theater, underscored that the public associated the royal family with values such as 'Britishness' and public duty. "The palace then used that to shape its strategy....

"It also introduced reforms to disarm the critics. 'The queen began to pay tax on her private income, reimbursed the government for the parliamentary annuities to members of the royal family, opened Buckingham Palace to pay for the repair to Windsor Castle following the fire, decommissioned the royal yacht and accepted greater parliamentary scrutiny of royal accounts,' wrote Prof. Prochashka in his book 'The Republic of Britain.'" [318]

Vanity Fair: 28 Apr 11 Article: **Jury Didn't Hear**:

"The story[a] goes back to 1992, which Queen Elizabeth II called the *annus horribilis*.... Ever since, the Queen has been at pains to ensure the survival of the monarchy in its current form. With that in mind, the then lord chamberlain, Lord Airlie, established a secretive discussion procedure called the Way Ahead Group, which is chaired by the Queen and consists of senior courtiers and senior working royals. (The working royals reportedly include the Queen and Prince Philip, Prince Charles, Princess Anne, Prince Andrew, Prince Edward, Prince William, and Prince Harry.) The Way Ahead Group convenes twice a year, doesn't keep minutes of its meetings, and deals only with such paramount issues as primogeniture, the feudal rule by which the Crown passes to the eldest male heir.

"After its initial meeting in 1992, the group made several precedent-shattering decisions. The Queen and Prince Charles volunteered to pay taxes on the private income from their vast estates. The Queen agreed to reimburse the government for its annual Civil List grants.... Buckingham Palace was opened to visitors in order to raise money for $65.6 million in repairs to Windsor Castle. And the royal yacht *Britannia*, with its 19 officers and crew of 217, was later decommissioned and turned into a tourist attraction." [319]

---

[a] Regarding issues over the role of Prince Andrew.

Comment: The evidence about the purpose of the WAG and content of discussion at the meetings is:[a]

- "to discuss literally the way forward, to produce a degree of coordination between their programmes" – Hunt-Davis to Burnett
- "to make sure that ... the central core of what the Royal Family was doing was properly coordinated" – Hunt-Davis to Burnett
- "it was really just to coordinate their programmes" – Hunt-Davis to Mansfield
- "the Way Ahead Group was to do with coordination.... The central theme was coordinating their public life" – Hunt-Davis to Mansfield
- "it was brought together as a coordinating group so that the activities, public activities, of the core members of the Royal Family ... were as purposeful and effective as possible" – Fellowes to Burnett
- "it was an attempt to render more pointful ... the public appearances of the Royal Family" – Fellowes to Mansfield[b]
- "typical topics considered included the coordination of Royal diaries; priorities for forthcoming Royal visits; work with the charitable section; and the creation of a Royal website" – royal household written response to coroner's question, confirmed by Hunt-Davis
- "[the WAG] has been discussing issues such as the succession and royal marriages to Catholics" – Washington Times, September 1996
- "the Queen and her children met in [a WAG] council ... in an effort to chart the future of the Royal Family" – The Spectator, September 1996
- "the Way Ahead Group summit ... [meets] to consider long-term issues" – The Independent, February 1998
- "the Way Ahead group ... [is running a campaign] intended to modernise the monarchy" – The Economist, March 1998
- "one of the first [WAG] decisions was that the Queen should pay tax" – BBC, August 1998
- "the efforts of Buckingham Palace's 'way ahead group' to try to reinvent and modernise the monarchy for the 21st century" – The Guardian, June 2000
- "that [public opinion] poll was commissioned by the Way Ahead Group" – The Mirror, April 2001

---

[a] The inquest accounts of Hunt-Davis and Fellowes – listed here – are what they directly said about the WAG. Other possible topics of conversation were put to them by Mansfield, and they both generally said they could not recall, but some of those topics put were possible or even likely. This is discussed later.
[b] Fellowes later confirmed evidence to Mansfield that conflicts with this. That is addressed below.

-   "the [WAG] makes the decisions which have shaped the Royal Family for the past decade or so" – Daily Mail, August 2006
-   "many topics were mundane, like the coordination of schedules, [but] at times the group tackled bigger questions like 'palace policy' and 'how they were going to defend themselves,' – Frank Prochashka[a], April 2011
-   "the Way Ahead Group ... deals only with such paramount issues as primogeniture, the feudal rule by which the Crown passes to the eldest male heir" – Vanity Fair, August 2011.

The evidence relating to the purpose and content of WAG meetings falls into five main categories:

1) The written response to the coroner from the royal household – confirmed by Hunt-Davis

2) Information that Robert Fellowes or Miles Hunt-Davis – who were both present in the meetings[b] – state they recall

3) Possible meeting agenda topics that were put to Fellowes or Hunt-Davis, but which they say they couldn't recall but wouldn't rule out – addressed later

4) Possible meeting agenda topics that Fellowes or Hunt-Davis say were never included – addressed later

5) Information that is in the public domain – through the media.

There is a huge conflict between what Fellowes or Hunt-Davis say they can positively recall and the information that has been provided or leaked to the media repeatedly over a period of 15 years.[c]

The positive recall evidence of Hunt-Davis and Fellowes basically matches.

Hunt-Davis said that the WAG was set up "really just to coordinate [the senior royals'] programmes". Fellowes was more wordy: The WAG "was brought together as a coordinating group so that the ... public activities of the core members of the Royal Family ... were as purposeful and effective as possible".

Both men appear to be singing from the same song sheet: The WAG was about coordination of the senior royals' activities and schedules.[d]

Mansfield put to Hunt-Davis: "Was [the WAG] not [discussing] the concerns that they all may have about how things may appear to the public?"[e]

---

[a] Monarchy expert, quoted in *Wall Street Journal*.
[b] Fellowes was the Queen's private secretary from 1990 to 1999; Hunt-Davis was Philip's private secretary from 1993 through to 2010.
[c] 1996 to 2011.
[d] At one point Fellowes conflicts with this – see point 2 below.
[e] Mansfield didn't put this directly to Fellowes. In the context of the WAG, he asked: "Worried about image, wasn't it?" Fellowes answered: "Yes, sure, but all public figures are."

Hunt-Davis replied: "To be honest, I cannot remember, but it is quite likely, I should think."

There are three media articles that indicate the WAG had actually commissioned public surveys to be taken:

- "the [WAG] discussed results of the Mori survey commissioned after the death of Diana ... at a cost of £20,000" – The Independent, 23 February 1998

- "the [WAG] has been considering ... results from focus groups that it secretly commissioned from MORI, an opinion-poll company" – The Economist, 12 March 1998

- "a survey by Mori ... was commissioned by the [WAG]" – The Mirror, 11 April 2001.

These articles indicate that the WAG commissioned and discussed surveys of the public in 1998 and 2001. Hunt-Davis said: "To be honest, I cannot remember".

I suggest that is unlikely.

Although at times there is some conflict – detailed below – the general evidence from Miles Hunt-Davis, Robert Fellowes and the royal household is:

- the WAG meetings were primarily about coordination of royal family member schedules and other administrative matters[a]

- there could have been some discussion of the public perceptions of the royal family

- Diana was not on the agenda in the 1997 WAG meetings.

The question is: Is this Fellowes and Hunt-Davis account true? Put another way: Did the WAG focus on administrative issues or major problems that the royal family faced?

There are several points that indicate Hunt-Davis and Fellowes may have lied in their evidence:

1) There is a glaring conflict between the media reports about the WAG – from 1996 to 2011 – and the inquest evidence from Hunt-Davis and Fellowes.

---

[a] The written royal household response focuses on administrative matters: "the coordination of Royal diaries, priorities for forthcoming Royal visits; work with the charitable section; and the creation of a Royal website". Although that could be seen as conflicting with the Fellowes and Hunt-Davis inquest evidence – they focused on the coordination of diaries and activities – the possible conflict is not significant. The issue really is whether the WAG meetings were focused on major issues facing the royal family or just administrative issues.

DIANA INQUEST: WHO KILLED PRINCESS DIANA?

The media has consistently indicated that the WAG focus is not primarily on coordination of schedules and activities – as stated by the private secretaries – but instead is:
- "discussing issues such as the succession and royal marriages to Catholics" – 1996
- "an effort to chart the future of the Royal Family" – 1996
- "to consider long-term issues" – 1998
- "intended to modernise the monarchy" – 1998
- "to try to reinvent and modernise the monarchy for the 21st century" – 2000
- "makes the decisions which have shaped the Royal Family" – 2006
- "'palace policy' and 'how they were going to defend themselves"[a] – 2011
- "paramount issues [such] as primogeniture" – 2011.

This is a major conflict and gets right at the very heart of why the WAG was set up. Was it just a group of royals discussing mundane administrative matters such as lining up schedules, or was it a top-level group that dealt with major issues facing the royal family?

If it was the latter then I suggest Miles Hunt-Davis and Robert Fellowes misled the inquest into the deaths of Princess Diana and Dodi Fayed.

2) At one point Mansfield quoted the July 1997 *Mirror* article to Fellowes: "'The Queen, Prince Philip, their four children and senior courtiers meet twice a year to discuss <u>new challenges facing the monarchy</u>.' Well, that is true, isn't it?" Fellowes answered: "Yes."

That is a significant conflict with Fellowes' general evidence that the WAG was about dealing with administrative issues – "it was brought together as a coordinating group".

There is a possibility that Mansfield caught Fellowes off guard. If Fellowes had answered "no", then it could have opened the door to Mansfield asking for an explanation. He may have decided "yes" was a better option.

Whatever Fellowes' reason for confirming the content of the article, his response is a major conflict in his evidence and he should have been challenged on it at the inquest. That didn't happen.

3) Hunt-Davis' responses to questions about possible WAG discussions on Diana.

Burnett asked Hunt-Davis: "Was 'Diana' discussed at all at the [20 July 1997[b]] meeting as an agenda item?" [a]

---

[a] This quote also does mention: "many topics were mundane, like the coordination of schedules". Given that this article appeared after the inquest, it may be that Frank Prochashka, who said this, was influenced by the inquest testimony from Miles Hunt-Davis and Robert Fellowes.

[b] This meeting was actually held on 23 July 1997 – see earlier.

Hunt-Davis replied: "I cannot remember. I think it would have been difficult to have done so with the senior officials there, if it was indeed a family discussion, but to be honest, I do not recall the details."

Burnett then asked: "Was the Way Ahead Group considering ... an issue arising from the divorce of" Charles and Diana?

Hunt-Davis confirms: "It is quite possible that it might have been. In terms of status, I would have thought that would probably be the meat of it, but I do not recall it at all." And then confirms he is talking about Diana's "Her Royal Highness" title.[b]

Now Miles Hunt-Davis knows that Diana's HRH title had been removed at the time of the divorce and her exile from the royal family in August 1996 – and there has never been any suggestion of that decision being reviewed.[c] That was around 11 months before this *Sunday Mirror* article.

Therefore, if Diana was the subject item in a July 1997 WAG meeting, it could not have been about her HRH title. And I suggest that Hunt-Davis has lied under oath when he indicated that was "quite possible".

Later it was put to Hunt-Davis that the "Royal Household"[d] had told the coroner in writing: "There is no truth in the *Sunday Mirror's* report of 20th July 1997 that 'top of the agenda for the next meeting is Diana'".

Hunt-Davis confirmed that, and also the household statement: "There were no discussions in relation to Princess Diana at these [1997 WAG] meetings." [e]

---

[a] Referring to a newspaper article that had said, regarding Diana: "Top of the agenda for the next meeting".

[b] The fact that Hunt-Davis is accepting that this discussion "quite possibly" occurred appears to conflict with his general evidence that the WAG meetings dealt with administrative issues.

[c] That is, while Diana was alive. She was reinstated as a member of the royal family immediately after her death – see Part 4.

[d] Which includes Hunt-Davis. He was still in the job at the time of the inquest – he retired in 2010.

[e] One of the arguments Hunt-Davis put for Diana not being on the agenda in the 1997 WAG meetings was: "I would very much doubt that Princess Diana would have come into the discussion in front of officials such as myself, for what was basically by then a family matter." That appears to conflict with another statement Hunt-Davis made to the inquest: "The Princess was no longer a member of the Royal Family after the divorce in August 1996": 13 Dec 07: 82.6. This was a sentiment Hunt-Davis expressed a couple of times and then at one stage said: "Once the divorce had happened, what Princess Diana did was not relevant to the mainstream of the Royal Family": 13 Dec 07: 86.25. So on the one hand, discussion about Diana "was basically by [1997] a [royal] family matter", but on the other hand: "[Diana] was no longer a member of the Royal Family" in 1997.

Hunt-Davis' confirmation of these statements is a conflict with his earlier suggestion that a discussion re the HRH title was "quite possible".

The general evidence was that the WAG kept their agenda documents. So when Hunt-Davis was asked at the inquest about the July 1997 agenda, it seems strange that he replied, "I cannot remember" – because the household[a] had recently received a list of questions from Baker, which included that issue in it.

Hunt-Davis appeared evasive when the specific topic of a possible 1996 WAG discussion of Diana's removal from the royal family came up.

Mansfield asked: "It was discussed at the Way Ahead Group, was it not, in 1996?" Hunt-Davis: "I do not think it was discussed in that detail, no." Mansfield again: "In some little detail then?"

Then Hunt-Davis: "I doubt it was even in that detail, a little detail. The Way Ahead Group was to do with coordination. It was not to do with personal affairs of members of the Royal Family." He went on to say: "I have no idea" who took "the decision to divest [Diana] of membership of the Royal Family".

So, on the one hand, we have Hunt-Davis suggesting to Burnett that it was "quite possible" that the WAG would have discussed Diana's HRH title in July 1997, 11 months after it was removed. Yet on the other hand, Hunt-Davis indicates to Mansfield that in 1996 – when these events did happen – he doubts Diana's removal from the royal family would have been discussed "even in that detail, a little detail". And he backs this up by saying: "[The WAG] was not to do with personal affairs of members of the Royal Family.... It was not an inner sanctum where the lives and behaviour of members of the Royal Family was discussed."

Then distancing himself and the WAG even further from the subject of Diana's removal, Hunt-Davis says: "I imagine Her Majesty the Queen took the decision, having taken advice, I presume. I have no idea."

I suggest that it is not credible that Miles Hunt-Davis – who at the time of this testimony had served 14 years as private secretary to the Queen's husband – would have "no idea" who would make "the decision to divest [Diana] of membership of the Royal Family".

There are three points here:

a) Hunt-Davis appears to have lied when he suggests to Burnett that the WAG could have been discussing Diana's HRH title in July 1997 [b]

---

[a] At the time of the inquest Hunt-Davis was still in the royal household and when one considers that he had been a prominent household attendee at WAG meetings for many years, it seems likely that he would have had input into the written household responses to the coroner's questions.

[b] Hunt-Davis indicates that the WAG didn't discuss Diana's removal from the royal family in 1996 – when it did happen – yet he said it was "quite possible" the WAG

b) the suggestion of discussing Diana's HRH title is a major conflict with the Hunt-Davis, Fellowes and written household evidence that Diana was not a subject of discussion in 1997 – "there were no discussions in relation to Princess Diana at these [1997 WAG] meetings"

c) Hunt-Davis appears to have lied again when he said, "I have no idea" who would make "the decision to divest [Diana] of membership of the Royal Family".

4) The name of the group.

The group is called the Way Ahead Group. I suggest this, in itself, indicates it is designed to discuss the "way ahead" for the royal family – i.e. discussing major issues of direction and facing up to challenges along that way.

Early in his evidence on this, Hunt-Davis said the purpose of the group was "to discuss literally the way forward, to produce a degree of coordination between their programmes".

Hunt-Davis equates discussing "the way forward" with producing "a degree of coordination between [the royals'] programmes".

When one considers the seniority of the people present – including the Queen and Philip – I suggest that this is not true. In other words, "the way ahead" in the context of the royal family cannot just simply be a matter of achieving "coordination between their programmes".

5) The WAG meetings were started in November 1992.

It may not be a coincidence that 1992 marked a major turning point in the relationship between Diana and the other senior members of the royal family – the Queen, Philip and Charles.[a]

The Andrew Morton book – with which Diana collaborated – was published in June 1992 and Squidgygate was published in August. On December 9 – the month following the first WAG meeting – the apparent royal family response to the Morton book was handed out: the announcement of the official separation of Diana and Charles.[b]

I suggest that following the publication of the Morton book it is possible that the Queen and Philip may have started considering Diana to be a major threat to the stability of the royal family.

The question must certainly be raised: Did the Queen set up the WAG so that major issues – initially, how to deal with Princess Diana – could be discussed in a group setting?

---

discussed Diana's HRH title removal in July 1997 – 11 months after it had taken place.

[a] See earlier Timeline of Events.

[b] The full analysis of the sequence, nature and significance of these events has been covered in Part 2 – the section on Diana and the Royal Family in Chapter 6.

Under analysis, the evidence does point to the Hunt-Davis, Fellowes and household inquest evidence – that the WAG was primarily about dealing with administrative issues – being false.

The media have written many articles over 15 years[a] saying that the WAG is about dealing with major issues facing the royal family – all of these articles would have to be wrong. When the articles are viewed in the light of the other points – and later discussion – it becomes clearer that they are true.

Both Hunt-Davis and Fellowes – the only inquest witnesses to the WAG meetings[b] – have provided conflicting evidence on this and have lied in their inquest testimony.

The WAG meetings commenced at an incredibly critical time in the Diana-Royal Family relationship – in fact, the month before the official separation decision was made public.[c]

Looking at it from a common sense viewpoint, it seems logical that if the WAG meetings were dealing with administrative issues – as Fellowes, Hunt-Davis and the household have said – then they wouldn't necessarily have

------

[a] Only a sampling of the articles has been shown above. A search of Google News archives reveals there are many more.

[b] Other witnesses should have been called, including the Queen, Philip and Charles – the failure to do this is addressed later.

[c] It may be significant that Hunt-Davis came across evasive on the timing: "To be honest, I do not remember when it was formed, but it was formed sometime in the 1990s". By the time Mansfield came to address timing with Fellowes, two months later, the inquest had found out that the WAG was set up in November 1992. Mansfield asked Fellowes: "Now that we have established the date, in November 1992, was it set up in the wake of the speech that the Queen made about – ". Fellowes never gave Mansfield a chance to continue with this – he instead butted in with: "It had no connection with that. I think it was – there was a feeling that there was a lack of coordination in programming...." And Fellowes continued on with the "coordination" mantra – see earlier. But why did Fellowes cut Mansfield off? What was Mansfield about to say? Was it something Fellowes didn't want the jury to hear? The earlier Timeline of Events reveals that on 24 November 1992 the Queen made a speech in which she declared 1992 as her "annus horribilus". It appears that Mansfield was about to refer to that speech. There is little question that Diana-related activities – the Morton book, Squidgygate – had a huge impact on the Queen's year. I suggest it is likely that there was a connection between these events and the birth of the WAG – and it is possible that Fellowes' speed in cutting Mansfield off midstream could be confirmation of that. It's interesting that just two questions later Mansfield commented: "It is just that there had been a series of events – well, you know what they are – that could be perceived as extremely damaging." Fellowes replied: "Yes, the Way Ahead Group was formed in the wake of those or some of those." One could suggest that that could conflict with Fellowes' comment just before that: "[The WAG] was an attempt to render more pointful ... the public appearances of the Royal Family".

required the presence of senior royals, with the Queen in the chair. One would think that administrative issues could be dealt with in meetings between the private secretaries, who would separately consult their respective royal family bosses.

Hunt-Davis was asked a simple question: "Do you remember who actually attended [the WAG meetings]?" He replied: "the Queen and Prince Philip, the Prince of Wales, the Duke of York, the Princess Royal and Prince Edward". When Mansfield pushed for more, Hunt-Davis conceded: "the Queen's private secretary, myself and possibly the Prince of Wales' private secretary".

Mansfield then asked more about this – "Were there any outside advisers present?"; "Was there somebody who liaised with outside advice?"

Mansfield was obviously seeking a full answer, but Hunt-Davis instead repeated his mantra: "I mean [the WAG] was really just to coordinate their programmes".

Two months later Burnett asked Fellowes the same simple question: "Who attended the Way Ahead Group meetings?"

Fellowes replied: "The Queen, the Duke of Edinburgh, their children, the Private Secretaries to the members of the Royal Family concerned, the Lord Chamberlain, who chaired it with the Queen, and the financial department, represented by the Keeper of the Privy Purse".[a]

Given that Hunt-Davis was still working as Philip's private secretary at the time of the inquest – and Fellowes had left nine years earlier[b] – it is surprising that it is Hunt-Davis who gave the most incomplete response.

Why did Hunt-Davis miss out the Lord Chamberlain – the co-chairperson – the Keeper of the Privy Purse[c] and the private secretaries of Anne, Andrew and Edward? [d]

Maybe he was told to.

I suggest that the less people that are present, the more it supports the false account that this was "really just to coordinate their programmes". The presence of the Lord Chamberlain, as co-chair, and the Keeper of the Privy Purse indicate a level of formality and significance that it appears Hunt-Davis

---

[a] I suggest it is also possible that the Queen Mother attended these WAG meetings in 1997.

[b] In 1999.

[c] The Keeper of the Privy Purse meets with the Queen once a week according to Wikipedia.

[d] Anne's private secretaries in 1997 were Peter Gibbs and Rupert McGuigan (there was a changeover during that year); Andrew's was Neil Blair and Edward's was Sean O'Dwyer. Source: Wikipedia, under Royal Households of the United Kingdom.

was not willing to concede.[a] In this light, it is important that Hunt-Davis fails to divulge that anyone chaired these WAG meetings.

It may have been considered by the Queen[bc] that Fellowes – who was cross-examined two months after Hunt-Davis – should admit to a truer make-up of the WAG meetings.

Another important factor omitted by Hunt-Davis was the existence of preparatory WAG meetings. Under questioning Fellowes said the July 1997 preparatory meeting was "chaired by the Lord Chamberlain, Lord Airlie[d], and it would have composed the Private Secretaries concerned and the Keeper of the Privy Purse".

Fellowes downplayed the significance of the preparatory meeting – "It was an agenda meeting really. No more than that."

But the point here is that the fact a preparatory meeting took place increases the significance of the WAG meeting that it is preparing for. In other words, if a meeting requires a "preparatory meeting" before it occurs, that indicates that the meeting itself is likely to be addressing very significant issues – not "it was really just to coordinate their programmes".

The question is: Why did Fellowes and Hunt-Davis lie about the nature of discussion topics at the WAG meetings?

As suggested earlier, this is another case of excessive distancing: If the WAG only discussed administrative issues then it is clearly not possible that an assassination of Diana could be on the agenda.

But, why the excessive distancing?

A related question is: Why is there a cover-up about the WAG discussion topics if there is nothing to cover up?

If the WAG meetings were only discussing major issues facing the royal family – even including the major challenge created by Diana's activities – there would not necessarily be a need for such information to be covered up.[e] I suggest that the discussions only need to be covered up when they involve the contemplation of possible illegal activity.

---

[a] In simple terms, knowing who attended these meetings helps one understand their nature and what issues might be discussed. I suggest this is why Mansfield would have asked Hunt-Davis the question in the first place. For Hunt-Davis to not fully answer the question indicates he is deliberately withholding information.

[b] Fellowes' direct boss.

[c] Bearing in mind what was already in the public domain by the time of the inquest. In 1998 the BBC had stated that "the Queen herself [was] in the chair"

[d] David Ogilvy. He played a significant role in post-crash events – see Part 4.

[e] There is a big difference between a discussion regarding Diana and a discussion regarding the elimination of Diana. The evidence from the Palace is that there was no WAG discussion of Diana in 1997 – see earlier.

So if there had been a WAG discussion – however brief – on 23 July 1997 regarding eliminating Princess Diana, then we could expect to see a cover-up of that.

There is no question that there has been a cover-up regarding the WAG discussion topics. There has to be a reason for that. Seen in the light of the other evidence in this section, this could indicate that the assassination of Diana was contemplated at the July 23 WAG meeting.[ab]

Coroner: Summing Up: 31 Mar 08: 125.18:

"You will remember that some time was spent in evidence with both Hunt-Davis and Lord Fellowes on something called the "Way Ahead Group" and especially its meeting on 20th July 1997.[c] A newspaper report had suggested that Diana was top of the agenda and that a file on the Al Fayeds was produced by the security services. It is true that Hunt-Davis thought it quite likely that there was some discussion at the meeting of the perceived damage to the Royal Family. I have seen both the agenda for that meeting and the minutes. They were produced through Fellowes. I have decided not to disclose their contents because they were irrelevant; that is to say they provided no support for the allegations contained in the newspaper report. Diana was not on the agenda, neither were the Al Fayeds."

Comment: The above paragraph was the coroner's sole mention of the WAG in his 2½ days of Summing Up.

It is notable that Baker fails to point out that the fact the *Mirror* was able to predict that a WAG meeting was coming up, indicates that they were receiving information from a valid and knowledgeable source – as Mansfield suggested to Hunt-Davis: "the newspaper had particularly accurate information, at least about the existence of the group and the date that it was meeting".[d]

---

[a] If MI6 were present at this meeting – and the 31 August 1997 *Mirror* article indicates that is a possibility – an order to carry out an assassination need not necessarily be overt. In fact I suggest it is likely not to be overt as there would then be no specific trail of evidence.

[b] The general evidence – particularly from the media articles – is that the WAG discussed major issues facing the royal family. It is common sense that Diana was a major issue facing the royal family – right from 1992 onwards – and therefore it is logical that she would have been a topic of WAG discussion. The fact that the Palace – through Hunt-Davis and Fellowes – has distanced itself from this indicates there has been a cover-up regarding WAG discussion topics.

[c] This date is wrong – the meeting was on 23 July 1997 (see earlier and later).

[d] Hunt-Davis failed to acknowledge this: "As I have not seen the article or don't remember seeing the article, I have no way of commenting."

What Scott Baker said raises several other serious concerns:[a]

1) Baker stated: "A newspaper report had suggested that Diana was top of the agenda [for the July meeting] and that a file on the Al Fayeds was produced by the security services."

Whilst it is true that the paper suggested "Diana was top of the agenda", Baker appears to have lied when he indicates the same newspaper report said "a file on the Al Fayeds was produced by the security services".

There was a later article on 31 August 1997 – the day of the deaths – where the *Mirror* claimed: "MI6 has prepared a special report on the Egyptian-born Fayeds, which will be presented to the meeting." This refers to a meeting planned for the first week in September 1997.

Baker has stated this as though the paper was claiming the event had occurred – "a file on the Al Fayeds <u>was produced</u>", past tense. In fact the article was referring to an event in the future – "a special report on the Egyptian-born Fayeds, which <u>will be presented</u>".

This is significant because the articles – which both refer to the contents of future WAG meetings – are quite different from each other:

-   the 20 July 1997 *Mirror* article claims: "Top of the agenda at the forthcoming meeting is Diana". This relates to a meeting that took place three days after the article, on 23 July 1997. There is no mention of the Al Fayeds.[b]

-   the 31 August 1997 article, also in the *Mirror*, makes claims about an expected WAG meeting "next week": "MI6 has prepared a special report on the Egyptian-born Fayeds, which will be presented to the meeting. The delicate subject of Harrods and its Royal warrants is also expected to be discussed". Regarding this meeting – which was scheduled to take place after the crash – there is no mention of Diana being on the agenda, only the "Fayeds" and the Harrods royal warrants. The article – which is reproduced below – makes references to Diana, but not in connection with the WAG meeting.

So we have a late July meeting where it is suggested Diana will be top of the agenda and we have an early September meeting where Diana is no longer mentioned – instead the subject is now the Fayeds and Harrods.

The key point here is that between the two WAG meetings Diana was assassinated.

Therefore it is significant that the August 31 article[c] makes no mention of Diana being on the agenda – it indicates that the source where Andrew

---

[a] Not all of the concerns are addressed here – some are in the later section on MI6 Report on the Fayeds.

[b] The St Tropez family holiday concluded the same day the article was published. The Diana-Dodi relationship didn't commence until straight after that holiday – see Part 2.

[c] Although written before the crash.

Golden from the *Mirror* was getting his information was already aware that Diana may no longer be around for the next WAG meeting in September.

There is a possibility that the Queen underestimated the depth of feeling for Diana and the effect that her death would have on the British nation.[a] It may well be that the Al Fayed-Harrods agenda for the September meeting was shelved – in fact the WAG meeting may have been shelved altogether, or instead changed to discuss the aftermath of the assassinations of Diana and Dodi.

The issue here is that Scott Baker appears to be aware of the significance of the two different articles – July 20 and August 31 – and has deliberately clouded it for the jury by merging them together in his Summing Up.

---

[a] This has been addressed in Part 4.

QUEEN 'TO STRIP HARRODS OF ITS ROYAL CREST'

By Andrew Golden

THE Royal Family may withdraw their seal of approval from Harrods as a result of Diana's affair with owner's son Dodi Fayed.

The top people's store — with its long and proud tradition of royal patronage — may be about to lose its Prince of Wales royal crest.

Senior Palace courtiers are ready to advise the Queen that she should refuse to renew the prestigious royal warrants for the Knightsbridge store when they come up for review in February.

It would be a huge blow to the ego of store owner Mohamed Al Fayed — and would infuriate Diana, who was yesterday understood to be still with Dodi aboard his yacht, near the Italian island of Sardinia. But the Royal Family are furious about the frolics of Di, 36, and Dodi, 41, which they believe have further undermined the monarchy.

Prince Philip, in particular, has made no secret as to how he feels about his daughter-in-law's latest man, referring to Dodi as an 'oily bed-hopper'.

At Balmoral next week, the Queen will preside over a meeting of The Way Ahead Group where the Windsors sit down with their senior advisers to discuss policy matters.

MI6 has prepared a special report on the Egyptian-born Fayeds which will be presented to the meeting.

The delicate subject of Harrods and its royal warrants is also expected to be discussed. And the Fayeds can expect little sympathy from Philip.

A friend of the Royals said yesterday: "Prince Philip has let rip several times recently about the Fayeds — at a dinner party, during a country shoot and while on a visit to close friends in Germany.

"He's been banging on about his contempt for Dodi and how he is undesirable as a future stepfather to William and Harry.

"Diana has been told in no uncertain terms about the consequences should she continue the relationship with the Fayed boy.

"Options must include possible exile, although that would be very difficult as when all is said and done, she is the mother of the future King of England."

She has also been warned about social ostracism. But Diana's attitude is if that means not having to deal with the royals and their kind, then she would be delighted."

There are some who believe Diana may be posturing and has decided to look towards those who can afford to keep her in the lifestyle to which she became accustomed.

The Fayed family have all the trappings of vast wealth... wherever it originated from.

And Dodi has told Diana what he has told many of his other beautiful girlfriends in the past: "It's my father's store and you can have what you want. Charge it to my account and I'll just sign the bill."

But now the Royal Family may decide it's time to settle up.

Figure 10

Article that appeared in the early edition of the *Sunday Mirror* on 31 August 1997 – the morning of the crash. It revealed that at the WAG meeting at Balmoral "next week" an MI6 report on the Fayeds would be tabled and Harrods royal warrants would be discussed. There was no mention of Diana being on the agenda. In his Summing Up, Scott Baker merged the information from this article into an earlier 20 July 1997 article that said Diana would be top of the July WAG meeting's agenda.

2) Baker stated: "It is true that Hunt-Davis thought it quite likely that there was some discussion at the [23 July 1997 WAG] meeting of the perceived damage to the Royal Family."

This is false.

Hunt-Davis made no mention of "discussion at the [July 23] meeting of the perceived damage to the Royal Family".

Instead, as discussed earlier, Hunt-Davis said it was "quite possible that [the WAG] might have been [discussing the divorce] in terms of [Diana's HRH] status".[a]

Baker has either made this up, or plucked it out of someone else's evidence – not Hunt Davis': see footnote.[bc]

3) Baker says: "You will remember that some time was spent in evidence ... [regarding the WAG] meeting on 20th July 1997.... I have seen both the agenda for that meeting and the minutes. They were produced through Fellowes. I have decided not to disclose their contents...."

Earlier in the inquest, Burnett had indicated the meeting took place on 20 July 1997 – he asked Hunt-Davis: "Are you able to confirm that, in 1997, [the WAG] met on ... 20th July?"[d] Burnett then went on to refer to the meeting as occurring on July 20.

Then later Mansfield mentioned the 20 July 1997 newspaper report, and continues: "Assuming that [July 20] was the [meeting] date...." – so that indicates there was an awareness amongst the lawyers that the 20 July 1997 date for the meeting could have been incorrect.

Then two months later, when Fellowes is on the stand, he says: "We met in late July [1997]". And Burnett then refers to "a letter that was written by the Treasury Solicitor when inquiries were made of the Palace". He indicates that the letter "suggested that the [WAG] met ... on a date which was clarified to be 23rd July." Fellowes confirmed that.

Next Burnett said to Fellowes: "Indeed, the Coroner received the agenda and minutes for the meeting on 23rd July and considered them."

---

[a] It has been shown earlier that Hunt-Davis appears to have lied when he said this.
[b] In a strange twist, it is possible Baker plucked this out of Sarah, Duchess of York's statement. Sarah was the next witness heard after Hunt-Davis vacated the stand, on 13 December 2007 – there was a lunch break in between. Sarah quoted from Michael Cole's statement, which read: "Diana and Sarah spoke about their fears of them both being killed because of the perceived damage that they had caused to the institution of royalty and to the House of Windsor in particular." Scott Baker said: "It is true that Hunt-Davis thought it quite likely that there was some discussion at the meeting of the perceived damage to the Royal Family." Source: 13 Dec 07: 105.13.
[c] Baker makes no comment on what would have caused "the perceived damage".
[d] Hunt-Davis replied: "I cannot recall the dates specifically".

From that point on, Burnett and Mansfield both correctly refer to the meeting as occurring on 23 July 1997.

Then on the last day of inquest evidence – 18 March 2008 – the Treasury Solicitor letter was read out: "During a search made for documents ... a memorandum dated 18th July 1997, and relating to the Way Ahead Group meeting on 23rd July 1997, was located. I attach a copy." [a]

That confirmed to anyone at the inquest that there was no longer any question over the date – it was definitely 23 July 1997. The coroner, Scott Baker, apparently had even more proof of that, because since before 12 February 2008[b] he had been given a copy of "both the agenda ... and the minutes".

Yet in his Summing Up Baker wrongly quoted the date of the WAG meeting as "20th July 1997", instead of 23 July 1997.

The question is: Baker appears to have had a copy of "both the agenda ... and the minutes" well before he prepared his Summing Up[c], so why does he get the date wrong? [d]

And the second question is: Why is the date Baker gave identical to the erroneous date put forward by Burnett earlier in the inquest – 20 July 1997?

The point is that one would presume Baker compiled his Summing Up with care.[ef] I suggest we could have expected him to check the minutes of the

---

[a] It could be significant that this document is used to confirm the meeting date, rather than the meeting's minutes or agenda documents. This could be further evidence that the content of the minutes and agenda documents contained information Baker did not want the jury to see or hear.

[b] The date that Burnett stated to Fellowes: "Indeed, the Coroner received the agenda and minutes for the meeting on 23rd July and considered them." Also Burnett, Baker and Fellowes appear to be looking at copies of the minutes during Fellowes' cross-examination – this is addressed below.

[c] It is my understanding that the inquest coroner is expected to prepare thoroughly for the Summing Up. The last day of evidence was Tuesday 18 March 2008 and there was a day with the lawyers on the 20th. Easter weekend then followed. The jury didn't reappear to hear the Summing Up until Monday 1st April. So Baker had somewhere between 8 and 13 days to put together the Summing Up.

[d] Burnett had a copy of the minutes in front of him when he referred to "the minutes of 23rd July".

[e] Given that the jury are expected to rely on its accuracy to help them arrive at a verdict.

[f] In a surprising and troubling twist, Baker repeated this same mistake – dating the meeting July 20 – in his "Reasons" for not calling for evidence from Philip or the Queen. See later section on Failure to Cross-Examine Suspects. This raises serious concerns on just how deeply Baker carried out his research before drawing significant conclusions.

meeting, before writing the date into his very short section[a] of the Summing Up that relates to the WAG.

Instead what seems to have happened is that Baker appears to have got the meeting date from the early transcripts involving Hunt-Davis – it is evident that Baker did not get this date from either the Treasury Solicitor's letter or the meeting's minutes.

This raises a couple of questions:

a) When Baker put together the WAG section of the Summing Up, did he even look at the transcript of Fellowes' evidence on the subject?

This is significant, in that only two witnesses gave evidence on this – Hunt-Davis and Fellowes. Baker only makes reference to what Hunt-Davis said[b] and makes no mention of Fellowes' evidence.

I suggest Baker did not look at Fellowes' testimony – because if he had, he should have come up with the correct date (see above).

b) When Baker put together the WAG section of the Summing Up, did he even look at the minutes of the 23 July 1997 meeting?

In his Summing Up, Baker says the agenda and minutes "were produced through Fellowes".

During the 12 February 2008 Fellowes cross-examination, Baker said: "I was not provided with page 5 [of the WAG meeting minutes] in the accompanying letter from the Treasury Solicitor".

That is an apparent conflict.

On February 12 the minutes came from the Treasury Solicitor, but a month later Baker says they "were produced through Fellowes".

The first we hear about Baker having these documents is from the inquest lawyer, Ian Burnett – "Indeed, the Coroner received the agenda and minutes for the meeting on 23rd July and considered them." Burnett is talking to Fellowes, but makes no acknowledgement that Fellowes played a role in the process. It comes across that Burnett is informing Fellowes – and the jury – that Baker has seen the agenda and minutes.

I suggest that in 2008 Robert Fellowes is not the first person one would go to for a copy of the agenda and minutes of a 1997 royal meeting, because by that time he had left the Palace employ nine years earlier.[c]

---

[a] 151 words out of over 80,000 in the Summing Up. By Baker's own admission in the Summing Up, during the inquest "some time was spent in evidence" on the WAG.

[b] As it turns out Baker lied about what Hunt-Davis said – see earlier.

[c] Fellowes was the Queen's private secretary from 1990 to 1999. After leaving the Palace in 1999, Fellowes became Vice-Chairman of Barclay's Private Banking.: Wikipedia, Robert Fellowes.

It would appear that the logical place to arrange to get these documents could be Buckingham Palace.

And that may be what happened and it could be that Baker was directed to the Treasury Solicitor.

I suggest that the involvement of the Treasury Solicitor's Department – "the legal advisors to the Crown and the State"[320] – in WAG documentation, indicates that these meetings were about more than coordinating the royal schedules (see earlier).

Are copies of the WAG documentation not kept at Buckingham Palace or in the royal archives?

Why didn't Baker simply ask Hunt-Davis – who was still working at the Palace until 2010 – for a copy of the agenda and minutes? [a]

4) Baker said: "I have seen both the agenda for that meeting and the minutes.... I have decided not to disclose their contents because they were irrelevant; that is to say they provided no support for the allegations contained in the newspaper report. Diana was not on the agenda, neither were the Al Fayeds.[b]"

Baker's basis for not passing on the agenda and minutes to the jury is "because they were irrelevant".[c] Why? Because "Diana was not on the agenda".

The point here is that a specific allegation had been made in an article published three days before the WAG meeting: "Top of the agenda ... is Diana."

That is what makes the agenda and minutes of that WAG meeting relevant – whether or not Diana is on the agenda. In other words, Baker's perception that "Diana was not on the agenda" does not make the agenda and minutes documents irrelevant.[d]

The moment the *Sunday Mirror* made the allegation on 20 July 1997, the agenda and minutes of that July 23 meeting became very relevant in the event of Diana's suspicious death.

---

[a] Another question could be: Why didn't Hunt-Davis offer to supply the inquest with a copy of the agenda or minutes after he was asked: "Was 'Diana' discussed at all at the [July] meeting as an agenda item?" and he replied: "I cannot remember."?

[b] It has been shown that the Al Fayeds were not mentioned in the July 20 article – they were the subject of a later article on August 31.

[c] One could argue that a more logical reason could have been for Baker to claim they were confidential, but that may have given rise to the suggestion that the information was more than about coordinating schedules.

[d] This is similar to a hypothetical situation where a witness may say they did not see an event. The fact they say they did not see the event does not make their evidence irrelevant. There may be a significant reason why the witness is saying they didn't see it.

The jury were expected to deliberate on the cause of the deaths of Diana and Dodi, yet withheld from them were the minutes and agenda of a meeting:

- that took place just six weeks before the deaths
- that was attended by several named suspects – the Queen (who was chairman), Philip, Charles and Fellowes
- before which it had been publicly alleged that one of the victims – Diana – was to be "top of the agenda".

I suggest that – in light of the Fellowes and Hunt-Davis evidence – the general nature of topics discussed at the WAG meeting was relevant to the jury. A question that the July 23 minutes may have answered would be: Was the meeting about coordinating royal schedules, or was there discussion of more serious challenges facing the royal family?

During the Mansfield cross-examination of Fellowes about the 23 July 1997 WAG meeting, Baker stated: "I was [possibly] not provided with page 5 [of the minutes] in the accompanying letter from the Treasury Solicitor".

Burnett then says to Baker: "given that I have [a copy of the minutes] with page 5. it must have arrived with page 5 but perhaps it has not been copied onto [your copy]".

And Baker told Mansfield: "I am sorry, Mr Mansfield, I gave you misleading information" about the minutes.

Taken together this evidence indicates that the minutes arrived by letter from the Treasury Solicitor and upon arrival at least one copy was taken. It is possible Burnett received the original and a copy was made for Baker – but whatever happened, it is clear that Mansfield was not provided with a copy, even though he was asking questions that related to the content of the minutes.

Earlier Burnett had given the impression that only the coroner had the minutes – "Indeed, the Coroner received the agenda and minutes for the meeting on 23rd July and considered them."

It is only because of the issue regarding the missing page 5 in Baker's copy that Burnett is forced into admitting he has a copy, or even possibly the original.[a]

---

[a] The evidence highlights the fact that Burnett received either the original or the main copy. Baker may have been embarrassed when this came to light and it is possible that led him to suggest something that is completely illogical: "I was not provided with page 5 [of the minutes] in the accompanying letter from the Treasury Solicitor or it may be that this is an error in copying at our end." I suggest that Baker's first option for not having page 5 is illogical because Burnett has just shown him page 5, which Burnett could only have obtained when it came with the Treasury Solicitor's letter. Burnett points out straight after this that it is a problem in the copying.

This appears to indicate that there was a lack of openness regarding documentation. Both Burnett and Mansfield questioned this witness – Robert Fellowes – about the 23 July 1997 WAG meeting, but only Burnett was provided with the minutes from the meeting.[a]

It is significant that the jury were shown absolutely no WAG documentation – nothing at all, and neither was Michael Mansfield. At one point, during Hunt-Davis' cross-examination, Mansfield said: "I do not have, as you don't appear to have either, access to any of the documentation relating to this group".

The question is: Why?

In summary, there are major problems in Baker's descriptions of the 23 July 1997 WAG meeting: he has the wrong date in his Summing Up; he says the minutes came through Fellowes even though Fellowes hadn't worked at the Palace for nine years; Baker's "irrelevant" comment lacks substance.

The key concern is that Lord Justice Scott Baker has used his claimed knowledge of the contents of the agenda and minutes of the July WAG meeting – "Diana was not on the agenda" – to neutralise the effect of the *Mirror* article – "Top of the agenda ... is Diana". But in doing this he has not allowed the Al Fayed lawyer, Michael Mansfield, or even more importantly, his own inquest jury, to view the minutes of the meeting.

This failure to show the minutes leads to the inescapable possibility that there could be truth in the article's account.

There are several ways this could happen: a) the WAG minutes could have been doctored before they are sent to the inquest;[b] b) Diana is included in the minutes and Baker has lied; c) Diana is included in the meeting's oral discussions but is deliberately omitted from the original agenda and minutes at the time they were written up.

I suggest that if the contemplation of Diana's assassination was discussed at the July WAG meeting, then there is a realistic possibility that a decision would be made to omit that subject from the record – given that assassination is an illegal act.

At the inquest Robert Fellowes said that the WAG "met twice a year, usually in the first two months, and then in the late summer".

Burnett stated that the Treasury Solicitor wrote to the inquest saying: "the [WAG] met twice in 1997, once on 20th January and then, again, on ... 23rd July".

Now July 23 is not "late summer" – it is mid-summer.

---

[a] It is possible that the contents of the minutes were suppressed because they would have revealed that the topics discussed at WAG meetings were more than dealing with the coordination of royal schedules.

[b] We are not told if the original minutes are loose-leaf – if they were, then they would probably be easier to doctor.

Fellowes' account appears to be supported by *The Spectator* article published on 17 September 1996[a]: "The Queen and her children met in council yesterday", referring to a WAG meeting.

The 1997 timing then does not fit. If it is usual practice for the second meeting to be "in the late summer", why was the second 1997 meeting on July 23?

This evidence raises the possibility that the WAG's second 1997 meeting was brought forward. In other words, it may have been originally scheduled for September 1997, but for some reason a decision was made to hold it two months early – in July.[bc]

The question is: What would trigger a decision of this nature – changing the scheduling of a WAG meeting?

The balance of the evidence has already indicated that the main purpose of the WAG was to discuss issues of importance facing the royal family.

Was there then an issue that had arisen at this time that was of urgent significance to the royal family?

Robert Fellowes gave testimony about a preparatory meeting that was held on 8 July 1997 "it was an agenda meeting really – no more than that" and was "chaired by the Lord Chamberlain, Lord Airlie ... [with] the Private Secretaries concerned and the Keeper of the Privy Purse".[d]

The earlier Timeline of Events reveals that significant events – from a royal family perspective – were happening around this time.

On 11 June 1997[e] Princess Diana wrote a letter to Mohamed Al Fayed confirming that she was intending to join – accompanied by the Queen's grandsons, Princes William and Harry – Mohamed in St Tropez in mid-July.

The preparatory meeting on July 8 was held just three days before Diana and the boys arrived in St Tropez on the holiday – and the day before the

---

[a] The year preceding the crash.

[b] In light of Fellowes' "late summer" comment, Baker should have sought the minutes from the 20 January 1997 meeting – they could have shown the expected date for the next meeting. I suggest that it would have been in September.

[c] Another factor that may point to this being an extraordinary meeting is that it was held on a Wednesday (23 July 1997). The only other known WAG meeting dates were both on Mondays – 16 September 1996 and 20 January 1997.

[d] Fellowes confirmed that there could be "a record of that particular agenda meeting" and Mansfield consequently requested Baker "if we might be provided" with that record. There is no evidence of Baker seeking the record of the 8 July 1997 meeting.

[e] Less than a month before the July 8 WAG preparatory meeting.

head of royalty protection, David Davies, apparently called Fellowes warning him of police concerns regarding the St Tropez holiday.[a]

The full WAG meeting was held on July 23, precisely three days after Diana and the boys returned from the St Tropez holiday, on July 20.

So July 8 is the preparatory meeting; July 11, Diana, William and Harry join Mohamed in St Tropez; July 20, Diana, William and Harry return to the UK; July 23, the special WAG meeting is held.

The preparatory meeting is three days before the holiday starts and the full WAG meeting is three days after the holiday concludes.

I suggest that this is not a coincidence.

I further suggest that from the Queen's viewpoint, taking Prince William and Prince Harry on a 10 day holiday with Mohamed Al Fayed was a major event.

This is supported by the reactions of other people to the news of this holiday:

- David Davies, representing the police view: "the matter gave us cause for concern"[b]

- Davies: "the holiday shouldn't go ahead"

- Davies: "I was concerned as to the consequence ... for ... the reputation of the Royal Family" [321]

- Davies: "the future King of England and his brother and the mother were going on holiday with a gentleman who ... I had some concerns about"[322c]

- Lucia Flecha de Lima: "Mr Al Fayed's bad reputation as a business man and the problem over his passport being refused" – statement

- Lucia: "I did not think it was a proper thing to do.... [Mohamed] is a bit of a controversial person" – inquest

- Rosa Monckton: "going on holiday with Mr Al Fayed ... was an inappropriate thing for [Diana] to do".[d]

---

[a] Davies described Fellowes' initial response, after he told him about the police concerns: "there was a silence as I recall". See earlier.

[b] Police commissioner, Paul Condon, and David Veness, Assistant Commissioner Specialist Operations, both disagreed with Davies' account, but I suggest Davies had no reason to lie, whereas Condon and Veness did. This has been addressed in an earlier footnote and other lies told by Condon at the inquest are covered in Part 2 (See Surveillance) and Part 6.

[c] Davies' concerns were qualified. He says: "I had some concerns ... because of [an] allegation" against Mohamed Al Fayed, who was the subject of a police investigation. Davies continued: "I don't think [the allegation] has been substantiated in any way.": 31 Jan 08: 115.18.

[d] Harold Brookes-Baker, editor of *Burke's Peerage*, was quoted in the *Sunday Mirror* at the time: "This is totally irresponsible of the Princess – particularly considering the problems people have faced with the Al Fayed connection. These problems are likely

Royal Motives[a]

What follows includes some speculation, but is also based on the known evidence.

When the preparatory meeting took place on 8 July 1997 it would have been obvious that the St Tropez holiday was going to occur. When the full WAG meeting took place 15 days later, on July 23, the holiday had occurred and Willam and Harry had been back at Balmoral for about three days.[b] By that stage the royals would have been in a position to fully consider what had occurred, review the media coverage of the holiday and plan their response.

There is a possibility that by July 23 the royals could have had information about a very early but developing relationship between Diana and Dodi. Debbie Gribble, who was stewardess on the *Jonikal* during that July holiday, has said "they seemed to fit as a couple".[323c] Certainly Diana was under intelligence surveillance[d] and both Paul Burrell and Michael Cole gave evidence at the inquest of Diana and Dodi seeing each other regularly throughout the first week after the St Tropez holiday.

The senior royals may have asked relevant questions of William and Harry after their return and I suggest they would have been receiving regular intelligence updates on Diana's activities. It is likely that the Queen and Philip would have been aware of an early but emerging Diana-Dodi relationship by the time of the WAG meeting on 23 July 1997.

Evidence of initial planning for future joint ventures between Diana, Dodi and Mohamed was heard at the inquest:

-   Diana, Dodi and Mohamed planned to set up a worldwide hospice network called "Diana Hospices" [e]

---

to go on for a lot longer – and so it is important that she and the family she married into should be completely removed from controversy. The controversy this is creating is unnecessary for a family that has already been through so much.": "This Is Diana Being Totally Irresponsible", *Sunday Mirror*, 13 July 1997.

[a] Evidence and comment in this section should be viewed in the light of Possible Motives (Section 1) in Part 2.

[b] Trevor Rees-Jones & Moira Johnston, *The Bodyguard's Story*, 2000, pages 36-37: "The Princess and Princes ... [would] have to separate as soon as they returned to London [on July 20] with the Princes going to Balmoral to spend August with their father."

[c] The fuller quote is included in Part 2 in the section on Eye-Witnesses to the Diana-Dodi Relationship.

[d] See Surveillance chapter of Part 2.

[e] This evidence came from Richard Kay and Rita Rogers. The detail is in the Future Activities section of Chapter 3 in Part 2.

-    Richard Kay, journalist and friend of Diana, confirmed that Diana had told him, Mohamed Al Fayed "had agreed to finance a charity for the victims of [land] mines".[a]

Given that Diana had spent ten days during the July holiday with Mohamed[b], I suggest it is quite possible that the seeds for these ideas – both the hospices network and the landmine charity – could have been sewn during that period.

Intelligence agencies monitoring Diana's calls also could have picked up on this.

So the *Mirror* article of 20 July 1997 may have been correct – that Diana was "top of the agenda" for the specially brought forward July 23 WAG meeting. The discussion could have focused on an appropriate response or punishment for Diana taking William and Harry on a holiday with Mohamed Al Fayed. These events could also have been looked at in the light of an awareness of a developing relationship between Princess Diana and Dodi Fayed and possible joint ventures involving his father, Mohamed.

In the meantime, I suggest that MI6 had been commissioned to find out as much as possible about Diana's intentions and movements – in response to the Mohamed holiday and Diana's anti-landmine activities, including the June 12 speech and the forthcoming Bosnia trip that commenced on August 8. In that direction, Rosa Monckton, around June 30 – acting on MI6 instructions – organised a boat trip with Diana, which was scheduled to take place between August 15 and 20.[c]

In short, Diana was continuing to cause headaches for the Establishment and given that her activities naturally at times involved her sons, Princes William and Harry – who were key members of the royal family – the Queen was going to be taking an intense interest.

There are reasons why the senior royals could react strongly against contact between William and Harry and Mohamed and Dodi Al Fayed.

In Part 2 it was shown that Philip is famous for making racist remarks.[d]

Added to this is the 31 August 1997 *Mirror* article – reproduced earlier – which stated: "The Royal Family are furious about the frolics of Di, 36, and Dodi, 41, which they believe have further undermined the Monarchy. Prince Philip, in particular, has ... made no secret as to how he feels about his daughter-in-law's latest man, referring to Dodi as an 'oily bedhopper'.... A friend of the Royals said yesterday 'Prince Philip has let rip several times

---

[a] Kay had originally written this in an article in the *Daily Mail* on 1 September 1997. See Future Activities section of Chapter 3 in Part 2.

[b] Six of those days with Dodi present – see Part 2 for timings.

[c] See earlier in the Rosa Monckton chapter.

[d] In the section on Philip's View of Dodi, there is a list of remarks Philip has made.

recently about the Fayeds.... He has been banging on about his contempt for Dodi and how he is undesirable as a future stepfather to William and Harry."[a]

This racist attitude of Philip's should be viewed in the light of other evidence in Part 2 – particularly from Diana's friend, Roberto Devorik – showing that Diana feared Philip. Devorik quoted Diana: "[Philip] really hates me and would like to see me disappear"; "Prince Philip wants to see me dead".[b]

Diana also told Devorik that she feared her brother-in-law, the Queen's private secretary, Robert Fellowes: "She told me three names that she feared – Nicholas Soames, Robert Fellowes ... and Prince Philip." [324]

These comments were all made well before the July 1997 St Tropez holiday.[c]

I suggest that when the factors are put together – the evidence that Diana feared Philip and Fellowes and felt that Philip wanted her dead; Philip was a racist and had "contempt for Dodi"; "the Royal Family ... believe [Diana's activities] have further undermined the Monarchy" – there is a potent mix.

The *Mirror* article also indicated the Al Fayeds were on the agenda for the September 1997 WAG meeting – see earlier.[d]

---

[a] Three weeks earlier than this *Mirror* article, the *Daily Mail* had asked this question: "Could an heir to the throne really have a stepfather who doesn't qualify to be British?": Public Unease at a Royal Romance, *Daily Mail*, 8 August 1997.

[b] This is covered in the Prince Philip section of the Fears and Threats chapter of Part 2.

[c] Diana also told her lawyer, Victor Mishcon, in 1995 that "efforts would be made if not to get rid of her ... then at least to see that she was so injured or damaged as to be declared 'unbalanced'". This note, written up by Mishcon, was shown in Part 2 and will be readdressed in Part 6.

[d] There is a possibility that – on top of the concerns regarding contact with Diana, William and Harry – the senior royals were not comfortable with Mohamed Al Fayed's control of Harrods. That could be suggested in the light of Philip's racism. Mohamed, who is Egyptian-born, has repeatedly been refused British citizenship starting in the early 1990s – this is despite the fact that he has four British children and is a major contributor of British taxes. There does not appear to be any logical reason for withholding citizenship.

Mohamed Al Fayed was a business enemy of Tiny Rowland, the head of Lonrho, throughout the mid to late 1980s and early 1990s. Their falling out appears to have occurred as a result of Mohamed's takeover of Harrods. Angus Ogilvy, husband of Princess Alexandra of Kent, first cousin of the Queen – and brother of the Lord Chamberlain at the time of Diana's death – was heavily involved with Rowland in Lonrho in the 1960s and early 1970s. On the surface this timing does not appear to suggest any connection between the Rowland-Al Fayed problems which started in 1984 and Ogilvy's interest in Lonrho, which was finished when Ogilvy resigned

In summary, I suggest that at the time of the 8 July 1997 preparatory meeting, the following was known to the British Establishment and particularly the most senior royals, the Queen and Philip:
- Diana had spoken out in London against landmines
- Diana was planning further anti-landmine overseas trips
- Diana was taking William and Harry to stay for 10 days with Mohamed Al Fayed.

By the time of the full WAG meeting, 15 days later, on 23 July 1997, additional information was now to hand:
- Diana had started spending time with Dodi
- there were plans for Mohamed and Diana to set up an international network of hospices called "Diana hospices"
- there were plans for Mohamed to finance a charity for the victims of landmines.

---

from the company in 1973. Sources: Sir Angus Ogilvy – Obituary, *The Telegraph*, 27 December 2004; Peter Rodgers and John Moore, Rowland-Fayed: Handshake in Harrods Food Hall Ends Eight-Year Feud, *The Independent*, 23 October 1993; Yasmine Shihata, Mohamed Al Fayed, *Enigma* Magazine, August 2000.

Table of Major Events: 1992 to 1997			
Activity By Diana		**Establishment or Royal Response**	
Date	**Event**	**Date**	**Response**
June 1992	Morton Book	June to December 1992	Ostracised by Royal Family; Travel and Other Restrictions Enforced; Formal Separation[a]
August 1992	Squidgygate		
November 1995	Panorama Interview	December 1995 to August 1996	Removal from Royal Family; Loss of "HRH" Title; Formal Divorce[b]
January to August 1997	Anti-Landmines Campaign	31 August 1997	Crash in Alma Tunnel, Paris
July to August 1997	Mohamed Holiday St Tropez[cd]		
	Plans for Diana-Mohamed Joint Ventures		
	Relationship with Dodi		

The above table reveals that after August 1996 – when the Queen successfully brought about the Diana-Charles divorce, removed Diana's HRH status, and effectively ousted Diana from the royal family – the Establishment had run out of legal options in dealing with the behaviour of Diana.[e]

---

[a] Separation requested by Charles on November 25 and announced in Parliament on December 9.

[b] Divorce requested by the Queen on 18 December and Charles on 19 December 1995.

[c] Diana brought sons, William and Harry, with her.

[d] According to James Whitaker, during Christmas 1996 "Diana took the boys for a meal at Harrods in preference to attending a private Buckingham Palace lunch".: James Whitaker, I've Done Nothing Sarong, *The Mirror*, 14 July 1997.

[e] This has been addressed in detail in Part 2 – see Diana and the Royal Family: 1992 to 1997 section in Chapter 6.

I suggest that Diana's activities – particularly her dealings with Mohamed and taking William and Harry to St Tropez, her relationship with Dodi – could have been deemed a threat to the stability of the royal family.[a]

The knowledge of the trip to St Tropez could have triggered the bringing forward of the WAG meeting from September to July. By the time the July 23 meeting was held, a lot more information – through surveillance – would have become known (see above). The situation may have been viewed as escalating out of control.

Concurrently, I suggest, the UK, French and US governments – particularly the US, who have never signed the anti-landmine treaty[b] – would have been increasingly concerned about the growing intensity of Diana's anti-landmine activities.[c]

I suggest that, at the very least, there would have been inter-governmental discussions about this issue – possibly from January 1997 onwards, after Diana's well-publicised trip to the minefields of Angola.[defg]

---

[a] There is a possibility that a foundation was being set, where at some future point Princess Diana – who had amazing levels of popular support – could have attempted to set up an alternative court, with the support of Mohamed Al Fayed. This is speculation as it is not supported by any concrete evidence, nevertheless it is a possibility. Part 2 showed that Diana's plans involved setting up a home with Dodi in the US and a second home in France. That evidence suggests that an alternative royal court – if it was being considered – would have been based off-shore. Certainly the assassination of Diana completely removed the possibility.

[b] Agreed in Oslo on 17 September 1997 – just 17 days after the crash. It was signed three months later in Ottawa, Canada.

[c] One has to bear in mind that Diana was a humanitarian and it is unlikely she would have stopped at landmines – she may well have progressed to cluster bombs and other weapons. This means that other Western governments – not just the US – would have ultimately been threatened by Diana's humanitarian activities.

[d] Mentioned in the excerpts of Diana's June 1997 London speech, shown earlier.

[e] In February 1997 Diana received a death threat over her landmines campaign from a Tory minister, Nicholas Soames – see earlier and Part 2.

[f] Diana's speech after arriving in Angola on 12 January 1997: "It is an enormous privilege for me to be invited here to Angola, in order to assist the Red Cross in its campaign to ban once and for all anti-personnel landmines. There couldn't be a more appropriate place to begin this campaign than Angola, because this nation has the highest number of amputees per population than anywhere in the world. By visiting Angola, we shall gain an understanding of the plight of the victims of landmines and how survivors are helped to recover from their injuries. We'll also be able to observe the wider implications of these devastating weapons on the life of this country as a whole. It is my sincere hope that by working together in the next few days we shall focus world attention on this vital but, until now, largely neglected issue."

[g] *The Mirror* editor, Piers Morgan, wrote in his diary: "Tuesday, 14 January [1997]: Diana has gone to Angola to continue her campaign against landmines, and the first pictures in today were amazing shots of her with ... local guys with various legs and

I further suggest that Diana's anti-landmine activities would have been a subject of discussion during the weekly meetings held between the British prime minister, Tony Blair, and the Queen.[a] It is likely that concerns from the US, France and maybe other countries would have been passed onto the Queen.

It is possible that there was an intelligence presence – MI6, MI5 or both – at the July WAG meeting.[b]

It is possible that plans were commenced to carry out the complete elimination of Diana, either at the 23 July 1997 meeting or in its direct aftermath.

Just 39 days after that WAG meeting, Princess Diana lay dead in a Paris hospital.

Tony Blair, British Prime Minister: 2010 Book: **Jury Didn't Hear**:
"[Diana] was ... strong-willed ... and was always going to go her own way....
"For sure, just as we[c] were changing the image of Britain, [Diana] was radicalising that of the monarchy; or perhaps, more accurately, her contrast with them[d] illuminated how little they had changed. For someone as acutely perceptive and long-termist about the monarchy and its future as the Queen,

---

arms missing, lost to mines. They were very powerful images and there is no doubt Diana is making a difference on this one. Nobody can fail to support her view that these mines have got to be banned.

"Wednesday, 15 January: Just when I thought I had seen it all, yesterday Diana walked through the live landmines herself, wearing a protective helmet. You've got to hand it to her, this takes balls, whichever way you look at it. The whole world is waking up to this issue entirely because of one headstrong young princess making it her business to highlight it.": Piers Morgan, *The Insider: The Private Diaries of a Scandalous Decade*, p143.

[a] The Official British Monarchy website states: "The Queen has a weekly meeting alone with the Prime Minister, when they are both in London (in addition to other meetings throughout the year). This usually takes place on Wednesdays at 6.30 pm. No written record is made of such meetings; neither The Queen nor the Prime Minister talk about what is discussed between them, as communications between The Queen and the Prime Minister always remains confidential." And: "The Queen gives a weekly audience to the Prime Minister at which she has a right and a duty to express her views on Government matters. If either The Queen or the Prime Minister are not available to meet, then they will speak by telephone." Official British Monarchy website: www.royal.gov.uk/MonarchUK The Queen's Working Day: Evening; Queen and Prime Minister.

[b] Earlier evidence indicated that there was an expectation of a September WAG meeting where an MI6 report would be tabled.

[c] Meaning, New Labour.

[d] The royal family.

it must have been deeply troubling. Above all, the Queen knew the importance of the monarchy standing for history, tradition and duty. She knew also that while there was a need for the monarchy to evolve with the people, and that its covenant with them, unwritten and unspoken, was based on a relationship that allowed for evolution, it should be steady, carefully calibrated and controlled. Suddenly, an unpredictable meteor had come into this predictable and highly regulated ecosystem, with equally uncertain consequences. [The Queen] had good cause to be worried." [325]

MI6 Report on the Fayeds

Did MI6 have an interest in Mohamed Al Fayed?

Richard Tomlinson, Ex-MI6 Officer: 13 Feb 08: 112.13:

Mansfield: Q. Is it right that in 1992/1993, when you were serving in MI6, you were aware or saw files or a file relating to Mohamed Al Fayed?

A. I was aware of – at the time I believe it was around that time when he had a great rivalry with Tiny Rowland and there was quite a lot of information about that, and Tiny Rowland had this dispute with Mr Al Fayed, I believe.

Richard Dearlove, MI6 Director of Operations, 1994 to 1999, UK: 20 Feb 08: 131.20:

Mansfield: Q. Mr Tomlinson said he saw a file relating to Mohamed Al Fayed. Was there one?

A. I do not think so, but I think this was probably established by the Paget inquiry[a], as far as I recall. I do not think there was, personally.

Q. You see, I am asking you because he said he saw one. Was there a MI5 file?

A. You cannot ask that question of me.

....Q. Now the basis for these questions is Mr Tomlinson said he saw a file. We have been told that there was a file in MI5 relating to Mohamed Al Fayed dated 1997. Are you saying that you did not know about that?

A. I did not know about that.

Q. Right. Really the question, you see, is: somebody plainly had their eye ... on Mohamed Al Fayed as a potential threat in 1997. Would that appear to be right?

A. That is a leap of imagination. I fear the truth is we were not very interested in him.

Q. Really? Well, I hear people laughing about it. You were not ... interested in him? He was regarded as persona non grata in 1997: no passport, cash for questions, Tory Government in trouble over sleaze. He was persona non grata and you were interested, weren't you?

A. Not in SIS.

---

[a] There is no mention in the Paget Report of checks being made at MI6 regarding files relating to Mohamed Al Fayed.

Q. Where then?

A. That is for others to say.

At 187.5: Burnett: Q. I would just like to read to you a letter written on behalf of SIS and the Security Service ... to see whether you can confirm its accuracy. The first question was this: "Were either the Security Service or the Secret Intelligence Service preparing a report or had they ever prepared a report (a) for consideration of the Way Ahead Group or any member of the Way Ahead Group, whether for meetings which were proposed in 1997 or otherwise concerning Mr Mohamed Al Fayed or Mr Dodi Al Fayed?" And the answer to that given in correspondence was no. Are you able to confirm that as far as SIS are concerned?

A. I am able to confirm that the answer, no, is correct.

Q. And do you have any reason to suppose that the answer regarding the Security Service is incorrect? [a]

A. I do not.

Q. The second question was: "Were either the Security Service or the Secret Intelligence Service preparing a report or had they ever prepared a report, otherwise than in 1997, in relation to Mr Mohamed Al Fayed or Mr Dodi Al Fayed?" The answer given was no, and that is correct as far as SIS is concerned?

A. I think that is correct, yes.

Q. And you have no reason to suppose that it is wrong as far as the Security Service is concerned?

A. Similarly.

Q. And then this question: "Are there any documents within the power, possession or control of the Security Service or the Secret Intelligence Service dated 1997 which show either organisation considering Mr Mohamed Al Fayed or Mr Dodi Al Fayed?" Answer: Mr Dodi Al Fayed, no. So, similarly, you can give the confirmations that you have just been giving?

A. Yes, I can confirm that.

Q. Mr Mohamed Al Fayed, no, in respect of the Secret Intelligence Service, so that you can confirm?

A. I can confirm.

Q. Yes, in respect of the Security Service.

Coroner: Now, I had to look into that from the point of view of relevance, and concluded that it was not relevant, having seen the underlying matter. [b]

---

[a] I suggest that it is pointless asking MI6 personnel about questions relating to MI5. If the inquest wanted to be thorough in their investigation they should have heard from an MI5 witness. That never occurred.

[b] This is another case of Baker determining that critical documentation is not relevant. This is discussed in the Comment.

Q. Sir, the letter went on: "So far as the affirmative answer ... is concerned, I am taking steps to make the documents available for information by the Coroner." As you have just indicated, that occurred. Sir, those are my questions.

Miss X, MI6 Administrator, UK: 26 Feb 08: 57.8:

Burnett: Q. As far as Mr Mohamed Al Fayed is concerned, I think it is right that Lord Stevens did not particularly ask about Mr Al Fayed Senior, but you nonetheless ran checks.

A. Yes. There was a question with regard to monitoring, so I checked in so much as to whether or not there was any monitoring and no, there was not.

Q. Did you also check to see if there was a file on him, a P file?

A. Yes, I did.

Q. And was there?

A. No, there is not.

Q. Did you check to see whether there was a card relating to him?

A. Yes, I did.

Q. Was there?

A. Yes, there is.

Q. When was it created?

A. May I just check back? It was in the 1980s.

....Q. Did you check its content?

A. Yes, I checked the content and also the Paget team had access to everything in relation to that card.

Q. Were there any entries at all for 1997?

A. No, not on the – no, there were not.

....Q. Did you show the Paget team the card and the related documents?

A. Yes, I did.

Q. Did you also search your system for Mr Al Fayed's name to see whether it appeared in other documents?

A. Yes, on our electronic filing system, yes I did.

Q. So, again, this would have been telegraphic material going back to 19 –

A. Early 1990s and any other correspondence post 2001.

Q. Did his name crop up?

A. Yes, it did.

Q. Are you able to tell us when the earliest reference was in that material?

A. Yes, I can. It was in July; July 1994.

Q. That is a date, just so that we are clear, that you have corrected. Originally in your statement you had indicated August 1998, but you have corrected that in your later statement to July 1994.

A. Yes. Would there be any mileage in just explaining why I have made that error, because it would take me a very little bit of time, for the jury –

Coroner: Yes.

Q. Please do.

A. Obviously I wrote this statement. I had help with it, but it was mainly my statement. When the Paget team came in to check everything, they saw everything going back to July 1994 or had access to. On our electronic system, when I went back to put in correct dates for my statement, I put the details in, "Mr Mohamed Al Fayed", et cetera, and the hits came up, but what I did not – I probably did it in too much of a hurry, and unfortunately, of course, I do not have my God's access anymore, so I should have pressed a button and then it would have shown me what the sort of potential hits were above, and so I just read the one in the top line and that was 12th August, but I think there were – I cannot be absolutely precise – very few above, the first of which was July 1994, hence the reason, but entirely my mistake.

Q. So far as any hits were concerned in 1997, so we are still looking at Mr Mohamed Al Fayed, did they post-date the crash or pre-date the crash?

A. They post-dated the crash.

At 121.12: Mansfield: Q. A letter which was read out to Sir Richard last week.... It is written on 12th October [2007] by the Treasury Solicitor to the Coroner because questions have been asked on this topic.... The specific question in the end that was posed to the security services was this question.... "Are there any documents within the power, possession or control of the Security Service or the Secret Intelligence Service dated 1997 which show either organisation considering ... Mr Mohamed Al Fayed or Mr Dodi Al Fayed?"... The answer as read out last week was this: "Mr Dodi Al Fayed [so dealing with him first], no; Mr Mohamed Al Fayed, no; in respect of the Secret Intelligence Service, no; in respect of the Security Service, yes."... Do you understand the reply?

A. Yes. I totally understand the reply, yes.

Q. Everyone understands the reply, but I want to suggest to you that it is economic with the truth, isn't it?

A. It is not possible just to have a look at that, is it, so that I can ...

Q. Yes, certainly. You can see my copy....

A. Thank you. I find it easier to answer that question now, if I may, sir?
Coroner: Yes.

A. If you were asking – if there was a question about were[a] there were any documents at all in 1997, yes, there were.

Q. Yes.

A. If the question is whether any documents in 1997 related to Princess Diana or Dodi Al Fayed, which goes on in the next two paragraphs, then no, there were not.

Q. I am going to be very focused. There were questions asking about other

---

[a] This probably should be "whether".

people. The question in relation to Mohamed Al Fayed was: were there any documents in the possession of the Secret Intelligence Service, MI6, dated 1997 vis a vis Mohamed Al Fayed? All right, that is the question –

Tam: Sir, with respect, that is not the question that was asked. The question that was asked is quite plain on the piece of paper that the witness now has. It has the word "considering", which is a word which my learned friend has avoided putting in the questions that he has put.

Q. Sir, that is just not right. I have just read it out. I am trying to shorten it. I have given the witness the letter, so that is absolutely not right.

A. I think in answer to the question, "Were the ..." – well, I can speak – "Were the Secret Intelligence Service considering Dodi Al Fayed or Mohamed Al Fayed?", my understanding of the word "considering" there is were they of operational interest, and my answer to that would be no, they were not of operational interest.

Q. I have not got to your answer yet. This is the answer that we were provided with; in other words, once again, unless the precise words are, the fact of the matter is, in 1997, the Secret Intelligence Service did have documents within their power and possession or control which did consider Mohamed Al Fayed, didn't they?

A. There are two documents I am thinking of in 1997, and if I was able to tell you what they were, it would really make it plain that they are not what you would consider to be intelligency kind of documents. The bottom line is they are both incredibly insignificant documents.

Q. I do not mean what was created after the crash, do you follow? What was in the possession of the Secret Intelligence Service in 1997, but not dated 1997, were documents relating to Mohamed Al Fayed; correct?

A. Were there any documents at all? Yes, there are documents.

Q. Yes. You see no one was told that in the letter, that "Sorry, we don't have any dated 1997, but we do have documents", and I will come to them now because you have been kind enough to indicate. In fact, first of all there was a card created for him, is that right, in 1980, or somewhere around then?

A. Yes, that was in my original statement.

Q. As you have already indicated a card is created when somebody is of interest to the Secret Intelligence Service; also correct?

A. Yes, to a certain degree, sir. What I also said was that often names will be carded, and, if you remember, just going back to my original showing you of the minute, where you get the index, names are underlined in red and that is still the case, although in a different form. You will find that we have a lot of names on the system. It does not mean that we are actively doing anything about it sort of thing.

Q. But the card was in existence in 1997?

A. The card was certainly in existence in 1997.

Q. And there were a number of entries on it, were there not?

A. There were a number of entries, all of which were shown to the Paget team.

Q. I dare say. Roughly how many, can you remember?

A. I hope I can remember roughly right. I think there were about 14.

Q. Were those spread over the years between 1980 and 1996?

A. I would not like to answer that entirely. I know that the card originated in 1980, but I could not tell you exactly what that last entry is on the card.

Q. I am going to ask you a very particular question. Were these 14 entries the result of focused or specific intelligence-gathering?

Tam: Sir, no. With respect, that is asking about specific SIS operations and that is too sensitive and should not be asked.

Coroner: Do you have any observations about this, Mr Burnett?

Q. Sir, there are two observations I would make. I am sure the witness is very conscious of the importance of neither confirming nor denying nor answering questions that give away any detailed operational matters, any sensitive matters or any detail of intelligence that might be held on any individual and it may be that the witness can say something. But, sir, a question that asks for the quality ornate of what is on the card would seem to me, with respect, to take us straight into the "neither confirm nor deny" territory, which Sir Richard Dearlove sought to explain to the jury last week. But it may be that the witness feels she can go a little way without transgressing any of where she knows where the boundaries are.

Coroner: Yes.

A. I think, if I can try to explain because I would really like to try to be helpful is that in relation to the references on the card, they were not in relation to what I would call directly looking at somebody, but were perhaps more insignificant, indirect references, but I do not think I can be any more helpful than that, I am afraid. Does that answer the question?

Q. I am not going to trespass into areas that are forbidden, so I do not. But could you help us in this way? Can you give us the date of the last entry now or not?

A. I can't unless you can find the spot in my statement where I have written that.

Q. It does not say.

A. Sorry, no, I can't off the top of my head.

Q. What you recall in the statement is that you showed the card and all of the documents to the Paget inquiry.

A. Yes.

Q. I am not going to trespass into areas that may be too difficult, but "related documents" means that there were documents relating to the 14 entries or some of them?

A. No, all of the entries. Each of the references on the card refers to a different piece of correspondence, and so each of those pieces of correspondence were attached to the back of the card and that was shown to the Paget inquiry when they came in.

Q. That was one – I do not know whether you call it a "database", but let's call it a database for the moment. That is one database, but then you also searched a file system. Did you search the file system electronically or did you have to do it by hand because of the restrictions you have already indicated?

A. No, I did it electronically because I believed that anything substantive would have been written telegraphically and therefore would have covered the period 1997, going back to the start of 1990.

Q. That is the restriction. It may be that you make assumptions and beliefs, and it is entirely understandable that you might do that, but of course there may be materials that are not telegraphically communicated. Is that right?

A. Yes, certainly we have letters, things like that.

Q. So they would not appear on the search that you did?

A. Not on the electronic search pre 2001.

Q. No. So, in fact, what you have come up with, which although you don't in fact identify the number – I have gleaned it from another source – it appears that on this search there were six entries of his name in the file search; two of them relate to 1997 and post crash, but the other four don't. But again, would there be documents relating to those other four?

A. To the other four, yes, there would be, yes.

Q. So whether or not there was other information on Mohamed Al Fayed that was not thrown up by this search, you are unable to help us. Is that right?

A. I would only be able to help you in as much as that our substantive way of communicating is by telegram, and that it would be highly unlikely that there would be a great deal of letters on a subject. Letters are used very much for something like "I attach a brochure", "I attach something", something like that.

Comment: Any MI6 interest in Mohamed Al Fayed is significant to this case because earlier evidence has indicated that there could have been Establishment concern over interaction between Diana, William, Harry and Mohamed.[a]

Did MI6 collect and retain intelligence about Mohamed Al Fayed?
The evidence is:
- "there was quite a lot of information [in MI6 files] about ... [the] Tiny Rowland ... dispute with Mr Al Fayed" – Tomlinson
- "I do not think there was, personally ... [an MI6] file relating to Mohamed Al Fayed" – Dearlove

[a] See earlier.

- "the truth is we were not very interested in [Mohamed]" – Dearlove
- "I checked ... whether or not there was any monitoring [of Mohamed] and no, there was not" – X
- "there is not ... [an MI6] file on [Mohamed]" – X
- "there is ... [an MI6] card relating to [Mohamed]" – X
- "there were not ... any entries at all [on Mohamed's MI6 card] for 1997" – X
- "I think there were about 14" entries on Mohamed's MI6 card – X
- Mohamed appears on MI6 "telegraphic material going back to ... [the] early 1990s[a] and ... post 2001" – X, confirmed to Burnett
- "were there ... any documents at all in 1997 [considering Mohamed]? Yes, there were" – X
- "no" to "had [MI6] ever prepared a report ... for consideration of the Way Ahead Group ... concerning Mr Mohamed Al Fayed ...?" – letter from Treasury Solicitor, confirmed by Dearlove
- "no" to "had [MI6] ever prepared a report, otherwise than in 1997, in relation to Mr Mohamed Al Fayed" – letter from Treasury Solicitor, confirmed by Dearlove
- "no" to "are there any documents within the power, possession or control of ... [MI6] dated 1997 which show [MI6 or MI5] considering Mr Mohamed Al Fayed ...?" – letter from Treasury Solicitor, confirmed by Dearlove
- "MI6 has prepared a special report on the Egyptian-born Fayeds, which will be presented to [the WAG] meeting" – *Sunday Mirror*, 31 August 1997.

There are several concerns that arise from the MI6 evidence – Dearlove, X – which primarily has been provided by X:

1) Earlier, during her evidence regarding the general MI6 filing system, an excerpt from X's statement was read out: "[The MI6 electronic carding system] contains the details of all individuals and organisations that the service has an interest in."[326] X confirmed this.[b]

When the subject of an MI6 card for Mohamed came up, X was reminded about this by Mansfield: "As you have already indicated a card is created when somebody is of interest to the Secret Intelligence Service – also correct?" Now X replied: "Yes, to a certain degree, sir."

X appears to have qualified her account – "to a certain degree" – to avoid making any admission that MI6 "has an interest in" Mohamed.[c]

---

[a] This was then changed to July 1994.

[b] "Yes, that is right."

[c] Dearlove had already said: "the truth is we were not very interested in [Mohamed]".

Yet based on X's statement account[a], the evidence seems clear: there are cards raised for people "[MI6] has an interest in". The inquest evidence revealed that Mohamed had a card with 14 entries on it. That should then indicate that MI6 has an interest in Mohamed.

I suggest that this also is common sense.

What is the point of MI6 creating a card for an individual if they have no interest in them?

2) Mansfield asked X: "Did you search the file system electronically or ... by hand?" X replied: "I did it electronically because I believed that anything substantive would have been written telegraphically".

When Mansfield pursues this, we find X admitting: "we have letters[b], things like that" that weren't searched if they were "pre 2001".

The point here is that the crash was in 1997 – so "pre 2001" includes the significant period.

This evidence shows that X failed to carry out a thorough search.

3) Dearlove and X repeatedly volunteered that information had been shown to Paget:[c]

- "I think this[d] was probably established by the Paget inquiry" – Dearlove

- "also the Paget team had access to everything in relation to that card" – X

- "the Paget team came in to check everything, they saw everything going back to July 1994 or had access to [it]" – X

- "all of which were shown to the Paget team"[e] – X

- "that was shown to the Paget inquiry when they came in" – X.

Why did Dearlove and X do this?

I suggest it comes across as though the comments are for the benefit of the jury, maybe to put them at ease – saying that the records have been subjected to investigation by Scotland Yard. It is not spelt out, but there appears to be an implication that if there was anything untoward, then Paget would have picked up on it.

It may be significant that Paget makes no mention of anything to do with MI6 records relating to Mohamed Al Fayed in the 832 page Paget Report.

---

[a] Made on 20 December 2007, just two months previously: 26 Feb 08: 3.21.

[b] X explains: "Letters are used very much for something like 'I attach a brochure', 'I attach something', something like that."

[c] It's interesting that both X and Dearlove only did this during answers on the Mohamed Al Fayed file search. There are no instances of either witness volunteering information regarding Paget on any other topic.

[d] That there was no MI6 file on Mohamed.

[e] Following this, Mansfield – who may have detected this strategy from X – said: "I dare say".

I suggest that it has been previously shown[a] that the Paget Report was so full of holes that it is no comfort whatsoever whether a document was viewed by Paget or not.

4) The intelligence agencies were asked in writing: "Are there any documents within the power, possession or control of ... the Secret Intelligence Service dated 1997 which show [MI6 and MI5] considering Mr Mohamed Al Fayed...?"[b]

The reply was "no", and this was confirmed by Richard Dearlove on 20 February 2008.

X revealed, under cross-examination six days later: "if there was a question about [whether] there were any documents at all [considering Mohamed Al Fayed] in 1997, yes, there were".[c]

X, who was speaking while looking at the intelligence letter, provided two qualifications to this:

a) that the Mohamed-related documents were not "related to Princess Diana or Dodi Al Fayed".

This appears to be irrelevant.

The issue, at least initially, is whether MI6 had an interest in Mohamed Al Fayed – not whether they had an interest in him in connection with the Diana-Dodi relationship.

So I suggest that evidence of any MI6 interest in Mohamed is relevant. According to the August *Mirror* article, there was an MI6 report on the Fayeds – not on the connection between the Fayeds and Diana.

b) X states: "my understanding of the word 'considering' there is, were [Mohamed and Dodi] of operational interest, and ... no, they were not of operational interest".[d]

---

[a] In the 2007 book *Cover-Up of a Royal Murder: Hundreds of Errors in the Paget Report*.

[b] This was in a letter from the Treasury Solicitor.

[c] See earlier transcript.

[d] X appears to have been alerted to this by a protest from the MI6 lawyer, Robin Tam, who had seconds earlier intervened during Mansfield's questioning. Mansfield – who had just given his copy of the Treasury Solicitor's letter to X, at X's request ("it is not possible just to have a look at that, is it") – restated the question, after X had been restating her own different versions of the question. Mansfield asked: "were there any documents in the possession of the Secret Intelligence Service, MI6, dated 1997 vis a vis Mohamed Al Fayed?" Tam intervened with: "That is not the question that was asked. The question that was asked [in the letter] ... has the word 'considering', which is a word which [Mansfield] has avoided putting in the questions that he has put." Mansfield protested against this – "that is absolutely not right". Tam had said that Mansfield "avoided putting ['considering'] in the questions that he has put". The reality is that Mansfield had included "considering" in his

In saying this, X appears to have come up with her own meaning for the word "considering". "Considering", in this context, means "look attentively at someone".[a] I suggest that is not necessarily the same as an "operational interest" by MI6.

In short, there is a conflict between the letter, apparently written by the Treasury Solicitor – there were no documents "considering Mr Mohamed Al Fayed" – and X – "yes, there were" documents.[b]

I suggest that the intelligence documents on Mohamed – including the MI6 card – should have been shown to the inquest jury. The evidence in this book has shown that intelligence perceptions of Mohamed Al Fayed may have played a key role in determining that Diana had to be eliminated. The jury were entitled to establish precisely what the intelligence perceptions of Mohamed were.

At one stage Scott Baker declares: "I had to look into [MI5 documents on Mohamed] from the point of view of relevance, and concluded that it was not relevant".

And X stated – referring to a different lot of MI6 documents: "They are not what you would consider to be intelligency kind of documents. The bottom line is they are both incredibly insignificant documents".

If they are that insignificant and "not intelligency", then why the secrecy?

Intelligence documentation on Mohamed Al Fayed should have been shown to the jury – they should have been allowed to determine the relevance of those documents.

The evidence from MI6 raises the question: Why did MI6 admit to having documents regarding Mohamed Al Fayed, while at the same time denying they had anything relating to Princess Diana? [c]

The following includes some speculation.

I suggest that it ostensibly gives some credibility to the MI6 claim to have nothing on – or no interest in – Diana. If MI6 just completely deny that they have anything on anybody, then it is easier for them to be accused of dishonesty.

But, on the other hand, if MI6 admits to having some documents[d], then it raises the possibility that they might be telling the truth when they deny having other documents.

---

questions and only replaced it once with "vis a vis", and that was after he had given his copy of the letter to X.

[a] Oxford dictionary.

[b] In support of X's account, Mansfield asked her: "The fact of the matter is, in 1997, the Secret Intelligence Service did have documents within their power and possession or control which did consider Mohamed Al Fayed, didn't they?" X replied: "There are two documents I am thinking of in 1997...."

[c] See earlier.

[d] And they openly showed it all to Paget – see above.

Admission of some documents on Mohamed may have been considered a safe option by MI6, because – even though Mohamed is a key player – documentation relating to him does not necessarily link MI6 to the assassinations.

Tomlinson supports the evidence from X. He said: "I was aware ... there was quite a lot of information [in MI6 files] about ... [the] Tiny Rowland ... dispute with Mr Al Fayed".

Then two years after Tomlinson had left MI6, the *Mirror* article stated: "MI6 has prepared a special report on the Egyptian-born Fayeds, which will be presented to [an early-September 1997 WAG] meeting".

That conflicts directly with the Treasury Solicitor's letter – confirmed by Dearlove: That letter said "no" to the question, "had [MI6] ever prepared a report ... for consideration of the Way Ahead Group ... concerning Mr Mohamed Al Fayed ...?"

Earlier and later evidence – including what follows below – indicates that there may have been a cover-up regarding the planned September 1997 WAG meeting.[a]

Baker told the jury in his Summing Up: "A newspaper report had suggested that ... a file on the Al Fayeds was produced [at the July WAG meeting] by the security services."

The newspaper actually said: "MI6 has prepared a special report on the Egyptian-born Fayeds[b], which will be presented to the meeting."

The inaccuracies in Baker's Summing Up are:
-   the article referred to a future September 1997 meeting, whereas Baker changed it to past tense and indicated it was referring to the July 1997 meeting – see earlier
-   Baker says "security services", whereas the article specifically named MI6
-   Baker says it was a "file", whereas the article said a "special report" had been prepared.

Baker's falsifications are significant.[c]

---

[a] It has also been shown earlier that intelligence witnesses – including Dearlove – have a proclivity to lie, even under oath.

[b] This could refer to the Fayeds, father and son – Mohamed, Dodi – or the two brothers – Mohamed and Ali. It was mentioned earlier that the reason Diana is not mentioned in the context of the September WAG meeting could have been because it was already known by the article's source that she could be dead. This could also be the case regarding Dodi, in which case I suggest that the "Fayeds" in the article refer to Mohamed and Ali.

[c] The first one has been dealt with earlier.

Changing "MI6" to "security services" – which means MI5 and MI6 – helps to confuse the issue for the jury. The evidence in this book has shown that it was MI6 which was involved in the assassinations of Diana and Dodi – not MI5. Even though "security services" technically means MI6 and MI5, in some people's minds they could equate the term to mean only MI5. This is because the other name for MI5 is the Security Service.

At the inquest the jury had heard a lot of evidence from and about MI6, but almost nothing about MI5. This is because no one has ever accused MI5 of involvement in the crash.

So when Baker in the Summing Up brings in the "security services", instead of MI6, it automatically distances what he is talking about – the "Al Fayeds" issue at the WAG meeting – from the crash in the Alma tunnel.

The point here is that the information the WAG was seeking on the Al Fayeds was going to come from the precise same organisation – MI6 – that was deeply involved in the Paris assassinations. Baker has assisted in preventing the jury from being able to understand that.

There is a major difference between "a file ... was produced" and "prepared a special report".

The latter means that a special report has been specially requested by someone or some group at an earlier time – and that requested report – which will have been put together after some investigation – is now going to be tabled.

A "file" generally refers to whatever is already on file – it does not infer that a special investigation has been made to produce a new document.[a]

This then indicates that MI6 have – at some point prior to 31 August 1997[bc] – been requested by the WAG, or someone within the WAG, to carry out an investigation on the Fayeds.[a]

---

[a] The Oxford definitions are: "report" – "an account given of a matter after investigation or consideration"; "file" – "a folder or box for keeping loose papers together and in order".

[b] The date of the article.

[c] The MI6 report on the Fayeds may have been requested after the July WAG meeting. According to evidence at the inquest – but not viewed by the jury – the July meeting's minutes read that "the next [WAG] meeting has been arranged for Monday 19th January 1998". This indicates that the September 1997 meeting – referred to in the *Mirror* article – was not planned for well ahead of time. The MI6 report may have been requested as more information about activities between Diana and the Al Fayeds became known – for example, the rapid escalation of the relationship between Diana and Dodi. The September WAG meeting may have been called in late July or sometime in August. When the issue of a possible September 1997 meeting was put to Robert Fellowes at the inquest, he initially replied, "No" and then apparently started looking through his "pocket diary". Fellowes' conclusion was: "I can see no reference in my pocket diary anyway to a Way Ahead Group meeting in September". There are a couple of points here: a) Fellowes stated: "I was on holiday

Baker – by replacing "prepared a special report" with "a file ... was produced" – prevented the jury from being able to deduce that.

I suggest that the punishment for Diana's actions – see earlier – was assassination. The punishment for Mohamed's involvement was the assassination of his son, Dodi, and I believe there were to be further consequences, which were scheduled to be discussed at the September WAG meeting. The MI6 report would have been tabled and the Harrods royal warrants may have been withdrawn, as indicated in the *Mirror* article.

The British public intervened.

The outcry and reaction to the death of Diana was overwhelming – I suggest, beyond the belief of the senior royals. If the September 1997 WAG meeting had taken any further action against Mohamed, the royals would have risked further alienation from the British public. It may also have increased suspicion amongst the public about possible royal involvement in the Paris crash – and strengthened public sympathy towards Mohamed.

I believe the plans for the September WAG meeting would have been put on hold – or if that meeting did occur, it would have been decided to postpone any further action against Mohamed Al Fayed.[b]

---

from early – well somewhere around the first week of August.... I went back to Balmoral on the following Sunday, I think, after the funeral.... I was at the Palace certainly until the end of July": 12 Feb 08: 111.13. If the September WAG meeting had not been called until August – we know it was called after July 23 – then it is unlikely Fellowes would have been around, if he was on holiday, and therefore may not have diarised the meeting. b) Fellowes uses the term: "my pocket diary anyway". Pages from Fellowes' full-size diary were produced in the inquest evidence, when Fellowes tried to refute David Davies' evidence – see INQ0060775 and INQ0060776. It is obvious that Fellowes has specifically brought his 1997 pocket diary along to the inquest into the death of his sister-in-law. The question is: Why didn't Fellowes offer to consult his main diary about this September 1997 WAG meeting?

[a] It is possible that the use of the word "Fayeds" could refer to Mohamed and his brother, Ali, not necessarily Mohamed and Dodi – see earlier footnote.

[b] The Harrods royal warrants were apparently removed in early 1998: 13 Dec 07: 90.16. Michael Cole has said: "Following the tragedy in Paris in August 1997 and, in February 1998, Mohamed's initial voicing of his long-held and considered conviction that the Duke of Edinburgh had conspired in the killing of his former daughter-in-law and his own son Dodi, Mohamed expressed to me among others that he wished the royal crests to be removed from the facade of Harrods. This was his firm intent.... After I retired from the company in March 1998, Mohamed decided to ... take them all down. Even before that, he had asked his chief designer ... architect, Bill Mitchell, to design a new device for the four corners of the store where the coats of arms were displayed. Bill came up with the design that you ... see on the facade today."

Prince Philip

Philip was a named suspect who was feared by Princess Diana.[a]

Miles Hunt-Davis, Private Secretary to Prince Philip: 13 Dec 07: 64.19:

Mansfield: Q. [Philip] was approached originally not by the Coroner, but by officers or – to be more precise – by Lord Stevens on behalf of the Stevens inquiry, wasn't he?

A. Correct.

Q. Lord Stevens wanted, at that stage just to know about one thing, didn't he? He wrote a letter which you saw in which he made note of the general allegations, but he said that there was a matter of particular concern. Do you remember? Do you need to see the letter or not or do you remember it?

A. I do not remember it.

Q. It was, in fact, to do with correspondence. You don't remember the letter?

A. No.

Q. All right. Never mind the letter that was written to you. You, in fact, sent a message back on his behalf on 11th October 2006. Do you remember that?

A. I do.

Q. I will just read it: "Brigadier Hunt-Davis telephoned the Paget office. The Duke of Edinburgh had seen the letter from Lord Stevens and initialled it. However, he did not wish to make any comment to Operation Paget." Is that what you wrote back?

A. That is correct. I did not write it. I spoke on the telephone.

Q. What was the reason given at that stage by the Duke of Edinburgh, as it were, refusing to cooperate with Operation Paget?

A. Would you like to rephrase that because I am not quite sure what you want?

Q. Sorry, it is not what I want. Did the Duke give you a reason for refusing to cooperate, ie not making any comment, in October 2006, barely two years ago – well, less than that, a year ago – for refusing to cooperate?

A. No, he did not give me a reason, no. There is no need for him to have done so. He asked me to convey a message, which I did, to Lord Stevens' staff.

Q. How close is the relationship between you and the Duke of Edinburgh?

A. As close as a private secretary is to a member of the Royal Family.

Q. Presumably, after this length of time[b], you would go beyond "Look, there

---

Michael Cole, Email to author, 5 December 2011. It seems likely that the removal of the royal warrants from Harrods in 1998 was mutual – the royals wanted them removed and Mohamed Al Fayed also wanted them removed. Mohamed later oversaw the burning of the royal warrants – this was filmed in the 2012 movie, *Unlawful Killing*.

[a] See earlier.

[b] At the time of the communication from Paget, Hunt-Davis had been private secretary for 13 years.

has been this request" and he says "No" and you just leave it at that. Surely it does not rest at that level, does it?

A. It depends on the subject.

Q. This is a rather important subject; an investigation conducted by the police and an approach by Lord Stevens, who heads it, where there are allegations as he made clear in the letter. Would you like to see the letter that was written to you? We can bring it up on screen.

....Q. "I seek your assistance in this investigation ..." Do you see that?

A. I do.

Q. "... specifically in relation to His Royal Highness the Duke of Edinburgh. There has been much speculation in the media since 1997 of the alleged fears of the Princess of Wales that she would meet an untimely death and also allegations made by Mr Al Fayed that His Royal Highness the Duke of Edinburgh was the prime motivator in the conspiracy. Mr Al Fayed, over the course of my investigation, has not produced evidence to support any of the allegations he has made publicly concerning His Royal Highness the Duke of Edinburgh, however there is one specific matter that I should address and this concerns allegations made by Mohamed Al Fayed that His Royal Highness the Duke of Edinburgh made threats to Diana, Princess of Wales, in letters sent to her. Mr Al Fayed supports this allegation only by reference to conversations he had with the Princess of Wales in the weeks before her death and a claim that New Scotland Yard are in possession of such letters. "I feel it is only right at this time to give you the opportunity if you so wish to address these allegations. I can confirm that any interview will be as a witness and as such his attendance at any meeting is completely voluntary." Now, do you remember this letter that was sent?

A. I do.

Q. This was plainly a serious matter, wasn't it?

A. Yes.

Q. So when a request comes from the person heading the investigation, Lord Stevens, it would have to be treated seriously, would it not?

A. I feel sure it was.

Q. All I am asking is whether there was more to the conversation than you have put in the reply, namely, "No comment"?

A. There was nothing more.

Q. I mean, if he were asked today to assist, asked by the learned Coroner to assist, would he be prepared to come?

A. I have no idea.

Q. Did you speak to him recently about your attendance here?

A. He knows I am attending.

Q. Yes.

A. I did not discuss what would happen here. I said that I had been asked to attend and he acknowledged that he had heard what I had said. There was not a discussion about it.[a]

Mohamed Al Fayed, Dodi's Father, UK: 18 Feb 08: 120.19:

Burnett: Q. That is a point also you have made about Prince Philip, isn't it, why has he not sued you?

A. Why Prince Philip haven't sued me, it is the same.

Q. And the same in respect of everybody?

A. Not everybody. If you are confronted with powerful people in Government or in power like Prince Philip, right, how can you get the evidence?

Q. But Sir Michael Jay has not sued you.

A. No, he has not sued me.

Q. And Lord Fellowes has not sued you.

A. No.

Q. And the Prince of Wales has not sued you.

A. No.

Q. And Prince Philip has not sued you.

A. Right. Why they didn't sue me? I am available. I am talking my mind, I am talking the truth. Because I am talking the truth, they cannot do it because they would get themselves in trouble.

Comment: Prince Philip – a named suspect – refused to assist the official police investigation into the Paris crash.

When asked to do so, Philip apparently responded: "No comment".

Michael Mansfield asked Miles Hunt-Davis, Philip's private secretary of 14 years: "Did [Philip] give you a reason for refusing to cooperate?" Hunt-Davis answered: "No, he did not give me a reason, no. There is no need for him to have done so. He asked me to convey a message, which I did, to Lord Stevens' staff." [b]

But "the message" Hunt-Davis refers to was: "No comment".

The question is: How can it be that a named suspect in a murder investigation can simply answer "no comment" and not be expected to be available for interview and to provide a sworn statement?

Hunt-Davis states: "There is no need for [Philip] to have" provided a reason for refusing to cooperate with the investigation into his ex-daughter-in-law's suspicious death.

The fact that Philip has been able to do this – and get away with it – indicates that he is above the law.

---

[a] Miles Hunt-Davis was awarded a CVO in the New Year's Honours announced 31 December 1997, just four months after the Paris crash.: New Year Honours: The Prime Minister's List, *The Independent*, 31 December 1997.

[b] Hunt-Davis initially answered: "Would you like to rephrase that because I am not quite sure what you want?"

There are really only three possibilities:

1) Philip is guilty of playing a role in the assassinations

2) Philip is not guilty, but possesses knowledge that could be helpful to the investigations

3) Philip is not guilty and has no knowledge that could be helpful.

The question must be asked: Why would a person say "no comment" when approached by police seeking information into the circumstances of the death of their ex-daughter-in-law?

Such a reply certainly does nothing to remove perceptions of possible guilt. I suggest it tends to have the opposite effect and leads to questions being asked in people's minds – questions like: Does this person have something to hide?

There are several points that indicate Philip may have a case to answer or could provide material assistance to the investigations:

- Philip was present in the WAG meetings – it has been shown earlier that the WAG may have played a role in the assassinations

- Philip's wife, the Queen, was the chairman of the WAG – see earlier

- there are five witnesses – Paul Burrell, Hasnat Khan, Susan Kassem, Roberto Devorik, Mohamed Al Fayed – who have indicated that there were problems in the Diana-Philip relationship – see Part 2[a]

- Devorik said that Philip was one of three people Diana feared – see Part 2

- Devorik and Mohamed both said that Diana had told them Philip wanted to "get rid of" her – see Part 2

- Devorik also stated that Diana had said: "[Philip] really hates me and would like to see me disappear"; "[Philip] blames me for everything"; "Prince Philip wants to see me dead" – see Part 2

- Simone Simmons stated that Diana had shown her letters from Philip which described Diana as a harlot, a trollop, a bad mother and said that she "was damaging the Royal Family". Simmons also said: "[Diana] had death threats which were worded nicer than [Philip's] letters" – see Part 2[b]

- statements made by Philip indicating he appears to be a racist – listed in Part 2[c]

- allegations in the *Sunday Mirror* published on 31 August 1997 – the day of the crash: "Prince Philip, in particular, has had made no secret as to how he feels about his daughter-in-law's latest man, referring to Dodi as an 'oily bedhopper'.... A friend of the Royals said yesterday 'Prince Philip has let

---

[a] Section on Prince Philip in the Fears and Threats chapter.

[b] Section on Post-1992 Letters in the Fears and Threats chapter.

[c] Section on Philip's View of Dodi in the Fears and Threats chapter.

rip several times recently about the Fayeds.... He has been banging on about his contempt for Dodi and how he is undesirable as a future stepfather to William and Harry" – reproduced earlier

- Philip's refusal to be interviewed by Scotland Yard
- Philip's failure to provide a statement or allow himself to be cross-examined at the inquest into the deaths.

There is evidently no justice in this.

The above 11 points all contribute to the perception that Philip may have been involved in the assassinations, or at the least, could provide information that could assist the investigations.

Yet we see that Philip has been able to avoid giving any evidence to any investigation into the death of his ex-daughter-in-law and his complete contribution to date is just two words: "No comment".[a]

"Dark Forces"

Paul Burrell, Diana's butler, described a conversation he had with the Queen on 19 December 1997 – just 3½ months after the crash. He says that the Queen warned him to be careful of powers "about which we have no knowledge".

Paul Burrell, Diana's Butler: 14 Jan 08: 85.24:

Burnett: Q. The discussions that you had with Her Majesty [on 19 December 1997] no doubt ranged over wide subject matters and I don't wish to trespass upon private discussions that you had. But there is one aspect of the discussion which it won't surprise you I do want to ask you about and no doubt others will ask you as well. I will take the record of what you say Her Majesty said from ... your book: "Be careful, Paul, no-one has been as close

---

[a] Michael Cole, who was the BBC royal correspondent assigned to Buckingham Palace from 1985 to 1988, said in his Paget statement – not heard by the jury: "Although these matters were not discussed in royal circles when I was the Court Correspondent, I knew that the Duke of Edinburgh was the person who liaised with the security services on behalf of the Royal Family. With his military background and seniority, he was the obvious person for the job. When The Queen or other members of the Royal Family were going to parts of the world where security considerations became significant, his role would become even more important. This was not just security in the sense of personal protection but on the wider political issues relating to visits abroad. It has been reported that the Duke was hurt by suggestions that he ordered the death of Diana, Princess of Wales. I have never encountered a man with a thicker skin and I cannot imagine him being dismayed by anything anyone might say.... "The Duke of Edinburgh would not have given any orders because that is not the way things are done in this country and certainly not the way M16 operates. Those security officers who met with the Duke on a regular basis would have been very aware of his prejudices and attitudes.": Michael Cole, Witness Statement, 6 July 2006, p25.

to a member of my family as you have. There are powers at work in this country about which we have no knowledge. Do you understand?"

A. Yes.

Q. Now, that is what you attribute to Her Majesty. Was that recollection one aided by a note that you made after the meeting?

A. Yes, it was.[ab]

Q. Now in your book you go to considerable lengths to explain that you don't know what Her Majesty meant by that.

A. One doesn't ask the Queen what she means by something.

Q. And you didn't ask her?

A. No.

Q. You give three possibilities, if I can summarise them. The media bosses and their editors?

A. Could be.

Q. The establishment generally?

A. (Witness nods)

Q. Or the security service?

A. Yes.

Q. Now what is it that you thought yourself you needed to be careful about?

A. I just think it was a general "be careful" warning over many issues. This was unprecedented times, and as the Queen said to me, "No-one has been as close to a member of my family" and this had never happened before. The Queen is a good, kind, devout lady and she looks after the members of staff who look after her on a daily basis. As I had done that to her, she extended me the kindness of looking after me and she said she was just looking out for me. That's how I felt that was meant, just be careful.

Q. Of course you carry around with you an enormous amount of private information concerning various members of the Royal Family; that's the special knowledge you have?

A. Yes.

Q. There are people who are interested in that, no doubt.

A. I am sure they are.

....Q. Now if that observation from Her Majesty were relevant for the purposes of these inquests, in other words the question of how Dodi and Diana came by their deaths, what sort of information do you think you would have to have that people would be interested in that should make you be careful? Have you any idea?

---

[a] It will be shown later that Burrell's recollection of this is false. He should have been asked to produce the "note ... made after the meeting".

[b] Later, when it suited him, Burrell said: "I didn't keep notes at that meeting". See section on Perceptions of the Relationship.

A. I have no idea. I have no idea what I would know. All I know is that – you know, the Queen is incapable of telling a lie[a], and what she said to me during that meeting indicated to me that she was just a wonderful lady.

Q. Of course if you knew anything that suggested that Dodi and the Princess had been murdered –

A. Yes, I would have to say.

Q. But if you knew anything of that sort, then perhaps you do need to be careful. Do you follow me?

A. I do, yes, but I don't.

Q. But you don't know anything of that sort? You know nothing, then, do you, to support the suggestion that they were murdered?

A. No. It's – I cannot begin to believe that. Knowing the members of the Royal Family as I do and knowing them so well, I think that's impossible.

Q. Also, if Her Majesty were giving you that warning in that context – I am just trying to think through what it must mean she knew; that she knew that they had been murdered and by her husband[b]?[c]

A. Do you honestly believe that? I don't believe that for a second.

Q. But you didn't understand her to be suggesting that you needed to be careful of Prince Philip or anyone who might be working for him officially or unofficially?

A. I think I know Prince Philip's shortcomings.

Q. They don't extend that far?

A. They don't extend that far.

Q. The phrase is one that is very arresting, Mr Burrell –

A. Yes.

Q. – and you must have thought about it endlessly since –

A. I have thought about it, but I genuinely believe that it was just a kindness, a "be careful"; just "be careful along your way".

Q. The language used by Her Majesty has from time to time been paraphrased or put into a shorthand in the media and so on.

A. Yes.

Q. You know what I am talking about?

A. Yes.

---

[a] I suggest that this evidence is beyond belief.

[b] Some might suggest that Burnett is referring to Charles when he says "her husband". I believe he is referring to Philip – Charles and Diana were no longer husband and wife at the time of the crash.

[c] This is a very strange suggestion from the inquest lawyer, Ian Burnett. Up to this point his questions appear to be logical, but there is no credible connection between the Queen's "powers at work" comment and an implication that "[the Queen] knew that [Diana and Dodi] had been murdered ... by her husband [Philip]". This is not to say that Philip wasn't involved, but just that there can be no logical suggestion of that from what Burrell said the Queen told him.

Q. What phrase is that?

A. Not the "annus horribilis"?

Q. No, no, no, "dark forces".

A. "Dark forces"?

Q. Yes.

A. Oh, I see. Yes, well, I have seen that certain times. It rather resembles something from Star Wars, doesn't it?

Q. Is that a phrase Her Majesty used?

A. Absolutely not.

Q. Is it a phrase you have ever used?

A. I have never used that word.

At 16 Jan 08: 56.18: Mansfield: Q. Interview, "Tabloid Tales, Paul Burrell, 27th May 2003"....: "I took it upon myself to think, well, there are people out there that would wish me harm and I found it since. When I saw the unused material for my trial ... I saw that 20 phone lines were tapped, so there are people listening to my telephone conversations and there are people, you know.... So I knew that people were listening to me and I know that people are watching me, and they are the forces to which Her Majesty referred." Do you remember saying that?

A. I do.

Q. That's the truth, isn't it, as far as you are concerned?

A. In my mind, yes.

At 98.21: Croxford: Q. The content of that discussion, the context of it, was the death of Her Majesty's former daughter-in-law –

A. It was included in the conversation, yes.

Q. – and the aftermath of that death, the circumstances as they then were and how things were to be carried forward. Is that right?

A. Yes, that's right.

Q. In that context, that was the context in which Her Majesty made an observation to you about being careful, which we have heard. Is that right?

A. That's right.

Q. As you have told Mr Mansfield, you understood that to be careful of the security services? [a]

A. Well, just to be aware of people around me.

---

[a] This appears to be misleading. Burrell confirmed three groups to Burnett: the media, Establishment and the security services. To Mansfield, Burrell confirmed: "There are people listening to my telephone conversations.... So I knew that people were listening to me and I know that people are watching me, and they are the forces to which Her Majesty referred." Burrell was not asked – and did not confirm – that that referred to the security services.

Robert Fellowes, Brother-In-Law of Diana; Queen's Private Secretary, 1990-99, UK: 12 Feb 08: 83.22:

Mansfield: Q. On December 19th 1997, Paul Burrell had a lengthy conversation with Her Majesty at Buckingham Palace.... Were you aware of it before it happened?

A. No.

Q. Were you there when it happened?

A. No.

Q. Were you aware that it had happened afterwards?

A. No, not until I read about it, whenever it was, very recently; relatively recently.[a]

....Q. He says that at the meeting, towards its close, something was said by Her Majesty to him about taking care because of forces that may be at work. On another occasion, he described it as "dark forces". You don't know anything about that?

A. Absolutely nothing, except that it sounds exceedingly unlike the Queen.

Q. It may do, of course, but the Queen is quite cautious about all sorts of things, including a request to investigate security services and so on.

A. I am not prepared to comment on the Queen's character or get involved in that sort of thing. I am merely saying that as a figure of speech, it is very unlike her to use terms like "forces" or "dark forces".

Q. What terms would she use if she was trying to say to Paul Burrell, "Be careful"?

Coroner: Mr Mansfield, really.

Q. Well, I appreciate that you were not there and you say it is not her turn of phrase, but it has become an apocryphal term in the sense that it is well known.

A. "Apocryphal" is probably the right word.

Q. The only person who can say whether it was said, seriously or not seriously or whatever because there does not appear to have been anybody else present, is the Queen herself.

A. Correct.

Paul Burrell, Diana's Butler: 15 Jan 08: 189.11:

Mansfield: Q. When it came to the Burrell note, as we see in the epilogue to your book ... who could you trust? Can I just ... remind you of how you put it in the epilogue to the book, "A Royal Duty", which is added in the American version?[327b] I will take it in stages...."If the Princess was justified in

---

[a] Burrell went public with it in November 2002 – so over five years before this cross-examination.

[b] The epilogue is only added in the 2004 revised edition – it is not in the 2003 editions, US or UK.

suspecting that forces out there were capable of such an act[a], in what potential danger did it place me as the guardian of such a letter?" That's how you put it –

A. Yes.

Q. – as a question. "Also in my mind was the Queen's subtle but clear warning to be careful about ...", and here you put "dark forces", your term, in there.

A. Does it say "dark"?

Q. Yes, it does.

A. Well, that's an error.

Q. Is it?

A. Yes.

Q. Whose error would that be?

A. The Queen never mentioned "dark forces".

Q. Well, I appreciate that's what you say, but the book doesn't put it that way. I will read it again. It's very clear: "Also in my mind was the Queen's subtle but clear warning to be careful about dark forces at work in the country. However irrational such a thought process may seem, I was armed with a chilling letter in the Princess's hand and clear advice from the Monarch." The letter that you had that the jury have seen part of, you clearly had connected with what had happened in Paris, hadn't you?

A. Yes, I had. It was an obvious connection.

....Q. You then go on and explain. "As a married man with two children, it hardly made me want to rush to the authorities, hand it over and expect an immediate inquiry to be announced." You are very, if I may put it, bold in what you then say. "Make no mistake, had I handed that letter[b] to Buckingham Palace, St James's Palace or the Metropolitan Police, the Princess's fears would never have been made public." That was your belief, wasn't it?

A. It was.

Paul Burrell: *A Royal Duty*: **Jury Heard Part Only**:

"As the meeting neared its end, the Queen said one more thing to me. Looking over her half-rimmed spectacles, she said: 'Be careful, Paul. No one has been as close to a member of my family as you have. There *are* powers at work in this country about which we have no knowledge,' and she fixed me with a stare where her eyes made clear the 'Do you understand?'...

---

[a] Referring to the Paris crash. The Burrell Note was written by Diana in 1995 predicting such a car crash could occur. This has been addressed in Part 2.
[b] The Burrell Note.

"What did she mean? All I know is what I heard. It wasn't quantified or expanded upon, neither was it melodramatically delivered. I walked away and accepted what had been said as it had been intended: as sound advice to be vigilant. In my opinion she was telling me to be careful of everyone because no one more than the Queen understood the position in which I found myself, and the closeness I had shared with the princess.

"The reference to the 'powers at work in this country about which we have no knowledge' has often played on my mind in the intervening years and, yes, I have worried about it too. The Queen might have been referring to the power base of media barons and editors who can topple individuals from their pedestals. She might have been referring to that unknown quantity called 'the Establishment'.... She might have been referring to the domestic intelligence service MI5 because, have no doubt, the Queen does not know of its secret work and darker practices, but she is aware of the power it is capable of wielding. Like the royal household, the intelligence services are given *carte blanche* to act in whatever way is considered to be in the best interests of state and monarchy....

"I have beaten myself up mentally many times over why I didn't ask her at the time what she meant." [328]

Paul Burrell, 27 Apr 06 Statement: **Jury Didn't Hear**:

"In my book I mention a discussion that I had with the Queen. I do not wish to talk about this further. It was private. However I will add that when she spoke about 'powers we know nothing about', I did not know to whom or what she referred and did not ask. You do not question the Queen when she talks to you as it is not my position to do so." [329]

Paul Burrell, Diana's Butler: 16 Jan 08: 143.23:

Burnett: Q. Do you remember having lunch with Mr Devorik and also Lady Bowker not very long after the Princess's death?

A. Yes, I do.

Q. I am not sure exactly when, but sometime after your conversation with the Queen?

A. Yes, I believe it was at Lady Elsa Bowker's apartment.

Q. Now, we have an account of that conversation from Mr Devorik....: "He ... told us about an audience he had had with the Queen."[a] Do you remember

---

[a] Up to this point Burrell had agreed with all of Devorik's recollections of the meeting:

From 144.8: Burnett: Q. I will do it bit by bit and ask you to confirm or tell us it's wrong and, if so, why: [Quoting from Devorik's statement]: "Following [Diana's] death, Lady Bowker and I, knowing how much the Princess respected him, invited Paul Burrell for lunch."

A. Yes, that's true.

Q. "Amongst other things, we wanted to make sure he was financially sound as Diana had mentioned in the past how poorly paid he was."

discussing the audience with Her Majesty –

A. Not at great length. I had told them that I had been to see the Queen. They were trusted, dear friends and I didn't see any harm in that.

Q. All right. I will read you the next two sentences in one go: "Lady Bowker asked him if he had asked the Queen if they killed her. He said that the Queen had replied to him something like 'We shouldn't awake forces we don't know'."

A. No, that's not true. I wouldn't ask a question such as that to Her Majesty.

Q. Let's just take it in stages, then. This is Mr Devorik not purporting to quote you precisely. He is giving what he recollects of the substance of a conversation that happened many, many years before. Did you discuss this subject at all with Mr Devorik and Lady Bowker, this part of – or aspect of the audience?

A. No, I would have remembered telling them that I had been lucky enough to meet Her Majesty at Buckingham Palace, but certainly I do not recognise that conversation. That did not happen.

Q. Now, I appreciate, Mr Burrell, that you worked very closely for Her Majesty for a number of years before you went into the service of the Prince and Princess of Wales. Is it conceivable that in your position you could ask a question of Her Majesty of that nature?

A. No. I wouldn't be so presumptuous.

Q. Did you ask her a question of that nature?

A. I did not.

Q. Now the reply that's recorded, "We shouldn't awake forces we don't know", first of all your evidence is that you didn't ask a question and you didn't get a reply.

A. No.... I would not ask Her Majesty the Queen such a personal, intimate question of her daughter-in-law.

Q. But if Mr Devorik is right at all about the discussion concerning the audience with Her Majesty, it would follow, wouldn't it, that you mentioned something of that part of the conversation that touched on "forces"?

A. That is true.

....Q. "Paul Burrell told me that he was concerned that the French had not found the white car ..."

A. Yes.

....Q. "... that [Burrell] had been told that the cameras on the tunnel were always working, but hadn't done so at the time of the crash."

....A. I was told that, yes.

....Q. "He was also concerned at the length of time it took for the ambulance to reach hospital."

A. Yes, I was.

A. There is a similarity, but remember, Mr Devorik has read my book since he made the statement.

Q. He might have done. I simply don't know.

A. I presume he has.

Roberto Devorik, Friend of Diana and Fashion Executive: 17 Jan 08: 161.11:

Hough: Q. Have you ever had cause to read Mr Burrell's books?

A. I bought them in – I live in the States. I bought them, I opened them and I closed them. Sorry.

Q. Did you cast your eyes over any pages before you closed them?

A. To be honest, no. The only book that I read thoroughly was Sally Bedell Smith, which was the first book ever written on the Princess after her death. Even Patrick Jephson, who I respect as a human being, I have it, but I never opened his book.

At 191.21: Q. A conversation you had with Paul Burrell at Lady Bowker's apartment after the Princess's death.

A. Correct.

Q. Do you remember a lunch with Mr Burrell?

A. Totally.

Q. Mr Burrell has already been asked about this and we have heard his evidence. He accepts that during lunch, as you say in your statement, he raised some concerns about the circumstances of the crash and you say that he then told you about an audience he had had with the Queen.

A. Correct.

....Q. What did [Burrell] say about the audience with the Queen?

A. He said that the Queen was very kindly to receive him and he was concerned about the whole thing went so quickly, so fast, blah, blah, blah, and he asked to the Queen her point of view. Precisely exactly the words I could not put in my mouth as I could on that day, but the sense was: we shouldn't disturb the forces we don't know or we shouldn't – something on the sort, told me Paul Burrell. I said to him, "What does it mean?" "That's what it means", he answers me, not to ask more questions.

Q. So can you remember at this time what the context for the Queen's remark was?

A. No, to be honest, no, because it was him with the Queen not me with the Queen. It was part of the conversation, as his financial situation, the funeral, the burial of the Princess, how her body was. We discussed many things over that lunch.

Q. No criticism of you, but just as you can't remember the context, you can't remember the precise words he used?

A. I think the words were like the Queen told him, "Let's not remove things" or something on the sort. "Let's not wake up forces we don't know or people we don't know" or something like on the sort. That's what he said to me. But I think – correct me if I am wrong – he said it in one of his appearances or whatever because I read it somewhere that he said it after he told me that. Then you can find it somewhere.

Q. Because Mr Burrell – and I have to put this to you as a matter of fairness – he recalls the lunch, but he says that you are wrong about him discussing the audience with the Queen and he suggests that perhaps you picked it up from his book, where it does appear, before you had that meeting.

A. No, he spoke that he went to see the Queen in front of Lady Bowker and myself, that's for sure, because I wouldn't know it if not.

At 195.19: Mansfield: Q. If you just follow [from your statement]: "He also told us about an audience he had with the Queen. Lady Bowker asked him if he had asked the Queen if they killed her. He said that the Queen had replied to him something like 'We shouldn't awake forces we don't know'." Do you follow?

A. Yes.

Q. You remember you have just been asked about the context. That was your recollection of the context in which Burrell was saying that the Queen had said something about not awaking forces. Is that right?

A. That was at the time what Paul Burrell mentioned to – because the question came from Lady Bowker, not from me.

Q. Quite. What he said is that he didn't say anything along these lines and that really you were saying that all because you had read it in his book.

A. I never read his book. I am sorry, I think he has mentioned me more in his life than me in his life. I am extremely sorry....

Paul Burrell: 13 Feb 08 Transcript of Meeting in a New York Hotel read out 6 Mar 08: 6.2:

Burrell: Perjury. Perjury is not a very nice thing to have to consider.

Contact: Not at all.... Do you think you committed perjury...?

Burrell: No, I didn't, I – well, I didn't tell the whole truth. When you swear on oath you swear an oath to tell the truth, the whole truth and nothing but the truth.... I told the truth as far as I could. But I didn't tell the whole truth.... But he put me in the most unenviable position the Coroner because he made me, he said to me I had to report the conversation I had with the Queen. That conversation was three hours long and I wasn't about to sit there and divulge everything she said to me. I wasn't going to do that. So I said, do I have to answer that question? And he said, yes you do. And I said, well. He said, what ... did the Queen say to you? I said, well she showed great concern. That was all I was prepared to say. And he still let me get away with it."

Robert Jobson, UK Journalist: 6 Nov 02 *Evening Standard* Article: **Jury Didn't Hear**:

Title: Queen and the Dark Forces.

"Serious questions are today being raised over the role of the intelligence services after butler Paul Burrell claimed the Queen warned him of 'powers at work' behind the scenes.

"Concern about possible covert surveillance of members of the royal family by MI5 and MI6 is mounting, after the former royal butler's claim that the Queen issued the warning to him in the course of a three-hour meeting.

"'Be careful Paul,' she told him, he claimed today. 'There are powers at work in this country about which we have no knowledge.'

"The possible allusion to 'dark forces' at work suggests the Queen was referring to the work of MI5 and MI6, the security intelligence services which have been accused of spying on the royal family.

"Claims of a pattern of covert and possibly unauthorised espionage against the most senior royals have been repeatedly made but widely dismissed as 'conspiracy theories'....

"Burrell made his potentially devastating claim as he told of the meeting between him and the Queen two months after Diana's death....

"'The Queen said, "Nobody, Paul, has been as close to a member of my family as you have",' Burrell told the *Daily Mirror*.[a] He claimed she followed this with the 'powers at work' warning, and he went on: 'She did not quantify it but she told me to be careful. She looked at me over her half-rimmed spectacles as if she expected me to know the rest. She fixed me with her eye and made sure I knew she was being deadly serious. I had no idea who she was talking about. There were many she could have been referring to. But she was clearly warning me to be vigilant. It was not a threat, it was sound advice. She had my interests at heart.'

"Palace sources have dismissed the idea that the Queen would discuss national security with Burrell and have claimed that his meeting with her lasted minutes, not the three hours he claims.[b] A senior member of the Royal

---

[a] The original article was in the *Mirror* which also quoted Burrell: "No-one had [ever] warned me like that. It made me suddenly realise the magnitude of the situation. It was obviously much, much bigger than I had ever thought.": Steve Dennis, Paul Burrell Revelations, *Daily Mirror*, 6 November 2002.

[b] Piers Morgan, the editor of *The Mirror*, the paper that conducted the Burrell interview, wrote in his 2005 book: "The BBC lunchtime news [on 6 November 2002] had Jennie Bond saying the Palace were dismissing Burrell's claims, saying the meeting with the Queen had been 'nearer three minutes than three hours'. The same line ran on the Press Association [PA] wire. I rang Penny Russell-Smith, the Queen's press secretary. 'This is outrageous and I'm not having it. Put out a correction on PA or you guys will regret it. Paul is not in the mood to be dicked around.'

"'What do you mean by that?' Penny asked.

"'I mean he can say a lot more than he intends to, including stuff about all you lot, so I would tread carefully.' She rang back fifteen minutes later to say PA were putting out a 'clarification'. 'What does it say?'

Household said: 'It is almost inconceivable that the Queen would discuss matters of national security such as the work of the secret services with a servant. This is the kind of subject she might discuss in total confidence with her Prime Minister, but not with a butler.'[a]

"Questions about the allegations are unlikely to go away, especially because of the claim that they come from the highest possible source." [330]

Comment: There are varying accounts of what the Queen said to Paul Burrell.

The evidence follows:

- Burrell: "'Be careful Paul,' [the Queen] told him ...'There are powers at work in this country about which we have no knowledge.'" – *Mirror* interview 6 November 2002

- Jobson: "the possible allusion to 'dark forces' at work suggests the Queen was referring to the work of MI5 and MI6" – article 6 November 2002

- Burrell: "I knew that people were listening to me and I know that people are watching me, and they are the forces to which Her Majesty referred" – interview, 27 May 2003

- Burrell: "the Queen said ... 'Be careful, Paul.... There are powers at work in this country about which we have no knowledge'" – in 2003 book[b], confirmed at inquest

- Burrell: "the Queen's subtle but clear warning to be careful about 'dark forces' at work in the country" – epilogue in 2004 revised edition of book

- Devorik: "Lady Bowker asked [Burrell] if he had asked the Queen if they killed her. He said that the Queen had replied to him something like 'We shouldn't awake forces we don't know'" – police statement, August 2005

- Devorik: "[Burrell] asked ... the Queen her point of view.... The sense was: 'we shouldn't disturb the forces we don't know'.... I said to him, 'What does it mean?' 'That's what it means', he answers me, not to ask more questions" – at inquest

---

"'It says that the meeting lasted up to an hour and a half, that is all our records can establish.'

"'Sorry, no good. I will accept "at least an hour and a half", but not "up to".'

"Ten minutes later, a clarification of the clarification ran on PA – an unprecedented climbdown by the Palace. They are terrified.": *The Insider*, pp361-2.

[a] This is based on the publicised Burrell account of the Queen's statement. It will be shown that Devorik's version is more accurate. That account could be viewed as primarily a discouragement to action – "we shouldn't awake forces" – rather than a discussion on "matters of national security".

[b] The book *A Royal Duty* was published in October 2003.

- Devorik: "the Queen told [Burrell],'Let's not remove things' or something [like], 'Let's not wake up forces we don't know or people we don't know'" – at inquest
- Fellowes: "as a figure of speech, it is very unlike [the Queen] to use terms like 'forces' or 'dark forces'" – at inquest.

There is a huge conflict between Paul Burrell and Roberto Devorik.

The differences in their evidence are:

1) Burrell is saying that the Queen gave him a warning – "Be careful Paul" – and it was not prompted by any question or remark from him.

Devorik – who was told by Burrell about the Queen-Burrell meeting at a luncheon "not very long after the Princess's death"[a] – has said that Burrell indicated to him that the Queen's remark was in response to a question or comment from Burrell.

2) Devorik's account directly connects the Queen's statement to the Paris crash. He says: "Bowker asked [Burrell] if he had asked the Queen if they killed her".

Burrell admits that the Queen's statement was in the context of the crash – "the context of it was the death of [Diana] and the aftermath ... [and] the circumstances ... and how things were to be carried forward"[b] – but the connection is not as direct.

3) Burrell has used the term "dark forces" – this is addressed below. Devorik only used the word "forces" – not "dark".

4) The key part of Burrell's main account is: "there are powers at work in this country about which we have no knowledge".

The key part of Devorik's main account is: "we shouldn't awake forces we don't know".

These two accounts have similarities and differences:

---

[a] That timing was confirmed by Burrell at the inquest. Given that the meeting with the Queen occurred 3½ months after the crash, this infers that the luncheon must have been fairly soon after Burrell's conversation with the Queen. Burnett asked Burrell: "I am not sure exactly when, but sometime after your conversation with the Queen?" but Burrell replied: "Yes", without providing anything further. Devorik was not asked about the timing. In his statement, Devorik described the reason for the luncheon, which was organised by Elsa Bowker and himself: "Amongst other things, we wanted to make sure [Burrell] was financially sound as Diana had mentioned in the past how poorly paid he was." Given that the concern about Burrell's finances probably would have been as a result of Diana's death, this would confirm that the luncheon is likely to have occurred fairly soon after the Burrell meeting with the Queen.
[b] Confirmed to Croxford.

a) Both Burrell and Devorik specify ignorance of the powers or forces – Devorik: "we don't know"; Burrell: "we have no knowledge".[a]

b) Burrell has "in this country", whereas Devorik's has no mention of a region.

c) Burrell says "powers at work"; Devorik says "forces".[b]

d) Burrell's is a statement indicating a belief by the Queen – "there are powers at work" – whereas Devorik's is a statement apparently aimed at discouraging action – "we shouldn't awake forces".

I suggest that point d is the most significant difference – this is discussed below.

The analysis of this evidence is difficult because Paul Burrell is a particularly unreliable witness – he has been shown to have lied in Part 2 and has admitted that he failed to tell the whole truth at the inquest (see above).

On the other hand, Roberto Devorik is an Argentinian fashion designer who was a friend of Princess Diana – he has no apparent reason to lie.[c]

The fact that Devorik has provided an account of the Queen's statement is what gives Burrell credibility – it removes the possibility that Burrell could have completely made this statement by the Queen up, for publicity or other purposes. In other words, Devorik's evidence – even though it conflicts with Burrell's – shows that the Queen did say something significant to Burrell.

The question is: What did the Queen say?

It is significant that during Burrell's cross-examination, he concurred with everything he was asked about out of Devorik's statement[d] – the invite details, the reason for the lunch, discussion about "the white car"[e], the tunnel cameras not working, the time-consuming ambulance trip, the Queen-Burrell meeting – until it came to the Queen's statement.

Burrell's reaction to Devorik's account of the Queen's statement is: "No, that's not true." Then he adds: "I wouldn't ask a question such as that to Her Majesty".[f]

---

[a] It may be significant that when Burrell was interviewed by the police all he admitted to was: "powers we know nothing about" – that is the main area of agreement between Devorik's and Burrell's account.

[b] Burrell has also said "forces" in another account – but not in his main account that he has consistently repeated. See above and below.

[c] Unfortunately Devorik does not appear to have strong English – it may be his second language – and this has to be considered when reviewing his testimony.

[d] See earlier footnote.

[e] This is the white Fiat Uno – see Part 1.

[f] With Burnett's help, this was Burrell's key argument – that he wouldn't have put a question like Bowker's to the Queen – "I wouldn't ask a question such as that to Her Majesty"; "I wouldn't be so presumptuous"; "I did not ... ask her a question of that

The question Burrell is referring to is: "Lady Bowker asked [Burrell] if he had asked the Queen if they killed her."

Devorik doesn't actually say that Burrell said he asked the Queen that specific question. Devorik says: "Lady Bowker asked [Burrell] if he had asked the Queen".

Devorik then says: "He said that the Queen had replied...."

Putting oneself in the position of Burrell, who had just recently lost his boss – Princess Diana – who he was close to, I suggest there has to be a possibility that Burrell did ask the Queen a question about the crash. He could have asked something like: "Do you think Princess Diana was murdered?" [a]

It is significant that at that time Burrell admits to having concerns along those lines. The inquest lawyer, Jonathon Hough, said to Devorik: "[Burrell] raised some concerns about the circumstances of the crash". That is what the Devorik statement shows, and that is confirmed by Burrell at the inquest – the list of concerns is shown above.[bc]

Burnett puts to Burrell that Devorik's account would indicate "that you mentioned [to Bowker and Devorik] something of that part of the conversation that touched on 'forces'?" Burrell replies: "There is a similarity, but remember, Mr Devorik has read my book since he made the statement."

This comment doesn't make sense. Burrell suggests Devorik read his book since the police statement – it is possible Burrell meant to suggest Devorik read the book before making his statement.[d]

Devorik denied reading Burrell's book, but even if he had, there is no logical explanation for why he would have changed Burrell's account of his conversation with the Queen. Devorik has no known motive to lie about this.

It is common sense that Burrell raised the subject of the meeting with the Queen at the luncheon – Burrell and Devorik both concur on that point.[e] I suggest that it is also common sense that once Burrell had divulged that information, then there would inevitably be an expectation that Burrell would tell them some of what transpired during such a significant meeting. It is natural that Bowker and Devorik could have had questions about what the Queen had said to Burrell.

---

nature"; "I would not ask Her Majesty the Queen such a personal, intimate question of her daughter-in-law".

[a] Burrell also could have made a comment about the crash – maybe saying he had concerns – that the Queen replied to.

[b] The detail is shown in the earlier footnote.

[c] There is a possibility that Burrell's concerns had increased after hearing the Queen's comment – and that is when he met with Devorik and Bowker.

[d] The book was published in 2003 and Devorik's statement was taken in 2005.

[e] Devorik: "[Burrell] ... told us about an audience he had had with the Queen"; Burrell: "I had told them that I had been to see the Queen".

This is indicated in Devorik's account, but it appears to be missing in Burrell's.

Burnett asked: "Do you remember discussing the audience with Her Majesty – ". Burrell cut Burnett off mid-question: "Not at great length. I had told them that I had been to see the Queen. They were trusted, dear friends and I didn't see any harm in that."

That answer then indicates that it was just, "I ... told them that I had been to see the Queen" – and that is the end of that subject in the conversation and there is no further discussion about it.

So Burrell is not saying "Yes, I did tell them about the 'powers at work' comment, but Devorik has remembered it wrongly".

Instead Burrell is saying that the topic of what the Queen said – warning to Burrell, or comment on the crash – did not come up. Burrell appears to also suggest that nothing at all of what the Queen said was discussed at the lunch.[a]

Burrell then effectively alleges that Devorik has taken what he says from his book[b], but has changed it to a question and answer related directly to the crash, and has submitted that in a signed statement to Scotland Yard.

Given that Burrell appears unable to provide a motive for why Devorik would do this[c], I suggest that it is unlikely – i.e. it is unlikely that Devorik would have done all of the following: a) read Burrell's book; b) deliberately changed Burrell's account; c) pretended that Burrell had told him this at the lunch; then d) put this falsification into a signed police statement as part of the investigation into the death of his friend, Princess Diana.

Devorik's statement account is fairly short and I suggest it has possibly been abbreviated – either by Devorik or the police. There are just two steps:

- the question from Bowker to Burrell: "Lady Bowker asked him if he had asked the Queen if they killed her"

- the reply from the Queen to Burrell: "the Queen had replied to [Burrell] something like 'We shouldn't awake forces we don't know'".

I suggest there is a step missing: the question or comment Burrell put to the Queen.[da]

---

[a] Burrell should have been challenged on this and asked specifically what he remembers was said at the luncheon about the audience with the Queen.
[b] Burrell made this allegation even though he didn't actually know whether Devorik had read his book – he said: "I presume he has".
[c] There is no record or suggestion of any falling out between Burrell and Devorik – certainly not pre-Paget or pre-inquest.
[d] This would have been what generated the Queen's response. In Devorik's statement all we are given is the question Bowker asked Burrell, but Burrell's communication to the Queen is possibly more significant.

Devorik was asked more about this at the inquest. He said: "[Burrell] asked to the Queen her point of view".

I suggest this is the step that is missing from the statement.

So from Devorik's evidence we can put forward a possible scenario of what was said at the Bowker-Devorik-Burrell lunch:

Bowker asks Burrell "if he had asked the Queen if they[b] killed her". Burrell says that "he asked ... the Queen [for] her point of view" regarding whether it was murder. Burrell then "said that the Queen had replied to him something like 'We shouldn't awake forces we don't know'." Devorik asks Burrell,[c] "What does [that] mean?" Burrell replies "That's what it means". Burrell tells Devorik and Bowker "not to ask more questions" about it.

This indicates that Burrell was uncomfortable about that subject – the Queen's comment.

The evidence shows that Burrell was the one who was raising the issues during the lunch conversation: "the white car", the tunnel cameras not working, the time-consuming ambulance trip, the Queen-Burrell meeting – all of these topics were initiated by Burrell.[d] But when it came to the Queen's significant statement, that is not initiated by Burrell – that instead arises out of the question from Bowker.

The indication is that if Bowker hadn't asked Burrell the question then he may not have divulged the Queen's statement. Devorik's recall that Burrell told them "not to ask more questions" confirms that he was uncomfortable around that issue.

The Queen's statement – "we shouldn't awake forces we don't know"[e] – is significant, for several reasons:

-   it indicates the Queen could be aware that Diana was murdered
-   it indicates a desire by the Queen to cover it up
-   it appears to be intended to discourage Burrell from attempting to establish what actually happened[f].

---

[a] There are also a couple of other steps at the end of the lunch conversation that have been missed in the statement but are in Devorik's inquest account. These are included in the scenario below.

[b] No lawyer asked Devorik who "they" were, but the context infers that Bowker was referring to either the royal family or British intelligence. There were early allegations that the royal family were behind the Paris crash. Libyan leader, Muammar Gaddafi, "pointed the finger at Britain's royal family" in a 23 September 1997 TV interview. Source: Ghadafi Now Blames Royals, Earlier Tied Agents to Death of Diana, *Philadelphia Daily News*, 24 September 1997.

[c] What follows is from Devorik's inquest account – see earlier.

[d] See earlier footnote which shows the transcript of this.

[e] As recalled by Devorik.

[f] In this sense, it could be viewed as a warning to Burrell to just leave the issue of Diana's death alone.

The question then is: Why would the Queen say something like this? [a]

I suggest it indicates one of two possibilities:

1) that the Queen was not involved in the assassinations, but knows who was and does not want them to be held accountable for it – in other words, the Queen wants it covered up

2) the Queen herself was involved in the assassinations and she is discouraging Burrell from seeking the truth.[bc]

Why did Burrell change the wording of the Queen's statement?

The timing is a key factor in Burrell's actions. Burrell publicly kept "mum" on the whole subject of the Queen's comment, until after the Queen had publicly confirmed that there was a meeting with Burrell in the aftermath of the crash. This occurred just before – and in fact triggered – the 1 November 2002 collapse of the trial of Paul Burrell on charges of theft of Princess Diana's possessions.[d]

Within a week Burrell had done a major interview with the *Daily Mirror*.[e] It was during this interview, on 6 November 2002, that Burrell divulged for the first time his account of the Queen's "powers at work" statement.

---

[a] Devorik is not saying these are the exact words, but it was words to that effect. Those words are from his earliest recall, which was the August 2005 statement, over 7½ years after the lunch. Devorik's inquest testimony wasn't until another almost 2½ years later, in January 2008. I suggest that it is most unlikely that Devorik would have remembered the precise words, and he admits this several times – "something like" (statement); "precisely exactly the words I could not put in my mouth as I could on that day, but the sense was"; "something [of] the sort" (twice); "I think the words were like" – but the general sentiment of a statement of this significance directly attributed to a person of the Queen's stature would not be difficult to remember. It is the sentiment that is important, not the exact words.

[b] It's interesting that in the initial November 2002 interview, when Burrell first went public with this, he said: "It was not a threat, it was sound advice." The question is: Why would anyone introduce the possibility of this statement being a threat, unless they believed the Queen either had knowledge or was herself involved?

[c] In his book Burrell says that the Queen's statement occurred "as the meeting neared its end". It is possible that the Queen could have been displeased with the comment or question from Burrell that triggered her statement, and terminated the meeting.

[d] The Queen said that she recalled a meeting with Burrell where he told her he was keeping Diana's possessions safe. It is not the purpose of this book to cover the detail surrounding that trial and its collapse – a lot of it is in the public domain in media articles. Part 6 does address some aspects of the trial evidence that are relevant to this case.

[e] Burrell was apparently paid £300,000 for this interview.: I'm Still Loyal to the Royals, Says Butler, IOL News, 21 November 2002.

It could be significant that the wording of what Burrell said, at that interview, the Queen told him – "be careful Paul, there are powers at work in this country about which we have no knowledge" – is identical to what was written in Burrell's book that was published 11 months later.[a]

It has been reported that in the same interview Burrell said that he "remained loyal to the royal family".[331]

There is a possibility that Burrell publicised this statement because it could be seen to increase his standing – the Queen has confided to him a statement of some significance. The statement – as reported by Burrell – is not as significant as what the Queen actually appears to have said (see above), but I suggest that it was not in Burrell's interests to reveal the actual statement.

I suggest Burrell had three options:

a) tell the truth publicly of what the Queen had said

b) adjust the Queen's statement to: i) make it of high interest[b], but ii) protect the Queen[c], and iii) enhance Burrell's public standing

c) omit the Queen's statement and not make it public.

I suggest Burrell chose option b. In so doing, he misled the public, protected the Queen and enhanced his standing as the revealer of a mysterious comment made by the Queen, the highest ranked resident in the country.

This was not the only time Paul Burrell has tried to prevent the full truth being made public, in order to protect the royals.

On 20 October 2003 Burrell publicly released Princess Diana's 1995[d] note to him through *The Mirror* newspaper – but it was amended. *The Mirror* editor, Piers Morgan, said in his 2005 book: "The letter[e] says 'Charles is planning an "accident" in my car, so he can marry again', but Burrell has insisted we alter the wording so Charles is not branded an assassin." [332f]

---

[a] In October 2003.

[b] The adjusted statement has a certain mystery about it – what are the "powers at work"?

[c] The true statement could be seen as implicating the Queen – see above.

[d] Burrell claimed that it was written in 1996, but it was shown in Part 2 to be from 1995.

[e] Burrell refers to it as a letter to himself, but it is not addressed to Burrell – it is a note that Diana gave to Burrell for safe-keeping. This is addressed in Part 2.

[f] In Burrell's 2003 book, he produced a transcript of the letter, but in place of the words "my husband" wrote: "[The princess then identified where she felt the threat and danger would come from]".: *A Royal Duty*, p322.

On 5 January 2004, Piers Morgan publicly named Charles as the person Diana was referring to. Morgan said it was because "Burrell has been asked to hand over all his evidence, including the letter, to the investigating authorities. This means ... it will inevitably leak." Morgan said Burrell "went potty" when told Charles would be publicly named.: *The Insider*, pp431-2.

The note, in the form Burrell first made it public, is shown below.

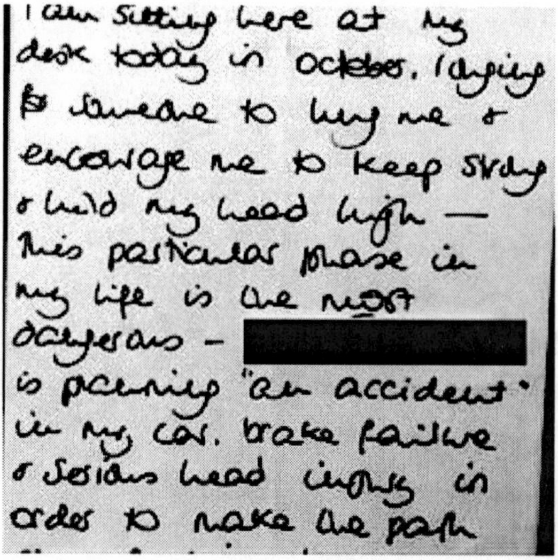

I am sitting here at my desk today in October, longing for someone to hug me & encourage me to keep strong & hold my head high — this particular phase in my life is the most dangerous — [redacted] is planning "an accident" in my car, brake failure & serious head injury in order to make the path

Figure 11

The Burrell Note as it was first made public by Paul Burrell in October 2003.

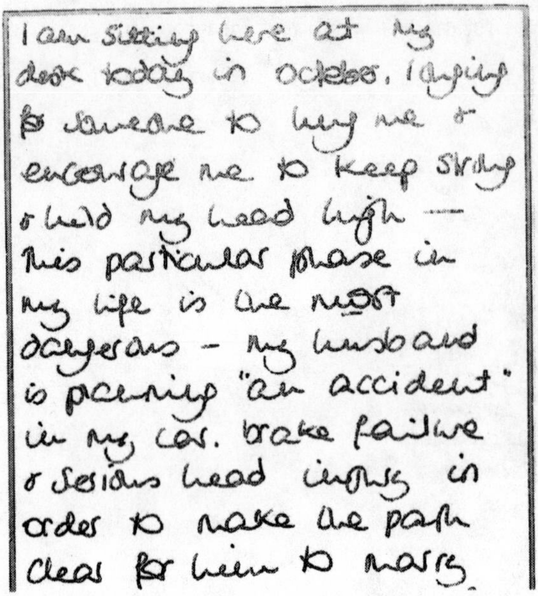
I am sitting here at my
desk today in October, longing
for someone to hug me &
encourage me to keep strong
& hold my head high —
this particular phase in
my life is the most
dangerous - my husband
is planning "an accident"
in my car. brake failure
& serious head injury in
order to make the path
clear for him to marry.

Figure 12

The Burrell Note excerpt in its undoctored state. In the image shown above Burrell had blanked out "my husband" and cut out the line saying "clear for him to marry". A fuller image of the note has been shown in Part 2.

When royal correspondent Robert Jobson wrote up the *Mirror* interview, he apparently decided to add an extra dimension to Burrell's comments. Not quoting Burrell, Jobson wrote: "The possible allusion to 'dark forces' at work suggests the Queen was referring to the work of MI5 and MI6".[a]

Jobson replaced "powers at work" with "dark forces at work".

I suggest that at some stage Paul Burrell read Jobson's article in the *Evening Standard*, and must have liked it. Because when the revised edition of Burrell's book *A Royal Duty* was published in 2004, he included that very term in connection with the Queen's statement – "the Queen's subtle but clear warning to be careful about dark forces at work in the country".

Then four years later, when Burrell is on the stand at the inquest into the death of his boss, he is asked by Burnett: "Is ['dark forces'] a phrase you have ever used?" and Burrell lies:[b] "I have never used that word."

When Mansfield, on the following day, reads out the relevant excerpt from his book, Burrell states: "That's an error". Mansfield asks: "Whose error

---

[a] In another part of the article Jobson had correctly quoted Burrell – see earlier transcript.

[b] Burrell has been shown to be a liar earlier and in Part 2.

would that be?" But Burrell doesn't answer that question – instead he says: "The Queen never mentioned 'dark forces'".

I suggest that the reason Burrell didn't say whose error it was – normally, publisher or author – is because it was not actually an error at all.[a] I suggest that Burrell had already changed the statement the Queen made – see earlier – and now it was no problem at all for him to latch onto Jobson's phrase, "dark forces".

Hough told Devorik: "I have to put this to you as a matter of fairness: [Burrell] ... says that you are wrong about him discussing the audience with the Queen and he suggests that perhaps you picked it up from his book ... before you had that meeting".[b]

There are two problems with this.

First, Hough has lied when he states: "[Burrell] ... says that you are wrong about him discussing the audience with the Queen" at the lunch.

Burrell said: "I had told them that I had been to see the Queen"; "I would have remembered telling them that I had been lucky enough to meet Her Majesty at Buckingham Palace".

These comments from Burrell are the opposite of what Hough has put to Devorik. Burrell admits talking about the audience with the Queen, whereas Hough indicated to Devorik that Burrell had said the audience with the Queen wasn't discussed.

Second, Hough told Devorik that Burrell "suggests that perhaps you picked [the audience with the Queen] up from his book".

This, again, is not what Burrell said.

Burrell did say, "Mr Devorik has read my book since he made the statement"[c], but the context was about what Burrell had told Devorik and Bowker at the lunch – not a suggestion that Devorik learned about the audience with the Queen from the book.[d]

Hough's false comments appear to be an attempt to undermine Devorik's evidence.[e]

---

[a] Devorik uses the word "forces" in his evidence, but not "dark". This is not particularly significant because Devorik has never claimed that each word is accurate – see earlier. Devorik's evidence is that he has given the "sense" of the statement made.

[b] It is not known what Hough is referring to by "that meeting". The suggestion from Burrell was that Devorik had read his book before he gave his Paget statement.

[c] Burrell said this without knowing whether it was true or not – see earlier.

[d] Burrell had already said he told Devorik and Bowker about the audience at the lunch – see above.

[e] This fits with pressure Hough applied to Devorik regarding his failure to precisely remember the exact words of the Queen's statement, even though Devorik was trying

It is Burrell's evidence that the Queen – at the end of her statement – asked him: "Do you understand?"

Burrell has since indicated that he didn't understand. One could then ask: Why didn't Burrell simply take the Queen up on this and ask her what she meant?

Burrell appears to have provided conflicting positions on why he didn't do that:

- "I have beaten myself up mentally many times over why I didn't ask [the Queen] at the time what she meant" – in 2003 book
- "you do not question the Queen when she talks to you as it is not my position to do so" – 2006 statement
- "one doesn't ask the Queen what she means by something" – inquest in 2008.

To the public, in his book, Burrell has indicated that he could have asked the Queen "at the time what she meant".

Yet, just three years later, in his police statement Burrell has changed his position on that – asking the Queen was now no longer an option: "you do not question the Queen". And he carried this same argument through to the 2008 inquest.

When Burrell first went public with this – in the November 2002 *Mirror* interview – he said: "[The Queen] looked at me over her half-rimmed spectacles as if she expected me to know the rest. She fixed me with her eye and made sure I knew she was being deadly serious. I had no idea who she was talking about."

11 months later, in the published book, this has changed to: "[The Queen] fixed me with a stare where her eyes made clear the 'Do you understand?'"

Burrell says that the Queen specifically asked him: "Do you understand?" But Burrell has never said what his reply to that question was.[a]

The "Do you understand?" fits okay with his book explanation for not finding out what the Queen meant – "I have beaten myself up mentally many times over why I didn't ask". In other words: "why didn't I answer 'no' to the 'do you understand?'"

But I suggest that Burrell's explanations to the police and inquest – "you do not question the Queen" – do not fit at all with the "Do you understand?"

---

to recall something that happened about 10 years previously – "So can you remember at this time what the context for the Queen's remark was?"; "No criticism of you, but just as you can't remember the context, you can't remember the precise words he used?". As discussed earlier, the key issue is the sentiment, not necessarily the exact words used.

[a] In Burrell's book, which is the fuller account, immediately after "Do you understand?", he starts a new paragraph, quoting the Queen: "Well, it has been fascinating talking to you again, Paul....": Paul Burrell, A Royal Duty, p318.

The point being that Burrell did not have to question the Queen, because she had put the question to him. All Burrell had to say was "No".

Burrell told the inquest, "one doesn't ask the Queen what she means by something", and the police, "it is not my position to do so".

Burrell had worked directly as footman for the Queen for ten years[a]. I suggest that if none of the people who work for the Queen – and there are around 1,200 in her household[333] – are able to "ask the Queen what she means by something" she says, then things would be very difficult at Buckingham Palace.

This is further evidence indicating that the statement made by the Queen was not the mysterious one that Burrell has promoted to the world – but instead was in response to a question or comment from Burrell and is along the lines of what Devorik said: "We shouldn't awake forces we don't know".

I suggest it was primarily a warning to Burrell to just leave the whole issue of Diana's death alone.

This also appears to fit with the: "Do you understand?" – the Queen ensuring Burrell has clearly received her message.

Mansfield quoted from Burrell's 2004 book:[b] "I was armed with a chilling letter in the Princess's hand[c] and clear advice from the Monarch. As a married man with two children, it hardly made me want to rush to the authorities, hand [the letter] over and expect an immediate inquiry to be announced. Make no mistake, had I handed that letter to Buckingham Palace, St James's Palace or the Metropolitan Police, the Princess's fears would never have been made public."

The key point here is that in his mind Burrell has linked the Queen's comment with the Burrell Note – which is Diana's written prediction that she could be involved in a car crash. This link becomes more evident when one realises that Devorik's account is the truer version of what the Queen actually said.

In the middle of reading this quote, Mansfield stopped and asked Burrell: "The letter that you had ... you clearly had connected with what had happened in Paris, hadn't you?" Burrell replied: "Yes, I had."

I suggest that it is just as significant that the context also appears to indicate that Burrell saw a clear connection between the Queen's comment and the crash – and this is made particularly obvious when Devorik's account is studied.[d]

---

[a] Between 1977 and 1987, when he was transferred to the Wales' household.
[b] The revised version.
[c] This is the Burrell Note – see Part 2. Burrell refers to it as a letter, but it is not a letter – it is a note.
[d] As has been done in this section.

The evidence indicates that Burrell held onto the Note until 2003 – and kept publicly quiet about the Queen's statement until late-2002 – at least partly out of fear: "as a married man with two children, it hardly made me want to rush to the authorities".

I suggest that Burrell's overall position comes across as being conflicted. He evidently felt a strong loyalty to Princess Diana when she was alive, and it is also clear – see earlier – that he had concerns about the nature of the crash.[a] Yet, despite all this, Burrell emerges loyal to and protective of the Queen. There is a possibility that Burrell has taken this approach – despite his concerns – because he is fearful of consequences if he doesn't.[b]

At one stage Burnett – in the context of the Queen's statement to Burrell – asked Burrell: "Of course if you knew anything that suggested that Dodi and the Princess had been murdered – ". Burrell doesn't let Burnett finish: "Yes, I would have to say".

Burrell has jumped to the conclusion that Burnett was going to suggest Burrell would have to speak up if he knew anything. This indicates that Burrell is nervous around this subject.

Burrell had jumped to the wrong conclusion – Burnett then finished the question: "But if you knew anything of that sort, then perhaps you do need to be careful." [c]

---

[a] Burrell was asked about this at the inquest:
At 16 Jan 08: 9.12: Mansfield: Q. May 2003, on 27th May, you appeared on television with Piers Morgan.... Mr Morgan said: "You don't subscribe to the theory that it was just a simple accident?" Then you answer: "I think there is more to it. I think there is really more to it, but I do not have the information to be able to judge that."
A. Yes.
Q. First of all, did you say that?
A. Yes, I did.
Q.... I want to, if I may, ask you whether that observation you still adhere to, that it wasn't a simple accident?
A. As I have said before, I do not feel that I have all the information to be able to judge that statement properly.
Q. All right. So it's a feeling that you had at the time of the programme?
A. I know what I witnessed on that dreadful day in Paris. I was there. I saw it. I was present.
Q. Yes?
A. I know what the Princess told me before she died because I was very close to her. But I don't know what happened in Paris and it would be very foolish of me to even guess or assume what happened in Paris.
[b] In this context it should be noted that Burrell moved to the USA in 2005.
[c] At this point, Burnett asked: "Do you follow me?" and Burrell answered: "I do, yes, but I don't." This is not clarified, but it is possible Burrell was saying: "I do follow you, but I don't know anything indicating Diana was murdered."

Burnett continued: "But you don't know anything of that sort? You know nothing, then, do you, to support the suggestion that they were murdered?"

Burrell's answer to this is significant: "No. It's – I cannot begin to believe that. Knowing the members of the Royal Family as I do and knowing them so well, I think that's impossible."

The point here is that Burnett had made no mention of the royal family – that has been introduced by Burrell in his answer.

Burnett's question is simple: "You know nothing ... to support the suggestion that they were murdered?" This has nothing to do with the royal family – this is straightforward: Does Burrell know anything that could indicate Diana and Dodi were murdered?

In Burrell's mind, he appears to have converted this question to: "Do you know anything to support the suggestion that the royal family murdered Diana and Dodi?"

Our question though is: Why has Burrell done this?

I suggest that Burrell's answers – this one and the earlier instance where he interrupted the question – indicate that he is nervous around this and could be hiding information. In other words, Burrell could have knowledge that he has not told the inquest. That notion is supported by Burrell's New York Hotel "interview": "I didn't tell the whole truth".

It may be that the true statement by the Queen – which Burrell withheld from the inquest – may have: a) raised or strengthened suspicions in Burrell about the real nature of the crash; or b) made Burrell suspicious that the Queen knew something sinister about the crash – and could have been involved in it or could be covering up for others.[a]

Coroner: Summing Up: 1 Apr 08: 5.16:

"Burrell's recollection of what the Queen said to him was, 'Be careful, Paul, no one has been as close to a member of my family as you have. There are powers at work in this country of which we have no knowledge. Do you understand?' He said he thought it was a 'be careful' warning over many issues. He had a lot of private information about many members of the Royal Family; it was just a kindness, a 'be careful along your way'. The phrase 'dark forces' was never used.

"Members of the jury, assuming something like those words were said, you may think it stretches one's imagination to breaking point to conclude that they have the remotest thing to do with a staged collision in a tunnel three and a half months before. I ruled that Her Majesty the Queen should not be

---

[a] This should be viewed in the light of the earlier evidence indicating that Burrell has significantly changed the content of the Queen's statement to him.

questioned on this and other matters, just as the Duke of Edinburgh should not be called to give oral evidence to you in this court.[a]"

Comment: The above is Baker's complete comments on this subject in his Summing Up.

What Baker says raises several serious concerns:

1) Baker has completely omitted Devorik's evidence.

There are two witnesses regarding the Queen's statement to Burrell – Burrell and Devorik – yet in his Summing Up, Baker has chosen to only record the evidence from one, Burrell.

The previous day[b] Baker had told the jury: "You will probably want to take with a pinch of salt many things that [Burrell] said in evidence because of the inconsistencies and, you may think, lies in what he told you, but that does not mean that nothing that he said can be of any value." [334]

Then[c] about four minutes before Baker covered Burrell's account of the Queen's statement – shown above – he launched a more comprehensive attack on Burrell's credibility.[d] Baker told the jury: "How should you approach [Burrell's] evidence, you may ask. You heard him in the witness box, and even without what he said subsequently in the hotel room in New York[e], it was <u>blindingly obvious,</u> wasn't it, that the evidence that he gave in this courtroom was not the truth, the whole truth and nothing but the truth? ... You may think that a thread running through his evidence was the impression that he thought he was giving and a consideration of the impact whatever he said might have on any of his future enterprises.... You may think that he is rather bitter about having been prosecuted.[f] It may be that having heard him give evidence in this court, you are left with a concern about whether what, if anything, he told you can be believed. I advise you to proceed with caution, especially when and if you are left with the impression that he only told you what he wanted you to hear.... The fact that he has not told the truth on some occasions does not mean that you cannot accept anything he has told you, but you should, as I say, proceed with caution." [335]

It has already been shown that – in the context of establishing who was behind the crash – the Queen's statement to Burrell could be significant.

Baker carried out two important actions:

---

[a] This failure to call members of the royal family is addressed in a later section in this chapter.

[b] 31 March 2008 – the Summing Up went on for 2½ days.

[c] On the next day, 1 April 2008.

[d] I am not suggesting Burrell is a credible witness – I am simply recording what occurred.

[e] An excerpt of that has been shown earlier.

[f] This is a reference to the trial over stealing Diana's possessions, which collapsed in early November 2002 – see earlier.

a) Baker completely undermined Burrell's credibility just four minutes before he presented Burrell's account of the Queen's statement[a]

b) Baker omitted Devorik's entire evidence on the Queen's statement.

These actions need to be viewed in concert.

Taken together, these manoeuvres by Baker have essentially removed any possibility that something of significance had been said by the Queen to Burrell.

Baker had the evidence of both witnesses, but with a major conflict between the two – see earlier.

It is not that Baker had a choice about whether to remind the jury about Burrell's or Devorik's evidence. There is no choice. If Baker was to provide an honest and balanced Summing Up – and that is his primary responsibility – then he had to include the accounts of both Burrell and Devorik.

Baker chose to reveal only the evidence from Burrell – the very person he had strongly indicated was dishonest – and deliberately omitted the evidence of Devorik, who was a credible witness.

The Queen's statement has been shown to be a key issue[b] – Baker should have given the jury both accounts and the fact he didn't is further evidence that he is a corrupt judge.

2) Baker said: "The phrase 'dark forces' was never used."

That is a lie.

It had already been shown that Burrell said in the epilogue to the 2004 revised edition[c] of his book: "the Queen's subtle but clear warning to be careful about dark forces at work in the country".

And that was addressed by Michael Mansfield at the inquest – see earlier.

Burrell did say at the inquest: "The Queen never mentioned 'dark forces'."[d] But Baker failed – I suggest deliberately – to point out that Burrell has provided conflicting accounts on this.[e]

3) Even though Baker only covered Burrell's account, he failed to include critical aspects of his evidence:

a) Baker missed out Burrell's reference to the Queen saying "dark forces" – see point 2 above

b) Baker missed out Burrell's references to the Queen meaning the "powers at work" being "media bosses and their editors ... the establishment generally ... or the security service" – confirmed to Burnett

---

[a] Baker reinforces this with: "assuming something like those words were said".

[b] See earlier.

[c] It was incorrectly stated at the inquest to be the American edition – see earlier.

[d] Burrell also said, "I have never used that word", referring to "dark forces" – that was shown to be false (see earlier).

[e] The issue of use of the term "dark forces" has been addressed earlier.

c) Baker missed out Burrell's: "There are people listening to my telephone conversations.... I knew that people were listening to me and I know that people are watching me, and they are the forces to which Her Majesty referred" – confirmed to Mansfield.

Instead Baker focused on Burrell's most innocuous evidence: "[Burrell] said he thought it was a 'be careful' warning over many issues.... It was just a kindness, a 'be careful along your way'."

Burrell has provided several conflicting possibilities of what the Queen was referring to – yet Baker basically focused on the one.

In doing this, Baker misled his own jury.

4) After misrepresenting Burrell's evidence and omitting Devorik's altogether, Baker then landed his knock-out punch to the evidence on the Queen's statement to Burrell: "Members of the jury, <u>assuming</u> something like those words were said, you may think it <u>stretches one's imagination to breaking point</u> to conclude that they have <u>the remotest thing</u> to do with a staged collision in a tunnel three and a half months before."

The evidence indicates that the message from the Queen was different to what Burrell has stated – see Devorik earlier – and the inquest did hear the words spoken. Those words[a] – in response to a question or comment from Burrell[b] – did clearly relate directly "with a staged collision in a tunnel three and a half months before".

Through his deft and dishonest manipulation of the jury, Baker was able to turn the evidence upside down and probably had the courtroom believing his emotive argument – "it stretches one's imagination to breaking point" – that the Queen's statement to Burrell had not "the remotest thing" to do with the Paris assassinations.

By the time Baker had finished – the removal of Burrell's credibility; the omission of Devorik's evidence; the omission of much of Burrell's evidence; drawing of manipulative conclusions – any possible link between the Queen's statement to Burrell and the Paris crash was dead and buried.[c]

Yet, I suggest, the actual evidence – see earlier – indicates that nothing could have been further from the truth.

---

[a] Along the lines of: "We shouldn't awake forces we don't know".

[b] This has been covered earlier.

[c] Next Baker stretched his strategy to justify his decision not to call the Queen to give evidence – "I ruled that Her Majesty the Queen should not be questioned on this". This is covered later.

Other Evidence

Arson Attack Against Burrell

Paul Burrell, Diana's Butler: 16 Jan 08: 57.19:

Mansfield: Q. You or your business were the subject of an attack, weren't you?

A. Yes, we were.

Q.... You say to Mr [Piers] Morgan [in May 2003[a]]: "The arson attack literally finished the business because we had to close it because of all the smoke damage and fire damage. Unfortunately the police were not able to find out who did it, but it was a little more sinister than we first thought because they told us it was a device that was pushed through the window, not just a piece of paper lit." Did you say that?

A. I did say that.

Q. Is that the truth?

A. That is the truth.

Q. A device. Now, can you help us, what was the device?

A. It wasn't explained to me. The way it was explained was it was not just a piece of lit paper through the letter box.

Q. Right. When did it happen, just roughly?

A. I am not very good with dates.

Q. All right. Can you give us a year, maybe? The interview is May 2003. You have had the trial in 2002.

A. Yes.

Q. You have had the arrest in 2001. So is it after the trial?

A. After the trial, December 2002.

Q. After the trial, December 2002?

A. Yes, just before Christmas.

Q. And the business, it was a flower shop business?

A. It was my wife's flower shop, yes.

Q. Which police were dealing with it?

A. That would be North Wales Constabulary.

Q. No-one presumably has been arrested as a result of any inquiries?

A. No.

Q. To this day, we don't know who was behind that?

A. No.

The Mirror: 2 Dec 02 Article: **Jury Didn't Hear**:

---

[a] TV interview: Tabloid Tales, Paul Burrell, 27th May 2003.

"Frightened Paul Burrell has been threatened by 100 menacing phone calls since he was cleared of theft [of Diana's possessions] a month ago, it was disclosed last night.

"All were made to his florist shop which was torched by a firebug early yesterday leaving £50,000 damage.

"One hate-filled caller has persistently warned father of two Paul: 'I'm going to get you and every single one of your family.'...

"In yesterday's 1a.m. arson attack the firebug smashed a window in Paul's shop in Holt, North Wales, then dropped a blazing item on the carpet.

"A family friend walking home spotted flames licking up an inside wall and raised the alarm. Two fire crews put out the blaze before it took hold of the entire building....

"The menacing phone calls began soon after his Old Bailey acquittal. Most were silent and were made from different locations. But a single caller, believed to be dialling from the North West, made a series of calls threatening to 'get' the family." [336]

Comment: The timing is possibly significant – it is the month following Burrell going public with the Queen's statement to him.[a] It was also possibly known that Burrell was working on a book – *A Royal Duty* – which was published in October 2003.

Was this action a royal warning to Burrell to be careful what he included in his forthcoming book?

Queen's Perception of the Diana-Dodi Relationship

Paul Burrell, Diana's Butler: 16 Jan 08: 55.5:
Mansfield: Q. It's page 315 [of your 2003 book] at the bottom....: "It seemed the Queen was under the same impression as the rest of the country, that the relationship was the start of a long-term union rather than a summer fling." Do you see that sentence?
A. I do.
....Q. Is that based on something that the Queen said?
A. That was my opinion, yes, at the time.
Q. So the answer is, so we are clear, that it is based on something that the Queen said?
A. Yes.
Q. Right. Do you happen to remember what it is that the Queen said that led you to be able to put that in the book? (Pause). If you can't remember, I am not going to press it. It is just in case you do.
A. No, I can't remember.
At 99.11: Croxford: Q. You have written that the Queen was under the same

---

[a] Burrell went public on November 6 and the arson attack was 3½ weeks later, on December 1, 2002.

impression as the rest of the country that the relationship was the start of a long-term union; that's with Dodi Al Fayed. What did she say?

A. My Lord, I would rather not discuss that any further.

Coroner: Well, you have told us part of this conversation.

A. Well, I think –

Coroner: I don't think you are in a position to tell us what you are going to tell us and what you are not going to tell us.

Q. I am much obliged, sir.

A. You want me to repeat the rest of the conversation?

Coroner: Yes.

Q. Please, Mr Burrell.

A. Her Majesty was concerned that the Princess was rather over-excited at the moment.

Q. She was at the start of a long-term union with Dodi Al Fayed. Is that right?

A. Yes.

Q. What did Her Majesty say about this long-term union?

A. Her Majesty was concerned about the future.

Q. And a marriage?

A. No. The Queen did not mention that.

Q. A "long-term union", was that the expression that she used?

A. A "relationship".

Q. Long-term?

A. I didn't keep notes at that meeting.[a] I couldn't tell you if that was exactly what Her Majesty said.

Comment: The evidence in Part 2[b] shows conclusively that the Diana-Dodi relationship was set to be long-term.

A lot of that came from witness and documentary evidence that has surfaced as a part of the investigations – both police and inquest.[c]

The question here is: How is it that the Queen is privy – in mid-December 1997, just 3½ months after the deaths – to information that led her to believe the relationship was long-term?

This raises the possibility that the Queen had access to intelligence gained from the pre-crash surveillance of Diana.[d]

---

[a] Earlier, on a different issue, Burrell confirmed that his "recollection [was] aided by a note ... made after the meeting". See "Dark Forces" section.

[b] See Chapters 1 to 4.

[c] These investigations started in 2004. This issue was not addressed in the earlier French investigation.

[d] See Surveillance, Fears and Threats (Section 2) in Part 2.

Post-Crash Treatment of Diana's Staff

Paul Burrell: *A Royal Duty*: **Jury Didn't Hear**:
On Monday 1 September 1997[a] "Michael Gibbins[b] came to see me, armed with a difficult task. 'Paul, I've been asked by St James' Palace to collect all back-door keys [to Diana's residence]....
"There was no way I was handing them over. I refused, and it wasn't challenged.
"The cold-hearted treatment of the princess's staff was evident later that day when I heard the fate of dresser Angela Benjamin – whom [Diana] had admired.... When she turned in for work like the rest of us, she had found herself being escorted off the premises by policemen. She was told to gather her belongings, and was even watched as she unloaded her laundry from the tumble-dryer. Her own grief didn't seem to matter. She was back on the train to Devon by lunchtime, wondering what on earth she had done wrong." [337]

Post-Crash Control of Diana's Belongings

Michael Cole, Director of Public Affairs, Harrods: 6 Jul 06 Statement: **Jury Didn't Hear**:
"After she was killed, the personal [belongings] of Diana, Princess of Wales were packed by a maid and her bags were brought back to London on Mr. Mohamed Al Fayed's aircraft. The Princess's bags were brought to Harrods. They were put in the dining room in the Chairman's suite of offices.... One of the secretaries in the Chairman's office called me on the internal telephone and asked me to go urgently to the reception area of the Chairman's office to deal with an incident that was developing there. The secretary sounded very worried....
"At the reception area, I was confronted by two large, well-built men who identified themselves as royalty protection officers.... Their warrant cards ... were produced and ... I looked at them though I cannot recall the names that I read. The one who appeared to be in charge demanded in forthright terms that the Princess's luggage should be handed over to him right there and then....
"The luggage had been put just inside the door of the dining room.... I said to the two men that they would have to wait while I found out what was happening and what should happen. I left the reception area to investigate.... I returned and told the two policemen that they could not have the Princess's belongings until I had clarified the situation. The two men were visibly taken aback, even angry at being rebuffed. One became quite flushed. It was clear they were not used to being refused by members of the public like me.... I asked them to come back in an hour while I tried to ascertain the situation.

---

[a] The day immediately following the crash.
[b] Diana's private secretary.

"I found out that they had arrived at Harrods and found their way to the Chairman's Office ... on the fifth floor only a couple of minutes after the bags themselves arrived. Thinking about it later, I concluded that the policemen must have followed the vehicle carrying the Princess's luggage from the aircraft to Harrods.... When I spoke on the telephone to Mr. Mohamed Al Fayed about the luggage ... he told me that the appropriate person to receive the Princess's belongings was Sarah ... her eldest sister. The Princess had told Mr. Al Fayed that Sarah was the sibling closest to her and that she was on good terms with her.... I knew the Princess's sister Sarah lived in Lincolnshire and found her telephone number. I called it. I cannot be sure but I think I spoke to the Princess's sister. At any rate, I conveyed the message that the bags and the briefcase would be coming to her by road later that day.... It was arranged with someone at Kensington Palace that the Princess's usual chauffeur ... would be coming to Harrods to collect everything....

"In the meantime, the two policemen had returned. Somehow, the one who had been the leader had managed to get beyond the reception area. He was standing in the dining room, next to the luggage, when I arrived. I think the other one was still in the reception area. The leader said without any opening pleasantries, 'I am commanded by The Queen to take possession of the Princess's luggage'. I found this a rather startling pronouncement. I said I was sorry but I could not allow him to do that. The policeman was clearly dissatisfied with this response. He looked at the luggage in a meaningful way but made no attempt to remove [it] after I told him he could not have it. After a short pause while nothing was said, he left reluctantly, empty-handed." [338]

Comment: Michael Cole has described a situation where royalty protection officers attempted to take control of Princess Diana's possessions – on behalf of the Queen – following her death.

At the time of her death Diana had been out of the royal family for around a year and had been without royalty protection for nearly four years.

So it is amazing that royalty protection should suddenly become involved in any dealings related to Diana straight after her death.

This appears to be further evidence[a] of the Queen taking control of key events immediately following the death of Princess Diana.

Queen's Request for Diana's Jewellery

Keith Moss: 22 Oct 04 Statement: **Jury Didn't Hear**:
"I have been shown a passage from the website www.wethepeople.la which claims to be[b] excerpts from the book *The Day Diana Died* written by

---

[a] Further to a huge amount of evidence in Part 4.

[b] The excerpt is an accurate record from the book.

Christopher Andersen[a], to which I am attributed the following: "'The Queen, the Queen" Consul General Moss blurted to [Nurse] Humbert as he rushed into the room where Diana still lay naked under a sheet. If there were any Royal jewels among Diana's effects, her Majesty wanted them returned to the Royal Family immediately. "Madam" said Moss, "the Queen is worried about the jewellery. We must find the jewellery quickly! The Queen wants to know, where are the jewels?'"

"I can say that this is a load of nonsense, and it is certainly not based on an interview with me." [339]

Christopher Andersen, US Author: 1998 Book: **Jury Didn't Hear**: Continuation after the above excerpt in Moss' statement:

"'But there wasn't any jewelry,' replied Humbert, somewhat stunned at the apparent callousness of the question. 'No wedding band, of course, no rings, no necklace.'" [340]

Comment: Christopher Andersen, who is a respected US writer and journalist, based this account on an interview with Béatrice Humbert, chief nurse at La Pitié Salpêtrière Hospital on the night of the crash.

It is significant that Humbert – who Paul Burrell said "handled the situation as a consummate professional"[341b] – has never been interviewed by any investigation and was not heard from at Scott Baker's "thorough" inquest.

This again appears to be a case of the Queen taking control of royal interests immediately after the death of Princess Diana. And again, as with Michael Cole's evidence, this information was withheld from the London inquest.

---

[a] Why are the police relying on a website for their information, when copies of this book are readily available in London? Had the police read the book, they would have realised that Andersen is basing his information on an interview with the chief nurse in the hospital on the night of the crash.

[b] Nine years later, Paget Officer, Philip Easton, said that "Doctor Béatrice Humbert" was Professor Bruno Riou's assistant and she was present during the Paget walk-through of the hospital on 7 March 2006.: Philip Easton, Witness Statement, 13 March 2006, reproduced in *The Documents* book, p373.

Failure to Cross-Examine Royal Suspects

Coroner: Summing Up: 1 Apr 08: 5.22:

"I ruled that Her Majesty the Queen should not be questioned on this[a] and other matters, just as the Duke of Edinburgh should not be called to give oral evidence[b] to you in this court."

Coroner: "Decision": 7 Mar 08: 220.13: **Jury Not Present**:

"Decision [after hearing arguments]

"In my judgment it is not expedient[c] to call the Duke of Edinburgh to give evidence, nor do I think the Queen should be asked to answer the questions posed by Mr Mansfield. Neither step will in my judgment further the inquest process."

Coroner: "Reasons" 12 Mar 08: **Jury Didn't Hear**:

"Throughout these inquests there has been an ongoing request that I should call His Royal Highness Prince Philip Duke of Edinburgh to give evidence. Having refused the request at an early stage, I said I would keep my decision under review as the hearing proceeded and this I have done. Eventually the point was reached where any remaining evidence was unlikely to have any bearing on the question and consequently I gave my ruling after hearing further argument on 7 March 2008....

"There was a suggestion that Her Majesty the Queen should also be called but this was modified into a request that she be invited to answer certain questions. I gave my ruling on this too on 7 March 2008, again after hearing oral argument.

"s.11(2) of the Coroners Act 1988 requires me to examine on oath all persons who tender evidence as to the facts of the deaths of Diana and Dodi and all persons having knowledge of those facts whom I consider it expedient to examine.... One of the functions of an inquest is to confirm or allay rumour or suspicion....

"There comes a time when a halt has to be called to calling evidence of marginal if any relevance. This is not ... an inquiry into the relationships between the late Princess and other members of the Royal Family....

"I am satisfied that calling the Duke of Edinburgh to give evidence ... would not advance the inquest process. Indeed it would be likely to be detrimental to it in reducing it to what has already been described in respect of some witnesses' evidence as a circus....

---

[a] The Queen's statement to Burrell – see earlier.

[b] Baker says oral, but no written evidence was heard either. There was no evidence from Philip. He has said only two words in the entire investigations – "no comment" to Paget: see earlier.

[c] Suitable or appropriate: Oxford.

"Simone Simmons ... was the only evidence that the Duke actually had any animus at all against the Princess of Wales and a good deal of evidence has been heard about the nature of the relationship between the two of them indicating that the Duke was caring and supportive. Mr Devorik gave evidence that the Princess had said that the Duke was hostile to her, but he firmly believed that those remarks simply indicated that the Duke was 'out of favour' at the time....

"Had there been ... a discussion [on perceived damage to the royal family at the 20 July 1997 WAG meeting[a]] it is very far from the matter for the jury to consider: how the deceased came by their deaths....

"Looking at the whole of the evidence and keeping firmly in mind that it is for the jury and not me to decide what evidence is to be accepted or rejected, nothing has emerged to persuade me it would be expedient to call the Duke of Edinburgh....

"Her Majesty [the Queen] is not, I think, a compellable witness[b] (although I emphasise that this has not been explored in argument). It is submitted that nevertheless these questions, should be put to Her Majesty and she can answer them if she wishes. What should be done thereafter would depend on the answers. I do not think I should go down this route....

"Mr Burrell said he was unclear to what the Queen was referring but this conversation, assuming it was as Mr Burrell described, must be seen against the backcloth that no evidence has emerged of involvement on the part of the British intelligence agencies in the collision.

"In summary, I have concluded that enquiries of Her Majesty the Queen should not be made as suggested by Mr Al Fayed, on the basis that they will not assist the jury to answer the statutory questions.[c]

"For these reasons I refused the applications." [342]

Mr Justice Gross & Mr Justice Walker: "Approved Judgement" 18 Mar 08: **Jury Didn't Hear**:

"This is the judgment of the Court

"On 18 March 2008 we heard and dismissed an application for permission to apply for judicial review of a decision of ... Lord Justice Scott Baker.... These are our reasons, published after the Coroner's jury have returned their verdicts.

---

[a] Baker again gets the meeting date wrong – it is July 23 – raising serious concerns about what evidence he was actually looking at to arrive at this judgement. Baker made the same mistake in his Summing Up – see earlier section on the WAG.

[b] Baker appears to be suggesting the Queen cannot be forced to give evidence. If this is the case, then that would mean she is above the law.

[c] The statutory questions are: "who the deceased was and how, when and where he or she came by their death".: Taken from page 1 of the "reasons".

"The hearings began in October 2007. One of the witnesses called, Simone Simmons, gave evidence that ... in her opinion the Royal Family would do nothing to harm Princess Diana.[a]

"On 13 December 2007 Brigadier Sir Miles Hunt-Davies[b], private secretary to the Duke of Edinburgh, produced copies of letters written by the Duke of Edinburgh to Diana, Princess of Wales and copies of her letters to him.... After his evidence was concluded, on 17 December 2007 the claimant's solicitors wrote to the solicitor to the inquests contending that there were a number of relevant issues about which Brigadier Hunt-Davies had been unable to assist the Coroner.... We should however notice that the fact that the Brigadier had been unable to answer questions posed by Mr Mansfield did not carry the consequence that the Duke of Edinburgh should be called instead. The statutory task for the Coroner was to decide whether it would be expedient for the purposes of the inquests for the Duke of Edinburgh to be called to give evidence on these topics....

"The Coroner made his decisions on 7th March.... On 12th March, he provided short reasons for his decision....

"The Coroner had already called a vast body of evidence before the jury....

"The question whether it was expedient ... for any evidence (from whomsoever) to be given on these or any other issues was pre-eminently a matter for [the coroner's] judgment. His analysis of the issues in his ruling demonstrates that there was nothing in the proposed evidence which would be of advantage to the jury when reaching their verdict. The stark reality was that enough was enough.

"The Coroner's approach was neither illogical nor unreasonable, and his conclusion was not flawed. He was required to make a judgment based on whether it was expedient in the particular context of the facts and issues relevant to these inquests. In that context he was entitled to have regard to the vast amount of evidence which had been called and the very limited evidence which remained to be called....

"In our judgment the contention that this court should interfere with these carefully considered decisions was unarguable. Accordingly the applications were dismissed. The claimant will pay the defendant's costs." [343c]

---

[a] The actual comment was: "Oh, the Royal Family wouldn't hurt Diana, not at all." Seen in the light of all Simmons' evidence – inquest, statement, book, articles – there is every reason to believe this was a facetious comment that has been taken here out of context. Source: 10 Jan 08: 98.16.

[b] Should be Hunt-<u>Davis</u>.

[c] The full transcript is locatable through Google Search by typing in: "Queen's Bench Division Case No CO/2706/08". Alternatively it is on the British and Irish Legal Information Institute (BAILII) website under "England and Wales High Court

Comment: At the inquest there was some debate – none of which was in front of the jury – about whether evidence should have been heard from the Queen and Philip.

The issue was discussed at length on the afternoon of 7 March 2008, after the jury had retired for the day.[a] Scott Baker judged that the senior royals' evidence would not be required – on 12 March 2008 he provided a five page document, which was not made public, entitled "Reasons".

Baker's judgement was challenged in the High Court – the case was heard and dismissed on 18 March 2008.

Excerpts from both Baker's "reasons" and High Court judgement appear above.

It should be noted that the High Court judgement appears to rely heavily on the information that was provided in Baker's reasons.

There are some areas of concern in Baker's reasons:

1) Baker stated: "Simone Simmons ... was the only evidence that the Duke actually had any animus at all against the Princess of Wales".

He also stated: "Mr Devorik gave evidence that the Princess had said that the Duke was hostile to her".

So Baker says that Simmons is "<u>the only evidence</u>" of animus[b] from Philip against Diana. In the same paragraph, he says Devorik said Diana "said that [Philip] was hostile to her".

Baker has just contradicted himself. Does he think no one will notice?

The truth is that there were five witnesses – Hasnat Khan, Susan Kassem, Roberto Devorik, Simone Simmons[c] and Paul Burrell – who recognised there were difficulties in the Diana-Philip relationship.

It is true that Devorik did say Philip was "out of favour"[d] but he also said at the inquest – and Baker doesn't mention this: "I think Prince Philip was coming in and out of favour on [Diana's] life quite often".[344]

(Administrative Court) Decisions", go to 2008, then April, then click on the Al Fayed case (10 April 2008). It also can be found by doing a "Case Law Search" on the BAILII website using "Citation" details [2008] EWHC 713.

[a] The transcripts of that are available on the inquest website.

[b] Hatred or hostility – Oxford.

[c] Simmons did not expressly state this, but her evidence regarding the Philip-Diana letters indicates it.

[d] Baker said: "[Devorik] firmly believed that those remarks simply indicated that the Duke was 'out of favour' at the time". What Devorik actually said was: "I think [Philip, Fellowes and Soames] were out of favour of the Princess." So there was no "at the time". Also, Devorik did not come up with "out of favour" – his comment was in response to inquest lawyer, Jonathon Hough's: "So you simply regard those comments about those people as being whether they were in favour or out?" The full context of this Hough cross-examination can be viewed in Part 2, section on Expression of Fears or in the inquest transcripts starting at 17 Jan 08: 173.18. It is possible for a person to conclude, from the Hough cross-examination, that Philip was

Devorik made several other comments that Baker fails to mention:[a]
- "[Diana] <u>always</u> had a very tough view on Prince Philip" [345b]
- "the Princess of Wales used to say, '[Philip] blames me for everything'" – statement [346]
- "[Diana] said 'I am sure that Prince Philip is involved with the security services. After this[c], they are going to get rid of me'" – statement, confirmed at inquest [347]
- "[Diana] pointed to the portrait of Prince Philip and said 'He really hates me and would like to see me disappear' – statement, confirmed at inquest [348]
- "[Diana] used to say, '[Philip] blames me for everything'" – statement[349]
- "[Diana] ... added, 'Prince Philip wants to see me dead'" – statement, confirmed at inquest [350]
- "[Diana] told me three names that she feared – Nicholas Soames, Robert Fellowes ... and Prince Philip" – statement, confirmed at inquest.[351]

2) Baker states: "Had there been ... a discussion [on perceived damage to the royal family at the 23 July[d] 1997 WAG meeting] it is very far from the matter for the jury to consider: how the deceased came by their deaths".

It has been shown earlier – in the section on the WAG – that circumstantial evidence indicates the July 1997 WAG meeting could have played a very significant part in the lead up to the crash.

Not least in the evidence is that the Queen's own men – Fellowes and Hunt-Davis – attempted to cover up the true nature of the WAG during their inquest cross-examinations.

3) Baker says: "Looking at the whole of the evidence and keeping firmly in mind that it is for the jury and not me to decide what evidence is to be accepted or rejected".

Baker has failed on both counts.

In his Summing Up – produced 19 days after this – and throughout his "reasons", Baker has completely failed to consider "the whole of the evidence".[a]

---

out of favour at the time when Diana made comments about Philip – but it is also possible not to conclude that. Devorik's evidence really must be taken on balance – including his statement and all his cross-examinations from the lawyers. Baker never did that. This subject is addressed in detail in Part 2.

[a] The context and significance of these comments is discussed in Part 2.

[b] The word "always" is in direct conflict with Baker's "at the time" – see previous footnote.

[c] Referring to Diana's *Panorama* appearance in late 1995.

[d] Baker said 20 July, but the meeting was actually on 23 July – see earlier.

Baker says that "it is for the jury and not me to decide what evidence is to be accepted".

But what actually happened is that Baker refused to call suspects who were central to this case – Diana's ex-in-laws: the Queen and Philip; and her ex-husband, Charles. In doing this Baker prevented his own jury from being able "to decide what evidence is to be accepted".

4) Baker says: "Mr Burrell said he was unclear to what the Queen was referring".

In saying this, Baker completely ignores Devorik's clear evidence on this – see earlier.

5) In arguing that the Queen's statement to Burrell has no significance, Baker says: "No evidence has emerged of involvement on the part of the British intelligence agencies".[b]

The main reason Baker is able to make a statement like this is because he failed to allow evidence that pointed to MI6 involvement to be heard. For example, Baker prevented evidence on the Gaddafi plot[c] – a high-level assassination attempt that took place in the year preceding the Paris crash.[d]

Baker failed to call key witnesses regarding the involvement of MI6 – in particular, Sherard Cowper-Coles and Valerie Caton.

This issue – about whether the Queen and Philip should have been called – actually appears to be very simple.

Are there people in the United Kingdom who are above the law?

The Queen, Prince Philip and Prince Charles have all been shown to be possible suspects in the deaths of two people, Princess Diana and Dodi Fayed.

The issue of whether they should have been required to give evidence does not rest on that – it is wider. The issue is: Do these people have knowledge that could assist the investigations into the deaths?

If there is a chance that they do have that knowledge, then they should have been summonsed to appear at the inquest.

The fact that there is evidence that suggests they may be suspects strengthens the requirement for their evidence to be heard.

The Queen, Philip and Charles should have each been required to shed light on one or more of the following issues:

- the statement the Queen made to Paul Burrell – see earlier

---

[a] Baker uses the word "looking". Looking at the evidence is useless if you don't then go on to consider it.

[b] It's interesting that Baker says, "Mr Burrell said he was unclear to what the Queen was referring", but nevertheless, in the same sentence, brings in, "no evidence ... [of] involvement ... [by] the British intelligence agencies" as a reason not to call the Queen.

[c] Baker said: "This is not an issue in these inquests". See earlier.

[d] This has been covered in Chapter 1.

- how did the Queen learn that the Diana-Dodi relationship was long-term – see earlier
- the nature and location of post-1992 letters sent from Philip to Diana – see earlier and Part 2
- the nature of their – Philip, Charles, the Queen – relationships with Diana – see earlier, Part 2 and Part 4
- the content of the Way Ahead Group meetings in July and September 1997 – see earlier
- the location and activities of Robert Fellowes on the night of the crash – see earlier
- contacts with MI6 regarding Princess Diana – see earlier
- their reactions to the July 1997 royal holiday at Mohamed's St Tropez property – see earlier
- their attitude towards and perceptions of Mohamed Al Fayed and Dodi Fayed – see earlier and Part 2
- the timing of their knowledge of the St Tropez holiday – see earlier
- their attitude towards Princess Diana and her actions throughout 1997 – see earlier and Part 2
- the reason why Diana would suggest that Charles would organise a car crash involving her – see Part 2
- the reason why the Queen – through her coroner – took illegal control over Diana's body on its return to the UK on 31 August 1997 – see Part 4
- the reason why samples for testing from the UK post-mortem were taken from a different body – not Diana's – see Part 4
- the reason for rushing Diana's body back to the UK within hours of her death – see Part 4
- the reason for organising an embalming in France within hours of Diana's death – see Part 4.

As it turned out, out of four possible royal suspects – Fellowes, the Queen, Philip, Charles – only one, Fellowes, was heard from at the inquest.

If this had been the death of an ordinary British citizen – and not Diana, Princess of Wales – and the evidence suggested that the person's ex-in-laws were suspects, then those persons would have been subjected to thorough interviews by the British police.

In the case of the assassinations of Princess Diana and Dodi Fayed, that has never occurred. And not only that, neither was their evidence sought by the coroner of the inquest, Lord Justice Scott Baker.

And, on top of that, the High Court ruled that their evidence was not required.

I suggest this means that these three people – the Queen, Prince Philip, Prince Charles – are above the law.

Conclusion

The question was: Were the royals involved in the August 1997 assassinations of Princess Diana and Dodi Fayed?

There is a substantial amount of evidence pointing to royal involvement:

- the post-war secret Anthony Blunt trip to Germany shows that royals have worked directly with British intelligence, both in the initial activity and in the ensuing cover-up [a][b]
- there was a major cover-up at the inquest around the nature of meetings of the Way Ahead Group (WAG) – Hunt-Davis and Fellowes, the only royal witnesses heard, both lied about this [c]
- evidence points to Diana being the subject of the July 1997 WAG meeting – which was brought forward by two months
- the timing of the July WAG preparatory and full meetings on either side of the 10 day St Tropez holiday, where Diana took William and Harry to Mohamed's villa
- the apparent calling of a special WAG meeting for early September 1997 to discuss "the Fayeds" and attempts to cover this up at the inquest
- the development of the relationship between Diana and Dodi [d] and the plans for Diana and Mohamed to work on joint enterprises including a worldwide hospice network and a charity for landmine victims
- Philip's racist attitude and reports of his antagonism towards the Al Fayeds
- witness evidence that Diana feared Philip and Robert Fellowes
- witness evidence of Diana's belief that Philip wanted her dead
- both the Mishcon and Burrell Notes indicate prior knowledge from Princess Diana of an orchestrated car crash directed by members of the royal family [e]
- the Queen's statement to Paul Burrell, as reported by Roberto Devorik – "we shouldn't awake forces we don't know" – and the subsequent cover-up of this at the inquest [f]
- Paul Burrell's misleading accounts of the Queen's statement to himself [g]

---

[a] This was supported by Richard Tomlinson's evidence which related to times closer to the Paris crash.

[b] It has been shown that British intelligence was involved in the orchestration of the Paris crash – see Chapter 1.

[c] This was another case of excessive distancing – see earlier.

[d] Including the perception that Diana may become pregnant.

[e] The Burrell Note is addressed in Part 2 and the Mishcon Note is in Parts 2 and 6.

[f] It was also completely ignored by Paget.

[g] Burrell may have been pressured by the royal family – there was an arson attack on his shop (see earlier).

- the failure of Robert Fellowes to provide a proper alibi for his movements on the night of the crash
- the failure of senior royals – the Queen, Philip, Charles – to provide any evidence, written or oral, to the inquest, despite being suspects
- the refusal by Philip to assist the Paget investigation, despite being asked to
- following the 1996 Charles-Diana divorce the Queen had run out of legal options in dealing with Princess Diana's behaviour.

All these points need to be viewed together. And when they are, they appear to implicate the senior royals over involvement in the August 1997 assassinations of Princess Diana and Dodi Fayed.

A key aspect of the case against the royals is the extraordinary lengths they have gone to cover up their actions:

- the blanket denials that the WAG had a focus of dealing with major issues facing the royal family
- the blatant denial that Diana could have been a discussion point at the July 1997 WAG meeting
- the efforts to cover up the nature of the Queen's statement to Burrell
- the absolute refusal for key personnel to have to provide any evidence at all.

Obviously the royals didn't personally carry the assassinations out, but it seems that the order – verbal or implied[a] – came from a senior royal, most likely the Queen.

The evidence – studied throughout this book – indicates that the order would have been given to MI6[b], who carried out the assassinations in conjunction with the CIA and French intelligence agencies.

---

[a] By implied I mean that it is possible there was no explicit instruction, but the Queen's wishes would have somehow been made known to senior officers from MI6.
[b] Who may have had a presence at the July 1997 WAG meeting – see earlier.

4 Role of British Government[a]

Coroner: Opening Remarks: 3 Oct 07: 15.25:
"The United Kingdom Government has maintained from the outset that it was entirely unaware of the presence of Diana in Paris on 30th/31st August 1997 and that it had no information with regard to her movements or the circumstances of the crash."

Comment: This was in Baker's Opening Remarks given before any inquest evidence was heard. Baker made no comment on this in his final Summing Up.

The reality is that, outside of staff in the Paris embassy, the police and MI6, no person from the government has ever been interviewed in either the French or British police investigations.

Baker doesn't tell us, and therefore it is not known, the source of this information – that the UK government has stated it was unaware of Diana's presence.

Baker contributed to the general ignorance on the British government's position by failing to call – or take statements from – any witnesses from its ranks during the inquest.

Role of Tony Blair[b]

There is evidence – not heard by the inquest jury – indicating UK Prime Minister, Tony Blair, could have had prior knowledge of the Paris assassinations.

Andrew Rawnsley, UK Journalist and Author: 2001 Book: **Jury Didn't Hear**:

---

[a] Appendix 3 records excerpts from an article written by a British MP on 9 August 1997 predicting the death of Princess Diana.

[b] British Prime Minister. He was at his home at Trimdon Colliery in his electorate of Sedgefield over the weekend of 30-31 August 1997.

"Shortly after one in the morning [of 31 August 1997], [Tony] Blair was woken by the bedside phone. Angus Lapsley, the Downing Street official on call over the weekend, briskly reported a communication from the British Embassy in Paris.... There had been a car crash involving the Princess of Wales. Details were sketchy at this stage, but it was believed that her summer lover, Dodi Al-Fayed, was dead. Diana was thought to be seriously injured.
"Blair woke his wife.... 'God. How could this happen?' He would repeat the same or similar phrases again and again in the small hours.... The phones were patched together so that he could take a conference call with Lapsley and Alistair Campbell. Blair was beginning to grasp what he was likely to be dealing with. He said to Cherie and to his aides: 'If Dodi is dead, then Diana is dead.'
"Blair received confirmation that his expectation was correct at around two in the morning. Diana had been killed." [352]

Alastair Campbell, Tony Blair's Press Secretary: 2011 Published Diary: **Jury Didn't Hear**:

"At around 2 [a.m.][a] I was paged by media monitoring: 'Car crash in Paris. Dodi killed. Di hurt. This is not a joke.' Then TB[b] came on. He had been called by Number 10 and told the same thing. He was really shocked. He said she was in a coma and the chances are she'd die. I don't think I'd ever heard him like this. He was full of pauses then gabbling a little, but equally clear what we had to do. We started to prepare a statement. We talked through the things we had to do tomorrow, if she died. By now the phones were starting from the press, and I didn't sleep. Then about an hour later Nick[c] called and said simply 'She's dead. The prime minister is being told now.' I went through on the call. Angus Lapsley was duty private secretary and was taking him through what we knew. But it was hard to get beyond the single fact of her death. 'I can't believe this. I just can't believe it' said TB. 'You just can't take it in, can you?' And yet, as ever with TB, he was straight onto the ramifications. By the end of the call we had sorted out all we had to do practically....

"TB had been late learning of the actual accident because he hadn't heard the phone and then when the cops were asked to wake him up, they thought it was a hoax. Number 10 had to go through Scotland Yard to get on to Durham and explain it was serious and the cops would have to bang on his door....

"TB and I agreed a statement to put out as soon as it was confirmed that she was dead. It was pretty emotional. TB was genuinely shocked. It was also

---

[a] On 31 August 1997.

[b] Tony Blair.

[c] Nick Matthews, senior duty clerk at 10 Downing Street.

going to be a test for him, the first time the country had looked to him in a moment of shock and grief. We went round and round in circles about what he should say, and also how.... The phones were going all the time and then at around 4 [a.m.] I got a rash of calls asking if it was true that she was dead, then the dreadful wait for the official announcement.... Just after 7 [a.m.] TB called again. He'd been working on the words for his [statement] and he was going over some lines he'd drafted. We agreed that it was fine to be emotional, and to call her the People's Princess.... We talked about the last time they met at Chequers and the letters she sent afterwards. She was a real asset, a big part of 'New Britain'. But somehow [Blair] knew it was going to end like this, well before her time." [353]

Tony Blair, Prime Minister: 2010 Book: **Jury Didn't Hear**:

"At about 2 a.m.[a], something most peculiar happened. Cherie is difficult to wake once asleep, but I woke to find a policeman standing by the bed, which as you can imagine was quite a surprise. As I struggled into consciousness he told me that he had tried the bell but I hadn't heard it; that Princess Diana had been seriously injured in a car crash; and that I should immediately telephone Sir Michael Jay, the British ambassador in Paris.

"I was fully awake now. Cherie had also woken up. I explained the situation to her, then rushed downstairs and Downing Street put Michael [Jay] through. It was clear from the outset that Diana was highly unlikely to survive. Michael went over her injuries, informed me that her boyfriend Dodi Fayed and the driver had been killed outright, and the bodyguard was alive but unconscious.

"I phoned Alistair. He had heard from media monitoring. We were both profoundly shocked. I couldn't believe it. She was such a force in people's lives, so much part of our national life, so clearly, indubitably[b] and unalterably alive herself, it was impossible to think of her dead.

"At 4 a.m. I was phoned again, however to be told that she was.... From that time onwards there was a constant round of calls and, through it all, we were trying to work out how it should be managed.

"I know that sounds callous. I was genuinely in grief.... I was the prime minister; I had to work out how it would work out. I had to articulate what would be a tidal wave of grief and loss....

"In addition to grief, I felt something else, which stemmed from the last meeting I had with Diana. It had not been all that easy.... We had been talking about what she could do for the country in a more formal way. It was self-evidently tricky to see what that might be, though she was enthusiastic to do something. She was undoubtedly an enormous asset and I also felt it was right that she be given the chance to shift the focus somewhere other than

---

[a] On 31 August 1997.

[b] Or, unquestionably.

exclusively on her private life; but I also felt – and I don't know, maybe I would be less punctilious[a] about it nowadays – that Dodi Fayed was a problem. This was not for the obvious reasons, which would have made some frown on him; his nationality, religion or background didn't matter a hoot to me. I had never met him, so at one level it was unfair to feel nervous about him, and for all I know he was a good son and a nice guy; so if you ask me, well, spit it out, what was wrong, I couldn't frankly say, but I felt uneasy and I knew some of her close friends – people who really loved her – felt the same way....

"Diana and I had a walk in the grounds. She reproached me gently but clearly for cancelling the June date.[b] I wonder how I would deal with her today, but then I just broached the subject of her and Dodi straight out. She didn't like it and I could feel the wilful side of her bridling. However she didn't refuse to talk about it, so we did, and also what she might do. Although the conversation had been uncomfortable at points, by the end it was warm and friendly. I tried my hardest to show that I would be a true friend to her, and she would treat the frankness in that spirit.... It was the last time I saw her.

"As I contemplated her death and what I would say, I felt a sense of obligation as well as sadness.... I sat in my study in Trimdon as the dawn light streamed through the windows, and thought about how *she* would have liked me to talk about her....

"I ... worked out what I wanted to say. I scribbled it on the back of an envelope and discussed it with Alistair....

"The phrase 'people's princess' now seems like something from another age.... But at the time it felt natural.... I also wanted to capture the way she touched people's lives...." [354]

Alastair Campbell: 2011 Published Diary: **Jury Didn't Hear**:
"Sunday, July 6 [1997].... TB was at Chequers entertaining Diana and William. We chatted about it briefly on Sunday, more extensively on ... Monday.... He admitted the conversation was hard and it might have been better had I been there to jolly things along.... She and TB went for a walk in the woods." [355]

Comment: Tony Blair describes the Chequers meeting with Princess Diana, but fails to give the precise date – he simply said it was in July 1997.[c] Alistair

---

[a] "Showing great attention to detail or correct behaviour" – Oxford.
[b] Blair had originally accepted an offer from Diana of a date in June1997 but this was changed to July because it was deemed inappropriate for Blair to meet with Diana before Charles: *A Journey*, p139. The meeting occurred on 6 July 1997 – see below.
[c] See earlier footnote.

Campbell, his press secretary, reveals in a book published a year later[a], that the meeting took place on 6 July 1997.

Blair provides details of the conversation he had with Diana and focuses on one subject: "I just broached the subject of her and Dodi straight out"; and this: "she didn't refuse to talk about it, so we did".

The problem with this is that the initial Diana-Mohamed holiday didn't commence until July 11 and Diana didn't meet Dodi until July 14 – this was eight days after the July 6 Blair-Diana meeting at Chequers.

This evidence reveals that Tony Blair has lied about the content of his conversation with Diana at the Chequers meeting. It couldn't have been about the Diana-Dodi relationship, because the relationship didn't commence until after 20 July 1997[b] and wasn't in the public domain until August 7.[c]

The question is: Why did Blair lie about this?

The answer may become clearer as this chapter develops.

Timing of Crash Notification[d]

There is a major issue around precisely when Tony Blair was notified about the Paris crash.

The evidence from the above book excerpts is:

- Blair: "at about 2 a.m.[e] ... I woke to find a policeman standing by the bed"
- Campbell: "at around 2 [a.m.] I was paged by media monitoring ... then TB came on"
- Rawnsley: "shortly after one in the morning Blair was woken by the bedside phone".

Blair and Campbell are in unison – "about 2 a.m." – that neither of them were notified about the crash until over 2½ hours after it occurred.[f]

Rawnsley – whose book was written around a decade earlier than the Blair-Campbell accounts – differs. He indicates that Blair was notified around an hour earlier than he has said – "shortly after one".

The question is: Is this plausible – that possibly the most significant car crash of the 20th century involving a British princess occurs in Paris and it is 2½ hours before the prime minister is notified?

Other key people, who were also in the UK at the time of the crash, have told of when they first heard about it:

---

[a] Blair's book was published in 2010 and Campbell's in 2011.

[b] The day Diana, William and Harry returned to London after the St Tropez holiday.

[c] See Part 2.

[d] This section should be viewed in the light of the earlier evidence showing that ambassador Jay lied about the timing of his notification of the crash.

[e] 3 a.m. in Paris.

[f] The crash took place at 12.23 a.m. in Paris, which was 11.23 p.m. on 30 August 1997 in London.

- Paul Burrell:[a] "<u>Shortly after midnight</u>, the telephone rang. It was Lucia Flecha de Lima.... She had been at home in Washington when Mel French[b], chief of protocol for President Clinton ... had rung to inform her about a car accident involving the princess. She had seen reports on CNN."[356c] – 2003 book

- John Macnamara:[d] "On Sunday 31 August 1997 <u>at 12.20 a.m.</u> I was telephoned at home by Paul Handley-Greaves, the head of Mr Al Fayed's personal protection team, who informed me that a car driven by Henri Paul ... carrying Diana ... and Dodi ... had been involved in a crash in Paris. He told me that Dodi and Henri Paul were dead and that Princess Diana was very seriously injured." [357]

- Michael Cole:[e] "I knew nothing about the tragedy in Paris until <u>approximately 12.45 a.m.</u> on Sunday, 31 August [1997]. I was in bed but awake. I received a telephone call from *The Sunday Times*.... As I swung my legs out of bed, the telephone rang again. This time it was Clive Goodman, Royal Editor of the *News of the World*.... He ... said he was sorry to have to tell me that there had been a car crash in Paris. The Princess had been badly hurt, he said, and Dodi had been killed." [358]

Burrell: "shortly after midnight"; Macnamara: "at 12.20 a.m."; Cole: "approximately 12.45 a.m."

These times are 1¼ to 2 hours earlier than the Blair and Campbell evidence.

Burrell – supported by Lucia[f] – states that Lucia called him after she had been notified about the crash by "Mel French, chief of protocol for President Clinton".

Burrell says this occurred "shortly after midnight". If we presume Burrell was called by about 12.15 a.m.[g] then it is possible Lucia was called by Mel French somewhere around midnight or soon after.

---

[a] Diana's butler.

[b] Mary Mel French.

[c] The basic circumstances of Burrell's account are supported by Lucia Flecha de Lima in her police statement: "When I heard about the accident I prepared to go to Paris. I heard she was injured but not dead. It was Mel French, Bill Clinton's head of protocol who told me.... I ... called Kensington Palace to get hold of Paul Burrell. He was not there but they got a message to him.": Lucia Flecha de Lima, Witness Statement, 1 September 2004, reproduced in *The Documents* book, p34.

[d] Harrods Head of Security.

[e] Harrods Director of Public Affairs.

[f] See above footnote.

[g] This is fairly close to Macnamara's 12.20 a.m.

Given that French was Clinton's "chief of protocol", this then indicates that Clinton would have been aware of the crash involving Diana at around midnight (UK time).

Returning to the Blair-Campbell "2 a.m." evidence – this in turn would mean that the US President was notified about the crash around two hours earlier than the UK prime minister – if Blair and Campbell are telling the truth.

This is despite the fact it was the British princess involved in the crash – not a US citizen.

Again, the question is: Is this plausible?

Philippe Massoni[a] – see earlier – stated: "I arrived at [the crash scene at] 0050 hours [12.50 a.m.]. During the journey[b], I alerted the Minister of the Interior, M Chevènement. When I got to the scene, I gave him a situation report.... At the same time as the Minister of the Interior was making his way to [the hospital], I notified the British Ambassador, as well as the office of the President, the office of the [French] Prime Minister and the Foreign Minister in person. These notifications were done on my behalf by Nicola Basselier.... There was frequent contact between my assistant private secretary and these high-level authorities. They were kept informed on a regular basis.... I believe that the British Ambassador to France was informed at the same time as the other high-level authorities that I just mentioned, as soon as we knew that the Princess of Wales was one of the victims of the accident."

Earlier evidence has shown that the British ambassador, Michael Jay, was notified by Massoni at around 12.50 a.m.[cd]

This evidence from Massoni indicates that the offices of the French leadership – president and prime minister – were notified about the crash at around the same time: "as soon as we knew that [Diana] was one of the victims".

This then reveals that the French leaders were informed about the crash just before midnight UK time – this again is approximately two hours earlier than Blair and Campbell have stated they were told: "about 2 a.m." (see earlier).

Keith Moss, the British consul general in Paris, said in his police statement "at around 0110hrs [1.10 a.m.][e] ... I received a telephone call"[f] that

---

[a] Paris Prefect of Police.

[b] To the crash scene.

[c] See British Embassy chapter.

[d] 11.50 p.m. on August 30 in the UK.

[e] This is 12.10 a.m. in the UK.

[f] Moss said the call came from Keith Shannon, but other evidence indicated it could have been from Michael Jay. Moss may have received calls from both people, but it

notified him of the crash. Moss then continues: "I immediately telephoned the Resident Clerk / Duty Officer at the FCO. I asked him to inform Buckingham Palace, number 10 Downing Street, and others, including the FCO News Department, and the Foreign Secretary who was at that time in Manila." [a]

If Moss called the FCO officer at around 1.20 a.m. – 12.20 a.m. in the UK – and the officer called Buckingham Palace first and then Downing Street, we could be looking at a call to Downing Street by 12.40 a.m. at the latest.

What was the response from 10 Downing Street when the officer phoned?

The FCO officer remains anonymous, has never been interviewed by police and wasn't heard from at the inquest.

No one from 10 Downing Street has ever been interviewed.

Other evidence – Burrell, Lucia, Massoni, Macnamara, – indicates that 10 Downing Street may have already heard about the crash before 12.40 a.m.

Campbell says: "[Blair] had been late learning of the actual accident because he hadn't heard the phone and then when the cops were asked to wake him up, they thought it was a hoax. Number 10 had to go through Scotland Yard to get on to Durham and explain it was serious and the cops would have to bang on his door...."

This could fit with Blair's account: "I woke to find a policeman standing by the bed". But Blair doesn't even admit that he has a phone by the bed – instead it is: "[the policeman] told me that he had tried the bell but I hadn't heard it".

I suggest it is unusual that the UK prime minister would either: a) not have a phone by the bed, or b) not have a phone in the bedroom that rings loud enough to wake him up.

But even if what Campbell says – that Blair was notified via Scotland Yard[b] – was credible, there are two additional problems:

1) There is a gap of 1 hour and 20 minutes – 12.40 to 2.00 a.m. – between Moss' account of Downing St notification[c] and the Blair-Campbell accounts. This means that for Campbell to be right, it needed to take 1 hour 20 minutes for: a) Downing St to phone Blair and realise they couldn't rouse him; b)

---

is likely that the 1.10 a.m. call was from Jay. This has been covered thoroughly in the earlier Embassy chapter.

[a] At the inquest Moss stretched the time out on this – he said: "I tried to collect my senses. I then sat down and worked out the immediate things that I needed to do". There are reasons for Moss' conflicts that were addressed in the Embassy chapter. I suggest the statement may be more accurate.

[b] The common sense method of notifying the prime minister would I suggest be a phone call directly from 10 Downing Street to his bedroom in Sedgefield.

[c] See above and earlier Embassy chapter.

Downing St to then phone the police security at Blair's residence and be told that the police believe it is a hoax; c) Downing St to call Scotland Yard; d) Scotland Yard to call the Blair security police; e) the police to arouse Blair.

I suggest that rather than the above five events taking 1 hour 20 minutes, they would have approximately taken 30 minutes – if they occurred at all.

In the meantime all that needed to happen was for the Blair security police to be told to switch on a television set, where the crash was being covered from around 12.54 a.m.[ab]

2) Campbell stated: "At around 2 [a.m.] I was paged by media monitoring".

Blair said: "At about 2 a.m. ... I woke to find a policeman standing by the bed".

Both have given a time of "around 2 a.m." but their sources of notification are completely different – Campbell from the media, Blair from the police.

Is this timing a coincidence? Or have their accounts been harmonised?

Campbell writes: "[Blair] had been late learning of the actual accident"[c], but fails to mention that in stating he was also woken "at around 2 a.m." Campbell was "late learning of the ... accident" as well.

Campbell, who was press secretary for the prime minister, hears about the crash from his media organisation 1¼ hours after Michael Cole was notified by a newspaper[d] – "approximately 12.45 a.m.". I suggest this is odd, bearing in mind that Campbell freely admits that media outlets had his home phone number – "the phones [at home] were going all the time and then at around 4 [a.m.] I got a rash of calls asking if it was true that [Diana] was dead.... The journalists calling were breathless with excitement. Eventually, I turned off the phone...."[359]

---

[a] This is actually 1½ hours after the crash (which occurred at 11.23 p.m. UK time). It is from an article by Richard Preston in *The Telegraph* published on the fifth anniversary of the deaths. It is possible there were earlier TV or radio reports than that. Ken Lennox, pictures editor for *The Sun* stated at the inquest that he was woken by a phone call related to the crash at about 12.10 a.m.: 27 Nov 07: 12.11. Article source: Richard Preston, News Flashes That Alerted the World, *The Telegraph*, 31 August 2002.

[b] Piers Morgan wrote: "Around 12.30 a.m. the [*Mirror*] news desk rang to say that Diana and Dodi had been involved in some sort of run-in with photographers in Paris and pranged their car.... I switched on the TV news.... By 1 a.m., the news was more serious.": Piers Morgan, *The Insider: The Private Diaries of a Scandalous Decade*, pp168-9.

[c] Discussed above.

[d] And almost two hours after Ken Lennox received his call at 12.10 a.m. – see earlier.

In summary, both Blair and Campbell have stated that they were first notified of the crash at a time – 2 a.m.[a] – that simply does not fit with the other evidence, or common sense.[b]

This indicates that Blair and Campbell may have harmonised their accounts.[cd]

---

[a] 3 a.m. in Paris.

[b] I suggest that it is common sense that in regard to a fatal car crash involving a British princess that the British prime minister would not be notified around two hours after the French and US presidents.

[c] Both books were published in a similar time frame – Blair's in 2010 and Campbell's in 2011.

[d] There is also a possibility that Blair and Campbell have harmonised their accounts of Blair's initial reactions to the news of the crash. It could be a case of over-emphasis:

- "[Blair] was really shocked" – Campbell
- "I don't think I'd ever heard [Blair] like this. He was full of pauses then gabbling a little" – Campbell
- "'I can't believe this. I just can't believe it' said [Blair]. 'You just can't take it in, can you?'" – Campbell
- "It was pretty emotional. [Blair] was genuinely shocked." – Campbell
- "We [Campbell and Blair] were both profoundly shocked. I couldn't believe it." – Blair
- "it was impossible to think of her dead" – Blair
- "I was genuinely in grief" – Blair
- "in addition to grief, I felt something else" – Blair
- "I felt a sense of obligation as well as sadness" – Blair.

Rawnsley though also appears to concur – quoting "private sources": "'God. How could this happen?' [Blair] would repeat the same or similar phrases again and again in the small hours." Rawnsley then provides a detailed and graphic account of an early post-death conversation between Blair and Campbell – for which Rawnsley doesn't give any source: "Both men ... were shell-shocked by the enormity of this event. As they talked there were long stunned silences, punctuated by expletives of incredulity. Blair said: 'God. This is unbelievable'. Campbell: 'Fuckin' hell. Just unbelievable.' Silence. Campbell: 'Fuckin' hell. What do we do with this?' Blair: 'God. This is big.' Campbell: 'It's too big. It's just too big a story.'": *Servants of the People*, p60.

If Blair had prior knowledge of the assassination – and I believe he did (see earlier and later) – I suggest he would be keen to promote the belief that he was genuinely shocked after hearing the news of the crash and Diana's death. There is not enough evidence to know whether Campbell had prior knowledge, and he may well not have. It is also not possible to judge whether a conversation like this could have occurred and Rawnsley doesn't claim any source. To put together a detailed word for word account of a private conversation like this, I suggest Rawnsley has sourced it from a recording, or from Blair or Campbell. The account in Campbell's book indicates that

But why would they do this?

I suggest the answer could be linked to the earlier question of why Blair lied about his July 1997 Chequers conversation with Diana.

There appears to be an effort on the part of Blair and Campbell to distance Blair from the circumstances of the crash.

Blair stated regarding his meeting with Diana at Chequers: "I ... felt ... that Dodi Fayed was a problem"; "I just broached the subject of her and Dodi straight out".

As shown earlier, this was a blatant lie.

Blair adds: "I felt uneasy"; "I ... [felt] nervous about [Dodi]".

But the effect of bringing up this Dodi-Diana issue in Blair's book is that it – without actually stating this – indicates that Diana was getting mixed up with Dodi and that was not a good move. There is, I believe, an implicit suggestion by Blair that this action by Diana in turn created a set of circumstances that led to the crash.

In other words, Blair appears to be implicitly suggesting his "uneasy" and "nervous" feelings ended up being justified – because within two months of this Chequers meeting Princess Diana died as a result of a car crash while she was in the company of Dodi Fayed.

I suggest it is amazing that Blair states he is unable to provide any reason for his unease and nervousness: "what was wrong [with Dodi], I couldn't frankly say". But he protects himself from allegations of racism: "his nationality, religion or background didn't matter a hoot to me".

Blair completely fabricated his Chequers discussion with Diana about Dodi[a] and he may have even made up his concerns – or at least the suggestion he had no reason for them – but the key issue here is that Blair is stating all this in the context of the Paris crash.[b]

The implicit link Blair has created – concerns over Dodi to the ensuing crash – has the effect of providing a background reason for the crash. In other words, if Diana had not been meddling with the "problem" Dodi, then she would still be alive today.

---

if he did not have prior knowledge of the crash, he has certainly helped cover for Blair in the aftermath. If both Blair and Campbell had prior knowledge, then it is unlikely a conversation of this nature would have taken place.

One could argue that Rawnsley's above account of a Blair-Campbell conversation that is alleged to have occurred after Diana's official death, doesn't fit with other comments (some listed in point 1 in the Prior Knowledge section below) that indicate Blair was expecting Diana's death.

[a] It took place before Diana had even met Dodi – see earlier.

[b] In his book Blair doesn't mention the July Chequers meeting until his discussion of the crash and its aftermath – in doing this, he draws a direct link between the two events.

In turn, this directs the reader[a] away from considering other possible causes – particularly, an orchestrated crash with the involvement of MI6, the royals and the British, French and US governments.[b]

Blair and Campbell's account of a 2 a.m. timing for learning about the crash provides additional evidence distancing them from the events.

This is strikingly similar to Michael Jay's: "I was woken at my residence ... at about 1.45 a.m." [c]

The point again being: If Blair didn't wake up until 2 a.m. – and Campbell's account supports this – then how could he possibly have been involved in the assassination crash which occurred at 11.23 p.m.[d], 2½ hours earlier?

The evidence indicates otherwise. It indicates that Blair woke up well before 2 a.m., possibly around midnight and at least before 1 a.m. The evidence also indicates that Blair and Campbell have harmonised their accounts before publishing their books.

As shown above, Keith Moss declared in his 2004 statement that he told the FCO duty officer "to inform Buckingham Palace, number 10 Downing Street, and others, including the FCO News Department, and the Foreign Secretary".

At the inquest Moss stated: "my first telephone call was to the ... Foreign Office ... duty officer ... to ... ask him if, through his channels, a range of contacts could be put in the picture, namely the Royal Household ... that the Foreign Secretary should be informed ... and probably a number of other contacts as well. I cannot remember the precise detail ... oh and the news department in the Foreign Office".

Missing in Moss' inquest list is any reference to Downing Street or the prime minister – even though he specifically mentions "the Foreign Secretary" and "the news department in the Foreign Office".

It is significant that Moss had his statement in front of him – and was accessing it – while he gave this inquest testimony (see footnote).[e]

Despite Moss' statement account being very precise on this[a], Moss now says at the inquest: "I cannot be precise"; "I am fairly certain"; "I cannot remember the precise detail".

---

[a] The readers of Blair's book.

[b] A scenario along these lines was addressed in the Royals chapter and will be detailed in the Conclusion chapter.

[c] See Embassy chapter.

[d] UK time.

[e] Moss says: "my statement says 10 past 1" – 22 Nov 07: 9.4; "I think in my statement I said that he did" – 10.7. Moss' answer about his call to the FCO duty clerk is immediately after both of these quotes, at 10.19.

675

It is no coincidence that even though Moss had four phone call destinations written down in the statement in front of him – "Buckingham Palace, number 10 Downing Street ... the FCO News Department, and the Foreign Secretary[b]" – he "recalls" three of them at the inquest and the one he misses out is "number 10 Downing Street".

This indicates that Moss has been told not to mention at the inquest that the UK prime minister was one of the initial persons notified after the Paris crash.

This appears to be further evidence of an attempt to distance Blair from the 31 August 1997 events in Paris.

Prior Knowledge of Crash

There are some points from the above book excerpts – Blair, Campbell, Rawnsley – that, when taken together, could indicate that Blair had prior knowledge of Princess Diana's assassination. One has to bear in mind that if Blair did know about the assassination in advance, he is hardly going to publicly put his hand up on that one – in fact, it is more likely that he would attempt to cover it up.

The following points should be considered:

1) There are statements regarding Blair's knowledge that could be significant:

-   "[Blair] said [Diana] was in a coma and the chances are she'd die" – Campbell

-   "[Blair] said to Cherie and to his aides: 'If Dodi is dead, then Diana is dead.'" – Rawnsley[c]

-   "it was clear from the outset that Diana was highly unlikely to survive" – Blair

-   "somehow [Blair] knew it was going to end like this, well before her time" – Campbell.

2) The accounts indicate that after hearing the news from Paris, planning started virtually straightaway, with very little, if any, hesitation:[d]

-   "[Blair] was full of pauses then gabbling a little, but equally clear what we had to do" –Campbell

-   "we started to prepare a statement" – Campbell, this was after 2 a.m.[a] about an hour before Diana's death[b]

---

[a] See Moss' full statement excerpt on this in the Embassy chapter, the Phone Calls and Missing Records section.

[b] Foreign Secretary, Robin Cook, was in the Philippines and went public with an early press statement after Princess Diana's death.

[c] Rawnsley quotes "private sources".

[d] This is even though the news arrived in the middle of the night when most people in the UK were asleep.

- "we talked through the things we had to do tomorrow, if she died" – Campbell
- "'you just can't take it in, can you?' [said Blair] and yet, as ever with TB, he was straight onto the ramifications" – Campbell
- "by the end of the [notification of death] call we had sorted out all we had to do practically" – Campbell
- "through it all, we were trying to work out how it should be managed" – Blair.

The evidence from point 1 (above) indicates that Blair had a post-crash expectation that Diana was doomed to die – "if Dodi is dead, then Diana is dead"; "somehow [Blair] knew ... [Diana would die] well before her time" [c]

The quotes from point 2 indicate that in the middle of the night there was little or no hesitation before Blair started working out what he had to do to deal with the aftermath of Diana's death – even before it was known she had died: "we started to prepare a statement" before Diana had died; "we talked through the things we had to do tomorrow, if she died".

The speed with which post-crash and post-death planning was initiated by prime minister, Tony Blair, is eerily reminiscent of the early actions of the Queen, who was up in Balmoral, as detailed in Part 4.[d]

Sue Reid, Investigations Editor, *Daily Mail*: 17 Jun 06 Article: **Jury Didn't Hear**:

"Mr Y was one of the security staff on duty at Tony Blair's Sedgefield constituency during the weekend that Diana died.[e]

"It was one of the first weekends the Labour Prime Minister had spent there with his family since his election....

"After delivering his 'People's Princess' tribute, he returned to London to receive Diana's body at Northolt airport at 5pm on the Sunday.

"The Prime Minister's wife and their three children were put on a scheduled British Midland flight from Teesside airport at tea-time for them to return to Downing Street. Normally, the Prime Minister would have travelled with them.

---

[a] Earlier evidence indicates this could have been well before 2 a.m. – see previous section – which could place this occurring over two hours before Diana's official time of death.

[b] Diana officially died at about 4 a.m. in Paris, which was 3 a.m. in London – see Part 2.

[c] Campbell stated this in the context of Blair's post-crash reactions.

[d] Early Royal Control chapter.

[e] It was also stated in this article: "*The Mail* understands that [Y] was interviewed at length by Lord Stevens's detectives recently." Neither Tony Blair nor Y is mentioned at all in the 832 page Paget Report.

"But instead, he boarded an RAF plane piloted by a crew based in Scotland which had flown to Teesside. Waiting on the tarmac for Mr Blair was Mr Y. "Idly chatting to the co-pilot, he was told something very strange. The co-pilot ... asked him: 'What's really going on? We've been on standby in Scotland since 5 p.m. on Friday [August 29] waiting to make this flight to Northolt with the Prime Minister." [360]

Comment: In late 2010 I spoke with this article's author, Sue Reid.

Reid explained the circumstances in which Y provided her with this information. Although I am not free to pass those details on, I am satisfied that the circumstances, as described by Reid, are credible.

Sue Reid stands by the above article excerpt and has complete confidence in the authenticity of her source.

This is further evidence indicating prior knowledge by Tony Blair of the Paris assassinations.

Conclusion

The evidence indicates that UK Prime Minister, Tony Blair, could have been involved – at the very least he had prior knowledge – in the assassination of Princess Diana:

-    no British-based[a] non-intelligence/police member of the UK government has ever been interviewed by any investigation and none were heard at the inquest

-    Blair clearly lied about the content of his conversation with Princess Diana at Chequers on 6 July 1997 – Blair says he warned Diana about her relationship with Dodi Fayed, when Diana and Dodi didn't actually meet until eight days after this

-    both Blair and Campbell, who appear to have harmonised their book accounts[b], lied about the time they first heard about the Paris crash – they said it was about 2 a.m., when the evidence shows it would have been well before 1 a.m. and possibly closer to midnight

-    Moss changed his inquest evidence to omit mentioning that Downing Street was called soon after 12.10 a.m. UK time

-    there are statements and quotes in the Blair, Campbell, Rawnsley books that indicate Blair appeared to be expecting the death of Princess Diana before it actually officially occurred

-    in the middle of the night Blair started planning what needed to be done in the event of Diana's death, before she had officially died [c]

---

[a] Some of the personnel in the Paris embassy were interviewed and cross-examined.

[b] On the subject of the immediate crash aftermath.

[c] Blair's speed of planning is reminiscent of the quick post-death action taken by the Queen, outlined in Part 4.

- there is credible evidence Blair organised an RAF plane to be on standby that weekend – he used it to travel from Sedgefield to Northolt to meet Diana's body.

It has already been shown – see The Royals chapter – that the Queen was involved in the assassination of Princess Diana.

The reality is that in the UK, the government of the day and the Monarchy are closely connected – weekly meetings are held between the Queen and the prime minister.[a] I suggest that these regular discussions are meaningful and relevant – i.e. they do not just discuss the weather.[b]

A scenario outlining what could have occurred is included in the following Conclusion chapter – Blair's possible role in the events should become clearer.

There was a general failure to address the issues that point to Blair's prior knowledge in the police investigations and the inquest.

The French investigation did not address involvement by any senior members of the British government and Tony Blair is not mentioned by name anywhere in the Paget Report.[c]

No one from the Blair government was heard from or cross-examined during the Baker inquest.

There is no evidence suggesting that the British government was the source of the assassination plot to eliminate Diana. Tony Blair was a newly elected prime minister[d] and under him the UK signed the 17 September 1997[e] treaty to ban landmines. That had not been the policy of the previous Conservative government and indeed one of their ministers, Nicholas Soames, had threatened Diana over her anti-landmine activities, in February 1997.[f]

Having said that, the UK is still a major arms dealer and it has been suggested earlier that Diana would not have stopped at an international ban

---

[a] See The Royals chapter.

[b] If they are unable to meet, they are still required to communicate – see earlier.

[c] There is a quote of an allegation from Mohamed Al Fayed against the "prime minister". Paget states that Mohamed alleged, in a 15 February 2006 letter to John Stevens: "There is no doubt that Messrs Langman, Spearman and Spedding have all been directly implicated, acting, I am sure, directly to the orders of the Royal Family, the Prime Minister and his senior henchmen." Paget failed to address this claim, merely stating: "There is no evidence at all to support this allegation.": Paget Report, pp747, 817.

[d] The Blair government came to power in the UK in May 1997 – the crash occurred just three months later.

[e] Agreed on that date – final signature was in Ottawa in December: see earlier.

[f] This is addressed in Part 2.

on landmines – she may have moved on to other weapons. So although there is no evidence of direct senior-level British government involvement, the government still could have benefited from the elimination of Diana.

The scenario in the next chapter will indicate that Blair – who met weekly with the Queen and was in regular contact with the US and French leadership[a] – may have acted as a central contact point between those parties.

I suggest that prior knowledge of the assassination in British government circles would have been extremely limited – possibly only Tony Blair and maybe Alistair Campbell.[b]

---

[a] France also signed the landmines ban treaty, but is nevertheless a huge arms dealer.
[b] It was shown in Part 3 – section on Hold-Up in Body Transfer – that Jack Straw, Home Secretary, could have been involved in discussions on 31 August 1997 over a post-crash misunderstanding in France about a UK investigation into the crash.

5   Conclusion[a]

Coroner: Summing Up: 31 Mar 08: 27.11:
"It is rare to have direct evidence of a criminal conspiracy because when people make agreements to commit crimes, they can be expected to do so privately and without committing themselves to writing."

Who killed Princess Diana and Dodi Fayed?

One factor this series of volumes has made clear is that the operation to assassinate Princess Diana was extremely complex and required huge resources and inter-governmental support and involvement – both in the operation itself and the massive ensuing cover-up.

The evidence points to the involvement of people from five different areas:

1) there is substantial evidence indicating MI6 carried out the orchestration of the Paris crash and the subsequent assassination of Princess Diana[b], with the assistance of the CIA and French intelligence agencies, DST and DGSE

2) there is substantial circumstantial evidence indicating the assassination of Diana was ordered by senior royals, principally the Queen[c], either at the 23 July 1997 Way Ahead Group meeting, or in the aftermath of that meeting

3) there is evidence indicating US interest in the death of Princess Diana as a result of her anti-landmine activities. President Bill Clinton agreed to sign the 17 September 1997 treaty, but then reversed that decision very soon after the death of Diana

4) the fact that the assassinations of Princess Diana and Dodi Fayed took place on French soil – and the fact the French government has been deeply

---

[a] This chapter should be viewed in the context of the Conclusion sections of the chapters throughout the book.

[b] Primarily carried out in the SAMU ambulance – see Part 2.

[c] The Queen was chairman at the WAG meetings.

involved in the ensuing cover-up – indicates French involvement for a reason similar to the US: Diana's increasing anti-landmine campaign[a]

5) there is evidence that at the very least UK Prime Minister, Tony Blair, had prior knowledge that the Paris crash was going to occur and that Princess Diana would be assassinated.

The general evidence indicates that the plot to assassinate Princess Diana is something that developed over a period of time. Diana believed she could be a target from around October 1995 onwards and there is substantial evidence of her fears – the Burrell Note; the Mishcon Note; her expressed fear of Philip, Fellowes and Soames.

The reasons to assassinate Diana mounted as each year passed – there was the *Panorama* interview in 1995, then the anti-landmines campaign that she launched publicly in Angola in January 1997.

Princess Diana was threatened by Nicholas Soames, over her anti-landmines campaign, in February 1997. That is clear evidence – along with public pronouncements by Conservative MPs at the time – that Diana's activities were causing more than disquiet in government circles.

Diana's landmine campaign grew through 1997 – there was the landmark speech in June and the trip to Bosnia in August.

I suggest that was an issue that was not just upsetting people in Britain – both the US and France are major arms dealing nations.

It would seem very likely that Diana's anti-landmine activities could have been the subject of discussion between the US and French Presidents, Bill Clinton and Jacques Chirac[b], and Tony Blair.

The evidence indicates that it was Princess Diana's decision to take Princes William and Harry on a holiday with Mohamed Al Fayed that really tipped the balance and possibly led to royal consideration of her assassination.

I suggest the ensuing relationship between Diana and Dodi Fayed[c] would have helped strengthen their resolve, or maybe it confirmed to the royals that Diana's elimination was the best or only option.

It appears that at some point after Diana's decision early in June 1997 to holiday with Mohamed, MI6 became directly involved in seeking intelligence – possibly with a view to preparing the groundwork for her assassination.

Rosa Monckton, an MI6 agent who had earlier befriended Diana, appears to have been assigned a mission aimed at learning more about Diana's intentions and upcoming activities. Around June 30 Monckton organised a

---

[a] Diana could have – in the future – moved on to campaigns to ban other weapons.

[b] President of France from 1995 to 2007.

[c] And the possibility of pregnancy – addressed in Part 6 – which could have produced a Muslim step-sibling to the future King of England.

boat trip with Diana off the Greek coast, scheduled to take place in mid-August – that trip concluded just 11 days before the Paris crash.

I suggest that Blair – and Major[a] before him – would have been discussing the anti-landmine campaign with the Queen at times during his weekly meetings through mid-1997.[b] Those meetings would have provided an opportunity to pass on concerns about the building campaign from the US and French leadership.[c]

---

[a] Conservative Prime Minister, John Major.

[b] There is evidence of royal involvement in the arms industry. The following was published in the *Guardian* in November 2010: "[Prince] Andrew accepted an invitation to tour the SFO's [Serious Fraud Office] headquarters in Elm Street, London on 9 December 2008. According to the palace, he ... discussed the state of the BAE case, which was still probing secret alleged payments to clinch arms deals in several ... countries.... US ambassador Tatiana Gfoeller reported back to Washington on her shocking encounter with the British royal [Prince Andrew] in Kyrgyzstan: '... He railed at British anticorruption investigators, who had had the "idiocy" of almost scuttling the al-Yamama deal with Saudi Arabia.'...
"Anti-corruption campaigners called on Andrew to resign as a special UK trade representative. Kaye Stearman of the Campaign Against the Arms Trade, said: 'It is wrong ... that Prince Andrew is seen to be supporting arms sales and accepting corruption. This report shows that the relationship seems to go even deeper, with Prince Andrew speaking out against a government agency attempting to investigate corruption and arms deals.'
"Andrew Feinstein, an anti-corruption campaigner and former South African MP who resigned in protest over BAE bribery allegations, said: 'I am amazed but not entirely surprised by the prince's comments. The royal family has actively supported Britain's arms sales, even when corruption and malfeasance has been suspected. For instance, the royal family was involved in trying to persuade South Africa to buy BAE's Hawk jets, despite the air force not wanting the planes that cost two and a half times the price of their preferred aircraft. As an ANC [African National Congress] MP at the time, I was told that £116m in bribes had been paid to key decision-makers and the ANC itself. The royal family's attitude is part of the reason that BAE will never face justice in the UK for its corrupt practices.'" Rob Evans and David Leigh, Wikileaks Cables: Prince Andrew Demanded Special BAE Briefing, *The Guardian*, 30 November 2010.
Sherard Cowper-Coles – Head of MI6 France at the time of the Paris crash (see Chapter 1) – has worked at BAE Systems since leaving the FCO in 2010.

[c] Because of Diana's background of 15 years, 1981 to 1996, in the royal family – and her position as mother of the future King – I believe that world leaders would have felt the need to pass on their concerns primarily to the Queen, as head of the royal family. Since Blair met with her on a weekly basis, I suggest it is natural that concerns would have been passed on through him.

DIANA INQUEST: WHO KILLED PRINCESS DIANA?

There was already a background of trouble between Princess Diana and the senior royals – the 1992 Morton book and the 1995 *Panorama* interview. Then came the very powerful anti-landmine campaign.

Events merged towards a "perfect storm", when added to the above came the St Tropez holiday involving Princes William and Harry.

The 23 July 1997 Way Ahead Group meeting – brought forward from September and held just three days after the conclusion of that holiday – may have included an MI6 intelligence report on Diana's activities.

It appears that either at that meeting, or very soon after it, the decision to assassinate Princess Diana was made. The order would have been passed to MI6 – not in writing and possibly not even a verbal direction.

But from the Queen – authorised by the Queen.

The Queen was the only person in the Establishment with the power to order the removal of the widely popular and much loved Princess Diana.

MI6 would have then set about the difficult task, but not alone. The United States and France had clear interests in this – and their intelligence agencies, the CIA, DGSE and DST would have quickly come on board.

Both Diana and Dodi would have been under close surveillance and the results of Monckton's work would have contributed to the necessary intelligence – necessary to work out future movements and possible locations where the assassination could take place.

What emerged was a very complicated – but extremely deniable – plan to assassinate Princess Diana in Paris' Alma Tunnel on the weekend of 30-31 August 1997.[a]

Prior to that, highly trained and very senior MI6 officers were moved into the British embassy in Paris – particularly Sherard Cowper-Coles, Valerie Caton and Richard Spearman.

Various undercover agents were employed by the intelligence agencies along the way, as required – including Claude Roulet, Henri Paul, Jean-Marc Martino, Arnaud Derossi, Jean Monceau, Dominique Lecomte, Gilbert Pépin.

The results of the activities of those intelligence agencies have been covered in detail in the preceding volumes of this series.

Just 39 days after the 23 July 1997 special Way Ahead Group meeting presided over by the Queen, Princess Diana lay lifeless in a Paris hospital.[b]

---

[a] The logistics of prior knowledge of the couple's movements has already been addressed in Part 1.

[b] There is a common thread that runs through the evidence of the few key players, with links to the perpetrators, who were cross-examined – they carried out excessive distancing. Rosa Monckton over her ignorance of SIS being MI6 and her ignorance of publicity over Philip's letters; Michael Jay over his ignorance of the missing log sheets; all but two of the embassy staff claimed ignorance of Diana's presence in Paris before the crash; Fellowes and Hunt-Davis' claims that the WAG was primarily about scheduling and didn't discuss major issues.

Appendix 1

Bonn Embassy Political-Economic Staff List Comparison: 1996 to 1997

Ambassador: Sir Nigel Broomfield, KCMG
Minister and Deputy Head of Mission:
R F Cooper, MVO
Defence Attaché: Colonel B R Isbell
Air Attaché: Group Captain S A Wrigley, RAF
Naval Attaché: Captain M Booth, RN
Counsellor (Economic): Dr P Collecott
Counsellor (Political): A Charton
Counsellor (Bilateral Relations): (Vacant)
Counsellor (Science and Technology): R W Barnett
Counsellor (Management and Consular): S C Johns
Counsellor (Labour): Miss R E Green
Counsellor (Defence Supply): R P Craine
First Secretary (Economic): Miss S J Hinds, MBE
First Secretary: (Information): M F Smith
First Secretary: (Economic): R Kershaw
First Secretary (Science and Technology):
D R Bacon
First Secretary (Agriculture): G Steel
First Secretary (Economic): Mr R E Deane
First Secretary (Management): R Milburn
First Secretary (Political): R E Meredith
First Secretary (Political): J S Smith
First Secretary (Political): A V Tucker
First Secretary (Political/Military): P A Jones
Assistant Defence Attaché: Major N C W Dunkley,
MBE
Second Secretary: M Hullands
Second Secretary (Press and Information):
Mrs S B Speller
Second Secretary (Management): E A Fearn
Second Secretary (Political): D C G London
Second Secretary (Political): J A Kraus
Second Secretary (Defence Supply): A Blackwell
Second Secretary (Political/Military): M Axworthy
Second Secretary (Bilateral Relations): J N Cox
Third Secretary: (Accounts/Personnel):
D M Lingwood
Third Secretary (Private Secretary): A J Battson
Third Secretary (Science and Technology):
A Woodcock
Third Secretary (Management): P Noon

Figure 13

Personnel list for the British Embassy in Bonn, Germany in September 1996.

Ambassador: Mr C J R Meyer, CMG
Minister and Deputy Head of Mission: Mr R F
Cooper, MVO
Defence Attaché: Brigadier B R Isbell
Air Attaché: Group Captain S A Wrigley, RAF
Naval Attaché: Captain M D Booth, DSC, RN
Counsellor (Political): Mr A Charlton CMG
Counsellor (Economic): Mr P Collecott
Counsellor (Management and Consular): Mr S C
Johns
Counsellor (Defence Supply): Mr P Watkins
Counsellor (Science and Technology): Mr R W
Barnett
Counsellor (Labour): Miss R E Green
First Secretary (Economic): Mrs S J Axworthy MBE
First Secretary (Press and public affairs): Mr M F
Smith
First Secretary (Agriculture): Mr G Steel
First Secretary (Science and Technology): Mr D R
Bacon
First Secretary (Management): Mr M F J Ryder
LVO
First Secretary (Economic): Mr R E Deane
First Secretary (Political): Mrs C H Smith
First Secretary (Political): Mr J S Smith
First Secretary (Political): Mr R E Meredith
First Secretary (Political/Military): Mr P A Jones
First Secretary (Economic): Mr S Muchall
Assistant Defence Attaché: Major N C W Dunkley,
MBE
Second Secretary: Mr M Hullands
Second Secretary (Press and Public Affairs): Ms S
B Speller
Second Secretary (Management): Mr E A Fearne
Second Secretary (Economic): Mr M Axworthy
Second Secretary (Private secretary to HMA): Mr
J A Kraus
Second Secretary (Bilateral Relations): Mr J N
Cox
Second Secretary (Defence Supply): Mr A
Blackwell
Third Secretary (Management): Mr P Noon
Third Secretary (Accounts/Personnel): Mrs C A
Schumann
Third Secretary (Political): Mr A D C Smith
Attache: Mr G Griffiths

Figure 14

Personnel list for the British Embassy in
Bonn, Germany in September 1997.

Table: Bonn Embassy Political and Economic Departments Comparison Between 1996 and 1997

Role	September 1996			September 1997		
	Rank	Person	In MI6 List?	Rank	Person	In MI6 List?
	a		b			
Counsellor Political	7	A. Charlton[c]	No	6	A Charlton	No
Counsellor Economic	6	P. Collecott	Yes	7	P. Collecott[d]	Yes
1st Secretary Economic	12	Miss S.J. Hinds	No	12	Mrs S.J. Axworthy	No
1st Secretary Economic	14	R. Kershaw	No		NO POSITION	
1st Secretary Political	17	R.E. Deane	No	17	R.E. Deane	No
1st Secretary Political		NO POSITION		18	Mrs C.H. Smith	No
1st Secretary Political	19	R.E. Meredith	No	20	R.E. Meredith	No
1st Secretary Political	20	J.S. Smith	No	19	J.S. Smith	No
1st Secretary Political	21	A.V. Tucker	No		NO POSITION	
1st Secretary Political/ Military	22	P.A. Jones	No	21	P.A. Jones	No

[a] Based on the Diplomatic List being ordered by seniority, as discussed earlier.

[b] Yes/No. This is the MI6 list on the internet – it is not complete so it is likely that a person could be an MI6 officer but not be included on the list.

[c] Reads as "A. Charton" on the List, but it should be "A. Charlton".

[d] Collecott and Charlton have switched rank numbers because by 1997 Charlton had been awarded a CMG, so became more senior.

DIANA INQUEST: WHO KILLED PRINCESS DIANA?

Role	September 1996			September 1997		
	Rank	Person	In MI6 List?	Rank	Person	In MI6 List?
1st Secretary Economic		NO POSITION		22	S. Muchall	No
2nd Secretary Political	27	D.C.G. London	No		NO POSITION	
2nd Secretary Economic		NO POSITION		27	M. Axworthy[a]	No
2nd Secretary Political	28	J.A. Kraus	No		NO POSITION	
2nd Secretary Political/ Military	30	M. Axworthy	No		NO POSITION	
3rd Secretary Political		NO POSITION		33	A.D.C. Smith	No

The above table relating to political and economic department personnel in the Bonn embassy should be compared to an earlier similar table for the Paris embassy.[b]

The Bonn table shows there were 12 staff in the two departments in September 1996 and a year later this had been marginally reduced to 11. In Paris there were 11 in both years – so the overall department numbers are similar between the embassies.

The Paris table showed that of the 11 in 1997, 6 had been newly employed in the preceding 12 months. In Bonn, that figure is 4 out of 11 – so only 36% in Bonn compared to 55%[c] in Paris.

Just focusing on senior staff – first secretary upwards – 6 out of 10, or 60%, were new staff in Paris, whereas in Bonn the figures are 3 out of 9, or just 33%.

In Paris the 4 top positions in the political and economic departments had been filled by new personnel. That is not the case in Bonn – of the top 4 positions, only one is filled by a new employee in September 1997.

---

[a] Not a new employee. In 1996 Axworthy was in the Political Department – see below on the table.

[b] See Embassy Tables section.

[c] 6 out of 11.

BONN EMBASSY STAFF COMPARISON

The staff who left in Paris in 1996 were all replaced by more senior personnel. In Bonn only one person was directly replaced and that was S.J. Hinds, ranked 12th in the embassy – she was replaced by S.J. Axworthy, who was also ranked 12th.

Appendix 2

Paris Embassy Political-Economic Staff List
Comparison: 1995 to 1996

Ambassador: Sir Christopher Mallaby, GCVO, KCMG
Minister: The Hon Michael Pakenham
Defence and Air Attaché:
Air Commodore C Adams, AFC, RAF
Military Attaché: Brigadier C D M Ritchie OBE
Naval Attaché: Captain D J Thomson, RN
Counsellor and Head of Chancery: M A Arthur
Counsellor (Cultural) (British Council Director):
D T Ricks, OBE
Counsellor: T R Ewing
Counsellor (Management): M A Price, LVO
Counsellor (Technology): Dr M A Darnbrough
Counsellor (Information): T V Fean
Counsellor (Financial and European Community):
P F Ricketts
Counsellor (Director of Trade Promotion and
Investment): R J Codrington
First Secretary and Consul-General: K C Moss
First Secretary (Labour): Ms M M Hartwell
First Secretary: E G Curley
First Secretary (Technology): Dr J Hodges
First Secretary (Commercial): N J Paget
First Secretary (Aviation and Defence Supply):
J K Clayton
First Secretary: J Bevan
First Secretary: G J Hendry
First Secretary: M A Runacres
First Secretary (Economic): R D Fitchett
First Secretary (Technology): Dr J Hodges
First Secretary and Consul: Miss A M Cowley
First Secretary (Economic/Financial): D G Roberts
First Secretary (Technology): G J Muir
First Secretary (COM/UNESCO): D O Hay-Edie
First Secretary (Management): B A Lane
First Secretary (Works): J I S Maclean, OBE
First Secretary (Agriculture): Mrs E M Morris
First Secretary (International Finance):
N J A Langman
Attaché (British Council Deputy Director):
P D R Ellwood
Assistant Naval Attaché (Technical):
Commander P A C Lockwood, RN
Assistant Military Attaché (Technical):
Lieutenant-Colonel M G Felton
Assistant Air Attaché (Technical):
Wing Commander S Gunner, RAF
Second Secretary (VISA) (Vice-Consul): F Jones
Second Secretary (Labour): S Ryan
Second Secretary (Commercial): B W West
Second Secretary (Private Secretary to
Ambassador): H E Powell
Second Secretary (Science and Technology):
K Shannon
Second Secretary: C Martin

Second Secretary: R M Hardy
Third Secretary (Chancery): P D Batson
Third Secretary (Information): S J Lucas
Vice Consul: Ms V S Jennison

Figure 15

Personnel list for the British Embassy
in Paris, France in September 1995.

Table: Paris Embassy Political and Economic Departments Comparison Between 1995 and 1996

Role	September 1995			September 1996		
	Rank	Person	In MI6 List?	Rank	Person	In MI6 List?
a	b		c			
Counsellor Political		NO POSITION			NO POSITION	
Counsellor Finance & Economic[d]	12	Peter Ricketts	No	12	Peter Ricketts	No
1st Secretary Political	16	Eugene Curley	No	16	Eugene Curley	No
1st Secretary Political/ Military		NO POSITION		18	Matthew Kirk	No
1st Secretary Political/ Internal	20	James Bevan	No	19	Mrs Anna Kirk	No
1st Secretary Political	21	G.J. Hendry	No	20	G.J. Hendry	No
1st Secretary Political/ Internal	22	Mark Runacres	Yes	21	Julia Nolan	No
1st Secretary Economic	23	Robert Fitchett	Yes	22	Robert Fitchett	Yes
1st Secretary Political		NO POSITION		23	Andrew Wightman	No
1st Secretary Economic[e]	26	David Roberts	Yes	25	Simon Fraser	No
1st Secretary Economic[f]	32	Nicholas Langman	Yes	31	Nicholas Langman	Yes
2nd Secretary Political[a]	40	Hugh Powell	No	34	Hugh Powell	No

[a] In the 1995 List the positions do not include the word political – i.e. "First Secretary Political" in 1996 reads "First Secretary" in 1995.

[b] Based on the Diplomatic List being ordered by seniority, as discussed earlier in Chapter 1B.

[c] Yes/No. This is the MI6 list on the internet – it is not complete so it is likely that a person could be an MI6 officer but not be included on the list.

[d] In 1995 shows as "Counsellor Financial and European Community".

[e] First Secretary Economic/Financial in 1995.

[f] Shows as "First Secretary International Finance" in 1995.

The above table relating to the comparison of political and economic department personnel in the Paris embassy between 1995 and 1996 should be compared to an earlier similar table for the same embassy between 1996 and 1997, the year of the crash.[b]

The 1995-6 table shows there were 9 staff in the two departments in September 1995 and a year later this had been increased to 11. In 1996-7 there were 11 in both years.

The 1996-7 table showed that of the 11 in 1997, 6 had been newly employed in the preceding 12 months. In 1995-6, that figure is 5 out of 11 – so 45% in 1995-6 compared to 55%[c] in 1996-7. Out of the 5 new staff in 1996, 2 were filling new positions that hadn't existed in 1995 – Matthew Kirk and Andrew Wightman.

Just focusing on senior staff – first secretary upwards – 6 out of 10, or 60%, were new staff in 1996-7, whereas in 1995-6 the figures are 5 out of 10, or 50%.

In 1996-7 the 4 top positions in the political and economic departments had been filled by new personnel. That is not the case in 1995-6 – of the top 4 positions, only two have been filled by new employees in September 1996.

The staff that left in Paris in 1997 were all replaced by more senior personnel. In 1996 the three staff that left were directly replaced by people on a similar rank – James Bevan (20) was replaced by Anna Kirk (19); Mark Runacres (22) was replaced by Julia Nolan (21); David Roberts (26) was replaced by Simon Fraser (25).

The political-economic staff movements between 1995 and 1996, although less than between 1996 and 1997, are still reasonably high – 45% compared to 55%.

It seems that the significant difference occurs in the most senior positions and rankings – in 1997 all top four positions had changed by September and the new people were significantly higher ranked.

That simply did not occur in 1996.

In 1995 the top 4 rankings of political-economic staff members were: 12, 16, 20, 21; then in 1996 the top 4 were: 12, 16, 18, 19 – very similar.

But just 12 months later in September 1997[d], the position was dramatically different – the top 4 rankings then were 6, 7, 13, 14.[e]

---

[a] Private Secretary to Ambassador in 1995.
[b] See Embassy Tables section.
[c] 6 out of 11.
[d] The month following the crash.
[e] See earlier.

Appendix 3

British MP's Prediction of Princess Diana's Death

Nicholas Soames and Alan Clark were both members of the preceding Conservative government that lost power in May 1997 – over three months before the crash.

Nicholas Soames, Minister for Armed Forces to May 1997: 12 Dec 07: 85.14:

Keen: Q. In the weeks preceding the crash in Paris in 1997, do you recall a political or ministerial colleague alluding to the prospect of the sudden death of the Princess of Wales in unexplained circumstances?

A. No.

Q. Perhaps this quotation may jog your memory: "... and still elusive, though occasionally one must assume in the telescopic sight, is the ultimate trophy, the most brightly plumaged of all, to accelerate and then to be the first to capture the sudden death of Diana, Princess of Wales in unexplained circumstances."

A. It means absolutely nothing to me.

Q. Those are the words of the late Alan Clark.

A. It could be, yes.

Q. Member of Parliament?

A. Yes.

Q. Minister of State in the Ministry of Defence?

A. A long time before that.

Q. Indeed so. Those words were printed and indeed published on 9th August 1997. Do you recall now their publication?

A. I do not recall their publication, but now you have told me they were by Alan Clark and listening to the words, I recognise them as being Clark, Clark literature.

Q. By style?

A. By style.

Q. And you would not have called him paranoid, would you?

A. I would call him lots of things but not paranoid, no.

Q. Not paranoid and yet, there we are some three weeks before the crash in Paris, and Mr Clarke anticipating that event in these words.

A. Again, Mr Keen, I am very sorry, but I cannot be held responsibility for what Alan Clark said.

Q. He was a close personal friend?

A. He was a very close personal friend, but I nevertheless cannot be held responsible for what he said. He did not consult me before he said it.

Q. No, but once he had said it, you became aware that he had said it?

A. I have never heard the words before in my life.

At 95.22: Burnett: Q. You were asked questions about what was said by Mr Clark in his article in *The Spectator* of 9th August 1997. Were you aware that the context of his remarks were denouncing harassment by the press of the Princess?

A. I was not. I did not see the article, Mr Burnett. I was not aware of the article until Mr Keen mentioned it.

Alan Clark, British Conservative MP: 9 Aug 1997 Article in *The Spectator* read out 17 Dec 07: 131.12:

The headnote reads: "After a Glasgow MP killed himself, Alan Clark on lethal journalists, and the person they most want to drive to suicide."

"The suicide of Gordon McMaster MP brings the press corps' body count up to three. 'Confirmed', as they used to say in Vietnam briefings. Congratulations, boys! The big one (see below) still eludes you, but I expect you will get her in the end. The deaths, by their own hand, in the last three years of Lady Green, Lady Caithness and poor fat Gordon are all of them directly attributable to press harassment over incidents or rumours that were intensely personal.... At present there is total collusion between police and media. Far from being protected, any citizen who, driven to distraction, might punch a cameraman is arrested on the spot. Anyone who has suffered bereavement – particularly from loss of a child in criminal circumstances – will be pressured to have a 'press conference' on television where, with a bit of luck, they will break down. In the Met, most stations seem to have a 'press liaison officer' whose principal function appears to be ringing round the tabloids the moment a potential subject hits a spot of bother. I am sure, of course, that no money ever changes hand in consideration of this service.... And still elusive, though occasionally one must assume in the telescopic sight of every editor, is the ultimate trophy, the most brightly plumaged of all: to accelerate, and then to be the first to capture, the sudden death of Diana, Princess of Wales in 'unexplained circumstances'."

Evidence, Maps, Diagrams & Photos

Figure 1 MI6 CX document detailing the plot to assassinate Muammar Gaddafi.. 123

Figure 2 Ritz CCTV still shot of two unidentified persons outside the hotel 227

Figure 3 Diplomatic List excerpt of Paris Embassy personnel in September 1997 245

Figure 4 Diplomatic List excerpt of Paris Embassy personnel in September 1996 273

Figure 5 Photo of *Della Grazia* – the boat used during the 1997 Aegean cruise ... 394

Figure 6 Photo of Diana and Rosa on Hydra during the Greek Islands holiday 395

Figure 7 Closing excerpt from Diana letter to Philip dated 12 July 1992 432

Figure 8 List of US Government assassination plots 1947 to 1999 465

Figure 9 Excerpt from CIA manual entitled "A Study of Assassination" 468

Figure 10 Article from early edition of *Sunday Mirror* 31 August 1997................ 586

Figure 11 Excerpt of the Burrell Note as made public by Burrell in Oct 2003 639

Figure 12 Excerpt of the Burrell Note before it was redacted by Paul Burrell....... 640

Figure 13 Diplomatic List excerpt of Bonn Embassy personnel in Sep 1996 685

Figure 14 Diplomatic List excerpt of Bonn Embassy personnel in Sep 1997 686

Figure 15 Diplomatic List excerpt of Paris Embassy personnel in Sep 1995 690

Bibliography

Books

Andersen, C., (1998). *The Day Diana Died*. New York: William Morrow & Co Inc.

Anderson, N., (2009), *NOC: Non-Officer Cover: British Secret Operations*, USA, Enigma Books

Andrew, C., (1986), *Secret Service: The Making of the British Intelligence Community*, Sceptre

Belfield, R., (2008), *The Secret History of Assassination: The Killers and Their Paymasters Revealed*, London, Magpie Books

Blair, T., (2010), *A Journey: My Political Life*, USA, Alfred A. Knopf

Bloch, J., & Fitzgerald, P., (1983), *British Intelligence and Covert Action*, London, Junction Books Ltd

Bloch, M., (1986), *Operation Willi: Plot to Capture the Duke of Windsor, July 1940* , Littlehampton Book Services

Blum, W., (1995), *Killing Hope: US Military and CIA Interventions Since World War II*, Common Courage Press

Burrell, P., (2003), *A Royal Duty*, Australia: Penguin Books

————,(2004), *A Royal Duty*, London, Penguin Books

————, (2006), *The Way We Were: Remembering Diana*, London, Harper Collins Publishers

Campbell, A., (2007), *The Blair Years*, London, UK: Hutchinson

————, (2011), *The Alastair Campbell Diaries: Volume 2: Power and the People*: *1997-1999*, Hutchinson

Collins, T., (1990), *Open Verdict*, UK, Sphere Books Ltd

Deacon, R., (1991), *British Secret Service*, London, Grafton Books

Delorm, R., Fox, B., & Taylor, N. (1998). *Diana & Dodi: A Love Story*. Los Angeles, USA: Tallfellow Press.

Dorril, S., (2001), *MI6: Fifty Years of Special Operations*, UK, Fourth Estate

Foot, M.R.D., *SOE: The Special Operations Executive 1940-46*, British Broadcasting Corporation

Foreign & Commonwealth Office, (1996), *The Diplomatic Service List 1996*, London, Her Majesty's Stationery Office

————, (1997), *The Diplomatic Service List 1997*, London, Her Majesty's Stationery Office

————, (1998), *The Diplomatic Service List 1998*, London, Her Majesty's Stationery Office

————, (1999), *The Diplomatic Service List 1999*, London, Her Majesty's Stationery Office

————, (2000), *The Diplomatic Service List 2000*, London, Her Majesty's Stationery Office

————, (2002), *The Diplomatic Service List 2002*, London, Her Majesty's Stationery Office

Green, A., (2003) *Writing the Great War: Sir James Edmonds and the Official Histories, 1915-1948 (Military History and Policy)*, Routledge

Higham, C., (1989), *Wallis: Secret Lives of the Duchess of Windsor*, Pan Books

Hollingsworth, M. & Fielding, N., (1999), *Defending the Realm: MI5 and the Shayler Affair*, André Deutsch Ltd

Hyde, H. M., (2001), *Room 3603: The Incredible True Story of Secret Intelligence Operations During World War II*, New York, The Lyons Press

Ingram M., & Harkin, G., (2004), *Stakeknife: Britain's Secret Agents in Ireland*, Ireland, The O'Brien Press

Jeffrey, K., (2011), *The Secret History of MI6*, Bloomsbury Publishing

Junor, P., (1998), *Charles: Victim or Villain?*, HarperCollins

King, J. & Beveridge, J., (2001), *Princess Diana: The Hidden Evidence*, New York, S.P.I. Books

Machon, A., (2005), *Spies, Lies and Whistleblowers: MI5, MI6 and the Shayler Affair*, UK, The Book Guild Ltd

Macintyre, B., (2010), *Operation Mincemeat*, Bloomsbury Publishing

Mansfield, M., (2009), *Memoirs of a Radical Lawyer*, London, Bloomsbury Publishing

Morgan, J., (2007), *Cover-Up of a Royal Murder: Hundreds of Errors in the Paget Report*, USA: Amazon

————, (2009), *Diana Inquest: The Untold Story*, USA, Amazon

————, (2009), *Diana Inquest: How & Why Did Diana Die?*, USA, Amazon

————, (2010), *Diana Inquest: The French Cover-Up*, UK, Lightning Source

————, Editor, (2010), *Diana Inquest: The Documents the Jury Never Saw*, UK, Lightning Source

————, (2011), *Diana Inquest: The British Cover-Up*, UK, Lightning Source

Morgan, P., (2005), *The Insider: The Private Diaries of a Scandalous Decade*, Ebury Press

Morton, A., (1997), *Diana: Her True Story – In Her Own Words*, Australia: Harper Collins

————, (2004), *Diana: In Pursuit of Love*, Michael O'Mara Books

Norton-Taylor, R., (1990), *In Defence of the Realm?: The Case For Accountable Security Services*, London, The Civil Liberties Trust

Pearson, J., (1966), *The Life of Ian Fleming*, UK, Jonathan Cape Ltd
Picknett, L., Prince C. & Prior, S., (2002), *Double Standards: The Rudolf Hess Cover-Up*, Time Warner
————, (2003), *War of the Windsors: A Century of Unconstitutional Monarchy*, Edinburgh, Mainstream Publishing
Rawnsley, A., (2001), *Servants of the People: The Inside Story of New Labour*, Penguin Books
Rees-Jones, T. & Johnston, M., (2000), *The Bodyguard's Story*, Warner Books
Simmons, S., (2005), *Diana: The Last Word*, London, Orion Books
Stevenson, W. (1977), *A Man Called Intrepid: The Secret War 1939-1945*, Sphere Books Ltd
Thomas, G., (2010), *Inside British Intelligence: 100 Years of MI5 and MI6*, London, JR Books
Tomlinson, R., (2001), *The Big Breach*, Edinburgh, Cutting Edge
West, N., (1990), *The Friends: Britain's Post-War Secret Intelligence Operations*, Coronet Books
Wharfe, K., with Jobson, R., (2002), *Diana: Closely Guarded Secret*, London, UK, Michael O'Mara Books Limited
Wright, P., (1987), *Spycatcher*, Australia, Heinemann Publishers

Websites

BBC News	http://news.bbc.co.uk
British Army Killings	http://britisharmykillings.org.uk
British Government Press Releases	www.gov-news.org/gov/uk/news
British Monarchy	www.royal.gov.uk
CBC News	www.cbc.ca/news
CIA Assassination Manual	www.whale.to/b/ciaass1.html
CNN	http://edition.cnn.com
Electronic Mine Information Network	www.mineaction.org
Executive Intelligence Review	http://www.larouchepub.com
Famous Speech Transcripts	http://thespeechsite.com
Diplomatic Service Interviews	www.chu.cam.ac.uk/archives
Funding Universe	www.fundinguniverse.com
Gaddafi Plot – David Shayler	http://cryptome.orh/shayler-gaddafi.htm
Halo Trust website	www.halotrust.org
Home Office	www.homeoffice.gov.uk
History Learning Site	www.historylearningsite.co.uk
International Court of Justice	www.icj-cij.org
International Criminal Court	www.icc-cpi.int
International Road Traffic and Accident Database	www.internationaltransportforum.org/irtad
IOL News	www.iol.co.za

BIBLIOGRAPHY

Judiciary of England and Wales   www.judiciary
Landmine Action website   www.landmineaction.org
Language Schools   www.languagecourse.net
Map Distances   http://distancecalculator.himmera.com
MI6   www.sis.gov.uk
MI6 Officer List   www.cryptome.org
Moyo Island Tourism   www.indonesia,travel
MPS   www.met.police.uk
MPS Paget Report   www.met.police.uk/news/operation_paget_report.htm
National Archives   http://yourarchives.nationalarchives.gov.uk
Official Inquest at National Archives
http://webarchive.nationalarchives.gov.uk/20090607230718/http:/www.scott
baker-inquests.gov.uk/
Onassis Foundation   www.onassis.gr/en/
PUSD Records   http://collections.europarchive.org.tna
Random House   www.randomhouse.com.au
Richard Tomlinson Affidavit:
http://www.conspiracyplanet.com/channel.cfm?channelid=41&contentid=88
Royal Albert Hall: www.royalalberthall.com
SAS Equipment   www.sasequip.com
SBS   www.specialboatservice.co.uk
South of France   www.south-of-france.com
Treasury Solicitor   www.tsol.gov.uk
UK Parliament Publications   www.publications.parliament.uk
White Pages Paris   www.pagesjaunes.fr/pagesblanches
Wikipedia   http://en.wikipedia.org/wiki/
Yachts   www.sailingpoint.com/yachting
                                                           www.greeceyachts.com
                                              www.charterworld.com/index.html
                                                         www.superyachts.com

Newspapers & Periodicals

Alderson, Andrew, Diana's Friends Confirm Duke's Account of His Letters, *Daily Mail*, 24 November 2002
Ansari, Massoud & Alderson, Andrew, Why Surgeon Could Not Marry Princess Diana, *The Telegraph*, 16 December 2007
Barak, Daphne, Building Up Confidantes, *Sunday Times*, 19 March 1995
Bennett, Richard, Assassination and the License to Kill, *Asia News*, 13 June 2003
Black, Ian, Files Show UK Backed Murder Plot, *The Guardian*, 28 June 2001

Bowcott, Owen, No Soldiers or Police to be Charged over Finucane Murder, Prosecutors Rule, *The Guardian*, 26 June 2007

Breakfast at Rosa's, *ES Magazine*, 10 November 2006

Britain Revokes Wedding Invite To Syria Envoy, *Wall Street Journal*, 28 April 2011

Bruce, Ian, Smash-and-Grab Rescue Comes After Fortnight Spying on Captors, *The Herald*, 11 September 2000

Buckley, Nick, Diana and, in the Aegean, Diana is Cruising Again, *Mail on Sunday*, 17 August 1997

Charles, Diana Attend Second Dinner Together, *The Star*, 30 April 1993

Clinton Backs Diana on Mine Ban, *Daily Mail*, 19 August 1997

Clinton Rejects Landmine Treaty, *Mail On Sunday*, 30 November 1997

Cockburn, Patrick, MI6 in Plot to Kill Saddam, *The Independent on Sunday*, 15 February 1998

Cohen, Nick, Secrets and Lies, *The Observer*, 12 March 2000

Collins, Laura, How Rupert Lost His Babykins to Big Willie, *Daily Mail*, 19 August 2006

Craig, Olga, John Le Carré, *Sydney Morning Herald: Spectrum Magazine*, 18 September 2010

———, John Le Carré: "We Carried Out Assassinations During the Cold War", *The Telegraph*, 28 August 2010

Daley, Paul, Media Gag on Alleged Plot to Kill Gaddafi, *The Age*, 10 October 2002

Dempster, Nigel, Baby Joy for Diana's Friend, *Daily Mail*, 24 October 1996

Dennis, Steve, Paul Burrell Revelations, *Daily Mirror*, 6 November 2002

———, 100 Threats: Burrell Menaced by String of Phone Calls to Arson-Hit Shop, *The Mirror*, 2 December 2002

Diana Eludes Media Again, *The Record*, 19 August 1997

Diana Plays It Cool, *The News Letter*, 21 August 1997

Diana: The Last Days; Part 8: Princess In Disguise, *Daily Record*, 24 August 1998

Diana Was A True Friend, Weeps [Diana's] Closest Confidante Rosa, *Daily Mail*, 14 December 2007

Elsworth, Catherine, Diana "Had First Affair with Personal Detective", *Daily Telegraph*, 25 October 1998

Evans, Rob & Leigh, David, Wikileaks Cables: Prince Andrew Demanded Special BAE Briefing, *The Guardian*, 30 November 2010

Fiat Uno Witnesses, *Hello! Magazine*, January 17 1998

Fisk, Robert, 'Abu Henry' and the Mysterious Silence, *The Independent*, 30 June 2007

Fricker, Martin, Scots Battalion The Black Watch on 24-Hour Standby to Enter Libya in Ghadafi Now Blames Royals, Earlier Tied Agents to Death of Diana, *Philadelphia Daily News*, 24 September 1997

Humanitarian Mission, *Daily Record*, 5 March 2011

Fryer, Jane, The MI5 Messiah: Why David Shayler Believes He Is the Son of God, *Daily Mail*, 15 August 2007

Gardham, Duncan, MI6 Boss Admits Differences in Values With US Over Torture, *The Telegraph*, 11 August 2009

Garner, Clare, House of Windsor Joins the PR Circus, *The Independent*, 23 February 1998

Golden, Andrew, Queen to Strip Harrods of Its Royal Crest, *Sunday Mirror*, 31 August 1997

Green, Michelle, Ping-Pong Princes, *People Magazine*, 6 September 1993

Gysin, Christian, Call Me Delores, Says MI5 Whistleblower David Shayler, *Daily Mail*, 16 July 2009

Hardcastle, Ephraim, So Apart from Tony Blair and Gordon Brown, Who Are the Other Notable Royal Wedding Absentees?, *Daily Mail*, 29 April 2011

Harding, Thomas, Intelligence Assets Listen In To Tehran, *The Telegraph*, 26 March 2007

————, Forgotten SAS Diary Reveals Mission to Capture Rommel, *Daily Telegraph*, 24 September 2011

Heap, Peter, The Truth Behind the MI6 Facade, *The Guardian*, 2 October 2003

Heatley, Colm, British Spies in Irish Parties, Claims Former British Spook, *Politico*, 5 January 2006

Hickman, Martin, Kill Gaddafi Plot Report Posted on Net, *The Independent*, 13 February 2000

Hollingsworth, Mark, Secrets, Lies and David Shayler, *The Guardian*, 17 March 2000

Jobson, Robert, Queen and the Dark Forces, *Evening Standard*, 6 November 2002

Kay, Richard, The Real Truth About Diana, *Daily Mail*, 29 November 2003

Richard Kay & Ian Cobain, Will He Phone Me?, *Daily Mail*, 20 August 1997

Kempster, Doug & Wingett, Fiona, Is Diana's Baby Clock Ticking?, *Sunday Mirror*, 20 July 1997

Kerr, Jane, Abolish Them: Two Thirds of Our Readers Want Rid of the Royal Family, *The Mirror*, 11 April 2001

Klein, Edward, The Trouble with Andrew, *Vanity Fair*, August 2011

Lashmar, Paul & Judd, Terry, Student Questioned Over Links to Shayler as Special Branch Investigates MI6 Leak, *The Independent*, 8 March 2000

Lashmar, Paul & McCann, Paul, Parliament: Speculation: Editor Named as MI6 Agent, *The Independent*, 17 December 1998

Lawson, Dominic, A Crucial Personal Detail ... and the Truth About Diana's Death, *Daily Mail*, 4 June 2006

Lowther, William & Lewis, Jason, Gadaffi Plot Credible, Say US, *Mail on Sunday*, 31 August 1997

Lyall, Sarah, Are Britain's Covert Operatives Messing Up? Don't Even Ask, *The New York Times*, 5 August 1998

Mackay, Neil, "My Unit Conspired in the Murder of Civilians in Ireland", *The Sun-Herald*, 19 November 2000

Maier, Timothy, The Bugging of the APEC in Seattle, *Insight Magazine*, 29 September 1997

Morrisroe, Clare, Diana's Last Secret: She Asked Me to Marry Her & Dodi, Says Priest, *The People*, 15 October 2000

Narayahan, K.S., 10 Questions: Nina Pillai, *Outlook India Magazine*, 11 June 1997

New Year Honours: The Prime Minister's List, *The Independent*, 31 December 1997

Norton-Taylor, Richard, MI6: The Nightmare Scenario as a Rogue Agent Goes Public, *The Guardian*, 13 May 1999

————, Rogue Agent Accused of Going Public on MI6 Names, *The Guardian*, 19 May 1999

————, Sir David Spedding: MI6 Chief Behind Post-Cold War Change of Role, *The Guardian*, 14 June 2001

————, Police Raid Riviera Home of Former MI6 Officer, *The Guardian*, 29 June 2006

Norton-Taylor, Richard & Pallister, David, MI6 Tries to Limit Internet Damage, *The Guardian*, 15 May 1999

Phoblact, An, History: British Spies in the 26 Counties, *Ireland's Own*, 27 December 2001

Plunkett, John, Profile: Dominic Lawson, *The Guardian*, 14 June 2005

Preston, Richard, News Flashes That Alerted the World, *The Telegraph*, 31 August 2002

Princess Diana Sparks Frenzy Of Sightings, *Daily Gazette*, 19 August 1997

Pritchard, Louise, A Harlot, a Trollop and a Whore...., *Mail on Sunday*, 10 November 2002

Public Unease at a Royal Romance, *Daily Mail*, 8 August 1997

Reid, Sue, Diana: The MI6 Mystery, *Daily Mail*, 4 December 2004

————, Revealed: Diana Inquiry's Tantalising New Questions, *Daily Mail*, June 17 2006

————, Diana: The Unseen Evidence Which Has Been Mysteriously Ignored Until Now, *Daily Mail*, 25 September 2007

Revamping the Royals, *The Economist*, 12 March 1998

Risen, James, FBI Probed Alleged CIA Plot to Kill Hussein, *Los Angeles Times*, 15 February 1998

Roberts, Laura, MI6 Chief Sir John Sawers Says Secrecy is Vital to Keep UK Safe, *The Telegraph*, 28 October 2010

Robinson, Eugene, Elizabeth II Offers to Pay Taxes: Queen Trimming Family's Costs, *Washington Post*, 27 November 1992

Rodgers, Peter & Moore, John, Rowland-Fayed: Handshake in Harrods Food Hall Ends Eight-Year Feud, *The Independent*, 23 October 1993

Rosa Monckton, *You Magazine*, 21 October 2007

Royal Family Gathers to Chart Its Future: Way Ahead Group Talks About Church Links, Rules for Succession, *The Spectator* (Toronto), 17 September 1996

Royal Family Rethinks Future Role for Survival, *The Washington Times*, 1 September 1996

Rufford, Nicholas, Revealed: Cook Misled Public Over Libya Plot, *Sunday Times*, 16 February 2000

Sharrock, David, No Charges Against Security Forces for Finucane Murder, *The Times*, 26 June 2007

Shihata, Yasmine, Mohamed Al Fayed, *Enigma Magazine*, August 2000

Simpson, Aislinn, Camilla: "I Won't Attend Princess Diana Service", *The Telegraph*, 27 August 2007

Singh, Kuldip, Obituary: Rajan Pillai, *The Independent*, 10 July 1995

Sir Angus Ogilvy – Obituary, *The Telegraph*, 27 December 2004

Sir David Spedding, *The Telegraph*, 14 June 2001

Smith, Michael, Cook Denies MI6 Plot to Assassinate Gaddafi, *Daily Telegraph*, 10 August 1998

Taylor, Peter, Six Days That Shook Britain, *The Guardian*, 24 July 2002

The Face: Rosa Monckton, *The Times*, 28 August 2007

The Media Swarm Greek Isles, In Search Of Diana, *Philadelphia Inquirer*, 18 August 1997

"This Is Diana Being Totally Irresponsible", *Sunday Mirror*, 13 July 1997

Travis, Alan, Support for Royal Family Falls to New Low, *The Guardian*, 12 June 2000

Traynor, Ian, MI6 Involved in Balkan Spy Plot, Says Croatian Paper, *The Guardian*, 27 August 2004

Traynor, Ian & Norton-Taylor, Richard, Editor "Provided Cover for Spies", *The Guardian*, 26 January 2001

Van Gelder, Lawrence, Chronicle, *The New York Times*, 19 August 1997

Walker, Tom, & Ivanovic, Milorad, Vengeful Serbs Betray Top MI6 Man, *Sunday Times*, 16 August 2004

Weathers, Helen, My Down's Daughter Changed My Life, *Daily Mail*, 14 November 2007

Whitaker, James, I've Done Nothing Sarong, *The Mirror*, 14 July 1997

White, Stephen, Diana 1961-1997: Last Goodbye: My Life Is Bliss, Bye Bye, *The Mirror*, 8 September 1997

Press Releases

Ahern, Dermot, Statement on N.I. Police Ombudsman's Report on McCord Case, 22 January 2007
International Transport Forum, Asia Needs To Act On Road Crashes, 22 September 2009
Press Office Downing Street, Change of Her Majesty's Ambassador to the Republic of Finland, 26 January 2006

Media Documentaries, Interviews and Transcripts

Associated-Rediffusion Television, *Unlawful Killing*, Documentary Film, 2012
Artline Films, *Requiem for a Princess*, Documentary Film, 2007
Barbara Walters, *Princess Diana's Best Friend*, Interview with Rosa Monckton, ABC 20/20, 5 September 1997
BBC, *The David Shayler Affair*, Panorama, 7 August 1998
Gordon Corera, *MI6: A Century in the Shadows*, BBC Radio 4 Documentary, 10 August 2009
Hallmark Entertainment, *Diana: Queen of Hearts*, TV Documentary, 1998
Independent Television News, *Diana: Her True Story*, Documentary, 1998
Paul Sparks, Interview with Richard Tomlinson, 2009
Tabloid Tales, Paul Burrell, TV Documentary, 27 May 2003

Official Reports

Guidelines on Special Branch Work in the United Kingdom, Home Office, Communication Directorate, March 2004
O'Loan, Nuala, Statement by the Police Ombudsman for Northern Ireland on her Investigation into the Circumstances Surrounding the Death of Raymond McCord Junior and Related Matters, 22 January 2007
Stevens, John, Stevens Enquiry: Overview & Recommendations, 17 April 2003
The Report of the Independent Commission of Inquiry into the Dublin and Monaghan Bombings, December 2003

Documents from Operation Paget Investigation File

Burrell, Paul, Witness Statement, 27 April 2006
Cole, Michael, Witness Statement, 6 July 2006
Easton, Philip, Witness Statement, 13 March 2006

Flecha de Lima, Lucia, Witness Statement, 1 September 2004
Jay, Michael, Witness Statement, 13 December 2005
Launay, Patrick, Witness Statement, 21 March 2006
Macnamara, John, Witness Statement, 3 July 2006
Moss, Keith, Witness Statement, 22 October 2004

Correspondence

Beamish, David, Clerk of the Parliaments (UK), Letter to Christopher
Monckton, July 2011: www.parliament.uk/business/news/2011/july
Cole, Michael, Email to John Morgan, 5 December 2011
Davies, Julie Ann, Email to John Young, 22 August 2000:
http://cryptome.sabotage
Klein, Frank, Email to John Morgan, 21 July 2011
Machon, Annie, Email to John Morgan, 25 April 2011

Reference Works

Soanes, C., & Hawker, S., (2005), Editors, *Compact Oxford English
Dictionary of Current English*, UK, Oxford University Press

Legislation

Official Secrets Act 1911
Official Secrets Act 1989
Intelligence Services Act 1994
Criminal Justice (Terrorism and Conspiracy) Act 1998

Court Rulings and Documents

Baker, Scott, Coroner's Inquests Into The Deaths Of Diana, Princess of
Wales and Mr Dodi Al Fayed, Reasons, 12 March 2008
Case No: CO/2706/08, In The High Court Of Justice, The President Of The
Queen's Bench Division, Mr Justice Gross and Mr Justice Walker, Between:
The Queen on the Application of Mohamed Al Fayed (Claimant) and
Assistant Deputy Coroner of Inner West London (Defendant), Hearing dates:
18th March 2008, Approved Judgement

Index

0

007............................68, See Bond, James

A

A Man Called Intrepid 81, 163, 698
A Study of Assassination 466
A4 Paper 113, 178
Abu Dhabi 145, 212
Accountability ... 35–38, 35, 36, 37, 38, 55, 66, 132
Adeane, Michael................................ 554
Aden 83
Aegean Sea . 387, 388, 389, 390, 391, 392, 393, 700
After Dark 69
Agenda 360, 547, 561, 562, 563, 564, 565, 566, 568, 574, 575, 576, 577, 578, 582, 583, 584, 585, 587, 588, 589, 590, 591, 592, 593, 596, 597
Ahern, Dermot................................97, 704
Airlie, Lord ... 562, 563, 571, 572, 582, 593
Al Fayed, Heini 368
Al Fayed, Mohamed 22, 44, 45, 46, 51, 52, 125, 150, 184, 185, 186, 187, 194, 195, 242, 251, 254, 255, 271, 328, 331, 360, 367, 368, 369, 370, 372, 373, 374, 375, 377, 378, 380, 381, 382, 383, 384, 385, 395, 396, 398, 433, 447, 455, 472, 523, 524, 526, 530, 547, 568, 593, 594, 595, 596, 597, 598, 599, 600, 602, 603, 604, 605, 606, 608, 609, 610, 611, 612, 613, 615, 616, 617, 618, 619, 652, 653, 661, 662, 668, 679, 682, 703, 705
accused MI6 ....45, 185
accused Philip..........................45, 185
alleged Rosa worked for MI6 329
joint ventures with Diana 595
letters from Diana 381
MI6 admitted it had documents on613
MI6 interest in......................... 608–13
not asked about source re Fellowes 526
punished by assassinating Dodi..... 615
Al Fayeds .... 367, 370, 372, 380, 382, 396, 533, 561, 567, 583, 584, 590, 613, 614, 662, See Fayed, Dodi
on WAG agenda 597
Albania................................333, 334
Alderson, Andrew 412, 413, 427, 428, 699
Alexandria.................................82, 83
Al-Hayat...............................111, 116
Alibis ... 241, 251, 303, 318, 319, 320, 321, 324, 467, 472, 504, 509, 515, 520, 525, 526, 527, 528, 530, 541, 544, 663
never checked 472
Allidiere, Jean-Pierre ..215, 216, 218, 221, 223, 224, 225, 226, 227
Alma Tunnel.... 3, 4, 16, 43, 105, 126, 132, 198, 202, 227, 247, 268, 303, 308, 309, 323, 324, 328, 448, 458, 480, 482, 491, 500, 501, 503, 514, 518, 525, 538, 539, 541, 548, 599, 614, 684
MI6 sightings 230
Althorp.. 369
Al-Yamama 683
Amanusa......................................351, 357
Amanwana..................................351, 357
Ambassador.. 36, 117, 234, 238, 239, 244, 249, 257, 262, 267, 268, 269, 270, 275, 278, 285, 290, 292, 294, 295, 296, 300, 301, 308, 310, 330, 337, 339, 340, 341, 350, 351, 356, 362, 369, 413, 415, 439, 443, 476, 477, 481, 484, 486, 487, 488, 490, 491, 494, 500, 506, 507, 508, 509, 511, 515, 519, 522, 524, 528, 529, 531, 532, 666, 668, 670, 692, 704, See Jay, Michael
Ambulance... 4
Amman 100, 145
ANA... 84
Andanson, James ...26, 286, 456, 457, 551

Andersen, Christopher 654
Anderson, Nicholas 67, 159, 166, 696, 740
Andrew, Christopher 38, 39, 160, 161, 162
Andros 388
Angola .190, 191, 205, 207, 208, 209, 210,
    211, 212, 328, 546, 548, 549, 600, 682
Annus Horribilus. 327, 360, 546, 572, 580,
    623
Answerphone 484, 489
Anti-Landmines Campaign ... 27, 192, 211,
    327, 328, 385, 449, 463, 469, 472,
    474, 546, 547, 596, 598, 600, 601,
    679, 681, 682, 683, 684, See
    Landmines
    June 1997 speech 548
Apocryphal 624
Appeal Court 134
Arab.84, 89, 108, 109, 110, 112, 113, 115,
    116, 119, 143, 145, 292
Archives.14, 113, 175, 305, 370, 478, 580,
    590, 698
Argentina 633
Aristocracy 340, 341, 344, 345, 346
Armaments .199, 210, 212, 474, 601, 615,
    679, 680, 682
Arthur, M.A. 275
Asia Times 89
Assassination
    CIA manual 66, 466–68
    history of British involvement in 80–
    180
    in MI6 training 54–80
    part of MI6 ethos 180
Assassination in Paris
    a joint intelligence operation 474
    allegations against MI6 185–98
    allegations of MI6 involvement 125
    CIA involvement 466–69
    conflicts in allegations 195
    evidence of MI6 involvement .. 471–72
    highly coordinated 26
    not independent operation 180–85
    possibilities involving MI6 195
    possibilities of how carried out 26
    royal involvement 662
    similarities to assassination manual
    467

Assassination Plots
    CIA list 465
    Gaddafi, Milosevic, Saddam plots
        compared 125–29
Associated Press 288
Athens ..173, 387, 388, 389, 390, 391, 392
Attenborough, Richard 397, 398
Australia 36, 136, 696, 697, 739
Austria 70, 136, 160
Authorisation ..31, 57, 101, 112, 113, 114,
    144, 145, 146, 147, 160, 167, 168,
    187, 193, 195, 475
Authorised Deceit 235, 294

B

Babysitter 248, 251, 252, 319
BAC 16
BAE 304, 683
BAE Systems 304
Baghdad 100
Bahamas 351, 358, 359
Baker, Scott.13, 16, 28, 29, 30, 32, 40, 41,
    44, 45, 46, 47, 48, 51, 52, 53, 54, 58,
    59, 61, 71, 75, 76, 77, 78, 102, 103,
    125, 126, 129, 130, 132, 149, 150,
    154, 155, 157, 158, 169, 172, 176,
    179, 183, 184, 185, 190, 205, 206,
    207, 209, 210, 211, 212, 218, 235,
    236, 237, 238, 241, 242, 244, 250,
    255, 256, 257, 258, 260, 262, 263,
    265, 266, 285, 291, 302, 318, 322,
    380, 400, 401, 407, 409, 415, 438,
    439, 440, 441, 445, 456, 457, 460,
    470, 471, 473, 476, 480, 496, 498,
    525, 527, 530, 531, 552, 563, 564,
    565, 566, 578, 583, 584, 587, 588,
    589, 590, 591, 592, 593, 594, 603,
    604, 605, 607, 612, 613, 614, 615,
    616, 617, 624, 629, 645, 646, 647,
    648, 651, 654, 655, 656, 657, 658,
    659, 660, 661, 664, 679, 681, 705
    a corrupt judge 194, 647
    attacked Burrell's credibility 646
    attacked Tomlinson 263
    chose Milosevic over Gaddafi plot
    125–29

concerns about Summing Up re WAG 584–92
concerns over his comments on Queen's statement 646–48
conflicting account re WAG minutes 589
deliberately undermined Tomlinson 263
described MI6 activities 52, 54
failed to call key witnesses 144, 230, 304, 496, 654–61, 664
failed to investigate foreign involvement 457
failed to seek out Philip-Diana letters 440
failed to seek truth .132, 496, 518, 525
falsely merged two WAG articles together 585
falsified information on Sep 97 WAG meeting 613
intervened inappropriately .52, 75, 78, 154, 156, 211, 553
lied about rogue element 184
lied at inquest 47, 48, 53, 77, 185, 442, 647
lied to protect royals from giving evidence............................. 658–60
manipulated his jury...................... 648
misled his jury 45, 46, 76, 78, 130, 158, 185, 265, 458, 646, 647, 664
misled his jury re WAG 584–92
misquoted Tomlinson..................... 263
refused to call senior royal suspects 654–61
refused to discuss Gaddafi plot 101, 125, 129, 145
said key WAG documents not relevant 590
suppressed argument......41, 129, 157, 212, 554
withheld evidence ..517, 543, 590, 660
wrongly stated crucial WAG meeting date 588
Bali 327, 350, 351, 353, 354, 355, 357, 358, 359, 360
Balkans . 32, 49, 61, 63, 69, 127, 150, 159, 166, 169, 178, 188, 201, 203, 318, 322, 332, 472, 703
Ball, Jonathan 56

Balmoral 186, 195, 351, 352, 403, 486, 523, 563, 568, 595, 615, 677
Banja Luka 331, 332
Bar Vendôme....... 214, 215, 216, 218, 228
8 witnesses in 218
MI6 sightings 214–28
Barker, Jackie.................19, 104, 131, 145
not heard.................................19, 131
Barrett, Ken 93
Bartholomew, Carolyn........................ 364
Bartlett, Richard 18, 104, 131, 144
not heard...................................... 131
Bashir, Martin 327, 406, 410, 546
Basselier, Nicola.... 20, 481, 489, 500, 506, 670
not heard.. 20
Bateau-Mouche 520, 521
Battle 212
BBC ... 37, 53, 68, 106, 107, 108, 113, 114, 115, 117, 133, 135, 231, 327, 446, 536, 546, 570, 573, 582, 620, 630, 698, 704, 740
BCA 23
Beatrice 337, 348
Bedhopper...........................568, 596, 619
Beirut....................................145, 288
Belfast............................89, 90, 97
Belfield, Richard....... 85, 88, 162, 164, 696
Belgium..............................87, 162
Belgrade 331, 332, 336
Benhamou, Serge 229
Benjamin, Angela
mistreated by royals...................... 652
Bennett, Richard..............89, 90, 162, 699
Berlin 557, 558
Bettles, Trevor 351
Bevin, Ernest....................................69, 82
Biographies. 161, 265, 267, 276, 278, 279, 282, 287, 288, 290, 292, 293, 301, 302, 304, 306, 307, 308, 309, 310, 311, 321, 323, 331
issues regarding List biographies306–8
Birthday 251, 316, 319, 328, 366, 367, 370, 372, 434, 547
Bishop, Andrew 483, 496
not heard....................................... 19
Bistro d'a Côte 248, 319
Black, Ian 87, 162, 699
Blackmail 53
Blair, Cherie 665, 666, 676

Blair, Tony 21, 186, 195, 385, 547, 581, 664, 665, 666, 667, 668, 669, 670, 671, 672, 673, 674, 675, 676, 677, 678, 679, 680, 682, 683, 696, 701
central contact point for Queen 680
concerns regarding Dodi 674
description of Queen's reaction to
Diana 601
distancing 674, 676
harmonised account with Campbell
.... 673
lied about Chequers conversation . 667
lied about crash notification timing
.... 668–76
not heard 21
prior knowledge of assassination ... 12, 664–80, 676–78
role in Paris crash 664–80
weekly meeting with Queen 601
Bloch, Jonathan .. 152, 153, 158, 163, 556, 696
Blum, William 466, 696
Blunt, Anthony ... 554, 555, 556, 557, 558, 662
royal mission to Germany 554–59
BMP-3 212
Bombs . 12, 82, 89, 91, 101, 105, 106, 107, 110, 111, 114, 117, 148, 161
Bond, James 68, 69, 109, 160, 630
Bonn Embassy 685
Boothby, Robert 83
Bordeaux 293, 295, 298
Bose, Chandra 69, 159, 161
Bosnia .. 190, 259, 328, 332, 334, 547, 596, 682
Bowcott, Owen 93, 700
Bowker, Elsa 191, 352, 364, 376, 397, 398, 626, 627, 628, 629, 631, 632, 633, 634, 635, 636, 641
Boy's Own 109, 111
Brady, Gerald 96
Brazil 36, 294, 327, 337, 339, 340, 341, 346, 347, 349, 351, 356, 374, 375, 426, 439, 443
Brazilian Embassy 341, 418
Brigade Criminelle 23, 229, 454, 456, 533, 534

Britannia 570, 572
British Ambassador. 238, See Jay, Michael
British Authorities 37, 134, 144, 336, 461, 525
British Consul General 477, 478, 488, 654, See Moss, Keith
British Consulate 529
British Embassy ....17, 19, 20, 32, 35, 68, 109, 183, 234, 237, 238, 240, 242, 244, 247, 249, 250, 256, 257, 258, 259, 263, 264, 268, 269, 270, 271, 279, 285, 288, 292, 309, 317, 318, 331, 335, 461, 476, 475–545, 476, 479, 480, 481, 483, 486, 489, 496, 500, 504, 505, 506, 507, 516, 523, 524, 525, 530, 531, 534, 535, 536, 537, 539, 665, 670, See Embassy
diplomatic personnel list September
1996 273
diplomatic personnel list September
1997 246
distancing of staff 539
involvement in assassination 544
knowledge of Diana's presence in
France 531–42, 543
missing phone call records 479–518
most staff not interviewed 537–39
phone calls 479–518
police statements re phone calls ... 510
post-crash reports 477–79
suppressed 479
pre-crash phone calls 518
problems with phone call evidence
.... 491–502
relationship to Consulate 476
staff comparison 1996 and 1997 ... 275
staff lied in evidence 479
British Government. 12, 20, 24, 25, 26, 31, 33, 34, 57, 85, 87, 106, 107, 116, 132, 134, 147, 148, 191, 193, 208, 233, 310, 475, 533, 664, 678, 679, 680, 698, See Blair, Tony
accountability **37**, 38
involved in Paris crash 12, 663–80
suppressed Shayler's evidence 132–35
British Intelligence .. 39, 54, 67, 68, 89, 90, 95, 97, 98, 99, 106, 110, 112, 115,

116, 117, 119, 135, 151, 161, 165, 175, 332, 378, 384, 385, 396, 447, 458, 462, 471, 528, 548, 554, 558, 656, 660, 662, *See* MI6; MI5
Anthony Blunt's royal mission . 554–59
involvement in assassination plots.. 12
British Investigations*See* Operation Paget; Inquest; Baker, Scott
delayed.. 11
flawed.. 11
British Landmines Trust 188, 189, 190
British Midland 677
British Security Coordination....23, 69, 81, 161, *See* BSC
British Taxpayers 109, 112, 570
British-Irish Rights Watch 95
BSC.................... 23, 69, 81, 159, 161, 163
Buckingham Palace.......20, 327, 340, 380, 410, 412, 414, 416, 429, 440, 441, 442, 443, 447, 486, 546, 566, 567, 568, 570, 571, 572, 573, 590, 599, 620, 624, 625, 627, 641, 643, 671, 675, 676
Buckley, Nick.......387, 389, 390, 391, 392, 393, 700
possibly influenced by MI6............ 391
problems over Greek holiday article
.... 391
Bulovka Hospital 81
Burnett, Ian.. 22
falsely introduced rogue element . 184
flawed questioning over assassinations 171
inadequate questioning of Dearlove
.... 552
inadequate questioning of Mohamed
.... 526
inadequate questioning of X 203
lied at inquest..........................194, 441
misled the jury......................257, 374
protected a false witness 374
provided answers to Curley........... 312
rescues Baker re Gaddafi plot 130
Burnham Market 524, 527
Burrell Note 643
Burrell, Paul 189, 190, 352, 353, 359, 375, 376, 386, 397, 398, 410, 411, 414, 425, 433, 434, 435, 437, 438, 442, 595, 619, 620, 621, 622, 623, 624, 625, 626, 627, 628, 629, 630, 631, 632, 633, 634, 635, 636, 637, 638, 639, 640, 641, 642, 643, 644, 645, 646, 647, 648, 649, 650, 651, 652, 654, 655, 656, 658, 660, 662, 663, 669, 671, 682, 696, 700, 704
arson attack.................................... 649
warning 650
conflict with Devorik 632–33
conflicted loyalties 644
conflicting evidence 642
connected crash to royal family 645
crash notification 669
had concerns re the crash 634
lied... 629
lied at inquest................................ 640
lied re Queen's statement........12, 643
misled the public 638
protected Charles over Burrell Note
.... 638
protected the Queen..............638, 644
Queen's statement.................. 620–48
suspicions regarding the Queen.... 645
withheld evidence 645
Burrell-Queen Meeting................ 620–48
Burrell admitted lying.................... 629
concerns over Baker comments .. 646–48
conflicting evidence 631
conflicts between Burrell and Devorik
.... 632–33
significance of Queen's statement 636
Bystanders...........................116, 230, 317

C

Cabinet Office......116, 124, 127, 128, 552
Cairo 84, 85, 86, 116, 118, 288, 292
Caithness, Lady 694
Cambridge 198, 232, 439
Cambridge Street................................. 401
Campaign Against the Arms Trade 683
Campbell, Alistair....21, 98, 665, 667, 668, 669, 670, 671, 672, 673, 674, 675, 676, 677, 678, 680, 696
distancing of Blair......................... 674
harmonised account with Blair 673
lied about crash notification timing
.... 668–76
not heard....................................... 21
Campbell, Menzies 117

Canada 463, 558, 568, 600
Canadian Initiative 463
Carpenter, Paul .. 216, 218, 219, 220, 221,
    222, 223, 224, 225, 226, 227, 228
    flawed investigator 225
    misled the jury 219–28
Carte Bleue................................. 216, 222
Castro, Fidel 69
Catholic Church 568, 573, 576
Caton, Valerie..... 271, 276, 280, 282, 306,
    307, 308, 309, 310, 318, 321, 323,
    471, 472, 475, 684
    arrived in Paris pre-crash 306–8
    List biography not updated............ 307
    not heard 17, 660
    transferred into Paris....................... 17
Cavalcade 101, 105, 106, 107, 110, 114,
    115, 116
CCTV....216, 217, 219, 220, 221, 222, 223,
    225
Central Intelligence Agency..... 23, See CIA
Century House 152, 153
Chancery 275, 278, 292, 308, 480, 481,
    482, 484, 487, 491, 493, 495, 499,
    507, 508, 510, 517, 525, 529
    daily occurrence log...... 480, 481, 482,
        483, 491, 493, 495
    desk.. 483, 529
Chapman, Adam................................. 564
Charing Cross Hospital .... 16, See Imperial
    College
Charlton, A. 687
Chequers 547, 666, 667, 668, 674, 678
Cheshire 411, 414
Chevènement............................. 480, 670
China 304, 306
Chios 387, 388, 391
Chirac, Jacques.................................... 682
Christmas 104, 131, 136, 191, 304, 558,
    599, 649
Chronology... 480
Churchill International Hotel............... 368
CIA... 23, 36, 50, 67, 68, 69, 82, 83, 84, 87,
    88, 99, 100, 101, 106, 112, 126, 163,
    166, 454, 455, 456, 457, 461, 462,
    463, 466, 467, 469, 473, 474, 550,
    663, 681, 684, 696, 698, 702

assassination manual66, 82, 160, 466–
    68
assassination plot list.................... 465
evidence of involvement 462–69
prior knowledge............................. 469
relationship with MI6 461
Cigars 217, 223, 225, 226, 227, 228
Circumstantial Evidence...... 125, 659, 681
Civil List 570, 572
Clair, Jean-François 456
Clark, Alan 693, 694
Clinton, Bill..387, 462, 463, 469, 474, 669,
    670, 681, 682, 700
    crash notification 670
Clinton, Chelsea 463
Clinton, Hillary.................................... 463
CNN 463, 469, 669, 698
Cobain, Ian 389, 390, 391, 392, 701
Cockburn, Patrick 99, 700
Cohen, Nick 118, 700
Cole, Michael 229, 368, 369, 370, 377,
    378, 587, 595, 615, 616, 620, 652,
    653, 654, 669, 672, 705
    conflict with Rosa Monckton 370
    crash notification 669
Coles, John 116, 304, 478
Collecott, P. 687
Collusion 66, 93, 94, 95, 96, 160, 166, 694
    between Baker and MI6 129
    between Carpenter and MacLeod219–
        28
    between embassy and police 542
    between French and British... 507, 522
    between MI6 and Paget.................. 44
Colonial Office................................ 82, 86
Colthurst, James................................. 327
Communications Centre 397, 523, 524,
    526, 528, 529
Condon, Paul378, 379, 382, 383, 559, 594
Confidante ..337, 338, 341, 345, 360, 361,
    446
Congo.. 87, 88
Congress for Cultural Freedom 462
Conservatives...........................See Tories
Conspiracy.......40, 44, 103, 109, 130, 139,
    140, 141, 150, 201, 203, 242, 455,
    456, 467, 476, 617, 630, 681

Consul General ...243, 276, 476, 485, 487, 532, 534, *See* Moss, Keith

Consular Report.................................... 477

Controllerate 61, 169

Convie, Gary 96

Cook, Robin 115, 117, 118, 119, 134, 136, 137, 138, 139, 140, 141, 142, 146, 147, 186, 195, 232, 233, 304, 486, 676, 703

   denied involvement re Gaddafi plot 114, 137

   misled the public 138, 142, 146

Cooper, Chester..................................... 83

Copley, Caroline.. 276, 280, 282, 306, 310, 318, 321

   could be Ms 1 310

   not cross-examined 17

Coptic... 288

Cornwell, David.....................67, 159, 166

Coroner...........................*See* Baker, Scott

Coroners Act 1988 655

Corruption . 11, 26, 37, 129, 194, 542, 647

Costello, Seamus 89, 90

Counsellor... 269, 270, 275, 276, 282, 286, 287, 289, 290, 291, 292, 294, 297, 300, 301, 302, 304, 307, 308, 321, 331, 336, 687, 691

Court of St James................................ 337

Courtiers 350, 357, 358, 566, 568, 569, 572, 576

Covert Operations 69, 152, 153, 161

Cover-Up. 4, 11, 13, 26, 27, 29, 48, 93, 95, 96, 197, 235, 302, 303, 317, 325, 458, 472, 473, 505, 507, 514, 520, 522, 541, 542, 544, 545, 559, 582, 583, 613, 662, 681, 682

   of MI6 officer movements............. 324

Cover-Up of a Royal Murder .4, 11, 44, 95, 228, 527, 611, 697, 739

Cowper-Coles, Sherard .17, 245, 267, 268, 270, 275, 280, 282, 283, 286, 287, 288, 289, 290, 291, 292, 293, 294, 295, 296, 297, 298, 299, 300, 301, 302, 303, 304, 305, 306, 308, 310, 311, 313, 314, 318, 319, 321, 323, 447, 471, 472, 475, 508, 533, 684

   2011 interview 304

      ignored Diana........................... 305

   arrived in Paris before crash.. 287–306

   comparison with Eugene Curley... 292, 295

   distanced from involvement 302

   involvement with BAE 683

   issues around Paris arrival....... 298–99

   List biography not updated 308

   mentions by Jay............................ 296

   no alibi request 319

   not heard. 17, 290, 297, 303, 304, 319, 323, 660

   reaction to news........................... 291

CPS... 103

Craig, Keith 334, 700, 740

Credit Cards 248, 319

Criminal Investigation Department 96

Criminal Justice Act...............70, 168, 705

Crinnion, Patrick 90

Croatia 100, 332, 703

Crocodiles 87

Crown Jewels 410, 411, 414, 434

Crown Prosecution Service 102, 127

Croxford, Ian....................................... 22

Curley, Eugene.... 276, 280, 282, 285, 287, 288, 289, 290, 291, 292, 294, 295, 296, 297, 298, 299, 301, 302, 303, 304, 310, 311, 312, 313, 314, 315, 316, 318, 319, 322, 324, 535, 691

   comparison with Cowper-Coles ... 292, 295

   evidence re officers on duty.... 314–20

   given answers by Burnett.............. 313

   identified as Mr 4 288

   left Paris before crash 296, 313

   lied at inquest.........292, 297, 301, 323

   not mentioned by Jay.................... 296

   participated in cover-up................ 302

   points regarding inquest evidence 291

   promoted in 1997 287

   protected Cowper-Coles 302

   reaction to the news 291, 294

   refused to carry out assassination 301

   replaced by Cowper-Coles before crash.................................. 287–306

Curtil, Christian 451, 452, 453

   assaulted 452

   not heard...................................... 453

CX 95/53452 Document .18, 19, 104, 115, 120, 121, 122, 123, 125, 131, 132, 139, 162

   authenticity 139–42

CX Reports...104, 109, 113, 116, 127, 128, 139, 140, 143, 144, 145, 146, 147, 168, 174
Cyprus 86, 87

D

Dadgar, Ahmad 164
Dail Chamber.. 90
Daily Mail 147, 217, 226, 345, 355, 357, 370, 392, 443, 446, 447, 462, 523, 525, 526, 571, 574, 596, 597, 677, 699, 700, 701, 702, 703
Daily Record 151, 388, 389, 390, 391, 392, 393, 700, 701
Dark Forces ...12, 620, 623, 624, 625, 629, 630, 631, 632, 640, 641, 645, 647, 651, 701
    originated with Robert Jobson.......640
Darlan, Jean-François 163
Dauzonne, Georges............................... 16
Dauzonne, Sabine 230
Davies, David...... 134, 378, 379, 380, 382, 383, 384, 547, 594, 615, 705
Davies, Julie Ann 134
DB 332
De la Mare, Tom.................................... 22
De Witte, Ludo 87
Dearlove, Richard....29, 30, 32, 33, 36, 40, 41, 42, 47, 48, 71, 72, 73, 74, 75, 78, 79, 99, 102, 129, 130, 138, 139, 150, 153, 154, 155, 156, 157, 158, 160, 166, 168, 169, 173, 174, 184, 188, 189, 190, 191, 192, 193, 202, 210, 211, 212, 268, 381, 383, 471, 473, 474, 475, 552, 553, 607, 608, 609, 610, 611, 613
    carefully questioned about assassinations........................... 168
    conflict with Ritchie 553
    cross-examination on strobe lights 202
    evasive at inquest 72, 211
    evasive on Angola 210
    knowledge of training policy............ 73
    mantra on landmines..................... 210
    not open at inquest 47
    presided over Gaddafi, Saddam and Diana 156
    reactions re questions on Increment 154–58
    refused to answer questions 47, 71, 212
    tried to undermine Tomlinson......473, 553
Deceit.................................. 449, 470, 473
Defence, Press and Broadcasting Advisory Committee................................... 231
Della Grazia..386, 388, 389, 391, 392, 393
Delorm, Rene 696
Dempster, Nigel 355, 356, 700
Denial....32, 193, 203, 204, 231, 232, 381, 384, 430, 457, 663
Denmark 232
Department of Trade 236, 368
Derossi, Arnaud....... 11, 26, 251, 474, 684
Devon.. 652
Devorik, Roberto 352, 353, 359, 360, 376, 397, 398, 436, 527, 597, 619, 626, 627, 628, 631, 632, 633, 634, 635, 636, 637, 641, 643, 646, 647, 648, 656, 658, 659, 660, 662
    conflict with Burrell 632–33
DGSE 23, 456, 457, 458, 461, 473, 474, 681, 684
    didn't deny involvement............... 457
Diana - Her True Story book 599
Diana, Princess of Wales .... *See* Princess Diana
Diana-Dodi Relationship 596
Diary....252, 296, 309, 310, 319, 368, 370, 378, 502, 504, 505, 508, 509, 510, 521, 522, 532, 540, 541, 562, 563, 600, 614, 615
Dictionary................................... 314, 705
Diplomatic List ... 235, 236, 240, 243, 244, 245, 247, 250, 251, 265, 266, 267, 268, 269, 270, 271, 273, 274, 275, 276, 278, 279, 280, 282, 288, 289, 290, 292, 296, 302, 304, 306, 307, 308, 311, 319, 321, 323, 472, 687, 691, 696, 697
    order of entries....................... 268–71
Diplomatic Pouch........ 415, 417, 422, 427

Direction Générale de la Securité .. 23, *See* DGSE

Directorate de Surveillance Territories 23, *See* DST

Disney 351, 352, 357

Disruptive Actions 151

Distancing ... 303, 324, 335, 424, 445, 494, 507, 541, 542, 578, 582, 662, 675, 684

Divorce 327, 335, 338, 341, 347, 360, 381, 406, 410, 413, 444, 533, 540, 546, 561, 577, 587, 599, 663

Dixon, Peter 85

D-Notice 233

Donnelly, Stephen 518, 534, 537, 538, 542, 544

   missing notes 518

Dordogne 285

Dorril, Stephen 33, 66, 68, 82, 85, 90, 100, 109, 139, 151, 152, 153, 158, 159, 160, 166, 462, 466, 696, 740

Dossier 119, 142, 187, 189, 190, 191, 208, 317, 328, 445

Double Agent 163, 558

Doucin, Philippe 218

Downing Street. 20, 21, 82, 308, 486, 523, 665, 666, 671, 672, 675, 676, 677, 678, 704

   crash notification 671

   missing in Moss' inquest evidence 675

Down's Syndrome 367

DPP 95

Drug Liaison Officer 287, 296

DST .. 23, 50, 134, 135, 456, 457, 458, 459, 460, 461, 473, 474, 681, 684

   didn't deny involvement 457

Dublin 89, 90, 165, 167, 704

Duke of Brunswick 556

Duke of Edinburgh ...... 44, 45, 46, 53, 183, 184, 185, 187, 188, 192, 193, 196, 380, 400, 402, 406, 407, 408, 411, 413, 415, 427, 435, 438, 440, 551, 559, 560, 581, 615, 616, 620, 646, 655, 656, 657, *See* Prince Philip

   not heard 654–61

Duke of Kent 556, 558

Duke of Windsor 555, 556, 558, 696

Dulles, Allen 82, 84

Dunbar, Graham 133

Durham 665, 671

Duty Officer 271, 301, 310, 311, 312, 314, 315, 316, 351, 481, 484, 485, 486, 487, 488, 493, 499, 509, 516, 517, 535, 675

Dyevres, Vianney 533

E

Easton, Philip 456, 704

Economic Counsellor 280

Economic Department 17, 40, 52, 54, 236, 247, 250, 269, 270, 275, 276, 277, 279, 280, 281, 282, 283, 287, 306, 307, 308, 310, 311, 318, 321, 323, 387, 479, 685, 687, 688, 690, 691, 692

   comparison 1996 to 1997 282

   disproportionate movements in 1997 279

   staff at 31 August 1997 284

Economic with the Truth 40, 236, 605

Economist 161, 569, 573, 575, 702

Eden, Anthony 82, 83, 84, 85, 86, 193

Edmonds, James 38, 39, 697

Egypt 13, 82, 83, 84, 85, 86, 105, 288, 569, 584, 597, 609, 613

Eichelberger, James 82

Eisenhower, Dwight 87

Elephants in the Room 305

   omission of Embassy occurrence logs from evidence 517

Elysée Palace .. 20, 23, 481, 482, 483, 484, 485, 486, 488, 489, 492, 493, 496, 498, 499, 500, 501, 503, 504, 505, 507, 509, 510, 511, 514, 515, 516, 517

Embalming 23, 542, 544, 661

Embassy ..... 238, 286, 287, 291, 296, 300, 341, 477, 478, 486, 487, 488, 529, 530, 533, 534, *See* British Embassy, *See* British Embassy

   communication with Scotland Yard 519

   communication with the FCO 518

Emperor Frederick III 556

Empress Frederick 555

English National Ballet 369, 370

English, Thomas 96

Ephemeral 149, 157, 158, 175

Esher, Lord 38

Espionage 84, 118, 630

Establishment ... 85, 92, 93, 139, 144, 194, 331, 350, 360, 382, 385, 396, 399,

449, 462, 470, 472, 494, 528, 596,
598, 599, 608, 621, 623, 626, 647, 684
alibis not checked 520
denial around St Tropez holiday 381
faced landmines campaign and St
    Tropez holiday 385
ran out of legal options 599
surprised by St Tropez holiday 378
Estonia 333
Étoile Limousines 23
Eustace, P.H. 275
Eveland, Wilbur 83
Evening Standard 446, 629, 640, 701
Ewing, Timothy 275
Executive Intelligence Review 232
Explosives Research and Development
    Establishment 86
Extradition 134
Extremist Leader 127, 177

F

Fantasy .. 68, 114, 115, 118, 119, 134, 137,
138, 142, 146, 231, 329, 368, 382
Far East 351
Farran, Roy 82
Farrell, Mairead 91
Fayed, Dodi ... 3, 11, 13, 27, 28, 30, 45, 49,
50, 71, 95, 96, 125, 156, 158, 169,
172, 174, 181, 187, 188, 192, 194,
195, 197, 230, 234, 247, 248, 249,
285, 298, 309, 317, 320, 322, 324,
423, 433, 444, 446, 449, 454, 455,
461, 462, 470, 473, 474, 486, 487,
488, 492, 498, 501, 502, 532, 533,
534, 535, 536, 537, 539, 542, 543,
548, 554, 568, 571, 576, 596, 603,
605, 606, 611, 651, 660, 661, 662,
663, 666, 667, 674, 678, 681, 682,
696, 705, 739, See Assassination in
Paris
assassinated 13
FBI 23
FCO 19, 20, 23, 120, 124, 127, 128, 132,
139, 140, 141, 142, 143, 144, 146,
147, 162, 167, 168, 193, 232, 233,
236, 238, 240, 241, 256, 257, 262,

265, 266, 268, 274, 275, 278, 292,
300, 301, 302, 304, 306, 308, 331,
336, 477, 478, 481, 482, 483, 486,
488, 490, 493, 495, 496, 497, 498,
499, 508, 514, 518, 536, 549, 555,
671, 675, 676
bypassed by royals 554
possible positions on Gaddafi plot. 139
posting policy 259
prior knowledge of Gaddafi plot 139
FCO Duty Officer 20
FCO News Department 487, 671, 675, 676
Federal Bureau of Investigation ..... 23, See
    FBI
Feinstein, Andrew 683
Fellowes, Jane 524
Fellowes, Robert 378, 379, 382, 383, 384,
385, 476, 523, 524, 525, 526, 527,
528, 530, 544, 547, 560, 562, 564,
566, 567, 568, 573, 574, 575, 576,
579, 580, 581, 582, 583, 587, 588,
589, 591, 592, 593, 594, 597, 614,
615, 618, 624, 632, 658, 659, 661,
662, 663, 682, 684
conflicting alibis 526, 527
distancing re St Tropez holiday 383
excessive distancing 582
factors pointing to being in Embassy
    530
feared by Diana 527, 597, 659
lied about WAG purpose 575–83
lied at inquest 580, 582
location on the night 522–30
no proper alibi 525, 527
no supporting evidence 528
secrecy regarding movements 527
suspect 527
Fergusson, Bernard 82
Fianna Fail 89
Fiat Uno 229, 456, 551, 633, 700
Fielding, Nick 103, 107, 110, 111, 134,
141, 697
FIG 106, 107, 144, 146
Finland 308, 310, 704
Finucane, Patrick 91, 92, 93, 94, 95, 98,
162, 700, 703
assassination 91–95

Fireworky 201

Fishwick, Nicholas 49, 50, 63, 99, 204

Fisk, Robert 288, 289, 700

Fitchett, Robert ..277, 279, 283, 310, 311, 318, 321, 691

Fitzgerald, Patrick 152, 153, 158, 163, 696

Flash Equipment 198–204

Flecha de Lima, Beatriz .17, 327, 340, 348, 349, 350–60, 350, 351, 354, 355, 356, 357, 359, 360

not heard 17, 348

presence on Bali holiday 355

Flecha de Lima, Lucia 17, 327, 330, 337, 338, 339, 340, 341, 342, 343, 344, 345, 346, 347, 348, 349, 350, 351, 352, 353, 354, 355, 356, 357, 358, 359, 360, 361, 362, 363, 364, 365, 369, 370, 374, 375, 376, 377, 382, 383, 387, 396, 397, 398, 413, 414, 415, 416, 418, 419, 420, 421, 422, 423, 426, 427, 430, 431, 432, 434, 435, 437, 438, 439, 441, 442, 443, 444, 445, 446, 448, 594, 652, 669, 671, 705

Bali and Moyo Island holiday .. 350–60

changed her account on the Philip-Diana letters 417, 418, 419, 431

changed reason for Diana-Rosa introduction 345

collaborated with Rosa 444

conflict with Rosa 346

conflicting evidence 343, 344

first meetings with Diana 340

gave date of first Philip letter 426

lied in evidence 349, 350, 354, 357, 358, 365

mentioned Secret Service 364

refused to answer questions 364

relationship with Diana 341

role in Philip-Diana letters 400–446

told to help Diana 349

withheld evidence from inquest ... 423

Fleet Street 352, 357

Fleming, Ian 68, 160, 161, 698, 740

Fletcher, Richard 50, 65, 172, 178

Florida .. 351, 352, 356, 357, 358, 359, 360

Flying Free 4, 739

Foot, Hugh 86

Foot, M.R.D. 69, 159, 161, 163, 166, 696

Force Research Unit .... 23, 92, 94, 95, *See* FRU

Foreign & Commonwealth Office ... 22, 23, 696, *See* FCO

Foreign Minister 481, 506, 670

Foreign Office ... 83, 84, 88, 104, 107, 109, 110, 112, 114, 115, 116, 118, 119, 124, 138, 140, 141, 146, 167, 231, 232, 242, 251, 332, 333, 334, 386, 486, 511, 523, 528, 549, 550, 552, 556, 675, *See* FCO

prior knowledge of Gaddafi plot ... 139

Foreign Secretary 19, 35, 36, 57, 70, 82, 87, 105, 112, 114, 115, 116, 117, 118, 119, 132, 134, 135, 136, 137, 138, 140, 142, 145, 146, 147, 160, 167, 168, 178, 186, 195, 232, 233, 238, 486, 487, 671, 675, 676

Fort Bar 55, 56, 76

Fortwilliam Drive 93

Fowlcrooke, Rick 259

Fox, Eamon 96, 696

France 4, 13, 16, 17, 34, 67, 132, 136, 163, 197, 223, 227, 234, 235, 236, 238, 239, 247, 259, 267, 268, 270, 271, 285, 288, 289, 290, 291, 292, 294, 298, 299, 300, 301, 302, 303, 305, 306, 310, 312, 314, 317, 318, 319, 321, 323, 324, 335, 367, 369, 374, 375, 381, 384, 385, 458, 459, 460, 461, 467, 472, 474, 478, 481, 484, 487, 490, 506, 507, 508, 511, 516, 519, 522, 524, 528, 531, 532, 533, 534, 535, 536, 537, 539, 540, 541, 543, 601, 661, 670, 680, 682, 684, 699, 740

Frankfurt 462, 555

Franz von Papen 558

Fraser, Simon 277, 280, 283, 310, 382, 691, 692

Freedom of Information Act 454

French Alps 460

French Authorities 235, 238, 267, 287, 292, 303, 324, 335, 458, 460, 478, 508, 511, 522, 532, 533, 539, 540, 541, 542, 543, 544

French Government

involved 11

involved in Paris crash 12

French Intelligence..... 458, 461, 473, 663, 681
   involved in Paris crash 461
   relationship with UK 458–61
French Investigation..4, 32, 49, 61, 63, 65, 66, 217, 221, 222, 223, 226, 286, 516, 517
   didn't address British involvement 679
French, Mary Mel............................... 669
Friedrichshof 556
Friends 118, 133, 191, 300, 309, 315, 328, 337, 339, 340, 341, 342, 343, 344, 345, 346, 347, 348, 349, 350, 352, 356, 359, 361, 362, 363, 364, 365, 370, 371, 372, 374, 375, 376, 377, 386, 398, 406, 409, 413, 414, 422, 432, 434, 446, 447, 448, 525, 526, 547, 569, 627, 635, 667
   lent Rosa boat........................ 386, 389
Frost, David 115, 116, 307
FRU.....23, 92, 93, 94, 95, 97, 98, 162, 175
Führer 555
Fulham Mortuary 16
Furnival-Jones, Martin 167

G

G6A/3..19
   not heard 131
G6A/5..19
   not heard 131
G6A3 .... 120, 125
G6A5 .... 120, 125
G9/0 .... 104, 144
G9/PT16 Meetings 104, 108
G9A/1.................... 18, 104, 108, 131, 144
G9A/15 .... 19, 104, 108, 131, 145
G9A5 .... 120, 125
Gabcik, Josef 81
Gaddafi Plot 18, 19, 102, 105, 125, 126, 127, 128, 129, 130, 131, 133, 143, 145, 146, 172, 174, 322, 475
   authorised by government 144–47
   MI6 involvement in......................143
   witnesses not heard.............. 130, 660
Gaddafi, Muammar.... 18, 19, 25, 61, 101, 102, 103, 104, 105, 106, 107, 108, 109, 110, 111, 112, 113, 114, 116, 117, 125, 126, 127, 128, 129, 130, 131, 133, 135, 137, 138, 139, 140, 143, 144, 145, 146, 147, 151, 156, 162, 165, 167, 171, 172, 173, 174, 176, 181, 187, 197, 198,젝 322, 461, 462, 471, 475, 636, 660, 698, 700, 701, 703
   assassination plot 101–47
Gadsby, A.C.J.............................. 275, 281
Gamble, C.................................... 275, 281
Gangsters 242, 255
Gardai 90
Gargan, Nicholas 244, 254, 268, 287, 296, 301, 518, 533, 534, 538, 539
Garland, Sean................................... 89
Garrec, Claude 15
Gate House 304
Gatwick Airport.............................. 133
GCHQ 23, 46, 105, 109, 114, 116, 120, 125, 128, 140, 141, 142, 523, 524
Gelli, Frank 397, 398
General Support Branch.................... 151
Geneva 104, 331, 460, 463
Germany 38, 69, 70, 85, 136, 159, 160, 163, 166, 281, 300, 458, 554, 555, 556, 557, 558, 569, 662
Gfoeller, Tatiana 683
Gibbins, Michael
   asked to collect Diana's door keys. 652
Gibraltar.. 91, 162
Gigou, Eric....................................... 229
Giles, Lewis....................................... 455
Goldsmith, Annabel ... 345, 353, 364, 376, 397, 398, 420, 434, 446
Goodman, Clive................................. 669
Gooroovadoo, Clifford 454
   followed after the crash 454
Göring, Hermann 81, 558
Gouyette 533
Government Communications
   Headquarters......... 23, 125, *See* GCHQ
Grand Floridian 357
Grater, Adrian 481, 495, 542, 543
Greece...86, 326, 328, 370, 371, 372, 373, 377, 378, 386, 387, 388, 389, 390, 391, 392, 395, 396, 397, 547, 683, 703

Greek Islands 326, 388, 389
Greek Islands Holiday
   conflicting media accounts..... 387–95, 390
   ideal surveillance conditions 386
   trip details 386
Green Light 470, 471
Green, Lady.. 694
Green, Michelle ..351, 353, 354, 355, 356, 357, 358
Green, Philip Kirby ..39, 87, 355, 360, 697, 701
Grivas, Georgios.......86, 87, 162, 165, 197
   assassination plot 86
Gross, Justice 656, 705
Grube, Joane..............................454, 455
Guardian. 87, 93, 118, 134, 137, 142, 143, 145, 164, 230, 231, 232, 295, 332, 333, 334, 336, 570, 571, 573, 699, 700, 701, 702, 703, 740
Guarente, Matt................................... 133
Gubbins, Colin....................69, 159, 166
Gunner, Steven....278, 536, 537, 538, 539
Gyppos... 83

H

Hamilcar 83
Handley-Greaves, Paul........................ 669
Hanover 556
Harbinson, John.................................... 96
Hare, David 571
Harkin, Greg..............93, 97, 98, 175, 697
Harrods229, 367, 368, 370, 388, 548, 567, 568, 584, 585, 597, 599, 615, 652, 653, 669, 701, 703
   Chairman's Office 652, 653
Harte, Christopher............................... 98
Harvey, William 69
Hastings, Stephen 87
Heap, Peter...................36, 294, 295, 740
Helicopter 50, 199, 204, 369
Hello! 230, 700
Hendry, G.J. 267, 277, 282, 283, 310, 311, 318, 321, 691
Henry, John... 85
Henry, M.. 456
Hereford 151
Hesse 555, 556
Hesse-Cassel 556

Hewitt, James 347, 453
Heydrich, Reinhard 81, 161
Hickman, Martin 116, 138, 140, 701
Hidden Agenda ... 360, 362, 363, 364, 365, 387
High Court 657, 658, 661, 705
   relied on false information from Baker 658–60
Higham, Charles...................555, 558, 697
Highgrove 547
Hill, Henrietta 22
Hilliard, Nicholas................................... 22
Hitler, Adolf 54, 81, 161, 177, 467, 556, 558
Hodges, Mark 455
Holborow, Jonathan 107
Hollingsworth, Mark...103, 107, 110, 111, 118, 134, 141, 142, 143, 697, 701
Home Office... 24, 107, 133, 555, 698, 704
Home, Lord 87
Hong Kong ... 302, 304, 306, 371, 373, 447
Horsfall, Robin 164
Horwell, Richard 22
   inadequate cross-examination 226
   lied at inquest...................53, 192, 194
   manufactured evidence 190
   misled the jury........................ 189–93
Hospices 595
Hot Potato 174
Hough, Jonathon 22
   lied at inquest............................... 641
   misled the jury............................... 641
   tried to undermine Devorik........... 641
House of Lords........................63, 135, 335
Houses of Parliament 37
Howarth, S.F. 275, 281
Howarth, Stephen 518
HRH Title...... 327, 546, 561, 577, 578, 579
Hughes, Lee 22
Human Intelligence 106
Humbert, Béatrice 20, 654
   not heard...............................20, 654
Hunt-Davis, Miles380, 382, 383, 384, 385, 409, 416, 425, 427, 428, 433, 438, 440, 559, 561, 565, 567, 573, 574, 575, 576, 577, 578, 579, 580, 581, 582, 583, 587, 589, 590, 591, 592, 616, 618, 657, 659, 662, 684
   distancing 578
   excessive distancing 582

lied about WAG purpose 575–83
lied at inquest 580, 582
responses regarding WAG Diana
    discussion 576–79
Hunter, Gary 230
Hussein, Saddam .. 99, 100, 101, 112, 126,
    127, 128, 129, 131, 145, 156, 163,
    165, 167, 171, 172, 173, 176, 177,
    181, 197, 466, 471, 700, 702
    assassination plot 99
Hutton Inquiry....................................... 36
Hyde, H. Montgomery........... 69, 159, 697
Hydra.................................. 388, 391, 392

I

I Spy... 55
IML 23
Immunity... 70
Immunity Certificate 91
Imperial College ...... 16, See Charing Cross
    Hospital
Increment31, 148–58, 148, 149, 150, 151,
    152, 154, 155, 156, 157, 158, 178
    Dearlove evasive over.............. 154–58
India 69, 159, 337, 348
Indonesia..................... 327, 353, 358, 361
Ingram, Martin 93, 94, 97, 98, 153, 175,
    697
Injunction 107, 108, 114, 133, 136
Inousses387, 388, 389, 390, 391, 392, 393
Inquest .... See Baker, Scott
    corrupt... 11
    day off during MI6 evidence 78
    relationship with MI6................. 42–48
Inquest Transcripts
    excerpts 15
Inquest Website 15
    closed down..................................... 13
Intelligence Agencies ... 12, 23, 24, 28, 40,
    48, 55, 100, 124, 147, 204, 241, 454,
    456, 473, 474, 549, 611, 656, 659,
    660, 663, 681, 684, See MI5, MI6
Intelligence Services Act .. 31, 35, 70, 160,
    167, 168, 705
Intelligence Services Tribunal................ 35
Intelligency.................................. 606, 612

Interior Ministry.......................... 287, 533
International Court of Justice........ 13, 698
    should conduct independent inquest
    13
Internet 115, 116, 117, 119, 124, 127,
    135, 136, 140, 231, 232, 233, 252,
    255, 267, 270, 275, 279, 282, 288,
    300, 306, 311, 321, 336, 353, 687,
    691, 739
    MI6 officer list.......................... 230–33
Investigation of Subversive Organisations
    118
IONEC.. 39, 56
IRA.........................89, 90, 91, 94, 98, 152
Iranian Embassy 164
Iraq.....82, 83, 99, 100, 101, 126, 270, 462
Iraqi National Accord 99, 100
Iraqi National Congress 101
IRD... 83
Ireland ... 66, 89, 90, 91, 92, 93, 94, 95, 96,
    97, 98, 152, 153, 154, 160, 162, 165,
    167, 697, 702, 704
Ireland's Own 89
Irish Assassinations 89–97
Irish Gardai... 90
Irrational 232, 361, 422, 625
Islam....103, 106, 108, 109, 110, 111, 112,
    114, 121, 122
Islamic Fighting Group 108, 111
Italy 69, 132, 556, 568

J

Jackson, Simon 487, 525, 529, 530
    not heard 530
Jay, Lady.. 519
Jay, Michael...20, 234, 235, 236, 238, 239,
    257, 262, 267, 268, 269, 270, 275,
    286, 290, 291, 292, 293, 294, 295,
    296, 297, 298, 299, 300, 301, 303,
    304, 305, 306, 310, 318, 319, 476,
    477, 478, 479, 481, 484, 487, 488,
    489, 490, 491, 493, 494, 495, 496,
    500, 502, 503, 504, 505, 506, 507,
    508, 509, 510, 511, 512, 513, 514,
    515, 516, 517, 519, 520, 521, 522,
    524, 526, 528, 529, 530, 532, 533,

537, 538, 540, 541, 542, 544, 618, 666, 668, 670, 671, 675, 684, 704, 705
alibi.....................................504, 509, 520
communication with the FCO 518
conflicting evidence 504, 521
cover-up regarding initial crash
    notification.......................... 514–15
crash notification............................ 670
diary entry re French and British
    knowledge of Diana's presence 540
diary for August 30 not read out ... 521
distanced himself from MI6 239
distancing 507
doesn't mention Curley.................. 296
early call from Massoni 505
evasive............................522, 528, 529
excessive distancing 494, 542
kept weekend free 521
lied at inquest.........292, 300, 323, 494
lied in evidence 239, 298, 301, 505,
    514
misappropriated resources 542
not linked to MI6........................... 300
possible involvement 508, 521
post-crash reports 477–79
prior knowledge 239, 521
received extra early information... 504
reports on events 477, 478
role of 508, 519–22
suspect 520
Jemelik...................................... 81
Jephson, Patrick...327, 379, 380, 385, 628
Jewellery...................................... 653
JIC 19, 120, 124, 127, 128, 141, 209
Jobson, Robert....629, 631, 640, 641, 698,
    701
    first to say dark forces 640
John, Elton 364
Johnson, Jeremy 22, 244, 254
Johnston, Paul 227, 278, 286, 287, 296,
    301, 509, 516, 517, 533, 535, 537,
    538, 540, 595, 698
    accounts of the events 516–17
    not heard..................................... 544
Joint Intelligence Committee 19, 116, 124,
    132, 209, See JIC
Jonikal. 367, 397, 399, 536, 540, 547, 548,
    595
Jordan 99, 100, 126, 128, 145

Journalists... 111, 117, 118, 214, 219, 220,
    454, 672, 694
Judd, Alan 174, 701
Judgement 37, 135, 658
Judicial Police... 24
Judiciary............................11, 13, 37, 699
    accountability................................. 38
    corruption in current case.............. 37
Judiciary of England and Wales 699
Jury 16, 478
    evidence withheld from 256, 257, 320,
        348, 354, 453, 479, 493, 507, 509,
        517, 522, 525, 543, 544, 591, 612,
        654, 660
    heard confusing evidence 72, 258
    information withheld from....173, 218,
        219
    misled at inquest............303, 472, 554
    not properly informed....194, 251, 256
    shown no WAG documents........... 592
Jury Didn't Hear 16, 29, 33, 35, 36, 37, 38,
    39, 42, 43, 44, 49, 53, 66, 67, 68, 70,
    81, 82, 85, 86, 87, 88, 89, 90, 91, 93,
    96, 97, 99, 100, 103, 105, 107, 108,
    113, 114, 115, 116, 117, 118, 151,
    152, 173, 174, 187, 212, 217, 230,
    231, 232, 238, 247, 249, 250, 268,
    286, 304, 331, 332, 333, 334, 340,
    341, 342, 350, 351, 352, 367, 369,
    370, 372, 387, 388, 414, 415, 452,
    458, 462, 463, 472, 477, 481, 482,
    483, 484, 486, 488, 489, 516, 518,
    522, 523, 524, 532, 534, 535, 536,
    548, 552, 554, 555, 556, 567, 568,
    569, 570, 571, 572, 601, 626, 629,
    652, 653, 654, 655, 656, 664, 665,
    666, 667, 677
Jury Not Present 16, 45, 655

K

Kaiser Wilhelm II................................. 556
Kassem, Susan 352, 353, 376, 397, 398,
    434, 446, 619, 658
Kay, Richard 345, 348, 349, 350, 353, 355,
    356, 357, 358, 359, 360, 370, 375,
    376, 388, 397, 398, 414, 416, 417,
    418, 419, 431, 438, 443, 595, 596, 701
Keen, Richard....................................... 22
    cross-examination re Gaddafi 129

Keeper of the Privy Purse..... 20, 560, 563, 581, 582, 593, *See* Peat, Michael
Kendwrick-Piercey, Maurice ... 49, 63, 173
Kennedy, John............... 69, 464
Kensington Gardens........................... 369
Kensington Palace 16, 327, 341, 346, 347, 362, 401, 414, 415, 417, 420, 438, 439, 449, 653, 669
Kenya 87
Kerr, Gordon 92, 93, 94, 95, 701
Khan, Hasnat...................... 453, 619, 658
    threatened...................................... 453
King Edward VIII 332, 556
King George VI............. 555, 556, 557, 558
King, Jon 385, 463, 464, 469
King, Martin Luther 464
Kiparissi.. 389
Kirk, Anna........... 276, 280, 282, 691, 692
Kirk, Matthew 276, 280, 282, 691, 692
Kirk, Matthew and Anna 280, 310
Klein, Frank 226, 536, 540, 701, 705
Klukker 217, 223, 227, 228
Knights, PC 351
Knightsbridge 568
Komsomolskaya Pravda 334
Korea........................... 366, 396, 397, 463
Kronberg 555, 556, 558
Kropje Chocolates 85
Kubris, Jan 81
Kukker 217, 223, 227, 228
Kurdistan.. 101
Kurgan.. 212
Kuwait 462
Kyrgyzstan.. 683
Kythera... 388, 392

L

L'Hottelier, Vincent 215, 218
    not heard 218
La Pitié Salpêtrière Hospital477, 481, 485, 486, 488, 501, 502, 654
La Rochelle ..285, 294, 295, 297, 302, 303, 312, 313, 314, 316
Labour Party276, 333, 368, 462, 601, 677, 698
Lambert, Brian 92, 98

Lancaster House.................................... 86
Land Mine Survivors Network............. 463
Landmines...187, 189, 190, 191, 192, 193, 205, 206, 207, 210, 211, 212, 331, 387, 447, 462, 463, 471, 474, 548, 598, 600, 601, 679, 680, *See* Anti-Landmines Campaign
    Angola trip 328, 546
    Bosnia trip............................. 328, 547
    charity for victims 596, 598
    Diana speech June 12 .... 328, 385, 547
    dossier 191, 328
    MI6 involvement in.................. 205–13
Landmines Eradication Group............. 547
Langley.. 106
Langman, Nicholas49, 194, 195, 239, 240, 241, 242, 243, 247, 249, 250, 251, 252, 253, 254, 255, 257, 258, 259, 262, 263, 264, 265, 266, 267, 277, 279, 283, 303, 310, 311, 318, 319, 320, 321, 679, 691
    accused by Mohamed.................... 242
    alleged to be involved................... 239
    issues over Paris departure date .262–67
    movements pre-crash.............. 239–72
    named suspect..................... 186, 251
    never acknowledged as MI6.......... 254
    not heard 251
    posting documentation 240
Language Schools....................... 293, 306
    distances from Paris.............. 293, 298
Language Training...... 241, 243, 247, 250, 260, 266, 291, 305
LanguageCourse.net 293, 306
Larouche, Lyndon............................... 230
Launay, Patrick.................................... 705
Lawson, Domenica 328, 367, 370
Lawson, Dominic.. 18, 331, 333, 334, 335, 336, 337, 367, 370, 372, 374, 386, 395, 408, 409, 414, 420, 423, 424, 425, 426, 428, 430, 431, 432, 444, 447, 702
    conflict with Rosa 372
    MI6 agent 336
    not heard 18
Lawson, Edmund.................................. 22

Lawson, Nigel.....................................333
Le Bourget 533, 534
Le Bourgogne.....................................453
Le Jeune d'Allegeershecque, Susan ... 239,
    240, 241, 242, 257, 258, 259, 260,
    262, 263, 265
Le Monde 328, 548
Lebanon 145, 304, 306
Lecomte, Dominique 11, 26, 154, 251,
    474, 684
Lefort, Bernard 453
    attempt to bribe...........................453
Leinster House 89
Lemos Family.......387, 389, 391, 392, 393
Lemos, Panagiotis 387, 388, 391
Lennon, John 464
LeQueux, William.................................. 38
Lethal Force 64
Leverton, Keith 705
LGC 24
Libya 18, 19, 101, 103, 104, 105, 106, 107,
    108, 109, 110, 111, 112, 113, 114,
    115, 117, 118, 121, 122, 123, 125,
    126, 131, 132, 138, 139, 144, 151,
    181, 636, 700, 703
License to Kill 68, 159, 166
Lille 291, 304, 305, 306
Littlejohn, Keith and Kenneth..........89, 90
LiveNote 58, 78
Livesey, Geoffrey 278
Livesey, Timothy ...20, 276, 278, 281, 486,
    487, 488, 489, 490, 491, 500, 502,
    504, 509, 510, 515, 536, 537, 538
    not heard................................20, 544
Lockerbie 104
Log Sheets... 484, 493, 494, 495, 496, 497,
    498, 499, 514, 684
    not properly scrutinised 496
London.. 3, 16, 43, 82, 85, 86, 89, 90, 100,
    106, 110, 111, 116, 124, 136, 145,
    164, 182, 212, 236, 238, 243, 250,
    262, 292, 294, 300, 301, 302, 304,
    306, 308, 327, 328, 331, 337, 339,
    340, 348, 349, 351, 353, 354, 356,
    357, 358, 366, 370, 401, 417, 420,
    439, 442, 젝 455, 472, 477, 478, 481,
    495, 523, 527, 536, 547, 563, 595,
    598, 600, 601, 652, 654, 668, 677,
    696, 697, 698, 705
Lord and Lady Palumbo 341, 345

Lord Chamberlain560, 562, 563, 571, 581,
    582, 593, 597
Los Angeles... 696
Los Angeles Times..................99, 100, 702
Lowther-Pinkerton, Jamie 22
Lumumba, Patrice....................87, 88, 162
    assassination plot............................ 87
Lyall, Sarah.....................................107, 702
Lyford Cay 351
Lyttle, Tommy....................................... 93

M

Macallan Whisky..................215, 223, 226
MacDonald, Alison.............................. 22
Macedonia..................................333, 334
Machon, Annie ... 10, 18, 34, 70, 103, 108,
    109, 110, 111, 124, 131, 132, 133,
    134, 138, 141, 143, 144, 145, 146,
    147, 154, 159, 166, 697, 705
    arrested by SB 133
    not heard..............................18, 131
MacLeod, Duncan................................ 22
    flawed cross-examination of
      Carpenter................................. 225
    misled the jury........................ 219–28
Macmillan, Harold 87
Macnamara, John186, 187, 194, 195, 197,
    669, 671, 705
    accused MI6 186
    crash notification 669
MacStiofain, Sean................................. 89
Mafia 69
Mahoney, Jerry.............18, 104, 131, 144
    not heard..............................18, 131
Mail on Sunday ... 105, 106, 107, 133, 391,
    392, 410, 412, 414, 422, 427, 429,
    430, 437, 442, 443, 463, 700, 702
Malicious 250, 263, 265
Manila.....................................487, 671
Mannakee, Barry 342, 343, 344, 453
Mansfield, Michael 22, 240
    introduced possibility of frightening
      target 51–53
    key evidence withheld from.......... 591
    questioned Dearlove over Increment
      154–58
    questioning of Dearlove on strobe
      lights... 202

questioning on MI6 landmine
    involvement...............................210
shown no WAG documents 592
tried to get evidence from senior royal
    suspects..............................654–61
Marala 388, 389
Marchwood..213
Marseille 293, 295, 298
Martino, Jean-Marc 11, 26, 154, 251, 474,
    684
Maskey, Alex..95
Massoni, Philippe. 20, 480, 481, 482, 483,
    484, 489, 490, 491, 492, 493, 495,
    496, 497, 498, 500, 505, 506, 507,
    508, 509, 510, 511, 512, 513, 514,
    515, 516, 517, 521, 529, 530, 534,
    536, 544, 670, 671
    conflict over phone call............490–91
    questioning by Paget 505, 507
Matthews, Nick 21, 665
    not heard 21
Maude, Francis.......................... 115, 117
McBain, Malcolm 305
McCann, Danny..................................... 91
McCann, Joe..........................89, 90, 701
McColl, Colin ...50, 66, 139, 171, 173, 174,
    178, 197
McCord, Raymond 96, 704
McCorquodale, Sarah... 22, 345, 397, 398,
    653
McDermott, Geoffrey............................ 83
McDonald's 352
McKenna, Sharon 96
McMaster, Gordon..............................694
McParland, Sean 96
McTasney, Peter 96
MECAS................................292, 304, 306
Media Monitoring 665, 666, 668, 672
Mediterranean...........................381, 547
Menzies, Kate.............. 351, 352, 356, 359
Menzies, Stewart 82
Mercedes 23
Mercedes S28011, 13, 26, 30, 52, 81, 154,
    214, 221, 474, 492, 508, 543
Mercenaries 208, 210
Metropolitan Police Service .....24, 43, *See*
    MPS; Operation Paget

Gaddafi plot investigation.............127
MI5.. 16, 18, 19, 23, 24, 34, 37, 38, 40, 41,
    43, 46, 67, 69, 70, 85, 86, 87, 88, 91,
    98, 102, 103, 108, 111, 112, 113, 114,
    116, 118, 119, 124, 125, 127, 128,
    131, 132, 133, 134, 135, 138, 139,
    140, 141, 144, 145, 146, 147, 148,
    149, 152, 154, 162, 167, 174, 175,
    182, 187, 195, 196, 234, 238, 239,
    245, 301, 333, 364, 453, 461, 471,
    519, 552, 553, 554, 555, 557, 558,
    601, 602, 603, 609, 611, 612, 614,
    626, 630, 631, 640, 697, 698, 701, 740
    followed MO5..................................38
    hid illegal operations from FCO 167
MI622, 23, 24, 25, 239, 300, 301, 381, *See*
    Rogue Element, *See* Accountability,
    See Increment, *See* Need to Know, *See*
    Secrecy
    "need to know"................................29
    accountability 35–38
    admits dishonesty...........................42
    admitted to having documents on
        Mohamed 613
    alibis not checked 318, 324
    allegations against 185–98
    allegations of involvement 125
    allegiance to Queen and country.....38
    assassinates people 53–180
    Baker falsified account re report for
        WAG 613
    capabilities...31, 47, 48, 149, 150, 154,
        155, 156, 158, 462, 466
    chief .20, 29, 36, 37, 49, 50, 53, 66, 68,
        74, 82, 87, 125, 131, 145, 151, 155,
        156, 168, 171, 173, 174, 175, 178,
        196, 197, 247, 252, 261, 268, 271,
        287, 296, 301, 533, 702, 703, 740
    clandestinity 31
    closed down questioning................44
    culture 29–42, 262
    culture of secrecy and deception 12
    database search........................42–48
    deniability 30–35, 30, 31, 32, 33, 34,
        42, 106, 149, 157, 209, 262
        car crash 34
        linked to lying 41

regarding Paris crash.................. 34
destruction of evidence....99, 174, 457
director of operations 31, 149, 156,
    See Dearlove, Richard
disinformation..........................40, 41
    re Paris crash............................. 41
distancing of Paris officers 324
doctored evidence.......................... 79
don't admit to assassination 30
ethos 61, 63, 65, 78, 99, 159, 166, 175,
    180
evidence not credible.................... 317
files...... 48, 50, 74, 169, 174, 194, 270,
    608, 613
founded on a lie 39
frightening targets...51–53, 51, 52, 53,
    182
God's access42, 74, 169, 263, 270, 605
helped by French and US.............. 473
in Paris................................... 213–325
    sightings around Ritz Hotel 214–30
independent operations.37, 157, 180–
    85, See Rogue Element
influence over media reports of Greek
    holiday 392
interest in arms industry 212
interest in Mohamed Al Fayed 608–13
internet officer list.................... 230–33
involved in Paris crash.......12, 27–475,
    314, 317, 471–72
involvement in assassination plots.. 12
involvement in landmines 205–13
key officers not heard 318, 322
licence 51, 67, 70, 159, 161, 166
lied at inquest................................ 316
lying........38–41, See National Interest
    in national interest.................. 174
    in training..............................39, 41
    linked to deniability 41
no one on duty in Paris............ 314–20
not open at inquest..............45, 47, 48
number of officers in Paris 266
officer movements pre-crash 233–321
officers refused to participate....... 301
perjury... 36
prior knowledge 259
recruits family members 335
registry 66, 160, 166, 174
relationship with CIA 461

relationship with French intelligence
    458–61
relationship with inquest 42–48
relationship with Paget 42–48
report on the Fayeds 608–13
secrecy 29
senior staff movements 12
sensitivity over Angola 209
should have sought answers post-
    crash.................................314, 318
shredding of documents 175
taradiddles 40
training.. 31, 37, 39, 48, 50, 54, 55, 56,
    57, 58, 60, 62, 63, 64, 67, 70, 71,
    72, 73, 74, 75, 76, 77, 78, 79, 80,
    132, 150, 198, 199, 200, 201, 202,
    203, 204, 206, 240, 241, 243, 247,
    256, 268, 290, 291, 292, 295, 298,
    299, 300, 304, 305, 306, 309
training manual . 57, 58, 60, 62, 64, 71,
    72, 73, 75
    conflicting evidence on 71
training re assassination............ 54–80
    conflicting evidence 73, 78
    order of witnesses...................... 78
undermined Tomlinson 79
use of flash equipment.......... 198–204
used day off.................................... 78
witnesses given green light 471
witnesses lied at inquest................. 75
witnesses not heard 17
would have had CIA help......... 466–69
wouldn't admit involvement......... 125
MI6 Internet List 136, 331
Middle East. 68, 69, 70, 83, 106, 109, 115,
    124, 125, 131, 138, 139, 145, 152,
    159, 160, 288, 304, 739
Mijatovic, Zoran.............................. 332
Mikynos 388, 392
Milosevic, Slobodan 32, 49, 50, 59, 60, 61,
    63, 66, 99, 101, 126, 127, 128, 129,
    130, 145, 148, 149, 156, 157, 162,
    165, 167, 170, 176, 177, 178, 179,
    180, 181, 197, 316, 318, 322, 472
    assassination plot 99
    identity of target 176–78
    assassination proposal 50
    different target............................. 61
    MI6 file search...................58, 179–80
Minister of the Interior........480, 490, 670

Ministry of Agriculture 236
Ministry of Defence 36, 95, 116, 124, 164,
    212, 693
Mirror ..229, 333, 547, 548, 563, 565, 566,
    567, 568, 571, 573, 575, 576, 577,
    583, 584, 585, 590, 592, 594, 596,
    597, 599, 600, 609, 611, 613, 614,
    615, 619, 630, 631, 637, 638, 640,
    642, 672, 700, 701, 703
    31 August 1997 article 586
Mischievous 176, 183, 250, 263, 265
Mishcon Note 662, 682
Miss X 29, 30, 41, 42, 44, 47, 61, 71, 73,
    74, 75, 78, 99, 102, 129, 130, 159,
    166, 169, 172, 173, 174, 175, 176,
    178, 179, 180, 193, 194, 202, 203,
    263, 551, 553, 554, 609, 610, 611,
    612, 613
    admitted Gaddafi plot more than an
        idea 130
    changed her evidence 609
    evasive in evidence 203
    failed to do thorough search 610
    knowledge of training policy 74
    lied at inquest 169, 179
    lied over Milosevic file search .. 179–80
    not open at inquest 48
    unfinished sentence 553
    unreliable witness 180
Mitchell, Paul 104, 144, 615
MO5 38
MoD95, 120, 124, 127, 128, 141, 152, 212
MODA/SO 49, 178
Monarchy 38, 182, 195, 196, 340, 341,
    344, 345, 346, 560, 565, 566, 568,
    570, 571, 572, 573, 574, 576, 596,
    597, 601, 602, 626, 679, 698, *See*
    Royal Family, *See* Queen Elizabeth II
Monceau, Jean .11, 26, 154, 251, 474, 684
Monckton, Anthony . 82, 85, 98, 193, 331,
    332, 334, 335, 336, 337, 365, 447,
    555, 558, 662
    List biography 331
    MI6 officer 336
Monckton, Christopher 332, 335, 705
Monckton, Rosa 17, 18, 326, 325–450,
    326, 327, 328, 329, 330, 331, 332,
    334, 335, 336, 337, 340, 341, 342,
    343, 344, 345, 346, 347, 348, 349,
    350, 351, 352, 353, 354, 355, 356,
    357, 359, 360, 361, 362, 363, 364,
    365, 366, 367, 368, 370, 371, 372,
    373, 374, 375, 376, 377, 378, 382,
    383, 385, 386, 387, 388, 389, 395,
    396, 397, 398, 399, 400, 402, 409,
    413, 414, 415, 416, 417, 418, 419,
    420, 421, 422, 423, 424, 425, 426,
    427, 428, 429, 430, 431, 432, 433,
    434, 435, 436, 437, 438, 439, 440,
    441, 442, 443, 444, 445, 446, 447,
    448, 449, 450, 472, 547, 594, 596,
    684, 700, 703, 704
    admitted MI6 connection 334
    Bali and Moyo Island holiday ... 350–60
    collaborated with Lucia 444
    collaborated with Philip 443
    communicated with Philip 429
    conflict with Lawson 372
    conflict with Lucia 346
    conflict with Michael Cole 370
    conflicting evidence 343, 377, 424,
        425, 427, 428, 431
    created image of emotionally
        befuddled Diana 444
    defended Philip 430, 436
    defended Philip against Diana's
        interests 437
    distancing 438, 444, 446
    evasive over MI6 334
    evasive witness 449
    excessive distancing 334, 445
    failed to answer questions 449
    final phone call to Diana 397–99
    gave account regarding Mannakee 343
    gave illogical evidence 424
    Greek cruise 326, 328
    Greek Islands holiday 371–97
    lied in evidence 349, 350, 374, 395,
        396, 435–38, 444, 445, 448
    lied to press 430
    lied to protect Philip 437
    made mistakes reading out Diana's
        letter 432

made to look like Diana's best friend 446

meeting Diana 337–50
    conflict over timing 342
    three possibilities 349

met Diana through Lucia 341, 342, 344, 349

MI6 agent 12, 335, 337, 377, 396, 448, 450

not a close friend of Diana 377, 378, 399, 434, 447, 448

organised Moyo Island holiday 359, 360

over-answered Philip letter questions 420

prepared answers........................... 421

promoted as Diana's best friend .. 446, 449

pushed evidence on Diana's
    emotional condition................. 422

quiet to police on Philip-Diana letters 418

radio silence 366–97, 366, 367, 370, 372, 373, 374, 375, 376, 377, 395, 396, 397
    conflicting evidence 395
    possibilities 375

received Philip letters from Lucia . 439, 443

relationship with Diana 341, 344, 361–65, 446

relationship with MI6 328–37

role in Philip-Diana letters 400–446

statement not heard 347

undermined Simmons 436

usurped Lucia's role re letters 444

working for Establishment 386, 682

Money Laundering.......................133, 134

Montpellier...........................293, 295, 298

Morgan, John........................1, 4, 705, 739

Morgan, Piers 600, 601, 630, 638, 644, 649, 672

Mori Surveys...............569, 570, 571, 575

Morocco 105

Morshead, Owen 555, 556, 557, 558

Mortimer, John............................524, 527

Morton, Andrew.327, 347, 349, 360, 398, 399, 441, 447, 546, 579, 580, 599, 684, 697
    office burgled 327

Moscow 333, 334

Moss, Keith. 240, 243, 245, 276, 476, 477, 478, 479, 485, 486, 487, 488, 489, 490, 491, 492, 498, 499, 500, 501, 502, 503, 504, 505, 507, 509, 510, 511, 512, 513, 514, 515, 517, 518, 529, 532, 534, 537, 538, 542, 543, 544, 653, 654, 670, 671, 675, 676, 678, 704, 705
    changed his evidence 511
    conflicting evidence 504
    disposed of notes 479
    distancing of Blair......................... 676
    lied in evidence 505
    post-crash report................... 477–79
    received extra early information... 504
    report on events....................477, 488

Mossman, James 84

Motorbike Riders....................11, 26, 474

Mountbatten, Lord 558

Moyo Island 327, 350, 351, 353, 354, 355, 357, 358, 359, 699
    compared to Paris holiday............. 354
    Diana had police protection 354
    questions regarding...................... 359

MPLA 208, 209

MPS 24, 25, 43, 44, 50, 53, 66, 91, 105, 127, 128, 130, 174, 187, 189, 219, 220, 221, 222, 354, 378, 379, 382, 384, 559, 699

Mr 4 .... 266, 271, 285, 288, 289, 291, 301, 303, 310, 311, 313, 316, 318, 322, 324, 535, 538, *See* Curley, Eugene
    identified as Eugene Curley........... 288
    lied at inquest.............................. 289

Mr 5 .... 251, 267, 309, 310, 311, 312, 314, 315, 316, 317, 318, 321, 535, 538
    alibi not checked 319
    could be Hugh Powell.................... 311

Mr 6 .... 32, 33, 34, 35, 131, 137, 183, 247, 251, 252, 253, 254, 255, 266, 267, 271, 310, 311, 312, 313, 316, 318, 321, 322, 461, 535, 538, 620, *See* Spearman, Richard
    identified as Richard Spearman251–54

Mr A.. 32, 61, 63, 64, 65, 73, 99, 102, 103, 129, 130, 173, 177, 192, 197, 203, 204, 318, 322
    knowledge of training policy 74

Mr E...42, 51, 52, 53, 63, 65, 99, 129, 130, 159, 166, 169, 170, 171, 172, 173, 178, 193, 197, 280, 283, 311, 318, 322
   confirmed MI6 frighten people........52
   lied at inquest 171, 173
Mr H 32, 33, 34, 42, 63, 73, 74, 75, 78, 79, 80, 81, 99, 129, 130, 159, 166, 169, 170, 173, 175, 176, 300, 318, 322, 697
   evasive 79
   knowledge of training policy............ 74
   training evidence doctored.............. 79
Mr I...........66, 99, 129, 171, 172, 173, 175
Ms 1 ....252, 267, 295, 297, 309, 310, 312, 314, 315, 316, 318, 321, 535, 538
   alibi not checked........................... 319
   could be Caroline Copley 310
Mufti of Jerusalem 69, 159
Mugabe, Robert 54, 165
Mukhabarat 84
Mulholland, Neil............................. 91, 92
Muller, Scott 455
Murder Gangs 69, 160
Murphy, Paul....................................... 186
Mussolini, Benito 83
Mykonos 388, 392

N

Nacional 332
Nasser, Gamal Abdel.... 82, 83, 84, 85, 86, 112, 162, 165, 167, 193, 197
   assassination plot 82–86
National Archives 14, 15, 88, 124, 162, 273, 699
National Interest 39, 41, 147, 174, 194, 302, 457, 470, 471
National Security.24, 37, 52, 54, 107, 108, 114, 117, 134, 155, 158, 194, 209, 231, 454, 455, 457, 470, 554, 630, 631
National Security Agency ....24, *See* NSA
Nazi Party 163, 555, 556
Nedeljni Telegraf................................ 332
Need to Know .29, 30, 31, 33, 41, 48, 143, 149, 155, 156, 168, 301, 341, 449, 469, *See* MI6
Neguib, Mohammed 84
Nejad, Fawzi....................................... 164

Nelson, Brian.................. 92, 93, 94, 95, 98
Nerve Gas...................... 85, 86, 106
Netherlands 557
New Britain 666
New York...16, 69, 81, 136, 159, 161, 232, 629, 645, 646, 696, 697, 702
New York Times........................... 107, 115
New Zealand 36, 136, 458, 739
News Letter.388, 389, 390, 391, 392, 393, 700
News of the World 669
Newsnight 133
Nice 293, 295, 298, 459
No Comment...................... 617, 618, 620
Nolan, Julia...277, 280, 283, 310, 691, 692
Norfolk 524, 527
Normandy 509, 516, 517, 535
Northern Ireland 93, 154
Northolt 677, 678, 679
Norton-Taylor, Richard 91, 118, 137, 145, 152, 153, 154, 158, 162, 230, 231, 232, 697, 702, 703
Norway.......................................35, 469
NSA 24, 454, 455, 456, 457

O

O'Loan, Nuala.................. 95, 96, 162, 704
O'Malley, Dessie 89
Obfuscation................. 58, 75, 77, 78, 384
Observer.............................. 118, 134, 700
Obukhov, Platon 333
Occurrence Logs. 482, 483, 484, 487, 493, 495, 496, 497, 498, 499, 500, 501, 503, 504, 508, 509, 510, 512, 514, 515, 517, 522, 525, 526, 529, 544
OCG 24
Official Secrets Act 50, 133, 134, 150, 233, 336, 456, 460, 524, 705
Oinousa 388, 391
Oldfield, Maurice 151, 174
Ombudsman's Report 95, 96, 97, 162, 704
On Call..309, 310, 314, 315, 316, 543, 665
On Duty 218, 301, 310, 314, 315, 316, 317, 318, 324, 335, 351, 472, 484, 488, 523, 525, 529, 677
Onassis Foundation.................... 387, 392

Opening Remarks 125, 242, 255, 256, 260, 262, 263, 322, 415, 438, 476, 664
Operation Paget 42, 43, 44, 48, 59, 74, 105, 127, 174, 194, 221, 228, 250, 253, 257, 258, 259, 263, 271, 313, 324, 443, 455, 467, 478, 481, 482, 496, 525, 526, 527, 530, 537, 543, 604, 605, 607, 610, 616, 704
   corrupt conduct............................ 542
   flawed investigation 537
   gave Donnelly Moss' statement.... 542
   relationship with MI6 42–48
Operational Support Branch................. 67
Orlando.............................351, 352, 357
Oslo..35, 469, 600
Ottawa................. 207, 463, 469, 600, 679

P

P File 61, 102, 129, 551, 604
Paget Report. 4, 11, 42, 43, 44, 48, 95, 99, 105, 110, 127, 129, 137, 177, 186, 221, 228, 229, 247, 249, 250, 251, 252, 254, 256, 257, 258, 259, 260, 261, 268, 271, 304, 319, 320, 331, 336, 341, 342, 344, 345, 347, 398, 415, 439, 443, 478, 480, 481, 482, 483, 495, 496,젝 497, 500, 501, 503, 505, 517, 522, 524, 526, 527, 536, 537, 602, 610, 611, 677, 679, 697, 699, 739, 740
   dishonest claim 539
   misquoted Tomlinson.................... 263
   neither here nor there 48
   on Gaddafi plot............................. 127
   regarding embassy phone records 496
Pakenham, Michael 275, 281, 476, 477
Palumbo, Lord and Lady 339, 341, 345, 350, 352, 355, 360, 376
Panorama ... 106, 108, 110, 113, 114, 131, 133, 138, 139, 141, 146, 327, 376, 406, 410, 436, 546, 599, 659, 682, 684
   Shayler interview..................... 108–13
Paparazzi....... 47, 214, 215, 216, 217, 219, 221, 223, 224, 225, 226, 227, 228, 229, 317, 388, 390, 454, 531, 533, 539, 543
Park, Daphne 68, 88, 159, 164, 166
Parker-Bowles, Camilla 347, 361, 414, 547, 568, 703

Parliament 60, 599, 693, 699, 701
Parliamentary Intelligence Security Committee 36
Parliamentary Oversight Committee.... 35
Part 1 .... 4, 14, 16, 17, 539, 739
Part 2 4, 13, 17, 26, 27, 53, 191, 192, 205, 211, 317, 326, 328, 342, 345, 353, 354, 359, 360, 374, 378, 384, 385, 397, 398, 400, 410, 422, 425, 436, 440, 443, 451, 453, 456, 467, 470, 474, 480, 481, 482, 485, 501, 503, 527, 540, 541, 547, 579, 584, 594, 595, 596, 597, 599, 600, 619, 625, 633, 638, 640, 643, 651, 658, 659, 661, 662, 668, 677, 679, 681
Part 3 .... 4, 11, 17, 27, 192, 221, 227, 235, 267, 303, 317, 324, 335, 458, 473, 507, 533, 539, 540, 541, 543, 544, 680
Part 4 11, 17, 27, 239, 259, 278, 292, 343, 381, 476, 479, 486, 487, 505, 507, 522, 523, 530, 542, 544, 559, 577, 582, 585, 653, 661, 677, 678, 739
Part 5 ....10, 14
Part 6 48
Parts 1 to 4 .... 17, 37, 298, 458, 466
Paul, Henri 3, 4, 11, 13, 15, 22, 26, 30, 49, 50, 53, 154, 187, 215, 216, 218, 221, 223, 224, 225, 227, 228, 249, 251, 254, 324, 448, 456, 457, 474, 475, 492, 501, 669, 684
   DGSE..456, 457
   DST 456
Peacetime Targets 55, 56, 72, 76
Pearson, John 68, 161, 698, 740
Peat, Michael.........................20, 568, 570
   not heard... 20
Peloponnesus 388
Pentagon 463, 469
People 351, 353
People's Princess 12, 666, 667, 677
Pépin, Gilbert... 11, 26, 154, 251, 474, 684
Perfect Storm 684
Perfect Stranger................................... 39
Perjury 36, 629
Permanence 20, 482, 485, 487, 489
Petty, Alan 50, 66, 171, 197
Philip-Diana Letters 400–446
   concerns regarding the evidence 420–46

draft replies .. 401, 402, 403, 404, 405, 407, 417, 419, 420, 423, 425, 426, 441, 442, 445, 446
   typed up prior to inquest.......... 445
   first Philip letter missing 440
   first Philip letter withheld 441
   Rosa and Lucia switched roles 431
   Rosa supplied faxed copies 438
   table 416
Philippines..................... 486, 676
Phoenix 557, 558
Picknett, Lynn..................... 556, 557, 698
Pillai, Nina 17, 337, 348, 349, 702, 703
   not heard 17, 348
Pincher, Chapman 462
Pittuck, Charles 84
Place Vendôme 229, 456, 531, 533
   MI6 sightings.................................. 229
Poland 81, 212
Police Commissioner.... 22, 43, 66, 81, 91, 378, 379, 380, 382, 559, 594
Political Counsellor...................... 280, 286
   changed just before crash...... 287–306
Political Department 35, 50, 67, 69, 83, 86, 89, 90, 112, 114, 132, 152, 167, 178, 240, 243, 245, 247, 267, 268, 269, 270, 275, 276, 277, 278, 279, 280, 281, 282, 283, 286, 287, 288, 289, 290, 291, 292, 294, 296, 297, 298, 299, 300, 302, 304, 305, 306, 308, 310, 311, 312, 318, 321, 323, 331, 336, 462, 466, 479, 533, 620, 685, 687, 688, 690, 691, 692, 693, 696
   comparison 1996 to 1997 282
   disproportionate movements in 1997 279
   staff at 31 August 1997 284
Pont d'Alma........ 287, 486, 488, 501, 533
Poole 151, 198, 204
Portman Square 368, 369
Porton Down................................ 85, 86
Portsmouth 39
Posner, Gerald............................... 40
Post-Mortem......................... 11, 16, 661
Powell, Hugh 278, 283, 310, 311, 318, 321, 691
   could be Mr 5................................ 311
Powell, Olga 351
Powers ..97, 133, 474, 620, 621, 622, 625, 626, 630, 631, 632, 633, 635, 637, 638, 640, 645, 647
Prague 81
Prefet de Police 480, 490, 508
Prendergast, John 87
President......22, 49, 69, 87, 100, 112, 148, 163, 178, 181, 462, 463, 469, 474, 481, 506, 536, 669, 670, 681, 682, 705
Press Association 231, 630
Press Complaints Commission 411, 429
Prime Minister ..12, 21, 82, 83, 87, 88, 91, 112, 116, 152, 164, 167, 174, 177, 186, 193, 195, 207, 481, 487, 499, 506, 571, 601, 618, 631, 664, 665, 666, 668, 670, 671, 672, 673, 675, 676, 677, 678, 679, 682, 683, 702, *See* Blair, Tony
   weekly meeting with Queen.......... 679
Primogeniture 572, 574, 576
Prince Andrew............. 560, 572, 581, 683
   not heard 20
Prince Charles .37, 98, 186, 195, 327, 335, 339, 340, 341, 342, 343, 344, 345, 346, 347, 349, 350, 351, 352, 357, 358, 360, 362, 366, 380, 383, 396, 400, 404, 413, 414, 415, 430, 478, 479, 516, 522, 533, 535, 536, 537, 546, 551, 560, 568, 569, 572, 577, 579, 580, 581, 591, 599, 618, 622, 638, 660, 661, 663, 667, 697, 700
   above the law 661
Prince Edward 560, 572, 581
   not heard 20
Prince Harry ...22, 328, 352, 547, 572, 594
Prince Philip 37, 45, 46, 184, 185, 186, 192, 193, 195, 196, 338, 341, 380, 400, 402, 403, 404, 405, 409, 410, 411, 413, 414, 415, 416, 417, 418, 419, 420, 421, 422, 423, 424, 425, 426, 427, 428, 429, 430, 431, 432, 433, 434, 435, 436, 437, 438, 439, 440, 441, 442, 443, 444, 445, 446, 447, 448, 449, 550, 551, 556, 559, 560, 561, 565, 566, 567, 568, 569, 570, 572, 574, 576, 579, 580, 581,

591, 595, 596, 597, 598, 616–20, 616, 618, 619, 620, 622, 654, 655, 658, 659, 660, 661, 662, 663, 682, 684, 704, *See* Duke of Edinburgh
above the law 618, 660, 661
collaborated with Rosa Monckton 443
communicated with Rosa Monckton
.... 429
correspondence with Diana . 400–446, 430
feared by Diana 527, 597
has a case to answer 619
may have been involved............... 620
named suspect 46, 185, 618
never came forward with Diana letters
.... 440
not heard...........................46, 618, 620
possibilities regarding guilt............ 619
racist... 596
refused to assist Paget 618
withheld evidence 440
Prince William.......22, 328, 341, 352, 398, 547, 572, 594, 696
Prince Wolfgang 556
Prince, Clive 556, 557
Princes William and Harry ..341, 342, 352, 358, 360, 369, 382, 384, 569, 593, 594, 595, 596, 597, 598, 599, 600, 620, 662, 668, 682, 684
Princess Anne 556, 560, 572, 581
not heard... 20
Princess Diana 3, 4, 11, 12, 13, 16, 26, 27, 28, 30, 34, 37, 45, 46, 49, 50, 53, 71, 80, 95, 96, 125, 132, 150, 156, 158, 165, 169, 172, 173, 174, 181, 185, 187, 188, 189, 190, 191, 192, 193, 194, 195, 196, 197, 201, 205, 207, 211, 230, 232, 234, 247, 248, 253, 260, 261, 262, 267, 287, 290, 293, 298, 301, 305, 309, 312, 317, 320, 322, 324, 325, 326, 327, 328, 329, 330, 331, 335, 337, 338, 339, 340, 341, 342, 343, 345, 347, 348, 350, 353, 354, 355, 357, 360, 361, 362, 363, 365, 366, 367, 368, 370, 371, 374, 377, 378, 381, 382, 384, 385, 397, 398, 399, 402, 405, 406, 413, 415, 416, 417, 418, 421, 423, 430, 434, 439, 440, 442, 444, 446, 448, 449, 450, 453, 454, 455, 457, 461,

462, 463, 466, 469, 470, 472, 473, 474, 475, 477, 478, 479, 480, 481, 485, 486, 487, 488, 492, 494, 498, 501, 502, 506, 507, 508, 516, 519, 521, 522, 524, 525, 531, 532, 533, 534, 535, 536, 537, 539, 540, 541, 542, 543, 544, 548, 550, 554, 561, 566, 569, 571, 576, 577, 579, 583, 593, 596, 601, 605, 611, 612, 616, 617, 620, 627, 633, 634, 635, 637, 638, 644, 652, 653, 654, 656, 657, 658, 659, 660, 661, 662, 663, 664, 665, 666, 667, 669, 670, 674, 676, 678, 679, 681, 682, 684, 693, 694, 696, 697, 699, 703, 705, 739, *See* Assassination in Paris
Bali and Moyo Island holiday .. 350–60
compartmentalised relationships 352, 353
correspondence with Philip.. 400–446, 430
death predicted............................ 693
early departure from Moyo Island
.... 356–59
feared three people 527, 597, 659
Greek Islands holiday 371–97
joint ventures with Mohamed....... 595
knowledge of Rosa's MI6 connections
.... 361–65
letters to Mohamed 381
mistreated in ambulance 26
relationship with Charles............... 341
relationship with Rosa......361–65, 446
removal of HRH title...............327, 546
survived the crash itself 26
threat to national security............. 470
told to become friends with Lucia 348, 349
under surveillance 378
unpredictable meteor 602
wanted to leave Moyo Island early
....358, 360
Princess of Wales.........*See* Princess Diana
Prior Knowledge 12, 19, 96, 127, 128, 139, 192, 262, 335, 383, 384, 396, 458, 469, 480, 481, 482, 536, 539, 662, 664, 673, 674, 676, 678, 679, 680, 682, 684
British Embassy 518
Tony Blair 676–78

Prior, Stephen 556, 557, 698
Prochashka, Frank............... 572, 574, 576
Professional Killers 152, 153
Prussia... 555
PT16 .... 108, 131, 138, 140, 143
PT16/B...18, 103, 104, 108, 109, 111, 112,
    113, 114, 131, 139, 140, 143, 144,
    145, *See* Watson, David
Public Domain 177, 245, 330, 335, 408,
    574, 582, 637, 668
Public Prosecution Service 93, 94
Public Record Office 88
Pulvertaft, David 231, 233
PUSD 120, 124, 699

Q

Queen Elizabeth II 4, 11, 13, 21, 22, 26,
    27, 37, 83, 174, 195, 327, 345, 360,
    378, 379, 381, 382, 383, 410, 413,
    415, 421, 439, 442, 522, 523, 524,
    546, 554, 555, 559, 560, 561, 565,
    568, 570, 572, 573, 574, 578, 579,
    580, 581, 582, 585, 589, 591, 593,
    594, 595, 596, 597, 598, 599, 601,
    602, 619, 620, 621, 622, 624, 625,
    626, 627, 628, 629, 630, 631, 632,
    633, 634, 635, 636, 637, 638, 640,
    641, 642, 643, 644, 645, 646, 647,
    648, 650, 651, 653, 655, 656, 658,
    659, 660, 661, 662, 663, 677, 678,
    679, 680, 681, 683, 684
    above the law 660, 661
    accountability 37
    and tax 570
    authorised assassination................ 684
    controlled Diana's body 27
    dark forces statement..................... 12
    discussion with Burrell 626
    involved in Paris crash 12
    not heard 654–61
    order to MI5 officer 555
    perception of Diana-Dodi relationship
    650
    requested Diana's jewellery post-
    death 654
    source of order 663

    statement to Burrell 620–48
        connected to crash 643
        response to a question 634, 636
    took control post-crash................. 653
    took control post-death................. 654
    tried to get Diana's belongings post-
        crash 652–53
    troubled by Diana 601
    warned Burrell to leave crash alone
        643
    weekly meeting with Blair 601
    weekly meeting with PM 679
Queen Victoria 555, 556
Quinn, Frank.................................. 84, 85
Quirk, Carol 351, 354, 355, 356

R

R/ME
    not heard 131
R/ME/C................. 18, 104, 120, 121, 125
Rabta... 106
Radio 4 .... 107, 704, 740
RAF..................................... 163, 678, 679
Range Rover 531
Rawnsley, Andrew...... 664, 668, 673, 674,
    676, 678, 698
Raynes, P.J.E....... 277, 280, 283, 310, 311,
    318, 321
Red Cross 188, 189, 190, 548, 549, 600
Rees-Jones, Trevor 13, 191, 215, 218, 451,
    452, 453, 486, 501, 504, 513, 533,
    595, 698
    received threatening calls.............. 452
Reichs Chancellery 558
Reid, Sue 217, 523, 525, 526, 677, 678,
    702
    not heard 525
Reilly, Patrick.................................... 84
Renault.. 229
Republican 89
Republican Guard............................. 101
Residence....483, 490, 507, 508, 509, 517,
    529
Revolutionary Warfare Wing 151, 153
Revolver 70
RG 24

Richards, Francis 477, 478

Ricketts, Peter 276, 280, 282, 306, 310, 691

Ricks, D.T. 275, 281

Ridde, John 49

Rifkind, Malcolm...19, 118, 137, 145, 146, 147

   not heard.................................19, 132

Rimington, Stella 104, 144, 154

Risen, James 99, 702

Ritchie, Charles...237, 275, 281, 317, 516, 531, 533, 535, 536, 537, 538, 539, 541, 553

   describes visit security 553

Ritz Hotel 4, 22, 23, 214, 215, 216, 217, 218, 220, 222, 223, 225, 226, 228, 229, 249, 253, 254, 428, 456, 531, 533, 536, 539

   MI6 sightings 214–30

Road Traffic Statistics 34

Roberts, Colin 270, 276, 280, 282, 283, 310, 311, 318, 321

   not heard.................................... 17

Roberts, David 691, 692

Roberts, Kenneth.................259, 334, 336

Roberts, Laura 703, 740

Rogers, Rita..................376, 397, 398, 595

Rogue Element 37, 182, 183, 184, 185, 314

Rommel, Erwin 163, 701

Room 3553 81

Room 470 111

Roulet, Claude ..11, 26, 30, 154, 225, 251, 254, 448, 453, 474, 536, 540, 684

Rowland, Herbert 81, 597, 598

Rowland, Tiny 602, 608, 613, 703

Royal Albert Hall 328, 369, 370, 699

Royal Archive 556

Royal Courts of Justice.......................3, 14

   closed inquest website.................... 14

Royal Crest...........................567, 568, 701

Royal Family......12, 25, 26, 186, 195, 327, 328, 338, 342, 345, 370, 379, 381, 383, 384, 411, 429, 436, 442, 447, 449, 455, 475, 523, 546, 548, 549, 551, 552, 553, 554, 555, 556, 558, 559, 560, 561, 562, 565, 567, 568, 569, 570, 571, 572, 573, 574, 575, 576, 577, 578, 579, 580, 581, 582, 583, 587, 591, 593, 594, 596, 597, 599, 601, 616, 619, 620, 621, 622, 630, 636, 638, 645, 646, 653, 654, 655, 656, 657, 659, 662, 663, 679, 683, 701, 703, See Queen Elizabeth II; Way Ahead Group, See Royals

   accountability..............................37, 38

   culture of secrecy and deception 12

   involvement in arms trade 683

   no evidence from 37

   prior knowledge of St Tropez holiday 384

   stability threatened by Diana 600

   suspects in...................................... 37

   workings of..44, 47, 48, 107, 271, 338, 339

Royal Family and Household 545–663

   links to intelligence agencies... 549–59

Royal Geographic Society 328, 385, 547

Royal Household. 486, 549, 550, 565, 566, 567, 577, 631, 675, See Royals

   direct contact with MI6................. 554

Royal Navy.....................................67, 153

Royal Ulster Constabulary ..92, 93, 94, 96, See RUC

Royal Warrant-Holders Committee 567

Royal Warrants ...548, 567, 568, 569, 584, 615, 616

Royal Website......................565, 573, 575

Royals

   assignment to Anthony Blunt........ 555

   Blunt mission to Germany....... 554–59

   involved in major cover-up 663

   involved in Paris crash................... 662

   links to intelligence agencies......... 384

   motives for assassination 595–602

   senior 11, 384, 558, 571, 574, 581, 595, 596, 597, 630, 658, 663, 681, 684

      list of concerns regarding Diana in July 1997 598

      list of evidence should have contributed 660

      surprised by public reaction to deaths 615

      tried to collect Diana's door keys post-crash.............................. 652

Royalty Protection 378, 384, 541, 547, 553, 594, 653

   ordered to collect Diana's belongings post-crash 652

Rubowitz, Alexander 82, 162
RUC 92, 96, 97, 165
Rufford, Nicholas........................ 115, 703
Runacres, Mark 691, 692
Russia 38, 85, 88, 109, 139, 167, 208, 212, 333, 462, 558

S

Sabotage ...25, 67, 69, 134, 151, 152, 153, 161, 705
Sadeq, Abu Abdullah 106
Sadiq, Abdullah Al 109, 110
Samoens.. 460
SAMU 13, 24, 25, 26, 467, 681
Sapeurs-Pompiers 24
Sarajevo 322, 334, 336
Saronic Gulf............................... 388, 392
SAS 49, 85, 91, 93, 148, 149, 150, 151, 152, 153, 154, 157, 158, 162, 163, 164, 178, 204, 471, 699, 701
   role in MI6 operations 148–58
Saudi Arabia 100, 270, 683
Savage, Sean 91
Sawers, John 29, 41, 703, 740
SBS 148, 149, 150, 151, 152, 153, 154, 157, 158, 198, 199, 201, 203, 204, 699
   role in MI6 operations 148–58
Scarlett, John........37, 42, 53, 68, 159, 166
Scenarios.50, 53, 157, 193, 314, 360, 431, 438, 558, 636, 675, 679, 680
   overall re the assassinations.... 680–84
   re British Embassy phone calls.......508
   re Philip-Diana letters 442
Schloss Friedrichshof................... 556, 557
Schloss Kronberg............................... 555
Scotland 678
Scotland Yard 24, 218, 232, 233, 350, 354, 355, 505, 518, 537, 539, 542, 610, 617, 620, 635, 665, 671, 672
Sea of People 539
Sea Sedan................................... 388, 389
Secrecy..10, 12, 29, 30, 31, 36, 41, 42, 44, 50, 83, 125, 233, 323, 336, 447, 448, 449, 470, 473, 527, 528, 572, 612, 703, 740

Secret Intelligence Service . 24, 28, 44, 47, 49, 61, 100, 102, 113, 114, 118, 129, 138, 234, 238, 244, 254, 340, 364, 365, 470, 550, 603, 605, 609, 611, 612, *See* MI6
Secret Service..38, 39, 160, 162, 330, 364, 365, 696
Secret Service Bureau 38, 39
Secretary of State... 57, 70, 160, 167, 306, 308, 454
Security Officer .. 480, 484, 486, 489, 525, 534, 536
Security Service...... 24, 43, 102, 124, 138, 139, 238, 245, 364, 552, 553, 603, 605, 614, *See* MI5
Security Services36, 45, 47, 107, 114, 117, 125, 150, 152, 185, 186, 187, 195, 197, 207, 210, 211, 229, 234, 235, 236, 237, 238, 245, 329, 330, 334, 364, 561, 567, 583, 584, 605, 613, 614, 620, 623, 624, *See* MI5; MI6
Sedgemore, Brian................................ 333
Seine 520
Separation...327, 338, 341, 344, 345, 346, 352, 358, 360, 400, 405, 546, 579, 580
Serbia .49, 63, 99, 126, 148, 177, 178, 332
Serious Fraud Office 683
Shannon, Keith..... 19, 278, 484, 485, 486, 487, 489, 490, 491, 492, 493, 498, 499, 500, 501, 502, 504, 505, 506, 507, 508, 509, 510, 511, 512, 513, 514, 515, 517, 536, 537, 538, 670
   lied in evidence.............................. 508
   not heard 19, 508, 544
Sharp, Dave 351
Shayler, David ...10, 18, 34, 102, 103, 105, 106, 107, 108, 109, 110, 111, 112, 113, 114, 116, 118, 119, 124, 125, 126, 127, 128, 131, 132, 133, 134, 135, 137, 138, 139, 140, 141, 142, 143, 144, 145, 146, 147, 154, 162, 187, 194, 195, 196, 198, 461, 697, 698, 701
   accused MI6 for Paris crash 187
   arrested and jailed in Paris 134
   convicted 135

evidence suppressed by British
    Government.................132–35, 144
not heard....................................18, 130
Panorama interview 108–13
told the truth.................................. 144
Shayler, Phil 134
Sheppard, Thomas............................. 96
Simmons, Simone187, 188, 189, 190, 191,
    328, 330, 331, 362, 363, 365, 375,
    376, 377, 387, 399, 409, 410, 412,
    414, 420, 422, 425, 427, 428, 429,
    436, 437, 442, 443, 453, 619, 656,
    657, 658, 698
    burnt documents........................... 191
    fallouts with Diana 376
Sinn Féin 95
Sirte 105, 110, 116, 123
SIS 238, 239, 300, See MI6
Slim, Paul 104, 144
    not heard..................................18, 131
Smallbrow.. 333
Smith, Howard...................................... 88
Smith, Martin.. 22
Snettisham... 527
Soaking Up...........................60, 62, 73, 74
Soames, Catherine.......351, 352, 356, 359
Soames, Harry 352, 356
Soames, Nicholas 328, 356, 381, 382, 527,
    547, 600, 658, 679, 682, 693
    feared by Diana 527, 597, 659
SOE 25, 68, 69, 70, 159, 161, 163, 177,
    696
    agent Alphonse 163
South Africa 683
South of France ..291, 292, 293, 319, 370,
    374, 540
Southampton...................................... 213
Soviet Union 88, 558
SPA..83, 85
Spain 91
Spearman, Richard ...32, 42, 49, 131, 145,
    183, 194, 195, 196, 197, 239, 240,
    241, 242, 243, 244, 245, 247, 250,
    251, 252, 253, 254, 255, 256, 257,
    258, 259, 260, 261, 262, 263, 264,
    265, 266, 267, 268, 270, 271, 276,
    280, 282, 283, 290, 298, 299, 303,
    308, 310, 311, 316, 318, 319, 321,
    322, 323, 461, 471, 474, 475, 535,
    538, 679, 684

accused by Mohamed 242
alibi not checked 319
alleged to be involved 239
arrived 5 days before crash 256
dealings with the Ritz Hotel 253
identified as Mr 6 251–54
identity withheld from jury 251, 322
internet listing 252
movements pre-crash 239–72
named suspect 186
never acknowledged as MI6.......... 254
not heard re Gaddafi plot.............. 131
not mentioned by name in Baker's
    Summing Up.............................. 255
personal secretary to Spedding..... 261
posted to Paris late-August 197, 322
posting date issues 256–60
posting documentation ..240, 256, 261
suspect 251
transfer to Paris table.................... 260
Special Air Service. 148, 152, 153, See SAS
Special Boat Service......93, 148, 151, 152,
    153, 200, See SBS
Special Branch .. 24, 25, 90, 92, 93, 96, 97,
    132, 133, 134, 135, 165, 459, 701, 704
Special Operations Branch.......25, 69, 161
Special Operations Executive ...25, 68, 69,
    161, 696, See SOE
Special Political Action....................67, 83
Special Service 85
Special Unpaid Leave..................280, 306
Spectator 333, 334, 568, 573, 593, 694,
    703
Speculation46, 52, 54, 107, 115, 149, 154,
    155, 182, 209, 239, 258, 264, 301,
    326, 359, 360, 385, 429, 442, 508,
    533, 559, 595, 612, 617
Spedding, David.... 49, 131, 145, 156, 195,
    196, 197, 242, 247, 252, 261, 474,
    475, 679, 702, 703
    named suspect 186
    oversaw Diana assassination......... 262
    presided over Gaddafi, Saddam and
        Diana 156
Spence, Jim.. 93
Spencer... 333
Spencer, Raine 370
Spetsai 388, 392
Spetses 388, 392
Spies of the Kaiser................................ 38

Spies, Lies & Whistleblowers 103, 132, 133, 134, 138, 141, 145

Spin-Doctors 570

Spy Catcher 85, 86, 174, 554

Squidgygate ..327, 360, 546, 579, 580, 599

SS *See* MI5

St Malo 304

St Tropez 328, 366, 368, 369, 371, 372, 373, 374, 375, 378, 381, 384, 385, 395, 396, 547, 584, 593, 594, 595, 597, 599, 600, 661, 662, 668, 684

St Tropez Holiday.

   prior knowledge 383, 384

   reactions to news 594

   triggered special WAG meeting 594

Stakeknife 93, 97, 98, 153, 175, 697

Star Wars 623

State Department 84

Stearman, Kaye 683

Sten 81

Stéphan, Hervé 99, 230, 247, 249, 269, 271, 296, 308, 459, 509, 516, 517, 533, 535, 540

   letter from Tomlinson 268

   not heard 230

Stephenson, William . 68, 69, 70, 159, 163

Stevens III 94, 95

Stevens. John 40, 42, 43, 65, 66, 91, 93, 94, 95, 150, 160, 162, 166, 170, 186, 254, 523, 524, 604, 616, 617, 618, 677, 679, 704, 740

   letter to Hunt-Davis 617

Stevenson, William 81, 161, 698

Stobie, William 92

Storey, Gillian 543

Strobe Light .....50, 99, 128, 170, 198, 200, 201, 202, 203, 204, *See* Flash Equipment

Succession 129, 488, 491, 568, 573, 576

Suez 82, 85, 86

Suez Canal Company 82

Summing Up 28, 40, 44, 46, 52, 53, 54, 183, 184, 185, 190, 250, 255, 263, 322, 415, 438, 445, 456, 470, 471, 476, 531, 583, 585, 588, 589, 592, 613, 614, 645, 646, 647, 655, 659, 664, 681

Sunday Herald 92, 95

Sunday Telegraph 67, 329, 333, 338, 352, 367, 408, 409, 411, 412, 414, 423, 427, 428, 429, 443, 446

Sunday Times 107, 115, 116, 161, 327, 332, 346, 349, 442, 555, 556, 669, 699, 703

Sunrise 387, 388, 389, 392

Sunshine 86, 87

SUPL 306, 307

Surrogates 105

Surveyor of the King's Pictures 555

Suspects 37, 45, 46, 52, 66, 82, 92, 104, 126, 129, 155, 158, 241, 251, 253, 254, 256, 262, 298, 314, 318, 320, 322, 324, 419, 423, 445, 459, 464, 471, 479, 520, 527, 591, 616, 618, 660, 661, 663

   royals not cross-examined 654–61

Swan Lake 328, 368, 369, 370

Swinburn, James 84

Switzerland 136, 231, 232, 459

T

Table 15 .... 215, 223, 228

Tables

   accounts of Elysée Palace call to Embassy 503

   comparison of 1990s MI6 assassination plots 128

   embassy staff comparison 1996 and 1997 275

   events re Diana and the Establishment 599

   MI6 officers in Paris 321

   Philip-Diana letters 1992 416

   political and economic department staff at 31 August 1997 284

   political and economic departments comparison 1995 and 1996 691

   political and economic departments comparison 1996 and 1997 282

   Richard Spearman transfer to Paris 260

   Rosa-Lucia evidence on the Philip-Diana letters 431

   the witnesses not heard 17

Tabloid Tales........................623, 649, 704

Tallin 333

Tam, Robin...... 22, 40, 41, 48, 61, 71, 150,
154, 158, 172, 173, 176, 178, 188,
193, 199, 205, 206, 207, 209, 210,
211, 212, 235, 237, 606, 607, 611
suppressed argument on landmines
.... 212

Tarr, Jack.. 351

Tawil, Camille...................................... 111

Taylor, Peter 164, 703

Technical Services............................66, 85

Teddy Bear... 342

Teesside...677, 678

Telegrams 477, 478, 514, 518, 528, 529

Telegraph......84, 145, 151, 163, 342, 343,
408, 411, 414, 417, 418, 422, 424,
430, 431, 434, 435, 436, 437, 441,
443, 446, 447, 598, 672, 699, 700,
701, 702, 703, 740

Tendil, François... 214, 215, 216, 218, 219,
220, 221, 223, 224, 225, 226

Thames House 111

Thatcher, Denis................................... 164

Thatcher, Margaret91, 152, 164, 165, 332

The Big Breach...... 36, 39, 54, 55, 56, 125,
132, 133, 135, 147, 178, 198, 300,
459, 698, 740

The Documents the Jury Never Saw..... 14,
297

The Friends 82, 86, 87, 174, 386, 698

The Independent... 99, 116, 138, 288, 332,
348, 569, 573, 575, 598, 618, 700,
701, 702, 703

Thomas, Gordon . 66, 82, 90, 98, 145, 151,
160, 162, 163, 166, 698, 701, 740

Thomas, Jane 104

Thomson, D.J. 275

Thoumieux Restaurant 252, 309, 311, 319

Tiffany's 337, 340, 341, 348, 349, 351,
356, 360, 406, 448

Timeline of Events327, 546, 579, 580, 593

Tippexing 175

Tomlinson, Richard . 10, 31, 32, 33, 34, 35,
36, 37, 39, 40, 41, 42, 43, 44, 47, 49,
50, 53, 54, 55, 56, 58, 60, 61, 63, 64,
65, 66, 67, 72, 73, 75, 76, 77, 78, 79,
99, 102, 125, 126, 127, 129, 130, 131,
132, 135, 136, 137, 147, 148, 149,
152, 153, 154, 158, 162, 169, 170,

171, 174, 175, 176, 177, 178, 181,
183, 184, 185, 186, 187, 194, 195,
196, 197, 198, 200, 201, 202, 203,
204, 206, 209, 210, 212, 231, 232,
235, 242, 243, 247, 249, 250, 251,
252, 254, 255, 256, 257, 258, 259,
262, 263, 264, 265, 266, 267, 268,
269, 270, 271, 288, 300, 308, 333,
334, 335, 336, 458, 459, 460, 461,
466, 471, 472, 473, 517, 552, 553,
554, 555, 602, 608, 613, 662, 698,
699, 704, 740
affidavit . 48–51, 49, 50, 61, 63, 65, 66,
99, 125, 169, 171, 178, 194, 204,
232, 252, 255, 258, 549, 550, 554
blamed for MI6 internet list ...232, 233
evidence tempered 198
evidence undermined by Baker.... 129,
472
evidence undermined by MI6 .79, 129,
472, 553
falsely undermined by Baker......... 263
highly educated............................. 198
issues over MI6 officer Paris departure
dates 262–67
letter to Stéphan 268
mistreatment by MI6 ....135, 198
not asked about Spearman 256
not asked about Spearman and
Langman.................................. 255
number two in MI6 France...... 268–71
pressured by MI6 198
shut down at inquest 212
told the truth...........................180, 336
training re assassination................. 75

Tories...... 83, 87, 112, 144, 146, 147, 174,
207, 232, 328, 333, 367, 547, 600,
602, 679, 682, 683, 693, 694

Toronto................................70, 568, 703

Toulouse 163, 293

Transcripts .... See Inquest Transcripts

Treasury Solicitor 562, 564, 587, 588, 589,
590, 591, 592, 605, 609, 611, 612,
613, 699

Trimdon 664, 667

Tripoli 106, 110, 121, 123

TRL... 25

Trote, Sébastien.................................. 218

Tunis 18, 103, 109, 116, 131

Tunworth 18, 104, 105, 108, 109, 111, 112, 113, 114, 116, 131, 139, 140, 141, 142, 143, 144, 147
  supplied intelligence to MI6 143
Tweeten, Thomas................................. 100
Tyrer, Robert 454

U

UDA 92, 93
UK Eyes Alpha 115, 117, 118, 124
UK/N... 47
UKDEL.. 331
UK-US Eyes Only.................................. 118
Ulster Defence Association 92, 95
Undeclared Officers 49, 234, 235, 237, 267, 311
UNITA................................ 208, 209, 211
United Arab Emirates......................... 212
United Nations 100
United States.............................. 455, 463
Urban, Mark 108, 109, 110, 111, 112, 113, 114, 139, 140, 141, 142, 146
US Embassy 455
US Government... 36, See CIA; Clinton, Bill
  involved in Paris crash 12
US Intelligence 55, 105, 106, 133, 144, 454, 456, 457, 464, 466

V

Valcik.. 81
Van Gelder, Lawrence 387, 389, 390, 391, 392, 703
Vanity Fair 572, 574, 701
Vauxhall Cross............................. 124, 231
Veness, David 379
Veres, Laslo 229

W

WAG .... See Way Ahead Group
  commissioned public surveys 575
Walker, Justice 656, 703, 705
Wall Street Journal 571, 574, 700
Wallis 555, 558, 697
Walters, Barbara 343

War of the Windsors 556, 557, 698
Washington.106, 107, 116, 292, 463, 546, 573, 669, 703
Washington Times 567
Watson, David.18, 19, 103, 104, 105, 108, 131, 144, 145, 146
  not heard 18, 131
Way Ahead Group.... 20, 25, 559–94, 559, 560, 561, 562, 563, 565, 566, 567, 568, 569, 570, 571, 572, 573, 574, 577, 578, 579, 580, 581, 583, 588, 603, 609, 613, 614, 661, 662, 681, 684, 703
  23 July 1997 meeting 12
  brought forward from September 593
  triggered by St Tropez holiday.. 594
  Baker falsified account on Sep 97 meeting 613
  concerns about Baker Summing Up 584–92
  conflicting evidence on 575–83
  contemplated Diana assassination 583
  dealt with major issues 575–83
  Diana on agenda 596
  discussion of Diana 576–79
  meeting..546, 547, 548, 577, 579, 582, 583, 584, 585, 588, 589, 590, 591, 592, 593, 594, 595, 596, 597, 598, 600, 601, 613, 614, 615, 656, 659, 662, 663
  meeting attendees......................... 581
  preparatory meeting..... 562, 563, 582, 593, 594, 595, 598
  purpose
    areas of evidence 574
    major conflict in evidence 574
  set up 327, 546
  timing of setup............................. 579
Weeders............................... 174, 194
Weekes, Robert...................................... 22
West, Nigel............. 82, 86, 162, 174, 386
Westminster Abbey 352
Westphalia 556
Westrick, Gerhard 163
Wharfe, Ken 350, 351, 353, 354, 355, 357, 358, 359, 448, 698

Whistleblower 118
White House 100, 463
White Pages... 227
White, Dick 83, 84, 223, 699
White, Jerry 463
White, Stephen....................388, 389, 390
Whitehall .. 32, 38, 88, 104, 109, 112, 113,
    116, 119, 140, 231, 523
Whiteman, Phil 19, 483, 496, 498, 499
    not heard... 19
Whomersley, Christopher....483, 495, 499
Wightman, Andrew 277, 283, 310, 311,
    318, 321, 691, 692
Wikileaks 683, 700
Wikipedia.......89, 275, 439, 581, 589, 699
Wilkinson, Nick 116, 117
Willaumez, Alain . 215, 218, 221, 223, 224,
    225
Willi Plot 556, 696
Williams, Lord 107
Wilson, Harold 98, 182, 196
Wimbledon 341, 346
Windsor Castle.... 403, 555, 556, 570, 571,
    572
Windsors.......................................558, 568
Wingfield, Kez...............................215, 218
Wingfield, Philippa.............................. 332
Witnesses
    inadequate questioning 218
Witnesses Not Heard.......................15, 17
Wright, Peter 10, 35, 37, 69, 85, 86, 87,
    135, 154, 162, 167, 174, 182, 194,
    333, 336, 555, 558, 698
    meeting with Adeane 554
WWII.................... 23, 25, 68, 69, 161, 167

Wyke, John 87
Wyman, John....................................89, 90

X

X   See Miss X

Y

Yacht... 326, 367, 373, 381, 386, 398, 536,
    568, 572
Yahoo! 14, 116, 124
Younes, George .. 480, 481, 482, 483, 484,
    486, 487, 488, 489, 490, 491, 492,
    493, 494, 495, 496, 497, 498, 499,
    500, 501, 502, 503, 504, 505, 506,
    507, 508, 509, 510, 511, 512, 513,
    514, 515, 516, 517, 525, 529, 530,
    534, 536, 537, 538, 539, 544
    lied in evidence 494, 508
    Massoni call never occurred ..508, 510
    reason for lying 511
    told to lie 510, 511
Young, George 82, 83, 98, 134, 705
Younger, Kenneth.................69, 159, 161
Yugoslavia................ 49, 63, 176, 178, 203

Z

Zagreb...331, 336
Zarb, James... 84
Zecha, Adrian...............................351, 360
Zimbabwe 165

Author Information

John Morgan was born in Rotorua, New Zealand in 1957, and has lived in Australia for the last 24 years. He and his wife currently reside in Redcliffe, on the shores of Moreton Bay, near Brisbane.

John is an investigative writer with a diploma in journalism from the Australian College of Journalism. He completed his first book titled *Flying Free* in 2005 – about life inside a fundamentalist cult. Information regarding that book can be viewed on the internet at: www.flyingfree.zoomshare.com

In his earlier life John was an accountant for various organisations in Auckland and Sydney. Later during the 1990s, he became a retailer operating a shop on Sydney's northern beaches. Since the 1980s John travelled widely throughout the Pacific, Asia and the Middle East.

He retired in 2003 at the age of 46, after being diagnosed with a severe neurological illness called multiple system atrophy. After a year or two of coming to terms with that devastating turn of events, he eventually found that the forced retirement created an opportunity to fulfil a lifelong ambition to write.

Following the death of Diana, Princess of Wales in 1997, John developed an interest in the events that had led to the Paris crash. Since 2005 he carried out extensive full-time research into those events and studied the official British police report after it was published in late 2006. John subsequently completed a book on that subject in September 2007 – it was titled *Cover-Up of a Royal Murder: Hundreds of Errors in the Paget Report*.

Throughout 2008 John Morgan continued his investigations into the crash and closely followed the British inquest into the deaths of Princess Diana and Dodi Fayed. That research resulted in the publishing of the initial volume of work on the inquest entitled *Diana Inquest: The Untold Story* – Part 1: *The Final Journey*. Six months later, during 2009, that work was followed up with the second volume *Diana Inquest: How & Why Did Diana Die?* The third volume, entitled *Diana Inquest; The French Cover-Up* was published early in 2010. It was followed by Part 4, published in 2011, entitled *Diana Inquest; The British Cover-Up*.

Those books have now been added to with this current fifth volume.

John can be contacted at: shining.bright@optusnet.com.au

Notes

[1] Laura Roberts, MI6 Chief Sir John Sawers Says Secrecy is Vital to Keep UK Safe, The Telegraph, 28 October 2010

[2] Stephen Dorril, MI6: Fifty Years of Special Operations, 2001, page 611

[3] Asia Needs To Act On Road Crashes, Press Release, International Transport Forum, 22 September 2009. Jack Short, Secretary General of the International Transport Forum, said: "In Asia over 2,000 people die on the road every day, accounting for 60% of casualties at [a] global level."

[4] Interview with Richard Tomlinson conducted by Paul Sparks at Arles, France on 5 April 2009.

[5] Interview with Richard Tomlinson conducted by Paul Sparks at Arles, France on 5 April 2009.

[6] Peter Heap, The Truth Behind the MI6 Facade, The Guardian, 2 October 2003

[7] Duncan Gardham, MI6 Boss Admits Differences in Values With US Over Torture, The Telegraph, 11 August 2009

[8] Richard Tomlinson, The Big Breach, 2001, page 58

[9] Richard Tomlinson, The Big Breach, 2001, pages 53-56

[10] Interview with Richard Tomlinson conducted by Paul Sparks at Arles, France on 5 April 2009

[11] 31 Mar 08: 67.17

[12] 29 Feb 08: 27.3

[13] 1 Apr 08: 83.17

[14] Duncan Gardham, MI6 Boss Admits Differences in Values With US Over Torture, The Telegraph, 11 August 2009

[15] Richard Tomlinson, The Big Breach, 2001, page 141

[16] Interview with Richard Tomlinson conducted by Paul Sparks at Arles, France on 5 April 2009

[17] John Stevens, Stevens Enquiry: Overview & Recommendations, 17 April 2003, p16. This was also quoted in the Paget Report, p810

[18] Gordon Thomas, Inside British Intelligence: 100 Years of MI5 and MI6, 2010, page 174

[19] Olga Craig, John Le Carré, Sydney Morning Herald: Spectrum Magazine, 18 September 2010, page 39; Olga Craig, John Le Carré: "We Carried Out Assassinations During the Cold War", The Telegraph, 28 August 2010

[20] Nicholas Anderson, NOC: Non-Officer Cover: British Secret Operations, 2009, ppiii-v

[21] Gordon Corera, MI6: A Century in the Shadows, BBC Radio 4 Documentary, 10 August 2009

[22] Duncan Gardham, MI6 Boss Admits Differences in Values With US Over Torture, The Telegraph, 11 August 2009

[23] Stephen Dorril, MI6: Fifty Years of Special Operations, 2001, pages 610-612

[24] John Pearson, The Life of Ian Fleming, 1966, pages 129 to 130

[25] Annie Machon, Spies, Lies and Whistleblowers: MI5, MI6 and the Shayler Affair, 2005, page 167

[26] 26 Feb 08: 3.10

[27] 19 Feb 08: 1.4

[28] William Stevenson, A Man Called Intrepid: The Secret War 1939-1945, 1977, pp364-380

[29] Nigel West, The Friends: Britain's Post-War Secret Intelligence Operations, 1990, pp41-2, 50

[30] Gordon Thomas, Inside British Intelligence: 100 Years of MI5 and MI6, 2010, pages 175-6

[31] Stephen Dorril, MI6: Fifty Years of Special Operations, 2001, pages 623 to 639

[32] Peter Wright, Spycatcher, 1987, pages 160-1

[33] Peter Wright, Spycatcher, 1987, pages 156-8

[34] Nigel West, The Friends: Britain's Post-War Secret Intelligence Operations, 1990, pp95, 102-3

[35] Ian Black, Files Show UK Backed Murder Plot, The Guardian, 28 June 2001

[36] Richard Belfield, The Secret History of Assassination: The Killers and Their Paymasters Revealed, 2008, pages 24 to 25

[37] Richard Bennett, Assassination and the License to Kill, Asia News, 13 June 2003

[38] An Phoblact, History: British Spies in the 26 Counties, Ireland's Own, 27 December 2001

[39] Gordon Thomas, Inside British Intelligence: 100 Years of MI5 and MI6, 2010, pages 207 to 208

[40] Stephen Dorril, MI6: Fifty Years of Special Operations, 2001, page 741

[41] Richard Norton-Taylor, In Defence of the Realm?: The Case For Accountable Security Services, 1990, pp64, 91-2

[42] John Stevens, Stevens Enquiry: Overview & Recommendations, 17 April 2003, pp7-10

[43] Martin Ingram & Greg Harkin, Stakeknife: Britain's Secret Agents in Ireland, 2004, pp197, 204

[44] Owen Bowcott, No Soldiers or Police to be Charged over Finucane Murder, Prosecutors Rule, The Guardian, 26 June 2007

[45] Nuala O'Loan, Statement by the Police Ombudsman for Northern Ireland on her Investigation into the Circumstances Surrounding the Death of Raymond McCord Junior and Related Matters, 22 January 2007, page 8

[46] Nuala O'Loan, Statement by the Police Ombudsman for Northern Ireland on her Investigation into the Circumstances Surrounding the Death of Raymond McCord Junior and Related Matters, 22 January 2007, pages 144 to 146

[47] Dermot Ahern, Statement on N.I. Police Ombudsman's Report on McCord Case, 22 January 2007

[48] James Risen, FBI Probed Alleged CIA Plot to Kill Hussein, Los Angeles Times, 15 February 1998

[49] Patrick Cockburn, MI6 in Plot to Kill Saddam, The Independent on Sunday, 15 February 1998

[50] Stephen Dorril, MI6: Fifty Years of Special Operations, 2001, pages 781-2

[51] Annie Machon, Spies, Lies and Whistleblowers: MI5, MI6 and the Shayler Affair, 2005, pages 165 to 172

[52] William Lowther & Jason Lewis, Gadaffi Plot Credible, Say US, Mail on Sunday, 31 August 1997

[53] Mark Hollingsworth & Nick Fielding, Defending the Realm: MI5 and the Shayler Affair, 1999, page 209

[54] Sarah Lyall, Are Britain's Covert Operatives Messing Up? Don't Even Ask, The New York Times, 5 August 1998

[55] BBC Screens Shayler Interview, BBC News, 8 August 1998

[56] Michael Smith, Cook Denies MI6 Plot to Assassinate Gaddafi, Daily Telegraph, 10 August 1998; Annie Machon, Spies, Lies and Whistleblowers: MI5, MI6 and the Shayler Affair, 2005, page 251

[57] Nicholas Rufford, Revealed: Cook Misled Public Over Libya Plot, Sunday Times, 16 February 2000

[58] Martin Hickman, Kill Gaddafi Plot Report Posted on Net, The Independent, 13 February 2000

[59] Shayler: Cook "Misled" Over Gaddafi Plot, BBC News, 15 February 2000

[60] Nick Cohen, Secrets and Lies, The Observer, 12 March 2000

[61] Mark Hollingsworth, Secrets, Lies and David Shayler, The Guardian, 17 March 2000

[62] 2 Oct 07: 79.22

[63] Annie Machon, Spies, Lies and Whistleblowers: MI5, MI6 and the Shayler Affair, 2005, page 213

[64] The Operation Paget Inquiry Report into the Allegation of Conspiracy to Murder Diana, Princess of Wales and Emad El-Din Mohamed Abdel Moneim Fayed, December 14 2006, page 746

[65] The Operation Paget Inquiry Report into the Allegation of Conspiracy to Murder Diana, Princess of Wales and Emad El-Din Mohamed Abdel Moneim Fayed, December 14 2006, page 762

[66] The Operation Paget Inquiry Report into the Allegation of Conspiracy to Murder Diana, Princess of Wales and Emad El-Din Mohamed Abdel Moneim Fayed, December 14 2006, pages 762-4

[67] Annie Machon, Spies, Lies and Whistleblowers: MI5, MI6 and the Shayler Affair, 2005, pages 279 to 280

[68] Annie Machon, Spies, Lies and Whistleblowers: MI5, MI6 and the Shayler Affair, 2005, pages 167 to 168

[69] Annie Machon, Spies, Lies and Whistleblowers: MI5, MI6 and the Shayler Affair, 2005, page 166

[70] Annie Machon, Spies, Lies and Whistleblowers: MI5, MI6 and the Shayler Affair, 2005, page 171

[71] Annie Machon, Spies, Lies and Whistleblowers: MI5, MI6 and the Shayler Affair, 2005, page 169

[72] Annie Machon, Spies, Lies and Whistleblowers: MI5, MI6 and the Shayler Affair, 2005, page 169

[73] Annie Machon, Spies, Lies and Whistleblowers: MI5, MI6 and the Shayler Affair, 2005, page 119

[74] Annie Machon, Spies, Lies and Whistleblowers: MI5, MI6 and the Shayler Affair, 2005, page 171

[75] Mark Hollingsworth & Nick Fielding, Defending the Realm: MI5 and the Shayler Affair, 1999, pages 179 to 180; Annie Machon, Spies, Lies and Whistleblowers: MI5, MI6 and the Shayler Affair, 2005, page 212

[76] Mark Hollingsworth & Nick Fielding, Defending the Realm: MI5 and the Shayler Affair, 1999, pages 176, 181

[77] Mark Hollingsworth & Nick Fielding, Defending the Realm: MI5 and the Shayler Affair, 1999, pages 176 to 177; Annie Machon, Spies, Lies and Whistleblowers: MI5, MI6 and the Shayler Affair, 2005, page 211

[78] Mark Hollingsworth & Nick Fielding, Defending the Realm: MI5 and the Shayler Affair, 1999, page 181

[79] Annie Machon, Spies, Lies and Whistleblowers: MI5, MI6 and the Shayler Affair, 2005, page 217

[80] Mark Hollingsworth & Nick Fielding, Defending the Realm: MI5 and the Shayler Affair, 1999, page 182; Annie Machon, Spies, Lies and Whistleblowers: MI5, MI6 and the Shayler Affair, 2005, page 217

[81] Annie Machon, Spies, Lies and Whistleblowers: MI5, MI6 and the Shayler Affair, 2005, page 217

[82] Mark Hollingsworth & Nick Fielding, Defending the Realm: MI5 and the Shayler Affair, 1999, pages 193 to 195

[83] Annie Machon, Spies, Lies and Whistleblowers: MI5, MI6 and the Shayler Affair, 2005, page 244

[84] Mark Hollingsworth & Nick Fielding, Defending the Realm: MI5 and the Shayler Affair, 1999, pages 213-4, 218-9, 226-8; Annie Machon, Spies, Lies and Whistleblowers: MI5, MI6 and the Shayler Affair, 2005, page 246

[85] BBC News, Timeline: Shayler Spy Row, 4 November 2002

[86] Annie Machon, Spies, Lies and Whistleblowers: MI5, MI6 and the Shayler Affair, 2005, page 276; Paul Lashmar & Terry Judd, Student Questioned Over Links to Shayler as Special Branch Investigates MI6 Leak, The Independent, 8 March 2000

[87] Annie Machon, Spies, Lies and Whistleblowers: MI5, MI6 and the Shayler Affair, 2005, page 277

[88] BBC News, Timeline: Shayler Spy Row, 4 November 2002; Annie Machon, Spies, Lies and Whistleblowers: MI5, MI6 and the Shayler Affair, 2005, page 321

[89] Annie Machon, Spies, Lies and Whistleblowers: MI5, MI6 and the Shayler Affair, 2005, page 324

[90] Annie Machon, Spies, Lies and Whistleblowers: MI5, MI6 and the Shayler Affair, 2005, page 326

[91] BBC News, Timeline: Shayler Spy Row, 4 November 2002; Annie Machon, Spies, Lies and Whistleblowers: MI5, MI6 and the Shayler Affair, 2005, pages 326-7

[92] Paul Daley, Media Gag on Alleged Plot to Kill Gaddafi, The Age, 10 October 2002; Annie Machon, Spies, Lies and Whistleblowers: MI5, MI6 and the Shayler Affair, 2005, pages 328-9

[93] BBC News, Timeline: Shayler Spy Row, 4 November 2002; Annie Machon, Spies, Lies and Whistleblowers: MI5, MI6 and the Shayler Affair, 2005, page 333

[94] BBC News, Timeline: Shayler Spy Row, 4 November 2002; Annie Machon, Spies, Lies and Whistleblowers: MI5, MI6 and the Shayler Affair, 2005, page 333

[95] Annie Machon, Spies, Lies and Whistleblowers: MI5, MI6 and the Shayler Affair, 2005, page 334

[96] Annie Machon, Spies, Lies and Whistleblowers: MI5, MI6 and the Shayler Affair, 2005, page 119

[97] Stephen Dorril, MI6: Fifty Years of Special Operations, 2001, page 760

[98] Annie Machon, Spies, Lies and Whistleblowers: MI5, MI6 and the Shayler Affair, 2005, page 272

[99] Richard Tomlinson, The Big Breach, 2001, page 74

[100] Stephen Dorril, MI6: Fifty Years of Special Operations, 2001, page 742

[101] Jonathan Bloch & Patrick Fitzgerald, British Intelligence and Covert Action, 1983, pp40,44-5

[102] Richard Norton-Taylor, In Defence of the Realm?: The Case For Accountable Security Services, 1990, p64

[103] Peter Wright, Spycatcher, 1987, page 310

[104] 26 Feb 08: 3.10

[105] 26 Feb 08: 171.22

[106] 29 Feb 08: 29.20

[107] 29 Feb 08: 28.18

[108] 29 Feb 08: 29.25

[109] 29 Feb 08: 31.13

[110] 29 Feb 08: 28.17

[111] Richard Tomlinson, The Big Breach, 2001, page 150

[112] Peter Wright, Spycatcher, 1987, pages 9-10

[113] Definitions for both words are from the Oxford Dictionary

[114] The Operation Paget Inquiry Report into the Allegation of Conspiracy to Murder Diana, Princess of Wales and Emad El-Din Mohamed Abdel Moneim Fayed, December 14 2006, page 747

[115] Annie Machon, Spies, Lies and Whistleblowers: MI5, MI6 and the Shayler Affair, 2005, page 213

[116] 16 Jan 08: 27.11

[117] Starting at 10 Jan 08: 93.20

[118] 10 Jan 08: 74.22

[119] 10 Jan 08: 74.14 – "4 to 6 inches"

[120] Chapter 2A

[121] 14 Feb 08: 134.24

[122] SAS Website: www.sasequip.com

[123] Wikipedia, Strobe Light, History

[124] Richard Tomlinson, The Big Breach, 2001, page 111

[125] Sue Reid, Diana: The MI6 Mystery, Daily Mail, 4 December 2004

[126] 3 Dec 07: 146.3

[127] Fiat Uno Witnesses, Hello magazine, January 17 1998, www.public-interest.co.uk/diana/dianafuwit.htm

[128] Richard Tomlinson, The Big Breach, 2001, page 302

[129] Richard Norton-Taylor, MI6: The Nightmare Scenario as a Rogue Agent Goes Public, The Guardian, 13 May 1999

[130] Richard Norton-Taylor & David Pallister, MI6 Tries to Limit Internet Damage, The Guardian, 15 May 1999

[131] Richard Norton-Taylor, Rogue Agent Accused of Going Public on MI6 Names, The Guardian, 19 May 1999

[132] Richard Tomlinson, The Big Breach, 2001, pages 302-3

[133] Michael Jay, Witness Statement, 13 December 2005, reproduced in Diana Inquest: The Documents the Jury Never Saw, 2010, pp633-5 (UK Edition)

[134] The Operation Paget Inquiry Report into the Allegation of Conspiracy to Murder Diana, Princess of Wales and Emad El-Din Mohamed Abdel Moneim Fayed, December 14 2006, page 765

[135] The Operation Paget Inquiry Report into the Allegation of Conspiracy to Murder Diana, Princess of Wales and Emad El-Din Mohamed Abdel Moneim Fayed, December 14 2006, page 767

[136] The Operation Paget Inquiry Report into the Allegation of Conspiracy to Murder Diana, Princess of Wales and Emad El-Din Mohamed Abdel Moneim Fayed, December 14 2006, page 769

[137] The Operation Paget Inquiry Report into the Allegation of Conspiracy to Murder Diana, Princess of Wales and Emad El-Din Mohamed Abdel Moneim Fayed, December 14 2006, page 829

[138] The Operation Paget Inquiry Report into the Allegation of Conspiracy to Murder Diana, Princess of Wales and Emad El-Din Mohamed Abdel Moneim Fayed, December 14 2006, page 767

[139] The Operation Paget Inquiry Report into the Allegation of Conspiracy to Murder Diana, Princess of Wales and Emad El-Din Mohamed Abdel Moneim Fayed, December 14 2006, page 767

[140] 29 Feb 08: 61.16

[141] 29 Feb 08: 65.9

[142] Richard Tomlinson, The Big Breach, 2001, page 151

[143] The Operation Paget Inquiry Report into the Allegation of Conspiracy to Murder Diana, Princess of Wales and Emad El-Din Mohamed Abdel Moneim Fayed, December 14 2006, page 753

[144] Foreign & Commonwealth Office, The Diplomatic Service List 1996, p223

[145] 29 Feb 08: 40.1

[146] The Operation Paget Inquiry Report into the Allegation of Conspiracy to Murder Diana, Princess of Wales and Emad El-Din Mohamed Abdel Moneim Fayed, December 14 2006, page 766

[147] Michael Jay, Witness Statement, 13 December 2005, reproduced in Diana Inquest: The Documents the Jury Never Saw, 2010, p638 (UK Edition)

[148] Michael Jay, Witness Statement, 13 December 2005, reproduced in Diana Inquest: The Documents the Jury Never Saw, 2010, pp632-3 (UK Edition)
[149] Foreign & Commonwealth Office, The Diplomatic Service List 1997, p161
[150] Foreign & Commonwealth Office, The Diplomatic Service List 1997, p161; Foreign & Commonwealth Office, The Diplomatic Service List 1998, p167
[151] Foreign & Commonwealth Office, The Diplomatic Service List 1998, piii
[152] Foreign & Commonwealth Office, The Diplomatic Service List 1998, p167
[153] Michael Jay, Witness Statement, 13 December 2005, reproduced in Diana Inquest: The Documents the Jury Never Saw, 2010, pp630-1 (UK Edition)
[154] Foreign & Commonwealth Office, The Diplomatic Service List 1997, p157
[155] Foreign & Commonwealth Office, The Diplomatic Service List 1997, p8
[156] Interview with Sherard Cowper-Coles conducted by Malcolm McBain on Friday 4 March 2011
in Cowper-Coles' office at BAE Systems, London
[157] Foreign & Commonwealth Office, The Diplomatic Service List 1998, p278
[158] Foreign & Commonwealth Office, The Diplomatic Service List 1998, p154; Foreign & Commonwealth Office, The Diplomatic Service List 1999, p154
[159] Foreign & Commonwealth Office, The Diplomatic Service List 2000, pp34, 157
[160] Foreign & Commonwealth Office, The Diplomatic Service List 2002, p168
[161] Foreign & Commonwealth Office, The Diplomatic Service List 2002, p40
[162] Foreign & Commonwealth Office, The Diplomatic Service List 1998, p154
[163] Press Office Downing Street, Change of Her Majesty's Ambassador to the Republic of Finland, 26 January 2006: www.gov-news.org/gov/uk/news
[164] Foreign & Commonwealth Office, The Diplomatic Service List 1998, p162
[165] Andrew Morton, Diana: In Pursuit of Love, 2004, pages 31-32
[166] Andrew Morton, Diana: In Pursuit of Love, 2004, page 35 and Andrew Morton, Diana: Her True Story – In Her Own Words, 1997, pages 14-15
[167] Andrew Morton, Diana: Her True Story – In Her Own Words, 1997, page 17 and Andrew Morton, Diana: In Pursuit of Love, 2004, pages 37,159
[168] Andrew Morton, Diana: In Pursuit of Love, 2004, page 49
[169] Andrew Morton, Diana: Her True Story – In Her Own Words, 1997, page 17
[170] Simone Simmons, Diana: The Last Word, 2005, page 185
[171] Simone Simmons with Ingrid Seward, Diana: The Last Word, 2005, page 170
[172] Simone Simmons with Ingrid Seward, Diana: The Last Word, 2005, page 196
[173] Foreign & Commonwealth Office, The Diplomatic Service List 2002, p261
[174] Tom Walker & Milorad Ivanovic, Vengeful Serbs Betray Top MI6 Man, Sunday Times, 16 August 2004
[175] Ian Traynor, MI6 Involved in Balkan Spy Plot, Says Croatian Paper, The Guardian, 27 August 2004
[176] Paul Lashmar & Paul McCann, Parliament: Speculation: Editor Named as MI6 Agent, The Independent, 17 December 1998
[177] Ian Traynor & Richard Norton-Taylor, Editor "Provided Cover for Spies", The Guardian, 26 January 2001
[178] Richard Tomlinson, The Big Breach, 2001, page 98
[179] Foreign & Commonwealth Office, The Diplomatic Service List 2002, p100

[180] Lucia Flecha de Lima, Witness Statement, 1 September 2004, reproduced in Diana Inquest: The Documents the Jury Never Saw, 2010, pp29-31 (UK Edition)

[181] Catherine Elsworth, Diana "Had First Affair with Personal Detective", Daily Telegraph, 25 October 1998

[182] Richard Kay, The Real Truth About Diana, Daily Mail, 29 November 2003

[183] Andrew Morton, Diana: In Pursuit of Love, 2004, pages 31-32

[184] Lucia Flecha de Lima, Witness Statement, 1 September 2004, reproduced in Diana Inquest: The Documents the Jury Never Saw, 2010, pp31-32 (UK Edition)

[185] Ken Wharfe with Robert Jobson, Diana: Closely Guarded Secret, 2002, page 214

[186] Richard Kay, The Real Truth About Diana, Daily Mail, 29 November 2003

[187] Michelle Green, Ping-Pong Princes, People Magazine, 6 September 1993

[188] Ken Wharfe with Robert Jobson, Diana: Closely Guarded Secret, 2002, pages 222 to 227

[189] Michelle Green, Ping-Pong Princes, People Magazine, 6 September 1993

[190] Paul Burrell, The Way We Were: Remembering Diana, 2006, pp53-54

[191] Ken Wharfe with Robert Jobson, Diana: Closely Guarded Secret, 2002, page 214

[192] Nigel Dempster, Baby Joy for Diana's Friend, Daily Mail, 24 October 1996

[193] Charles, Diana Attend Second Dinner Together, The Star, 30 April 1993

[194] Ken Wharfe with Robert Jobson, Diana: Closely Guarded Secret, 2002, page 224

[195] Ken Wharfe with Robert Jobson, Diana: Closely Guarded Secret, 2002, page 208

[196] Ken Wharfe with Robert Jobson, Diana: Closely Guarded Secret, 2002, page 214

[197] Daphne Barak, Building Up Confidantes, Sunday Times, 19 March 1995

[198] Dominic Lawson, A Crucial Personal Detail ... and the Truth About Diana's Death, Daily Mail, 4 June 2006

[199] Michael Cole, Witness Statement, 6 July 2006, p4

[200] Lucia Flecha de Lima, Witness Statement, 1 September 2004, reproduced in Diana Inquest: The Documents the Jury Never Saw, 2010, p29 (UK Edition)

[201] Dominic Lawson, A Crucial Personal Detail ... and the Truth About Diana's Death, Daily Mail, 4 June 2006

[202] 13 Dec 07: 144.16

[203] Lucia Flecha de Lima, Witness Statement, 1 September 2004, reproduced in Diana Inquest: The Documents the Jury Never Saw, 2010, p29 (UK Edition)

[204] Simone Simmons with Ingrid Seward, Diana: The Last Word, 2005, pages 10, 58

[205] Simone Simmons with Ingrid Seward, Diana: The Last Word, 2005, page 68

[206] 31 Jan 08: 114.25

[207] 31 Jan 08: 113.14

[208] Paul Burrell, A Royal Duty, 2003, pxi

[209] Paul Burrell, A Royal Duty, 2003, pxi

[210] Nick Buckley, Diana and, in the Aegean, Diana is Cruising Again, Mail on Sunday, 17 August 1997

[211] Lawrence Van Gelder, Chronicle, The New York Times, 19 August 1997

[212] Richard Kay & Ian Cobain, Will He Phone Me?, Daily Mail, 20 August 1997

[213] Diana Plays It Cool, The News Letter, 21 August 1997

[214] Stephen White, Diana 1961-1997: Last Goodbye: My Life Is Bliss, Bye Bye, The Mirror, 8 September 1997

[215] Diana: The Last Days; Part 8: Princess In Disguise, Daily Record, 24 August 1998

[216] www.sailingpoint.com/yachting; www.greeceyachts.com

[217] Sunrise and Marala: www.charterworld.com/index.html; Sea Sedan (renamed Huntress) www.superyachts.com

[218] Princess Diana Sparks Frenzy Of Sightings, Daily Gazette, 19 August 1997

[219] Diana Eludes Media Again, The Record, 19 August 1997

[220] The Media Swarm Greek Isles, In Search Of Diana, Philadelphia Inquirer, 18 August 1997

[221] Quote in the third person from People interview: Clare Morrisroe, Diana's Last Secret: She Asked Me to Marry Her & Dodi, Says Priest, The People, 15 October 2000

[222] 28 Jan 08: 108.9

[223] Diana: Her True Story, Independent Television News, Documentary, 1998

[224] Diana: Queen of Hearts, TV Documentary, Hallmark Entertainment, 1998

[225] 18 Jan 08: 189.8

[226] 14 Jan 08: 31.8

[227] 14 Jan 08: 38.10

[228] Andrew Morton, Diana: Her True Story – In Her Own Words, 1997, page 279

[229] Andrew Alderson, Diana's Friends Confirm Duke's Account of His Letters, Daily Mail, 24 November 2002

[230] Richard Kay, The Real Truth About Diana, Daily Mail, 29 November 2003

[231] Louise Pritchard, A Harlot, a Trollop and a Whore…., Mail on Sunday, 10 November 2002

[232] "Prince Philip Branded Diana a Harlot", IOL News, 11 November 2002, also reported by CBC News: New Scandals for Royal Family, CBC News, 12 November 2002

[233] Andrew Alderson, Diana's Friends Confirm Duke's Account of His Letters, Daily Mail, 24 November 2002

[234] 13 Dec 07: 56.3

[235] 17 Dec 07: 5.25

[236] 17 Dec 07: 6.1

[237] 18 Dec 07: 165.10

[238] 13 Dec 07: 52.10

[239] 13 Dec 07: 46.14

[240] What Were You Doing When …?, BBC News, 31 August 1997. This article is dated 30 August 1997, but it was clearly written after the crash.

[241] Breakfast at Rosa's, ES Magazine, 10 November 2006

[242] Aislinn Simpson, Camilla: "I Won't Attend Princess Diana Service", The Telegraph, 27 August 2007

[243] The Face: Rosa Monckton, The Times, 28 August 2007

[244] Rosa Monckton, You Magazine, 21 October 2007

[245] Diana Was A True Friend, Weeps [Diana's] Closest Confidante Rosa, Daily Mail, 14 December 2007

[246] Massoud Ansari & Andrew Alderson, Why Surgeon Could Not Marry Princess Diana, The Telegraph, 16 December 2007

[247] Ephraim Hardcastle, So Apart from Tony Blair and Gordon Brown, Who Are the Other Notable Royal Wedding Absentees?, Daily Mail, 29 April 2011

[248] 14 Dec 07: 6.15

[249] Trevor Rees-Jones & Moira Johnston, The Bodyguard's Story, 2000, pages 356-7

[250] Trevor Rees-Jones & Moira Johnston, The Bodyguard's Story, 2000, page 356

[251] Interview with Richard Tomlinson conducted by Paul Sparks at Arles, France on 5 April 2009

[252] Richard Tomlinson, The Big Breach, 2001, page 191

[253] Stephen Dorril, MI6: Fifty Years of Special Operations, 2001, page 89

[254] Stephen Dorril, MI6: Fifty Years of Special Operations, 2001, page 475

[255] Stephen Dorril, MI6: Fifty Years of Special Operations, 2001, page 710

[256] Stephen Dorril, MI6: Fifty Years of Special Operations, 2001, page 710

[257] Stephen Dorril, MI6: Fifty Years of Special Operations, 2001, page 736

[258] Clinton Backs Diana on Mine Ban, Daily Mail, 19 August 1997

[259] US Agrees to Soften Stance on Land-mine Ban, CNN, September 15 1997

[260] Worldwide Ban on Landmines Approved, Without US, CNN, September 17 1997

[261] Clinton Rejects Landmine Treaty, Mail On Sunday, 30 November 1997

[262] Jon King & John Beveridge, Princess Diana: The Hidden Evidence, 2001, pages 54-55

[263] Jon King & John Beveridge, Princess Diana: The Hidden Evidence, 2001, page 56

[264] William Blum, Killing Hope: US Military and CIA Interventions Since World War II, 1995, p453

[265] 20 Feb 08: 114.24

[266] 20 Feb 08: 115.2

[267] 20 Feb 08: 115.3

[268] 20 Feb 08: 115.4

[269] 20 Feb 08: 118.6

[270] 20 Feb 08: 122.2

[271] 20 Feb 08: 122.16

[272] 20 Feb 08: 122.17

[273] 20 Feb 08: 140.13

[274] 20 Feb 08: 140.21

[275] 20 Feb 08: 145.4

[276] 20 Feb 08: 176.9

[277] 20 Feb 08: 177.5

[278] Keith Moss, Witness Statement, 22 October 2004, reproduced in Diana Inquest: The Documents the Jury Never Saw, 2010, p648 (UK Edition)

[279] Michael Jay, Witness Statement, 13 December 2005, reproduced in Diana Inquest: The Documents the Jury Never Saw, 2010, pp630-1 (UK Edition)

[280] The Operation Paget Inquiry Report into the Allegation of Conspiracy to Murder Diana, Princess of Wales and Emad El-Din Mohamed Abdel Moneim Fayed, December 14 2006, page 610

[281] Keith Moss, Witness Statement, 22 October 2004, reproduced in Diana Inquest: The Documents the Jury Never Saw, 2010, pp648-9 (UK Edition)

[282] Michael Jay, Witness Statement, 13 December 2005, reproduced in Diana Inquest: The Documents the Jury Never Saw, 2010, pp631-3 (UK Edition)

[283] The Operation Paget Inquiry Report into the Allegation of Conspiracy to Murder Diana, Princess of Wales and Emad El-Din Mohamed Abdel Moneim Fayed, December 14 2006, page 610

[284] 17 Dec 07: 108.13

[285] The Operation Paget Inquiry Report into the Allegation of Conspiracy to Murder Diana, Princess of Wales and Emad El-Din Mohamed Abdel Moneim Fayed, December 14 2006, page 612

[286] Inquest website: INQ0008320

[287] The Operation Paget Inquiry Report into the Allegation of Conspiracy to Murder Diana, Princess of Wales and Emad El-Din Mohamed Abdel Moneim Fayed, December 14 2006, page 611

[288] The Operation Paget Inquiry Report into the Allegation of Conspiracy to Murder Diana, Princess of Wales and Emad El-Din Mohamed Abdel Moneim Fayed, December 14 2006, page 611

[289] Michael Jay, Witness Statement, 13 December 2005, reproduced in Diana Inquest: The Documents the Jury Never Saw, 2010, p630 (UK Edition)

[290] From 11 Feb 08: 102.8

[291] Michael Jay, Witness Statement, 13 December 2005, reproduced in Diana Inquest: The Documents the Jury Never Saw, 2010, p640 (UK Edition)

[292] Sue Reid, Revealed: Diana Inquiry's Tantalising New Questions, Daily Mail, June 17 2006

[293] 17 Dec 07: 109.4

[294] Keith Moss, Witness Statement, 22 October 2004, reproduced in Diana Inquest: The Documents the Jury Never Saw, 2010, p648 (UK Edition)

[295] The Operation Paget Inquiry Report into the Allegation of Conspiracy to Murder Diana, Princess of Wales and Emad El-Din Mohamed Abdel Moneim Fayed, December 14 2006, page 611

[296] Inquest website: INQ0008320

[297] The Operation Paget Inquiry Report into the Allegation of Conspiracy to Murder Diana, Princess of Wales and Emad El-Din Mohamed Abdel Moneim Fayed, December 14 2006, page 611

[298] The Operation Paget Inquiry Report into the Allegation of Conspiracy to Murder Diana, Princess of Wales and Emad El-Din Mohamed Abdel Moneim Fayed, December 14 2006, page 610

[299] The Operation Paget Inquiry Report into the Allegation of Conspiracy to Murder Diana, Princess of Wales and Emad El-Din Mohamed Abdel Moneim Fayed, December 14 2006, page 610

[300] The Operation Paget Inquiry Report into the Allegation of Conspiracy to Murder Diana, Princess of Wales and Emad El-Din Mohamed Abdel Moneim Fayed, December 14 2006, page 607

[301] The Operation Paget Inquiry Report into the Allegation of Conspiracy to Murder Diana, Princess of Wales and Emad El-Din Mohamed Abdel Moneim Fayed, December 14 2006, pages 607 to 613

[302] Andrew Morton, Diana: Her True Story – In Her Own Words, 1997, page 17

[303] Simone Simmons, Diana: The Last Word, 2005, page 185

[304] Princess Diana, Responding to Landmines: A Modern Tragedy and Its Consequences, Keynote Address at Royal Geographic Society, 12 June 1997. Transcript at: http://thespeechsite.com in English – Famous Speeches By Famous People

[305] Interview with Richard Tomlinson conducted by Paul Sparks at Arles, France on 5 April 2009

[306] 12 Feb 08: 143.14

[307] Peter Wright, Spycatcher, 1987, page 223

[308] Charles Higham, Wallis: Secret Lives of the Duchess of Windsor, 1989, pp446-7

[309] Lynn Picknett, Clive Prince & Stephen Prior, War of the Windsors: A Century of Unconstitutional Monarchy, 2003, pp193-200

[310] Royal Family Rethinks Future Role for Survival, The Washington Times, 1 September 1996

[311] Royal Family Gathers to Chart Its Future: Way Ahead Group Talks About Church Links, Rules for Succession, The Spectator (Toronto), 17 September 1996

[312] Clare Garner, House of Windsor Joins the PR Circus, The Independent, 23 February 1998

[313] Revamping the Royals, The Economist, 12 March 1998

[314] Paul Reynolds, Royal Family's Changing Guard, BBC News, 31 August 1998

[315] Alan Travis, Support for Royal Family Falls to New Low, The Guardian, 12 June 2000

[316] Jane Kerr, Abolish Them: Two Thirds of Our Readers Want Rid of the Royal Family, The Mirror, 11 April 2001

[317] Laura Collins, How Rupert Lost His Babykins to Big Willie, Daily Mail, 19 August 2006

[318] Britain Revokes Wedding Invite To Syria Envoy, Wall Street Journal, 28 April 2011

[319] Edward Klein, The Trouble with Andrew, Vanity Fair, August 2011

[320] Treasury Solicitor's website – www.tsol.gov.uk/about_us.htm

[321] 31 Jan 08: 115.14

[322] 31 Jan 08: 115.16

[323] Christopher Andersen, The Day Diana Died, 1998, page 80

[324] 17 Jan 08: 174.17

[325] Tony Blair, A Journey: My Political Life, 2010, pp135-6

[326] 26 Feb 08: 7.11

[327] Mansfield mentioned he was reading from page 407

[328] Paul Burrell, A Royal Duty, 2003, pp318-9

[329] Paul Burrell, Witness Statement, 27 April 2006, reproduced in Diana Inquest: The Documents the Jury Never Saw, 2010, p23 (UK Edition)

[330] Robert Jobson, Queen and the Dark Forces, Evening Standard, 6 November 2002

[331] I'm Still Loyal to the Royals, Says Butler, IOL News, 21 November 2002

[332] Piers Morgan, The Insider: The Private Diaries of a Scandalous Decade, 2005, p419

[333] The Royal Household, The Official Website of the British Monarchy, www.royal.gov.uk/TheRoyalHousehold

[334] 31 Mar 08: 131.4

[335] 1 Apr 08: 1.23

[336] Steve Dennis, 100 Threats: Burrell Menaced by String of Phone Calls to Arson-Hit Shop, The Mirror, 2 December 2002

[337] Paul Burrell, A Royal Duty, 2003, p292

[338] Michael Cole, Witness Statement, 6 July 2006, pp27-28

[339] Keith Moss, Witness Statement, 22 October 2004, reproduced in Diana Inquest: The Documents the Jury Never Saw, 2010, p659 (UK Edition)

[340] Christopher Andersen, The Day Diana Died, 1998, p20

[341] Paul Burrell, A Royal Duty, 2003, p288

[342] Coroner's Inquests Into The Deaths Of Diana, Princess of Wales and Mr Dodi Al Fayed, Reasons, 12 March 2008

[343] Case No: CO/2706/08, In The High Court Of Justice, The President Of The Queen's Bench Division, Mr Justice Gross and Mr Justice Walker, Between: The Queen on the Application of Mohamed Al Fayed (Claimant) and Assistant Deputy Coroner of Inner West London (Defendant), Hearing dates: 18th March 2008, Approved Judgement.

[344] 17 Jan 08: 178.23

[345] 17 Jan 08: 172.25

[346] The Operation Paget Inquiry Report into the Allegation of Conspiracy to Murder Diana, Princess of Wales and Emad El-Din Mohamed Abdel Moneim Fayed, December 14 2006, page 108

[347] 17 Jan 08: 173.7

[348] 17 Jan 08: 178.12

[349] The Operation Paget Inquiry Report into the Allegation of Conspiracy to Murder Diana, Princess of Wales and Emad El-Din Mohamed Abdel Moneim Fayed, December 14 2006, page 108

[350] 17 Jan 08: 174.21

[351] 17 Jan 08: 174.17

[352] Andrew Rawnsley, Servants of the People: The Inside Story of New Labour, 2001, pp59-60

[353] Alastair Campbell, The Alastair Campbell Diaries: Volume 2: Power and the People: 1997-1999, 2011, pages 124-6

[354] Tony Blair, A Journey: My Political Life, 2010, pp138-141

[355] Alastair Campbell, The Alastair Campbell Diaries: Volume 2: Power and the People: 1997-1999, 2011, page 83

[356] Paul Burrell, A Royal Duty, 2003, p284

[357] John Macnamara, Witness Statement, 3 July 2006, reproduced in Diana Inquest: The Documents the Jury Never Saw, 2010, p518 (UK Edition)

[358] Michael Cole, Witness Statement, 6 July 2006, p10

[359] Alastair Campbell, The Alastair Campbell Diaries: Volume 2: Power and the People: 1997-1999, 2011, pages 125-6
[360] Sue Reid, Revealed: Diana Inquiry's Tantalising New Questions, Daily Mail, June 17 2006

CPSIA information can be obtained at www.ICGtesting.com
Printed in the USA
LVOW060135170512

282107LV00001B/321/P